Human-Computer Interaction Series

Human-Computer Interaction is a multidisciplinary field focused on human aspects of the development of computer technology. As computer-based technology becomes increasingly pervasive – not just in developed countries, but worldwide – the need to take a human-centered approach in the design and development of this technology becomes ever more important. For roughly 30 years now, researchers and practitioners in computational and behavioral sciences have worked to identify theory and practice that influences the direction of these technologies, and this diverse work makes up the field of human-computer interaction. Broadly speaking it includes the study of what technology might be able to do for people and how people might interact with the technology.

In this series we present work which advances the science and technology of developing systems which are both effective and satisfying for people in a wide variety of contexts. The human-computer interaction series will focus on theoretical perspectives (such as formal approaches drawn from a variety of behavioral sciences), practical approaches (such as the techniques for effectively integrating user needs in system development), and social issues (such as the determinants of utility, usability and acceptability).

Author guidelines: springer.com > Authors > Author Guidelines

Also in this series

Satinder Gill

Editor

Cognition, Communication and Interaction

Transdisciplinary Perspectives on Interactive Technology

 Springer

Satinder Gill
Senior Research Fellow
School of Computing
Middlesex University
UK

British Library Cataloguing in Publication Data
A catalogue record for this book is available from the British Library

Library of Congress Control Number: 2007936184

Human-Computer Interaction Series ISSN 1571-5035
ISBN: 978-1-84628-926-2   e-ISBN: 978-1-84628-927-9

Printed on acid-free paper

9 8 7 6 5 4 3 2 1

Springer Science+Business Media
springer.com

Preface

This book examines the theoretical and methodological research issues that underlie the design and use of interactive technology. Present interactive designs are addressing the multi-modality of human interaction and the multi-sensory dimension of how we engage with each other. The writings contribute to the growing trans-disciplinary research for interaction design. The analysis directs attention to three human capacities that our engagement with interactive technology has made salient and open to constant redefinition. These capacities are human cognition, communication, and interaction.

The collection is a celebration of the 21 years of the foundation of the AI & Society Journal. Over the years, a wide horizon of researchers, practitioners and scholars have contributed to shaping a transdisciplinary debate on cognition, communication and interaction. The discussions represent this ongoing debate by bringing together timeless and historical papers on some of the fundamental issues that the journal's life has travelled through.

It brings together work by researchers and practitioners from a wide range of discourses that are pertinent to understanding the boundaries and possibilities produced by the intervention of interactive technology in all spheres of human social life. The authors come from philosophy, human-centred design, interactive art, participatory design, computer supported cooperative working (CSCW), human-computer interaction (HCI), dance, opera, theatre, interactive multi-modal design, cognitive technology, knowledge management, ambient interactive design, immersive and responsive technology, presence research, communications, linguistics, social science, psychology, engineering, and computer science.

2 Navigating the Transdisciplinary Debate

Interactive technology has now entered every sphere of human life, from the most private (e.g. the home, the 'presence' Amigo Project) to the most public spaces (e.g.

RCA's Presence Project, Buxton 2001; Immersive responsive media projects, Topological Media Lab, Concordia University, Sha 2005). The conceptual separation of mind and body, so prevalent in early work on AI and information systems (Fodor, 1976, 1981, Simon, 1985), has given way to the concepts of embodied cognition (Varela, Thomson, Rosch, 1993). The user model is questioned with a shift from the user being an individual, to the user being part of a community of practice (Wenger and Lave, 1991). Designers now include performance artists, interactive artists, as well as social scientists, philosophers, engineers, physicists, mathematicians, and computer scientists. This is a far cry from the days of computer scientists trying to elicit and explicate expertise to create autonomous expert systems. These changes of the cross-disciplinary make-up of designers (their motivations, perceptions, backgrounds, cultures) and the adaptation and sometimes unexpected use of their applications across contexts, necessitates taking a step back to make sense of this complexity and its implications. The writings in this book are a collection of reflections, concepts, methodologies, and applications, that address the fundamental bases on which we can understand these changes and harness the issues they raise for designing technologies to be symbiotic with human capacities and qualities.

The book is divided into three parts: Part I, on "Communication and Interaction", provides an analysis of those aspects of human communication and interaction that computer mediated communication, immersive, and interactive technology impacts upon. Part II of the book covers the impact of interactive technologies on the conceptions and performance of human knowledge and cognition. It presents issues pertaining to this impact and provides design concepts for interaction design. In Part III, on Ethics, Aesthetics, and Design, the understanding of the tacit dimension of human communication and human knowledge for designing interactive technologies is extended to consider the ethical and aesthetic aspects.

3 Part I: Communication and Interaction

Part I, on "Communication and Interaction", provides an analysis of those aspects of human communication and interaction that computer mediated communication, immersive, and interactive technology impacts upon. These impacts in turn cause us to rethink the distinctions between human-human communication and that impacted upon by the machine artifacts we increasingly use to mediate or even substitute that communication. The effects on our interaction practices also asks us to consider the nature of our relation with the machine and try to define what 'machine' means (Negrotti).

- whether it is a tool and what does 'tool' mean. (Mey), on the relationship between cognition and tool in "Cognitive Technology")

- whether it is an augmentation and what does that mean in the context of communication.

- whether it is a simulation and what does that mean in contrast to say going to the theatre and engaging with a simulation of everyday life.

This analysis unravels fundamentals of human communication that are necessary to take into account when considering design and application of such technologies. For example:

- the effect upon how we negotiate and make decisions.
- on how we relate to others and perceive ourselves.
- on the rhythmic synchrony of our engagement with each other and our environment. (SP Gill on communication and knowledge transformation in "Cognition, Communication, and Interaction")
- on conceptions of collaboration, cooperation, and coordination (Fruchter reflects on "Degrees of Engagement in Interactive Workspaces" with practical applications of collaborative interfaces).
- on conceptions of learning (Binder "Designing for Workplace Learning")
- on what it means to be in a community (Memmi proposes that virtual communities of abstract relationships are evolution of modern society).

In considering these fundamentals of communication, design itself involves these very aspects in its process of creating the machine artefact. The complexity of designing the shape and possibilities of communication and interaction necessitates a complex of perspectives that can encompass it. In the 1980's the complexity of information or expert systems threw up a concern for participation in the design process by potential users to ensure that 'design' and 'use' would meet. The present day concern with interactive multi-modal and multi-sensory technology is to involve numerous disciplines, kinds of expertise, as well as potential users, to ensure that 'design' and 'use' meet for human communication. The multiplicity of perspectives becomes problematic when commonly held conceptions of say, 'use', are rooted in different cultural traditions of design practice (Allwood and Hakken on "Use Discourses in System Development"). This added complexity of perspectives within the design process engages a multi-layering of language games that need to find common ground (Borchers, on "Pattern Approach to Interaction Design"). This multi-layering is intricate in global communication where interactive technologies increasingly intervene. Their intervention lies outside of cultural practices that need to find some translation. Addressing this in design of interactive technology involves the consideration of one's relation to others and perception of self, and one's existence in a community.

The nature of global communications is not just about individuals communicating with other individuals. It is about how we, as individuals, communicate from within our communities of practice or cultures (Banerjee, on cross-cultural communication and the management of language, "Narration, Discourse, and Dialogue".). This conception of global communication is described as the communication between cultural architectures or holonic structures within which we as individuals engage (KS Gill, on "The User and the Interaction Architecture"). Cross-cultural communication becomes a communication matrix of cultural holons (e.g. cultures, for instance, Japanese and British). Inevitably, as different cultural holons have different architectures, there are gaps in their communication. KS Gill proposes that such gaps in global communication necessitate 'cross-appropriation' and not just 'common ground', which is a Western concept of mutual understanding.

The design of interactive multi-modal and multi-sensory technology has the challenge to both sustain and shape a concept of the global that is sustainable at the local community level, in order that individuals can sustain their everyday communications with those they live, walk, play, learn, and work with.

The shape that such designs take will be determined by the motivations of those involved in their design. Negrotti, in "Towards a Theory of the Artificial", takes us through the possible motivations through history of man's creation of the artificial, which are to simulate, reproduce (imitate), and control nature, and now human behaviour. He proposes that 'control', rather than simulation or reproduction, offers the possibility for technology to be adaptive to human purpose.

4 Part II: Knowledge and Cognition

Part II of the book covers the impact of interactive technologies on the conceptions and performance of human knowledge and cognition. It presents issues pertaining to this impact and provides design concepts for interaction design. In particular it covers the relationship between the tacit and explicit dimensions of 'knowing' in human skill acquisition, multi-modal communication, and multi-sensory human engagement.

The tacit-explicit knowledge discussion was salient in the 1980's amongst proponents of knowledge based interactive systems who,

- assumed implicit knowledge to be something that could be made explicit
- designed structures of definition and causation for its representation and application.
- created masses of data and faced problems of processing it.

Tacit/implicit knowledge became termed a bottleneck in knowledge based interactive systems design. The model of the neuron as an alternative to causal propositions, for moving and processing knowledge, seemed to alleviate the 'bottleneck' problem as technologists built hybrid neural-network/knowledge based interactive technologies. However, the explication of the tacit was to simulate human knowledge in order to achieve one of many possible functions of technology. Some basic ones are cited in Part I, namely, to augment, to simulate, to replicate (imitate) human action, human decision-making, human judgement, and human communication. In Part II, Dreyfus on "The Socratic and Platonic Basis of Cognitivism", and Noble (Cockpit Cognition) provide us with the historical and conceptual bases of the Cognitivist paradigm of human knowledge and skill, and give insights into the problems of representation. Noble, directs our attention to the evolving notions of 'intelligence' and education technologies. FT Evans provides a historical understanding of how man's creativity shapes technology and reflects on how this technology can in turn affect human creative capacity.

The discussions here on the tacit in relation to the explicit provide definitions, frameworks, and contextual exemplars to explain what constitutes the tacit and why it is related to the explicit. One reason that technologists faced the 'bottleneck' problem above, is that they separated the tacit from the explicit by assuming the latter subsumes the former. This is to assume that you can separate the wood from the trees and focus on the trees and still see the wood. As Cooley puts it in Part III, ("On Human Machine Symbiosis), these are mutually exclusive. It is the problem Polanyi addressed in the Tacit Dimension, when he said, to paraphrase, that you can attend from the picture to the parts that constitute it, but you cannot attend from the parts and see the picture. A bottleneck was bound to happen if you did as you would never reach the whole.

But the design problem has two dimensions to it, of 'design' meeting 'use'. The design involves assumptions about what it is to 'know' and 'have knowledge'. The use part is where the humans interact with the representations of 'knowing' and 'having knowledge' as embedded in the machine interaction. In her work, Josefson ("The Nurse as an Engineer") presents concerns for nurses' tacit knowing when the language they are required to use in their practice is imported from medical practice, in order to make their 'profession' scientific. In this example, language becomes technology that is not rooted in experiential and personal knowing, leading to a gap between knowing and having knowledge.

Early work on interactive technology focused on the written word and mathematical representations and sometimes included speech. These representations impacted on human cognition, one of the most troubling outcomes being that skilled experts could doubt their own judgements and pass on decisions to machines (Goranzon, "The Practice and Use of Computers"). This is of concern as skill and innovation in any organization is dependent on 'tacit knowledge' (Senker, on the "Contribution of Tacit Knowledge to Innovation") that is rooted in personal interaction, mutual construction, and managing uncertainty. It is necessary for us to understand the cognitive impact of our engagement with representations of our skilled performance and the designs of interactive interfaces that are based on these.

Present interactive designs are addressing the multi-modality of human interaction and the multi-sensory dimension of how we engage with each other. The illusion of 'intelligence' now extends to the sphere of human communication where machines such as interactive embodied virtual agents and robots, are assigned human-like qualities that cause in us affective responses, and a perception of a 'social intelligence' (SP Gill, "On Tacit Knowing").

At the heart of both the present and previous forms of interactive technologies lies the conception of 'rule' but not 'rule-following'. The latter lies in the performance of human knowledge and the former the abstraction of it (Johannessen, "Tacit Knowing and Rule-Following"). The former is embedded in the machine and guides the machine interaction. The latter lies in human interaction and guides human dialogue.

The performance domains such as dance, opera, theatre, music, are helpful, almost vital, for analyzing and experiencing how we achieve rule-following or 'practical knowledge', giving us awareness that this is constituted by the human imagination, human senses, the body, and personal and experiential knowing. Ikuta ("The Role of Craft Language in Learning 'Waza'") provides an example of this with the embodiment of the traditional Japanese artistic performance, in this case Noh or Kabuki, by the performer through metaphor, imagination, experience, and the immersion of self. Interactive technologies can place an emphasis on the visual and textual representations of human knowledge and cognition, but if one is blind, such emphasis is of little 'use' and it may be more appropriate and more universal to develop conceptions of 'knowing how', 'knowing when' and 'knowing what', around action, the body, and emotion (Saha and Gangopadhyay, on "Building a Pedagogy around Action and Emotion: Experiences of Blind Opera of Kolkata"). Developments in responsive media technologies, (Sha, in Part III) take us in this direction, and the enrichment of the performance arts is opening up the possibilities for the multi-modal and multi-sensory dimensions of human knowing. This perspective of human knowing as skilled performance allows for the movement from 'seeing-as' (an instruction in a Noh dance lesson) to 'seeing' (embodied skilled performance) (Tilghman).

As well as looking closely into design assumptions and design processes, the technics of design, it is important to reflect back on the design motivations behind the representations of human knowing, as raised by Negrotti and KS Gill in Part I.

5 Part III: Ethics, Aesthetics and Design

And this takes us to Part III, on Ethics, Aesthetics, and Design, where an understanding of the tacit dimension of human communication, human knowledge, for designing interactive technologies, is extended to consider the ethical and aesthetic aspects. If we synthesise the essence of the tacit as being, 'we know more than we can tell' (Polanyi, 1966), then ethics and aesthetics are part of the tacit dimension and it is not insignificant that as we enter the complexity of human communication and interaction, that these aspects of human knowledge are becoming of greater importance as interactive design criteria. The writings in Part III unravel the critical ethical questions that target both design and use, and provide examples and analyses of how the narrative domains redefine the aesthetic quality of both the design experience and applications of design. The challenge for interactive technology designers is to achieve both the ethical and the aesthetic requirements for a symbiosis of human and machine which ensures the human capacity for being together with other humans, in social and cultural co-existence, as discussed in Parts I and Part II. This suggests that aesthetics within the sphere of interaction design would need to be in balance with the ethics of sociality.

The ethics of interactive design are concerned with the following conceptual and methodological issues:

- the distinction between causality and purpose - the constraints of defining the complexity of human communication in terms of 'one-best-way' (Rosenbrock, "Ethics and Intellectual Structures")

- defining human relations with machine metaphors (Hirose, "Organisational Spaces and Intelligent Machines: A Metaphorical Approach to Ethics")

- understanding the human social capacity of 'normal responsible behaviour', essential for the formation and functioning of any community (Leal, "Ethics is Fragile, Goodness is Not")

These methodological issues underlie the design considerations for human-machine symbiotic interaction, and are developed by Cooley ("On Human Machine Symbiosis"). Understanding how a designer thinks and being able to shape that for ethical design is part of the methodological framework (Ostberg, "What Goes on When a Designer Thinks?").

The ways designers think will also be determined by who the designers are, what their backgrounds are, their skills. An artist will have a different way of thinking about design than a computer scientist. In Part I we discussed the complexity of finding shared ground in the communication amongst multi-disciplinary designers that is now essential because of the complexity of the arena of interactive technology that impinges on the relations between human cognition, communication, and interaction. In this section, we are given an insight into how artists conceive and create databases and how their aesthetics and artistic practices shape these processes of design meeting use (Vesna, "Databases are Us").

When aesthetics is abstracted from the ethics of social norms, for example in exploring genetics for creating living art forms (Gigliotti, 2006), then this destabilizes 'normal responsible behaviour' (Leal). The consequences of this are a separation of how we judge action in the virtual representations of human life and how we judge human life in the social everyday co-existence. The symbiosis between the artificial and the real needs the symbiosis between aesthetics and ethics, in order to design socially sustainable interactive technology. In his work on responsive media technologies, Sha provides an example of the way forward for exploring this symbiosis of the ethical and the aesthetic. In engaging with his art works people find they touch something in each other and in themselves that goes beyond words and words' boundaries, to make contact and sense the other as a part of oneself.

The breadth and depth of the discussions around cognition, communication, and interaction, by these authors confronts the complexity posed by the permeation of interactive technologies in our everyday lives. The nature of our engagement with these technologies presents a challenge to develop fundamental transdisciplinary frameworks for understanding the human-system interface. It is hoped that these chapters will contribute to an increasing dialogue across the disciplines and research networks.

I have enjoyed bringing this book together and re-discovering the richness of the writings in AI & Society over the years. It has been rewarding to be in touch with the authors and find their enthusiasm for this collection. The decision for this book emerged in a discussion of the Journal's Editorial Board at the Springer headquarters, where Beverly Ford gave her commitment to support us. On behalf of the Editorial Board, I would like to thank her and Springer, who have consistently supported the humanistic and societal commitment of the Journal and its founders, Karamjit S. Gill, Mike Cooley, David Smith, Janet Vaux, Jim Finkelstein, Ajit Narayanan, and Massimo Negrotti.

Satinder P. Gill

Contents

PART I

COMMUNICATION AND INTERACTION

Knowledge as Embodied Performance

Satinder P. Gill[1]

[1] Middlesex University, School of Computing, London, NW4 4BT, UK. sattisan@yahoo.com

Abstract. This chapter presents an analysis of knowledge as a process of tacit knowing embodied in dialogue rather than as a process of information transfer embodied in signal processing (Shannon and Weaver 1949). Within dialogue we acquire knowledge (experiential knowledge, tacit knowing, practical knowledge) through our embodied performance of 'how ' and 'what' we know about the communication situation we are in. This embodied performance includes utterances, gestures, movement and modulation of body and voice, as well as mediating artefacts, such as interactive technologies. This chapter explores the implications of this perspective of knowledge for the conception and design of interactive technologies that seek to facilitate joint action and joint attention.

1 Introduction

The last twenty years have seen a transition in the ways in which designers think about human cognition, communication, and the role of the body in their conception of knowledge (from residing in an autonomous individual to being distributed across individuals [e.g. distributed cognition, Hutchins 1995]), intelligence (from individual to social), and being human (from being a black box to being multi-modal and multi-sensory (Sha 2002)). This transition is a fundamental shift from a focus on cognition as disembodied to being embodied (Andersen 2003) as, evident in the definitions and inclusions of the social (embodied cognition, gesture) and emotion, in the field of cognitive science and designs of interactive AI, Art, and Robotics technologies. Part of this shift has been motivated by the engagement of the artistic and performance narrative domains that have reflected on the nature of public, home, and entertainment spaces by using technology to explore and extend our engagement spaces (e.g. Topological Media lab, http://topologicalmedialab.net/joomla/main/index.php [Sha 2005]). Art demands a consideration of our senses and the aesthetic, and performance arts demands a consideration of the communication environments and performance structures (e.g. mixed media dance). Technology's appropriation by the narrative domains has created possibilities of analogue and digital symbiotics (e.g.

Sponge, TGarden; Infomus Lab, http://www.infomus.dist.unige.it [Camurri]) beyond the boundaries of the typewriter and TV screen metaphor that most of us work with and communicate through.

There is one fundamental conception that frames the design of human-machine interaction and that is the information theoretic signal transmission model (Shannon and Weaver 1949). This involves a speaker as being distinct from a listener at any moment in time, and where information is passed from speaker and received by listener. This is a linear model of feedback. The limitations of this conception and implications for human-machine symbiosis will be explored in this chapter, drawing on a theory of Body Moves and the concept of entrainment. In human interaction, entrainment is the coordinating of the timing of our behaviours and the synchronising of our attentional resources (Clayton, Sager, and Will 2005; Cross 2007). Body Moves are periodic rhythmic synchronizations of the movements and modulations of our bodies and voices as we engage with each other. They constitute an important dimension of the conception of knowledge as being embodied in performance (Gill SP, Kawamori, Katagiri, Shimojima 2000).

A focus on knowledge as embodied performance questions the information theoretic conception of knowledge. It asks questions about the meanings that interactive technology may take when we engage with it, for example, as a tool, as augmenting our capacities, as simulation. These meaning of technology are influenced by, or influence, our conceptions of collaboration, cooperation, and coordination, in human-machine interaction. The analyses in this chapter of communication and interaction include situations of negotiation, of learning, of misunderstanding and of repair. Performance of embodied knowledge involve how we relate to others and perceive ourselves, e.g. within a group, within a society, and within and across cultures (Gill, KS 2007).

Early work on interactive technology focused on the written word and mathematical representations and sometimes included speech. These representations impacted on human cognition, one of the most striking outcomes being that skilled experts could doubt their own judgements and pass on decisions to machines (Goranzon 1993). This is of concern as skill and innovation in any organization is dependent on 'tacit knowledge' (Senker 1993; von Krogh, Ichijo, Nonaka 2000) that is rooted in personal interaction, mutual construction, and managing uncertainty. It is necessary for us to understand the cognitive impact of our engagement with representations of our skilled performance and the designs of interactive interfaces that are based on these.

Present interactive designs are addressing the multi-modality of human interaction and the multi-sensory dimension of how we engage with each other. The illusion of 'intelligence' now extends to the sphere of human communication where machines such as interactive embodied virtual agents and robots, are assigned human-like qualities that cause in us affective responses, and a perception of a 'social intelligence' (Gill SP 2004).

At the heart of both the present and previous forms of interactive technologies lies the conception of 'rule' but not 'rule-following'. The latter lies in the performance of human knowledge and the former the abstraction of it (Johannessen 1988). The former is embedded in the machine and guides the machine interaction. The latter lies in human interaction and guides human dialogue.

The performance domains such as dance, opera, theatre, music, are helpful, almost vital, for analyzing and experiencing how we achieve rule-following or 'practical knowledge', giving us awareness that this is constituted by the human imagination, human senses, the body, and personal and experiential knowing. Ikuta (1990) provides an example of this with the embodiment of the traditional Japanese artistic performance, in this case Noh or Kabuki, by the performer through metaphor, imagination, experience, and the immersion of self. Interactive technologies can place an emphasis on the visual and textual representations of human knowledge and cognition, but if one is blind such emphasis is of little 'use' and it may be more appropriate and more universal to develop conceptions of 'knowing how', 'knowing when' and 'knowing what', around action, the body, and emotion (Saha and Gangopadhyay 2006). Developments in responsive media technologies (Sha 2005) take us in this direction and the enrichment of the performance arts is opening up the possibilities for the multi-modal and multi-sensory dimensions of human knowing. This perspective of human knowing as skilled performance allows for the movement from 'seeing-as' (an instruction in a Noh dance lesson) to 'seeing' (embodied skilled performance) (Tilghman 1988).

2 Knowledge as Embodied Performance

This paper analyses the relationship between knowledge and cognition within communication and interaction processes. It presents questions and challenges that interactive technology needs to address. The analysis questions the model of information transfer and feedback of communication theory rooted in Shannon and Weaver (1949) conception. This model describes human knowledge in terms of representations of context, content, and processing. Within this chapter, knowledge is described as being embodied in performance of everyday communication and interaction. Meaning comes with 'experiential knowing and the imagination' and the 'experiencing' is outside of the information theoretic linguistic patterns.

The tacit-explicit relationship and the role and nature of experiential knowledge is illustrated with two exemplars of practice. The first is an example of 'consultancy' performance, and the second is an example of underwriters evaluating insurance applications.

2.1 Knowledge as Performance: Example of Consultancy

A group of four upper-middle and senior management practitioners (experts in their fields) are giving a presentation of about 20 minutes each. They are seated around a table and are provided with an overhead projector to use. Each is given the task to present themselves to the others as a consultant and talk about what a consultant is, and sell the idea of consultancy to them. The group is chaired by another senior manager who sits at the table with them. A doctoral researcher (the author) was invited to observe the proceedings of the workshop.

The first 'consultant' stands facing the group and presents a 'tool kit' of consultancy using the overhead slides. This toolkit essentially consists of a list of propositional statements - descriptors, definitions, and rules. After a few minutes this consultant has to stop giving his presentation, saying he had lost the thread of information, i.e. the connection between himself and the information he has been presenting.

The second 'consultant' also stands and speaks of how consultants 'pull rabbits out of hats' whilst presenting hand drawn overheads of a rabbit being pulled out of a hat and one with the word 'magic' in large letters. His forms of expression disturb his 'clients' who accuse him of mocking their profession and expertise in what they see as his portrayal of them as insincere or dishonest. His expressions make them unreceptive to his 'content'.

The third consultant stands and speaks about rules or conduct and emphasises the good things a consultant does. His handwritten overheads are measured and consistently paced. He is perceived as sincere and the others feel he understands and supports them.

All these three 'consultants' have stood and presented overheads. The fourth consultant remains seated, but places himself on the other side of the table to the other three, facing them. He begins to tell them a confidential story of some political rumblings at the top of their corporation. This consultant is very high up in the organisational structure hence he has an authentic voice on these matters. The others become troubled and deeply involved in unravelling the story trying to find out as much as they can and work out the nature of the problem. After 20 minutes, this fourth consultant breaks the illusion of reality and tells them it was all a story. This is a disorienting experience for the others and they are very impressed by what he had done with them.

The fourth consultant has fully engaged his 'clients' in the performance of practical knowledge, where their experiential knowing was immersed, each with each other's. It was powerful acting with audience co-performance.

This performance session of consultancy takes place as part of a week-long workshop by a company that was reshaping its identity from being an 'expert' organisation to a 'consultancy' firm, for economic competitive purposes. The chairman of the consultancy workshop had invited me to join the workshop in order to elicit tacit knowledge of the formation of this corporate identity.

The second consultant who is seen to offend the others' moral well-being has in fact given a sound presentation at the level of content. The chairman of the workshop session later showed the doctoral researcher the copy of the overheads by this consultant pointing out that there was actually nothing offensive or wrong in what he was saying. The problem had lain in how he had presented the content and how he was perceived as a person. The third consultant provided the feeling of safety and comfort in his use of moral and ethical forms of expression and a calm, paced voice. He was described as genuine.

In all these performances, the posture, position, and presentation of the performers in relation to their 'clients' set the stage. If the forms of expression were not embodied (e.g. first consultant), the performance failed, and if the forms of expression did not meet the perceptions of self (e.g. of the moral position of the client, as in the case of the second consultant), there was breakdown in the communication process. The performance of the forms of our expression influences the perception and meaning of the content the forms carry.

This example illustrates the need to study the tacit dimension of knowledge as a process within dialogue, where knowledge is embodied in the performance of communication.

2.2 Cognition in Communication: Example of Underwriters' Performance

This example is concerned with the development of a data-base for underwriters that could process applications for life insurance policies. The work on the data-base was becoming cumbersome and the processing of all the possible data input categories was creating bottlenecks. As an observer, the doctoral researcher took part in one of the data-base development session involving a senior and a junior underwriter. The underwriters had brought along a set of application forms with them and were curious about the researcher's presence. The researcher told them that she was not there to extract any information but wanted to learn about what they do and she spoke a bit about her interest in the tacit and experiential dimension of human knowledge and skill. They began to chat about their skill and began to go through each form, thinking aloud in order to explain to her what they do. The session emerged as a senior expert teaching and imparting his skill to the junior (and to researcher). As they worked through the information on the forms they built up pictures of the people they had in front of them and imagined their past and future lives. On the basis of this they formed judgements as to whether this was someone who could or could not qualify for a certain type of life insurance policy. The experiential knowledge and imagination of the senior underwriter was made available to the junior who could then follow and work with him to understand the personality and life-style of their applicants.

It was clear that there was no one salient procedure of data processing as each person (each applicant) had a different picture of salient information. It could be problematic to assume predefined categories with predefined processing rules that are rooted outside the meaning of 'relevant' data - i.e. outside how it is meaningful to the underwriter in building a picture of a person. There are two problems and they relate to the idea of not being able to see the wood for the trees. If one functions at the level of data and procedures, then one builds composites, but these composites may not form a wholeness, instead they may simply remain a collection of parts. It is the human who can make the wholeness by applying experiential knowing and imagination but the skill of achieving that may become lost if the system automates the expert's creation of the applicant into the composition of parts. There are undoubtedly corporate factors (around risk and profit) which shape the imaginative construction of the client, but these are not the foci of the analysis.

This example raises the question of what role imagination and experience plays in human knowledge, and it questions the explication of this human knowing into representations of content, context, and procedure.

The above two examples present an understanding of human knowing as the interrelations of the tacit and explicit within the performance of content, context, and procedure. This is not a matter of representation but of communication.

3 Experiential Knowledge and the Distributed Setting

This next example, works through a problem where there is a breakdown in communication of knowledge. This breakdown illustrates the relationship of cognition, communication and interaction as the complexities of knowledge as embodied performance.

In the winter of 1996/1997, Gordon, an apprentice landscape architect with company 'BETA', sent a set of completed coloured maps that he had made at the company's Welsh office, to John, a senior architect based at its headquarters located in North England. The company was going to make a bid for project work to reshape a major road in North Wales where the frequency of traffic accidents was high, and these coloured maps were part of the depiction of the changes to the road design and effects upon the landscape. For example, colours depicted old woodland and new woodland. To Gordon's surprise, John judged the colours that he had used to be 'wrong' and that the maps needed to be correctly recoloured. Company BETA had barely two weeks left to submit their bid and recolouring all these maps was no small task. John brought in other experienced landscape architects at his branch to help, and asked Gordon to travel up from Wales and recolour the maps with them. It was felt that Gordon lacked experience and the only way he was going to get it was by experiencing the doing of colouring in a shared practice.

The problem of 'seeing' the colours was partly due to the company's economic condition. BETA was downsizing, as a result of which Gordon was the sole landscape architect left at the Welsh branch. Architects, however, do not interpret the material in isolation when they first handle it. In talking aloud and moving pens over paper, they engage the other person(s) in their conceiving. This, it is suggested enables one person to adapt upon another person's view, producing the conditions for a coherent development of the design (Gill SP 1996), and a process for 'seeing-as' (interpretation) until they come to 'see' (unmediated understanding) (Tilghman 1988). This is likewise with colouring activity: as the apprentice colours with the team and more experienced architects, he/she learns how they select, for example, a specific shade of blue to set against a particular shade of green ('seeing-as') to create a 'pleasing effect' that 'looks professional' (Gill SP op.cit).

Because of the distance between the two branches and because of their commitments, John had been unable to visit Gordon and work with him. Instead, he had sent him a set of previously coloured maps (examples of experience), colour coded keys, and a set of instructions. These are descriptive and propositional forms of expression, all located in the experience of the architects at the North England Branch. For Gordon, they are outside his experience, and he brings his own to bear in interpreting these fragmented representations of practice.

In his study of how a team of geophysicists judge when material fibres in a reaction vat are jet black, Goodwin (1997) shows how simply saying 'jet black' is not sufficient for helping an apprentice measure and make this judgement competently. Rather, the 'blackness of black' is learnt through physically working with the fibre, and in talking about the experience, "transforming private sensations and hypotheses into public events that can be evaluated and confirmed by a more competent practitioner". Geochemists use their bodies as 'media that experience the material' being worked with through a variety of modalities. In the case of the apprentice, Gina, in Goodwin's study, her interlocutor's ability to recognize and evaluate the sensation she is talking about requires co-participation in the same activity.

The example of Gordon's 'failure' to correctly interpret the forms of expression sent to him, is an example of how breakdown can take place when co-participation is missing from the interpretation process, and how essential it is for repair within a distributed apprenticeship setting. Knowledge becomes clearly more than a matter of applying learnt rules, but of learning 'rule-following' (Johannessen 1988) within the practices that constitute it. The need for Gordon to colour with the other architects in order to be able to correctly interpret any such future fragments that might be sent to him, shows that experiencing in co-presence has powerful tacit information. Gordon's acquired knowledge will be evident in his skillful performance of these forms of expression.

The equivalence in meaning of 'forms of expression' and 'representations of practice' denotes a range of human action, artifacts, objects, and tools. Human action includes cues, which may be verbal, bodily, of interaction with a physical material world (tools, e.g. pens, light tables, etc.), and construction of the physical boundary objects (e.g. colour, maps, sketches, masterplan sketches, masterplans, plans, functional descriptive sketches, photographs, written documents, etc.).

The dilemma of this distributed setting is that even in the future, any interpreting or understanding that Gordon, as an apprentice, does of similar or different fragments of knowledge, will still take place in isolation. The feedback from his local colleagues will be based on their 'seeing-as' (Tilghman 1988) (interpretation based on their experience) and not 'seeing' (as they lack sufficient skill in this domain to 'understand' without interpreting).

John, the senior architect was posed the question, that suppose it were possible for his team and Gordon to colour maps together in a distributed setting with the help of some hypothetical computer mediated technology, would he be interested in exploring this possibility? John declared that this was not a matter for technology but quite simply that Gordon 'lacks experience' and that the only way he will acquire it is by colouring with them in the same space. His conviction made me reflect on what it means to share a space and be present as a precondition to acquiring experience; experience that would have helped Gordon to interpret the examples of previously coloured maps for similar bids, colour keys, and instructions, that had all been sent to aid him in understanding how to colour the maps.

John was certain that once Gordon had this experience of colouring with him in the same physical space, he would have no trouble in the future in aligning his aesthetic 'seeing-as' with theirs when given such materials or representations (exemplars) to interpret and 'see', wherever he might be. Seeing-as requires interpretation and Tilghman terms this, 'mediated understanding'. Once you have the skill to see, you can understand without interpretation and just perform. The tacit knowing that Gordon had acquired would be 'retrieved and made active by sensing' (Reiner and Gilbert 2004) in his act of seeing. The role of mind and imagination is important for such retrieval in sensing that brings together past (memory), present, and future. In such sensing, our minds draw upon our bodies: 'wherever some process in our body gives rise to consciousness in us, our tacit knowing of the process will make sense of it in terms of an experience to which we are attending' (Polanyi 1966. p.15).

This is an example of the acquisition of knowledge as embodied performance. The constraints placed upon acquisition by the disembodied communication of the distributed setting, necessitates the analysis of the body for experiential knowing in shared physical space.

The problems of presence and sharing in a joint activity in a distributed setting are challenging conventional design paradigms. Further research into the design of interfaces may overcome these problems. In the UK, research projects of the PACCIT (People at the Centre of Communication and Information Technologies) investigate the psychological, social and organisational characteristics of individuals and groups as they relate to, and interact with, information technologies [http://www.paccit.gla.ac.uk/public/project.php]. The focus is to feed this knowledge back into evaluation and design of more effective IT systems and products. Research into designing interfaces that may overcome these problems is also being undertaken at MIT and NTT by Ishii (1991, 1992, 1994).

4 Multi-modal Systems: Complexity of Knowledge as Embodied Performance

Interactive multi-modal technology gives further insights into the complexity of knowledge as embodied performance in communication and interaction.

In the last few years, work in gesture has shown many features of gesture speech coordination that is being fed into interactive agent technology design (Cassell, Sullivan, Prevost and Churchill 2000). Designs of life-like agents, as in the case of the REA, (http://www.media.mit.edu/gnl/projects/humanoid/index.html the MIT Real Estate Agent) are full bodied and gesture at the appropriate prosodic speech moments. They also follow patterns of gesture and speech cue timing that is being discovered in gesture research. In the case of REA a camera is used to passively sense the user. REA plays the role of a real estate salesperson who interacts with users to determine their needs, shows them around virtual properties, and attempts to sell them a house. Cassell [http://www.soc.northwestern.edu/Justine/jc_research.htm] describes her Embodied Conversational Agent (ECA), as "a virtual human capable of interacting with humans using both language and nonverbal behavior". She introduced the rule-governed, autonomous generation of non-verbal conversational behaviours in animated characters. In a similar vein to the work at NTT and ATR, the embodied conversational agent is capable of generating and 'understanding' both propositional components of speech and synchronized interactional components such as back-channel speech, gestures and facial expressions. Work on gesture has shown that we begin a gesture movement prior to our speech action, and that our gestures have a structure called a 'stroke' (McNeill 1992; Kendon 2004) that is quite precise in its phases and works with speech content. A gesture may accompany a speech utterance and be its embodied representation. Work by former members of the Chicago school of gesture that was headed by David McNeil, and included Cassell and Kita, have investigated representational and conversational gestures and produced findings that are important for understanding the relation between hand and mind (McNeil 1992).

Other artistic approaches to gesture, such as in Tosa's interactive art/media projects [http://www.tosa.media.kyoto-u.ac.jp] focus on the emotional sensation of movements of the body and voice in creating attachment and care. At ATR, Tosa had developed an emotion matrix that she used to develop her artworks of 'neurobaby' that moves and coordinates its non-verbal body and voice actions in response to the movements (prosody, pitch, and modulation) of the sounds of our voices.

The domain of embodied agent designs is a large one, and here we focus on one aspect, that of the representation of communication processes (procedures) and semantics (content) of communication acts. The representation of the communication process is based on sequential turn-taking structures, and that of semantics is based on the affordances of computational structures. The turn-taking acts are pre-programmed responses to the feedback that the user provides (such as when users modulate the pitch and tempo of their voices when trying to calm the crying neurobaby) - and the user has to be predictable in giving the feedback (otherwise the emotion structure of the user's voice would not be recognized). The timing of any turn is bounded by the computational constraints of processing the data input and responding to it. The complexity problem for computing interaction/conversation is that if one tries to represent the human interaction and replicate it, then this necessitates making human interaction explicit. The problem of representation is similar to the problem faced by the bottleneck of 'implicit' or 'tacit' knowledge for the expert system. The interaction is definitely made more engaging when using human-like agents with programmed human voices as these elicit emotional (sensory) and imaginative responses that enable the illusion of contact with the artificial.

At a basic level, all these designs are a further development upon the Eliza system developed in the 1970's by Weizenbaum at MIT (1966, 1976), which asked the kinds of questions that people expected to hear from a therapist and gave the illusion of contact and understanding with the artificial. The multi-modal agent system extends interaction from speech (content and organization of content), to including the body, gestures, and modulation of the voice in eliciting a stronger embodied response. This we now know from work on mirror neurons (Rizzolatti, Fogassi, Gallese 2001; Ferrari, Fogassi, Gallese, Rizzolatti 2003), and work on music and motor neurons (Large and Jones 1999, on dynamics of attending), trigger both these neurons.

What interactive technologies would need to be able to achieve, in order to perform as co-performers with us, is adaptability and grounded meaning in communicative situations. This is not computationally possible and it is not clear if this is desirable.

At the moment, feedback patterns are based on a variety of methods, one of which is to aggregate and average the types and frequencies of an action, e.g., of a gesture with a speech action, and another is to simulate the communication setting and model it. The aim of simulations can be to discover a grounded ideal patterning of query and response by running through a large number of subjects who will entrain to the most prominent coordinated pattern (this is never predictable as it depends on the personalities and behaviours of the subjects) (e.g. Gill SP and Kawamori 2002). This grounded pattern is then taken as the normative case for computational purposes, and for human users to then engage with.

5 Limits of Presence in the Distributed Setting

The relation of self to other in a distributed setting is different from that of being face-to-face. But the issue has been to gain more understanding of the limits of presence in the distributed setting that had proven so problematic for the junior architect to 'see', discussed in the preceding sections.

At an experiment at NT Communication Science Labs (Gill SP and Kawamori 2002), an analysis was undertaken on how multi-modality, particularly the body, operates in communication. The aim was to identify the contingencies of adaptation for grounding meaning in a non face-to-face setting, where people cannot see each other but can talk to each other through a microphone. This involved exploring the synchronization of body and speech movements (prosody) the a non-face-to-face setting to further understand the functions of the body and voice for the self and for the other in grounding meaning.

In gesture research on face-to-face communication, coordinative gestures had already been identified (Bavelas 1994, 1995; Ekman and Friesen 1969, 1972) as functioning as a signal for the interlocutor. Ekman and Friesen had produced a semiotics of gesture, such as the 'OK' sign with the thumb, calling them illustrators and emblems, whilst Bevelas working on interactive coordination, showed, for example, how we may gesture with a hand, pointing it to the person we are talking with, to indicate something we are referring to in relation to that person. In contrast, in the non face-to-face setting, where speakers cannot see each other, there is no visual information that such gestures can carry. This implicates that their function, if they occur, in this setting will differ from that of the face-to-face setting. Alibali's findings (1999) of reduced but still high levels of representational gestures (topic based) in non face-to-face settings, and their proposal that these may have a function for the speaker which is independent of their function for the listener, supports the idea that there may be a difference in the functions of gestures in the two settings.

If coordinative gestures (not just the kinds cited above that are more clearly intended to be seen) require the presence of the interlocutor in a face-to-face setting, it is unlikely that they would occur in the non face-to-face communicative setting. Bavelas (1994) had found that 'interactive gestures' do occur in non face-to-face settings but that they are significantly reduced. As gestures still occur in this interaction, do they still presuppose the interlocutor, given that he or she cannot be seen, or is this not a necessary condition for the act?

In order to answer these questions NTT Communication Science researchers (Gill SP and Kawamori ibid.) conducted a couple of experiments. The gestures that research team focused upon, nodding gestures, were described as having a meta-communicative function, i.e. considered as signals for the interlocutor, carrying information, and thereby enabling coordination. (At this period, the notion of signalled information transmission was still a dominant concept). It was expected that if these gestures still occurred in the non face-to-face setting, then the presupposition of the interlocutor is not a necessary condition, in which case it was proposed that they embody an additional self-oriented function.

Of the two experiments, one consisted of British subjects and the other of Japanese subjects. The task in both cases was identical. The gesture that was focused on most was the head nod which is a frequent gesture in Japanese communication, and the team expected a cultural comparative analysis to identity common and essential coordinative characteristics of this gesture.

The experiment was of the communication of information between information provider and information seeker. Note the speaker-listener model of information. It is a web searching task, where the web-searcher is the information provider, and the person seeking information is the information-seeker. The experiment takes place in a laboratory setting. Subjects are placed in separate sound proof rooms. 4 video cameras were used, 2 in each room. These take a synchronised view of both subjects at two angles: of the upper torso, head and arm movement from a frontal view; of hand movement on the desk from an overhead view. All participants knew in advance that they were being video-taped. The main topic is about eating out in the Tokyo area. Questions are asked by both subjects, for example, about the price range of the restaurants, and the kind of food the subject wants to eat, directions on how to reach the place, and contact details. Each session lasts a few minutes.

Coding involved recording the timings of the picture frames of each nod, which person is nodding at the time, at which place in an utterance or turn the nod occurs, whether the person nodding is speaking at the moment they nod or the other person is speaking. The research team also noted which utterances and nods occurred just prior to or just after the nod coded. This included backchannels, endings of turns or phrases, pauses, simultaneous nodding, and prompts. Coding also involved functions, e.g. question, inform, suggest, propose, self-expression, emphasis, evaluate, request, listing, repair, confirm, topic shift, prompt, closure, initiate. This was to check for any relations between the gesture and the function of the speech as well as the category of the speech, for example, as filler or backchannel, etc. The frequency of nods per session, and for information-provider and information-seeker, were also coded.

Other gestures among the British subjects were also coded, but it was found the most frequent one in this communication setting to be the nod, and nods serve a co-ordinative function which does not directly serve to engage the interlocutor by the action itself. Three significant findings emerged which indicated a self-oriented function of the gestures.

Firstly, nods do occur in silence without the accompaniment of speech in a backchannel-like action. Although nods also occur in conjunction with speech in backchannel speech acts, the silent nod questions the claim that gesture and speech form a composite whole in the backchannel where the gesture functions as a signal for engaging the listener. In the case of silent nodding, this claim cannot be made. Rather, the claim of a self-oriented function to this interactive but non-communicative silent nodding is more applicable. In this case, we propose that gestures that do occur with backchannel speech are not performing the same function as speech. Here begins a questioning of the signal as an appropriate ascriptor for the body.

Secondly, it was found that nods occur with intonation and emphasis, when describing something, during the utterance itself. This backed up work on synchrony and coordination undertaken by Kendon (1990). They also occur with repetition. The nodding action when describing something is rather like a rhythmic beat and tends to occur at the beginning or middle of the specific word for British subjects speaking in English, and at end of the specific word for the Japanese subjects speaking in Japanese. The researchers had expected to find cultural differences of prosody of body and speech sounds in the different languages and cultures. For both groups of subjects, nodding can occur at the end of a phrase. It does not appear to perform any communicative function, but rather seems to be a necessary part of what would be termed as the internal autopoieitic rhythm of the speaker. The frequency and trajectory of the nods vary with the speech rhythm.

Thirdly, and surprisingly, given that the speakers cannot see each other, simultaneous nodding takes place. This would appear to suggest that the internal autopoietic rhythms of these two independent systems (speakers) are the same at that moment. The situations of this simultaneous gesturing vary. They can involve silent nods, or both information provider and information seeker speaking at the same time, either producing exactly the same utterance or different utterances, and can occur with simultaneous laughter. In the case of Japanese subjects, producing the same utterance is more likely to result in a simultaneous and same gesture (nod), than for the British subjects, who may produce differing gestures (for example, nod and body sway, or nod and a sideways head movement). The frequency patterns of the simultaneity for both experiments varies with differing situations. The simultaneity does not appear to be arbitrary and it is synchronised. Whether it is entrainment as in the case of the Parallel Coordinated Body Move, we could not be certain.

These three cases of nodding would suggest that nodding entails an additional function to the communicative function (signal for the interlocutor), which is coordinative and interactive. This is the self-orienting function essential for sustaining the interaction. The face-to-face theories do not provide us with an explanation for why such gestures take place in a non face-to-face setting. These are not iconic gestures, i.e. they are not representational. They occur as a person is speaking in a rhythmic manner, or in silence whilst the other person is speaking, or during a pause, and in a simultaneous manner. Hence the proposal for considering an autopoietic (Maturana and Varela 1980) internal mechanism of each person, which is coordinated by the feedback (but not information transmission) in the communication, provides a plausible theory to explore for the functionality of these gestures.

In comparing their findings with that of Bavelas' taxonomy of interactive gestures, Gill and Kawamori found that nodding did occur when giving information, seeking, and in turn-taking in the non face-to-face situation. Nodding occurs when seeking to check if the listener has understood and in turn the listener nods when confirming this. It occurs when releasing and taking turns. However, although there is an apparent similarity with the face-to-face situation, their findings suggest that the interactive function of gestures in human interaction necessarily involves both a self and other oriented dimension, which in the non face-to-face condition is predominantly self rather than other oriented. It has been suggested (Alibali 1999) that even in the case of representational gestures, they may perform dual functions, for self and for other. Hence Gill and Kawamori's proposal for a self and other function in the case of nodding, and other coordinating gestures has some precedent in gesture research.

Considering the idea of imaginative sociability (Fridlund 1991), it may be that feeling the presence of another is a necessary condition for performing metacommunicative (signalled conveyance of information about the communication) gestures. We could say that we perform certain gestures in the need to affirm the communicative situation to ourselves, thereby reinforcing this feeling of presence, and in this case, the expression 'metacommunicative' may not be suitable. This self-affirming may be a need on the part of the speaker as a self-referencing act. The autopoietic theory proposes that a system maintains it's own defining organisation, and regenerates its components. The self-referential gesturing actions may be part of the system's (persons') maintenance process.

In the autopoietic vision of communication, this is described as orienting behaviour. The interactions orient the listener within their 'cognitive domain', and if these oriented domains are similar on the part of both participants, consensual orienting interactions are possible, as each becomes subservient to the maintenance of both. Consensual orienting interactions are coordinating interactions. What we term self-referencing may be what autopoietic theory terms orienting.

Autopoiesis opposes the idea that communication involves the transmission of information, proposing instead that interaction serves to orient us within our 'cognitive domain'. This would support the idea that the function of the gestures in the non face-to-face setting is not for the interlocutor, but rather are a self-orienting mechanism, triggered off by the verbal feedback. As we orient towards similar cognitive domains, our gestures will be coordinated with our interaction. It would be expected, then, that some gestures will occur simultaneously as a result of being oriented in similar cognitive domains and not as a chance occurrence.

At this point we would like to take a step back, and before embarking on the explanation and examples of Body Moves, reflect on another technological space for the engagement of the body and co-presence. This is the virtual space.

6 Communication and Presence in the Virtual Environment

Whilst at Stanford Centre for the Study of Language and Information (2000-2003), the author ran a seminar series of Gesture and will give an example of engaging in a virtual space from one of these occasions. Steve Di Paola (2001) and his former colleagues had developed and worked with an avatar-based 3D virtual community that emulates many natural social metaphors but has extended and adapted many of these metaphors as its very tight-nit community of users has evolved over the years. OnLive Traveler [http://www.dipaola.org/sig99/sld002.htm, http://www.dipaola.org/steve/vworlds.html] and its communities use voice based emotive head avatars in online 3D virtual environments of their own creation. The community has evolved a very specific gesture and expression language that uses voice and 3D space in a socially complex manner.

The original design goals of creating this system were for a commercial start-up, and these goals succeeded and failed over the years, but ultimately the community members independently evolved expressively rich conventions of gesture, expression and emotional creation for their own personal inter-relationship needs and were running it as part of their daily lives.

In Di Paola's demonstration of OnLive Traveler, seminar participants had the chance to interact with the community members online and bring their thoughts of expression and gesture into our discussion. Being co-present in virtual space threw up some interesting issues, about how we project onto the virtual space and are able to engage with communication cues of proximity, of gestural nuances, of social performance cues of courtesy, offence, emotion, with people who can simulate these using the artificial theatre space. In interactive artwork this can become extended as we use more of our physical body (gesture, body motion, and voice) to cause the effect in the virtual environment to create social and emotional contact within it with other persons and their represented agency (of textures, colours, shapes, sounds, touch sensations, smell).

The author's research on how co-presence in virtual space can be mediated by representations of communication (agents, the written word, cartoons, etc) was triggered by an experience recounted to the author by a Japanese colleague who used on-line methods for teaching distributed groups of long-distance students. These students had never met face-to-face and she never met them. The on-line discussions were mainly functional and the information expressed in a very narrow bandwidth of modality, namely the written word within the context of the study task set to the students. So there was no social discourse. After a year of teaching, she made a decision to shuffle the members of the groups around without consulting them, and was astonished at their emotional responses to this action. They expressed disorientation and felt she should have asked at least informed them of her intention and asked them about it. Awareness of another presence over time, regardless of whether one can see the other or not, builds a feeling of sharing or inhabiting a space together, of being co-present. The Japanese colleague did not recount the details of the study activities of the student groups in the online space, however, there is no doubt that the awareness over time must have involved forms of expression, style of conveying expressions, and timing of expressions, that gave form for identities or personalities to be formed. Just the timing itself of another person's actions can give one a sense of the other in relation to oneself.

Here is another example of distributed communication, this time, with video-conferencing. A colleague from the author's group at NTT was sent to work in the International division based in Tokyo, where he was involved in numerous video-conference based meetings with clients and colleagues in the USA. This colleague is one of those special people whom you know understands what you are saying and can finish off your half uttered sentences. But in the video conference situation he was unable to understand what was being 'said'. Yet his Japanese colleagues had no problems. It was quite a dilemma. Here was one of the most brilliant of communicators with whom you could discuss Kant, finding himself having difficulties in communicating about relatively functional and mundane matters. It emerged in conversation that his colleagues spoke very good English whereas this colleague's English is not so perfect and his grammar is not great. However, he is uncanny in building trust and rapport face-to-face. The video conference had reduced the bandwidth of communication to the 'words' and 'grammatical fluency'. It had not offered the colleague the other cues of co-present physical space that he uses to be with another person when they speak and think. It was these 'other cues' that this research seeks to better understand, for these must be the same kinds of cues that the junior landscape architect, discussed further above, was missing when he tried to colour in the maps with the explicit representations he had in front of him. It is these other cues that are critical for gaining 'experience' of the other and building 'tacit knowing' and 'trust' that goes deep for sustainable knowledge.

This brings us back to relationship between embodiment and the tacit dimension in communication, and a return to Body Moves.

7 Body Moves: Rhythmic synchrony and coordination in interaction

Body moves are periodicities of rhythmic synchrony of body and speech entrainment across persons who are engaged in interaction. During these periodic moments the distinction between being a speaker and listener is not able to capture the nature of the dynamics (Gill SP 2004). We have seen from the non face-to-face nodding and gestural coordination study that thinking in terms of signal and information transmission (that underlies the speaker-listener distinction), does not appropriately explain the function of such gestures for one's own self-regulation or self-synchrony in relation to the other person.

It was mentioned at the beginning of this paper that the analysis of the movement of the body in the transfer and formation of knowledge has two conceptual layers, one from linguistics and one from the rhythmic synchrony of entrainment. Both have importance in Body Moves which are movements of both the body and the voice. However, the linguistic layer inhibits the fuller understanding of the operation of the other, to the extent that in the early work on Body Moves (Gill SP et al. 2000), one of the movements (Parallel Coordinated Movement) was placed aside, although the author was convinced it was significant but could not explain with linguistics, until it could be investigated much later (Gill SP 2002).

In search of a coherent framework to talk about Body Moves in the early stages and handle this multi-layered problematic picture, the analysis drew upon joint action (Clark and Schaefer 1989, Clark 1996)) theory (pragmatics of communication) and this seemed to work. However, joint action theory is based on information transfer and signaled information and has a sequential turn-taking structure. This still left a problem to resolve. In work on gesture in joint action the gesture itself becomes part of this sequential structure of human communication. Yet joint action theory did seem helpful in two ways. Clark's pragmatics acknowledges that there are multiple layers of sounds and semantics that constitutes a communicative act, and proposes that in cooperating to communicate, we express commitment to negotiate and understand each other, and this is necessary to arrive at grounded meanings. The author has now drawn on joint attention theory (Tomasello, Carpenter, Call, Behne & Moll 2005; Eilan, Hoerl, McCormack, Roessler 2005; Franco 1997) to help advance upon the problems of the linguistic structure underlying joint action.

At this point it would help to describe Body Moves in some more detail. The identification and conceptualisation of Body Moves emerged during a one month period (1997) spent by the author at ATR (Adavanced Telecommunications Research) Media Lab, located between Kyoto and Nara, with a group of computational linguists. This group were designing various multi-modal conversational agents, and the author sat in on their analyses of feedback and fillers. Although not fluent in Japanese, the author had experienced enough of the sound of the language and contexts of use to feel the meanings that were intended in the prosodic quality. The author reflected on the ethnographic video data collected from the landscape architecture study to analyse the movement of the body within different design situations. For example architects position themselves around a table and engage with their bodies very differently when discussing what happened in a recent meeting with a client than they do when they are sketching out a conceptual idea together on a sheet of paper. As the latter kind of scenario (sketching together) revealed a great deal of bodily activity and one could observe the expression of the architects' ideas as they used their hands, pens, and bodies, this design stage was selected as the data for analysis.

The analysis of the body in communication drew upon the Wittgensteinian discussion on action-reaction (Philosophical Investigations 1953) as underlying language games. It also drew upon the ATR research on feedback in communication, research in gesture and cognition (Kita 1993), conversation moves (Carletta, Isard, Doherty-Sneddon, and Anderson 1997). The concept 'move' in conversation analysis denote something that moves the information and conversation forwards. This gave rise to the expression 'Body Moves'. Here is a description of the activity in that video clip of the landscape architects sketching together. The background to the activity is explained first.

The selected video excerpt is of the landscape architects working on one design task of the daily practice in this firm. The senior architect is fully qualified and director of the company, whilst the other is being trained and due to qualify in a year's time. They are both familiar with each other and share a mutual respect, despite the difference in their status and experience (empathic relationship). Their task is to produce a plan for the car park of a site, as well as the site itself. Some time earlier, they had produced a sketch plan for the client. The site is to be transformed from being an old derelict brewery to a headquarters of this client. The client has produced a version of their sketch plan, largely following their ideas, and wants them to take this further. Part of the discussion between A (senior) and B (junior) is whether to go for something radical or generally remain within the bounds of what they have in front of them. They, or rather, A, decide that changing it would not greatly improve on what they have. Hence they decide upon the latter option.

There is a great deal of body interactions in this design activity. Their mutual respect means that B is able to express disagreements and produce his own suggestions. However, the discrepancy in status is evident in the take-turns and keep-turns that A performs. This activity is illustrated in the following sketch of the action unfolding, of gestures, movements, and entrainment taking place:

The two architects are developing a sketch plan for a client, one is senior and one is junior. They communicate at different levels of design - the senior architect is focusing on the ' conceptual structure' of the entire landscape, where as the junior architect is focusing on 'one position' within that 'conceptual structure'. Their gestures and body movement correspond to the level of the design. The senior architect makes large sweeping hand and arm gestures across the table. The junior architect makes small finger and hand pointing gestures. They never 'meet' although they do try- as one enters the space the other leaves it or shifts their position within it - until the senior architect 'mimics' the junior architect's gesture and posture, by focusing on one alternative location within the design to that which was the focus of the junior architect. The moment the senior architect's finger point indicates this intention, the junior architect moves down into the space as well. The moment the junior architect touches the paper with his finger and moves it in one stroke across the area of his proposed position, the senior architect moves his finger as well - back and forth - across his alternative proposal. During this parallel coordinated action, they are finally synchronised and entrained within each others' body motion and voice prosody. The moment the junior architect leaves and lifts his body out of the design space the senior architect's hand motion continues across into the junior architect's space and in one pen stroke acknowledges his proposal. This all happens within a period of three seconds. How we know that this has led to knowledge transformation is that the junior architect then explicitly proposes a topic shift and moves his body position priming this shift.

In the discussion that now follows, we explain the Body Moves that are hinted at above. These occur where the architects 'try to' meet and where the parallel coordinated action takes place.

Body Moves are essentially coordinated rhythms of body, speech, and silence, performed by participants orienting within a shared activity. These rhythms create 'contact', i.e. a space of engagement between and take two forms, sequential and parallel. They are kinds of behavioural alignments (Scheflen 1974; Bateson 1955) and interactional synchrony (Birdwhistle 1970, Condon and Ogston 1966, Kendon 1970), and metapragmatic (Mey 2001). Drawing upon the idea of the composite signal (Clark, 1996, Engle, 1998) that denotes an individual's composite act of speech and gesture, Body Moves were conceived as Composite Dialogue Acts where the idea of 'composite' denotes the various combinations of possible combinations of gesture, speech, and silence (Gill SP et al. 2000) across the persons engaging with each other (i.e. not of the individual's act). And as they occur Body Moves indicates the construction/establishment of mutual ground within a space of action. Ascribing an act as being a 'Body Move' does not refer to, and is not defined in terms of, the physical movement, rather, it targets the act that the movement performs.

Body Moves that were identified in the five minute video clip of the two landscape architects above are [please see Gill et al. 2000 for more detail]:

Attempt-Contact
Dem-Ref
Take-turn, Keep-turn, Release-turn
Body-Check (B-check)
Acknowledge (Ack)
Focus

An example of the Body Moves Attempt-Contact is:

Function - Draws person's attention and involvement
Effect - Increases engagement or commitment
Gesture - 'looking' gesture, or hand and arm gesture

The analysis of the body moves drew upon the concept of meta-communication (Allwood et al. 1991, Shimojima et al. 1997) in linguistics, where meta-communication is the conveyance of information about the conversation, as opposed to being about the topic situation of the conversation itself (i.e. content). Allwood's (1991) work was particularly helpful as it provided wider cognitive or behavioural categorizations of prosodic information that other linguistic theories could not account for, such as contact, perception, understanding, and attitudinal reactions are. He stated that these are requirements of human communication because they describe how we relate to each other when communicating, whether we are committed, whether we are positive or negative, whether we are perceiving the expression or are interpreting and showing how we understand, and what assumptions we are making. In linguistics, the conveyance of information is described as being triggered by cues that inform about the conversation situation for example, fillers and responsives (fillers: 'uhh, mmm, uhm'; responsives: 'uh huh, ok'). These function as 'discourse markers' and can be identified by prosody and 'phoricity' (Kawamori, Kawabata and Shimazu 1998). These interjections in speech determine discourse structures and the nature of the coordination taking place (Schiffrin 1987, Kawamori et al. 1998).

The idea of such conveyance cues or communication acts was applied to body movements that are occurring in response to each other, whether this is related to a verbal utterance or independent of it. However, such conveyance cues could not apply to what was described at that time as the 'exception', the Parallel Coordinated Move. In the context of gesture, Body Moves are distinct from representational or iconic gestures of the verbal utterance as these serve primarily to illustrate it. Where in conversation, a 'move' is described as being a verbal action that causes the conversation to move forward (Carletta et al. 1997), the body move is a bodily action which initiates or responds to a bodily action or verbal utterance. However, the body move is wider in its scope as it can be a response or an initiation, and in the case of the Parallel Coordinated Move it is both in the same moment as the bodies and speech of the participants move together. And we come back to this when reflecting on the speaker-response model.

The building of the categories of Body Moves (BM) draws upon dialogue acts and features of dialogue acts, which bear parallel to the phenomena observed. Some features of dialogue acts are specific to speech and are not embodied in Body Moves, such as intonation, and asking questions or making commands. Some Body Moves have required the development of new terms in order to either demarkate between the bodily actions and their Communication Act (CA) counterpart, such as 'check', which as a body move becomes b-check, or because there appears no clear counterpart in Communication Act theory, for instance dem-ref, attempt-contact and focus. As Body Moves are Composite Dialogue Act (CDA) across more than one person, a BM can be accompanied by a CA, or accompanied by no speech; and there may only be silence or stillness, e.g. as in a pause.

It is significant that right at the outset, in distinction from conversation acts, it was held that BMs cannot be said to embody specific intentions although they could be said to embody an intention for communication itself (Gill SP et al. 2000). Body Moves could now be described as expressions of mutually manifest intentions to understand the other (drawing on Sperber and Wilson 1986).

It was mentioned above that Body Moves create contact, a 'space of engagement'. An engagement space is the composite of the participants' body fields of engagement. Hence we can call the engagement space, the body field of engagement.

The body field of engagement is set as the communication opens and the bodies indicate and signal a willingness to co-operate (This linguistic description draws on Allwood's theory 1991). The body field of engagement is a variable field and changes when participants are comfortable or uncomfortable with each other. For instance, in the case where one person moves their hand over into the other's space, and that person withdraws their hand, this indicates that the 'contact' between these persons is disrupted. There are also examples where the participants hold their bodies back from entering either's field of engagement, indicating disagreement or discrepancy in the communication, and distance rather than contact. The degree of contact or nature of distance is described in terms of commitment and attitude. Hence an immediate space of engagement involves a high degree of contact and commitment to the communication situation, whereas a passive distance is less involved and committed, and disagreement, is very distanced and commitment is withheld. Disagreement or discrepancy can necessitate a reconfiguration of the body field of engagement.

Body Moves serve to sustain our commitment to engage with each other, to transform our states of tacit knowing such that we are able to arrive at agreements and achieve topic shifts. They are moments of empathic connection.

In summary, there are two forms of Body Moves.

a) Parallel Coordinated Moves, that are moments of simultaneous coordinated autonomy. These are evidence of intersubjectivity, and where knowledge transformation occurs.

b) Other Body Moves (for present purposes shall still be called sequential), that are moments of coordinated autonomy. They serve to build common ground, and enable knowledge flow

In this next section, the empathetic connection that the Body Moves embody is analysed.

8 Musicality and Entrainment in Human Interaction

The body moves have been described as being moments of empathetic connection. Drawing on the musical term 'accent', these moments may be expressed as being 'accents' of affect (emotion), and the most heightened one is that of the Parallel Coordinated Move where the accent is of empathy. Drawing on the concept of entrainment, these accents may be described as moments of 'convergence' that culminate in the strongest moment of convergence, where transformation takes place. Body Moves are emergent beats from the interactive structures they are embedded within. These beats are pulse periodicities. In the example of the two landscape architects we can see the emergence and movement of these pulse periodicities. The affective natures of Body Moves are indicative of how the participants are relating to each other. We spoke of this dimension of affect when talking of 'contact' in the engagement space that Body Moves shape. They are expressive structures through which we sense our relationship to each other. In a talk given at the Interacting Bodies conference in 2004, the author describes these emergent beats as 'salient phenomenal beats'. And we would like to explain what we mean by this.

To do so, we need to reconsider the application of the word 'signal' to Body Moves as denoting phenomena that has phenomenological experience already embodied (Tolbert 2001). The origins of this embodiment may be seen as being shaped in motherese, the interaction between a mother and her baby. Studies of motherese (mother-infant interaction) shows how the poetic sounds/rhythms of a mother's utterances and bodily engagement differ from ordinary adult interaction, by being simplified, rhythmically repeated, exaggerated and elaborated. This, uttered universally with a high, soft, and breathy voice, and phonetic foregrounding of salient utterances, attracts and sustains attention (Miall and Dissanayake 2003). The mother exhibits alternative patterns of intimacy and observation, empathy and commentary. The aesthetics in this poetic engagement facilitates emotional attachment. They propose that evidence of the sensitivity of infants as young as 6-8 weeks old to indications (vocal, visual and kinesic) of social contingency of mothers/fathers/partners, is evidence of design in neural organization. They argue that this supports the view that mutuality or intersubjectivity - the coordinating of behavioural-emotional states with another's in temporally organized sequences - is a primary human psychobiological endowment. Mutuality is dependent on a fundamental dyadic timing matrix. Disorders of emotion, and learning in early childhood are traceable to faults in early brain growth of neural systems underlying this capacity (Trevarthen 1994, 2005).

Hence the expression 'signal' does not mean 'information', but an experientially grasped iconicity of bodily states of the movements of body and sound. With the origins rooted in motherese, each person's experiential reference system is different but there will be some shared cultural base. Predictability or tacit knowing, lies in sharing this cultural base, these points of reference in order to come together in joint attention (Tomasello 2005). Music provides a framework for thinking about this. Music's model is that in order to grasp it you have to engage with it. Musical concepts such as tempo may need to be considered to understand this dynamics, as people have different personal time-frames, and it is possible they may articulate the same temporal patterns at different rates (turn-taking, sequences), that periodically come together (i.e. the Body Moves). Also after they have reached the end of a point of negotiation as in the parallel coordinated move, the personal tempos are sychnronised. They are entrained. Entrainment is coordinating the timing of our behaviours and rhythmically synchronising our attentional resources.

This proposal that personal tempos become synchronised would support the basis on which the author identifies the body moves as being salient movements of bodies and voices playing off each other and with each other, and describing these moves as being distinct from linguistic 'turn-taking'. If one considers music performance, we can further say these movements are distinct because the participants are co-performers i.e. they are both speaking and listening to each other as performers at exactly the same time, not in terms of turn-taking as in speech. This 'musical' communicative structure is essential to arrive at parallel coordinated action.

It is proposed that this synchronisation of temporal rhythms is how two people can come to share an idea (or acknowledge each others' recognition of a mutually-manifest [Sperber and Wilson 1986] state of affairs), and through parallel and coordinated motion, they reach a heightened form of co-regulation and convergence. The use of artefacts (interactive technologies, mediating technologies, pens and paper, overhead slides, smart collaborative technologies) can influence these rhythmic coordinations and even disrupt them, and this has implications for how we manage knowledge transformation.

The examples given above of the architects coming to share an aesthetic judgment about colours, and of the participants in the simulation of query-answer web-search session of where to eat out in Tokyo, involved the shaping of a group norm of ways of doing, talking, sensing, and perceiving information. These shared norms emerged from the entrainment of their individual tempo, pitch, phrasing, of embodied experience, carried in their rhythmic synchronization, that they brought to bear on the situation, grounding and accommodating its meaning in relation to themselves and each other. In a study of beat entrainment by Himberg (2006), where two people are tapping to a metronome (the artificial beat), their tapping drifts from the metronome as they tap to the beat of each other. After some time their tapping realigns with the metronome, and then it drifts off again to each other's beat. All this happens with no awareness on the part of the 'tappers' who think they have been tapping to the metronome (the artificial beat) all along. It is not an accident that each branch of the distributed architects' firm had its own shared sense of colour, as any shared norm emerges from the movements of those that ground it.

Collective action is seen as being shaped by the movement between the individual and social situation. We achieve collective action through our understanding of the performance of representations of the tacit dimension in our communication, such as gestures, non-verbal cues, speech, and pauses, as well as artefacts of practice, including technology, evident in how we perform with them. This understanding mediates the constant transition between individual and social states. (Gill, SP 2004). The Body Moves are transitions in body and speech sound movement [Body Prosody] and these transition states appear to be associated with different types of rhythm where the sound and body motions of the participants becomes coupled, if only for a very brief moment. This coupling is considered to be part of the process of understanding, and it is expressed at a level of the social. Rhythm, tempo, pulse are our personal expression of relating with another human being and our environment, and are in that sense, social. The coupling in this picture of knowledge formation is therefore considered as being part of the social understanding of tacit knowing. It is akin to music performance. In a choir for example, singers and musicians are 'collectively engaged in the synchronous production and perception of complex patterns of sound and music' (Cross 2007, Arom 1991, Blacking 1976). In collective musical behaviour, the individual behaviours are likely to be coordinated with time and be more or less predictable in relation to each other. This collective activity therefore has a high degree of coherence which is likely to help establish a strong sense of group identity ((Stobart and Cross 2000, Cross 2007). This work from music support the idea of collective action as entrainment in the case of Body Moves. These are points of convergence in interaction, where features of musicality are drawn on in terms of interpersonal performative cues - each participant 'signalling' to the other their mutuality of understanding by 'sharing time' - the mutual sense of shared meaning that is a feature of musicality in interaction (Cross, 2007) is foregrounded and confirmed in the sharing of time.

In musical terms, body moves (of body and vocal sound) are salient and explicit and phenomenal 'beats', that are emergent from accentual structures in terms of the articulated interactive structure (interactive gestural structure such as the engagement space), i.e. the structure of the interaction embodies cues as to structural accent (some events are more salient, more differentiated, more referential in respect of the dimensions that the interaction employs) that are experienced (by an experienced observer) as phenomenal or veridical accents. Each person has different phenomenological experience embodied.

Conclusion: Cognition and Knowledge Transformation in Communication

Body Moves can be summarised as being rhythmic spontaneous coordinations of at least two people that indicate the nature of contact, resonance, and commitment within a communication situation. They span more than one body (are collective). They shape and constantly configure the engagement space of action. Body Moves enable the formation and transformation of tacit knowing and intersubjectivity (Polanyi 1964, 1966). In performing Body Moves we engage with the representations of the tacit dimension of another's actions and move with them, for example, in a design activity, or to form a shared identity. Action is the performance, whilst its tacit dimension, is its basis that is sensed, grasped, responded to, rather like music. Going back to the consultancy practice study and the colouring of the maps to share aesthetic judgment, the representation of the tacit dimension of action is the structure of the form of its expression. In engaging with the representation of the tacit dimension of another's actions, we are resonating with the communicative structures being performed. In order to be able to do so, we both draw upon experience and are experiencing in the same moment. The bodily dimension of this resonance is critical for presence. In his work on "Keeping Together in Time", (McNeill 1995) speaks of visceral and emotional sensations that come with shared movement, that he proposes endows groups with the capacity to cooperate". The Body Moves are coordinated autonomy, essential for sociality.

In the 'Tacit Dimension', Polanyi described a relation between emergence and comprehension, as existing when 'an action creates new comprehensive entities'. Parallel Coordinated Moves are multi-activity gestural coordinations, where different but related projects are being expressed in the body actions of the participants at the same time. This fusion provides the conditions for tacit transformation in a new plane of understanding from the prior periodicities that revolve around one idea, and as a result they create new comprehensive entities, expressed in the simultaneous rhythmic sychronisation of bodies and speech. The collaborative features of these moves enable the participants to negotiate and engage in the formation of a common ground (Gill SP 2002) whilst expressing different perspectives. In the 'engagement space' it is the one moment where the body fields can overlap without disturbance and co-regulation is at a heightened affective state.

For Polanyi, the body is the 'ultimate instrument of all external knowledge', and 'wherever some process in our body gives rise to consciousness in us, our tacit knowing of the process will make sense of it in terms of an experience to which we are attending'. In performing Body Moves, the ability to grasp and sense someone's motions, and respond to them appropriately (skillfully) is based on experience (tacit knowing of the process) and experiencing (experience to which we are attending). It is spontaneous action.

Hence the architects can come to see colours with shared (not same) aesthetic judgements. Knowledge or a concept is an emergent property of being engaged with another. It is a point in the knowledge flow where transformation occurs, and this emerges through, for example, acknowledging and demonstrating understanding of what someone is trying to say in the same "language" expressing mutually shared intention to understand. The concept of sharing an idea of a colour as being of a 'right shade of blue' to work with a particular shade of 'green' is borne in practice with the other's expression of experience in making judgements. The formation of concepts have underlying them a temporal flow of prosodic and modulating events (gestures, body motion, vocal sound) that is entrainment. Entrainment is coordinating the timing of our behaviours and rhythmically synchronising our attentional resources.

The identification of body moves has contributed to the conception of 'pragmatic acts' by widening the 'narrow conception of strict natural language pragmatics' (Gill SP et al. 2000; Mey 2001) and the analysis needs to be taken deeper to understand the entrainment processes in human interaction.

Non-verbal communication has already gained strong ground in different disciplines and in its significance for understanding the 'human interface, the point at which interaction occurs' (Gill SP et al. 2000). As part of this shift from cognition to communication, the international gesture society was founded in 2002. The increasing focus on the non-verbal has been reflected in the design of interactive multimodal systems, some of which was referred to above. The performance arts domains are exploring the relation between sounds (from the spectrum of recognizable speech to recognizable music) and movement in dance performance and take this understanding beyond the 'paralinguistic'.

Body moves are being applied to performance environments, e.g. dance, where they are described as a-linguistic pragmatics, emerging in the sound and visual system of the performance space (Sha and Gill SP 2005). Although they were initially coded (described or explained) within a linguistic context, this has proven to be problematic as linguistics separates the speaker (sender) and the listener (receiver).

Sender and receiver are connected through information transmission which allows for the conception of the autonomous cognitive entity, the autonomous expert, functioning with explicit knowledge. However, Body Moves are necessarily sensory couplings of engaged persons and by working with performance arts domains, their analysis has evolved to discover their essential qualities as performance periodicities of the body that are self and other oriented.

Body Moves give us a further insight into the nature and operation of 'co-presence' (Good 1996), which is an essential component of human understanding, denoting how we are present to each other, be this in the same physical space or in differing physical spaces (e.g. computer mediated spaces, virtual, or mobile technology mediated spaces, computer augmented performance spaces). Being present is described as a precondition for committed communication, but the nature of this precondition affects how we coordinate with each other and make sense and meaning. Work on the body and experiential knowledge suggests that the design of technology needs to work with these affordances of entrainment.

9. Reflections

The human-machine interface needs to afford us the resonance of structures in communication operating at multiple dimensions. As we exist within our bodies, the body may be seen as a mediating interface for the tacit and explicit interrelationship of human communication, carried through the body's movement, breath, and vocal sound; gesture, silence, and speech. This mediating interface needs to operate in the human engagement sphere and the human-machine interface needs to afford us this capacity necessary for entrainment.

It is important to root the methodology and design in a conceptual framework for the relationship between entrainment, experiential knowledge, the body, tacit knowing, and communication. Such a framework is needed for analyzing and understanding the current and future impacts on our engagement with each other and our environments when we interact with various forms of interactive technologies. This framework will always be incomplete as each new form of technology causes us to rediscover (in a long historical sense) what makes us human. However, because it is about the very fundamental layers in which culture and semantic meaning is rooted, it can evolve with the technological developments and keep apace of them.

References

Alibali, M.W.& Heath, D.C. (1999), Effects of visibility between speaker and listener on gesture production: some gestures are meant to be seen. Source of reference was this pre-published paper. (Later publication of this article: Alibali, M. W., Heath, D. C., & Myers, H. J. (2001) in Journal of Memory and Language, Vol. 44:169-188.)

Allen, J. and Core, M. (1997). DAMSL: Dialog Act Markup in Several Layers. Unpublished manuscript.

Allwood, J., Nivre, J.,& Ahlsen, E. (1991). On the Semantics and Pragmatics of Linguistic Feedback. Technical Report No. 64. Gothenburg Papers on Theoretical Linguistics.

Anderson, M.L. (2003) Embodied cognition: A field guide. Artificial Intelligence 149(1): 91-130.

Arom, S. (1991). African Polyphony and Polyrhythm: musical structure and methodology. Cambridge: Cambridge University Press.

Bateson, G. (1955). "The Message. 'This is the Play.'" In Schaffner, B. (ed.) Group Processes. Vol.II. New York: Macy.

Bavelas, J.B. (1994). Gestures as Part of Speech: Methodological Implications. Research on Language and Social Interaction. 27(3): 201-221.

Bavelas, J.B., Chovil, N., Coates, L., Rose, L. (1995). Gestures Specialized for Dialogue. In PSPB, 21(4): 394-405.

Bekerian, D.A. and Dennett, J.L. (1990). 'Spoken and Written Recall of Visual Narratives', Applied Cognitive Psychology, 175-187

Birdwhistle, R.L. (1970). Kinesics and Context. University of Pennsylvania

Blacking, J. (1976) How Musical is Man? London: Faber

Carletta, J., Isard, A., Isard S., Doherty-Sneddon, G, & Anderson, A. (1997). The Reliability of a Dialogue Structure Coding System. Association for Computational Linguistics. 23(1):13-31.

Cassell, J., Sullivan,J., Prevost, S., Churchill, E. (2000) Embodied Conversational Agents. MIT Press.

Clark, H.H. and Schaefer, E.F. (1989). Contributing to Discourse. Cognitive Science. 13:259-294.

Clark, H.H. (1996). Using Language. Cambridge: Cambridge University Press.

Clayton, M., Sager, R., and Will, U. (2005). In Time with the Music: The Concept of Entrainment and its Significance for Ethnomusicology. In European Meetings in Ethnomusicology II, ESEM CounterPoint Vol.1.

Condon, W. S., & Ogston, W. D. (1966). Sound Film Analysis of Normal and Pathological Behavior Patterns. Journal of Nervous and Mental Disease, 143:338-347.

Cross, I. (2007 in press). The Evolutionary Nature of Musical Meaning. In *Musica Scientiae*

Di Paola, S. (17th April, 2001) Gesture and Narrative Creation in Avatar-Based 3D Virtual Communities). Invited paper at Gesture and Dialogue Seminar, CSLI, Stanford University.
http://www.dipaola.org/sig99/sld002.htm

Ekman, P. and Friesen, W.V. (1969). The Repertoire of Nonverbal Behaviour: Categories, Origins, Usage, and Coding. In Semiotica. 1:49-98.

Ekman, P. and Friesen, W.V. (1972). Hand Movements. In Journal of Communication. Vol. 22: 353-374.

Eilan, N., Hoerl, C., McCormack, T., Roessler, J. (2005). Joint Attention: Communication and Other Minds. Issues in Philosophy and Psychology. Oxford: Oxford University Press.

Engle, R.A. 1998. Not Channels But Composite Signals: Speech, Gesture, Diagrams and Object Demonstrations Are Integrated in Multimodal Explanations. In Proceedings of the Twentieth Annual Conference of the Cognitive Science Society, pp. 321-327.

Ferrari P.F., Fogassi L., Gallese V., Rizzolatti G. (2003) Mirror neurons responding to the observation of ingestive and communicative mouth actions in the monkey ventral premotor cortex. European Journal of Neuroscience, 17 (8):1703-1714.

Franco, F. (1997). The Development of Meaning in Infancy: Early Communication and Social Understanding. In S. Hala (Ed.) The Development of Social Cognition. Hove: Psychology Press.

Fridlund, A.J. 1991. Sociality of Solitary Smiling: Potentiation by an Implicit Audience. In Journal of Personality and Social Psychology. 60.2: 229-240.

Gill, J.H. (2000). The Tacit Mode. Michael Polanyi's Postmodern Philosophy. New York: SUNY Press

Gill, K.S. (2007) (in this volume). Rethinking the Interaction Architecture. In SP Gill (Ed.) Cognition, Communication and Interaction. London: Springer.

Gill, S.P. (1995) Dialogue and Tacit Knowledge for Knowledge Transfer. PhD Thesis, University of Cambridge.

Gill, S.P. (1996) Aesthetic Design: Dialogue and Learning. A Case Study of Landscape Architecture. AI & Society, Vol. 9(3).

Gill, S.P. (1998). Body Language: The unspoken dialogue of Bodies in Rhythm. In Proceedings of the ESSLI Workshop on Mutual Knowledge, Common Ground and Public Information.

Gill, S.P., Kawamori, M., Katagiri, Y., Shimojima, A. (2000). The Role of Body Moves in Dialogue. In RASK, Vol.12: 89-114.

Gill, S.P. (2002). The Parallel Coordinated Move: Case of a Conceptual Drawing Task. Published Working Paper: CKIR, Helsinki. ISBN.

Gill, S.P., and Kawamori, M. (2002). Coordination of Gestures in a Non Face-to-Face Setting. In M.Rector, I.Poggi & N.Trigo (Eds.) Gestures, Meaning and Use. Porto: Fundacao Fernando Pessoa.

Gill, S.P. and Borchers, J.O. (2004). Knowledge in Co-Action: Social Intelligence in Collaborative Design Activity. AI & Society, 17(3).

Gill, S.P. (2004). Body Moves and Tacit Knowing. In Gorayska, B. and Mey, J.L. (Eds.) Cognition and Technology. John Benjamin.

Gill, S.P. (2005) Pulse Periodicity in Paralinguistic Coordination. Presented at International Conference, Interacting Bodies, Lyon, 2005.

Good, D.A. (1996). Pragmatics and Presence. AI & Society Journal. Vol.10 (3&4):309-14.

Goodwin, C. (1997). The Blackness of Black: Colour Categories as Situated Practice. In Lauren B. Resnick, Roger Saljo, Clotilde Pontecorvo, & Barbara Burge (Eds.), Discourse, Tools and Reasoning: Essays on Situated Cognition (pp.111-140). Berlin, Heidelberg, New York: Springer.

Goranzon, B. (1993). The Practical Intellect: Computers and Skills (Artificial Intelligence and Society). Springer-Verlag.

Guberina, P. (1985). The role of the body in learning foreign languages. Revue de Phonetique Applique: 37-50.

Guimbretiere, F., Stone, M., Winograd, T. (2001). Stick it on the Wall: A Metaphor for Interaction with Large Displays. Submitted to Computer Graphics (SIGGRAPH 2001 Proceedings).

Himberg, T. (2006). Co-operative tapping and collective time-keeping - differences of timing accuracy in duet performance with human or computer partner. Presentation at 9th International Conference on Music Perception and Cognition, Bologna, Italy.

Hutchins, E. (1995) Cognition in the Wild. MIT Press: Masachusetts
Ikuta, K. (1990) The Role of 'Craft Language' in Learning Waza. AI & Society, Vol. 4(2): 127-147.
Ishii, H. and Arita, K., (1991). ClearFace: Translucent Multiuser Interface for TeamWorkStation, In Proceedings of Second European Conference on Computer-Supported Cooperative Work (ECSCW '91), Amsterdam, 25-27 September. pp. 163-174.
Ishii, H. and Kobayashi, M. (1992). ClearBoard: A Seamless Media for Shared Drawing and Conversation with Eye-Contact. In Proceedings of Conference on Human Factors in Computing Systems (CHI '92), ACM SIGCHI, Monterey, pp. 525-532.
Ishii, H., Kobayashi, M. and Arita, K. (1994). Iterative Design of Seamless Collaboration Media," Communications of the ACM (CACM), Special Issue on Internet Technology, ACM, Vol. 37, No. 8.pp. 83-97.
Jeannerod, Marc. 1997. The Cognitive Neuroscience of Action. Oxford: Blackwell.
Johannessen, K.S. (1988) Rule Following and Tacit Knowledge. AI & Society, Vol. 2(4): 287-303.
Kawamori, M., Shimazu, A., Kogure, K. (1994). Roles of Interjectory Utterances in Spoken Discourse. Proceedings of the International Conference on Spoken Language Processing.
Kawamori, M., Kawabata, T., Shimazu, A. (1998). Discourse Markers in Spontaneous Dialogue: A corpus based study of Japanese and English. In Proceedings of 17th International Conference on Computational Linguistics (COLING-ACL98).
Kendon, A. (1970). Movement Coordination in Social Interaction: Some examples described. In Acta Psychologia, 32:100-125.
Kendon, A. (1972) Some Relationships Between Body Motion and Speech: An analysis of an example. In A. Seigman and B. Pope (eds.) Studies in Dyadic Communication. Elmsford, NY: Pergamon Press.
Kendon, A. (1990) Conducting Interaction. Cambridge: Cambridge University Press
Kendon, A. (2004). Gesture: Visible Action as Utterance. Cambridge: Cambridge University Press.
Kita, S. (1993). Language and thought interface: A study of spontaneous gestures and Japanese mimetics. Ph.D. thesis. Chicago, Illinois: University of Chicago.
von Krogh, G., Ichijo, K., Nonaka, I. (2000). Enabling Knowledge Creation: How to Unlock the Mystery of Tacit Knowledge and Release the Power of Innovation. OUP: Oxford
Large, E. and Jones, M.R. (1999) The Dynamics of Attending: How People Track Time-Varying Events. Pyschological Review. Vol.106(1): 119-159
Maturana, H. and Varela, F. (1980). Autopoiesis and Cognition: The Realisation of the Living. Dordecht: D. Reidel Publishing Co.
McNeill, D. (1992). Hand and Mind. Chicago: University of Chicago Press.
McNeill, W. H. (1995). Keeping together in time. London: Harvard University Press
Mey, J. (2001). Pragmatics. An Introduction. Oxford: Blackwell.
Miall, D. S., & Dissanayake, E. (2003). "The Poetics of Babytalk." Human Nature 14: 337-364.
McNeill, D., Cassell, J., McCullough, K-E. (1994). Communicative Effects of Speech-Mismatched Gestures. Research on Language and Social Interaction. 27.3: 223-237

Polanyi, M. (1964). Personal Knowledge: Towards a post critical philosophy. N.Y.: Harper and Row.

Polanyi, M. (1966). The Tacit Dimension. Doubleday. Reprinted version, 1983, Gloucester, Mass.: Peter Smith.

Pylyshyn, Z.W. (1984) Computation and Cognition. Toward a Foundation for Cognitive Science. Cambridge: CUP.

Reiner, M. and Gilbert, J. (2004) The Symbiotic Roles of Empirical Experimentation and Thought Experimentation in the Learning of Physics. International Journal of Science Education, 26:1819-1834.

Rizzolatti G., Fogassi L., Gallese V. (2001). Neurophysiological mechanisms underlying the understanding and imitation of action. Nature Reviews Neuroscience, 2: 661-670.

Saha, B. and Gangopadhyay, S. (2006) Building a Pedagogy around Action and Emotion: Experiences of Blind Opera of Kolkata. AI & Society, Vol.21: 57-71.

Scheflen, A.E. (1974). How Behaviour Means. Exploring the contexts of speech and meaning: Kinesics, posture, interaction, setting, and culture. New York: Anchor Press/Doubleday.

Schiffrin, D. (1987). Discourse Markers. Cambridge: Cambridge University Press.

Sha, X.W. (2002) Resistance Is Fertile: Gesture and Agency in the Field of Responsive Media, in Makeover: Writing the Body into the Posthuman Technoscape, Configurations, 10(3): 439-472.

Sha, X-W and Gill, S.P. (2005). Gesture and Response in Field-Based Performance. In the ACM Proceedings of Creativity and Cognition 2005, Goldsmiths College, London

Sha, X.W. (2005) "The TGarden Performance Research Project." In Modern Drama, Special Issue: Technology. 48(3):585-608.

Shannon, C. and Weaver, W. (1949). The mathematical theory of communication. Urbana, Il: University of Illinois Press.

Shimojima, A., Katagiri, Y., Koiso, H. (1997). Scorekeeping for Conversation-Construction. In Proceedings of the Munich Workshop on Semantics and a Pragmatics of Dialogue

Simon, H. (Ed.)(1982) Models of bounded rationality. Behavioral economics and business organization, 2: 424-443. Cambridge, MA: MIT Press.

Simon, H. (1969). The sciences of the artificial (1st ed). Cambridge, MA: MIT Press.

Simon, H. (1983). Reason in human affairs. Stanford, CA: Stanford UniversityPress

Sperber, D. and Wilson, D. (1986). Relevance: communication and cognition. Oxford: Blackwell.

Stobart, H. and Cross, I. (2000) The Andean Anacrusis? rhythmic structure and perception in Easter songs of Northern Potosí, Bolivia. British Journal of Ethnomusicology, 9(2): 63-94.

Tolbert, E. (2001) Music and Meaning: An Evolutionary Story. In Psychology of Music, Vol. 29, No. 1, 84-94.

Tilghman, B.R. (1988). Seeing and Seeing-As. AI & Society Journal, Vol.2(4): 303-319 London: Springer.

Tomasello, M., Carpenter, M., Call, J., Behne, T., & Moll, H. (2005). Understanding and sharing intentions: The origins of cultural cognition. Behavioral and Brain Sciences, 28: 675 - 691.

Trevarthen C., Aitken K.J. (1994): Brain development, infant communication, and empathy disorders: Intrinsic factors in child mental health. In: Development and Psychopathology, 6: 597-633. (zit. nach Trevarthen, 1996)

Trevarthen, C. (2005). "Disorganized rhythm and synchrony: Early signs of autism and Rett syndrome". In Brain & Development, 27: S25-S34.

Trevarthen, C. (2005). "First things first: infants make good use of the sympathetic rhythm of imitation, without reason or language". In Journal of Child Psychotherapy, 31(1):91-113.

Weizenbaum, J. (1966) ELIZA--A Computer Program For the Study of Natural Language Communication Between Man and MachineCommunications of the ACM. Volume 9(1) (January 1966): 36-35.

Weizenbaum, J. (1976). Computer Power and Human Reason. San Francisco: WH Freeman.

Wittgenstein, L. (1953). Philosophical Investigations.

AI & Soc (1996) 10:226–232
© 1996 Springer-Verlag London Limited

Cognitive Technology – Technological Cognition[1]

Jacob L. Mey

Institute of Language and Communication, Odense University, Denmark

Abstract: Technology, in order to be human, needs to be informed by a reflection on what it is to be a tool in ways appropriate to humans. This involves both an instrumental, appropriating aspect ('I use this tool') and a limiting, appropriated one ('The tool uses me').

Cognitive Technology focuses on the ways the computer tool is used, and uses us. Using the tool on the world changes the way we think about the world, and the way the world appears to us: as an example, a simple technology (the leaf blower) and its effects on the human are discussed.

Keywords: Technology; Cognition; Computers; Language; Pragmatics; Mind and Brain; Tool; Leaf-blower

Technology, in a very broad sense, has to do with the desire and need of people to externalize themselves (Gorayska and Mey, 1996).

The human essence obtains the birthright of existence only by externalizing itself in its products, that is, the various ways and means that people have devised to deal with their environment, the world. The common denominator for this externalizing activity, this going out of oneself, is to become 'another'; that is to say, to alienate oneself in order to become a true human self.

One of the main ways in which this alienation happens is by the creation of tools. Tools can be many things, from the simple stone that a Neanderthaler picks up to batter his rival over the head, to the extremely sophisticated machinery that modern humans surround themselves with.

Common for all tools is that they are both necessary and insufficient. That is to say, they contain always two dimensions, along one of which we realize ourselves in alienation, while along the other we lose ourselves in the otherness of the world, we become 'alienated', in a popular parlance that used to go the rounds in the 'sixties and 'seventies.

---

[1] Closing address at the First International Cognitive Technology Conference, Hong Kong, 24–29 August 1995.

Consider the following passage from Virginia Woolf:

"Let us consider letters – how they come at breakfast, and at night, with their yellow stamps and their green stamps, immortalized by the postmark – for to see one's own envelope on another's table is to realize how soon deeds sever and become alien.

Then at last the power of the mind to quit the body is manifest, and perhaps we fear or hate or wish annihilated this phantom of ourselves, lying on the table. ... Ah, but when the post knocks and the letter comes always the miracle seems repeated – speech attempted. Venerable are letters, infinitely brave, forlorn, and lost.

Life would split asunder without them (Virginia Woolf, *Jacob's Room*. Harvest ed. p. 92–93)

I think this quote shows the double dimension of alienation, in particular of technological 'otherness', in an admirable way. Letters are a kind of tool: we use them to communicate with other people, enter their otherness, so to speak, as well as to communicate our inner selves to the outer world. In doing so, we 'sever our deeds', such that they become alien, like our own letter we imagine lying on the breakfast table. The 'speech' that we 'attempt' in our letters is, in a way, always 'forlorn', doomed to remain outside ourselves, like a limb that is cut off; yet, it is the only way we have to enter the communion of human beings, 'losing our souls in order to gain them' (Matthew 16:25).

Of course, in the process of gaining ourselves, of 'saving our souls', we prefigure the final separation of the mind and the body, the eternal 'S.O.S.' that humans incessantly emit during their entire lifetimes. This final dilemma is not one that we can solve: for how could we live with a 'final solution' that only is final in the sense that it ends not just the problems, but even all the solutions?

If cognitive technology is that by which we create our cognitive tools, that by which we go 'out of our minds' to imprint ourselves into othernesses, then we must try to bridge the gap that technology creates, by focusing on the technology from a human point of view. To do that, we must deliver our 'limbs' to be 'severed' on the operating table, just as we place our letters on the chest of drawers in the hallway to be opened and read. But there must also be a counterpart to this analyzing and severing, to this opening up, viz., a human activity by which we put the severed limbs together again; not only open, but read, understand, and absorb the letters we have written to ourselves. Dealing with technology is then not just a matter of understanding it, analyzing it from its technical outside in: we must understand the technology from its human inside out, so to speak. (Gorayska and Mey, 1996).

Let's consider a concrete example of how technology affects the mind. I will talk about a rather pedestrian form of technology, one that many of us are at least passively familiar with: the leaf blower. For those who are not acquainted with this masterpiece of technological innovation, a leaf blower is simply a piece of tube with a power blower at one end; the air stream that is generated can be directed by pointing the one end of the tube at the stuff I want to move: leaves, twigs, loose gravel and sand, and all sorts of garden related detritus. Basically, what the leaf blower does is what the broom used to do, except that the moving force no longer is the human muscle but an air stream generated by a technological gadget, a fan joined to a gasoline powered motor.

In our suburban society, leaf blowers are the object of much controversy, mainly because they make so much noise. On any normal Saturday or Sunday, their monotonous drone is always present, and most of the time rather annoying, especially when you have perfectionist neighbours who want their driveways to resemble their living room floors after the wives have been there with the vacuum cleaner. But since you are probably the proud owner of such a wondrous instrument yourself, you put up with it, and inflict the same punishment on your neighbours when your time comes to clean the porch, the driveway, the sidewalks, and of course the precious lawn.

From the point of view of the result obtained, the leaf blower is certainly a more effective instrument than its predecessor, the broom. The dirt gets removed more quickly, more efficiently, and more explicitly: you certainly are letting the surrounding humanity know that you are busy doing your garden chores. On the negative side we have, of course, the infernal noise (people should wear hearing protection while operating this instrument, just like the ground traffic controllers in an airport).

But there is another effect which is truly 'mind-blowing', if you will excuse the pun: we start thinking differently about the operation itself of yard-cleaning, which the new tool allows us to carry out in a novel way. And it is here that technology has its true impact on the mind: it affects our mental attitude towards ourselves and our environment. As Gavriel Salomon has remarked (in another, educationally-oriented setting – he is commenting on the well-publicized but rather disappointing results of training programs such as LOGO), "working with tools does not teach much in and of itself. It is the thinking that accompanies [tool]-afforded activities that may have an impact." (1992:13)

Which is precisely the point here. While technology changes the world, in that it allows us to perform certain, familiar operations in another, novel way, the effects of this change operate on us, in their turn, and change our way of thinking about the world; in this particular case about garden rubbish and how to remove it, and why – not to speak of the 'where to' problem, the old question already raised by Ján Neruda trying to dispose of a straw mattress in nineteenth-century cholera-ridden Prague (1853).

Leaf blowing is usually a typical case of sweeping things under the rug, if one can say that: you don't pick up the small heaps of dirt that your blower has created, but you try to blow them out of sight, if not out of existence (your existence) altogether, over to the neighbours' or the city's sphere of responsibility. What earlier was an object of collection upon removal, is now just an object of removal. We think about garden rubbish in a different way.

Consequently upon this thinking, another innovative thought process is taking place: we start to see the entire operation of garden upkeep in a different manner. Whereas we earlier might have tolerated a certain level of unorderliness (say, a certain number of leaves on the grass would be permitted, since it would be near-impossible to get them all out, using a hand-held rake or a broom), the leaf blower forces us to think of a garden lawn as a living room carpet on which even the tiniest white thread is a thorn in the eye and the possible igniting fuse of violent, domestic dispute. 'I gave you this vacuum cleaner, so why don't you use it properly?', a model husband would feel entitled to say. Similarly, the consensus of the neighbourhood is that a man who doesn't know how to wield a leaf-blower to create that spotless lawn is a blemish on the environment, a blot on the streetscape.

To illustrate this, let me recount a personal anecdote.

In the early morning hours of August 13, 1995, a Sunday, I saw a man at Caddo Lake State Park, in a place called Uncertain, Texas, use a blower to clean Park Road

#2, which is the road that connects the park to Texas 2315, and on to the campsites and cabins. This road goes nowhere; it is strictly a 'park road', that is, it is wholly within the confines of a nature reservation where you, among other things, cannot carry a loaded firearm, display alcohol or pornography, and so on.

The one fact that struck me immediately was the bizarreness of this person clearing a road, going through the woods, of all woodsy remnants such as leaves, twigs, sand, branches and other natural debris that might have collected during the night (or maybe week, if this was a typical Sunday morning operation).

One used to make fun of the Dutch for 'washing the streets', referring to their custom of cleaning their porches, the so-called 'stoops', with buckets of water, pails and brooms, every Saturday. The picture of maids in bonnets bending over the blue sandstone that was the favorite material for these structures, and scrubbing to their masters' hearts' delight is one of my earliest childhood memories. That work seemed to me, even at that time, to be a hard to rationalize use of human labor ('nigger' labor, as we were wont to say). Now why was this park employee (and he wasn't even black) seemingly happily doing this kind of slave work; and even more poignantly, why was he in such an absurd way trying to clean the forest of leaves and branches?

Naturally, the man was not doing all this on his own instigation; he was a park employee having been given orders to do precisely that. But suppose the park authorities had given this same man an old fashioned broom and dustpan, to perform what was exactly the same chore: cleaning a forest road for traces of nature. He probably would have balked at this assignment, and said that, in the old days, they would call this nigger work, and he wasn't going to do it. What's more, he would probably not have been able to see the point of doing it at all.

That point, finally, is relative to the instrument he was supposed to use, a blower instead of a broom, and can be formulated as follows: the nature of his tool changed his outlook on the labor to be performed. What had been classified as slave labor, now became ennobled because of the blower. The leaf-blower changed the mind of the worker, so that while earlier, he would have had nothing to do with the business if he wanted to keep his self-respect, now, with the help of the blower, he was happy to perform this absolutely idiotic task with a good conscience, and perhaps, God knows, even with pride.

Technology as such is unspecific as to its aims, and it has no roots in society. Technology as such is not plagued by associations of slave labor; no ghosts of housewife chores are left to deal with. By contrast, real 'human' labor is always anchored in some specific tradition, and as such is part of a societal whole (whether one likes it or not) – as in the case of my Norwegian neighbour, who once remarked, when he saw me hang up clothes after a bout of laundering: 'Women's work'. Had I had an automatic clothes distributor and -suspender, he probably would have admired my technological innovative prowess.

To sum up what we have been discussing so far:

While technology and its applications change the world, its effects on the world change the mind, but do this on the rebound, so to speak. We should, therefore, properly distinguish between these two kinds of effects as being of different orders: the first order representing the effects of technology on the world, the second order of technological innovation comprising the (indirect) effects of these changes on the mind.

Borrowing Herbert Simon's (1982) famous car example, I want to distinguish between the mere introduction of the automobile as a technological device (the horseless carriage' replacing the horse-driven vehicle)[1] and the adoption of the car as the device that allows us to 'Discover America: Best By Car' (as a US Mail stamped slogan had it in the 'sixties), or our second home-on-wheels, or a place of making out when you are a teenager, or an instrument of defining yourself in the eyes of your colleagues and neighbours, or even a spare bedroom on four wheels, as Salomon (1992) has put it.

This second order of effects is where the technology defines us, such that driving an old car around a posh neighbourhood may result in your being pulled over and questioned by the police (as happened to me once in Larchmont, N.Y.); parking your blue Ford Torino 1976 station wagon on the nice street in Evanston, Ill. where you happen to have lived on and off for three years or so, will sooner or later result in the police sticking one of those red notices on your window telling you to remove your jalopy within 7 days, or else...

Thus, not only is one man's pride his neighbour's eyesore: if beauty is in the eye of the beholder, then technology is, in a strict sense of the word, in the mind of the user. It is those *mind effects* of technology that are of the greatest interest to us in connection with cognition. We turn therefore now to the intricate question of the cognitive tool and what it does to the mind.

What defines a cognitive tool, as opposed to other tools? And how does the cognitive tool specifically influence our thinking? These are the two questions that circumscribe the domains of cognitive technology, and technological cognition respectively (on these terms, see Gorayska and Mey, 1996; Gorayska and Marsh, 1996). The specificity of the cognitive tool, as opposed to, say, a hammer or a car, is that it directly affects, and operates upon, the workings of our mind. In general, purely reproductive tools have little cognitive interest: a Xerox copier is not by itself a cognitive tool (in the normal case, and barring certain imaginative uses), while the typewriter, inasmuch as it interacts with our mind in forming our thoughts on paper, is a cognitive tool (albeit a primitive one, compared to a computer).

Of course, the distinction between cognitive and non-cognitive tools is by no means a watertight one. I could easily imagine some cognitive effects arising from, say, using an ax to clear virgin forest; after all, every tool is an expression of the human mind in the surrounding material world, as we saw earlier. But the cognitive tool is specialized for mental functions, as one sees easiest by contemplating the tool for thought by excellence, the human wetware a.k.a. as the brain.

I must emphasize that the brain by itself wouldn't be anything but a complicated, rather uninteresting collection of cells and intricate wiring. It is by using the brain in a cognitive activity that the effects of its typical mode of operation become apparent. Which is when we can start speaking of the influence that the activities of the brain as a cognitive tool have on our cognitive activity, on our thinking.

Here, too, the limitations of the analogy (so popular in our days) between the brain and a computer become clear. As a tool for cognition, the brain 'is' a kind of computer; but it is through its cognitive use that it becomes a true carrier of human

---

[1]Actually still the name of a small automotive business in Thrall, Texas (45 miles out of Austin on US 79): 'The Horseless Carriage Company'.

cognitive technology. And vice versa, this use spawns a cognition which is no longer 'general purpose', indiscriminate as to origin and effects, but is a specifically technological one: one that is geared to, and dependent on, the particular tools that the human brain has produced. Brains are always custom-made: but the customizing is not done by some computer company, or even God Himself as the super computer software creator and systems support person. The brain's customized design depends entirely on what we, as users, do with it and how we choose to weight and assign its essential functions.

Incidentally, as to the computer itself, the analogy operates in the same fashion. The computer is also what we make it: its functions arise not out of the software alone, but through the feedback effects of software (and hardware, of course) on the user.

Cognitive technology thus turns necessarily (although not automatically) into technological cognition (Gorayska and Marsh, 1996). I said: 'not automatically', because the necessity is one that we need to realize and make our own. The conditions for using technology are not in the technology alone, but in the minds of the users. To vary Kant's famous dictum, cognition without technology is empty, but technology without cognition is dangerous and blind. Our minds need the computer as a tool, but we need to consciously integrate the computer into our minds before we start using it on a grand scale. In this way (and in this way only), rather than being a mindless technological contraption, the computer may become a true tool of the mind.

Technology creates gadgets that can be put to use without regard for their essential functions. What, in the end, such gadgets do to ourselves and to our environment, however, is not necessarily anybody's concern in their actual conditions of use, in which the mind-captivating (not to say mind-boggling) fascination of advanced technology allows us to focus on the intermediate stage between intent and effect, the purely technological one.

To take a simple example, pressing a button is, in itself, a neutral activity; yet it can in the end cause a door bell to ring just as well as it may detonate a nuclear explosion. 'I just pressed a button', the pilot who launched Fat Boy on Hiroshima could have said. And if Timothy McVeigh (one of the three persons indicted in the 1995 Oklahoma City bombing of the Federal Building that took 165 lives) would have had to kill all those 165 people by hand, he never would have gotten beyond the first two or three, especially if he had started out with the babies. Now he could just connect some wires, and leave it at that. Technology does the work; our minds are at rest.

Garrison Keillor, in his program Lake Wobegone, 12 August 1995, offered a philosophical reflection on Halloween pranks. His point was that you are responsible even for the unknown, and unintended, effects of the fun you have (the example was of some boys at Halloween disconnecting a box car and sending it out on the tracks). What determines your responsibility is the outcome; he called this a strictly 'outcome-based morality'.

Applying this to our subject from a slightly different point of view, one could talk of a pragmatic view of technology and cognition. The pragmatics of cognitive technology (CT) deals with technology's effects on the users and their environment; a pragmatic view of technological cognition (TC) implies that we inquire into the conditions that determine that cognition, that is the conditions under which users can cognize their technology, in order to realize the effects of their technological efforts.

We need pragmatics in our CT so that it can be environmentally correct; we need pragmatics for our TC to be morally sound.

References

Gorayska, B. and Marsh, J. (1996). Epistemic Technology and Relevance Analysis: Rethinking Cognitive Technology. In Gorayska and Mey (eds.) *Cognitive Technology: In search of a humane interface.* Amsterdam/New York: North Holland/Elsevier. (*Advances in Psychology,* 113)

Gorayska, B. and Mey, J. L. (1996). Of Minds and Men. In Gorayska and Mey (eds.) *Cognitive Technology: In search of a humane interface.* Amsterdam/New York: North Holland/Elsevier. (*Advances in Psychology,* 113)

Neruda, J., (1854). *Kam s ním?* Prague: Melantrich. ['How to get rid of it?']

Salomon, G. (1992). Computers' first decade: Golem, Camelot, or the Promised Land? Invited talk at the AERA Meeting, April 1992, San Francisco. (Draft MS)

Simon, H. (1982). *The sciences of the artificial.* Cambridge, Mass.: MIT Press.

Correspondence and offprint requests to: Jacob L. Mey, Institute of Language and Communication, Odense University, DK 5230 Odense M, Denmark. E-mail: jam@language.ou.dk

AI & Soc (2003) 17: 322–339
DOI 10.1007/s00146-003-0286-6

ORIGINAL ARTICLE

Satinder P. Gill · Jan Borchers

Knowledge in co-action: social intelligence in collaborative design activity

Received: 29 January 2003 / Accepted: 21 July 2003 / Published online: 11 October 2003
© Springer-Verlag London Limited 2003

Abstract Skilled cooperative action means being able to understand the communicative situation and know how and when to respond appropriately for the purpose at hand. This skill is of the performance of knowledge in co-action and is a form of social intelligence for sustainable interaction. Social intelligence, here, denotes the ability of actors and agents to manage their relationships with each other. Within an environment we have people, tools, artefacts and technologies that we engage with. Let us consider all of these as dynamic representations of knowledge. When this knowledge becomes enacted, i.e., when we understand how to use it to communicate effectively, such that it becomes invisible to us, it becomes knowledge in co-action. A challenge of social intelligence design is to create mediating interfaces that can become invisible to us, i.e., as an extension of ourselves. In this paper, we present a study of the way people use surfaces that afford graphical interaction, in collaborative design tasks, in order to inform the design of intelligent user interfaces. This is a descriptive study rather than a usability study, to explore how size, orientation and horizontal and vertical positioning, influences the functionality of the surface in a collaborative setting.

Keywords Coordinated autonomy · Graphical interaction · Knowledge in co-action · Parallel coordinated moves · Social intelligence

S.P. Gill (✉)
Center for the Study of Language and Information (CSLI), Stanford University, USA
E-mail: sgill@csli.stanford.edu

J. Borchers
Department of Computer Science, ETH Zentrum, Switzerland

This paper is a revised version of the paper "Knowledge in co-action: social intelligence in using surfaces for collaborative Design Tasks', presented at the International Workshop on Social Intelligence Design, Royal Holloway College, London, 5–7 July 2003

1 Introduction: knowledge in co-action

In this paper we focus our analysis on how we engage with the representations of another's actions and move with these representations when interacting in a joint design activity using various types of surfaces. Particular emphasis is on the rhythmic patterns in this coordination, and observations of how the use of artefacts can influence these. The motivation behind this focus is to understand the formation and transformation of knowledge in communication. It is located within a framework that sees cognition as a dynamic system that co-evolves and emerges through the interaction of mind, body and environment. This co-evolution includes body moves (kinesics and kinaesthetics) that give the cognitive dynamic system meaning. Previous work on the metacommunicative[1] body dynamics of the engagement space (Gill, Kawamori, Katagiri, Shimojima 2000) showed that composite dialogue acts, of gesture, speech and silence (body moves), play an important role in the flow of information in interaction. Body moves are forms of behavioural alignments.

Skilled cooperative action seems to depend on specific types of behavioural alignments between actors in an environment. These alignments allow for a degree of coordination or resonance between actors that constitutes the knowledge they have available to them, both explicitly and implicitly. Knowledge is seen here as a process that is dynamically represented in actors' behaviours and the tools, technologies and other artefacts within an environment. These behaviours involve the sense of touch, sound, smell and vision. We will focus on touch, sound and vision in this study. Coordinated structures of these behaviours and artefacts—structures which can be extended and transformed through technology—form the interactional space in which the process of knowledge creation through co-action takes place. This analysis of coordinated structures in skilled cooperative action involves understanding what constitutes the socially intelligent behaviour that we takes so much for granted in our everyday behaviour. As a framework, the idea of social intelligence has been defined[2] as the ability of a collection of actors/agents to learn and to solve problems as a function of social structure, and to manage their relationships with each other through intelligent actions. Our study of such intelligent action is presented in this paper, through a study of body moves of designers collaborating and negotiating. It lies within the scope of social intelligence design that involves the detailed understanding of interpersonal actions exhibited during the course of computer-mediated or conventional communication environments in search for better design of communication media.

---

[1] Scheflen (1975) on the relation between kinesics (movements) and language: the former can "qualify or give instructions" about the latter in a relation that Bateson (1955) called metacommunicative, whereby the "movement of the body helps in clarifying meaning by supplementing features of the structure of language. Body moves do just this, and contribute further to the idea that the structure of language lies in its performance.

[2] Toyoaki Nishida's summary of the idea of social intelligence in his paper at the close of the Social Intelligence Design Conference, at the Royal Holloway, London, 2003.

324

Fig. 1 Physical contact enabled at surfaces

In the analysis that follows, we have found that certain behavioural alignments (e.g., the body move showing acknowledgement,[3] and suggestions (Fig. 1) operate upon the surface of the interfaces, e.g., by touching, pointing actions and suggest that touch influences the implicit formation of ideas. This haptic dimension of knowledge is part of the body move and other salient behavioural alignments that we will present here. The relation between touch and implicit knowledge has been investigated by Reiner (2003, 1999). She studies, for example, how the touch language learnt by surgeons who acquire this through experience, linking patterns of touch with interpretations in a non-symbolic manner. Related to this, she also studies how gestures are part of physics learning.

Our research also shows that design activities take place in zones of interaction within the configurations of the space of engagement around the surface(s), to reflect, negotiate and act. We note how these zones are blurred when physical contact is enabled at surfaces (as in Fig. 1), but demarcated when they are not enabled. This is not always evident in speech, but is visible in the spatial and movement orientation around the surface(s) and between participants.

2 The studies

The analysis in this paper is taken from an experiment and an observation study, to explore how people coordinate their interaction in a shared task. Students in pairs (dyads) and groups were asked to undertake collaborative conceptual drawing tasks, and student design projects, using the following affordances:

---

[3] "Acknowledge (Ack). The acknowledge move gives an idea of the attitude of the response, i.e., how the person hears and understands and perceives, what is being discussed. It shows continued attention. In the discourse act (DA) "acknowledge", this aspect of acknowledge, which was raised by Clark and Schaefer (1989), has not been included because it leaves no trace in a dialogue transcript to be coded. However, it is a part of the body move. The hearer or listener demonstrates, with his gesture, how he is acknowledging the other's proposal or request for agreement. The body move occurs in response to the other's verbal information reference or suggestion, and their body release-turn or bodily placeholder. Its associated DA is the speech act "ack" or "accept. The movement creates a change in the *degree* of contact which indicates the nature of the acknowledgement or acceptance." (Gill, Kawamori, Katagiri and Shimojima 2000)

a) paper and pens b) a shared white board c) SmartBoards (electronic white-boards for Web browsing, typing up session notes, drawing mock-ups, and viewing their work). In the student projects using the multiple SmartBoards a range of activities were recorded and some salient categories identified as fol-lows: device interface, interaction dance, attention control, team communication and personal work.[4] We have sought to capture the management of both the body and speech spaces within a task where you need to produce something together and agree upon it, i.e., in the performance of knowledge in co-action.

The experiment involved two drawing surfaces, used by different sets of subjects, a whiteboard and a SmartBoard. This is a large-scale computer-based graphical user interface, and is touch-sensitive (an electronic whiteboard). "Smart" technology does not permit two people to touch the screen at the same time. The contrast between drawing at the "smart" and the whiteboard was expected to reveal whether or not there are particular differences in body moves and gesture and speech coordination at these interfaces. Preliminary analyses[5] reveal that the participants' commitment, politeness and attention to each other becomes reduced at a single SmartBoard, showing behaviours that are in marked contrast to those of users at a whiteboard. Furthermore, the quality of the resulting design is lower when using the SmartBoard.[6]

Acting in parallel, e.g., drawing on the surface at the same time, involves a degree of autonomy that is coordinated, i.e., where the designers are aware of where and how they are in relation to the other. *The management of coordinated autonomy is culturally determined.* In our study we observe patterns of move-ment from sequential (e.g., turn taking) to parallel actions, as part of this design activity, and suggest that *coordinated autonomous action is part of sustainable collaborative activity.*[7] The role of autonomy within collaboration is an idea that lies at the heart of this research and has implications for any kind of collabo-rative activity, including cross-cultural collaboration. For instance, in the study, when a group of four users has three SmartBoards available to them, there appears to be a transposition of the patterns of autonomy and cooperation that one finds between a pair of users working on a whiteboard.

The focus of our analysis is of the gestures participants use to manage their interactions with each other and the interface during collaborative activity. This activity takes place in the "iRoom", which is the laboratory of the Stanford Interactive Workspaces project[8] (Guimbretiere, Stone and Winograd 2001). The study will raise issues for designing mediating interfaces that could support collaborative human activities to involve sustainable and committed engage-ment of the self and the interpersonal self.

---

[4] Some examples of behaviours are: device interface: right clicking, marker fixing, dragging, reaching, tapping, comparing, referring to paper, erasing; interaction dance: side stepping, pacing, stepping back, hand waving, cutting in, waiting, bumping, peeking, touching (others); attention control: pointing, asking permission, directing, teaching, concurrent control, pos-turing, calling out; team communication: reading aloud, catching up, filling in, talking, swag-gering, sharing, taking turns, role-playing; personal work: reading, note-taking, scanning, browsing, watching, concentrating, viewing, drawing and pointing.

[5] For a preliminary discussion of this research, see: Borchers, Gill and To (2002).

[6] This could in part be due to the awkwardness of the interface for producing smooth drawings.

[7] The relationship between autonomy and sustainable collaboration is being developed in a forthcoming paper by the author.

[8] http://graphics.stanford.edu/projects/iwork/

3 Parallel coordinated moves and collaborative activity

In 2001, whilst exploring the affordances of SmartBoard technology, we found that a SmartBoard's inability to allow for parallel action at the surface of the task being undertaken by participants, made for a useful case bed of data to analyse how such action affords collaborative activity. In the process of our observations, we also discovered that the use of multiple SmartBoards produced similar patterns of behavioural alignments of body moves and parallel actions (see Borchers, Gill and To 2002), but in a very different form, to those undertaken at a whiteboard or over a sheet of paper on a horizontal surface (table). When one has to wait one's turn to act at the surface, it may (a) take longer to build up the experiential knowledge of that surface than if one could move onto it when one needs to, and (b) there is a time lag for the other person working with you to experience with you, in a manner of speaking, your experience of the situation, i.e., there is an awareness lag. The former and the latter difficulties are, we suggest, linked because of this experiential dimension of tacit or implicit knowledge. With multiple boards in parallel use, awareness of the experience seemed more fluid than that of a dyad at the one board, evident in the movements around the boards to gather and disperse where rhythms in behavioural alignment were halted.

The interest in parallel coordinated action first arose during a study of landscape architects working on a conceptual design plan. The study focused on analysing the metacommunicative dynamics of body and speech coordination, and identified various body moves (Gill, Kawamori, Katagiri and Shimojima 2000). These are a kind of interactional synchrony (Birdwhistle 1970). One of these body moves was coded as the parallel coordinated move (PCM). This contrasts in rhythm to the other body moves whose action-reaction rhythms maintain the flow of information in the communication situation by participants. It was further analysed (Gill 2002) to understand its quality. During a five-minute video excerpt of architects working on a conceptual design plan, this PCM occurred only once and lasted 1.5 seconds. It was salient because it was the first time in that session that the disagreement between two architects was able to find a resolution, and it involved both their bodies acting on the surface at the same time, even whilst presenting alternative design plans. One of them was silent and the other speaking. It enabled the grounding in the communication to come into being (see Gill 2002 for a deeper analysis of the PCM) by enabling an open space for the negotiation of differences and possibilities for creative co-construction. The opening and closure of the PCM is by action-response body moves. For example, the "focus" move involves a movement of the body towards the area the "speaker" or "actor" is attending to, i.e., space of bodily attention, and in response causes the listener or other party to move his or her body towards the same focus.

In order to understand the PCM further, and to gather more examples for analysis, a number of configurations for a similar task were set up to collect further video data. These are the studies reported here. One task set was for dyads of students to design shared dorm living spaces. We also collected data and made a preliminary analysis of group activity where students are using multiple large-scale surfaces, i.e., SmartBoards (Borchers, Gill and To 2002).

The PCM is explored as a category of body move that has its own set of variable configurations, where the basic common defining feature is that participants act at the same time. In this paper, we concentrate on such actions taking place upon the surface of the interface, and the contexts within which these occur. Such actions, for example, can be to indicate ideas or proposals with a pen or finger or hand. We also consider the cases where only one participant has physical contact with the surface in order to glean some understanding of what the function of touching is, and reflect on that back to the case of parallel action.

4 Examples from the case studies

We will consider examples from two settings: a) using felt pens and standing at a whiteboard, b) using electronic pens, fingers and hands (tools that can produce representations on the surface) and standing at a SmartBoard, and marginally draw upon two other settings for reflection, namely: c) using paper and pen, and seated at a table; d) using paper and pen, and standing at a table. Using these examples, we will compare alignments and indicate salient phenomena that need deeper exploration for an understanding of how the configuration and affordances of surfaces influences collaborative activity.

4.1 The haptic connection

There is something about the contact that is made when standing at a horizontal surface that may alter the possible modes of configuration to communicate information, from the situation of standing at a vertical surface. When standing at a horizontal surface, the eye contact between participants is available without departing from the particulars in the locus of the surface. In the following examples (Figs. 2, 3, 4), we consider a case where one person is looking at the other. In Fig. 2 the person at the whiteboard (A) has to turn his head from the surface to see the person (B) who is standing back from it. There is neither a haptic connection via the artefact nor is the representation visually available to him, at that moment. (A) is discussing the location of a fireplace in the design of a room, which he has touched with a pointing hand gesture before he turns his head away. The use of deictics and his contact with the surface, enables (A) to locate the idea both for himself and for (B) who maintains a gaze on it, such that he (A) does not need it in front of him at that moment. This pattern is repeated by other dyads at whiteboards.

In the case of the architects (Fig. 3) standing at the drawing-table, the person to the left (P) has his hand on the drawing surface and is holding a pen (in this case, he is holding a position or idea), whilst his speech acknowledges ("yeh") what the person to his right (W) is saying. (W) is pointing to another particular place on the drawing and making a design suggestion. P is holding an idea and W proposing an idea. The contact on the surface allows for both acts simultaneously.

At the SmartBoard, pointing or touching acts at the surface, operate upon it causing marks. Hence, when such acts do occur, it is to explicitly suggest an idea by drawing it, or if it is not intended as an operation the result is an unintended

Fig. 2 A touches the surface, then turns his head to see B

Fig. 3 Surface contacts allowing for simultaneous acts

Fig. 4 Pointing over the surface combined with looking at another to communicate an idea

mark or two.[9] Acting on the surface seems to be to make things clear, e.g., in seeking confirmation or to emphasise a position. In this case, we find that instead of pointing directly on the surface, pointing combined with looking at the other person to whom one is communicating an idea, is done by keeping the hand hovered over the place one is referring to (as in Fig. 4).

---

[9] Work at Berkeley on Transient Ink is a potential solution, leaving marks that disappear after a while (Everitt, Klemmer, Lee, and Landay, 2003)

The haptic dimension in these examples seems to be important in its combination with vision, for touch surfaces that permit non-operational contact. Compensation for not being able to use the surface of the SmartBoard is to hold one's hand over the specific point or idea being proposed for a specific location. We do know from work by Gregory (1963) on touch and creativity, that there is a direct relation to being able to create conceptual designs and having the ability to tactilely feel our world. Although that work primarily concerns the individual's experience, it bears upon the collaborative experience in these design tasks given the physical role of the body, and where physical autonomy within coordinated parallel action constitutes a form of joint action. This cohesion between the virtual or imaginary, the tactile and the physical connection of coordinated movement involves social intelligence, i.e., it requires us to be able to use our bodies in rhythmic coordination with speech to share and co-create knowledge.

So far, in Figs. 2, 3, 4 we have considered three surfaces, all involving standing positions, and the making or holding of a specific design idea by a designer(s) at a specific location on a conceptual design plan. We made observations about how looking at another person and away from the surface, whilst touching it (the drawing-table), and after touching it (the whiteboard), involves certain kinds of behavioural alignments that differ from the use of pointing gestures held above the surface during the period of looking away from it (the SmartBoard).

4.2 Narrative and virtual space

Let us consider the case of zones, which were introduced earlier in the paper. In Fig. 3 (the drawing-table) one architect is acting on the surface and the other reflecting on the surface. *The narrative space lies in between the bodies and the surface, where the surface provides a mediating point of contact within it.*[10] In Fig. 2, neither are acting upon the surface of the whiteboard, but are negotiating and reflecting. The *narrative space lies in a virtual space between the bodies*, and the point on the surface that is being discussed, has been identified with a prior touch. The person to whom it was indicated (B) can look at it and at the proposer (A). In the case of the SmartBoard (Fig. 4), neither are acting on its surface, but are negotiating and reflecting with a hand held over the part on the surface being discussed. The hand position is needed whilst the idea is clarified in the mind of the person proposing it,[11] and they do not move into a virtual narrative space away from the surface until the idea becomes clear enough for such discussion.[12]

4.3 Engagement space

At this juncture, it may be helpful to situate this discussion about zones, and the use of hands and eyes to make contact, in the context of the engagement space (Gill et al. 2000; Gill 2002). The engagement space has been defined as the arena within which coordinated body movements take place in interactive settings.

---

[10] This is work in progress in a forthcoming paper by Satinder Gill.
[11] This could be another category of body move.
[12] This is a hypothesis and not a statement of fact, but is under analysis.

These movements take place within shifting spaces of engagement. An *engagement space* may be defined as the aggregate of the participants' body fields of engagement. An engagement field is based on some commitment in being bodily together. Hence we can call the engagement space, the *body field of engagement*. In defining this space, it was most useful to draw upon Allwood et al.'s theory of communicative acts (1991) where they speak of participants signalling and indicating their orientation to each other.[13] In so doing they can increase commitment by increasing contact.

The body field of engagement is set as the communication opens and the bodies indicate and signal a willingness to co-operate. The body field of engagement is a variable field and changes depending on the participants being comfortable or uncomfortable with each other. For instance, in the case where one person moves their hand over into the other's space, and that person withdraws their hand, this indicates that the 'contact' between these persons is disturbed. The degree of contact and the nature of distance are expressed in terms of commitment and attitude. Hence an *immediate* space of engagement involves a high degree of contact and commitment to the communication situation, whereas a *passive distance* is less involved and committed, *disagreement*, is very distanced and commitment is withheld.

Disagreement or discrepancy can necessitate a *reconfiguration* of the body field of engagement due to a disturbance in the relationship between the speakers, so that a feeling of sharing an engagement space is re-established. This reconfiguration is a rhythmic bodily reshaping of the field of engagement. This category of action occurs because there is a problem in the overlap in one body's field of engagement with the other body's field. Note that if there is no problem in the overlap of their respective fields, the participants can undertake parallel co-ordinated moves.

4.4 Engagement space and zones of interaction

The spatial fluidity of the zones (reflection, negotiation and action) of interaction makes it challenging to provide a definitive demarcation of their boundaries in terms of simply physical space, as such a demarcation does not help to explain how the zones work together when the designers are in more than one zone at the same time. Further, we need a framework to understand the movements from one zone to another. The zones were initially observed as being in distinct physical areas as depicted in Fig. 5: from left to right—reflection, negotiation, and action:[14]

---

[13] Allwood, Nivre and Ahlsen (1991) pay special attention to the context sensitivity of feedback. Aspects of their theory were adapted for the body situation, such as 'contact'. The four basic communicative functions are: 1) *Contact*; 2) *Perception*, 3) *Understanding*; 4)*Attitudinal reactions*. Winograd and Flores (1986)emphasise 'the need for continued mutual recognition of commitment' (p.63) that we find expressed in the maintenance of the 'engagement space' and they speak of communication as 'dance', a metaphor suited for Body Moves. Further, their argument for 'sufficient coupling' to ensure freguent breakdowns and a standing commitment by [participants] to enter into dialogue in the face of breakdown, is helpful for understanding the role of parallel coordinated motion for sustaining collaborative activity.

[14] This emerged when reflecting out loud with Renate Fruchter, Stanford University, in the Spring of 2002, about Donald Schon's work, in relation to this study.

Fig. 5 Reflection, negotiation and action

1. Reflection zone: if one person is acting at the surface, and the other person is standing further back and silently observing this action then he or she is reflecting. If both are standing back and looking at the surface, then both are reflecting. This state does not involve any immediate intent to act.
2. Negotiation zone: If both are engaging about an idea and there is some movement or indication to access the surface, then this occurs in the negotiation zone.
3. Action zone: this takes place upon the surface and involves direct physical contact with it.

The categorisation of zones does, however, provide a helpful description of a base level pragmatic activity above that of the metacommunicative (e.g., body moves) and we can see how the latter work in relation to them. By drawing upon the framework of the engagement space, we can see how the metacommunicative level of communication carries the fluidity of the zones, as it operates within movement, time, and space.

In Figs. 2, 3, 4, when looking away from the surface, the engagement space alters and bodily contact increases with the act of (A) opening the frontal part of his body and eye contact to the other person (B). In the case of the whiteboard, engaging (B) involves two steps on (A)'s part; first to touch the surface to indicate the idea and to hold its location for himself, and then turning to look at (B) and engage him in a discussion about it. In the case of the drawing-table, the (P) increases contact in two steps. He enters the floor space of the drawing by placing one hand down upon it, holding a pen, with his gaze on the place he has an idea about. His fingers and pen are moving in his hand in rhythm with the speech and motion of the other architect (W), but his hand is in a fixed position. After touching the surface, (P) looks at (W) to acknowledge his action and gauge it. The increase in contact using the SmartBoard, involves two steps. First, the designer (C) locates the idea with his hand gesture, and then opens his frontal body and eye contact to the other designer (D) whilst holding his hand gesture.

All three examples indicate or invite increased commitment in the engagement space, and make for increased contact. The body fields of the designers are not overlapping.

When a designer is making contact with the surface to act upon it, whilst the other person is doing so too, there is an attempt to engage with the body field of the other person, as in the case of the architects. It also happens in the example that Fig. 1 is taken from. In Fig. 6 the designer on the right side, close to us (E),

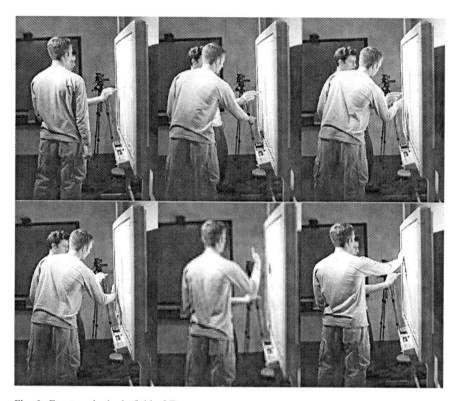

Fig. 6 E enters the body field of F

enters the body field of the other one (F) who is currently drawing (the action zone), and uses his index finger to trace out a shape that denotes a bed. He is proposing this idea to (F) who is drawing and getting his opinion (the negotiation zone). Both zones are operating at the surface.

The body field of the person drawing (F) is not disturbed, and as we know from the discussion of the engagement space, this indicates a high degree of contact and is identifiable as a PCM.

(F) acknowledges (E)'s proposal, after tracing the proposed idea above the surface of the board with his pen whilst (E) taps a position of one bed with the back of his hand on the surface. After tracing (E) continues to draw, and his pen touches the surface at the same time as (E) begins to lift his hand away. There is no break in the fluidity of the rhythm of the coordination between them (of body and speech).

4.5 Parallel coordinated actions

The following examples are of more parallel coordinated actions. During the studies, we note many instances of parallel actions taking place at the surfaces of the table and whiteboard, and attempts to do so at the SmartBoard when only one such board is available.

Fig. 7 A silent parallel shift

Fig. 8 Waiting for D to end his turn

In Fig. 7, (E) is standing back, watching and talking, and (F) is drawing on the whiteboard. (F) has his body positioned to accommodate (E) by slightly opening it, slanted to the right, to share the engagement space with (E). At some point, (E) looks to the left of (F) to an area on the whiteboard and moves towards it. He picks up another felt pen and begins to draw as well. As (E) touches the surface, (F) shifts his body and alters his posture so that it is now open slanted to the left, and increases contact with (E). Both are now acting in parallel. This shift occurs in silence.

At the SmartBoard (Fig. 8), C is standing back whilst D is drawing. He looks and moves to a position to the right of D, on the SmartBoard. He leans into the surface but cannot draw because he has to first wait for D to end his turn.

D, without looking up, speaks, and his utterance causes C to turn his body back to look at him. As he cannot yet act, C moves back from the surface and waits, and as he is doing so, he breathes in deeply in frustration. C notices him, pauses his drawing, turns to look at him and moves back from the zone of action, allowing D to move into it (Fig. 9).

Once C is acting, i.e., drawing, D continues with his drawing on the Smart-Board (Fig. 10). The result is a disturbance on the board, and a jagged line cuts across from D's touch point to C's, causing them both surprise and laughter (Fig. 10). D momentarily forgot that you cannot touch the surface at the same time. The need to act whilst another is acting is not a conscious one. This autonomy in co-action seems to be part of the coordinated collaborative process but at a metacommunicative level.

In Figs. 8 and 9 we see an attempt to act, causing frustration until the need to act is noticed, at which point the turn to act is offered to C by D. It is significant

Fig. 9 Allowing D to move into the zone of action

Fig. 10 A disturbance on the board

that they recognise each other's need to act, and signal this need (moving body away, distancing) and respond to it (speech and body), and further, that they forget the limitations of the surface to afford them this need. In contrast, the whiteboard permitted (Fig. 5) a more fluid movement around the surface, as there was no enforced pause by the surface, and no turn-taking required on one designer's part to permit the other person to act.

These examples are of parallel coordinated actions that involve autonomy, where *autonomy involves awareness of and attendance to the state of engagement in the space between participants and the surface(s)*. When a designer at the SmartBoard does not easily give the turn to the other one, we see various strategies to force it. These include, moving close to the board and inside the visual locus of the drawing space in a quick motion, or moving back and forth, or reaching for a pen, or looking at the pen, or simply reaching out and asking for the pen the other person is currently using, or just moving right in front of the body of the person currently drawing, thereby forcing them back, and taking a pen from the pen holder. As either person can act at the whiteboard, there is no need for such strategies.

In contrast to the SmartBoard, at the whiteboard an autonomous performance by one person that is not occurring in co-action can bring a reaction to regain co-action. In an example below, (Fig. 11) (E) looks up and stands to draw something higher up on the board, just after (F) has knelt down to draw beside him. (E) altered his position such that the contact within the engagement space became too low for (F) to be aligned with him in order to act.

(F) attempts to regain contact so that he can work with (E), first by speech and when that fails, by using body moves to *attempt contact* and *focus* (Gill et al. 2000).

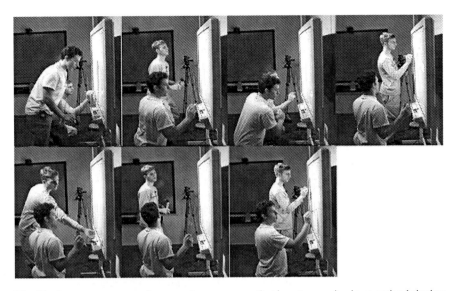

Fig. 11 An autonomous performance by one person that is not occurring in co-action bringing a reaction to regain co-action

5 Discussion

The ability to engage at the surface results in strategies for managing autonomous behaviour through various body moves. These strategies differ when using the SmartBoard and the whiteboard. At the former surface, for example, body moves such as take-turn are used, where the body field of the person acting is disturbed by the other one's entering it, and a reconfiguration of the engagement space is required. At the whiteboard, body moves such as attempt contact and focus are used, to increase contact.

In all the dyads working at the SmartBoard we observed moments where one person stands back in silence waiting (in contrast to the whiteboard where the person standing back sometimes speaks); or turning away to look at other parts of the surface and looking back at the person drawing because they cannot act; looking at the pens indicating an interest to act; or moving around the person drawing, and using the body field disturbance strategies listed above to intercept and take the turn or force it. If the SmartBoard were a horizontal surface there would be further inhibitors to natural actions such as that of bringing one's hands into the drawing space to increase contact, as in the example of the landscape architects (Fig. 3).

The SmartBoard makes those actions that are invisible, or are extensions of ourselves, when acting at a whiteboard, visible. Winograd and Flores (1986) speak of how 'structure' in communication 'becomes visible only when there is some kind of breakdown' (p.68). For instance, acts of rubbing something out whilst another is drawing, checking something by pointing on it, or touching the surface with a finger or hand to think about an idea, etc. When all these aspects are inhibited or have to be negotiated, the fluidity of sharing an engagement space in an interactive drawing task becomes altered by the kinds of communication strategies available to participants to achieve collaborative activity.[15]

The simultaneous synchrony of PCM in drawing or being able to touch the surface together provides for a certain kind of awareness of states of contact within an engagement space. This synchrony allows for the multi-dimensional expression of ideas in combinations of zones of activity using a pen, hand or finger, to sketch ideas.

These ideas can be rubbed out, located in one's self and made clear for the other person. Contact with each other's ideas can be made with gestures as well as speech. This is tacit bodily knowledge of self and intra-self.

We have noticed that in group activity using multiple SmartBoards, the patterns of rhythmic coordination of sequential movements and parallel coordinated actions, bear similarity to those in using a single whiteboard, with additional characteristics due to the increased complexity of the task, the larger numbers of participants and more surfaces. The locus of action in our study takes place around three SmartBoards, seen in the figures, and around the table in the centre of the room. A common pattern of motion activity between the boards is to have all three in use, or two boards in use, with one or two persons at each. When problems are noticed, either by pauses in body action at a surface, or by someone saying something, the other group members migrate towards the problem space, and try to help resolve it. As they cluster around a board, they frequently take turns by moving in and out of the problem focal spot to the outer rim, and once the problem is solved, they disperse to the separate boards.

This interactional dance happens when all the participants are at the boards, as this enables an awareness that allows them the fluidity of movement within each other's problem spaces. The fact that there are four students to three boards, may help this fluidity as one person will, at any time, not be acting on the surface, and hence have a sense of actions occurring elsewhere. However, other patterns occur in this configured room. Take Fig. 12, where two students at the centre SmartBoard are having some difficulty in erasing something they have drawn over the photographic image that they are working on by using Photoshop.

The student to the left of the centre SmartBoard has asked his partner to try to "take it (the pen stroke) away" using the rubber. He is overheard by another student who is standing at the table. (facing us in the picture). She breaks off her communication, stands straight and turns to look at the dyad, observes and asks them if they are having problems "deleting from the image". The dyad attempt to open the image from another board but that proves temporarily unfruitful. The "research observers", who are standing in the background behind the camera, hint to the student who is watching the pair at the board, to try using the third SmartBoard on the right. This hint is acted upon when she is gestured at with a pointing arm directed at it. All three SmartBoards are then used.

This is a different dynamic to the sequential-parallel movement transitions as the participants undertake different activities in spaces that separate them. Hence there is a lag in awareness. In the case above the observer has intervened

---

[15] The whiteboard is slightly unsteady if one person moves heavily upon its surface, but that is well handled and managed by the participants. In the example, where E taps the surface with the back of his hand, F has to momentarily lift his pen, yet the rhythmic coordination between them is maintained.

Fig. 12 A different dynamic to the sequential-parallel movement transitions: the overhearer and the mediator

to help because of difficulties in using the surface functionalities. We have discussed the limitations of the desktop metaphor for such design surfaces and design activity in Borchers, Gill and To (2002). The proximity of participants to each other within the space facilitates overhearing,[16] which is significant in helping the awareness and maintenance of the engagement space of the group.

The analysis being undertaken in this paper is work in progress. As part of a design effort to better understand how providing more contact affordances at the surface can improve collaboration in joint activity, we have been designing the software to permit the simultaneous operation of multiple functions at the surface.

6 Conclusions

Collaboration and cooperation in joint activities is analysed as having three basic elements: the skill to grasp and respond to the representations of the tacit dimension of our actions (e.g., in body moves, gestures, sounds), the ability to coordinate this grasping and responding in a rhythmic synchrony of sequential

---

[16] The SANE Project at Royal Holloway, London, shows that people who overhear others talking in work environments are participants of a kind within that space and constitute part of the organisational knowledge.

and parallel actions and coordinated autonomy that occurs within parallel coordinated movements, and involves awareness and attendance to the state of engagement in the space between us and interfaces.

The analysis of PCMs shows the importance of coordinated autonomous behaviour for sustainable collaborative activity, as it facilitates cooperative behaviour. Without it, the designers use disturbance strategies or behaviours. These ensure that the design task is completed, but with less engagement at the conceptual level.

The disruption of parallel coordinated action makes it problematic for participants to achieve a tacit awareness of their state of contact within the engagement space at the surface of the board. The fluid coordination of their rhythmic synchrony of body and speech, that would normally be invisible, i.e., not something they are consciously aware of doing, is made visible to them and they have difficulty in getting it back.

Parallel coordinated actions occurring at the surface have a physical touch dimension. There is an additional value to being able to touch the surface. We have found that touch enables the designers to create narrative spaces between their bodies and the surface of the interface, where the surface becomes a mediating point of contact within that space as virtual and imaginary. Where we cannot touch the surface to indicate an idea that we are talking about, for example, deciding on the location of a fireplace in the room we are drawing, we use our hands and arms to hold that place, above the surface, until we are ready to shift away from the surface to the virtual narrative space.

This study of the complexity of body moves of pairs and groups of designers collaborating and cooperating on design tasks shows how they learn and solve problems as a function of communicative and social structure, and manage their relationships with each other through intelligent actions. By intelligence, we mean the skill of grasping and responding to the representations of the tacit dimension of our actions and knowledge, appropriately for the purpose at hand. We call this the performance of knowledge in co-action. A challenge for designing mediating interfaces is for them to afford us our human skills of engaging with each other, communicating information and forming knowledge.

Acknowledgements Thanks and acknowledgements to Ramit Sethi and Tiffany To for their help in this research, and to Terry Winograd for his support of this work in the iSpaces Project at Stanford University. Thanks also to Syed Shariq for his encouragement to develop the framework of "knowledge in co-action", originally as a theoretical frame for the Real Time Venture Design Lab (ReVeL) at Stanford University. Thanks also to Renate Fruchter, Duska Rosenberg and Toyoaki Nishida for their comments on the paper.

References

Allwood J, Nivre J and Ahlsen E (1991) On the semantics and pragmatics of linguistic feedback. Gothenburg Papers. Theoretical Linguistics, 64

Bateson G (1955) The Message. 'This is the Play'. In: B Schaffner (ed) Group Processes. Vol. II. New York: Macy

Bavelas JB (1994) Gestures as part of speech: methodological implications. Res Lang Soc Inter 27(3):201–221

Birdwhistle RL (1970) Kinesics and context. University of Pennsylvania Press, Philadelphia, PA

Borchers J, Gill S and To T (2002) Multiple large-scale displays for collocated team work: study and recommendations. Technical Report. Stanford University

Clark HH, Schaefer EF (1989) Contributing to discourse. Cog Sci 13:259–294

Everitt KM, Klemmer SR, Lee R, Landay JA (2003) Two Worlds Apart: Bridging the Gap Between Physical and Virtual Media for Distributed Design Collaboration. Proceedings of CHI 2003, ACM Conference on Human Factors in Computing Systems

Gill SP (2002) The parallel coordinated move: case of a conceptual drawing task. Published Working Paper: CKIR, Helsinki

Gill SP, Kawamori M, Katagiri Y and Shimojima A (2000). The role of body moves in dialogue. RASK 12:89–114

Gregory R (1963) Recovery from blindness. A case study. Experimental Psychology Society Monograph No 2

Guimbretiere F, Stone M, Winograd T (2001) Stick it on the wall: a metaphor for interaction with large displays. Submitted to Computer Graphics (SIGGRAPH 2001 Proceedings)

Reiner M (1999) Conceptual Construction of Fields with a Tactile Interface. Interactive Learning Environments 6 (X), 1–25

Reiner M and Gilbert J (in press) The Symbiotic Roles of Empirical Experimentation and Thought Experimentation in the Learning of Physics. International Journal of Science Education

Scheflen AE (1975) How behaviour means. Anchor Books, New York

Winograd T and Flores F (1986) Understanding Computers and Cognition. A New Foundation for Design. Norwood NJ, Ablex Corporation

AI & Soc (2005) 19: 8–21
DOI 10.1007/s00146-004-0298-x

ANALYTICAL APPROACHES

Renate Fruchter

Degrees of engagement in interactive workspaces

Received: 9 February 2003 / Accepted: 15 April 2004 / Published online: 28 July 2004
© Springer-Verlag London Limited 2004

Abstract This paper presents a new perspective of the impact of collaboration technology on the degrees of engagement and specific interaction zones in interactive workspaces. The study is at the intersection of the design of physical work spaces, i.e., *bricks*, rich electronic content such as video, audio, sketching, CAD, i.e., *bits*, and new ways people behave in communicative events, i.e., *interaction*. The study presents: (1) an innovative multi-modal collaboration technology, called RECALL (patented by Stanford University), that supports the seamless, real-time capture of concept generation during project brainstorming and project review sessions, (2) the deployment of RECALL in an interactive workspace that supports real project review sessions, called FISH-BOWL, and (3) the observations of the impact of RECALL and the interactive workspace on degrees of engagement and interaction zones as it is deployed in the specific FISHBOWL sessions.

Keywords Collaboration · Teamwork · Interaction · Interactive workspace · Multi-modal · Multi-media technology · Capture · Sharing

1 Introduction

The former chief executive of HP, Lew Platt, was quoted saying, "*If HP would know what HP knows, we would be three times more profitable*" (Davenport and Prusak 1998). Managing and reusing knowledge can lead to greater competitive advantage, improved designs, and more effective facility management. However, reuse often fails, since knowledge is not captured—it is captured out of context, rendering it not reusable, or there are no formal mechanisms from both the information technology and organizational viewpoints for finding and retrieving reusable knowledge. The digital age holds great promise to assist in knowledge capture and reuse. Nevertheless, most digital content management today offers few solutions to capitalize on the core corporate competence, i.e., to capture, share, and reuse business-critical

R. Fruchter (✉)
Project Based Learning Laboratory, Department of Civil
and Environmental Engineering, Stanford University, Stanford, CA94305-4020, USA
E-mail: fruchter@stanford.edu

knowledge. They are limited to digital archives of formal documents (CAD, Word, Excel, etc.), and support only search by keyword, date, and originator. These ignore the highly contextual and interlinked modes of communication in which people generate and develop concepts, and reuse knowledge through *verbal discourse* and *sketching*. We argue that, in order for knowledge to be reusable, the user should be able to see and understand the context in which this knowledge was originally created and interact with this rich content, i.e., interlinked discourse and sketches.

While traditional product documentation captures explicit knowledge such as requirements, specifications, and design decisions, the contextual or tacit knowledge of the design group is often lost. Concept generation and development occur most frequently in informal media where design capture tools are the weakest. This statement has strong implications for the capture and reuse of design knowledge because conceptual design generates the majority of initial ideas and directions that guide the course of the project. Sketching is a natural mode for designers, instructors, or students to communicate in highly informal activities, such as brainstorming sessions, project reviews, lectures, or Q&A sessions. Often, the sketch itself is merely the vehicle that spawns discussion about a particular design issue. Thus, from a knowledge capture and reuse perspective, capture and retrieval of both the sketch itself and the discussion that provides the context behind the sketch are important. It is interesting to note that today's state-of-practice or best practices are not captured and knowledge is lost when the whiteboard is erased or the paper napkin sketch is tossed away.

Current tools to index and publish rich media content (e.g., Sketch, PowerPoint slide, CAD image) and audio:

– Require a production stage in which a user must manually go through and set up indexes and links into the digital documents. This is a very time consuming task that takes three to four times the length of the original event.
– Produce published material that is static and the consumer of the content cannot interact with it.
– Require very high cost and special expertise to publish multimedia material on the Web.

The study proposes the following hypotheses. The first hypothesis asserts that a primary source of information behind design decisions is embedded within the verbal conversation among designers. Capturing these conversations is difficult because the information exchange is unstructured and spontaneous. In addition, discourse is often multi-modal. It is common to augment speech with sketching and gesturing. Audio/video media can record these activities, but they do not provide an efficient means with which to index the captured information.

The second hypothesis asserts that any collaboration technology that engages multiple participants in communicative events and tasks in an interactive work space will determine specific interaction zones and degrees of engagement of the participants.

The objective of this research is to *improve* and *support* the process of knowledge capture and reuse in the architecture, engineering, construction industry, and provide corporations with leverage to capitalize on their core competence.

The study focuses on:

- How one can capture with high fidelity, and least overhead to the team members, the knowledge experience that constitutes conceptual design generated during informal events, such as brainstorming or project review sessions
- What are these interaction zones and degrees of engagement and how they are supported and impacted by the affordances of a specific collaboration technology, RECALL (Fruchter and Yen 2000), and the configuration of the interactive workspace

The paper briefly presents the multi-modal collaboration technology, called RECALL, developed in the Project Based Learning Laboratory (PBL Lab) at Stanford University that supports (1) the ubiquitous, seamless, real-time capture of concept generation during project brainstorming and project review sessions, (2) the deployment of RECALL in an interactive workspace that supports real project review sessions, called FISHBOWL, and (3) the observations of the impact of RECALL on degrees of engagement and interaction zones as it is deployed in a specific interactive workspace for FISHBOWL sessions.

2 "Bricks & Bits & Interaction"

Today's information technology and communications–intensive environment challenges designers of buildings, human interaction, and technology, as well as organizations to understand the impacts on the workspace, content that is created and shared, and social, behavioral and cognitive aspects of work, play, learning, and community. The study builds on the *Bricks & Bits & Interaction* principle (BBI) (Fruchter 2001) that is at the intersection of (1) the design of physical spaces, i.e., *bricks*, affordances and limitations of typical preset physical, spatial configurations of workspaces, (2) collaboration technologies and rich electronic content such as video, audio, sketching, CAD, i.e., *bits*, and (3) new ways people behave in communicative events using affordances of IT augmented spaces and content, i.e., *interaction*. The BBI principle is based on two hypotheses:

- *Brick & Bits & Interaction hypothesis*: if we understand the relationship between *bricks*, *bits*, and *interaction*, we will be able to:
1. Design workspaces that better afford communicative events.
2. Develop collaboration technologies based on natural idioms that best support the activities people perform.
3. Engage people in rich communicative experiences that enable them to immerse in their activity and forget about the technology that mediates the interaction.

- *Change hypothesis*: any new information and collaboration technology will require change and rethinking of:
1. The design and location of spaces in which people work, learn, and play.

2. The content people create in terms of representation, media, interrelation among the different media, the content's evolution over time so that it provides context and sets it in a social communicative perspective.
3. The interactions among people in terms of the individual's behavior, interaction dynamics, communication protocols, collaboration processes, relation between people and affordances of the space, and interactivity with the content.

The BBI case studies were launched in 1998 in the PBL Lab at Stanford University, and led to valuable findings both from a theoretical and practical perspective. (For more information about PBL Lab, see http://pbl.stanford.edu).

3 High fidelity ubiquitous knowledge capture and reuse

To test the first hypothesis, we designed, developed, deployed, and tested a tool called RECALL.

The issue of how to capture knowledge in project design teams has received extensive attention from researchers in design theory and methodology. The value of contextual design knowledge (process, evolution, rationale) has been repeatedly recognized, but so has the additional overhead required of the designer in order to capture it. This research focuses on the informal, unstructured knowledge captured through informal multi-modal channels, such as sketching, audio for the verbal discourse, video for the gesture language, and artifacts that support the discourse. The RECALL system builds on Donald Schön's concept of the reflective practitioner paradigm (Schön 1983). Research studies of design have focused on either the sketch activity, i.e., learning from sketched accounts of design (Tversky 1999; Stiedel and Henderson 1983; Olszweski 1981; Kosslyn 1981; Goel 1995) or verbal accounts of design (Cross et al. 1996; Cross and Roozenburg 1992). Some researchers have studied the relation between sketching and talking (Eastman 1969; Goldschmidt 1991).

RECALL is a drawing application, written in Java, that captures and indexes each individual action on the drawing surface. The drawing application synchronizes with audio/video capture and encoding through a client–server architecture. Once the session is complete, the drawing and video information is automatically indexed and published on a Web server that allows for distributed and synchronized playback of the drawing session and audio/video from anywhere at anytime. In addition, the user is able to navigate through the session by selecting individual drawing elements as an index to the audio/video and jump to the part of interest.

Figure 1 illustrates the different devices, encoders, and services of RECALL, such as video/audio capture, media encoding module, sketch capture device, such as Tablet PC or SmartBoard, sketch encoding module, sketch and media storage, and RECALL serving Web media applet that runs off the RECALL server.

Figure 2 illustrates the RECALL user interface during real-time production—that is, during a communicative session. The participants can create freehand sketches or import CAD images and annotate them during their discourse. They have a color pallet, and a "tracing paper" metaphor that enables

Fig. 1 RECALL production
and service modules

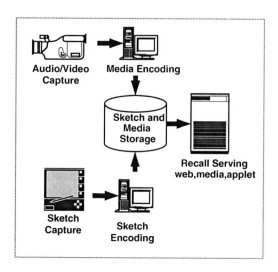

Fig. 2 RECALL-producer
user interface

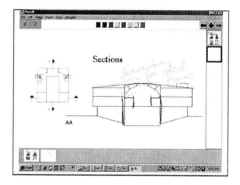

them to reuse the CAD image and create multiple sketches on top of it. The right side bar contains the existing digital sketch pad pages, which enables quick flipping or navigation through these pages. At the end of the brainstorming session, the participants exit and RECALL automatically indexes the sketch, verbal discourse, and video. This session can be posted on the RECALL server for future interactive replay, sharing with geographically distributed team members, or knowledge reuse in other future projects.

Figure 3 illustrates the interactive replay of a RECALL session. The user can interactively select any portion of the sketch and RECALL will replay the sketch from that point on.

The RECALL technology invention is aimed at improving the performance and reducing the cost of knowledge capture, sharing, and reuse. It provides the following benefits:

– Transparent graphical, audio/video indexing.
– Zero overhead and cost for production, i.e., editing/indexing.
– Zero overhead and cost for publishing, sharing, and streaming rich Web content.

Fig. 3 RECALL interactive replay with sketch and video window for playback

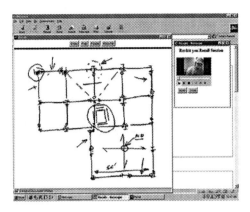

– Interactive and immediate access and retrieval of knowledge and information, i.e., sketch, audio/video on demand.

The RECALL system has been tested and deployed in different user scenarios, such as:

– *Individual brainstorming*, where a project team member has a "conversation with the evolving artifact" enacting Schön's "reflective practitioner" and using a Tablet PC augmented with RECALL then sharing his/her thoughts with the rest of the team by publishing the session on the RECALL server.
– *Team brainstorming* and project review sessions, using a SmartBoard augmented with RECALL.
– *Best practice capture*, where senior experts, such as designers, engineers, and builders, capture their expertise for the benefit of the corporation.

The following scenario illustrates RECALL in action during a special project review session, called the FISHBOWL.

4 The FISHBOWL scenario

The FISHBOWL project review scenario is inspired from the medical school learning environment, where it is typical to see special operation rooms with glass walls where world expert surgeons operate on patients (e.g., open heart surgery) and medical students watch. This learning experience brought to mind the *fishbowl* metaphor. More importantly, my goal was to emulate this learning experience in the school of engineering, specifically in the project-based design teamwork that I teach in the PBL Lab, at Stanford University. In addition, my goal was to capture the activity during the project-based review session for future reuse, either by the student team in the FISHBOWL session, or by future generations as a learning opportunity. RECALL was a perfect fit for this knowledge capture and reuse purpose.

The result was what is now known as the FISHBOWL session. The FISH-BOWL session is a project review session that is intended to act as a role modeling, mentoring and apprenticeship opportunity. It takes place in the architecture, engineering, and construction global teamwork course (A/E/C) I teach at Stanford University (Fruchter 1999). This course is a project-based, geographically distributed, collaborative teamwork experience. Each year, there are six to twelve A/E/C teams in the class. Each team: (1) has an architect, an engineer, and a construction manager; (2) is geographically distributed, and (3) has an owner/client with a building program, a location, a budget, and a time line.

The FISHBOWL session takes place after the teams have worked on their concepts for three months and face some key challenges. Each student team prepares for a FISHBOWL session in which they present, in 10 min, the status of their project and their key three to five challenges. They then hand over their project to a full team of A/E/C industry mentors who work on the challenges in front of the students for an hour.

The actors and their roles are the following: (1) the A/E/C "*team Fish* that brings the *patient*—that is, *their project.*" This is a geographically distributed team of students, e.g., composed of an architect at Georgia Tech, a structural engineer at Stanford University in the US and a second at Bauhaus University in Germany, and a construction manager who can be at Stanford University and a second at KTH in Sweden; (2) the industry mentors who are the "*mentor Fish*", composed of an architect, an engineer, and a construction manager from companies in the Bay Area; (3) the rest of the students in the A/E/C class. These are the *spectators* watching the "*fish*" in the project review FISHBOWL session interactions. They are from all the partner universities in the A/E/C class that are distributed worldwide. Consequently, there are collocated spectators who are in the PBL Lab, and geographically distributed spectators. Figure 4 illustrates a FISHBOWL session in the PBL Lab.

The collaboration technology and knowledge capture used consists of (Fig. 5): (1) a SmartBoard in the PBL Lab at Stanford University for direct manipulation and sketching through the RECALL application; (2) a Webcam that enables the remote students to see the interactive workspace in the PBL Lab that covers the FISHBOWL area, i.e., the SmartBoard, the *mentor Fish* and *team Fish*; (3) projectors and screens for the virtual auditorium video streams that enable the *mentor Fish* in the PBL Lab to see all of the remote students; (4) RECALL that runs on the SmartBoard and enables the sketching and capture in real-time of the FISHBOWL session; (5) NetMeeting videoconference for

Fig. 4 FISHBOWL session in the PBL Lab at Stanford University

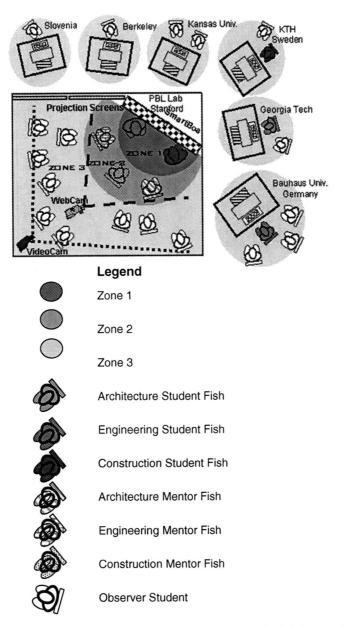

Legend

Zone 1

Zone 2

Zone 3

Architecture Student Fish

Engineering Student Fish

Construction Student Fish

Architecture Mentor Fish

Engineering Mentor Fish

Construction Mentor Fish

Observer Student

Fig. 5 The FISHBOWL configuration in the PBL Lab and the Global Teamwork Partner Universities

application sharing, i.e., RECALL, with all the remote sites; (6) a teleconference bridge for high quality audio; and (7) a microphone for audio capture that feeds into the SmartBoard computer that runs RECALL.

5 Data collection and analysis

The data for this study was collected in the following way:

- Indexed and synchronized sketch and discourse activities were captured through RECALL.
- Interactions, movement, and use of collaboration technology within the PBL Lab workspace was captured with the video camera (Fig. 5).
- Interaction and engagement of remote students was captured through a screen capture application that recorded all of the virtual auditorium video streams concurrently for future parallel analysis.

We performed a temporal analysis of the data by integrating the information about the speech-acts, discourse, movements, use of collaboration technologies, and workspace in the PBL Lab. The result was a temporal spreadsheet with the following rubrics: (1) time stamp, (2) verbal discourse used to identify the speech-acts, (3) video snapshots of the PBL Lab configuration showing the participants' movements, (4) RECALL snapshots of key sketch actions, (5) screen snapshots of concurrent virtual auditorium streams of remote sites showing the participants' movements, (6) screen layout of applications on remote PCs, (7) field notes, and (8) data analysis observations. Example snapshots of the temporal analysis are illustrated in Fig. 6.

This data analysis enabled us to observe and understand the relationships between the spatial configuration and technology in the PBL Lab, i.e., *bricks*, the effectiveness of the RECALL collaboration technology as a natural idiom to explore and share design ideas seamlessly, i.e., *bits*, and the *interaction*

Time	Discourse Transcript	Speech Act	PBL Lab config. and participants' engagement	Global participants' engagement	RECALL™ Replay
12:42	A: What can we do to reduce the slab height? - student G: you should consider a PT slab. Then you can install the ducts this way (sketches) - mentor	*Question* *Explore*		 Germany Kansas Sweden Stanford	
12:44	D: How do the two building wings work together? - mentor G: The best solution would be to think of the two building wings as two separate buildings, one of steel and one of concrete. mentor	*Question* *Problem solving*		 Germany Kansas Sweden Stanford	
...	...	...	...	...	...

Fig. 6 Temporal analysis schema for the FISHBOWL configuration in the PBL Lab and the Global Teamwork Partner Universities

mediated by the space and technology, i.e., movement, sharing of workspace, discourse, attention retention of remote participants, and their engagement in the communicative event. The following section describes one of the key findings related to degrees of engagement and corresponding zones of interaction.

6 Degrees of engagement and zones of interaction

The aim of the analysis was to understand better the nature of engagement in a specific interactive workspace during FISHBOWL communicative events, the sharing of these workspaces, and the impact of the collaboration technologies. The analysis resulted in the definition of three interaction zones and degrees of engagement, as well as how the participants are using the collaboration technology and other artifacts to best explore and convey their ideas. The three interaction zones and corresponding degrees of engagement are (Fig. 5):

Zone 1   Defined as the *action zone*, since it is in this zone that most speech-acts, interactions among participants, and the digital content, i.e., the *bits*, takes place, as the participants annotate, sketch, explore, explain, and propose ideas.

Zone 2   Defined as the *reflection zone*, since it is in this zone that the participants in the FISHBOWL reflect on proposed ideas that are presented in zone 1. In this zone, questions are asked, clarifications are requested, and negotiation and what-if scenarios are brought up. As Donald Schön so well defines in the reflective practitioner, we see an interplay between zone 1 and zone 2 as the participants become reflective practitioners across disciplines, building common ground and understanding of the artifact and its potential evolutions.

Zone 3   Defined as the *observation zone*, since the spectators, either collocated in PBL Lab or remote participants, observe the activities and discourse in the FISHBOWL. Rarely did we observe that participants from zone 3 move into zone 2 or zone 1 with a proposal or question.

The temporal spatial and movement analysis indicated the effect of the location of the collaboration technologies—more specifically, the SmartBoard and RECALL—in the use of the workspace, watching carefully the disposition of the participants in the space. In the 20 FISHBOWL sessions studied, the presence of the SmartBoard and RECALL determines a circular disposition of the participants during most of the interaction with back and forth movement between the mentor fish and student fish participants between zones 1 and 2. It is important to note that the participants in zone 3 are students who work on similar projects as the ones in the FISHBOWL. They participate in the session as active observers. This provides valuable peer-to-peer learning and legitimate peripheral participation opportunities (Lave and Wenger 1991). Zone 3 students engage in the FISHBOWL discussion by suggesting ideas related to the problem at hand, or posing questions about the proposed solutions in the FISHBOWL by the mentors, which they can relate to their own problems in their projects.

7 Preliminary observations

The data supports the hypothesis that concept generation and development occurs most frequently in informal design activities, such as brainstorming sessions. While it is possible to record notes and sketches, often, the contextual information that is conversed and debated verbally is lost. The RECALL system provides a benefit for both the designer and the researcher, since they can both use the same space (i.e., technology and knowledge archive). For the designer, the RECALL system is a tool that facilitates communication and improves productivity. For the researcher, RECALL is an instrument robust enough to collect and study the team interaction and designer behavior, rationale, and work habits. By capturing and indexing more of the informal media of design collaboration, important design decisions that capture not only the final product, but the context and design rationale behind the product, can be documented, shared, and archived.

The FISHBOWL sessions organized over the past five years in both academic and industry settings engaged small groups (three to five participants) and large groups (10 to 15 participants) of participants in zones 1 and 2 of the FISHBOWL. The key aspect in facilitating either small or large numbers of participants resides in applying the BBI principles that pay attention not only to the technology or the number of participants interacting in a session, but also the flexibility of the workspace in relation to the technology and interaction that responds to the different needs in the various scenarios. A workspace configured for a workspace where there are three participants will differ from a workspace that engages 15–20 participants. For instance, in the case of three collocated participants, they can choose to sit around two large monitors; one for video sharing of faces and the second for content sharing, whereas in the case of 15–20 participants, a hybrid solution, such as the one in the PBL Lab with Smart-Boards and projection screens, would work best.

From the temporal spatial and movement analysis in the context of the FISHBOWL sessions, a set of needs emerge for social intelligence design in the three dimensions—workspace (*bricks*), collaboration technology (*bits*), and communicative events (*interaction*), in order to best leverage their interplay. For instance:

- Acapability to reconfigure the workspace on-the-fly for and, dynamically during, FISHBOWL sessions as a function of the tasks and communication needs of the participants, as well as to facilitate a higher degree of engagement; for instance, of the zone 3 spectators.
- Improvement of visibility and awareness of remote and collocated participants. Visibility in this discussion is related to the affordance of the workspace configuration and communication technology to make all participants visible to all sites. In past years, participants were not visible to all sites, which decreased the engagement and social interaction. This is why, this year, the PBL Lab was reconfigured to include a Webcam to make the FISHBOWL activity visible to the remote participants, and the virtual auditorium prototype was used to make all the remote participants visible to the PBL Lab participants. This has increased the social and cognitive interactions. The awareness in this discussion is related to the viewing and

direct manipulation of digital capabilities, as well as viewing physical artifacts, such as building models that are used by architects. The RECALL system and the Webcam address both needs. An interesting observation related to the degree of engagement in zone 3 indicates that participants who are in zone 3 of remote sites are virtually closer to the content than collocated participants in zone 3 in the PBL Lab. This fact is dictated by the proximity to the hardware device, i.e., SmartBoard in PBL Lab vs. desktop PC in remote sites. This prompts an interesting question for future research on how to increase the engagement of zone 3 participants who are both collocated and remote.

- Hybrid workspace and collaboration technology solutions provided a smoother transition between private and public workspaces that lead to more effective communication, interaction, and common ground building. More specifically, in the present PBL Lab configuration (Fig. 5), the SmartBoard and RECALL provide direct manipulation of *bits* for both collocated and remote participants. The project screens can be used to share ideas and content from private wireless Tablet PCs in zone 3 and zone 2, which each participant has, to the public space in zone 1.
- Finally, as participants immerse into these interactive workspaces, they need to acquire new social and behavioral skills, from interaction dynamics, to use of collaboration technologies and sharing workspace, both physical and digital. From the preliminary analysis of spatial and temporal movement between zones 1 and 2 and the sharing of the workspace in zone 1, a concept of "dance" emerged in which the participants acquired a skill to tacitly negotiate the space by moving back and forth with respect to the other participants and the technology (SmartBoard) that facilitates content sharing and exploration. And, as with any dance, the partners have to learn the steps, otherwise they step on each other's toes, as we observed in many instances when multiple participants moved into zone 1 with the objective to perform specific uncoordinated actions on the shared digital artifact.

8 Discussion

This study contributes to the social intelligence design (SID) field through the following:

- The BBI principle that emphasizes the relation between the design of workspaces, collaboration technologies, and interaction experiences.
- The FISHBOWL experience as an instance of a designed computer mediated interaction and workspace that yields new and effective collaboration processes.
- RECALL collaboration technology as an instance of a ubiquitous collaboration technology that facilitates the externalization of tacit knowledge. The RECALL technology presented in this paper addresses the need for high fidelity non-intrusive real-time, contextual capture, sharing and retrieval of the sketch, and corresponding verbal discourse that encapsulates the knowledge externalized during the creative computer mediated FISHBOWL collaborative experience.

– A temporal analysis methodology to study, in an integrative way, the impact of collaboration technology on social interactions among participants, their degree of engagement in the discourse, and on the workspace and its affordances.

The quality of the product is improved by both the FISHBOWL process and computer mediated RECALL technology. The FISHBOWL experience brings together and engages all project stakeholders and facilitates:

– Effective collaboration
– Rapid building of common ground
– Timely input from different discipline perspectives by having all of the team members/stakeholders present and contribute, in real-time, ideas and solutions
– Participants to interact with the project material that is discussed and to track the discussion
– Joint exploration of ideas and concepts
– Effective identification of problems and key issues
– Joint problem solving for the benefit of the client

From an end user's point of view, feedback from industry practitioners expressed during the many FISHBOWL debriefs identify the value and benefits for both the product and process as:

– "Great accomplishment of the technology as a valuable aid in project design meetings and a great technology to engage people in dialogue."
– "This experience allowed us to accomplish in 3 h what would take, in a typical project, three months. It was amazing how much material the team went over in such a short time and the time spent in substantial problem solving."
– More than that, the process changed from sequential to concurrent interactions that provide timely input from other disciplines, as industry practitioners indicated that "usually, the process is incremental and, for instance, the landscape designer is brought in later on in the project. The FISHBOWL process brings all stakeholders together and all can contribute from the start. It allows a higher level of design."

It is important to note that the FISHBOWL is not only a valuable experience during the project meeting session, but the captured RECALL rich multi-modal and multimedia content, i.e., sketch, discourse, and video, serves as a learning resource over time. The session content is reused in multiple ways: (1) by the students or project members in the FISHBOWL project team, as they replay specific parts of the proposed solution details; (2) by the students or project members who were in zone 3 and find relevant ideas that they can use in their own projects; and (3) future generations of students or project members who have access to this rich learning resource, leveraging knowledge from past projects.

The RECALL technology and the FISHBOWL experience have been successfully deployed in academic and industry project scenarios over the past five years in over 50 project teams. This has served as a valuable testbed for both the technology and the social intelligence design studies of the BBI interdependence. These studies continue to reveal valuable insights and new research and development directions in the PBL Lab at Stanford University.

References

Cross N, Christiaans H, Dorst K (1996) Analysing design activity, 1st edn. Wiley, West Sussex, England

Cross N, Roozenburg N (1992) Modelling the design process in engineering and architecture. J Eng Des 3(4):325–337

Davenport T, Prusak L (1998) Working knowledge: how organizations manage what they know. Boston Harvard Business School Press, Boston, Massachusetts

Eastman CM (1969) Cognitive processes and ill-defined problems: a case study from design. In: Walker DE, Norton LM (eds) Proceedings of the international joint conference on artificial intelligence (IJCAI'69), Washington, DC, May 1969, pp 675–699

Fruchter R, Yen S (2000) RECALL in action. In: Fruchter R, Roddis K, Pena-Mora F (eds) Proceedings of the ASCE ICCCBE-VIII conference, Stanford, 14–16 August 2000

Fruchter R (1999) Architecture, engineering, construction teamwork: a collaborative design and learning space. J Comput Civil Eng 13(4):261–270

Fruchter R (2001) Bricks & bits & interaction. In: Terano T, Nishida T, Namatame A, Ohsawa Y, Tsumoto S, Washio T (eds) Special issue on exploring new frontiers on artificial intelligence, Lecture notes on artificial intelligence (LNAI) vol 2253. Springer, Berlin Heidelberg New York

Goel V (1995) Sketches of thought. MIT Press, Cambridge, Massachusetts

Goldschmidt G (1991) The dialectics of sketching. Creativity Res J 4(2):123–143

Kosslyn S (1981) The medium and the message in mental imagery: a theory. Psychol Rev 88:46–66

Lave J, Wenger E (1991) Situated learning: legitimate peripheral participation. Cambridge University Press, Cambridge, UK

Olszweski EJ (1981) The draughtsman's eye: late renaissance schools and styles. Cleveland Museum of Art, Indiana University

Schön DA (1983) The reflective practitioner. Basic Books, New York

Stiedel RF, Henderson JM (1983) The graphic languages of engineering. Wiley, New York

Tversky B (1999) What does drawing reveal about thinking?. In: Gero JS, Tversky B (eds) Proceedings of the conference on visual and spatial reasoning in design, Sydney, Australia

AI & Soc (2006) 20: 288–300
DOI 10.1007/s00146-005-0020-7

ORIGINAL PAPER

Daniel Memmi

The nature of virtual communities

Received: 25 February 2004 / Accepted: 10 August 2005 / Published online: 1 February 2006
© Springer-Verlag London Limited 2006

Abstract The impressive development of electronic communication techniques has given rise to virtual communities. The nature of these computer-mediated communities has been the subject of much recent debate. Are they ordinary social groups in electronic form, or are they fundamentally different from traditional communities? Understanding virtual communities seems a prerequisite for the design of better communication systems. To clarify this debate, we will resort to the classical sociological distinction between small traditional communities (based on personal relations) and modern social groups (bound by looser, more impersonal links). We will argue that the discussion about virtual communities is often vitiated by a simplistic assimilation to traditional communities, whereas they may be in fact quite different and much more impersonal. Virtual communities are often bound by reference to common objects or goals, and not by personal relations. In this respect, virtual communities are just another example of a long-term evolution of modern society toward more abstract social relationships.

Keywords Virtual communities · Community · Gemeinschaft · Gesellschaft · Cyberspace · Groupware · Collaborative software · Social networks.

1 Introduction

The impressive development of electronic communication techniques in the past twenty years has totally changed the overall picture of social communication methods. E-mail, instant messaging or chat, forums and newsgroups, discussion lists, co-ordination by means of Web pages and other computer-mediated communication methods on the Internet have greatly accelerated the speed, size and ease of human communication. Internet is beyond doubt a major phenomenon of our time.

D. Memmi
Department d'Informatique, UQAM,
C.P. 8888 Succ. C.V., H3C 3P8, Montreal, QC, Canada
E-mail: memmi.daniel@uqam.ca · Tel.: + 1-514-987-3000 · Fax: + 1-514-987-8477

One may ask whether the telephone should be included among electronic communication techniques. Technically, yes, but telephones have been around for a much longer time and do not constitute a new phenomenon (in spite of the recent spread of cell phones). And telephone communication is spoken, mostly one-to-one, with frequent emotional overtones, so that it probably belongs to a category in itself, to be differentiated from other recent techniques.

Because communication is one of the foundations of social groups (social cohesion requires communication of some sort between group members), the development of new communication techniques is apt to cause social changes. These new electronic techniques have thus given rise to new social groups, which now usually go by the name of *virtual communities*.

The expression itself deserves some preliminary comment. Those communities are presumably called *virtual* because they function without actual physical contact, in "cyberspace" (Kollock and Smith 1999). But is this really a crucial defining characteristic? Some traditional communities (e.g. ethnic or religious communities) do not necessarily imply physical contact between all group members but may be defined by common experience, awareness, beliefs or values. So let us say *virtual communities* has now become a set phrase referring to computer-mediated communities, and let's leave it at that for the time being.

The central question is probably the following: are virtual communities simply an extension of classical social groups (in electronic clothing so to speak), or are they a fundamentally new type of social grouping? The data so far is ambiguous enough to accommodate both points of view and the issue requires careful scrutiny. The issue is important because the exact nature of virtual groups is probably relevant to the design of good communicative or collaborative software. To better accommodate these new communities, we must first try to undersand how they function.

In the literature on virtual communities one can notice a marked tendency to equate them with communities of the most traditional kind, imbued with positive moral values. However, when the actual functioning of virtual communities is examined more closely, it is far from evident that they really conform to the traditional kind of social groups based on close personal relations between group members.

On the contrary, we will argue here that it is generally a mistake to equate virtual communities with traditional communities, because computer-mediated groups actually show novel characteristics and tend toward looser, more impersonal forms of interaction. The familiar image of traditional communities thus obscures the reality of the new electronic groupings, which requires a fresh approach to the subject.

As a matter of fact, there has been a long-term evolution at play in modern society toward more impersonal, functional social relations. In this respect, the recent development of impersonal electronic forms of communication is in perfect agreement with a general tendency of our society, which brings about more and more abstract social links. The question now becomes: how can we make sure that these new associations do function in a coherent way?

After this introduction, we will first describe the main types of social communities in Sect. 2. In Sect. 3, we will emphasize recent social trends. Virtual communities will then be analyzed more closely in Sect. 4. Finally, the diversity of social groups will be discussed in Sect. 5, before reaching a conclusion.

2 Types of communities

Before examining virtual communities in more detail, it would be relevant to analyze the very concept of social community. This is of course a central theme in sociology, and the issue has been discussed at length ever since the birth of this discipline in the nineteenth century. There is now a received set of concepts and distinctions on this subject.

2.1 The notion of community

We would like first to try to describe a frequent usage of the term *community* in everyday language. This common-sense notion implicitly permeates the debate about virtual communities, although it may not be really adequate. Analyzing this notion would clarify the issues and help improve the pertinence of the debate.

Though usage varies somewhat, it appears that in the most usual sense, a *community* refers to a particular kind of social group, defined by strong personal links. Such a group will be fairly small, so that it is possible for each member to know personally everybody else in the group. Relations are supposed to be direct, face-to-face, frequent and stable. Relations are strongly tinged with affectivity, which is often presented in a positive light. In a rosy version of the picture, relations are warm, cordial, well-meaning and kind. Everybody can count on the sympathy and solidarity of other group members in case of need or mishap.

Although we all know that real human relations are much more ambivalent, and that power struggles and village feuds are probably just as common as group solidarity, this ideal world is felt to be secure, reassuring, comforting. Everybody knows their place in a global relational network, and everybody is recognized personally by everybody else.

This type of community is often described with warmth and emotion in the mass media, such as television and the movies. This is a cliché which recurs regularly in television fictions set in the countryside or in small towns. Such an image obviously enjoys wide popular appeal.

Yet it does not take much thought to realize that this is all largely a myth by now (though a very common and powerful myth). It might be the case that such communities could still be found in Amazonian tribes or in remote villages of India, but they simply do not exist any longer in modern countries. When such communities do occur in our society, they are unstable, fragile and usually temporary.

There is then a strong flavor of nostalgia about this idealized picture of a community. The emotional appeal of traditional communities tends to blind people to the reality of social groups they are likely to encounter in modern life. Computer-mediated groups are inevitably confronted with this ideal picture, making it difficult to analyze their real functioning.

2.2 A classical distinction

Sociology has fortunately elaborated finer and more realistic descriptions of social groups for more than a century now. The general view is that modern societies tend toward more and more abstract social groupings, away from the personal links of traditional communities.

German sociologists such as Tönnies, Simmel, and Weber have proposed a fundamental distinction between traditional community (*Gemeinschaft* in German) and modern society (German *Gesellschaft*). Tönnies was probably the first to formulate it clearly at the end of the nineteenth century, but Weber is the most often quoted when this distinction is mentioned; Simmel also illustrated it repeatedly in his analyses of modern urban life (Tönnies 1963; Weber 1956; Simmel 1989).

The older *Gemeinschaft*-type community is based on strong personal links within small, fairly stable social groups (e.g. a tribe or a small village). This is close to the common-sense notion of community we have outlined above, but the sociological concept is more complex and less romantic. The life of such a group is usually associated with a limited territory and the group is structured by direct person-to-person relations and obligations. These relations are inflexible, and group pressure to conform is heavy and inescapable. Group identity is therefore obvious and strong.

One may see *Gemeinschaft*-type communities as psychologically reassuring, but they are also closed, oppressive, unchanging societies, where nobody can escape their allotted place.

On the contrary, in modern *Gesellschaft*-type society, links are much more impersonal, temporary and functional (as is typical in city life). In larger modern associations, function and social roles replace personal relations as the basis of social status. The increasing size of these organizations makes it impossible anyway to know all other group members on a personal basis, and social functioning is guided by rules, regulations and contracts, rather than by traditional custom and personal obligations. Individual members may well belong to several groups and group identity is much weaker.

Modern society is obviously much freer and more flexible, at the cost of increased loneliness, fragility of social structure, and potential psychological insecurity.

One can find a similar distinction in Durkheim: the difference between *mechanical* solidarity and *organic* solidarity (Durkheim 1960). The former is characteristic of traditional groups in primitive societies, whose members are poorly differentiated and strongly linked. But the "organic" solidarity of modern society is looser and more abstract. It is based on the complementarity of different social roles due to the increasing division of labor in modern economies, which has made personal bonds obsolete.

A more recent, but very similar distinction has been put forward by Granovetter: the difference between *strong ties* and *weak ties* (Granovetter 1973). Strong ties involve frequent contacts, emotional intensity and solidarity. They tend to form densely linked groups, such as family and friends. On the contrary weak ties are casual, superficial and do not form communities, but are nonetheless very important for the circulation of new information.

Whatever the names used, there has been a clear evolution from the former toward the latter form of association throughout the last century. There is a general trade-off between security and freedom, and social evolution has gradually favored mobility over belonging. As a matter of fact, traditional communities have by and large disappeared in developed countries, even if there is still widespread nostalgia for older times. Industrial and bureaucratic societies have replaced personal links with contractual relations.

Similarly, the rise of the merchant economy, with its finely differentiated products which require the use of money for their allocation, has gradually replaced many personal relations with monetary transactions. Simmel has analyzed in great detail the corrosive effect of money on traditional relationships and their replacement in modern society by more abstract links.

This general evolution is a fundamental fact of recent social history, due to a powerful conjunction of factors: cultural (the rise of individualism), economic (the increasing division of labor), technical (the development of modern transportation and communication methods). The trend is therefore massive and inescapable, and it would be naive to ignore this historical background when discussing modern social groups.

3 Recent social evolution

One can also observe a marked acceleration in the past twenty years of this long-term trend toward more flexible associations and network organizations (Castells 1996; Shapiro and Varian 1999). This is clearly correlated with the development of electronic communication techniques in the same period (although it seems that recent organizational changes have preceded by a few years the increased availability of modern telecommunications).

From a sociological point of view, flexible group membership is becoming more and more common. A typical modern behavior has emerged, where group membership is constantly re-evaluated and renegotiated. The modern individual belongs to several groups (professional, cultural, political...) at the same time but doesn't identify too closely with any of them. He or she views the association with any given group as potentially temporary, to be discarded without trepidation when circumstances have changed.

This type of person switches with ease between different social circles as his interests evolve or new opportunities arise, and doesn't burden himself with an obsolete identity. He is quite ready to renegotiate his status and membership to improve his situation, and carefully maintains a large social network in order to facilitate such changes.

One may witness in our time the emergence of a typical personality: affable, easy-going, pleasant and flexible. But this is often a superficial personality, cold and shallow behind the surface geniality. Such an individual is actually self-centered and calculating, ready to ditch obsolete causes in favor of newer, more profitable interests. His social engagements are usually loose, temporary and unemotional. This profile is more prevalent in the urban upper-class, but it somehow sets the tone for the whole society.

This personality type enjoys a relatively high degree of freedom, as he may surf from one social group to the next according to his plans. But he has lost the psychological comfort and emotional wealth of a unique identity, and it takes some fortitude or experience to deal with ever-changing circumstances.

A similar evolution is also evident in recent management fashions and practices (Veltz 2000). Various phenomena all point in the same direction: goal-oriented management, the emphasis on flexibility and autonomy, temporary work-teams, subcontracting and outsourcing, hollow firms... These are but different manifestations of an organizational structure where group membership has become temporary, groups are frequently reorganized, and flat networks have become the dominant structural paradigm.

These organizational changes have in turn been triggered or fostered by an economic evolution giving more and more weight to innovation and differentiation, product quality, adaptability to the market, lean production... There is an obvious parallelism between the social evolution toward looser associations and these recent economic and managerial changes. One may speculate as to which is cause or effect, but they are probably all entangled together, reinforcing each other.

This general evolution may also be observed in non-profit organizations, which are presumably less influenced by managerial discourse. Within a time-span of thirty years, the stereotypical militant, with his one-track mind, dogmatical discourse and intolerance to dissent, has given way to much more flexible and diversified behavior. Today's association members often belong to several associations and move freely between different associations. Their interests and ideology are more varied and there is much more tolerance for individual opinions. Many associations have accordingly evolved toward a network structure.

Anti-globalization movements for example are much more loosely structured than traditional unions or parties used to be. There is now a marked distrust of rigid hierarchical structures, and various groups and subgroups within the global movement are deliberately organized as flexible networks, bound together by modern communication techniques such as the Internet.

4 Computer-mediated communities

Given this description of the global sociological background of modern communication techniques, it is now time to examine more closely the actual functioning of virtual communities. Opinions vary as to the proper way to describe these communities, and a fresh view would be useful.

4.1 A common approach

When one begins to survey the literature about virtual communities, it is striking to see how frequently electronic groups are described as if they were *Gemeinschaft*-type communities, with strong personal relations between members. Pioneers and practitioners of early versions of forums, chats and similar computer-mediated communications systems insist that such systems are apt to give rise to real communities with rich human relationships, which are otherwise too often lacking in today's society (Rheingold 2000; Wellman 1999).

There is obviously an element of idealism or nostalgia in many of those high-tech experiences. Rebuilding or fostering meaningful human relationships appears to be a strong motivation among the early proponents of electronic communication systems. Though the evidence cited is usually anecdotal, we believe the use of some systems did in fact help create or maintain social groups with strong interactions and real personal contacts.

We doubt, however, that this picture would be generally valid. Some specific conditions seem necessary for electronic systems to give rise to tightly-linked communities: the number of members should be small (let's say, less than a hundred members), they should come from a similar socio-economic background, share similar interests, and spend sufficient time together on the network. Open, casual participation doesn't fit the picture.

This communal approach has also been the inspiration for a more formal and systematic research domain: collaborative software systems known as *groupware* (Favela and Decouchant 2003). Such systems aim at facilitating communication between members by raising the awareness level about common goals and data and about other network members. Various methods are used, such as posting the identity, history and goals of each participant, as well as common goals, tools and work in progress of the group. In this way, group cohesion and efficiency can be increased markedly on the network.

Different groupware systems have been designed for e-learning, collaborative diagnosis, sharing work information, etc., but they obviously assume a fairly small number of participants (typically about ten to thirty members). It is also common for virtual group members to know each other already at work, or to meet face-to-face sooner or later. It is then possible to try to turn the virtual group into a tightly-knit community.

This is a perfectly legitimate and interesting research field, and applications in real life are probably to be expected soon. But it should be clear that groupware techniques are designed for small groups and would not be adequate for a higher number of participants, or for more casual, open participation patterns.

In short, we do not believe this conception of small, tight communities to fit all electronic groups. This picture may be adequate at times, but it will also be false more often than not.

4.2 Typical virtual characteristics

There is in fact a variety of virtual communities, depending in the exact communication technique, the system users, the discussion theme, the task at hand... Techniques such as e-mail or instant messaging are used mainly for one-to-one communication, but may include several participants (although communication quickly becomes awkward with a number of participants). Discussion lists (by e-mail) can accommodate a higher number of participants. Newsgroups, forums and wikis have been designed for many-to-many interactions, and do attract large numbers of participants. Public documents such as Web pages or weblogs are read passively, but may be used to co-ordinate many users.

Empirical sociological surveys of actual usage are sorely needed, but the domain is a moving target: techniques and practices are in constant flux. This is why we will not attempt here a thorough description of current methods. No wonder that the literature on this subject is still poor and contains much anecdotal evidence rather than systematic studies.

One may easily notice, however, some characteristic features of computer-mediated communities (Gensollen 2004). We do not claim that those features are common to all such communities, nor even to a majority of them. But those characteristics are often found in virtual communities, and are typical of electronic communities as opposed to traditional communities.

Here are some of the most salient features of virtual communities:

- participation is often occasional, or a one-off occurrence,
- participants are frequently anonymous or use pseudonyms,
- groups may be quite large, with hundreds or thousands of participants,
- there are active participants, but also many passive readers,
- group membership is often temporary,
- there seems to be little group awareness,
- group structure is highly flexible,
- contributions to the discussion are often addressed to no one in particular,
- many contributions are apparently ignored,
- there are few personal relationships, and they are unstable,
- the discussion style is usually cold and unemotional, (except for some aggressiveness which serves social control purposes),
- interactions are not between persons, but revolve about a common object, goal or task,
- interactions contribute to the construction of a common workspace,
- contributions are mostly goal-oriented.

In short, interactions tend to be instrumental and impersonal. They contribute to common objects rather than to personal relations. The underlying conception might be called a *blackboard* model: interventions are posted in a public workspace in order to further some common goals, but the individual origin of interactions is less important than their effect on the state of the common discussion or task.

This may be seen as a form of distributed or situated cognition. Interactions are determined by a common environment, which they continuously modify. But explicit collaborative activity between individuals is minimal, as most interactions take place indirectly through the common public workspace.

Again, this is the picture of an ideal type. One doesn't always observe all these characteristics at the same time or to the same degree. But they are typical of a new kind of group where a common task supersedes interpersonal relations.

There are differences according to the particular communication method. In this respect, forums and newsgroups are probably the most typical of computer-mediation techniques. But discussion lists or wikis are usually not anonymous, and e-mail is clearly used for more personal interactions. Most techniques are asynchronous, making communication less personal, except for chats or instant messaging.

One may object that such impersonal communities are degenerate cases, and that virtual communities are normally closer to traditional social groups. In defense of this line of thought, it would certainly not be difficult to find examples of computer-mediated communities with a high degree of social cohesion, group awareness and personal interactions. However, the kind of instrumental communities we have just outlined has become very frequent by now, perfectly functional for a range of uses and in constant progression. In fact the impersonal nature of virtual communication often proves rather beneficial.

4.3 Benefits of virtual commmunication

In our experience, virtual groups are quite efficient to launch a research project, to organize a seminar or a workshop, to put together a journal issue, to solve technical problems, to work on open-source software... It is perfectly possible to work with people one has never met (and possibly will never meet), with the pleasure of getting things done while fulfilling a common goal. The list of possibilities is wide open and new application domains come to light repeatedly. Such endeavors are usually successful with a minimum of fuss: general emotional overhead is low and personal conflicts are rare.

Virtual communities present very interesting advantages indeed for social communication. The factual character of written interactions, the timelag required to respond, the lack of affective overtones are very useful to solve technical problems without undue emotional noise. Electronic communication is a "cool" medium. Personal conflicts are also rare because of the temporary nature of group membership, whereas members of real groups must perforce stay together, making power struggles unavoidable. Virtual communities are generally more flexible and constructive, and adapt easily to new circumstances.

Features of ordinary face-to-face communication would in fact prove harmful for typical virtual groups. The attention given to personal interactions is irrelevant for many technical tasks, and the expression of emotions would only complicate the task resolution process. Moreover, the lack of vocal intonation, facial expressions and body language makes it difficult to express emotional attitudes unambiguously. Subtleties are apt to cause misunderstandings and should best be avoided in favor of a simple, direct style.

Of course, there is a typology of tasks which are well suited to computer-mediated interactions. The narrow bandwidth, slow rate of interaction and (mostly) written exchanges are inadequate for vague, poorly defined and open-ended problems. In such cases, face-to-face meetings and telephone conversations are necessary till a common context of goals and rules has been agreed upon and the precise nature of the problem or task has been defined. Virtual groups are efficient when there is already a common cultural context and a clear awareness of the common goals. It is important in practice to understand when electronic communication is likely to be fruitful and when it will only lead to frustrations.

Lastly, it should be obvious by now that virtual communities are well adapted to the general social trend toward more impersonal relations that we have described above. Temporary, open, flexible social links, on a goal-oriented rather than a personal basis, are typical of modern society as well as of virtual communities. In this way, computer-mediated communities participate in social evolution.

---

5 Discussion

The picture of communities, either real or virtual, that we have just outlined is too simple, however, and deserves further discussion. We have assumed so far a binary opposition between community types, but there is in fact much more diversity, calling for various practical recommendations according to social context.

5.1 Diversity of social groups

Following a classical sociological distinction, we have contrasted here two opposite types of social association, closed traditional communities and more open modern groups. We have placed virtual communities squarely with the latter type, emphasizing the impersonal and flexible nature of virtual relations.

This is of course a simplification, both for ordinary social groups and for computer-mediated communities. Real communities fall somewhere in between closed *Gemeinschaft*-type communities and more modern *Gesellschaft*-type communities. Even if the general evolution of modern society tends toward the latter, there are elements of both in many social groups.

When one examines real communities more closely with an open mind, it appears that the typical features of community types are not always present at the same time. For example in traditional *Gemeinschaft*-type communities, some of the features usually mentioned (small group size, frequent physical contact, stable personal links, emotional aspects, group solidarity...) might well be absent and there is in fact much variation (Brint 2001). The notion of traditional community is a convenient fiction, an ideal type.

Modern *Gesellschaft*-type communities also show enormous variation. They usually include both weak impersonal links and islands of stronger, denser personal relationships (among a background of general flexibility). Personal links and emotional ties have certainly not totally disappeared from modern life (Luckmann 1970) and can still be found in families, circles of friends, and small work groups (e.g. in a workshop, office, store...). It would be absurdly dogmatic to deny the persistence of close relationships in modern society.

In the same way, there is a diversity of virtual communities. Some of them are in fact very close to traditional communities, of which they are just an electronic translation. Pre-existing communities (a circle of friends for example) may turn to electronic communication as an additional medium without changing their fundamental nature. There is for example a fairly common use of e-mail to maintain family or friendship ties, in the same way that cell phone are often used mostly to maintain pre-existing family ties.

Virtual communication techniques may also serve to establish links between people which could not easily meet otherwise (because of disabilities for example), with the explicit intent to create strong personal relations and a close community. The members of such virtual communities usually meet face-to-face sooner or later. This kind of motivation has been the source of quite a few experiments in electronic sociability, and an incentive to the development of new communication techniques on the Internet.

Conversely, many virtual communities do not require any group awareness to function correctly and do not usually lead to personal relationships. The enormous success of peer-to-peer file exchange systems such as Napster or KaZaA is based on common goals (downloading free music) but do not require personal links. In fact system users may be blissfully unaware of the participation of other members of the network (Memmi and Nérot 2003).

5.2 Practical recommendations

What are then the concrete recommendations one may offer system designers? Although virtual communities are diverse, they often are quite different from traditional, tightly-linked social groups. Designers of communication software should be conscious of this social diversity before attempting to formulate appropriate design guidelines.

More generally, one may think that any social group requires both operational and integrative activities (Mintzberg 1979; Zacklad 2003). To survive, a group must act upon the outside world and solve external problems, but also devote a variable proportion of its time and energy to maintain its internal cohesion. Although common goals and common activities go a long way toward ensuring a minimum of cohesion, social communication, common norms and group rituals are probably indispensable for efficient co-operation within the group.

There should probably be a minimum of shared references, values and goals for a group to function in any meaningful way (even mere communication for communication's sake cannot take place without a shared world to talk about). One must make sure that this minimal togetherness is already present to start with, or care should be taken to bring it about somehow. The function of traditional group rituals is to promote social cohesion, and virtual equivalents must be found in cyberspace.

Yet, if virtual communities with impersonal *Gesellschaft*-type characteristics are so common, the question arises as to the right communication tools for such communities. Software designed for smaller groups will not be adequate and will probably prove too cumbersome for larger communities. For example, posting and maintaining user identity is basically irrelevant when participation is occasional and there may be hundreds of participants. Forcing users in this case to post their identity by filling in a questionnaire may simply turn people away.

Some of the discussion tools available nowadays do offer interesting features. Forums and newsgroups are organized around specific themes rather than on a personal basis. Discussion threads inform users when a new message has been posted on a given theme, but not necessarily from a particular person. The recent *wiki* technique (a kind of interactive discussion panel) is probably inadequate for too many participants, but it emphasizes the common discussion theme rather than personal interactions. Such features seem, however, to have been designed by trial and error rather than from fundamental considerations about the nature of virtual communities.

In short, we feel that the necessary co-reference to a common world and togetherness of purpose is often achieved in cyberspace without the need for elaborate software tools. Still, it is very important to offer easy access to a common base of shared constructs (such as texts, programs, discussion threads...). This is a form of situated cognition: implicit co-ordination by a common environment which is constantly updated by a whole community.

5.3 Social networks

There is nevertheless a research domain which is better grounded in sociological theory and mathematical modeling: structural sociology or network analysis (Degenne and Forsé 1994; Wasserman and Faust 2004). This domain is both interesting for its own sake and relevant to the study of virtual communities. It dates back to the 1940s and has developed mostly in the past 30 years (in line with recent social evolution).

Structural sociology has elaborated formal models of social groups seen as networks of relations. The complexity of real social interactions is deliberately simplified so as to represent a group by a graph, in which nodes are actors and links are relations. Social interactions are reduced to simple relations, such as collaboration, advice or influence. This is clearly a drastic simplification, which makes it possible to develop computer models of social groups.

The structure of the network is both a resource and a constraint for individual actors. Social links give access to information, but some positions in the network are more favorable than others and this can be precisely quantified (notably by measures of centrality, influence or autonomy). The behavior and strategy of actors can then be explained or at least analyzed by reference to their position within a social network (Burt 1992).

Without going into more details, the point is that structural sociology is well formalized and sufficiently advanced to offer relevant representation tools for larger communities. Representing groups with hundreds of members is not a problem and the abstract nature of links (edges in a graph) is suitably impersonal. For larger modern communities, these formal methods would be a better source of inspiration than current groupware techniques. By shifting attention from personal relations toward group structure, network analysis is a more revealing approach to describe the functioning of impersonal *Gesellschaft*-type communities.

From a practical point of view, structural methods could be used to map the current state of a community and to show participants their position in the network, the coherence of the structure, what the sub-groups are, and the dynamic evolution of the network. This would be another way to raise group awareness, not in personal terms but from a structural, more abstract perspective. The relevant methods are readily available as software packages.

Still, when participation is only occasional or unique, and when interactions are totally impersonal (following the blackboard model), the notion of structural network loses significance. If all interactions take place through a common workspace, the most one could probably hope for is to make it easy for users to enter the system and to deal with common objects. A good blackboard design and convenient access and modification procedures are then necessary. And in practice, a dedicated and experienced moderator or co-ordinator is crucial for a virtual group to function properly and to keep course over time.

6 Conclusion

We have tried to investigate the nature of virtual communities which emerge from the use of recent electronic communication techniques. When examined as objectively as possible, it appears that computer-mediated communities may differ markedly from traditional communities, or rather from the idealized image of small, tightly-knit communities based on strong personal relationships. This image permeates popular discussion, but is inadequate to describe modern social groups in general and virtual communities in particular.

Virtual communities are often large, and show casual, impersonal relations. Group membership is mostly goal-oriented, frequently temporary, and group structure may evolve rapidly. Designers of communication software should be aware of these typical characteristics in order to tailor their products to the real needs of virtual communities. Allowing easy access to a common blackboard structure is usually more important than fostering personal relations. As a matter of fact, various collaborative methods do take such features into account, but more haphazardly than from a systematic perspective.

The rise of these virtual communities also illustrates and accompanies a long-term social evolution which dates back to the nineteenth century (at least) and which has accelerated in the past quarter century: the general transition from strong personal relationships toward more abstract and flexible social links. In this respect, recent technical developments are just another manifestation of fundamental social trends. Virtual links are simply the electronic version of modern social relations.

Acknowledgment We thank Bruno Oudet for useful information and discussions.

References

Brint S (2001) Gemeinschaft revisited: a critique and reconstruction of the community concept. Sociol Theory 19(1)

Burt RS (1992) Structural holes: the social structure of competition. Harvard University Press, Cambridge

Castells M (1996) The rise of the network society. Blackwell, Oxford

Degenne A, Forsé M (1994) Les Réseaux Sociaux. Armand Colin, Paris

Durkheim E (1960) De la Division du Travail Social. PUF, Paris

Favela J, Decouchant D (eds) (2003) Groupware: design, implementation and use. Springer, Berlin

Gensollen M (2004) Biens informationnels et communautés médiatées. Revue d'Economie Politique

Granovetter MS (1973) The strength of weak ties. Am J Sociol 78:1360–1380

Kollock P, Smith M (eds) (1999) Communities in cyberspace. Routledge Press, London

Luckmann B (1970) The small life-worlds of modern man. Social Res 37(4):580–96

Memmi D, Nérot O (2003) Building virtual communities for information retrieval. In: Favela J, Decouchant D (eds) Groupware: design, implementation and use. Springer, Berlin, Heidelberg, Newyork

Mintzberg H (1979) The structuring of organizations. Prentice Hall, NJ

Rheingold H (2000) The Virtual Community. MIT Press, Cambridge

Shapiro C, Varian HR (1999) Information Rules: A Strategic Guide to the Network Economy. Harvard Business School Press, Cambridge

Simmel G (1989) Philosophie des Geldes. Suhrkamp, Frankfurt

Tönnies F (1963) Gemeinschaft und Gesellschaft. Wissenschaftliche Buchgesellschaft, Darmstad

Veltz P (2000) Le Nouveau Monde Industriel. Gallimard, Paris

Wasserman S, Faust K (1994) Social network analysis: methods and applications. Cambridge University Press, Cambridge

Weber M (1956) Wirtschaft und Gesellschaft. Mohr, Tübingen

Wellman B (ed) (1999) Networks in the Global Village. Westview Press, Boulder

Zacklad M (2003) Communities of action: a cognitive and social approach to the design of CSCW systems. GROUP'03, Sanibel Island, Florida

AI & Soc (2001) 15:169–199
© 2001 Springer-Verlag London Limited

'Use' Discourses in System Development: Can Communication Be Improved?

Carl Martin Allwood[1] and David Hakken[2]

[1]*Department of Psychology, Lund University, Lund, Sweden*
[2]*Department of Sociology and Anthropology, State University of New York Institute of Technology at Utica/Rome, Utica, NY, USA*

Abstract: This paper aims to provide a basis for renewed talk about 'use' in computing. Four current 'discourse arenas' are described. Different intentions manifest in each arena are linked to failures in 'translation', different terminologies crossing disciplinary and national boundaries non-reflexively. Analysis of transnational use discourse dynamics shows much miscommunication. Conflicts like that between the 'Scandinavian System Development School' and the 'usability approach' have less current salience. Renewing our talk about use is essential to a participatory politics of information technology and will lead to clearer perception of the implications of letting new systems becoming primary media of social interaction.

Keywords: Computers and society; Computing; Information System Development; International perspectives; Use; Users

1. Introduction: 'Use': Useful or Useless?

Computing talk increasingly involves 'use' – the 'usefulness' of software, or 'putting users at the centre' of computing systems. At the same time, several professionals in the field have raised questions regarding the value of any 'use' talk. Sceptics point to the recent appropriation of 'use' discourse by virtually every vendor and text in the field, the emergence of a discourse critical of what 'use' perspectives have actually accomplished in the Nordic countries (e.g., Bansler and Kraft, 1994a), and critiques of existing approaches to usability like those discussed below (e.g., Booth, 1989; Grudin, 1993). Indeed, some computing people (e.g., Svanaes, quoted in Allwood and Hakken, 1995a) refuse to speak of 'users' at all any more. The transformed political conditions of the 1990s, and the substantial changes in the scale of the systems being developed (e.g., from simple process automations to building international information infrastructures), both contribute to the hesitancy about using 'use'.

83

Actually, there are several different ways of talking about computer 'use'. While they may involve different contexts and intellectual traditions, these discourses overlap, but in confusing ways. Still, use discourses in our opinion have had several salutary consequences for computing, helping to move it away from the narrowly technical to the more broadly socio-technical. In the face of the opposition cited above, is it still advisable to foster use discourses? If not the entire discourse, which parts of it should be refashioned?

We are of course aware that 'discourse' is a much-discussed issue in contemporary scholarship, but it is not our aim here to engage in this debate. Rather, in the context of this paper, by 'discourse' we simply mean a historically placed and socially and culturally dependent communicative tradition, with at least some assumptions implicitly or explicitly taken for granted among the people communicating via the discourse. Being historically placed means that discourses are unstable and subject to change.

Our aim in this paper is to provide a basis for renewed use talk in computing. We describe and analyse four main 'discourse arenas' in which use talk takes place. Our primary goal is to make sense of the talk, to comprehend it and place it in illuminating contexts, in the hope that such activity makes a 'useful' contribution to use discourse in the future. Different intents can be linked to failures in 'translation' due to different terminology characteristic of non-reflexive boundary crossings.

The practice patterns we highlight are drawn from varied sources. While we treat them as distinct, the arenas, and the actors within them, actually overlap somewhat. Likewise, most speakers may be assumed to have access to at least parts of more than one of the discourses. We are less concerned with how well this talk reflects what is actually happening than with clarifying the claims, whether implicit or explicit, being made by talkers. Thus, we ask that the way we make these differentiations be judged more for their heuristic than their ethnographic value. Such a charitable posture is of some necessity if transdisciplinary terrains like social informatics are to be traversed successfully.

Once the similarities and differences in each arena – the presumptions, preoccupations, and preferred rhetorical styles – are sorted out, we return to general use discourse dynamics. From here, it is possible to see how much of what appears to be serious disagreement is actually miscommunication following from misapprehending the discourse presumptions made in different arenas.

A reconnected, less segmented and therefore more effective general discourse on use in computing is possible and worth striving for. Conflicts like that between the 'Scandinavian System Development School' and the 'usability approach' have real historical roots. However, changing social and technological contexts – for example, 'user' rhetoric becoming more widespread in North America and 'off-the-shelf' software more available in Scandinavia – lessen their current salience.

Similarly, some efforts to institute broad participation in decisions about computing have fallen short of their goals. This has been interpreted as evidence that information technology is less compatible with broadly democratic political goals. General talk about use is essential to a participatory politics of information technology, an important dimension of a democratic approach to technology. Clearer understanding of past use discourses and practices will lead to clearer perception of the current power implications of the new systems becoming primary media of social interaction.

1.1 The Four Use Discourses

There are many different computing use discourses, which share a focus on computing in context, not just on the machines themselves. We[1] find it useful to abstract out four. Where they differ is in the constraints on the use context which they presume or to which they draw attention.

For example, discourse #1, *everyday practice*, is the talk that occurs in the context of the daily activity of working system developers. It is constrained by, for example, contracts specifying costs and deadlines.

In the Nordic countries, a second distinctive discourse about system development (SD) emerged among some academics, the #2 discourse we call *the Scandinavian School* (sometimes also the 'Nordic' school). This discourse has professionalised computing in specific ways, as it also was manifest in distinct rhetorics, such as formulating end-users' political interest in socialist terms.

The often more commercial *usability approach*, discourse #3, focuses quite narrowly, typically on individual users' interaction with a system. The goal of the approach is to produce systems that are highly 'usable'; that is, according to one author, systems which a user can work successfully (Shackel, 1991). For example, 'usability testing' refers to the execution of formal procedures to measure how well an information system performs.

Discourse #4 is that of *social and political theorists* concerned about both the dynamics of organisations and the broader implications of new information technology systems for social reproduction. Some sociologists, anthropologists and political scientists, for example, have argued that worker/user involvement in information SD can lead to important extensions of social democracy, while others have tried to evaluate seriously the popular notion that use of computing induces a social revolution. As with the other discourses, the arguments of these theorists, especially about users, have fed back into the other arenas and complicated their use discourses.

2. Discourses on Use Among Practising System Developers

In this section, we present some data on the nature of use discourses among working system developers, people preoccupied with trying to create information systems that work.[2] Since such individuals are often employed by for-profit organisations, economic considerations are obviously important. However, they also share a professional identity as experts in SD, an identity that they are generally proud of but which also means they have a professional territory to defend.

2.1 Extensive Discourse on Users

In the proper circumstances, one can elicit a rich discourse about users and 'use' among such practitioners. Professional developers in a 1995 Aarhus, Denmark workshop reported that they were 'involved in talking about users every day', much more frequently than 10 years ago: 'Now, everybody wants to be user-centred.' They encountered users in many different contexts: dealing with those experiencing 'user anxiety', selected by marketers, or formed into focus groups.

These Nordic informants were concerned about the occasional negative comments about users – 'users don't know what they want' – among their professional colleagues. They tended to use such comments as examples not of 'bad' users but poor uses of a 'use' perspective – e.g., as a way for unprofessional systems developers to 'sluff off' responsibility for difficult design decisions: 'Sometimes, you have "users" just so you can make them go away'; or 'such programmers talk about users only when they have hit a design problem'.

2.2 Discourse Intensive and Cumulative as Well

To avoid such pitfalls, these professional system developers talked about what one referred to as 'a need to rethink the user' – to be more specific about users and to 'deconstruct' 'user' and 'user needs' as categories. One source of this need is 'confusion about who the "user" actually is – the purchaser, the end user of the system, or the consumer of information produced by the system? (See also Grudin, 1993.) Aarhus participants wanted to distinguish users from customers. One talked about distinct user types – e.g., 'current', 'super' and 'real' users, while another differentiated among primary, secondary and tertiary users. They also distinguished among talking about 'users', 'usability' (see below) and 'marketability'.

The fundamental thrust of comments about change in their own user discourses was quietly positive. Some described themselves as starting to see users as, in an important sense, their own developers. This view in turn led them as developers to question the role of the expert and to problematise expertise. Discourse over users had led to new standards, such as evaluating as successful only those systems in which 'user' can be adequately imagined. While such changes could undermine their authority as developers, they also led to valuable new perspectives:

- 'Super users' became perceived as necessary 'effective ambassadors for new systems' within the organisation; indeed, working with such users helped developers resolve some of their conflicts with theorists.
- Learning how to 'use' users – e.g., while one can learn from users both through talking and watching, talking was most effective.
- While 'teaching the user' was in some ways an acceptable default conception of their role, it could also be a misrepresentation of actual practices, for developers themselves must also be seen as 'learners'.
- Sensitivity to social dimensions like gender enhanced working with users; e.g., female users may want to work with female system developers, because they wanted a reliable relationship.

These perspectives are indicative of a deepening appreciation of the need for complexity in professional use talk. Talkers spoke with pride of their personal involvement in projects in which user involvement had been an important success factor. The effort and creativity that they had expended in building effective relationships with users, in spite of the difficulties which this entailed, was impressive. Moreover, despite the complications, informants strongly endorsed the argument in much of the Scandinavian SD commentary (e.g., Sandberg et al., 1992) that substantive user involvement probably means better systems (see e.g. Heinbokel et al., 1996).

One informant summarised his understanding of user involvement in SD in the following terms: user involvement was a necessary but not a sufficient condition for good SD.

2.3 Factors That Make it Harder to Involve Users

These professionals also draw attention to factors making use talk more difficult. In pilot interviews by Allwood before a 1984 study, informants stressed how the bargaining situation experienced by consultants at the time of negotiating a contract with the customer complicates user talk. For example, in a competition situation with other consultants, it is not always wise entrepreneurship to bring up costs for user participation in the projects. Similarly, the Aarhus participants stressed that the 'user' is often 'socially constructed' through the market, and variations in how this is done add many complications to working with 'users'.

In the past, the first responsibility of the systems developer was understood to be system specification, coming up with a specific sense of what the system is supposed to do. Informants spoke of how they had come to see this process in more active, 'use' terms. In addition to talking about the frequent need to educate the user, some talked of systems specification as an interpretive act, a few even describing it as 'hermeneutic'. This language of course indicates that at least some in this discourse are quite aware of social science as well as natural science discussions. At the same time, these usages are reflective of a growing awareness that system specification involves extended conversation, understanding and shared learning. The contemporary developer often spends more time writing, describing systems orally, and even teaching, than simply writing code or 'programming' per se.

Moreover, development projects nowadays are now more likely to involve revision or replacement of existing IT systems than design of new ones. Decisions made some time ago substantially limit the possibilities that current users can consider. Moreover, the typical design project now involves integrating information systems across organisational units or even organisational boundaries, requiring much more sophisticated group theory, information hardware and software. To create effective information technology actor networks in the face of such complexity, substantial organisational change is likely to be involved, the decisions regarding which are unlikely to be made by a single SD team.

More complex projects reduce the influence that any particular user or users can have. Informants referred to 'complexity constraints' on involving users, conditions being described as markedly different from those obtaining in the 1970s. At that time, choices were more likely to involve a simpler selection between two ways – one computer automated, the other manual – of doing the same task. In the contemporary situation, developers described themselves as needing to be able to project themselves into the subjectivity of multiple users, build relationships and transfer skills of negotiation as well as knowledge of complex hardware and software.

Informants also drew attention to changes in the external context of relationships with users. Organisations like Oslo's Norwegian Computing Centre (NR), which used to be able to account for work with users under a 'research' rubric, have less leeway now, being more subjected to disciplines like 'billable hours'. Increasingly, NR developers found themselves working on end-of-year small projects, an eventuality that also militates against the creation of long-term relationships of trust with users. Such restrictions are even more important for those in private firms.

In Sweden, the existence at the beginning of the 1990s of a conservative government intent on privatising and cost cutting also meant tighter budgets for SD projects funded by the state. Since work with users is very resource consuming and difficult to predict, it is structurally discouraged. Several informants wondered whether, given such external constraints, it made sense any longer to speak of a distinct Scandinavian approach to SD (see section 3).

2.4 Wide Diversity in Actual User Involvement

By and large, these comments were prompted by interviews with and fieldwork among professional system developers at Nordic institutions. Such informants, arguably among those most committed to involving users, nonetheless paint a mixed picture of actual user participation: some projects have a great deal, some very little. Because the same developer often experienced both situations, the extent of user involvement appears less dependent upon the desire of the developer than on other factors.

Some researchers feel less importance is currently given to users. Jonas Löwgren at Linköping University, Sweden, worked for six months as one of two usability professionals in a project employing a total of over 30 developers (Löwgren, quoted in Allwood and Hakken, 1995a). The most striking feature of this project for him was the total absence of use- or user-perspectives. (This finding has continuity with Allwood's (1984) report that some of the consultants he interviewed appeared to see the users as an obstacle to the development process. Indeed, some consultants' initial interpretation of usability design (see below) was user interface programming!) Other practices which de-centred users included 'socially promoting' developers who had talked with customers to ersatz 'user representatives', making users 'hostages' in severe marketing situations.

Allwood (1984) interviewed SD professionals in Sweden, selected to be representative of companies of various sizes and locations in the country. He found great variation in the informants' view of the users. Some saw them as assets and resources in the SD project, whereas others saw them as obstacles and threats. During 1995, Kalén (personal communication) sent out a questionnaire to 300 Swedish system developers randomly selected out of an official register covering the whole country. Forty-one per cent of the responding developers reported that they never conduct any user testing of a program, nor of its manual.

Norwegian Trond Knudsen (1993a, 1993b) has been looking into different concepts that developers have regarding what constitutes what users know about their work and systems' use. He also perceives a broad range of actual user involvement. Most developer groups think in terms of a 'skill' or 'ability' type of knowledge, while a few may have a more complex, research- or evaluation-based 'reflective knowledge' conception. These different categories seem to Knudsen to correlate with different ways of limiting user participation in systems development.

In sum, there is a vibrant and nuanced use discourse among at least some working professionals – a discourse which they apparently have no intention of abandoning. Nonetheless, the extent and character of actual user involvement in computing development seem to vary widely even in relatively auspicious Scandinavian circumstances.

3. The Use Discourse of Academic Theorists: The Scandinavian School

There has also been an important use discourse among theorists of/researchers on SD, particularly Nordic academics who teach in this area and intellectuals who write for this academic audience (e.g., Ehn, 1988; Dahlbom and Mathiassen, 1993; the various authors in Greenbaum and Kyng, 1991). Especially important has been the idea that theoretical SD talk has travelled along different paths in different world regions, the special roles for users being a key factor differentiating Nordic SD theory. While in some ways academics' use discourse echoes that of the practitioners discussed above, in other ways – e.g., as a more self-conscious, reflexive, 'meta-discourse' – it is different.[3]

3.1 'Use' and Nordic vs. American Theoretical Discourses on System Development

Systems development theorists, especially but not only Nordic ones, tend to characterise non-Nordic approaches to SD as predominantly technology- or machine-centred. For many years, it certainly was the case that the design ideal projected to and by US systems analysts, the managers given responsibility for SD, was the 'turn key' system. In this narrative, a system analyst takes from a customer a short statement of system specifications – functions that the system is supposed to perform. She then uses resources – her professional knowledge, existing hardware, and the skills of programmers – to develop a system that is delivered complete to the customer, who need only 'turn the key' to make the system fully operational. (Although possibly a useful ideal in some contexts, previous research in many diverse contexts of SD shows that this 'turn key' idea is often not realistic (Allwood and Kalén, 1993a, 1994).)

The theoretical discourse in the Scandinavian countries in general, and in the Scandinavian School in particular, has been more 'use-centred' than this American discourse. Rather than merely seeking out a set of specifications, the good Nordic systems developer (the term preferred over 'systems analyst') is to embrace users' knowledge dialogically. Often, the dialogue is presented as best taking place in groups. It should also incorporate users in the making of decisions about the nature of the system to be developed. Such participation or 'action research' is presented as the natural and humane, and therefore the appropriately Nordic, way to change organisations: 'Of course we participate', said Norwegian Bjoerg Aasa Soerensen at the 1994 Participatory Design Conference, 'We are civilised.' Users' knowledge of information technology is often deliberately enhanced as part of the process; users can be incorporated into developing and testing prototypes of the system, providing feedback for redesign, and so forth.

The greater presence of users in this standard Scandinavian School account can be traced to a number of sources. One is the commitment to users that was part of the work of early informatics/computer science specialists in Scandinavia like Börje

Langefors (1966) and Kristen Nygaard (Nygaard and Soergaard, 1987). A second source is the greater influence exercised at the point of production by workers in Scandinavia as opposed to the United States, often through social structures erected through social democratic efforts (Ehn, 1988). As a formal matter, this influence was extended explicitly to SD through a series of laws and agreements among employers, unions and the Nordic states in the 1970s.

User involvement was also an important feature of a series of important and well-known research projects that explored its possible contribution to SD, beginning in Norway in the 1960s and spreading to the rest of the Nordic countries, through, for example, the Sydpol project. (See Allwood and Kalén, 1993b, for a short review of earlier human–computer interaction (HCI) and SD research in Scandinavia.) These projects have continued into the 1990s. They are described as demonstrating, among several things, that extensive user involvement can be beneficial, because involved users tend to be more satisfied with systems than those not involved. Moreover, being involved in a good development project can lead an individual to develop a more radically democratic attitude toward both work in general and other aspects of her life (Sandberg et al., 1992). In Scandinavian School talk, these projects often index a common rhetorical pattern or trope: that the projects were a manifestation of a more general pattern, a Scandinavian/Nordic 'model' or alternative approach to social issues. This alternative is described as more participatory, more democratic and therefore more effective, resulting in a kind of social synergy.

3.2 Theorists' Reflexive Critiques of the Scandinavian School

It is the rhetoric of this Scandinavian School to which the working professionals of Section 2 occasionally took exception. A critical attitude is also manifest among many thought to be at the school's centre. Gro Bjerknes and Tone Bratteteig are influential Norwegian SD researchers. Like others who identified with the Collective Resource Approach (CRA) sub-school, Bjerknes and Bratteteig (1995) see a quest for democracy as a constant in the texts and research initiatives of the Scandinavian School. In the 1970s, research projects originating from within the school had an explicit political agenda, as arguments for structural regulation to control resources, enforce rights to · influence and participate, and to produce alternative knowledge with which workers would obtain increased power. For example, acquiring knowledge was to lead to choice of different technologies – ones more likely to service workers' goals.

Subsequent changes in Scandinavian School talk about *how* democracy is to be attained are what provoke Bjerknes' and Bratteteig's ire. The developer replaced the group at the centre:

From the middle 80's, the quest for democracy was left to the individual system developer, the creator of liberating technology. The responsibility of a professional system developer changed towards being a facilitator of a morally – and legally – 'correct' system development process ... [a] shift from emancipation to professionalism ...

The snag here is that the individual system developer [must] undertake a rather impressive personal responsibility for the systems s/he is developing, without a professional organization to support them when running into problems or conflicts (unlike, e.g., physicians or trained nurses Bjerknes and Bratteteig, 1995: 85).

Bjerknes and Bratteteig recognise that this shift was a consequence of the changing social context of the SD process, not of intentional actions by professionals in SD.

Still, they characterise this 'shift from the political to the ethical system developer' as inappropriate, leaving the individual developer with too much responsibility and insufficient power.

At least some participants in the Third Decennial Conference of the Scandinavian System development School in Aarhus wished to de-emphasise politics even more. Political marginalisation is necessitated by the factors (similar to those referenced by practitioners) complicating practice since the early 1970s. An example of this discourse was a presentation by Kai Gronbaek et al. (1995), which advocated Cooperative Experimental SD (CESD) to replace the more militant CRA. CESD emphasises that SD is a highly professional activity. One overhead displayed during their talk contained the statement 'There are no politics here' – a statement not included in the printed conference paper.

Sensing that politics have been lost, Bjerknes and Bratteteig (1995) would reintroduce them into SD. However, this requires rethinking the centrality of 'use':

The challenge for future research is to contribute to democracy in a changing working life and workplaces. To achieve this it is not obvious that user participation in system development activities is a means or the only means ... Further discussion and experiments on other kinds of institutions and local actions different from the ones we know from the Collective Resource Approach are necessary to *reintroduce* the democratic dimension into system development research (Bjerknes and Bratteteig, 1995: 91; emphasis added).

This reintroduction cannot be accomplished simply by having systems developers work with users. 'The lesson to learn from history is that techniques aimed at user participation in system design should be accompanied by means and strategies aimed at other levels of influence' (p. 88), particularly what they refer to as 'global strategies' (p. 91).

Further, Bjerknes and Bratteteig state that 'it is no longer obvious that trade unions are the most strategic institutions through which democracy can be achieved' (p. 90). While noting that user involvement is institutionalised in Sweden in the form of trade union representation, Allwood and Kalén (1993a) are similarly sceptical about current forms of trade union-based user involvement. However, their concern is more with the effectiveness of the trade unions as agents to promote system usefulness than with democracy per se. They followed a system development project of a patient administration project at a university hospital radiology clinic. The trade unions of the staff were represented but made no contributions to usability.

Perhaps the most sustained scepticism about the value of Scandinavian School use talk is that of Bo Dahlbom (1990). After listing 'some examples of what theoreticians say system developers in the field are doing or should be doing ...' (p. 127), including democratic design in real cooperation with users, Dahlbom asserts: 'As we all know, system developers do very little of this sort in their practical work – at least knowingly.' He goes on to ask rhetorically, 'And the theories of system development that take up so much of our discussions, are they only so much "syntactic sugar?"' (p. 128). He traces this lack of fit to the fact that 'The typical Scandinavian approach to system development seems to be an attempt to change traditionally 'action-oriented' organisations into 'political' ones. In the process the system designer gives up her 'action-oriented' expert role in favour of a 'political' user-oriented approach' (p. 140). Here, the use of the term 'user' is taken as a marker of an overt political purpose.

Dahlbom argues further that a change in the organisation of SD work, from craft to something more industrial, has rendered the perspectives of the theoreticians even less relevant. Indirectly, he questions the compatibility of the 'user'-oriented commitment to politics with the need to assert professionalism more strongly:

A democratic approach to system design does not in itself have any practical implication for the design methods to be used. Rather, our willingness to accept such an approach is an indication of uncertainty. Realizing the complexity of our task, working with human beings and complex organizations, we find comfort in sharing responsibility or even getting rid of it altogether (Dahlbom, 1990: 133).

If evaluating her work primarily in relation to democracy, the system developer becomes involved in an attempt to create an ideal (Habermasian) speech situation or public sphere, which Dahlbom describes as 'a clever solution to a virtually impossible problem' (p. 133).[4] Dahlbom develops a specific critique of Scandinavian School rhetoric:

The increasing attention on the 'user' has meant a shift from the system developer designing systems, to the users using the technology to design, from the design of systems to applications used for design. The term 'user' has served well to force this shift of attention, but once the shift is made, the term loses its force. The term 'user' is much too passive in its connotations, and much too general, to support an understanding of the detailed use of current and future computer applications.

In an interesting footnote, he adds:

In the meantime, the use [of the term] is spreading. In current advertising, drivers, tenants, etc. ... are beginning to be called 'users.' The changes in relations between the individual and the state, expressed by such a terminological change as that from 'subjects' to 'citizens' to 'users' is well worth reflecting on? [sic] (Dahlbom, 1990: 140–141).

As an alternative to the use mantra in SD research, Dahlbom proposes a concentration on the nature of 'really existing' information technology in organisations: 'If research in system development has the potential to contribute to an understanding of the ongoing, changing, construction of organizations, it can only be by concentrating on the role of information technology in this process' (pp. 135–136).

In sum, Dahlbom more or less rejects the rhetoric of 'use' practised by the Scandinavian School. As an alternative to centring on users, he recommends that system developers concentrate on understanding the implemented technology in its own terms, a descriptive discourse (like ethnography?) rather than a prescriptive one.

3.3 Continuing Research in the Tradition of the Scandinavian Approach

If existence of a common discourse is taken as an indication of a 'school', then there remains something of a Scandinavian School, with use talk sounding quite like that of section 2. In his work at the Centre for Human–Computer Studies at Uppsala University, Mats Lind concentrates on articulating neglected prerequisites for successful user participation. One is how to create settings that allow users to utilise their repertoire of subconscious domain- (i.e., not computer-) related skills (see Allwood and Hakken, 1995a). Another is getting specific about the cost/benefit side of user participation through summarising the considerable number of projects with participating users. (On the cost/benefit issue, see also Bias and Mayhew, 1994 – a book developed out of the usability tradition described below.)

Toomas Timpka, Cecilia Sjöberg, and Birgitta Svensson pursue similar projects at IDA, the Department of Computer Science at Linköping University, Sweden (quoted in Allwood and Hakken, 1995a). Users participated in the development of MEDEA/Goesta's Book, a medical informatics hypermedia system. To avoid the problem of having systems developers thought of as 'outlaws' demanding total organisational redesign, participation from all practitioner categories was negotiated into the product development process. Because qualitative studies of work practices were performed before any design activity, very few 'surprises' with regard to work practices arose during the later design phases. Also, a respectful attitude was taken towards the existing hierarchies, decision structures and communication channels.

Perhaps the most important characteristic of the project may have been that 'users' were separated from 'customers', and that separate product development activities were performed with each group. Moreover, the MEDEA project produced a product and thus 'succeeded' as more than a mere local process.

An SD approach in the United States much influenced by the Scandinavian School is Participatory Design (PD). Randy Trigg, a proponent of PD from Xerox Palo Alto Research Center, doesn't think of practitioners of PD as having a single approach, but they do share a fundamental respect for the user (Allwood and Hakken, 1995a).

While Bjerknes and Bratteteig (1995) see the main problem as finding a way to remove one form of politics from ISD (Information System Development) research and put back another one elsewhere, Dahlbom (e.g., 1990) and his Danish counterparts want to abandon, even excise, politics. Nonetheless, they all share a frustration with the way 'use' is used, which leads to a revulsion toward most use talk. However, their frustration is with past political appropriations of use talk, not with use itself. Other not so frustrated practitioners, such as Lind, Timpka et al. and Trigg and his fellow PD advocates still look for and find ways to foster users' perspectives in research to improve SD.

This theorists' talk was a substantial presence in the discourse of the professional systems developers described in section 2 above. Some practitioners were good performers of, for example, the linguistic forms through which theorists evoke 'users' – e.g., through interviews and other techniques. These professionals also performed analogues of the theorists' critiques. They pointed out how, when 'user' was conceptualised at the beginning of a project, this was done primarily through an 'interest' perspective, users being treated as a distinct interested party. Use was thus politicised, even a bit dogmatically.

With good reason, they felt strongly that the original Scandinavian School tropes were 'burnt out'. Some satirised a construction of 'user' as 'merely' a research concept. While real users should be engaged in talk in order to open up conceptual structures, all too often this was not aided by the theorising, because academics had an idealised conception of 'users'.

4. The Usability Approach to Information System Development

Already we have described a complicated SD use discourse dialectic, between a professional and a related academic practice. This professional/academic dialectic is complicated by comparative/national differences and by considerable discensus over the appropriate role of politics.

We now complicate the picture further by describing a third SD discourse: that over usability. Practitioners felt that the Scandinavian School deliberately marginalised this third discourse. As an evaluatory perspective, usability first emerged to complement functionality, i.e., whether a program's functions effectively carry out intended tasks (e.g., Goodwin, 1987). There are many definitions of usability, but a common denominator is that the presence or absence of usability is revealed only when a system is actually employed in some task.

4.1 Typical and Possible Usability Discourses

Concern with usability originated in the USA, emerging as an 'approach' in the 1980s. Many of the pioneers within the usability approach were closely connected with the computer industry: John Gould and John Carroll, for example, were connected with IBM for a long time, while John Whiteside worked with DEC. They thus encountered SD problems from a practical/commercial point of view. While, on the one hand, there was commercial interest in creating systems that the customer likes, there was on the other a clear empirical orientation.

Usability talk has centred more on the artefacts and their qualities as tools than on the social context of work, yet other aspects of the total use situation can also be part of it. These include users' competence for using the program, their acceptance of the system, and how such factors interact with each other and the programming (see Allwood and Kalén, 1993a).

In the usability research literature on HCI, for example, there has been a debate between formal and empirical methods. The empirical approach to usability talk is more conducive to concern with social issues than the formal. On Whiteside's reading, usability is associated with a concern for hermeneutics: being open to surprises from reality and being prepared to see multiple influences as interacting in complex ways. Whiteside et al. (1985), for example, argue that the efficiency of each type of interface depends substantially on context – including other features of the program within which an interface is located – rather than on the characteristics of the interface alone.

Typically, however, usability talk manifests a more formal, engineering orientation. One can see this in, for example, the pervasive concern with usability goals – the idea that development projects should formulate exact, measurable goals for the usability aspects of a program. (A usability goal might be, for example, that secretaries after specified hours of training should be able to use a program to perform a particular task in less than a preset time frame.) The reason for measurable goals is the perceived need to be able to judge unambiguously whether or not the program fulfils the goal. If a usability goal is not reached by a pre-established point in time, a project should similarly have 'planned ahead' measures to be taken.

4.2 Critiques of Usability Use Talk

Although it need not, such formal usability discourse tends to conflict with listening carefully to users. Among the critiques summarised by Booth (1989) is the idea that usability discourse does not give any attention to who it is that sets usability goals. Because there is no methodology for talking about goals, if they are inappropriate, the system will not be a good system even if they are met. Nor is there a discursive way to improve the system if usability goals are not met. In the words of Booth, '... it does not provide a full framework for understanding HCI' (p. 128). As also argued by Booth, some definitions of usability such as Shackel's (1991) have been criticised for overstressing quantitative aspects at the cost of qualitative aspects.

The way usability testing has been performed in usability laboratories has also been criticised. Nyce and Löwgren (1995) identify usability testing as one of the two major roles of psychology in the broad field of HCI, the other being production of general human/machine interface models. (This distinction seems to us to parallel that between the empirical and formal approaches to usability noted above). They are critical of the initial role psychology played in usability testing:

Given the experimental heritage, it is not surprising that laboratory studies of usability tended to be unrepresentative or oversimplified in order to yield 'scientifically valid' results ... [such as] ... using undergraduates in the place of programmers or studying organized versus disorganized menus in order to obtain statistically significant results (Nyce and Löwgren, 1995: 37).

In studies of this type, the application problem – that is, going from theory to practice – is insufficiently addressed.

As indicated above, many systems developers – e.g., Randy Trigg and the PD variant of the Scandinavian School – find no respect for users in usability work. True co-design means being open to deep surprises arising in discussions with users. Usability testing, in contrast, often precludes users (one's 'testees') from having their own agenda for the discussion. Connected to a preference for an experimental approach to research, this approach reinforces existing power relations. Once again, talk of use turns political.

Similarly, while Aarhus workshop professionals identified positively with usability discourses, they also had several criticisms. In its US form, usability involves too much 'behaviouristic testing,' as well as continuing struggles over, e.g., how to do it and what to do it for. Usability testers are too often faced with choosing between quick information and 'good' information, quite small groups sometimes being sufficient to get information valuable for the SD practice (Nielsen, 1994). Thus, in usability debates over things like sample size, it is necessary to distinguish studies primarily about getting practically useful ISD information from those aimed mostly at attaining scientific validity. The dialectic between practitioner and theoretical orientations is as evident within usability as 'Scandinavian School' discourses.

Further, workshop participants felt that usability discourses lack a necessary aesthetic dimension. They questioned the adequacy of ISO standard 93401 – limited to the effectiveness, efficiency, and satisfaction of specific users in specific contexts, contrasting it to other possible standards, like Norman's 'user experience' or 'user satisfaction.' (This criticism appears to mirror tensions within the usability camp, of which both ISO Standard 93401-bearers and Donald Norman can be seen to be members.) Given its lingering heritage of lab experiments and its connections more to mainstream cognitive psychology and industrial design than even cognitive science, the relevance to the actual use situation of even 'empirical' usability testing was something about which workshop participants expressed doubts.

4.3 Some Innovative Usability Approaches

Jonas Löwgren, together with colleagues at Linköping University, Sweden, industry representatives and research students, has carried out several research projects to investigate the uptake, use and adaptation of usability-oriented development techniques in professional SD. They used 'close', contextual methods to study real development processes in depth and have interesting data on changes in how the developers regard the users. In one project, the view changed from a pessimistic 'nothing we couldn't have guessed' during the analysis phase to an over-romanticised 'providers of all the right answers' during design (see, for example, Carlshamre, 1994).

On the basis of his earlier research with Lisbeth Hedelin at Göteborg University, Sweden, Allwood (1995) stresses the importance of obtaining an understanding of the *information needs* of the user independent of the system. In his view, a good discourse on usability must necessarily address these needs as well as functionality, effectively broadening the way in which users are conceived and involved in the development process.

Indeed, Allwood's list of general usability problems echoes many of the concerns present in both system developer practitioner and Scandinavian School discourses. Users may lack knowledge of their own best interests and what is technically feasible, and it is not easy to decide which categories of users to involve and how to involve them most effectively. As noted already, user involvement is inversely correlated with at least some indicators of product quality (Heinbokel et al., 1996). His conclusion that '[u]ser involvement in itself may not be the solution to the problem of how to arrive at effective usability' nicely parallels that of Bjerknes and Bratteteig.

Aarhus workshop participants identified other elements of a more desirable approach to usability. One was to focus fulsomely on 'usability', as opposed to mere 'utility' – e.g., computers in use, not just controlled studies of technical properties, and studies of real people being creative vs. studies which merely demonstrate whether or not the actual use corresponds to what was intended. To get usability exercises to go further, participants wanted a usability discourse where the notion of 'interface' is conceived more broadly, as permeating the development as well as the use process. They accepted the pragmatic quality of usability discourses, but they insist that this need not be equated with the 'immediately useful' only. While usability has ties to HCI and cognitive science, it also has them to Heidegger and Habermas, as in the more complex forms of discourse (e.g., Whiteside et al., 1985) .

Further, they argued that, in the current 'anti-political' climate, basing use discourses in usability has distinct advantages. User testing offers an empirical alternative to formal modelling. A formal stress on usability can also lead to recognition that usability is too often not a high enough priority. Usability can be broadened beyond interface to justify early involvement of users, early testing and prototyping. Even in the lab, a shift is possible (and desirable) from hypothesis testing to more 'open-ended' testing – something like 'ethnography' can be used to identify issues and construct a basis for a discourse with users.

Nyce and Löwgren (1995) describe a recent approach to usability in which 'the realities of designing for complex, changing patterns of work, need, and context have become more and more evident'. They describe 'contextual design' as a usability approach whose key feature is creation of designs 'developed so that they reflect both the users' and the developer's current understanding of the context' (p. 38). Because it presumes a model of users' understandings, this approach takes usability testers in the direction of ethnography.

4.4 Ethnography among Practitioners, Scandinavian Theorists and Usability Researchers

Indeed, one finds considerable discussion about ethnography in practitioner and Scandinavian School SD discourses as well as usability (e.g., at the 1995 Aarhus conference and in papers submitted to the various HCI conferences). Several user-oriented research projects (e.g., early like the Florence Project in Norway and later projects run out of Lucy Suchman's anthropology group at Xerox PARC (e.g., Blomberg et al., 1994) attempt to integrate an anthropological ethnographic moment into SD. Such projects convinced Scandinavian School theorist Pelle Ehn to describe his preferred SD approach as anthropological, e.g. as design oriented to and built around the actual work life (work culture) of the workers (cf. Hakken, 1990a). Perceived as useful in usability perspectives as well, ethnography helps professional system developers as they work with everyday problems, providing insight into both 'old' and new, computer-mediated work processes. An ethnographic moment in SD makes sense, in that some mechanism must be found to transfer user knowledge into the system.

By and large, ethnography talk takes place in separate discourses, however. Those anthropologists most visible in SD (especially the Xerox PARC group; despite some effort an interest in SD has not been barely sustained among Nordic social anthropologists) remain highly sceptical of the usability tradition. They also feel it has been difficult to construct the effective transdisciplinary cooperation among system developers, ethnographers and users that effective ethnography in SD would require. Lucy Suchman (1994) and Ina Wagner (1995) both argue that such cooperation in building systems requires more open orientations toward basic epistemological issues than those currently characteristic of most professions, including SD.

On the usability side, Nyce and Löwgren (1995) are sceptical that the appropriation of ethnography in usability will be simplistic. They believe ethnography has only been used to describe action and behaviour, not for analytic perspectives or what they call 'foundational analysis'. Such analysis 'starts with questions about categories, meaning, and intention' (p. 39) in order to move beyond description. Nyce and Löwgren are equally critical of the few ethnographers who publish in the HCI/usability literature, who 'also seem to ignore foundational issues' (p. 41). Hakken (1999) also perceives a tendency for choosing 'quick and dirty' approaches to work ethnography as another important limitation of this epistemology's contribution to usability.

Our point is to highlight the extensive parallels between both the negative and positive evaluations regarding ethnography in these still separate discourses. At the same time, our workshop participants drew attention to certain undesirable consequences following from what they see as the overdeveloped critique of the usability perspective – a critique that in their view dominates much of Participatory Design. PD has, as a consequence, been developed as a competitor to, rather than to complement, usability – a situation that reinforces 'duelling', mutually undermining, use studies.

5. Social and Political Analyses of the Nordic Approach to System Development

To this point, we have sketched three overlapping but also contradictory ways of talking about use in SD. The discussion of ethnography is a useful example of a main point we wish to make, about the existence of parallel discourses with much overlap in content but which also manifest antagonism, at least some of it unnecessary. Before turning to what is to be done, it is necessary to take into account a fourth, further complicating discourse – that of social and political analysts outside of SD who have made their own, often influential readings of use discourses.

Aarhus workshop participants were very much aware of how SD use discourses are echoed in multiple philosophical debates, including those of phenomenology (e.g., Idhe, 1990) and Frankfurt school critical theory (Calhoun, 1995) as well as others already alluded to. Contemporary technology scholars like Andrew Feenberg (1991), Richard Sclove (1995) and Langdon Winner (1994), for example, have all turned to the discourse on user participation, especially in Scandinavian SD, for experience relevant to the future of democracy. Recent popular management theories of empowerment and organisational development similarly place considerable emphasis on user participatory IT. Finally, these developments have been seen by some (reviewed in, for example, Hakken, 1990b) as indicative of the profoundly different characteristics of the coming 'information society'.

These intellectuals largely followed early Scandinavian School theorising. Their appropriation of use discourse has impacted both the debate in the Nordic countries over technology policy and the more general discussions of intellectuals – discussions that have percolated back into intra-Nordic practitioner discussions and usability testing.

Some intellectuals maintain a positive view of the importance of 'use' measures. Aake Sandberg, sociologist at the ex-Centre for Working Life, and his colleges (1992) argue that, despite problems, user influence in Scandinavia has been and continues to be uniquely substantial. The national policies which support user involvement are claimed by Andersen and Kraemer (1994) to have had, at least in Denmark, important consequences, both as an important intermediary in the IT/organisation relationship and on general computing practice. Other's diction suggests that a 'use' focus is now general in IT development. In her discussion of difficulties encountered in promoting use of Lotus Notes, for example, Helena Karsten (1995) comments:

the requirements for new applications and the ideas of novel ways to use existing applications cannot be discerned fully by communication and co-ordination during conventional requirements analysis ... *but only as emerging in the use process.* As the application is used, its requirements are re-created (Karsten, 1995: 29; emphasis added).

5.1 Recent Critiques of User Involvement

Partly out of reaction to earlier effusive enthusiasm, a more critical view of what has actually been achieved has recently developed among such intellectuals. This critique encompasses both how much user involvement actually takes place and what it accomplishes. Because this critique echoes many of the points raised in the earlier discourses, we present merely a sampling of some of its forms.

Controversy over the actual extent and effectiveness of user influence is not restricted to system developers, nor is it only a recent phenomenon. In Sweden the law of co-determination that demanded workplace negotiation prior to introduction of new technology, especially information technology, stimulated such a debate. In a 1984 article, Sven Jonasson, a researcher at the then Swedish Centre for Working Life, describes how in Sweden:

> The Law on co-determination was received with great expectations. Many people believed that after its coming into force, industrial democracy would soon be a reality. This belief was an illusion. People have learned that negotiations not necessarily to be terminated with an agreement are no real negotiations. They have also learned that the fact that such negotiations are the last stage, according to provisions in collective agreements on co-determination, implies that real co-determination does not exist in Sweden (Jonasson, 1984: 21).

Jonasson goes on to argue that nonetheless, even without decisive influence on decisions, participation has consequences for employees that were at the time still considered to be important by unions in Sweden (p. 21).

Controversy has heated up recently among other social observers of the SD scene. Joergen Bansler is a Danish social theorist who has published several influential articles and books on systems development, while Philip Kraft is an influential American work sociologist. In a paper to the 1992 Participatory Design Conference in Cambridge, Massachusetts (Bansler and Kraft, 1994a) they argued that national-level corporate institutions of industrial relations in Scandinavia effectively pre-empted the substantive effectiveness of user involvement in SD.

Bansler and Kraft directly confront those like Hakken (1994) and Winner (1994), who have made much of the way in which participation has been institutionalised in the Scandinavian countries. To North Americans, whose public institutions have been de-illegitimated, institutionalisation of participation had appeared to be a major political accomplishment. However, Bansler and Kraft's view of this institutionalisation is perceived by, for example, some researchers at the Institute for Work Research in Oslo, as one of the prime inhibitors of the general transformatory potential implicit in worker participation. They described the 'social partners' – the national organisations of employers and of employees – as being as likely to use their formal participatory powers to impede as support the generalisation of transformative practices fostered in local sites. Successful local projects tend to be perceived as threats to the reproduction of the power of both large firms and the trade unions built around existing craft and skill demarcations.

5.2 Mixed Views: The Extent and Impact of Users Varies

Others 'outside the profession' argue for a more balanced evaluation of the extent and character of user involvement. Joern Flohr Nielsen and Niels Joergen Relsted from the Institute of Management at the University of Aarhus in Denmark call for 'A New Agenda for User Participation' (Nielsen and Relsted, 1994). They begin by asserting that there is a considerable degree of user participation in current Scandinavian SD and implementation – indeed, that participation is institutionalised and constructed socially as necessary. Yet their experience has convinced them that practitioners 'face severe problems in defining the right way of involvement'. Their survey research led them to conclude that the usefulness of participation is highly dependent on user type and organisational function; specifically, that participation is of little use if organisational issues, as opposed to strictly technical ones, are not on the participation agenda. They argue, moreover, that the recent penchant for decentralisation in organisations has actually broadened opportunities for user participation. They echo sociologist Knudsen (1993b), who finds evidence of substantial user involvement, but primarily in work sites where users already have substantial influence, often due to their professional status and prestige being at least comparable to that of systems developers. The quality of participation, in other words, follows more from factors internal to the specific work process than either national tradition or legislation.

Morton Kyng, an important Danish systems development theorist belonging to the Scandinavian School, argues (Kyng, 1994) that the critics of the actual importance of users in Nordic ISD like Bansler and Kraft both exaggerate the claims of proponents and over-simplify the discourse on users. Yet even in critiquing Bansler and Kraft, Kyng acknowledges that what was accomplished through user participation in decisions regarding technology was limited. In their rejoinder to Kyng, Bansler and Kraft (1994b) concentrate primarily on why little can be expected from participatory design in the USA, again because of the particular relations of social forces and the cultural construction of the current economic crisis. In his most recent work, Sandberg (1994) has drawn attention to the willingness of 'Swedish' capital to abandon participation in pursuit of globalisation – e.g., the rundown of Volvo's 'participatory' workplaces. These comments must be taken as moderating to some extent the claims he has previously made about the long-term importance of user involvement.

At the time of writing, something of a consensus has emerged in this 4th discourse: use perspectives are somewhat incorporated into SD and user involvement is associated with some changes in social process (mostly in organisations), but less of the former takes place, and much less of the latter, than was implied by earlier characterisations. In social theory discussions of issues like technology and democracy, as in a 1997 Oslo Conference on this theme, the Nordic SD experience is evoked less frequently than previously and, in one case at the conference, excised from a plenary presentation. Muted and tentative regarding broader impacts, these less optimistic assessments of use in SD echo current professional, Scandinavian School and usability commentaries.

6. Reconstructing Use?

Thus far, we have indicated the rhetorical presence of each of these discourses in the international SD community. Significant differences in the discourses' characteristic tropes continue to be performed. Moreover, while a particular discourse may frame one other discourse in oppositional terms (e.g., practitioner vs. theorist, or Participatory Design vs. Usability), such binary framings ignore the other discourses in the 'use' conceptual space. The result is confusing, even cacophonous – an important reason why several of the authors we quoted above experience frustration and despair of further use discourse. The misunderstandings and silences among these four discourses are an important reason for the lack of consensus over the proper role of user participation.

6.1 Is it Advisable to Attempt to Rescue the 'Use' Discourse?

Yet heightened awareness of the specificity of the distinct discourse modes also makes possible a reconstructed, more unified and consequently more effective general use discourse. Would this be a good idea?

One argument against rescue is that the concept of 'user' is so broad that nobody knows what it means, from people actually pressing the keys on the keyboard to people who are dependent on the result. Surely, however, such difficulties can be addressed by a complexifying meta-discourse through which what one means by 'users' and 'usability' is clarified and differentiations are introduced among types.

More difficult to deal with are the arguments that 'use' discourse is compromised. In this view, whether because of 'Big P' party political/ideological or 'small p' professional/political appropriations, the meaning of 'use' terms has been bankrupted, so thoroughly appropriated by other discourse dynamics, that there is no real hope of getting people to use 'use' in ways which further knowledge, understanding or practice.

Yet much of the preceding parts of this article documents the many ways in which professionals maintain a meaningful use discourse despite all the miscommunications at which we have pointed. Practitioners will continue to talk about 'use', 'users' and 'usability' irrespective of the pronouncements of theorists. Indeed, some continuing discourse, under 'use' or some other rubric, is compelled by the profound difficulties that continue to follow from acting as if computing artefacts can be considered in isolation from their use contexts. Moreover, arranged in parallel, the discourses manifest considerably more convergence now than in the past. Current assessments support users having substantive roles in the SD process, albeit for different reasons, while discourse participants are less willing to claim social transformation.

Besides, as Markussen (1995) points out, to act as if we can speak of computers without 'users' and 'use' is to treat the machines as independent entities and thereby reinforce technicist (unreflective technological determinist) views. Hakken finds it important, for example, to refer to his work as focusing on 'computing' rather than 'computers' precisely because it forces attention to the broader technology actor network, not just the artefact.

To accept the need for Knowledge Networking or Computer-Supported Cooperative Work – e.g., the idea that, since substantial proportions of both understanding and work are executed by groups rather than individuals, computing systems should support groups rather than individuals alone – is tantamount to accepting the need for a continued discourse on users. Again, however, the traditional use concept must be questioned and new formulations demanded. Even the discourse over the difficulties of constructing transdisciplinary SD teams can be used to justify a continued use discourse. Suchman (1994), for example, has outlined a program for reorienting epistemology through a continued cooperation with users in which ethnographers, systems developers and users cultivate simultaneous discourses over both work process and knowledge generation.

For all these reasons, rather than abandoning use discourse, those involved in SD should continue talking about those using computer systems. What might such talk emphasise?

6.2 Principles on which to Reconstruct Use Discourse #1: Users, not User

At least some professional developers are anxious to keep users a presence in SD discourse – we would say, to attribute ontological status to users, or to see them as an important element of the computing actor network. However, the term 'user' is used in SD discourses to refer to very different groups. Recognising the multiple uses of the term, Markussen (1995) suggests, will help deconstruct the historical roots and embedded assumptions about the nature of SD and different views of the politics of intervention. She argues that this deconstruction needs to focus on the different social constructions of the relations between users, designers and technologies as well as on the different conceptions of users.

One aspect of the deconstruction Markussen suggests involves recognising the double bind of 'users' in some cooperative design projects. That is, they are both expected to be 'subjects' in the sense of active agents in making decisions and 'subjected to the technology' – really, objects. There is a parallel double bind for system developers in cooperative design – that is, they are to be 'subjected' to the joint decisions of the group. Yet, as the 'design experts', they are held responsible for ultimate system success or failure.[6]

6.3 Principle #2: Take the Limits of System Development into Account and Differentiate User Participation

Like Markussen, Petersen Yoneyama (1995) uses a social constructivist perspective to address the issue of reconstructing a discourse on use. He emphasises a difference between the users brought into a design project and the eventual end users. In a project, the latter group are 'invented' by both 'domain expert' users and developers. Since 'real' users are likely to be different, it makes more sense to think of use in terms of 'continuous co-adaptation' or 'designing for tailorability'.

There are good reasons for seeing participation as a more complex task than some initially conceived it to be. This recognition should prompt us to be more specific about what we expect from any particular participation event, not abandon our efforts altogether. Among the important complexifying factors that a renewed use discourse would have to incorporate in that most contemporary SD is indeed system *re*development. It involves the expansion or modification of a pre-existing electronically mediated information system, not the development of a new one. Even systems that may be thought of as replacing existing systems will in fact be built, at least initially, on the practices characteristic of the old. Moreover, current development efforts are generally more complex than they used to be. Rather than simply automating an existing, relatively simple manual or electric process, a contemporary system is more likely to aim at reconfiguring whole complexes of practices – often practices which take place in different locations and/or different organisations. In such larger-scale efforts, the problem is no longer how to involve users in making a set of discrete choices about relatively discrete existing processes; rather, it is about how to integrate different generations of actor networks – indeed, how to transform highly complex organisational (inter- as well as intra-) relationships.

Andrews and Hakken's informants' comments also suggest the need for more clarity over the long-term objective of SD. For at least some adherents of the

Scandinavian School (e.g., adherents of the 'Collective Resource Approach'), user participation in SD had a fundamentally political purpose. It was in effect a 'non-reformist reform' – a practice intended to start a fundamental social transformation with a socialistic objective. For others, participation was primarily about generating better systems (both more efficient and more effective), whereas for still others it was primarily about increasing the likelihood of system acceptability. These goals may not be mutually exclusive in particular development situations, but ignoring their conceptual diversity has added additional elements of ambiguity into use discourses.

Given the great disparity of opinion regarding what the political consequences of user participation should be, let alone what they are, it seems wise to try to separate out, relatively and in time, discussion of the political correlates of user involvement from the efficiency and acceptability correlates. Questions about the implications of user participation in SD both for democracy and for efficacy/acceptance remain important, but we don't see why they can't be pursued separately.

Indeed, the hesitation characteristic in discourse #4 presents an opportunity to pursue such a programme. The Aarhus conference workshop developers supported resituating 'users' primarily in a research, not a political practice, discourse. This necessitates distinguishing among several ways 'users' are used:

1. Models are built out of them (as in software engineering).
2. Decisions are made by, even forced out of, them (organisational development).
3. System development professionals become involved with them so that users' work can be understood (ethnography).
4. They test systems for usability (e.g., creation and proofing of prototypes).

Complex historical relations exist among all these research appropriations of 'use', each with its own conferences, etc. For this particular developer group, understanding work and testing usability were the research appropriations of users with the most current value. The critiques of attempts to foster 'user participation in SD' discussed above constitute better arguments for changing how participation is encouraged and takes place – many, indeed (although by no means all) justify increasing such efforts – than for abandoning them.

They have less interest in abandoning 'usability'. Many of the problematic aspects of this discourse (such as its individualist and commercial framing) would be addressed by a more inclusive 'use'-type usability discourse – one which married concern with 'user participation' with 'usability'. Sharper, more contextualised differentiation of the types of users could, for example, increase the utility of usability testing.

6.4 Principle #3: Differentiate Expectations in Relation to Differentially Relevant National/Cultural Contexts

A group of US system developers might have more interest in jettisoning usability, which has had a higher profile in general use talk. Coming to terms with national differences in use talk is particularly taxing.

The difficulties of assessing the legacy of Nordic user participation are further complicated by global changes in thinking about SD. Interest in 'soft' SD, JAD

(Joint Application Development), CSCW (Computer-Supported Cooperative Work) and even some more humanistic interpretations of BPR (Business Process Re-engineering) has continued to grow around the world. While different from the original 'Scandinavian model' – e.g., with regard to the role of the state – these approaches were in part stimulated by it. Thus, Nordic practice appears to be less distinctive because it is: the world has become a bit more like Norden.

At the same time Scandinavians participate more fully in the global culture. Future attempts to promote effective use discourse will have to come to terms with additional 'universalist/globalist' factors (Hakken, 1993). Even in Norway and Sweden, most systems are erected today on the same Microsoft/Intel platforms, purchased 'off the shelf' and then used, with some modification. This leaves less scope for user-influenced, in-house customised systems, but it also means that the user is less dependent upon the professional system developer. Flattening of hierarchy and decentralisation of decision making can also expand the scope for user input.

Rather than simply automating an existing, relatively simple manual or electric process, developing a contemporary system is more likely to involve reconfiguring whole complexes of practices – often practices which take place in different locations and/or organisations. Hence, the problem is no longer how to involve users in making discrete choices but to involve them in the transformation of highly complex inter- as well as intra-organisational relationships (a point accepted by, for example, JAD and BPR).

For such reasons, a commitment to the 'old' Scandinavian approach to user involvement is no longer really possible. Still, the fact that most SD is really re-SD paradoxically means that some differences in national context remain relevant despite globalisation. In the 1970s, several of the Nordic countries developed social policies that aimed to promote user involvement in IT system development as important means to achieve social goals. These efforts, which mobilised relatively powerful social resources (enterprises, the state, social movements, ideologies), constitute one of the comparatively most sustained national attempts to intervene deliberately to influence the social correlates of technological change, let alone the specifics of the IT/organisation relationship. No such social policy was developed in the USA, although there were important public economic policies (e.g., support for techno-science through the National Science Foundation and the military) with major SD consequences. Thus, Scandinavian public debates over IT have had a different, more overtly social policy-oriented quality from those in the USA. In conjunction with the general American insensitivity to national difference, this actual difference enlarges the Nordic/US differences in discourse patterns.

Moreover, such national differences are not always present. In natural science, ideas are articulated in abstract, general, absolute language. Like others socialised into a positivist perspective, Nordic SD informants tended to avoid making cultural observations in their direct responses to questions about SD. However, descriptions of specific user participation situations were often connected to nations. Sometimes talk was policy connected, referring, for example, to Co-determination or Work Environment legislation. More frequently, it was more diffuse, as when invoking things like 'a Nordic habit of participation'. When asked whether in their experience the special features of Scandinavian IT systems had to do with specific social policies (e.g., work environment legislation) or with general features of Nordic culture, informants stress the latter. (We remind the reader that the character of specific social policies is itself connected to such cultural factors.) Both in Norway and in Sweden, when Hakken became (generally peripherally) involved in particular development projects, it was difficult for him to see any impact of formal entities (e.g., trade union negotiations over technology) mandated by social policy. Indeed, the strongest 'structural' argument for the importance of such policy came from a Swede who identified strongly with management and who had opposed the 1970s legislation. He argued that the formal structures had created the sense that the possible negative impacts of technological change 'had been dealt with', resulting ultimately in more immediate acceptance of technological change than might otherwise have been the case!

In one way or another, most of the ethnographically derived and published accounts discussed above draw attention to particular regional (Scandinavian) or national contexts (the individual Nordic countries) in developing their account of user involvement in SD. (The apparent exception is Bansler and Kraft, who are as pessimistic about the ultimate impact of user involvement in the USA, through, for example, PD, as in Scandinavia. However, they base their pessimism on different industrial relations institutions in the USA (essentially the weakness of working-class organisations) and thus for them national difference is still important as an explanatory mechanism in accounting for similar outcomes.)

Thus, the correlates of the discourses over user involvement in Scandinavian SD described above reflect more than policy. They also reflect broader 'endowments', describable in terms of culture, which go beyond the objectives of specific policies. Both these kinds of factors are captured in the notion of 'national technology style'. Put most simply, the argument for the importance of national technology styles is that one cannot make sense out of the way in which computing has been constructed in real situations without paying attention to national differences. The different conditions for systems development in the USA and Norway, for example, are illustrated by Hakken's informants from the faculty at the University of Oslo Department of Informatics. According to these informants, Norwegian students tend to begin their education with a strong ideological commitment to user involvement, as well as a naive enthusiasm for it. As their education progresses, however, awareness of the difficulties of achieving effective user involvement tends to displace some of the enthusiasm and temper, although by no means eliminate, the commitment.

In the USA, Hakken has witnessed a very different educational trajectory. There, students begin with the idea that the form and substance of a technological system are 'given'; they have to be convinced, and it takes time, that it is even possible for any non-technologist, let alone an ordinary employee, to influence technological development.

This inter-regional difference is directly related to some of the unease that Scandinavian School theorists expressed about American enthusiasm for 'Participatory Design'. In explaining her hesitation at using this term, for example, one informant said that PD sounded too much like 'yet another American "product" to be marketed'. Instead, she preferred to speak of 'user involvement in system development'.

Thus Scandinavians often talked of use with one eye on social policies that were important devices for constructing national/cultural difference, while Americans tended to ignore or otherwise misapprehend both the social policy stakes and the distinct national/cultural dimension. As traceable to different expectations based on different national experiences as they are to substantive differences of value or technical experience, miscommunications based on such dynamics were also likely substantial sources of frustration.

The differences between Scandinavian and American discourses on user involvement, paralleling those between 'user involvement' and 'usability', may be linked to the different endowments, histories, institutional structures and habitual practices of people in these different social formations, as well as different policies. It is only recently that calls for user involvement have moved from the margins toward the centre of American discourse, and their place is still ambiguous (as in Scandinavia, although from the opposite direction). Americanist calls for worker empowerment through business process re-engineering coexist with powerful calls for letting information technology (not people!) determine the proper shape of all business processes. As in the older discourse over Total Quality Management, the empowerment of individual workers is presumed to be quite compatible with the elimination of any vestige of collective influence based on pre-existing work practices. In contrast, Dahlbom (1990) seems to feel that the developments referred to immediately above mean that computing technology has gone so far toward materialising the role of users that a discourse on use is no longer necessary.

In these ways, nations mediate the social construction of computing. Despite globalisation developments, it is likely that important parts will remain of the historical consciousness, as well as the local cultural consciousness that is much a part of Scandinavian discourse. Even the typical Swedish discourse, which often minimises the cultural distinctiveness of Swedes, is itself extent a distinct national discourse. (While the authors share a sense of the importance of differences between US and Nordic use discourses, we differ somewhat regarding the importance of intra-Nordic differences.)[7] There are important reasons to maintain an analytical and critical national discourse; in North America, failure to cultivate a sense of national history has often left that history open to deliberate distortion and manipulation.

6.5 Principle #4: Acknowledge the Impact of Professional Politics

A final comment on politics, this time of the occupational, lower case 'p' variety: the general discourse in computer science is, as pointed out above, an abstract, internationalist one. Nationally/culturally related miscommunications follow as easily from failure to acknowledge difference (e.g., presuming that the state takes similar roles in both Scandinavia and the USA) as from exaggeration of it (e.g., presuming that corporations in the USA, because of their great power, would have no interest in worker participation). One consequence of past misappropriations is Nordic Systems theorists' ambivalence to the way Americans have responded to the Scandinavian discourse. While appreciating the attention of American scholars, Scandinavians even express annoyance at Americans who appear to be trying to tell them how to appropriate their own experience. While they appreciated the privileged attention to Scandinavian practice in the 'PD' and CSCW communities, these Nordic informants still wished to foster a separate SD discourse, as in the annual IRIS (Information system Research In Scandinavia) conferences. As researchers, they are particularly suspicious of what they feel is an American tendency to see PD as so much about product development and marketing as to exclude social impact.

Their caution may be justified; there is, for example, an important sense in which American culture emphasises the 'performance' of participation over its substance, confusing enthusiastic language for substantive commitment. One Swedish informant who had worked for several years for an American computer company, including some time as a manager in the USA, gave up on pursuit of a management career. He was particularly irked by organisational failure to 'follow through' on campaigns for which loud public endorsement was demanded of employees; as a consequence, he never quite knew what to take seriously. He contrasted the apparent American preference for showy public display and easily shifted enthusiasm with the Swedish preference for understatement coupled with long-term connections and commitments. To the extent that successful user involvement depends upon cultural predilection, especially as ensconced in an interventionist state, there is reason to be dubious, like Bansler and Kraft, regarding the long-term fate of PD in the USA.

This means that Nordic SD theorists find themselves performing their competence in an overtly abstract international discourse, expressed in English and therefore subtly inclined toward the USA. The impact of the notion of a distinct 'Scandinavian approach', with specific, rather fixed properties, continues to be paradoxical. It serves as a resource for Nordic researchers as they develop their careers but is also a limitation. This is both because it is a form of distinctiveness in a practice that prefers universality and because previous constructions of the approach constrict understanding of current practice. Adding to the paradox is the mixture of place of origin, national identification and political standpoints that occurs when the label the 'Scandinavian model' is applied.

There are consequences for Nordic SD theorists, whether they choose to *perform* the notion – as the notion of a special Scandinavian attention to, for example, safety, helps to sell Volvos – or if they choose to *critique* it, pointing out its shortcomings. What is most difficult is to try to ignore the notion of a distinct Scandinavian perspective. Indeed, there were several occasions in Hakken's field interviews when informants seemed to be of two minds, drawn on the one hand to perform the distinctive 'Scandinavian approach' discourse, while on the other wishing to be freed from it. One informant expressed his frustration in terms of 'this wretched English language discourse over systems development in Scandinavia'. There was a noticeable pattern of 'performing uniqueness' in English, while critiquing actual practice in a Nordic language. (It is of course also possible that the distaste for 'PD', shown by some Scandinavians, follows less from actual content than from its American heritage.) Following Irving Goffman, we should not expect a perfect correlation between 'backstage' and 'public' performance. Still the complex 'political' problem of having to develop a professional career simultaneously on national, regional and internationals stages has surely added another layer of complexity to interpretation of use discourses.

6.6 Principle #5: Anticipate the Likely Continued Relevance of Policy

While the rapid abandonment of many instruments of national policy is evident in both North America and Scandinavia, policy will retain at least some importance to use discourse in the future. Of the Nordics, Sweden may now be the least able to pursue nationalistic policy. Yet both Sweden and the USA have recently experienced major national IT policy initiatives – national information infrastructures (NIIs).

One can, moreover, hope that, unlike the present, future approaches to NIIs will take other social values, like democracy and the environment, more into consideration. Hanseth et al. (1994) argue that trans-organisational information sharing is really most likely to take place when the individuals who are supposed to share have a concrete sense of the value of sharing. One way to get this sense is to build NIIs 'from the ground up' – e.g., out of the specific suggestions of end-users about the kinds of information they need in order to carry out their activities. Hakken (1993) has extended this argument by contrasting it with the technology-centred, 'build the highway/infobahn and they will drive' approaches to national information infrastructures popular in the USA and Sweden (see also Allwood and Hedelin, 1996).

7. Summary

In sum, we reject the position of those who would give up the talk on use. After appropriate deconstruction, we should aim to reconstruct, not destroy it. Given the intimate link between advanced technology, organisation and society, some discourse on use is an inevitable part of SD. Many of the problems in existing discourses can be traced to the unrecognised presumptions of speakers. Once the different tropes are recognised and miscommunication eliminated, a more unified discourse is possible. Indeed, the four discourse arenas we identified are actually quite similar, especially more recently.

Moreover, there are obvious ideas on which a 'reconstructed' discourse on use can be built. We find that the argument about user involvement made in some of the early forms of the Scandinavian approach – that user involvement should be seen as primarily about transforming society – is, for various reasons, increasingly less viable. At the same time, arguments for use discourses based solely on efficiency grounds are also less persuasive, because the social effects of technology need to be considered as well. More complex arguments for a user discourse, however, remain persuasive – arguments such as those drawing attention to the contemporary imperatives for more information sharing, CSCW or the value of 'bottom-up' information infrastructure development.

An approach to usability that expands to encompass the whole SD process – from early phases of the design process and to implementation and re-engineering, not just design – is what is required. A usability approach that, like too many current ones, fails to include a perspective on the social reality in which SD processes occur is also not sufficient. Rather, usability discourses must incorporate robust models of the social contexts in which SD occurs.

References

Allwood, C.M. (1984). En kartläggning av psykosociala aspekter i systemutvecklingsprojekt ur datakonsultens perspektiv. (A report on psycho-social aspects in system development projects from the perspective of the computer consultant.) Syslab Report, No. 25, Stockholm University.
Allwood, C.M. (1995). On the way to effective usability. In Allwood, C.M. and Hakken, D. (eds) *Position Papers, Workshop on (De-) (Re-) Constructing 'Use': Diverse Evaluations of 'Users' and 'Usability' in Information Systems Development.* Prepared for the 'Computers in context' Conference, Aarhus, Denmark, August 1995.

Allwood, C.M. and Hakken, D. (1995a). Proposal for a Workshop on (De-) (Re-) Constructing 'use': Diverse Evaluations of 'Users' and 'Usability' in Information Systems Development, for the 'Computers in Context' Conference, Aarhus, Denmark, August 1995.

Allwood, C.M. and Hakken, D. (eds) (1995b). Position Papers Workshop on (De-) (Re-) Constructing 'Use': Diverse Evaluations of 'Users' and 'Usability' in Information Systems Development'. At the 'Computers in Context' Conference, Aarhus, Denmark, August 1995.

Allwood, C.M. and Hedelin, L. (1996). Information Administrative Support of Decision Processes in Organizations, *Behaviour and Information Technology*. **15**. 352–362.

Allwood, C.M. and Kalén, T. (1993a). User-Competence and Other Usability Aspects when Introducing a Patient Administrative System: A Case Study, *Interacting with Computers*. **5**. 167–191.

Allwood, C.M. and Kalén, T. (1993b). Using a Patient Administrative System: A Performance Evaluation after End-User Training, *Computers in Human Behavior*. **9**. 137–156.

Allwood, C.M. and Kalén, T. (1994). Usability in CAD: A Psychological Perspective, *International Journal of Human Factors in Manufacturing*. **4**. 145–165.

Andersen, K.V. and Kraemer, K.L. (1994). Information Technology and Transitions in the Public Service: A Comparison of Scandinavia and the United States, *Scandinavian Journal of Information Systems*. **6**(1). 3–24.

Bansler, J. and Kraft, P. (1994a). The Collective Resource Approach: The Scandinavian Experience, *Scandinavian Journal of Information Systems*. **6**(1). 71–84.

Bansler, J. and Kraft, P. (1994b). Privilege and Invisibility in the New Work Order: A Reply to Kyng, *Scandinavian Journal of Information Systems*. **6**(1). 97–106.

Bias, R. and Mayhew, D. (eds) (1994). Cost-Justifying Usability. Academic Press, Hillsdale, NJ.

Bjerknes, G. and Bratteteig, T. (1995). User Participation and Democracy: A Discussion of Scandinavian Research on System Development, *Scandinavian Journal of Information Systems*. **7**(1). 73–98.

Blomberg, J., Suchman, L. and Trigg, R. (1994). Reflections on a Work-Oriented Design Project. In Trigg, R., Anderson, S.I. and Dykstra-Erickson, E. (eds) *PDC'94: Proceedings of the Participatory Design Conference*. Computer Professionals for Social Responsibility, Palo Alto, CA, 99–109.

Booth, P. (1989). An Introduction to Human–Computer Interaction. Erlbaum, Hillsdale, NJ.

Calhoun, C. (1995). Critical Social Theory. Blackwell, Oxford.

Callon, M. (1986). The Sociology of an Actor Network: The Case of the Electric Vehicle. In Callon, M. et al. (eds) *Mapping the Dynamics of Science and Technology*. Macmillan, London, 19–34.

Carlshamre, P. (1994). A Collaborative Approach to Usability Engineering: Technical Communicators and System Developers in Usability Oriented Systems Development. Thesis No. 455, Department of Computer and Information Science, Linköping University, Sweden.

Carroll, J.M. (ed.) (1991). Designing Interaction. Cambridge, UK: Cambridge University Press.

Dahlbom, B. (1990). Using Technology to Understand Organizations. In Bjerknes, G. et al. (eds) *Organizational Competence in System Development: A Scandinavian Contribution*. Studentlitteratur, Lund. 127–148.

Dahlbom, B. and Mathiassen, L. (1993). Computers in Context: The Philosophy and Practice of Systems Design. NCC/Blackwell, Cambridge, UK.

Ehn, P. (1988). Work-Oriented Design of Computer Artifacts. Almqvist & Wiksell, Stockholm.

Feenberg, A. (1991). Critical Theory of Technology. Oxford University Press, New York.

Garsten, C. (1994). Apple World. Stockholm University Studies in Social Anthropology, Stockholm.

Goodwin, N. (1987). Functionality and Usability, *Communications of the ACM*. **30**. 229–233.

Greenbaum, J. and Kyng, M. (eds) (1991). Design at Work: Cooperative Design of Computer Systems. Erlbaum, Hillsdale, NJ.

Gronbaek, K., Kyng, M. and Mogensen, P. (1995). Cooperative Experimental System Development: Cooperative Techniques Beyond Initial Design and Analysis. In *Proceedings from the Third Decennial Conference Computers in Context: Joining Forces in Design*, Department of Computer Science, Aarhus University, Aarhus, Denmark, 20–29.

Grudin, J. (1993). Interface: An Evolving Concept, *Communications of the ACM*. **36**. 110–119.

Hakken, D. (1990a). Review of Pelle Ehn's Work-Oriented Design of Computer Artifacts, *Anthropology of Work Review*. **10**(4). 14–15.

Hakken, D. (1990b). Has there Been a Computer Revolution? An Anthropological View, *Journal of Computing and Society*. **1**(1). 11–28.

Hakken, D. (1993). International Information Infrastructure, *Telektronikk*. **89**(4). 106–110.

Hakken, D. (1994). An American at IRIS, *Scandinavian Journal of Information Systems*. **6**(2). 81–83.

Hakken, D. (1999). Cyborgs@cyberspace?: An Ethnographer Looks to the Future. Routledge, New York.

Hanseth, O., Thoresen, K. and Winner, L. (1994). The Politics of Networking in Health Care. Norwegian Computing Centre, Oslo.

Heinbokel, T., Sonnentag, S., Frese, M., Stolte, W. and Brodbeck, F. (1996). Don't Underestimate the Problems of User Centeredness in Software Development Projects – There Are Many!, *Behaviour and Information Technology*. **4**. 226–236.

Idhe, D. (1990). Technology and the Lifeworld: From Garden to Earth. University Press, Bloomington, IN.

Jonasson, S. (1984). Computers and Society in Sweden, *Information Age*. 6(1). 19–24.

Karsten, H. (1995). It's Like Everyone Working Around the Same Desk: Organizational Readings of Lotus Notes, *Scandinavian Journal of Information Systems*. 7(1). 3–32.

Knudsen, T. (1993a). The Scandinavian Approaches. In Bansler, J. et al. (eds) *Proceedings of the 16th IRIS*, 29–38. University of Copenhagen, Copenhagen, Denmark.

Knudsen, T. (1993b). Conception of Knowledge, Work Organization, Roles and Tasks in Three Systems Development Teams. Department of Information Science, Bergen University.

Langefors, B. (1966). Theoretical Analysis of Information Systems. Studentlitteratur, Lund.

Kyng, M. (1994). Collective Resources Meets Puritanism, *Scandinavian Journal of Information Systems*. 6(1). 85–96.

Markussen, R. (1995). Cooperative Design and Politics of Intervention. In Allwood, C.M. and Hakken, D. (eds) *Position Papers Workshop on (De-) (Re-) Constructing 'Use': Diverse Evaluations of 'Users' and 'Usability' in Information Systems Development*. At the 'Computers in Context' Conference, Aarhus, Denmark, August 1995.

Nielsen, J. (1994). Estimating the Number of Subjects Needed for a Thinking Aloud Test, *International Journal of Human–Computer Studies*. 41. 385–397.

Nielsen, J.F. and Relsted, N.J. (1994). A New Agenda for User Participation: Reconsidering the Old Scandinavian Prescription, *Scandinavian Journal of Information Systems*. 6(2). 3–20.

Nyce, J. and Löwgren, J. (1995). Toward Foundational Analysis in Human –Computer Interaction. In Thomas, P.J. (ed.) *The Social and Interactional Dimensions of Human–Computer Interfaces*. Cambridge University Press, Cambridge, UK, 37–47.

Nygaard, K. Soergaard, P. (1987). The Perspective Concept in Informatics. In Bjerknes, G., Ehn, P. and Kyng, M. (eds) *Computers and Democracy*. Avebury, Aldershot, UK.

Petersen Yoneyama, J.(1995). Users Now and Then. In Allwood, C.M. and Hakken, D. (eds) *Position Paper Workshop on (De-)(Re-) Constructing 'Use': Diverse Evaluations of 'Users' and 'Usability' in Information Systems Development*. At the 'Computers in Context' Conference, Aarhus, Denmark, August 1995.

Sandberg, A. (1994). 'Volvoism' at the End of the Road? Is the Closure of Volvo's Uddevalla Plant the End of a Human-Centered and Productive Alternative to 'Toyotaism'? Working Paper #12, Centre for Working Life, Stockholm.

Sandberg, A., Broms, G., Sundström, L. et al. (1992). Technological change and co-determination in Sweden. Philadelphia: Temple University Press.

Sclove, R. (1995). Democracy and Technology. The Guilford Press, New York.

Shackel, B. (1991). Usability: Context, Framework Definition, Design and Evaluation. In Shackel, B. and Richardson, S. (eds) *Human Factors for Informatics Usability*. Cambridge University Press, Cambridge, UK, 21–37.

Suchman, L. (1994). Working Relations of Technology Production and Use, *Computer Supported Cooperative Work*. 2. 21–39.

Timpka T., Sjöberg, C. and Svensson, B. (1995). Five Years of Participatory Design in the MEDEA Project, *Computer Methods and Programs in Biomedicine*. 46. 175–186.

Wagner, I. (1995). Telespace: Boundary Confusions and Embeddings. Paper prepared for the International Workshop 'The Mutual Shaping of Gender and Technology', University of Twente.

Whiteside, J., Jones, S., Levy, P. and Wixon, D. (1985). User Performance with Command, Menu, and Iconic Interfaces. In Borman, L. and Curtis, B. (eds) *Proceedings of CHI' 85 Human Factors in Computing Systems*. ACM, San Francisco, 185–191.

Winner, L. (1994). Political Artifacts in Scandinavia: An American Perspective, *Scandinavian Journal of Information Systems*. 6(2). 85–94.

Endnotes

1. Our perspectives are shaped by involvement in research on various aspects of HCI and the SD process, especially in Scandinavia. Carl Martin Allwood is Professor of Psychology at the Department of Psychology, Lund University, Sweden. He has an interest in the conditions for development and use of human understanding (the anthropology of knowledge), especially on the individual and meso levels. He has done research on various aspects of HCI since the beginning of the 1980s. This research ranges from the specific computer interaction of a single user to

research on how usability is affected by events in the SD process and other factors affecting system quality in use. Two recent research projects concerned the introduction of a patient administrative system into a hospital and the development of databases for communication and collaboration. The applied context for the latter research projects was the computer system used by the Swedish employment service (8000 users).

For about twenty years, David Hakken has been studying computing as an anthropological ethnographer, teaching computing in a manner informed by ethnography, and developing and evaluating information systems. Hakken has (together with Barbara Andrews) done research on computerisation at the national level in the Scandinavian countries, especially Norway and Sweden, funded by the US National Science Foundation. This research grew out of a previous research experience in Sheffield, England, in 1986–87, where national state hostility seriously enfeebled the ability of the local Labour state and its social movements to pursue social policy, including promotion of user involvement in SD, with regard to technology. Hakken is also involved as a consultant in several IT projects.

2. Data on talk among practising system developers are drawn primarily from three sources. Such discourse has been studied by ethnographers like Hakken, who engage in the sustained study and analysis of human practices in their 'natural' contexts. Because they had heard some of the criticisms of the use discourse described above and in order to get closer to how this approach was actually implemented, Hakken and his co-worker Barbara Andrews incorporated a series of interviews on use issues into their 1993–94 project on the cultural construction of computing in Norway and Sweden. Many of these interviews were executed with colleagues in the IT In Practice (ITIP) and related groups at the Norwegian Computing Centre (NR) – an important practice site of the Scandinavian School, as well as with socially oriented systems developers in Sweden.

Other data are drawn from the comments of a group composed largely of practising systems developers, some of whom also had university affiliations and some of whom were doing research. They participated in a workshop, at the 'Computers in context' Conference, August 1995, Aarhus, Denmark, on '(De-) (Re-) constructing "Use"' organised by us. The intent was to explore the possibilities for reinvigorating the discussion of 'use' in information SD. The morning, deconstruction part of the workshop tried to get away from the hype about 'user perspectives' by specifying concretely what has been learned about use and users from three kinds of activity: attempts to involve users directly in information SD, ethnographic studies of the systems development process and 'richer' forms of usability testing. Position papers on each of the three types of data had been written and circulated to participants (these have been collected in Allwood and Hakken, 1995b). The afternoon, reconstruction part of the workshop aimed to create a more sophisticated conception of the role of 'use' perspectives, both in a general understanding of IT SD and in each of the three data areas. To foster a constructive discussion, participants were urged to move beyond advocacy of a particular approach to evaluation of practice and to articulation of their view of a proper use/user/usability perspective in information SD (Allwood and Hakken, 1995a).

111

   The perspective of these groups is supplemented by what Allwood, Hakken and colleagues, mostly using interviews and other observation techniques, learned from several studies of systems developers in Sweden, and by other observers of the SD scene.

3. The data for this and the subsequent two sections are derived from publications, conferences presentations, interviews and fieldwork with appropriate Scandinavian School, usability and social theorists/academics. Also relevant is our personal practice, since both of us have participated in system development and are social practitioners and theorists.

   One is tempted to be sceptical of the importance of researchers' discourse, perhaps because it is less tied to the practical world of systems development than is that of practitioners. Still, some theorists are also practising developers. More importantly, systems development as a distinct profession, like other science-based practices, is heavily dependent upon research-based activities for its legitimacy. These intellectuals provide many of the terms of the SD discourse of great importance to the professional standing of systems developers everywhere.

4. Nor is Dahlbom convinced of the possibility of appropriating the knowledge base of 'organisational studies' as a sufficient grounding for professional systems developers, primarily because of what he sees as this field's possibly permanent state of intellectual underdevelopment.

5. However, there is a debate on this issue in the usability literature; many of the chapters in Carroll (1991) provide examples. While Nyce and Löwgren (1995) associate some compatible tendencies only with later developments in the usability approach, such tendencies have arguably been part of the perspective from the beginning.

6. In essence, Markussen argues for a more resolutely constructivist perspective on the technology. She uses Latour's notion of technology development as being an act of translation, which she claims 'requires the capacity of reading/interpreting not just the workplace, but the technology as an actant taking part in a redistribution of boundaries'. (p. 6). She concludes, 'The concept of users may emerge not just as an empirical but as a formal category, as a question of distribution of actants' (p. 6). Implicit in these observations is the preoccupation of those committed to Technology Actor Network (TAN) theory with the distribution of 'actorship' (the quality of agency, of actually leading construction of an alliance to institute a particular technology actor network) among those participants (actants) in the network. For example, can we execute SD in a way so sufficiently complexified that designers, users and technology are all recognised appropriately as actors, albeit in different ways?

7. In his ethnographic experience (see also Knudsen 1993a, 1993b), Hakken perceived significant differences among the Nordic discourses on use. The particular histories of the nations have led to significant differences in national discourses and social reproductive careers. For example, participation is complicated by particular contradictory myths/practices about each of the Nordic countries. In Norway, these include the idea that there has never been an indigenous ruling class and that there is reason to be sensitive to the dangers of foreign domination. There is a particular contradiction within Norwegian notions of participation – the pride in

egalitarian practices contrasts with suspicion that these are more often ritual than substantive – 'when we do consult, we never get anywhere'. This latter reflects the tension between Norwegian celebrations of the individual, the active creator, whereas participation implies collective responsibility.

For such reasons, Hakken feels that insufficient attention has been given to how such intra-Nordic differences influence SD talk. Allwood in general thinks it is difficult to draw conclusions of this kind about whole entities at the national level.

Correspondence and offprint requests to: *Carl Martin Allwood, Department of Psychology, Lund University, Box 213, SE-221 00 Lund, Sweden. Tel.: 46-46-222 9281; Fax: 46-46-222 4209; Email: Carl_Martin.Allwood@psychology.lu.se*

AI & Soc (2001) 15:359–376
© 2001 Springer-Verlag London Limited

A Pattern Approach to Interaction Design[1]

Jan O. Borchers

Computer Science Department, Stanford University, Stanford, California, USA

Abstract: To create successful interactive systems, user interface designers need to cooperate with developers and application domain experts in an interdisciplinary team. These groups, however, usually lack a common terminology to exchange ideas, opinions and values. This paper presents an approach that uses pattern languages to capture this knowledge in software development, human–computer interaction (HCI) and the application domain. A formal, domain-independent definition of design patterns allows for computer support without sacrificing readability, and pattern use is integrated into the usability engineering life cycle. As an example, experience from building an award-winning interactive music exhibit was turned into a pattern language, which was then used to inform follow-up projects and support HCI education.

Keywords: Design methodologies; Education; Exhibits; Interdisciplinary design; Music; Pattern languages

1. Introduction

To design systems that fulfil today's high expectations concerning usability, human–computer interaction (HCI) experts need to work together very closely with team members from other disciplines. Most notably, they need to cooperate with application domain experts to identify the concepts, tasks and terminology of the product environment, and with the development team to make sure the internal system design supports the interaction techniques required.

However, these disciplines lack a common language: it is difficult for the user interface designer to explain his guidelines and concerns to the other groups. It is often even more problematic to extract application domain concepts from the user representative in a usable form. And it is hard for HCI people, and for application domain experts even more so, to understand the architectural and technological constraints and rules that guide the systems engineer in the design process. In general,

---

[1] An earlier version of this paper appeared in the *Proceedings of the DIS 2000 International Conference on Designing Interactive Systems* (16–19 August 2000, New York) and appears by permission of the ACM Press.

people within a discipline often have trouble communicating what they know to outsiders, but to work together well disciplines must learn to appreciate each other's language, traditions and values (Kim, 1990).

1.1 Pattern Languages as *Lingua Franca*

Simply stated, a pattern is a proven solution to a recurring design problem. It pays special attention to the context in which it is applicable, to the competing 'forces' it needs to balance, and to the positive and negative consequences of its application. It references higher-level patterns describing the context in which it can be applied, and lower-level patterns that could be used after the current one to further refine the solution. This hierarchy structures a comprehensive collection of patterns into a *pattern language*.

The central idea presented here is that HCI, software engineering and application domain experts in a project team each express their expertise in the form of a pattern language. This makes their knowledge and assumptions more explicit, and easier for the other disciplines to understand and refer to. Such a common vocabulary can greatly improve communication within the team, and also serve as a corporate memory of design expertise.

The next section briefly explains the concept and history of pattern languages. A critical component of these languages, however, is the cross-references that help readers find their way through the material. To facilitate creating and navigating through patterns, possibly with computer support, a formal syntactic definition of patterns and their relations is presented that is independent of the domain they address. It is also shown where in the usability engineering life cycle patterns can be applied. A final section shows a pattern language for interactive music exhibits as an example, and summarises some initial empirical studies concerning the usefulness of pattern languages in HCI courses.

2. A Brief History of Pattern Languages

This section briefly outlines where the pattern idea comes from, and how it has been adapted to other disciplines.

2.1 Patterns in Urban Architecture

The original concept of pattern languages was conceived by architect Christopher Alexander in the 1970s. In Alexander (1979), he explains how a hierarchical collection of architectural design patterns can be identified to make future buildings and urban environments more usable and pleasing for their inhabitants. In Alexander et al. (1977), he presents 253 such patterns of 'user-friendly' solutions to recurring problems in urban architecture. They range from large-scale issues ('COMMUNITY OF 7000', 'IDENTIFIABLE NEIGHBOURHOOD'), via smaller-scale patterns ('PROMENADE', 'STREET CAFES') down to patterns for the design of single buildings ('CASCADE OF ROOFS', 'INTIMACY GRADIENT'). Finally, in Alexander et al. (1988), the architect uses his pattern language to define a new planning process for the University of Oregon as an example.

It is less known that Alexander's goal in publishing this pattern language was to allow not architects, but the inhabitants (that is, the *users*) themselves to design their environments. This is strikingly similar to the ideas of user-centred and participatory design, which aim to involve end users in all stages of the software development cycle.

Pattern languages essentially aim to provide laypeople with a vocabulary to express their ideas and designs, and to discuss them with professionals. This idea of creating a vocabulary implements well-known results from psychological research about *verbal encoding*: 'When there is a story or an argument or an idea that we want to remember …, we make a verbal description of the event and then remember our verbalization' (Miller, 1956). The idea can be recalled when its short name is remembered.

Each of Alexander's patterns is presented as several pages of illustrated text, using a very uniform structure and layout with the following components (Alexander et al., 1979: x):

A meaningful, concise *name* identifies the pattern, a *ranking* indicates the validity of the pattern, a *picture* gives a 'sensitizing' and easily understood example of the pattern applied, and the *context* explains which larger patterns it helps to implement. Next, a short *problem statement* summarises the competing 'forces', or design tradeoffs, and a more extensive *problem description* gives empirical background information and shows existing solutions.

The subsequent *solution* is the central pattern component. It generalises the examples into a clear, but generic set of instructions that can be applied in varying situations. A *diagram* describes this solution and its constituents graphically, and *references* point the reader to smaller patterns that can be used to implement this pattern.

It must be stressed that Alexandrian patterns are, above all, a didactic medium for human readers, even (and especially) for non-architects. This quality must not be lost in a more formal representation or extension of the idea to other domains.

2.2 Patterns in Software Engineering

Around 1987, software engineering picked up the pattern idea. At the OOPSLA conference on object orientation, Beck and Cunningham (1987) reported on an experiment where application domain experts without prior Smalltalk experience successfully designed their own Smalltalk user interfaces after they had been introduced to basic Smalltalk UI concepts using a pattern language. It is interesting to note that this first software pattern experiment actually dealt with user interface design and user participation.

The workshop started a lively exchange about software design patterns. An influential collection of patterns for object-oriented software design was published by Gamma et al. (1995). The annual Pattern Languages of Programming (PLoP) conferences have established an entirely new forum for exchanging proven generalised solutions to recurring software design problems.

The overall format of patterns has not changed very much from Alexander to software engineering examples such as those published by the so-called Gang of Four (Gamma et al., 1995): name, context, problem, solution, examples, diagrams and cross-references are still the essential constituents of each pattern.

The goals, however, have changed in an important way, without many noticing: software design patterns are considered a useful language for communication *among software developers*, and a practical vehicle for introducing less experienced developers to the field. The idea of end users designing their own (software) architectures has not been taken over. On the one hand, this makes sense, because people do not live as intensely 'in' their software applications as they live in their environments. On the other hand, though, a good chance to push the concept of participatory design forward by introducing patterns has not been taken advantage of. This was one of the reasons why, at OOPSLA'99, the 'Gang of Four' were put before a mock 'trial' for their work. (See the article by Tidwell, 1999, for an interesting commentary.)

2.3 Patterns in HCI

The pattern idea was referenced by HCI research earlier than most people expect. Norman and Draper (1986) mention Alexander's work, and in his classic *Psychology of Everyday Things* (Norman, 1988: 229), Norman states that he was influenced particularly by it. Apple's *Human Interface Guidelines* (Apple Computer, 1992), quote Alexander's books as seminal in the field of environmental design, and the Utrecht School of Arts uses patterns as a basis for their interaction design curriculum (Barfield et al., 1994).

But it was only recently that a first workshop dedicated to pattern languages for interaction design took place within the HCI community. It showed that the ideas about adopting the pattern concept for HCI were still very varied, and that 'as yet, there has been little attention given to pattern languages for interaction design' (Bayle et al., 1998). The patterns reported by this workshop were necessarily not strictly design patterns, but rather activity patterns describing observed behaviour (at the conference), without judging whether these represented 'good' or 'bad' solutions. Like the Utrecht curriculum designers (Barfield et al., 1994), it identified the temporal dimension as making interaction design quite different from architectural design. The workshop also stressed the often underestimated fact that patterns, to a large extent, represent the *values* of their author, i.e. the qualities that the author considers important in the artefacts he designs.

Subsequent workshops at UPA'99 (Granlund and Lafrenière, 1999a), INTERACT'99 (see Borchers et al., 2001b) and at CHI 2000 (Borchers et al., 2000) have confirmed the growing interest in pattern languages within the HCI community, and helped to shape more precisely the notion of HCI design patterns and their use. A preliminary definition of HCI design patterns and suggestions for structuring HCI design pattern languages, as well as a sample format for an HCI pattern, were given at the INTERACT workshop. The CHI 2000 workshop refined these findings and definitions, and the pattern idea has also been linked to other related concepts of usability engineering, such as *claims* (Sutcliffe and Dimitrova, 1999).

Meanwhile, a number of concrete pattern collections for interaction design have been suggested. The language by Tidwell (1998), for example, covers a substantial field of user interface design issues. Interaction design patterns have found their way into the PLoP conference series, even becoming a 'hot topic' at the ChiliPLoP'99 conference (Borchers, 2000a).

Less research, though, has gone into formalising pattern languages for HCI, to make them more accessible to computer support. Even Alexander (Alexander et al., 1979: xviii) admits that, 'since the language is in truth a network, there is no one sequence which perfectly captures it'. The hypertext model of a pattern language presented here makes it possible to create tools for navigating through the language, similar to those for interface design guidelines (Alben et al., 1994; Iannella, 1994).

2.4 Patterns in the Application Domain

Patterns have been a successful tool for modelling design experience in architecture, in software design (with the limitations discussed here) and, as existing collections such as Tidwell's show, also in HCI. Other domains have been addressed by patterns as well. Denning and Dargan (1996), in their theory of action-centred design, suggest a technique called *Pattern Mapping* as a basis for cross-disciplinary software design. Referring to Alexander's work, they claim that patterns could constitute a design language for communication between software engineers and users, just as Alexander's pattern language does between builder and inhabitant. Granlund and Lafrenière (1999b) use patterns to describe business domains, processes and tasks to aid early system definition and conceptual design. They also note the interdisciplinary value of patterns as a communications medium and the ability of patterns to capture knowledge from previous projects.

Indeed, there is no reason why the experience, methods and values of any application domain cannot be expressed in pattern form, as long as activity in that application domain includes some form of design, creative or problem-solving work. This brought the author to the idea that not only HCI professionals and software engineers, but also application domain experts, could express their respective experience, guidelines and values in the form of pattern languages.

The history of pattern languages in architecture, software engineering and especially HCI is described in more detail in Borchers (2001a).

3. Using Pattern Languages in Interdisciplinary Design

The following sections give a general model of pattern languages, and show how to integrate those pattern languages into the usability engineering process.

3.1 A Formal Hypertext Model of a Pattern Language

A formal description of patterns makes it less ambiguous for the parties involved to decide what a pattern is supposed to look like, in terms of structure and content. It also makes it possible to design computer-based tools that help authors in writing, and readers in understanding patterns. We first give a formal syntactic definition:

- A *pattern language* is a directed acyclic graph (DAG) $PL=(P,R)$ with nodes $P = \{P_1,\dots,P_n\}$ and edges $R = \{R_1,\dots,R_m\}$.
- Each node $P \in P$ is called a *pattern*.
- For P, $Q \in P$: *P references Q* $\Leftrightarrow \exists\, R =(P, Q) \in R$.

- The set of edges leaving a node $P \in \mathbf{P}$ is called its *references*. The set of edges entering it is called its *context*.
- Each node $P \in \mathbf{P}$ is itself a set $P = \{n, r, i, p, f_1 \dots f_i, e_1 \dots e_j, s, d\}$ of a name n, ranking r, illustration i, problem p with forces $f_1 \dots f_i$, examples $e_1 \dots e_j$, the solution s and diagram d.

This syntactic definition is augmented with the following semantics:

- Each **pattern** of a language captures a recurring design problem, and suggests a proven solution to it. The language consists of a set of such patterns for a specific design domain, such as urban architecture.
- Each pattern has a **context** represented by edges pointing to it from higher-level patterns. They sketch the design situations in which it can be used. Similarly, its **references** show what lower-level patterns can be applied after it has been used. This relationship creates a *hierarchy* within the pattern language. It leads the designer from patterns addressing large-scale design issues, to patterns about small design details, and helps him locate related patterns quickly.
- The **name** of a pattern helps to refer to its central idea quickly, and build a vocabulary for communication within a team or design community. The **ranking** shows how universally valid the pattern author believes this pattern is. It helps readers to distinguish early pattern ideas from truly timeless patterns that have been confirmed on countless occasions.
- The opening **illustration** gives readers a quick idea of a typical example situation for the pattern, even if they are not professionals. Media choice depends on the domain of the language: architecture can be represented by photos of buildings and locations; HCI may prefer screen shots, video sequences of an interaction, audio recordings for a voice-controlled menu, etc.
- The **problem** states what the major issue is that the pattern addresses. The **forces** further elaborate the problem statement. They are aspects of the design that need to be optimised. They usually come in pairs contradicting each other.
- The **examples** section is the largest of each pattern. It shows existing situations in which the problem at hand can be (or has been) encountered, and how it has been solved in those situations.
- The **solution** generalises from the examples a proven way to balance the forces at hand optimally for the given design context. It is not simply prescriptive, but generic so that it can generate a solution when it is applied to concrete problem situations of the form specified by the context.
- The **diagram** supports the solution by summarising its main idea in a graphical way, omitting any unnecessary details. For experts, the diagram is quicker to grasp than the opening illustration. Media choice again depends on the domain: a graphical sketch for architecture, pseudo-code or UML diagram for software engineering, a storyboard sketch for HCI, a score fragment for music, etc.

With these definitions, a formal model for pattern languages is in place. However, formalisation must not impede readability and clarity of the material. The process of writing patterns should not be hindered by the formal notation, and the results should still be accessible in a variety of formats, including linear, printed documentation (which most people still prefer for sustained reading for well-known reasons). Each part of a pattern, and its connections to other patterns, are usually presented as several paragraphs in the pattern description (see, for example, Alexander et al., 1979). Other media, such as images, animations and audio recordings, are used to augment the pattern description as described above.

3.2 Using Patterns in the Usability Engineering Life Cycle

It is not necessary to follow a specific design method to use this pattern language approach. As Dix et al. (1998: 6) point out, 'probably 90% of the value of any interface design technique is that it forces the designer to remember that someone (and in particular someone else) will use the system under construction'. Nevertheless, the design process must emphasise usability, and therefore include programmers and user interface (UI) designers as well as end users (Tognazzini, 1992: 57). Also, as with most usability methods (Dix et al., 1998: 179), patterns will not be used in just a single design phase, but throughout the entire design process. A suitable process framework for this is Nielsen's *usability engineering life cycle model* (Nielsen, 1993: 72). Patterns fit into each of the 11 activities that this model suggests:

1. Know the user.

If the application domain of an interactive software project involves some designing, creative or problem-solving activity, then its concepts and methods can be represented as a pattern language in the sense of the above definition. The development team, after explaining the basic idea of patterns to user representatives, can begin eliciting application domain concepts in the form of patterns from those experts. Those patterns do not need to be perfect in terms of their timeless quality. They just give a uniform format to what needs to be captured anyway, but explicitly state problems, forces, existing solutions and references within these 'work patterns'. Also, patterns for user interface and software design will have the same format, making all the material more accessible to all members of the design team, and helping users to recognise their work patterns in user interface concepts of the end product.

2. Competitive analysis.

Here, existing products are examined to gather information and hints for the design of the new system. The internal architecture of competing products is usually not accessible, but user interface design solutions of successful competing systems can be generalised into HCI design patterns for the new product.

3. Setting usability goals.

The various aspects of usability, such as memorability and efficiency of use, need to be prioritised. They can, however, be used as forces of abstract HCI design patterns that explain how these forces conflict, and how this conflict is to be solved for the current project. A design for a system used intensively by expert users, for example, will put the balance between the above goals more towards efficiency of use than first-time learnability.

4. Parallel design.

Several groups of designers can develop alternative user interface prototypes to broaden the 'design space' explored. HCI design patterns can serve as a common ground, working as design guidelines to be sure that the usability goals from the last phase are fulfilled. These patterns can also come from external sources such as HCI design books.

5. Participatory design.

This technique involves user representatives, or application domain experts, in the design process to evaluate prototypes and participate in design discussions. These users will have few problems understanding the pattern language of their application domain (which they have probably helped to create themselves). But knowing this format will also help them understand the HCI patterns that the user interface design team has collected, and which represents their design values, methods and guidelines. Conversely, the UI design team can use the application domain pattern language to talk among themselves and to users about issues of the application domain, in a language that users will find resembles their own terminology. A common vocabulary for users and user interface designers emerges from the combination of other languages.

6. Coordinated design of the total interface.

Coordinated design aims to create a consistent interface, documentation, on-line help and tutorials, both within the current product and with previous versions of this and other products within a product family. HCI design patterns, especially those addressing lower-level, concrete design guidelines, can serve as vocabulary among design teams, to help ensure this consistency. Of course, additional methods such as dictionaries of user interface terms are required to support this process.

7. Apply guidelines and heuristic analysis.

Style guides and standards are the ways to express HCI design experience that are closest to HCI design patterns. Patterns can improve these forms through their structured format and contents, combinations of concrete existing examples and a general solution, and an insightful explanation not only of the solution, but also of the problem context in which this solution can be used, as well as the structured way in which individual patterns are integrated into the hierarchical network of a pattern language. This coverage of multiple layers of abstraction and expertise is similar to the distinction between general guidelines, category-specific rules which are derived from previous projects and product-specific guidelines that are developed as part of an individual project (Nielsen, 1993: 93).

8. Prototyping.

Prototyping puts concrete interfaces into the hands of users much earlier than the final product, albeit limited in features, performance and stability. In this more software-oriented area of usability engineering, software design patterns play an important role. If the development group members express their architectural standards and components, as well as specific project ideas, as patterns, the user interface design group can relate to those concepts more easily, and will better understand the concerns of the development team. For example, the HCI design group could change the feature set in a prototype to make it easier to implement without compromising its usefulness for testing.

9. Empirical testing.

Prototypes, from initial paper mock-ups to the final system, are tested with potential users to discover design problems. While patterns cannot help the actual evaluation

121

process, the set of HCI patterns can be used to relate problems discovered to the patterns that could be applied to solve those problems, as shown in the next phase.

10. Iterative design.

Prototypes are redesigned and improved iteratively based upon feedback from user tests. In this activity, patterns of HCI or software design experience are an important tool to inform the designer about his options. Contrary to general design guidelines, which are mainly *descriptive*, and merely state desirable general features of a 'good' finished interactive system, patterns are *constructive*: they suggest how a problem can be solved. Naturally, patterns evolve over the course of a project, reflecting the progress in understanding the problem space and improving the design. Successful solutions serve as examples for existing patterns, or initiate the formulation of a new pattern. Subsequent projects will relate more easily to patterns with such well-known examples. The result is a post hoc 'structural' design rationale which keeps the lessons learned during a project accessible for the future. Patterns are less suited to documenting good and bad design decisions in the form of a 'process' design rationale, although the concept of *anti-patterns* of tempting but bad solutions could be used to model discarded design options.

11. Collect feedback from field use.

Studies of the finished product in use, help line call analysis and other methods can be used to evaluate the final product after delivery. Here, the application domain pattern language serves as an important tool to talk to users. HCI design patterns point out design alternatives for solutions that need to be improved. Similarly, feedback can strengthen the argument of those patterns that created a successful solution, and suggest rethinking those that led to suboptimal results.

4. Example: Designing Interactive Music Exhibits

As a proof of concept, we used our experience from designing an interactive, computer-based music exhibit, to start building a pattern language about the musical, HCI and software design lessons learned from the project. We will briefly present the original project's goals and its design, and then give some examples of resulting patterns from the various disciplines, and at various levels of abstraction.

4.1 The WorldBeat Project

The *Ars Electronica Center* in Linz, Austria (Janko et al., 1996) is a technology museum 'of the future', an exhibition and venue centre where the arts and new technology merge. Our research group designed one floor within this centre, addressing future computer-supported learning and working environments. Apart from an electronic class/conference room (Mühlhäuser et al., 1996), we designed several exhibits showing the use of computers in specific learning subjects and working situations. *WorldBeat* was one of these exhibits, designed by the author.

Briefly, *WorldBeat* allows the user to interact with music in various new ways. The entire exhibit is controlled using just a pair of infrared batons. They are used to navigate through the various pages of the system, and to create musical input, from playing virtual instruments like drums or a guitar, to conducting a computer orchestra playing a classical piece, to improvising to a computer blues band – without playing wrong notes. Furthermore, users can try to recognise instruments by their sound alone, and locate tunes by humming their melody. The system is described in more detail in Borchers (1997), and in the video proceedings of that 1997 CHI conference. The goal of *WorldBeat* was to show visitors that computers may open up entirely new ways of interacting with musical information, many of which they can expect to see implemented in future consumer products.

To design a system for such an environment, we had to take into account a number of factors that do not usually have to be considered in such detail when designing an interactive system. However, instead of listing our findings as a loose set of guidelines, we used the pattern format described above to summarise our experience in all three disciplines. We will show what musical concepts we identified to address in our exhibit, describe our user interface patterns specific to this scenario, and present software design solutions that we found for this system.

We will not describe the patterns in full detail; that would typically require several pages per pattern. Instead, we show the network of patterns identified so far, and look in more detail at the main issues of context, problem, solution, examples and references, for a small but representative selection. The actual patterns are written in a more detailed textual form without explicit labels for 'Context', 'Problem' and so on: instead, they use implicit typographical structuring to clearly show the components of each pattern. The complete pattern languages can be found in Borchers (2001a).

4.2 Musical Design Patterns

We will begin by describing the musical concepts and 'guidelines' that musicians use when they compose or improvise music. Our point is that this process can be considered a 'design' activity as well, and that it is feasible to structure the rules and values of this design process into patterns.

At the most abstract level we consider useful, a certain style of music is chosen. Our exhibit features various musical styles in different parts of the system, but we will restrict ourselves to the presentation of the BLUES STYLE. The patterns below are referenced by that top-level style pattern. Downward links are 'references' relations (see Fig. 1).

4.2.1 Twelve-Bar Progression

Context: Playing a BLUES STYLE piece.

Problem: Players need to agree to a common sequence ('progression') of musical chords to create harmonically coherent music. A progression is useful to avoid a too static, boring impression, but it should be simple enough to be easily remembered while playing.

Solution: Use the following blues progression of chords, each lasting one bar (in C major, I = C major, IV = F major, V = G major):

I-I-I-I-IV-IV-I-I-V-V-I-I

123

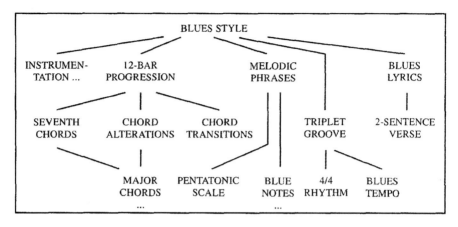

Fig. 1. A pattern language for blues music.

Examples: The above is the simplest form of any blues piece, and most blues music adheres to it. It is found in countless recordings and sheet music.

References: The sequence is built from basic MAJOR CHORDS. Many variations of this basic progression are possible that make the music more interesting. A simple one is to use SEVENTH CHORDS instead of the simple major chords. The sequence can be varied further by replacing chords with more complex CHORD TRANSITIONS.

4.2.2 Triplet Groove

Context: Playing a piece in the BLUES STYLE. The concept is also used in other styles like swing, and jazz in general.

Problem: Players need to create a swinging rhythmic feeling. The straight rhythm from other styles does not create this. At the same time, sheet music cannot include all rhythmic variances because it would become too complex and unreadable.

Solution: Where the written music contains an evenly spaced pattern of eighth notes, shift every second eighth note in the pattern backwards in time by about one third of its length, shortening it accordingly, and make the preceding eighth note one third longer. Instead of a rhythmic length ratio of 1:1, the resulting pattern is alternating notes with a length ratio of 2/3:1/3. Two straight eighth notes have been changed into 2+1 'triplet' eighth notes. This rhythmic shift creates what musicians call the 'laid-back groove' in a performed piece. Figure 2 shows this concept in traditional notation.

Fig. 2. From straight notation to triplet groove.

Examples: Any recorded blues piece will feature this rhythmic shift, although the actual shift percentage varies very widely. Usually, the faster a piece is, the less shifting takes place.

References: TRIPLET GROOVE always modifies an underlying straight beat, typically a 4/4 rhythm.

These examples show what issues musical patterns may address, and how they can be formulated. We will now look at HCI design patterns that could create an interface dealing with such musical concepts.

4.3 Interaction Design Patterns

This section describes our collection of patterns for HCI design. We have focused on issues particularly important for interactive exhibits, but they are of equal importance to 'kiosk' and similar public-access systems where typical users are first-time and one-time users with short interaction times and no time for a learning curve.

The outer graph (see Fig. 3) shows most of them, with top-down links again representing 'references' relations. We will go into more detail for two of these patterns.

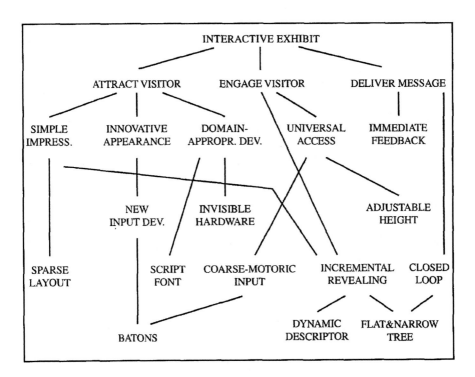

Fig. 3. An HCI pattern language for interactive exhibits.

4.3.1 Attract Visitor

Context: An INTERACTIVE EXHIBIT that should attract and engage its visitors to deliver a message.

Problem: In an exhibition centre, many exhibits are 'competing' for the visitor's attention although they should rather 'cooperate' to inform the visitor, without one system becoming too dominating in its appearance. On the other hand, people will never discover the message of an exhibit if they are not drawn towards it in the first place, or if it looks too complicated. After all, there is usually nothing that forces the visitor to use any of the exhibits.

Solution: Make the exhibit look interesting by creating an innovative-looking interface that promises an unusual experience, but make it appear simple enough to scare off neither computer or application domain novices. Use an appearance and interaction technique that is adequate for the domain of the exhibit (which is usually not computing).

Examples: At the *WorldBeat* exhibit, there is no mouse, keyboard or computer visible; all that the user sees is a pair of infrared batons, and a monitor with a simple, inviting start-up screen (see Fig. 4).

References: The SIMPLE IMPRESSION pattern shows how to build a system that does not scare off visitors. INCREMENTAL REVEALING conveys initial simplicity without limiting the depth of the system. Use DOMAIN-APPROPRIATE DEVICES on the exhibit and its periphery to reflect its subject area.

Fig. 4. A user at the *WorldBeat* exhibit.

4.3.2 Incremental Revealing

Context: Designing a computer exhibit interface that attracts visitors with its initial SIMPLE IMPRESSION, but that still ENGAGES VISITORS for a while with sufficient depth of functionality and content.

Problem: A simple appearance, and presenting the system's depth are competing goals.

Solution: Initially, present only a very concise and simple overview of the system functionality. Only when the user becomes active, showing that he is interested in a certain part of this overview, offer additional information about it, and show what is lying 'behind' this introductory presentation.

Examples: *WorldBeat* is structured into a short introductory screen, followed by a simple main selection screen with only names and icons of the main exhibit components (conducting, improvising, etc.) If the user moves the pointer towards one of the component icons, a short explanation appears (first revealing stage). Then, if he selects it, a separate page opens up that explains the features in more detail (second revealing stage).

References: Most information systems reveal their content incrementally through a FLAT AND NARROW TREE structure. The DYNAMIC DESCRIPTOR pattern also implements incremental revealing. It can be found in Apple's Balloon Help, Windows ToolTips, and has also been identified in Tidwell (1998).

4.4 Software Design Patterns

As Gamma et al. (1995) suggested, domain-specific software design patterns are important to supplement the general ones. There are many general software patterns that could be identified in our system, but we will concentrate here on those patterns that relate specifically to software design for music exhibits. We will describe one of these patterns below. More details of these patterns can be found in Borchers (2001a).

4.4.1 Metric Transformer

Context: Musical performance adds many subtle variations to the lifeless representation of a written score, in the harmonic, melodic and rhythmic dimensions. To model these variations, a system will follow the TRANSFORMER CHAIN pattern, where a sequence of transformations is applied to an incoming stream of musical data. Owing to its one-dimensional nature, the rhythmic dimension is especially accessible for computer modelling.

Problem: An incoming stream of musical events needs to be modified in its timing: some events need to be delayed for a short period. The delay may follow a deterministic algorithm, or a random distribution.

Solution: A number of objects need to interact for such a functionality. A Creator supplies the raw, straight musical material, and a Metronome the raw, straight rhythm. A Modulator models the metric transformation, i.e. the deviation from the uniform

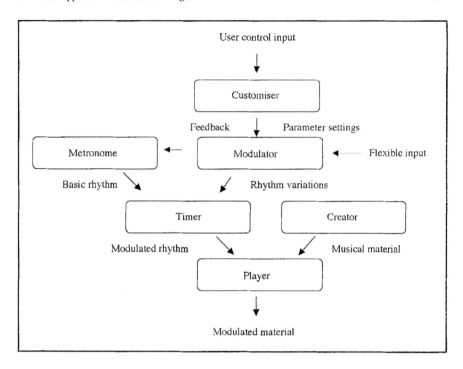

Fig. 5. The METRIC TRANSFORMER pattern.

beat. It captures the musical idea behind the transformation. It may feed overall gradual tempo changes back to the Metronome. A Customiser lets the user change the Modulator parameters in real time. A Timer takes the basic Metronome beat, and modifies it with the Modulator output. A Player component finally outputs the rhythmically transformed musical material as a new sequence of musical events (see Fig. 5).

Examples: The *WorldBeat* exhibit features a *Groove* slider that lets the user change the swing feeling of a blues and while playing (see below). Other examples of such variations that the pattern could implement are the random variations of human performance when interpreting a written score, or the conducting process where the conductor makes subtle changes to the existing tempo and dynamic structure of a orchestral piece.

References: This pattern works best with a representation of the musical material as MUSICAL EVENTS; an example is the widely used Musical Instruments Digital Interface (MIDI) standard.

4.5 Reusing the Pattern Language

In a follow-up project, we designed an interactive music exhibit to learn about the concept of the classical *fugue*. The musical domain here is quite different from jazz, and only a few musical patterns carried over into the new project. However, we identified many HCI and software engineering patterns in our language that carried over very well to this new task. In particular, these patterns helped us communicate our previous experience to new members of the design team.

Recently, we finished work on two other projects in a similar domain for the HOUSE OF MUSIC VIENNA, including a system to conduct the Vienna Philharmonic Orchestra (Borchers et al., 2001a), and have been able to again reuse and refine many of the patterns that were identified through *WorldBeat* and improved in the *Interactive Fugue* project.

4.6 Pattern Use in Education

HCI patterns were also used by the author to teach user interface design to first-year computer science undergraduate students. Although these students only received a pattern collection to refer to for their first design projects, it was surprising to see how quickly they discovered patterns that were applicable to their current design situation, how they used those proven solutions in their own project context, and how a vocabulary of patterns was used quickly to discuss options and solutions within and between the design groups.

In an ad hoc quiz and poll at the end of the term, students were able to recall 1.6 patterns by name on average (although patterns had only been used for a short period of the course), and judged their usefulness with an overall 1.9 (1 = will absolutely reuse them, 5 = will absolutely not reuse them). The findings of this study are described in more detail in Borchers (2001a).

5. Conclusions and Further Research

Communication in interdisciplinary design teams is a major problem for HCI practitioners. We suggested that all team members – especially HCI people, software engineers, and experts from the application domain – formulate their experience, methods and values in the form of pattern languages, as originally introduced in urban architecture. For a uniform representation and computer support, we proposed a formal representation of patterns and their relations.

As an example, we created pattern languages from our experience in creating an interactive music exhibit. Our results are promising, and indicate that such patterns help people from outside the respective disciplines to understand our findings. They have proven useful to create subsequent exhibits with a similar background, and HCI patterns have served well in an HCI course. Currently, we are extending and refining our language by identifying additional patterns and relations. First steps have also been undertaken in designing the Pattern Editing Tool (PET), a system to support creating, reviewing and browsing pattern languages. A complete version of the HCI and other pattern languages for interactive exhibits and similar systems, as well as a description of PET, can be found in Borchers (2001a).

Applying the pattern technique to entirely new application domains could further strengthen our argument that structuring them into patterns is a generally valid approach, and a more intensive use of HCI patterns in user interface design courses will hopefully give us more detailed findings about their usefulness in education.

Acknowledgements

The author would like to thank his former colleagues at the Telecooperation Group at Darmstadt University of Technology, the Telecooperation Research Group at the University of Linz, and the Distributed Systems and Multimedia Computing Groups at the University of Ulm, particularly Max Mühlhäuser at Darmstadt, for their help in working on the projects that created the necessary basis of this work.

References

Alben, L., Faris, J. and Sadler, H. (1994). Making it Macintosh: Designing the Message when the Message is Design, *Interactions*. 1(1). 10–20.

Alexander, C. (1979). The Timeless Way of Building. Oxford University Press, Oxford.

Alexander, C., Ishikawa, S., Silverstein, M., Jacobson, M., Fiksdahl-King, I. and Angel, S. (1977). A Pattern Language: Towns, Buildings, Construction. Oxford University Press, Oxford.

Alexander, C., Silverstein, M., Angel, S., Ishikawa, S. and Abrams, D. (1988). The Oregon Experiment. Oxford University Press, Oxford.

Apple Computer (1992). Macintosh Human Interface Guidelines. Addison-Wesley, Reading, MA.

Barfield, L., van Burgsteden, W., Lanfermeijer, R. et al. (1994). Interaction Design at the Utrecht School of the Arts, *SIGCHI Bulletin*. 26(3). 49–79.

Bayle, E., Bellamy, R., Casaday, G., Erickson, T. et al. (1998). Putting it all Together: Towards a Pattern Language for Interaction Design, *SIGCHI Bulletin*. 30(1). 17–23.

Beck, K. and Cunningham, W. (1987). Using Pattern Languages for Object-Oriented Programs. Technical Report CR-87-43, Tektronix, Inc., September 17, 1987. Presented at the OOPSLA'87 workshop on Specification and Design for Object-Oriented Programming.

Borchers, J.O. (1997). WorldBeat: Designing a Baton-Based Interface for a Interactive Music Exhibit. In *Proceedings of the CHI'97 Conference on Human Factors in Computing Systems*, Atlanta, GA, 22–27 March 1997. ACM, 131–138.

Borchers, J.O. (2000a). CHI Meets PLoP: An Interaction Patterns Workshop, *SIGCHI Bulletin*. 32(1). 9–12 (Workshop at ChiliPLoP'99).

Borchers, J.O. (2000b). Interaction Design Patterns: Twelve Theses. Position Paper for the workshop Pattern Languages for Interaction Design: Building Momentum, CHI 2000, The Hague, Netherlands, 2–3 April 2000.

Borchers, J.O. (2001a). A Pattern Approach to Interaction Design. Wiley, New York.

Borchers, J.O. and Mühlhäuser, M. (1998). Design patterns for interactive musical systems, *IEEE Multimedia*. 5(3). 36–46.

Borchers, J.O., Griffiths, R.N., Pemberton, L. and Stork, A. (2000). Pattern Languages for Interaction Design: Building Momentum. Workshop at CHI 2000, The Hague, Netherlands, 2–3 April 2000 (Report to be published).

Borchers, J.O., Samminger, W. and Mühlhäuser, M. (2001a). Conducting a Realistic Electronic Orchestra. *Proceedings of UIST 2001*, Orlando, FL, 11–14 November 2001, 161–162.

Borchers, J.O., Fincher, S., Griffiths, R., Pemberton, L. and Siemon, E. (2001b). Usability Pattern Language: Creating a Community. Report of workshop at INTERACT'99, Edinborough, UK, 30–31 August, 1999. (Appendix to this article).

Denning, P. and Dargan, P. (1996). Action-Centered Design. In Winograd, T. (ed.) *Bringing Design to Software*. Addison-Wesley, Reading, MA, 105–119.

Dix, A.J., Finlay, J.E., Abowd, G.D. and Beale, R. (1998). Human–Computer Interaction (2nd edn). Prentice-Hall, London.

Gamma, E., Helm, R., Johnson, R. and Vlissides, J. (1995). Design Patterns: Elements of Reusable Object-Oriented Software. Addison-Wesley, Reading, MA.

Granlund, A. and Lafrenière, D. (1999a). A Pattern-Supported Approach to the User Interface Design Process. Workshop report, UPA'99 Usability Professionals' Association Conference, Scottsdale, AZ, 29 June–2 July 1999.

Granlund, A. and Lafrenière, D. (1999b). PSA, A Pattern-Supported Approach to the User Interface Design Process. Position paper for the UPA'99 Usability Professionals' Association Conference, Scottsdale, AZ, 29 June–2 July 1999.

Iannella, R. (1994). Hypersam: A Practical User Interface Guidelines Management System. In *Proceedings of QCHI'94 Second Annual CHISIG (Queensland) Symposium*, Bond University, Australia.

Janko, S., Leopoldseder, H. and Stocker, G. (1996). Ars Electronica Center: Museum of the Future. Ars Electronica Center, Linz, Austria.

Kim, S. (1990). Interdisciplinary Cooperation. In Laurel B. (ed.) *The Art of Human–Computer Interface Design*. Addison-Wesley, Reading, MA, 31–44.

Miller, G.A. (1956). The Magical Number Seven, Plus or Minus Two: Some Limits of our Capacity for Processing Information, *Psychological Review*. **63**. 81–97. http://www.well.com/user/smali /miller.html

Mühlhäuser, M., Borchers, J.O., Falkowski, C. and Manske, K. (1996). The Conference/Classroom of the Future: An Interdisciplinary Approach. In *Proceedings of IFIP Conference 'The International Office of the Future: Design Options and Solution Strategies*, Tucson, AZ. Chapman & Hall, London, 233–250.

Nielsen, J. (1993). Usability Engineering. Morgan Kaufmann, San Francisco.

Norman, D.A. (1988). The Psychology of Everyday Things. Basic Books, New York.

Norman, D.A. and Draper, S.W. (1986). User-Centered System Design: New Perspectives on Human–Computer Interaction. Erlbaum, Hillsdale, NJ.

Sutcliffe, A. and Dimitrova, M. Patterns, Claims and Multimedia. In *Human–Computer Interaction: INTERACT '99*, Edinburgh, UK, 30 August–3 September 1999. IOS Press, Amsterdam, 329–335.

Tidwell, J. (1998). Interaction Design Patterns. PLoP'98 Conference on Pattern Languages of Programming, Illinois, extended version at http://www.mit.edu/~jtidwell/interaction_patterns.html

Tidwell, J. (1999). The Gang of Four Are Guilty. http://www.mit.edu/~jtidwell/gof_are_guilty.html

Tognazzini, B. (1992). TOG on Interface. Addison-Wesley, Reading, MA.

Correspondence and offprint requests to: Jan O. Borchers, Computer Science Department, Stanford University, Gates Building, Room 201, 353 Serra Street, Stanford, CA 94305-9020, USA. Email: borchers@cs.stanford.edu

AI & Soc (2001) 15:200–215
© 2001 Springer-Verlag London Limited

CSCW Design Reconceptualised Through Science Studies

Casper Bruun Jensen

Information and Media Science, Aarhus University, Aarhus, Denmark

Abstract: This paper points out the need for an analytical and ontological reorientation of the field of computer-supported cooperative work (CSCW). It is argued that even though this field is heterogeneous it is marred by general problems of conceptualising the co-constitutive relations between humans and technologies. This is demonstrated through readings of several recent CSCW analyses. It is then suggested that a conceptual improvement can be facilitated by paying attention to newer scientific studies, here exemplified by Pickering, Haraway and Latour.

Keywords: CSCW; Ontology; Normativity; Performativity; Representation; Science and technology studies

1. Introduction

STS could pose some critical questions about this dichotomy between the realm of human work and the realm of technological, instrumental rationality. If we grant that human work is not well depicted in terms of calculability, predictability, efficiency, and so forth, what about technology? Are we not replacing one category mistake when we assume that technology can be described in this way? (Berg, 1998: 474).

The aim of this paper is to show some of the ways in which such category mistakes are at play in computer-supported cooperative work (CSCW) discourse. In order to alleviate the propensity for some of these mistakes I discuss and offer three conceptual tools, which I call performativity, representation and normativity. Through applying these concepts to a range of recent CSCW analyses I will suggest that they point in the direction of a need for what I term an *ontological reorientation* of CSCW. In CSCW there is a common assumption that humans and technologies are *ontologically* or *constitutionally separated*, and thus that there are different spheres of analyses to apply to each set of entities. Newer STS (science, technology and society) studies would problematise such an assumption. By ontological reorientation I am therefore pointing in the direction of analyses towards a monistic framework in which humans and machines are *ontologically on par* or *constitutively intertwined*. I also hope to make an initial indication of how this matters in practice.

132

The paper is structured as follows. I start off with a short exposition of Bucciarelli's (1994) conception of *design as narrative*. I argue that while his analysis works well as an initial move from determinist accounts of design, it could be fruitfully complemented with developments from recent STS literature. I then discuss the concepts of performativity, representation and normativity from such a perspective. These concepts could offer insights into how one analyses design processes without recourse to the ontological dualism invoked above. I offer them as analytical tools for a CSCW audience.

Why do I aim these considerations specifically at CSCW? After all, it could be argued that they are of general interest to designers. I discuss this relevant question in an intermediary section, before moving on to the interpretive instantiations of the use of the above-mentioned concepts. In the final part of the paper I analyse several newer CSCW articles.

The insights gathered from these analyses are used to specify some ways in which CSCW might gain new theoretical and, perhaps, practical vitality by reorienting its ontology.

2. Design Process: Anti-Technicist Version

In *Designing Engineers*, Bucciarelli (1994) launches an attack on two *deterministic conceptions* of design. One is the *savant* perspective, which views design process as a fundamentally scientific matter. The second is the *utilitarian* perspective, which sees design as the outcome of the struggle of the market place. The overwhelming problem with both perspectives is that their focus is wrong. They focus on the end-object of design. Because of this focus they can convince themselves retrospectively that the *process* leading to this object was rationally determined. A particular goal is matched by the correct method for achieving it. This Bucciarelli calls the object-world view. His book points in another direction, towards viewing design as a social process. Seeing design as a social process is very different from seeing it from an object-world perspective. The process perspective shows us that design is a messy affair. Surely economic factors and scientific factors are involved. But there are also political, organisational, personal and psychological ones. And they do not add up rationally. Whereas rational engineers' stories about design are better with *fewer elements*, social process stories are better the *more* elements they include. This is because there are multiple spheres of interaction and they defy our usual categorisations. We don't know beforehand what elements will be most important, so none should be excluded *a priori*. To design, one must be simultaneously logical, political, rhetorical, shrewd and, of course, deft at handling various aspects of the material world. When multiple and differently interested actors participate in design one can picture a giant complex web or, perhaps, a game of cat's cradle consisting a multiplicity of materials and humans (Haraway, 1994). The ontologically relevant elements of design are multiplied in such an account.[1]

---

[1] See also Whalley and Barley (1997).

Ultimately, Bucciarelli's vision of design takes the shape of a story telling. Design is a story unfolding. Sometimes the narrative of this story is smooth, sometimes rough, and sometimes there is no story at all. This is when design dies. There are, however, two differences between design as story and regular stories. First, clearly this is a material story. Story of design involves pens and computers and drills and wrenches that may help them unfold or may, unmercifully and abruptly, stop it. Second, the story of design is not told by a single narrator. There are many voices and they may not always agree on the plot. For Bucciarelli design is a story, but the story is negotiated. This negotiation has lots of different actors – some human, some material. Getting design to work on these terms is finding a way in a landscape that is a

dense, interwoven fabric that is, at the same time, dynamic, thoroughly ecological, even fragile. (Bucciarelli, 1994:131).

3. Design Process: Further Specification

While Bucciarelli's formulation of what design is about is plausible, there is still a need for further specification of the problems of design. This is not so because of a lack in Bucciarelli's analysis itself but rather because of its focus. That is, because his primary aim is to demythologise the idea of rational design (savant and utilitarian), he does not spend as much time formulating a more positive conception of design. Taking our clue from STS studies, however, it is possible to complicate Bucciarelli's conception of *design as narrative*. It could be a good idea to complicate our stories of design, because design itself is such a complicated affair. Below I suggest the concepts of performativity, representation and normativity as tools that will enable us to span the ontological gap between humans and technology, and thus enhance our understanding of design as complex material-semiotic processes.

4. Performativity, Representation, Normativity

4.1 Performativity

What does performativity mean? Here, I turn to Andy Pickering (1995).[2] His claim is that STS studies have been immersed in problems of meaning, symbols and representation to the extent that it has been unable to account for actual physical encounters between materials and humans. The tradition has been steeped in a 'representational idiom'. Pickering wants to focus on the overlooked 'performative idiom'. One can survey the differences in focus between the representative and performative idioms through comparing the two following series of relevant factors.

Some of the most important concepts of the representative idiom are theory, cognition, introspection and retrospection. The performative idiom concerns itself rather with practice, hands-on experience, real-time action and activity.

---

[2]For a completely different understanding of performativity I recommend Butler (1993).

Pickering wants to know how scientific invention takes place in real time.[3] This is not a matter of theory – it is a matter of extensive, sometimes frustrating, interactions with a variety of more or less cooperative materials.[4] Gooding (1992, 1994) points in the same direction, emphasising agency in the world of things:

Much of what experimenters do involves non-verbal doing as well as saying. Such activity is often skilled and unpremeditated, especially at the frontiers where new experience is elicited, represented, and fashioned into empirical evidence (Gooding, 1992: 66).

What this quote suggests is that while it is certainly true that meaning and representation are involved in the innovative process (scientific or design innovation) it is not in any way prior. Before representation is *activity*. The human participant is certainly active. Her activity consists in, for instance, writing code to be used in a new prototype. But what is more, the material world is also active and unpredictable. While the programmer's job is to accommodate this non-human activity, the computer may resist this attempt. The code does not work, the machine crashes and days of work are lost. The material world intervenes in the processes in unpredictable ways. At a certain point we have a prototype. We have reached a level of agreement between human and non-human agencies that we deem 'good enough'. Pickering (whose vocabulary I am employing here) says that the programmer and the machine have been *tuned* to each other. This tuning process is design. The interactive stabilisation that results is the prototype. In the scientific world it is this ability to reach agreement with materials in the world that makes us believe in correspondence between our theories and the real world:

Convergence engenders belief in the correspondence of representations to things in the world (Gooding, 1992: 104).

This may not sound as controversial to designers who are supposed to *create artefacts*, as it has sounded to scientists who are supposed to *find facts* about the world. But the theoretical point that is worth making is that it is the prolonged interaction with an obstinate material world, the work of *interactive stabilisation* or what Gooding calls *convergence* that *leads to* the belief in representation.

This means that innovation does not follow from rational plan making and rule following.[5] It follows from a continuous creative tuning process with heterogeneous materials. The consequence of this is the realisation that design is an inherently unstable process, that the occurrence of unexpected events is inevitable, and that we must expect the absence of any linear, logical structure. Elements that we traditionally ascribe to many different ontological realms are involved. And thus it suggests that we should relativise our understanding of the design process.

4.2 Representation

Pickering and Gooding launch an attack on the problems of understanding design solely as a matter of meaning and representation. We should also take into account

---

[3]As opposed to scientists' retrospective rationalisations of it.

[4]For other perspectives on this interaction see Hacking (1983), Gooding (1992, 1994) and Galison (1997).

[5]As is also the conclusion to Suchmann's (1987) well-known study.

the tinkering dimension of design. The ways materials actively interfere with the design process in unexpected ways, *material agency*, should be better understood. But if the aim is to understand design processes in a more complex way the *meaning dimension* of design should not be forgotten. So this section is about the representations that happen as agencies converge or tune in, in the sense discussed above. Representation can refer to several different things. It can refer to the representation, on a computer, of some real-life domain. It can also refer to the designer's representation of the user – the implied user one could say. What are we assuming about our users? What is a user anyway? Cooper and Bowers (1995; see also Berg, 1998) show how the category 'user' came to be constituted and attributed quite specific properties within human–computer interaction (HCI) discourse. There were no 'users' before HCI needed that category as a legitimation for its own existence. What would HCI be without a user in need? Perhaps nothing; surely a very different discipline. Therefore the representation of the user suddenly became very important to this particular group of people. Are users smart or stupid, slow or fast? How would they interpret this screen or message; how would they act upon that interpretation? Different implied users point towards radically different types of design.

Finally, and perhaps most silently, we are representing ourselves. On this point we can track a certain concurrence between designers and scientists. Scientists are supposed to be strictly invisible with regard to the knowledge they produce. Transparency is the ideal. Anyone should *in principle* be able to do what it just so happened that this particular Nobel prize winner did *in practice*. The long arduous and *specific* path to discovery is forgotten. What about designers? We also don't hear about their choices and their long arduous paths of converging – even though these are also contingently instrumental in defining what are relevant goals, tools and designs under specific circumstances. Markussen (1996), for instance, tells of a project for which prototyping happened on Macintosh computers. Here there was a tension – because, while the designers preferred Macintosh and felt most at home with these machines, it was certain that the users would be working with PCs afterwards. In such ways designers imprint historico-specific marks that, henceforth, are invisibly represented in the user's working lives.[6] A pertinent question then becomes how this tension between designers' choices and end-users' 'needs' is handled in design. This is a tough question because it is not a matter of representing the user, but of making possible real-time tuning processes between heterogeneous materials.

4.3 Normativity

The representation problematic, in all the manifestations I discussed above, has strategic and political implications. As any design represents a specific vision of the work process it is supposed to support, it suppresses other visions of the same process. In this sense design is a perception of what a job is all about. When a design is implemented in a real work setting it will therefore also strengthen its

---

[6]On invisibility and silent work see also Star (1991a, 1991b).

implied perspective. This means, specifically, that this particular vision of the work gets stabilised by means of the material world (such as hardware and software). Hardware and software add power to a specific view of the work process. Getting one's design implemented can thus be seen as bootstrapping one's own version of the reality of that workplace or process. This is by no means a simple or uni-linear process and neither is it one that can be transparently enforced 'top-down'. Latour (1993) urges us to think of processes as partial translations. Goals, plans and hopes are always *transformed in action*, by each of the other actors it affects. Actors mediate the actions of each other, and these mediations always subtly transform the entire process of which they are part. This is important to bear in mind because it prevents falling into any narratives of, say, 'design as conspiracy-against-the worker'. Berg (1998) claims that CSCW can be understood as 'design as critique'. Even if a conspiracy was intended it *could not* be borne out without partially translating the original plot. Partial translations or transformations are more words with which to talk about the interrelated tuning process of design materials and humans. Conspiracy theories work precisely by forgetting the tunings and translations and thus:

technology is conceptualized as a mere 'projection screen' in which the social is reflected, and upon which social struggles are played out (Berg, 1998: 466).

This means that while normative and political implications of design should not be forgotten, purely social explananda cannot do the explanatory job expected of them. While technologies are not neutral they are not fully controllable either. Therein lies the 'slight surprise of action' which Latour (1999) has analysed. Performativity, representation and normativity are interweaved in complex ways *between and through* people and technologies. They cannot be separated in practice.

5. CSCW and Design

Before I can move on to analyse some of the ways such concerns *are* in practice separated with unfortunate results, I need to situate the article with regard to the intended CSCW audience. I also need to indicate why I do not direct the analyses made here at a wider design audience.

The points made above may seem old to people within the CSCW tradition.[7] *Performativity* involves the idea that *real-time activity* is at least as important to think about as representation. Within CSCW this is acknowledged; both the designers' and the users' activities have long been of prime concern to the tradition – a concern coming out of, for instance, *activity theory* (Engeströem, 1990). Thinking about *representation* means concurring that how one represents one's (1) domains, (2) users and (3) selves has vital implications for design. CSCW is well aware of this, at least the first two points.[8] Traditional misrepresentations of users have even been a key problematic; this is why the focus is so often said to be on designing for the

---

[7]CSCW tradition is, of course, a problematic notion, since CSCW is not a homogeneous field. Nevertheless I risk using it here for reasons of brevity.

[8]As mentioned above, point 3, designers' self-invisibility might be a problem (Markussen, 1996).

end-user! What about *normativity*? This problematic is so closely related to the one of representation that it almost goes without saying; *of course* when one tries to represent end-users better it is for a normative reason (such as empowerment of the worker). Thus, initially it seems as if the analysis above has been futile, except in order to reiterate points already well taken. Nevertheless, there is a tension here.[9] It consists in this: what is, within CSCW, said to be known (espoused theory) and what is actually and performatively known (theory-in-action) are two quite different things. Thus many of the ideas pointed out above are, in fact, ignored or trivialised when actual analysis and subsequent design are carried out.

There is no doubt that CSCW is a very heterogeneous field of investigation. This might even be taken as an indication of its health as a discipline. Therefore one might well counter the above accusation (of ignoring or trivialising important insights) in the following way. It is surely true that not all writers within CSCW seem to take notice of all the theoretical niceties pointed out above, in all their design efforts. However, this merely signals that some CSCW practitioners are more practically or 'directly' design oriented than others. The ones, on the other hand, that are seriously implicated in theoretical debates are already well aware of the points made. Thus, to some CSCW readers this analysis would be a matter of no concern and to part it would be old news. I would like to suggest that this is not the case. Rather, I would claim that these theoretical concerns are not secondary to actual design as if it was a case of an additional layer of analysis one could add, if time and interest were available. The stronger claim is that these problems are inherent in *any* design process, whether acknowledged by the actual designers or not. If, as suggested here, theoretical concerns and practical accomplishments are not two sides of a dualism but constitutively intertwined in the design activity, there is no room in the design world for practically ignoring the matters discussed above. But if *any* designer would have something to learn from these sorts of considerations, why direct them towards a CSCW audience in the first place? This is a reflexive question to which I will suggest some answers. First, I *am* interested in (while at the same time finding problematic) the general emancipatory project that has been an integral part of CSCW and the Scandinavian tradition since its inception. If such a project seems somewhat stalled at the present moment it suggests the need for renewed conceptual innovation to put it back on track. Another angle, which Hughes, Randall and Shapiro suggested in 1991, is that CSCW is not a discipline at all:

Since all work is socially organised, it would seem that all work potentially falls within the CSCW domain...We defend these consequences, and argue that CSCW is therefore more akin to a paradigm shift for its contributing disciplines than a particular subdiscipline in itself (Hughes et al., 1991: 309).

But if all design can be understood from a CSCW point of view, this does not entail that all designers would be equally thrilled by the proposition that design should be understood in much more analytically complex terms, instead of simpler ones. In

---

[9]To some extent the same tension that Suchmann (1998) relates when reading Morten Kyng's defence for the degree of D.Sci. (defended 16 August 1996, printed in the *Scandinavian Journal of Information Systems* 10(1–2), 1998.

this sense the direction of this paper to CSCW is tactical. It is not that *it could not* be directed at a broader audience (following the CSCW as paradigm idea). But as an effect of CSCW's own contingent history I would suggest that such theoretical initiatives have a specific pertinence, and could be more efficient within this forum. If I have a hope for the continued use of the concepts discussed in this text, they should *at least* prove to be relevant to a CSCW community that historically has been open towards theoretical as well as emancipatory initiatives.

6. The Analyses[10]

Below I analyse four recent CSCW pieces of very different orientation, in order to demonstrate the efficacy of (combinations of) the series of concepts I have presented. First I discuss Bertelsen and Nielsen's (1999) application of activity theory for analysing a wastewater treatment plant. I pick up on their highly problematic and reductive theoretical assumptions. Second, I take a look at Hayashi, Hazama et al.'s (1999) presumed CSCW analysis which, however, turns out to be a functionalist account. I show how some of its many problems can be put into focus by considering performativity, representation and normativity. Third, I discuss Ruhleder and Jordan's (1999) article on communication by video-conferencing. While these authors are quite theoretically subtle when discussing their own problematics of *meaning-making*, they become too sceptical, because they ignore the performative aspects of the technology. In their humanist analysis people are still radically separated from machines, which are conceptualised as stable and inert. They forget the *tuning process of interactive stabilisation* argued for above.

Finally I examine the claim that theoretically savvy CSCW designers already acknowledge the performative, representational and normative dimensions of their design projects. Such an assumption turns out to be problematic, as the analysis of Benford et al. (1999) aims to show. This article is co-written by, among others, John Bowers, whose brilliant article with Geoff Cooper (Cooper and Bowers, 1995) has been part of the inspiration for this paper. Nevertheless, in this instance many of the previous insights of his work are forgotten when we encounter a certain *naïveté* and exuberance as Benford et al. participate in the creation of CVEs (collaborative virtual environments).

Thus, it would seem worthwhile to examine again how selective theoretical blindness unfolds within various types of CSCW. As will be evident, the chosen pieces are highly differentiated with regard to level of sophistication as well as approach. This is part of the point I want to make, however. That point is that in year 2000 one can investigate a very broad variety of CSCW analyses, with quite simple theoretical means, and find deep-lying and problematic assumptions. I take this to be a good indicator of the productivity of reconceptualising CSCW design through STS studies.

---

[10]All the texts used in the analysis above is from *ECSCW '99: Proceedings of the Sixth European Conference on Computer Supported Cooperative Work*, Bødker, Kyng and Schmidt (eds).

7. Activity, Activity Theory, CSCW

In a standard exposition of activity theory, Engeströem (1990) puts forth three methodological principles. First, one should take as a unit of analysis no less than the entire activity system. The activity system thus 'integrates the subject, the object and the instruments into a unified whole' (p. 79). Second, historicity is the basis of classifications. In other words classifications are not stable, they are to be historically and contextually determined. Third, being dialectically inclined Engeströem views inner contradictions as the source of change and development. He then posits his well-known triangular structure (with tools, subject, rules, community, division of labour, object, etc.) dialectically related as the basic structure of human activity. Having carried out a number of analyses with this conceptual tool he feels ready to challenge certain 'radical constructivists', such as Latour:

the object of activity and cognition often becomes something to be constructed purely by the actors, not having any identity and dynamics of its own (Engeströem, 1990: 126).

Unfortunately this is a misreading of Latour, probably stemming from a propensity for believing that all constructivists are *social* constructivists. However, when Latour speaks of actors, these also include what Engeströem calls the *object of activity*. Both act *together*. The implication of this is that Latour *does* allow the object its own dynamic voice, and does so on much less deterministic terms than Engeströem, who has, *a priori*, drawn up his famous triangle with categories for insertion of the *at all times relevant factors* that determine the outcome of human (and non-human) activity.[11] Now where does this lead us in relation to CSCW? It leads us to Bødker et al. (1999: 277–291), where Bertelsen and Nielsen use activity theory in an analysis of a wastewater treatment plant and the problem of formalisation at this site. In this analysis Bertelsen and Nielsen distinguish 'five symmetrical levels of dynamics in complex technical work' (1999: 277); i.e., these levels are suggested as conceptual tools not only in this specific case, but also as transferable to other sites. These are: the technical process, people moving around, technical rearrangement, flexible routines and transformation of the domain. This is problematic. In Engeströem's activity triangle there are 10 variables whose interrelationships must be brought out in analysis. But in Bertelsen and Nielsen the number of variables to keep in play is randomly halved. Even within Engeströem's framework this seems reductionistic, not to mention theoretically unfounded. But Engeströem's frame itself is so too, only at a more abstract level.[12] My suggestion is that, in order to take heed of the real dynamics and performativity of activity, we must be *more aware* of possibilities for change in praxis and display less tendency to random generalisation. Interaction between humans and complex technical equipment is surely too multitudinous to be subsumed under a few predetermined variables (as Latour, 1993, 1999, also shows).

---

[11]In Engeströem activity is developing and dynamic and historical – *on Engeströem's terms*, since the basic structure of the activity is determined from now to eternity. This is what is meant by Engeströem's reductionism (see below).

[12]Since he has already established the relevant types of factors that would be relevant, and the way they are interrelated; i.e., the universal triangular analytical structure.

8. CSCW and Technicist Tendencies

The next example is the article by Hayashi et al. from the same volume. At first this article might seem to have a keen eye for the kinds of problems discussed above, since its manifest concern is developing the idea of an *activity awareness* for making sense of workers' collaborative activities (Hayashi et al., 1999: 99). But in practice this is not what emerges. If anything, they move in the wrong direction from where the above-mentioned concerns with a subtler understanding of design would take us. Hayashi et al. take us deep into technicist territory. While we might blame Bertelsen and Christensen for a certain reductionism in their proposal of a framework, at least they were concerned with issues such as 'how are we to understand what an activity involving humans and technical objects might mean?' This is nowhere near the focus of Hayashi et al. Their concern is solely technical. We thus experience in a pure form the ontological separation that Berg (1998) warned us against. Here it is possible to avoid concerning oneself with any but the most superficial interest in the users; superior technical skill will make the design work anyway. What is an activity for Hayashi et al.?

In this model we use the word *activity* to mean a human process of a worker to achieve some specific goal (e.g. writing a specific report). Generally, each worker will execute more than one activity (Hayashi et al., 1999: 101).

There are several comments one might make about a statement of this sort. First, it seems to suggest as its epistemology a sort of naïve realism. We can view a worker writing a report and then we can model a computer so that others can monitor that activity as well, *without any loss*. Secondly, it seems to view human activity (*contra* Bucciarelli, Markussen, Pickering, Suchmann etc.) as primarily *goal rational*. The authors believe they know what report writing is, since it is *fully defined* by typing words on a keyboard into a system. It is also this same goal rationality that shines through in the sentence above where workers are seen to *execute* their activities. This analysis can be connected back to the three keywords. Thinking about performativity it is noted that the essential ambiguity, the realisation that everything will always necessarily change slightly during the process of tuning, is overlooked. This system is supposed to be implemented and used *strictly as intended*. Thinking about representation we see that the domain of work is represented as transparent, users as goal rational and the designers as invisible. This is standard technicism. Finally, thinking about normativity we find a slight internal textual tension. It is this. Each worker is supposed to have an individual workspace instead of a large shared one. So there is privacy. Nevertheless:

A means to edit others' workspaces is needed. Since an individual workspace belongs to a specific worker, we have not allowed other members to alter the states of an individual's workspace ... We should relax this restriction (Hayashi et al., 1999: 108).

But in the discussion again:

In our model, we have carefully avoided imposing rigid restriction on workers' ways of using workspaces since each individual workspace belongs to the user (Hayashi et al., 1999: 115).

One can ponder why it is that we find such opposing statements (of privacy vs. public accessibility). From a representative and normative perspective it is plain to see. It has not been considered that there will be inherent problems with a system thought to be a mirror display of the actual work process. There *will be* different views of what is going on, who should do what and how it should be done (notwithstanding the problem with the suggestion that an activity is simply 'writing a report' and that this is transparent as such). And there will certainly be problems if one is given an individual workspace ('my own') which other people (superiors or otherwise) are then allowed to edit. Hayashi et al. represents a part of CSCW that is marred by a too heavy emphasis on the technical aspect of designing. This emphasis must necessarily be coupled with an understanding of the *interactive aspect* of human–technology relations, which have been analysed above.[13] A feel for the inherent *ambiguity* of design is needed.

9. CSCW and Performativity

The focus and problems of the third example (Ruhleder and Jordan, 1999: 411–431, in Bødker et al., 1999) are of a different kind. This is not least the case because the authors display a much higher degree of reflexive subtlety with regard to the issues of concern than the ones previously discussed. That is, their concern is precisely to show how representation may become problematic when people try to accomplish '*meaning-making across remote sites*'. The focus of the paper is communicating by video-conferencing and, specifically, how the technological mediation of communication might hinder meaning-making. This happens because of transmission delays (of up to a few seconds). In human face-to-face communication certain *turn-taking* rules apply. These rules are based on bodily as well as linguistic gestures that the speakers exhibit. The problem with video-conferencing, then, is that bodily gesturing is unclear because of insufficient resolution or blur, whereas the linguistic markers that guide face-to-face communication are delayed. This, the authors claim, has implications for attaining successful communication. Three different types of communicative delay problems are found. First, *collision and swaps*: this refers to the case when statements are uttered so that an answer temporally refers to the wrong question (or sentence). Second, *unnecessary rephrasings*: this happens when delay causes speakers' sentences to interrupt each other. Thus, there is a need for continual repair of sentences. Third, *misapplied feedback*: this is also a case of interruption. Here, a response or acknowledgement of some statement (such as 'I see' or 'OK'), which would fit at certain points of conversational turn-taking, is delayed, and enters instead at places where it makes no sense. Such situations are thoroughly analysed by the authors, who

identified 32 episodes within the 19 minute interaction which exhibited these characteristics (Ruhleder and Jordan, 1999: 416).

The question is how to interpret such findings. There are two different points to make. First, Ruhleder and Jordan's analysis displays much awareness of problems of representation (communication is not neutral or self-explanatory, technology is

---

[13]In the last instance I would, of course, prefer to get rid of the ontological and analytical distinction between the human and the technical realm altogether – this, again, following Berg (1998).

not transparent) and develops a typology of breakdowns due to delay. They also point towards certain normative issues these breakdowns might occasion:

Delayed or inappropriate responses could indicate the other party is not paying attention ('is Bill listening?') (Ruhleder and Jordan, 1999: 420).

If the possibility of disbelieving Bill's attention prevails, surely it might be consequential in relation to the perception of him by his boss. On the other hand, the analysis seems so clearly focused on representation and meaning-making, that it overlooks the imperative *performative* dimension of communication. Thinking performatively, one would necessarily question the *seriousness* of the problem pointed out above. As an analogy no one seem to have much trouble handling long-distance phone calls and their delays after a few attempts. In short, there seems to be no particular reason to disbelieve that people might *tune in* with this mediating technology after a short while; which would certainly diminish the dire normative consequences for Bill. In Ruhleder and Jordan's study, the users were indeed beginners. Performatively, it would be interesting to compare this with experienced users and their handling of delay problems. This is not to say that the analysis is not worthwhile. Specifically, in 'conclusions and implications', the authors point to some of the ways in which the analysis can better the necessary tuning processes of humans and technology ('How these findings can guide meeting strategies' and 'How these findings contribute to development efforts'). The problem is that the technology and the humans are seen as ontologically separate, which makes it too easy to analyse the technology as reductive compared to 'pure' human interaction.

10. CSCW and Representing the Other

The fourth and last discussion is of Benford et al.'s (1999) 'Broadcasting on-line social interaction as inhabited television' (in Bødker et al., 1999: 179–199). Their experiment is meant to investigate the following question: Is it possible to broadcast fast-paced social interaction on CVEs (collaborative virtual environments) (p. 179). Their tentatively optimistic conclusion after four different experiments (with a poetry performance and different versions of game-shows) is that it is indeed possible. First, it is worth pointing out a number of positive features of this analysis. After the first three experiments which came to be seen as preliminary to the fourth on-line game show, 'Out of this World', there were extended considerations of pros and cons of the deployed approach. That is, users, performers and producers were engaged in a reflexive exercise to determine the degree of success and the various problems that were encountered under these experiments. From the performative perspective this is good, since it acknowledges the real-time problems and developments that will always defy *a priori* planning.

Second, even in the instance where we may find problems with this experiment, the authors have helped us point them out themselves. As such this is an example of a successful design approach. Nonetheless if one wants to be critical it is possible to pick up at the very points the authors point out for us. These problems have to do with representative and by implication normative aspects of the game-show that was deemed successful: 'Out of this world'. This show splits up the inhabitants of the world in two sex-based teams. Women were 'aliens', men 'robots'. These two teams then had to compete in games of 'flipping frogs', 'falling fish', 'culture quiz', 'space-car race', 'wobblespace' and 'the end of the world'. In 'wobblespace' the losing team had to make a case for why their particular lives should be spared, after which the viewers chose a single person from the losing team for survival – the rest being left at the imploding space station. This was 'the end of the world'. The authors acknowledge that this is a cheesy outer space theme (p. 184), implying that we should not take it too seriously. Nevertheless, from a representative and normative perspective it is worth pondering what is happening in this scenario. First, the sex-based teams were pinpointed as problematic by viewers:

'I thought it was sexist the way there were two sexes' (Benford et al., 1999: 195).

Furthermore one can ponder why it is that women were rendered 'alien' and men 'robots', with all the connotations these two categories carry. Secondly, some viewers were intimidated by having to kill the losing team by voting for their lives, at the end of the show:

'I felt somewhat uncomfortable about consigning someone to oblivion [audience member]' (Benford et al., 1999: 194).

One (common-sense) response to this kind of critique is that it is paranoid and over the top. Another response might be, as the authors' note, that

'The subject matter was simplistic but the technology was interesting' (Benford et al., 1999: 196).

To the first kind of response, one answer might be that perhaps this reading is, indeed, over the top; but I would not be too sure. One need not read too far in Haraway's (1997) meditation, on how sexist and war metaphors infiltrate discourses as different as evolutionary biology and information superhighways, and how these metaphorics are performative in shaping those fields, to doubt the innocence of hooking up violence and gender stereotypes with the newest and fanciest broadcasting technologies.[14] To acknowledge that a certain stereotyping took place and that the concept was 'cheesy', as the authors do, is not enough. This is taking for granted that technical matters can be purely separated from their semantic contents – that there is, indeed, a cold technical realm (which is interesting) and a warm human one (which, perhaps, was represented simplistically). But with the levelled ontology for which I have made an argument, such easy dichotomisations become untenable and we must realise the extent to which our technologies and ourselves are always co-implicated, that we are, as Haraway (1997) would say, 'material-semiotic knots'.

11. Conclusion

Following Bucciarelli (1994) design is narrative. But it is a materialised narrative – and materials are themselves active and unpredictable agents. During design materials are continually redefined and recategorised. But so are designers and

---

[14]Another relevant reference here is the *AI & Society* 7(4), 1993 theme number on gender, technology and culture.

users. To take design as a complex phenomenon seriously one should not prioritise humans or technologies.

What could it mean to overcome such an ontological dualism in CSCW analyses? First, let me say what it does not mean. To trouble standard ontological categories does not mean that it makes no difference whether a given task is performed by a human or a machine, or how that task is to be carried out. For example, a levelled ontology cannot be used for arguing that since entities are all on par, we cannot decide which is better: ergonomic design or command-line interfaces.[15] But the reason for choosing the ergonomic design would not be found on the human side only. One would have to consider a double tuning process between the heterogeneous materials of design. One should think simultaneously about how oneself tunes in with specific design tools rather than others, how this might affect the resulting system, and what possibilities and hindrances such systems might entail for the end-user. The key point is to remember *possibilities* as well as *hindrances*. Both of these can take many forms. Command-line interfaces could be an improvement over typewriters, for example, since data could be integrated centrally. On the other hand, such data integration could be used for intensive monitoring of labour.[16] Furthermore, bad monitors might cause unnecessary eye-strain, and it could be a labour-intensive task to become skilled in using the commands. While this type of technology can tune in with some aspects of human, organisational work-life quite well, it surely *resists* many others.

Ergonomic designs alleviate several problems, especially related to the physiological components of the human–machine tuning processes. They would probably often be preferable to command-line interfaces because they are able to accommodate these aspects to a far higher degree than non-ergonomic designs.

Nevertheless, the process of tuning goes both ways: the human also needs to change to fit with the machine. Of course, achieving fit is not solely dependent on ergonomics or interfaces; the system could be badly structured or badly connected to external ones. Trying to facilitate tuning processes, *designing*, is a multifaceted task.

Thus, I suggest that disregarding this distinction means realising that humans and technology, and the simultaneous evolution of both of these types of agencies are connected much more complexly and intimately than we have been used to thinking. If design means trying to facilitate complex tuning processes between heterogeneous materials, deterministic approaches are bound to miss half the story. They always place all of the action or agency on one side of the human–technological divide. Partial translations or processes of tuning remain invisible.

With a levelled ontology one would have to keep in mind performative, representative and normative aspects of the design process at the same time, when carrying out CSCW design. It would become necessary to remember the performative aspects of design, and their convergence or *tuning* towards specific representations *simultaneously* and *continually*.

To take seriously that while neither humans nor technologies *determine* each other, they are always partially translating each other, has consequences. The design

---

[15]I thank a referee for probing me on this point. I use his example here.

[16]See, for example, Zuboff (1988, chapter 9) and Lyon (1994).

world can be understood as open and flexible, but also uncertain and ambiguous. We cannot always know what is emancipatory and what is repressing. Materiality might trick us in practice. Designers within CSCW have a special responsibility to take the processual ambiguities and tuning processes seriously, in theory and in practice. Designing for better practices, in an uncertain and complex world, is not an easy job. But understanding these irreducible conditions, at least, should not be unhealthy. Relativising our ontology might help us to revitalise our designs.

References

Benford, S., Greenhalgh,C., Craven,M. et al (1999). Broadcasting On-Line Social Interaction as Inhabited Television. In Bødker, S., Kyng, M. and Schmidt, K. (eds) *ECSCW '99: Proceedings of the Sixth European Conference on Computer Supported Cooperative Work*. Kluwer, Boston, MA.

Berg, M. (1998). The Politics of Technology: On Bringing Social Theory into Technological Design, *Science, Technology and Human Values*. **23**(4). 456–491.

Bertelsen, O.W. and Nielsen, C. (1999). Dynamics in Wastewater Treatment: A Framework for Understanding Formal Constructs in Complex Technological Settings. In Bødker, S., Kyng, M. and Schmidt, K. (eds) *ECSCW '99: Proceedings of the Sixth European Conference on Computer Supported Cooperative Work*. Kluwer, Boston, MA.

Bødker, S., Kyng, M. and Schmidt, K. (eds) (1999). *ECSCW '99: Proceedings of the Sixth European Conference on Computer Supported Cooperative Work*. Kluwer, Boston, MA.

Bucciarelli, L.L. (1994). Designing Engineers. MIT Press, Cambridge, MA.

Butler, J. (1993). Bodies that Matter: On the Discursive Limits of Sex. Routledge, London.

Cooper, G. and Bowers, J. (1995). Representing the User: Notes on the Disciplinary Rhetoric of HCI. In Thomas, P. (ed.) *Social and Interactional Dimensions of Human–Computer Interfaces* (Cambridge Series on Human–Computer Interaction no. 10). Cambridge University Press, Cambridge, UK.

Engeströem, Y. (1990). Learning, Working and Imagining: Twelve Studies in Activity Theory. Orient-Konsultit Oy, Helsinki.

Galison, P. (1997). Image and Logic: A Material Culture of Microphysics. University of Chicago Press, Chicago, IL.

Gill, K., Finkelstein, J., Smith, D. et al (eds) (1993). *AI & Society*. **7**(4). 275–280

Gooding, D. (1992). Putting Agency Back into Experiment. In Pickering, A. (ed.) *Science as Practice and Culture*. University of Chicago Press, Chicago, IL. 65–113

Gooding, D. (1994). Experiment and the Making of Meaning: Human Agency in Scientific Observation and Experiment. Kluwer, Boston, MA.

Hacking, I. (1983). Representing and Intervening: Introductory Topics in the Philosophy of Natural Science. Cambridge University Press: Cambridge, MA.

Haraway, D. (1994). A Game of Cat's Cradle: Science Studies, *Feminist Theory, Cultural Studies. Configurations*. **2**(1). 59–71.

Haraway, D. (1997). *Modest_Witness@Second_Millennium.FemaleMan©_Meets_OncoMouse™*. Routledge, London.

Hayashi, K. Hazama, T. Nomura, T. Yamada, T. and Gudmundson, S. (1999). Activity Awareness: Framework for Sharing Knowledge of People, Projects and Places. In Bødker, S., Kyng, M. and Schmidt, K. (eds) *ECSCW '99: Proceedings of the Sixth European Conference on Computer Supported Cooperative Work*. Kluwer, Boston, MA.

Hughes, J., Randall, D. and Shapiro, D. (1991). CSCW: Discipline or Paradigm? A Sociological Perspective. In Bannon, L., Robinson, M. and Schmidt, K. (eds) *ECSCW '91: Proceedings of the Second European Conference on Computer Supported Cooperative Work*. Kluwer, Amsterdam.

Latour, B. (1993). We have Never been Modern. Harvard University Press, Cambridge, MA.

Latour, B. (1999). Pandora's Hope: Essays on the Reality of Science Studies. Harvard University Press, Cambridge, MA.

Lyon, D. (1994). The Electronic Eye: The Rise of Surveillance Society. University of Minnesota Press, Minneapolis, MN.

Markussen, R. (1996). Politics of Intervention in Design: Feminist Reflections on the Scandinavian Tradition, *AI & Society*. **10**. 127–141.

Pickering, A. (1995). The Mangle of Practice: Time, Agency and Science. University of Chicago Press, Chicago, IL.

Ruhleder, K. and Jordan, B. (1999). Meaning-Making across Remote Sites: How Delays in Transmission Affect Interaction. In Bødker, S. Kyng, M. and Schmidt, K. (eds) *ECSCW '99: Proceedings of the Sixth European Conference on Computer Supported Cooperative Work*. Kluwer, Boston, MA.

Star, S.L. (1991a). Invisible work and Silenced Dialogues in Knowledge Representation. In Eriksson, I.V. Kitchenbam,B.A. and Tijdens, K.G. (eds) *Women, Work and Computerization*. Elsevier Science, Amsterdam.

Star, S.L. (1991b). Power, Technology and the Phenomenology of Conventions: On being Allergic to Onions. In Law, J. (ed.) *A Sociology of Monsters*. Basil Blackwell, Oxford. 26–58

Suchmann, L. (1987). Plans and Situated Actions: The Problem of Human Machine Communication. Cambridge University Press, Cambridge, UK.

Suchmann, L. (1998). Comment on Kyng, Morten, Users and Computers: A Contextual Approach to Design of Computer Artefacts, *Scandinavian Journal of Information Systems*. **10**(1–2). 45–52.

Whalley, P. and Barley, S.R. (1997). Technical Work in the Division of Labor: Stalking the Wily Anomaly. In Barley, S.R. and Orr, J.E. (ed.) *Between Craft and Science: Technical Work in U.S. Settings*. ILR Press, Ithaca, NY, 23–53.

Zuboff, S. (1988). In the Age of the Smart Machine. Basic Books, New York.

Correspondence and offprint requests to: Casper Bruun Jensen, Information and Media Science, Aarhus University, Niels Juulsgade 84, DK-8200 Aarhus N, Denmark. Fax: 89421952; Email: cirdan@imv.au.dk

AI & Soc (1995) 9:218–243
© 1995 Springer-Verlag London Limited

Designing for Work Place Learning

Thomas Binder

Institute of Technology and Social Science, Technical University of Denmark, Lyngby, Denmark

Abstract: The use of computers to support learning at work has for long been propagated. Although a large bulk of experience exists in this field, it is still an open question what role computer applications play and can play in the process of learning. It can even be questioned if the learning processes themselves are sufficiently well understood to enable designers and others to provide relevant support. In this article these questions are addressed with reference to experience gained with two projects on computer support for shop floor learning. The projects involved the future users actively in the design process and it is argued that this involvement reached far beyond the mere shaping of the learning artefacts.

Keywords: Learning; Participatory design; Multimedia

Introduction

The aim of this paper is to present and discuss experience gained with two projects on computer support for shop floor learning. The first project was concerned with information support for operators and technicians at automatic letter sorting machines.[1] The aim of the project was to improve efficiency of preventive maintenance, fault finding and repair by improving access to the relevant technical information for all team members around the machine. The second project had as its objective to design and evaluate an all-European multimedia based training package that could improve the in-house training of machine setters in the spring industry.[2]

---

[1] This project called the POSTI project was initiated by the Danish Postal Services and was carried out by a group of consultants at the Danish Technological Institute, dept. for Human Resource Development. The group consisted of Annemarie Holsbo, Linda Passarge, Caroline Simonsen, Niels Stockmarr, Carsten Andersen and Thomas Binder.

[2] This project called the SPRING project was initiated by a group of manufacturers associations and com panies in the European spring industry. The project was financed by the EC Force program and was carried out by a group of consultants at the Danish Technological Institute, dept. for Human Resource Development. The group consisted of Linda Passarge, Per Sommer, Karsten Bøjesen Andersen and Thomas Binder. Evaluation of the project has been made by Flemming Meier and Thomas Binder.

In both projects we established user groups which together with our design team should develop the form and contents of these systems. Viewed in retrospect it appears to me that this user involvement turned out to be much more than a mere asset in our design process. Rather than helping us in our design work, the users engaged in what I will call a prototypical learning process, developing and trying our the types of discourse that they and their colleagues would like to take part in. Fair to say this discussion also benefited our work as designers, but more than that it stimulated an interest on our side in understanding what learning at work really is, and what role our systems play in this everyday learning.

What is Learning Work?

It is widely accepted that we all gain experience while working, and this experience by and by makes us more competent in managing the tasks we are engaged in. This is however, not what we in general, consider learning. Learning is rather the stage we must go through before we are able to perform a certain task. In recent years it seems to become more obvious that the simple sequence of learning, exercising and performing is being stressed by the fact that not only learning to perform new tasks but also gaining experience from work already done becomes increasingly important. The typical machine operator will have to learn how to operate an increasing number of machines in still newer versions and the typical maintenance technician will have a growing stress upon him to register and evaluate data about machine failures in order to prevent future breakdowns. For a while it might be possible to provide more vocational training to the operator and supply more check lists to the technical but very soon this probably will turn out to be an unhealthy overloading of both.

Not least for these reasons learning in the workplace is getting increasingly popular as something to be enhanced and supported. Summing up very roughly on the mainstreams of attempts in this direction, I can see three groups of propagators: the educationalists, the organisationalists and the informationalists giving more or less different directions to go.

The educationalists are occupied with the question of how to provide efficient and comprehensive teaching in an environment where the topics to teach are growing, and the time for teaching is getting shorter. The answers have been to parcel the curriculum and move as much as possible of the teaching to the immediate surroundings of the people to learn. In this direction we have seen the renewal of interest in distant learning and computer based training, which however, does not question the distinction between learning and practice.

The organisationalists on their side, are taking the loading of informal learning needs on the work force as the fact to be dealt with. They are consequently advocating an opening up of the rigid and often individualised organisation of work which makes cooperation and sharing of experience difficult. In this direction we see suggestions for teamwork, quality circles and other cooperative types of organsational renewal.

Finally we have the informationalists, who more or less seem to circumvent the whole question of learning. Their vision is to bring all relevant information needed to perform a certain job right to the time and place where the job shall be done.

149

Correspondingly they want to formalise and even automate the collection, processing and feedback of information, to ensure that new actions can be taken based on past experience.

Let me quickly admit that my description of these positions are far from being fully-fledged or fair. The point I want to make and elaborate in this paper, is however, that we are likely to waste a lot of time and energy if we are not being more accurate about what learning really is or rather when the essentials of learning, the gaining of ability to do new things, actually take place.

Instructional Learning, the Problem of Context and Contextualisation

When we worked with information support for postal workers and technicians operating automatic letter sorting machines, one of the key issues for the postal services was to reduce "down-time". A letter sorting machine typically breaks down during rush hours where time schedules are very tights, and the amount of letters to be sorted is at its maximum. This means profound stress on the technicians, who are basically alone to sort out the problem.

With this type of tasks it is not surprising that both machine designers and postal management are searching for systems which can provide technicians with accurate and instructional information about not only what is wrong but also about what to do. The vision shared by management and machine designers is that a full description of faults and their repair can be derived from the detailed specification of technology and work processes. Learning for operators and technicians within the framework of this vision will be limited to the questions of reading and following instructions as they are displayed by the information systems.

We were urged to pursue this vision in the sense that we were asked to document best practice of fault finding and repair, roughly estimated to account for 90% of the time used on this type of task. This required learning more about two questions. First we needed an understanding of what is best practice for a competent service technician. Secondly we needed an idea of what reading and following instructions could mean for a group like the technicians. Both these questions highlighted the problems in instructional trouble-shooting.

We entered the world of trouble shooting from different angles. First we spent some evenings together with technicians and operators. We saw the two groups operating quite separately. The operators took care of the machine under normal operation. They loaded the machine with letters and removed the sorted mail. The technicians, located in their own staff room, were doing minor repair jobs on exchanged parts, keeping the place tidy and waited for the "crash" to happen. And when it happened an alarm on the machine loudly informed that a fault had occurred. The technicians rushed from their premises, while the operators turned themselves into a not too engaged audience, lighting cigarettes and engaging in small talk. The technicians did not approach the operators to learn what had happened. Rather they arrived like a doctor to see his patient. Now the machine was theirs, and "life and death" was on their shoulders. Usually the whole episode lasted only a short time. A fault was detected and a repair was made. The technicians went back to their room, cigarettes were squeezed and operation went back to normal. The technicians protocolled the episode in a log book for the colleagues and turned to waiting for the next alarm to sound. It seemed hard to imagine these "lonely cowboys" waiting for the alarm to turn on the computer and go through instructions for systematic trouble shooting, and even harder to see the operator seeking information and taking part in this "mastery of doctors".

We examined the technical documentation for clues for competent trouble shooting in discussion with the experienced technicians. We certainly found a lot. The machines are equipped with a delicate monitoring system. This system reports a wide variety of faulty states, and both the type and location of faults can be read from the appropriate control panels and lead displays. What we also found, however, was that the manuals documented the build up and technical interconnections of this monitoring system, but did not, to any large extent, organise or connect this information to real life instances of machine break down.

When discussing with the experienced technicians this mis-match, between the design logic and monitoring system and the trouble shooting logic, inherent in the experiences practice of the technicians, became even more apparent. Taken merely as a means of roughly typifying and localising machine faults the monitoring system was an important tool for the technicians, but when we tried to extend the underlying schemata of systemic fault finding to encompass the link between effects and causes, a number of serious problems occurred.

First the relations between effects and causes were more than troublesome. Not only could several causes be attributed to the same effect, but even to the same root cause of break down. The effects detectable to the technicians could vary depending on which of several effects was first detected by the monitoring system. Depicting a step by step procedure even for fault diagnosis therefore turned out to involve numerous repetitions and hints for possible repercussions of faults not normally (but after all even sometimes) associated with the particular trace of symptoms in question.

Secondly the inevitable hierarchical nature of associating effects to causes was not fully comforting to the technicians. Their point was not to object to the structuring of causal relations in itself, but rather to emphasise that practical importance fault finding tended to be distorted by the hierarchical approach. From their experience, the real problems in trouble shooting have more to do with imagining and searching for the very specific local causes at the bottom of the hierarchy than with employing a structured approach. As we sketched our documentation of best practice fault finding, they felt we would use too much time on stepping in to the target area, where problems in their understanding really begin.

Third, the whole idea of stepping through the process of trouble shooting maintained a flavour of linearity which did not fit very well to the self image of the competent technician. In the instructional terminology it is difficult to capture more open-ended reflection and reasoning, and this was exactly what seemed to be the mental practice of the experienced technician. Where instructions tend to address a person being an operator in the very literal sense of the word, we came to see the trouble shooters much more as detectives searching for clues and developing hypotheses. The technicians searched their clues in different directions, and they did not necessarily conclude on what they found. Rather the process of gathering information and developing ideas about possible explanations seemed to be a parallel process, where "old" information could gain new importance in the light of other clues and new ideas of their interrelations.

To sum up only a few arguments could be put forward for a pure instructional approach to support competent trouble shooting. It was in reality possible to prescribe all relevant actions to such a degree of detail that these could be used to guide actual actions. Furthermore, a step-by-step prompting of actions could not be said to actually mirror the procedures of the competent trouble shooter. This is not necessarily a problem, but would at least raise the question of how this type of support over time can be internalised. Last but not least the social context of trouble shooting, with the profound stress and the conventions of "firefighting" and "mastery" made it more than unlikely that technicians or operators would like to see themselves as careful followers of instruction.

We concluded to relax our aspirations. Following Suchman we reconceptualised our understanding of the actions that we were supposed to support. We gave up the idea that information support could in any way surpass or prompt the mental framing of the fault finding situation. Like Suchman, we turned to seeing any action as basically situated and the plan or instruction not a prerequisite but as a sort of general reflection of the localised actions to be taken (Suchman, 1990). We did not totally give up an instruction-like documentation of best practice. In accordance with Fischer, we also found evidence that the process of trouble shooting could be facilitated by providing tools for organising and maintaining experience (Fischer et al., 1993). Furthermore, we could, as Orr (1990) has also described it, see stories of best practice as vehicles for passing on experience. What we did was therefore to document typical cases of trouble shooting as animated sequences of words and pictures, enabling the viewer to follow a performer of competent practice. We silently renounced on our expectations concerning the usefulness of our support in the most stressful situations of trouble shooting, but turned our attention more to the other instances of preparation or afterthought. This made us more free to encompass new fragments of information, which could turn our support system into a resource of additional clues, rather than keeping us stuck with the idea of depicting and prescribing a world of competent actions.

Formalised Learning, the Problem of Practice and Participation

For the major group of postal workers, more than information support seemed necessary if this group should be able to take on more technical tasks. Form discussion with postal workers even with several years of experience of the letter sorting machines, we found that most of them had only a very limited understanding of the basic functionality of the machines. Reflecting on the rigid division of labour between operators, supervisors and technicians it appeared to us that the operators in general had a highly restricted outlook to the machine system, which is clearly confined to the physical aspects of their working area. The Postal Services wanted to change this situation, because they believed that a higher level of involvement and technical competence on the part of the operators was important for overall efficiency of the sorting job. Furthermore, they wanted the postal workers to take over part of the work involved in maintenance and fault finding.

Here a more educationalist approach was intended. The postal workers should at least for a start, have an introductory course at a vocational training centre, and in our training and information system entries should be designed specifically for giving the workers the basic training for these new types of tasks. Precisely what tasks the workers should carry out was not decided. It was an important objective for the Postal Services to stimulate a gradual and open ended transfer of tasks from the technician to the operator, and the initial training was in this context meant to create the preconditions for such a transfer rather than actually defining its scope. The problem of defining in clearer terms what the learning objectives should be for this initial training, was however, far from resolved.

Several possibilities were at hand. As seen from the perspective of the machine supplier and reflected in the technical documentation, understanding the technical function and interdependencies of the various functional units was a relevant starting point. Viewed from a conventional standpoint of the vocational training system, an introduction to and basic understanding of the theoretical principles employed in the machine system such as OCR-reading, barcode printing and light barrier control could be similarly relevant, with focus on slightly turning from the specificity of the machine to the underlying generality of principle. At last a problem-oriented approach disclosing basic principles from exemplary presentations of relevant cases of problem solving, also seemed worth considering.

For the part of the training we were involved in, it was clear that the educational element should be integrated into the work environment, and thereby enabling the learning situations to be somehow situated in the daily time schedule of the operators. We held workshops with operators and technicians where we sought a better under-standing of learning needs, from discussing specific tasks as examples of what in the future could be part of the operators' jobs. These discussions were in themselves difficult because organisational elements and skill elements were hard to separate, and furthermore, that borderlines between various groups tended to be internalised and explained by the participants in broader terms of e.g., gender and profession. The majority of female operators for example, appeared to clearly separate themselves from tasks which involved tools and typical technical machine elements such as belts and bearings. But even within the horizon of the narrowly defined operator jobs it seems as if the operators lacked an understanding of even quite essential machine parts. At one workshop were we presented a sequence of pictures describing the functionality of the light barriers which play a very important role in monitoring the letter flow, an operator said that this was the first time she realised what the light barrier actually was. The pictures we presented were very much every day pictures from the work area of the operators, but apparently it was quite typical for the operators to simply abstain from interpreting and associating meaning to the artefacts that surrounded them.

We suggested to make this kind of focusing and naming of artefacts in the work area the core of the educational entries in the information system. This approach was supplemented by small problem-oriented exercises, where the users could test their terminology and understanding of causal relations. At the workshops this educational design was well received. The prototypical users could more or less immediately use the insights gained in their daily work of implementing a new work organisation around the letter sorting machines.

Two questions should however, be raised both to the framing of policy and the approach to the problem of operator learning. First, we did not go more deeply into why the operators in the existing organisation of work took on the described alienating attitude to the artefacts in their work area. We accepted the premises given that the operators lacked "knowledge" in order to be able to "understand" these artefacts. Second, we correspondingly took for given that acquiring this knowledge and turning it into new practices of work, would more or less be a straightforward process for the users. I will return to the problematic answers to both questions later in the paper.

Informal Learning, the Problem of Dialogue and Reflexivity

To organise learning processes externally, for later implementation in particular communities of practice has often been criticised. Both with an informationalist and with an educationalist approach learning in itself tends to be kept external to the practice for which it is meant to provide access. One alternative here termed – the organisationalist approach – is simply to rely on the informal learning processes at work. Several authors have recently stressed the importance of learning through experience, also for new and technically complex tasks such as operation of CNC machines (e.g. Böhle, 1993). Böhle has in contradiction to other authors emphasising the new and more symbolic type of skills involved in e.g. programming. Zuboff (1985) pointed to the fact that sensitivity towards materials and processes is in fact of increasing importance when operators have to use technology with complex "interfaces". Böhle sees the acquisition of these types of skills as intimately related to the informal learning which takes place over time while actually working. I will not question Böhle's arguments in general, but from our work with machine setters a few additional questions will be raised.

As already mentioned, I took part in a European project aimed at preparing all European multimedia training packages for shop floor workers in the spring industry. In this project, we focused on the training and machine setters, working in more or less identical setting in the four countries involved: Denmark, Germany, Holland and the UK. Machine setting in the spring industry is a rather complex and time consuming task. In Denmark and Germany the setter will typically have a background as skilled machinists whereas the Dutch and British setters will more often have a more informal qualification obtained through different types of jobs in the sector. In the companies we visited in the four countries the experience with qualifying new setters were rather similar. In all companies training was dealt with informally in the sense that the new setter was placed together with a more experienced colleague to enable him to learn by watching and doing. In Denmark and Germany all companies reported that it would typically take between one and two years before a new setter could be said to have gained an all round level of competence. The estimates from other countries were comparable when taking into account the differences in formal education. For setting of spring coiling machines a typical set up procedure will take from 4 to 6 hours. The setter will typically work alone and he will in most cases also be responsible for monitoring production. In recent years lot sizes have decreased dramatically, and it is not unusual to use 6 hours for setting a machine which will only run production for two hours.

In the design team we were from the outset in doubt about how to approach the whole topic of supporting this type of worker. From the representatives of the spring industry backing the project the main attitude was that something had to be done about the increasing costs of training, but only a few companies had expertise of machine setting outside the workshop to draw upon, for qualifying the feasibility of such a claim. We as designers had difficulties in believing that building up training external to the workshop would in any way reduce costs or improve performance. To gain an insight into the training issue, we entered into a cooperation with an informal group of 6 machine setters in a Danish spring company.

We started out following one machine setter for three days. We quickly learned that there were many parallels between machine setting and the detective-like practice of service technicians described earlier. Machine setting can roughly be divided into three stages: basic setting, diameter adjustment and compensation, but what is more important than these stages is the iterative way in which correct setting is sought for and accomplished. Coiling springs is less exact than turning or milling, for example, because the shaping of coils in a complex way depends on the setting of tools, the specific properties of the material and the speed and synchronisation of machine movements. After a first day of merely watching, listening and asking questions, we started to video record the full setting process. We did not only register what happened, we wanted to understand what was going on, so we also asked for and recorded all the explanations which we found were necessary to keep us on track. This process turned out to be extremely fruitful. First of all the whole process of recording forced us to really go into the subject matter. We could not stop simply be noting the overall linearity of the process, but needed to follow every consideration that the setter made when going over and over again the same type of adjustment. Secondly the machine setter was brought to explain and thereby reflect upon his actions in a way in which by far exceeded his usual self-reflection. We came back from three days in the workshop convinced that setting could be learned at no other place than the workshop, but also with a growing feeling that the kind of explanation we provoked from the setter could be turned into clues and stories for use by the newcomer.

From the tapes we brought back we made a short 8 minute video, summarising the set-up process. With this video we entered into the first workshop session, where ideas and suggestions for a training package could be discussed with a group of setters. We suggested that the training package should be seen as a supplement to the well known "sitting-by-Nelly" type of training, enabling the trainer and trainee an access to pictures to discuss. This opening was well received and for the next months we prepared and presented a series of small videos following the various segments of the setting process. What we learned in this period was for us, quite surprising. The discussions on the workshop disclosed quite a wide variety of methods used during setting. It also seemed to be quite common that setters, even after several years of experience, would still avoid the employment of certain procedures which were fairly basic in the work of others and would provide an easier way forward.

One could think that "excavating" such heterogeneity would be conflicting and difficult. This was, however, not the case. Rather, the group of setters seemed increasingly confident in the usefulness of the video material produced and smoothly settled conflicts about which alternative procedures to present. Near the end of the project the setters discussed the benefits for the companies in using the training package produced. In this discussion dealing with a training package of 72 screen displays and 21 sequences of video with a total length of 36 minutes, the setters were very optimistic about the benefits and suggested reductions in time for training as high as 50%. This does not represent in any way a hard fact, but even as a loose and uncommitting comment, it was highly surprising, not least when taking into account the typical pride and self reliance among this type of worker.

A closer look at work practice and learning culture might to some extent explain these reactions. First of all it should be said that there is a lot of evidence for a notion of machine setting as experience based work in the sense of the word that is suggested by Böhle. Any attempt to describe in detail systematic procedures or possible instances of irregularities would, as we have all seen this work, be deemed to failure. The setter needs to rely on analogies with earlier cases and will try out different ways to go when encountering ever new possible setting problems. What should then also be said is however, that dealing with his job, the setter is extremely isolated. Not only does the setter formally work alone, he is also situated in an environment where the individual ability to solve problems is decisive for the status and autonomy that the setter can obtain from supervisors and fellow workers. So far setting of spring coiling machines only comply very well with the work of machinists in general, as described by Kern and Schumann (1985). Seen from within the workshop this means that common language and dialogue is almost absent in the community. When we interviewed the setters about how they dealt with atypical problems, if they were stuck with the problems themselves, they answered that they called on a colleague. We noted this example of informal cooperation and asked further if they then discussed the problem. They did not, as one of the setters explained, "I usually go for a walk, and hope my colleague has solved the problem before I am back".

If this could be said to simply represent the opposite case of what Orr reports as common sharing of experience for technicians repairing photocopiers (Orr, 1990), due to the shared interest in keeping customers happy, the positive reactions on the training package indicate that there is more to it than that. Returning to the large variety of procedures employed by the setters and the apparent inefficiency of the methods used by at least some of the setters, I will try to add another dimension to this question. When springs are coiled the wire is bent over a so-called cutter mandrel by coiling fingers. The positions and shape of the fingers and the mandrel determines the diameter of the spring. When coiling compression springs the coil furthermore has to be dragged apart to enable the spring to be compressed. In this last process the initial diameter of the coils will decrease slightly. To obtain a cylindrical spring, this decrease must be compensated for, and for this reason the machines are equipped with a delicate arrangement of compensating cams that can retract the coiling fingers accordingly. Precisely the use of this arrangement is a good example of a procedure which seems to be avoided by quite a number of setters. What they do instead is to grind, e.g. the mandrel or other of the tools in a way which produces the same effect. The springs are just as good when produced in this way, and this procedure is at least as difficult to learn as the one foreseen by the machine designers.

One could deductively conclude that this procedure must be better. From our discussions with the setters I will suggest another explanation. The use of the cam arrangement represents something rather special to this type of machine (not the use of cam arrangements as such but the specific way it is used here). If the setters are never comprehensively introduced to this procedure, it is very likely that they will never be able to master it. Grinding tools on the other hand is part of the standard vocabulary of every skilled machinist. Therefore the path that most machinists would follow is to focus attention on the area where the material meets the tools. Here individual creativity can draw upon the full spectre of skills embedded in the machinist profession, whether acquired in the spring company or elsewhere.

How come then that the setters at the workshop sessions reacted so positively to the access to learning materials while they did not themselves start talking at work. I think the answer is that conventions of the Taylorist factory regime has largely deformed workshops like in the spring companies by excluding and oppressing dialogue and reflexivity. This is widely internalised by the shop floor workers in their work practice, but represents also a profound barrier for gaining and sharing experience. This situation cannot be dramatically changed without loosening this factory regime, but on the other hand, such loosening in itself will depend on the emergence of a new and richer language of the workshop. I believe the positive feedback from the setters shall be understood precisely as an acknowledgement of this possibility inherent in materials such as the training package. In relation to discussions about informal and experience-based learning this case shed light to the fact that not only building on but also building up existing learning cultures might contribute to the development of shop floor skills.

Community Learning and Ladders of Reflection

So far I have tried to highlight some of the problems which to me seem important for dealing with learning at work. I have used examples from my own work, but as I see it these examples hint to problems of a more general nature. To summarise I have used the case of the service technicians, to point to problems in an instructional approach to learning. I have used the case of the postal workers and their alienated attitude towards the technical artefacts in their work environment, to discuss the problems of separating the questions of skills and skill acquisition from the questions of work organisation and community culture. Lastly, I have used the case of machine setting in the spring industry to illustrate the shortcomings in informal learning within the well known environment of the skilled machinist. I will end this listing of problems with a brief discussion on how a framework dealing with this problem can be conceptualised and I will try out the possibilities of combining Schön's concept of reflective practitioners with Lave and Wenger's concept of communities of practice.

In the debate about learning the relation between theory and practice as well as between knowledge and action has been widely discussed. Mainly in the debate on cognitive approaches in which a number of authors have questioned the role of abstracted knowledge for the competent practitioner as well as for the newcomer. Dreyfuss and Dreyfuss (1986) have suggested to see learning as a five step process from novice to expert. They see abstracted knowledge of rules and procedures to be an important starting point for the novice, guiding him into the domain of action, but argue that rules and procedures in later steps are internalised and expanded far beyond what can be inscribed in an abstracted bulk of knowledge. As an example, they argue that the novice driver to a large extent will rely on abstracted knowledge on e.g. the relations between car speed and appropriate gearing, whereas the more competent driver will master these relations without consciously dealing with formalised rules. They also point to the fact that the competent driver might even see their performance deteriorate, if they are for one reason or another, forced to relate their behaviour to the still not forgotten abstracted rules of "correct" action.

Even though the example in itself is convincing, the picture of the driver does not seem to fit very well with the problems encountered with instructional learning in an industrial setting, as illustrated earlier in this paper. Here Suchman's discussion about plans and situated action comes closer to explaining the role of abstracted knowledge. Suchman directly addresses the question of how instructional information relates to action. She argues that seeing plan whether in the form of instructions or in other formats as preceding and prescribing actions, neglects the basically situated nature of actions. She does not exclude the possibility that a plan exists in the mind of the actor before acting, but she argues that actions actually taken, mirrors reflections on the situation as it evolves during the course of the particular actions in question. As a general understanding of plans, she suggests to see these more as reflections on actions perceived or previously completed, and hereby clearly rejects the cognitivist idea that actions are merely an implementation of plans. From studying the use of instructional information by users operating photocopiers, she argues that the user enters into a dialogue with the artefact, making actional moves and reflecting on the response. The instruction in this context does not in any simple sense, guide actions but tends to create a point of reference, for the user's own framing of the situation. Using Suchman's notion of actions as always situated, and her rejection of the idea that plans and actions are intertwined, makes it tempting to simply give up the concept of knowledge as something separable from action, and replace this concept by the much more dynamic and procedure-oriented concept of reflections and reflexivity.

To move away from the static notion of knowledge and towards the more dynamic notion of reflexivity is taken by Schön (1987) in his study of architectural education. Schön discusses the nature of competence in the field of design in architecture, and he explores especially the architectural studio in order to find out how this competence is achieved. Like Suchman and Dreyfuss and Dreyfuss, he finds that competence cannot be ascribed to the acquisition of a certain body of abstracted knowledge. The competent architect like other professionals such as lawyers, medical doctors and engineer, in Schön's terminology is a reflective practitioner who constructs the world of problems and solutions. When the architect approaches a certain task of designing, e.g. a school for a particular site, he is not applying generalised knowledge of schools and sites, but is entering into a constructive dialogue of reflective action, where designing in terms of sketching and modelling lets the site talk back to the designer about possibilities and problems. Acting in terms of constructing design suggestions, or for the lawyer or doctor constructing a chain of arguments or narrative conceptualising the case in question is complemented by reflecting on the constructions to improve or redirect additional acting. For the competent professional the complementarity between action and reflection is embedded in the skilful practice. Schön speaks of reflection-in-action as the label best describing competence in what Suchman would call situated action.

Schön does not in any way deny that we can talk in more general terms about design, or even construct a generalised stock of resources to bring into play in the localised instance of design. Actually Schön points to the existence of a repertoire of such generalised resources as one of the core elements in the design profession. But what makes Schön in line with Suchman and others stressing the situatedness of action, is his strong emphasis on the point that these resources only come into play through reflection-in-action and reflection-on-action. The resources themselves must be understood as reflections on design, and their value for the designer will fully depend on his or her ability to relate these reflections to the localised reflections on the situated actions in question.

When discussing how newcomers enter the design profession, Schön develops this argument. He points to the paradox that competent designing with its interwoven patterns of localised reflection-in-action cannot be taught but only learned through the student's own actions and reflections-on-actions, at the same as doing and reflecting on design moves cannot be safeguarded on the road to competence, as long as the student does not know what competent designing is. For the newcomer he argues there is no other way out of this paradox, than engaging inaction, and relying on coaching from someone capable of competent design. Any attempt to appropriate generalised knowledge of design principles, techniques or standard solutions will remain barren to the student as long as these efforts cannot be related to a personal experience of acting and reflecting on action in the domain of design. Focusing on recorded dialogue between coaches and students he illustrates how the coach is neither able to fully guide nor follow the steps taken by the student. The student acts and reflects and the coach can reflect on the actions and reflections using his own professional experience of designing. If the coach however, directly intervenes in the work of the student by forcing upon him an imitative style of actions and reflections, the student will very likely be cut off from his essential dialogue with the subject matter. What coach and student can do according to Schön, is to seek to follow each other's moves. In doing so they can work inductively along what Schön calls the ladder of reflection. When the student acts, student and coach reflect on the action. The coach can respond to the student's reflection-on-action by acting or reflecting on the student's reflections. The student can seek to follow the coach by reflecting on the coach's reflection and so on. The important point to note here is that even though the student and coach can, in principle, remove themselves from the concrete action to a level of meta-meta reflection, their dialogue remains rooted in the context of the specific design tasks in question.

To adopt Schön's description of competent designing to the work of service technicians or machine setters seems to me attractive in several ways. First of all, the concept of competence as competent reflection-in-action fits well to the detective-like style of reasoning described earlier, and to the embeddedness of competence in the ever new context of trouble shooting, posing so harsh resistance to abstracted generalisations. Secondly, the unresolvable interrelations between acting and reflecting which puts action first in Schön's concepts of learning offers a framework for understanding learning processes much closer to stories of gaining experience in an industrial setting, than that of Dreyfuss and Dreyfuss. Thirdly, Schön's idea of a repertoire of resources as a constitutive element of professional competence, and his emphasis on the ladder of reflection as the inductive mediator between newcomer and professional, give more relevant hints for disclosing and discussing learning cultures than, e.g. Suchman's concept of situated action.

There are also problems in adopting Schön to the worlds of letter sorting and spring making. Schön has his attention focused on the mastery skills of the professional or would-be professional. His examples evolve around committed relations between coach and student, and his arguments are flavoured by the unquestioned competencies and individuality of professionals such as architects, doctors and lawyers. Hereby he avoids questions of the social structuring of the field of practice visible in the alienation of the postal worker towards her surrounding artefacts or in the persisting inadequacies of the practice of the tool grinding machine setter. To deal with these questions I would like to turn to the relation between learning and participation as discussed by Lave and Wenger.

Where Schön addresses and criticises the dualism between knowledge and action at the individual level and puts emphasis on the situatedness of action, Lave and Wenger focus on the broader categories of learning and practice as social processes in themselves situated in particular community settings (Lave and Wenger, 1994). They have studied apprenticeship relations in different socio-cultural settings and what they have found in these studies is mainly two things.

First, they find that across differences in setting, competence cannot be attributed to the individual but must be seen as embedded in what they call a community of practice. In their empirical studies they are not able to identify a core of this community, but define a broad spectre of rules, procedures, norms and resources commonly recognised by the participants as constitutive for competent action. They elaborate these findings by claiming that competence must be localised to communities commonly sharing the same understanding of competent action, and furthermore that the individual when confronted with a new task will rely on the acknowledgement of his competent actions, as it is accessible to him through his participation in the community of practice.

Second, they show how learning cannot be separated from participation in a community. To learn is, according to Lave and Wenger, to enter into a community of practice, and to separate the newcomer's accommodation to social norms and values from the acquisition of skills will even as an analytical separation violate the fundamental principle of rootedness of competence. To state their point clearer, they simply identify learning with that they call legitimate peripheral participation. With this notion they want to stress that the newcomer has to participate in order to learn, but also that this participation necessarily must involve a legitimate access to the periphery of the community of practice.

Lave and Wenger offer in this way, a better point of reference for understanding how the organisation of work will influence the structuring of competence and learning. With the example given earlier about the postal workers abstaining from any type of involvement with technical matters, the line of thought suggested by Lave and Wenger can turn attention to questions of what the communities of practice are, and how legitimacy for participation is distributed. For the machine setters the concept of communities of practice as the coreless domain of expertise can give explanations as to why a harder centre of setting skills cannot be identified and purified of the traces from a socially constructed context of individualised trouble shooting.

Even though Schön on the one side and Lave and Wenger on the other, conceptualise learning differently, it seems to me both possible and fruitful to combine them rather than choosing one instead of the other. Whereas Lave and Wenger give a better framework for catching the social aspects of learning, Schön on the other hand provides a more open ended conceptualisation of the individual learning process with his example of didactic dialogues up and down the ladder of reflection. When trying to bring the two together, it seems to me relevant to focus on the idea of a repertoire of resources constituting in Schön's terminology the profession, and in Lave and Wenger's terminology, a community of practice.

This idea stands rather central in both contributions but is also quite vaguely defined. The reason for me to focus precisely on the resources for action is that building up and maintaining these resources in the professional community seems to pose a weak point in the arguments put forward so far. The weakness stems from two questions poorly answered. First, how can these resources gain stability in time and space if they are fully embedded in the situated practice of a community. And second, through which social mechanisms can a repertoire of resources evolve and develop, and explain the growth of the overall competence of the community/ profession.

For me the most obvious path to take in order to shed light on these questions is to link the competence of the reflective practitioner and the community of practice through a more elaborated concept of human interaction. Even though Schön stresses the individual task of learning as part of the reflective practices of the profession, he also maintains that this task must be accomplished through the dialogue with competent practitioners. Similarly although Lave and Wenger emphasis that the community is established through practice, their argument relies on the ability of community members to communicate and establish common grounds for action. Taking such a step with relaxed references to Habermas (1981), and thereby introducing Hambermas' concept of communicative action as grounded in the localised world of language, would offer a better analytical tool for understanding the inner life of the community of practice and provide a basis for discussing transcendents and change.

I have discussed elsewhere the use of Habermas's line of thought for understanding learning processes in an industrial setting (Binder, 1993) and directly addressing the question of work place learning. A similar discussion has been put forward by Markert (1994). I will not however, develop arguments for such an expansion of the Schön/Lave and Wegner framework here, but instead try to explore the consequences of such an expanded framework for the type of projects I have been engaged in.

Learning with Computers

The different notions of computer based training, computer aided learning and programmed learning have all be framed by the view that the computer program in some way could be brought to mirror or even replace the cognitive processes necessary to perform a set of practical tasks. This has meant that the mainstream of debate on learning with computers has been heavily engaged in pointing to and developing the unique possibilities of isolating and purifying learning processes to unfold when the trainee engages with the computer. When this view is being fundamentally contradicted with arguments such as the ones put forward in this article, one might ask what has been accomplished with all the practical attempts to realise CBT, and what relevance does it have to go on engaging in supporting learning with computers. To the first question about what has been accomplished I think it is important to be pragmatic when seeking the answers. Even though CBT programmes have been designed for structuring and encompassing particular learning processes there is nothing certain about how the programs are read, when adopted in specific social settings. Furthermore in a pragmatic interpretation the social connotations associated with the introduction of new artefacts for learning such as the acknowledgement of learning needs and the modalisation of learning practices, might contribute as much to community life as the particular contents of the training package. So while the critique posed to the relevance of a cognitivist approach to computers and learning also finds support in empirical evaluations of the outcomes of implementing CBT, such as in the US report on worker training by OTA (1990), it would be wrong not to pay attention to the possible emergence of new social practices induced by the introduction of computers for learning in the workplace.

Going from the first question to the second of the relevance of using computers as part of a learning environment, the pragmatism in dealing with computers as an artefact (among others) for learning, suggested above, already suggests relaxation. When the view of the computer as the purifier of learning is rejected, what we have to discuss is really not if the computer has any particular role to play in learning, but rather how the computer programme as one media amongst others, can be brought into the workplace to facilitate learning. It is within this pragmatic perspective that I will return to my own work with postal workers and machine setters.

Computers as the Materialisation of Legitimate Learning Opportunities

When the Postal Services initiated the development of POSTI, it was part of a larger project of implementing 24 new automatic letter sorting machines at 8 regional postal centres where only one centre had previous experience with automatic letter sorting. The central office of the Postal Services had the responsibility for specification of the new technology, technical installation of the machines and preparation of the associated training schemes including the development of POSTI. Based on evaluation of experience with an earlier generation of letter sorting machines, the central office saw the establishment of teamwork and a softening of demarcation lines between operators and technicians as important elements in the organisation of work to be implemented in the regional centres. The responsibility for organisational questions was however, decentralised to the individual centres so the central office could only signal to the centres that teamwork and new job profiles were desirable.

By initiating the development of POSTI the central office sent out a clear signal for organisational renewal. The POSTI system should support both operators and technicians in handling technical maintenance and repair. The POSTI system should be placed physically in the immediate surroundings of the letter sorting machines, and should be open to everyone without constraints in terms of passwords or tests.

This meant that the use of the system was supposed to be integrated in the daily routines of operators and technicians. Finally the central office sanctioned the involvement of operators and technicians in the development of the system (and not the supervisors) and were hereby signalling a participative open approach also to the questions of organisational change.

These signals were sent at the time when the new machines had still not arrived at the centres, and the organisational question had hardly been opening locally. The POSTI system was launched almost parallel to the installation of the machines and the hardware and software was introduced during the initial training of operators and technicians at a vocational training centre before installation on the centres. Despite this timing the process of organisational work turned out to be rather conflictual, and the formal organisation of work varied considerably from centre to centre.

Given this setting it is obvious that POSTI simply for its symbolic value was constructed to have an impact, but what did this mean for the emerging communities of practice? We did not have the opportunity to evaluate systematically what happened after the implementation, but through our cooperation with operators and technicians during the design and test of POSTI at two of the eight centres, we got some idea of the role the system could play in these communities. We worked with two user groups consisting of four operators and two technicians. The first user group was recruited from the postal centre which had had letter sorting machines for some years, and the second was recruited from the centre being first to have the new generation of machines installed.

In the first group discussion about the form and content of POSTI could build on actual experience from working with the machines. This meant that possible changes in tasks as indicated by the whole objective of developing the POSTI system was treated by the users in the light of how this would affect social practices already established. In the early stages of the design it is my impression that the users tried to interpret the intentions of the design in terms which would make it fit into the well known practice. The operators were very reluctant to accept any major enlargement of their responsibilities and the technicians would hardly acknowledge that information support would be at all relevant for their tasks. These positions could however, not be maintained if the design should go on, and despite the scepticism it seemed as if the users on a more general level would like to respond positively to the offer for involvement posed to them by the central office of the Postal Services. So the design work slowly started with the basic question of final use of the system being left more or less unresolved.

As already described it was part of the specification of the POSTI system that best practice for maintenance, fault finding and repair should be documented. Together with the users we decided to start with a relatively uncomplex and well known case: cleaning of the light barriers to try out what this could mean in practice. We documented the cleaning operation with photos and organised a sequence of photos to be displayed together with a short oral explanation. We associated to this sequence a few blueprints which could be displayed on the screen showing the physical build up of the light barriers and their location in the machine. At last we prepared a so-called notebook function where the user could enter whatever they found relevant to remind them or their colleagues when returning to this sequence.

With this suggestion for a standard exemplar we played out to the users our first interpretation of intentions in the light of their initial reactions. This interpretation did not represent an acceptance of the first reactions from the users but could rather be seen as an argument that tried to take into account some of the objections that we heard or expected to hear. The example solely addressed the operators as the potential future user. The cleaning operation was by far too simple to be justified if the addressee had been the technician. At the same time, we knew that the cleaning job was not regarded as attractive to the technicians. By being fairly detailed in the documentation we did not only signal that this was a potential job for the operators, but also that the operators could (and should) expect from POSTI a background to act on that exceeded what could be acquired while actually acting. This meant that we signalled that POSTI should be seen as a means for preparation and general upgrading of competence. Furthermore, the attachment of blueprints was an attempt on our side to redefine which types of information the operator should regard as relevant. We deliberately sought to break down the de facto monopoly of the technicians over the technical documentation. At last the notebook function with general access for reading and writing indicated an element of shopfloor control over the system, which should envisage the users appropriation of the system also after the design had ended.

Our suggestion was by and large well received by the user group. We, of course, asserted the notion of questioning of what tasks should be carried out by the technicians. However, the technicians clearly felt that the example did not contest the type of competencies on which their jobs were built. Secondly, they also seemed to see positive aspects in the possibility that the operators would be more informed about the technicalities of the machines. The operators appeared to appreciate the implicit acknowledgement of the time needed to learn and could thereby open up potential advantages in an enlargement of their responsibilities. For the operators the role of the supervisors absent in the user group but highly present in their daily work, remained a key question to be dealt with, although this could not be done within the design work.

We continued the design work by working closely with two technicians, in order to build up the contents of POSTI along the lines suggested by the first paradigmatic example. During this work we renounced more and more the purely instructional approach, and tried to develop informational fragments well suited for preparing the operators to engage in maintenance and repair of the machines. The technicians we worked with kept a very open line to the remaining group of technicians. Topics that we dealt with were concurrently discussed by the technicians and topics were excluded or changed according to this discussion. We also followed a number of the technicians' suggestions. As work progressed we felt increasingly sure of the importance of developing POSTI also as an aid for the technicians. If the technicians excluded themselves as users beforehand, we feared that POSTI would turn out to define operator tasks rather than supporting them. At the same time we felt that the technicians although undoubtedly competent could gain from reflecting more on technical principles underlying the specific functionality of the machine. This need seemed to be mainly associated with principles less familiar to the basic profession of the technicians such as optics, pneumatics, and hydraulics. We pushed these types of topics quite hard despite some resistance by the technicians, and were successful in involving them in the actual design work, because we could point to the fact that the use of these topics should be seen as an option for learning and not as a suggestion for a new practice of work. Part of this could also be explained by the fact that we also included information essential to the technicians and difficult to find in the existing documentation.

The second group of users was involved in the design in the later stages, and had a different starting point. Both operators and technicians were recruited locally at the regional centre and both groups had a background as postal workers although the technicians also had some sort of skilled background. At this centre work organisation was about to be settled while the group took part in the design work and the local management had made it clear that they wanted the technicians to take part in operator tasks whenever possible. The information formats and a large part of the contents had already been implemented in POSTI and the second user group therefore was more involved with modifications and adjustments. In the group the discussions also took another direction. As no communities could be said to exist the users tended to use the topics dealt with in POSTI as an a la carte list from which the two groups could pick tasks and forward an argument concerning their role in the work involved. We experienced how discussions about the documentation of different tasks almost immediately was brought in to the parallel discussion about work organisation and how especially the operators deliberately used arguments put forward in the former discussion to reach out for new tasks in their daily work. The technicians quite obviously felt intimidated by the open access to information which for them was still new and troublesome to deal with. Their reactions were correspondingly ambiguous and shifted periodically between excluding themselves from the system (and also from dialogue with the operators over the topics enclosed in the system) and excluding the operators from the system.

I cannot give a full account of what happened later at the centres. We know that at some centres the technicians were able to move the POSTI system into their staff room and thereby in a very illustrative way underline who should be the user of the system. We also know that POSTI never made a big impact on the centre with previous experience in automatic letter sorting because the system was maintained in the work area and was never accepted from the still present supervisors. It is our impression, however, that POSTI induced learning and gradual changes in both the work of technicians and operators in some centres.

What is however more important to note is that POSTI with smaller or greater success presented the technicians and operators with a legitimate opportunity to learn during everyday work and to reflect upon and discuss topics arising. The extent to which this learning was directly sustained by the contents of the POSTI system is hard to estimate, but there is in my mind no doubt that the pure presence of POSTI both as a concrete physical space for learning and as an open catalogue of tasks to discuss, created opportunities for learning going far beyond what had existed in the postal centres before.

Computers as Resources for Dialogue

In the previous section I have tried to take what could be called an outward look at the role that computers might play for learning. I have chosen not to discuss the specific role which the POSTI system played or could play in the actual instances of use but rather to show that the computer in the physical and symbolic shape created at least temporary chances for learning, by the mere fact that it was there as an accessible requisite for the communities of practice. In this section I will take a more inward look by discussing how the idea of the computer as an additional source of clues for the detective like practitioners can be developed and extended to a more comprehensive concept of computer-based materials as potential language resources to be activated and expanded through dialogue. To do this I will use our experience with machine setting, but it should be said from the start that basically the same arguments could have been put forward from detailing the POSTI story.

I have already described how the machine setters resemble Schön's reflective practitioners in their search for ways of accomplishing the specific goals set out for the particular springs they are preparing for production. I have described them as detectives, because they seem to engage in an open minded search for clues that can lead them through the various steps of the setting task, and I have suggested that the competence that they draw on should rather be seen as a repertoire of resources brought into play through reflecting-in-action, rather than as an abstracted bulk of knowledge. The repertoire of resources are in my phrasing constructed in the common language of the community of practice. It is in the acknowledgement of the individual by the community and in the mirroring of individual actions towards collective experience in the community that competent action is established.

The case of machine setting of spring coiling machines is however, not a simple case within this framework. As described earlier, the setting strategies vary considerably, and the common dialogue on technical matters is rudimentary and rare. I have used the example of tool grinding to illustrate that there are even signs of a kind of regress to communality in the larger and more established community of skilled machinists. We entered the community from this particular point with the intention to use our task of developing computer-based learning aids to see if we could stimulate what could be called a particular technical discourse of spring making.

Through video documentation of the setting process, prototyping of information elements and extensive discussions with the setters at work and at workshop sessions we developed a learning material focusing on naming and framing of artefacts and work processes. The learning material was dedicated for use on the shopfloor, creating opportunities for reflection during the newcomer's introduction to the community as well as for dialogue among experienced coilers concerning methods and procedures used. Throughout the material we used video film of the shopfloor and the spoken word as close to shopfloor language as possible. Machines and hands on the video were deliberately kept just as oily as we found them in the real shopfloor environment, and also in the way we dealt with the different topics of spring making we sought to keep the material as contextualised as we could. The process of developing this material was in itself an important learning process for both us and the setters. I will discuss this in more detail in the concluding part of this article. Here I will instead jump directly to the question of how the material was adopted by the community of setters, as we have followed this process through three months of introduction to the newcomer.

A computer with the learning material was placed on the shopfloor in the company where it was also developed. All 40 blue-collar workers were given a brief introduction to the package and the computer was placed on wheels in the work area where the machine setters work. The supervisor and the production manager were actively promoting the use of this package also for occasional browsing and everyone was free to use the package during work hours. For the first two months there was no planned use of the package; it was mainly used by people who wanted to see "what was in it". After this introductory period a newcomer had to be trained for machine setting. It was decided that they should use the package alongside conventional learning-by-watching and learning-by-doing type of training. We followed the newcomer by joining them for a full working day every week for the first eight weeks of his training.

We knew the newcomer because he had been an occasional participant in some of the workshop sessions. He had been several years in the company and had also gone through his apprenticeship as a skilled machinist and dye maker. He had however never taken part in machine setting. The setting up job was both for him and the other setters regarded as a new task to master. His training was organised slightly differently from the usual training practices. Instead of starting by monitoring and adjusting the machines already set for production he had engaged in setting from the start. He followed an experienced setter and was supposed to take as many of the setting tasks as the experienced setter found relevant. He was given six weeks for initial training, where he would be expected to contribute to production. After this period his training should be evaluated and the continuation should be planned in detail.

The training went quite well. At the end of the first week he carried out a full setting operation under supervision by the experienced setter. After two weeks he worked mostly on his own, only calling on the experienced colleague occasionally when he encountered a problem. After four weeks he started to deliberate himself from the role as a learner by abstaining from use of the package as well as from questioning his colleagues. His results surprised everyone in the company, and when his training period was evaluated the supervisor concluded that he had learned in eight weeks what would usually take at least six months. But what happened during these eight weeks.

In the first weeks he took on the attitude of a true newcomer. He was guided through the setting process by the experienced setter, and was frequently brought to the package to go over details alone or in discussion with his colleague. He apparently took over the vocabulary and even the phrases from the package, when he explained to use how he went along in his work. He related his own procedures directly to procedures as they were described in the learning material. At the same time he was taken into the community as the new man to learn the game. He was tested both by colleagues and the supervisor. The supervisor tried to make him run like the "boy in the repair shop" he used to be and the colleagues watched to see if he could take care of himself as a true setter. His colleagues teased him when he was in trouble and pushed him back to do the job at the machine whenever they could. He seemed quite eager to meet the test and almost as a ritual he was included in the setters daily raffle.

He reacted to the pressure by retracting to his setting and his package. In the next weeks the did almost everything on his own, and used the package to find ways out of problems. He entered into conversations with the machine, trying out something and waiting for the machine to talk back. He browsed through the videos of the package to find the picture that could give him a clue of what was wrong and he read the stories of faulty springs to find parallels to what he was experiencing at the machine. The experienced setter encouraged him to go on in this way, and even pushed him back to the package when he thought he could find solutions on his own.

After four weeks had passed he began to feel more confident and it was also acknowledged by his colleagues. He even made fairly complex settings on his own and could describe in detail how he had done them, and how he wanted to proceed further. His growing self-confidence also meant that he started to distance himself from the package. He said, "OK, the package is good, but now I can find my own way". He clearly wanted to demonstrate his new gained competence by not being seen at the computer and to blend into the community without exposing himself to the visible learning site.

We went through the learning material with him afterwards and also discussed the whole training period. He was obviously very well acquainted with the package and had detailed opinions about every look up video. It was clear that in one sense he had been even more alone with his tasks than what would have been the case without the package. The dialogue among colleagues did not emerge, even though such a dialogue had started at the workshop sessions. Despite this he maintained that he had had a good training period and that the possibility for going into problems by using the package had an important influence on what he had learned.

We had expected more technical discussions when the package was introduced and we also thought the dialogue between newcomer and experienced would have been intensified. This did not happen, but on the other hand it was clear that the user community did not in any way reject the package. Actually the experienced setters frequently turned up at the learning site to see if the package was just rubbish. They joined the discussion where they were most sure of their own expertise and they loudly commented and made known what they thought of the package. In general the reactions were positive. Even though this can hardly be called a dialogue it seemed obvious that these signs of approval were crucial for the newcomer's own use of the package.

To conclude, I think the type of multimedia materials described here and in the previous sections enhance learning both by materialising and thereby symbolically acknowledging the need for reflexive sites and by giving the learner access to context related instances, exemplars and stories to relate to and reflect upon when engaging in the tasks at hand. These learning materials are just one among other ways of legitimising and stimulating ladders of reflection, but by building such computer based materials, a path is open for creating learning environments rather than attempting to program cognition.

Educational Design as Prototypical Learning

I will end this article by returning to a point already made in the beginning. In the projects described in this article we developed learning materials together with the future users. This turned out to be very fruitful for the design tasks we were to accomplish, but much more than that the dialogue with users and among users in itself appeared to evolve as new learning processes prototypical for the kind of reflexivity and dialogue that the learning materials could stimulate.

The involvement of competent practitioners in the design of learning materials for newcomers could simply be seen as an appropriate technique for gaining access to information concerning competent action. That is also true in the sense that involvement of practitioners will be inevitable as long as competence cannot be abstracted from the community in which it is rooted. The rootedness of competence is however, of a more exclusive nature than what is grasped by a mere methodological approach of user involvement. As I have tried to spell out along the lines of argument put forward by Schön and Lave and Wenger rootedness of competence does also mean that competence cannot be acquired without actually participating in the communities of practice, and that not only the potentials of competent action but also its limits must be understood as inscribed in the communality of the specific community. The dialogue among practitioners and designers described in this article attempted in different ways to widen the scope for competent action. The practitioners did not only express concepts and approaches already present as common tacit knowledge, they actually developed discourses that were either absent or rudimentary in their communities. In this sense the dialogue induced by our design tasks opened up for a possible transcendent in line with the suggestions for transcendents in language and through language (Markett, 1994).

(More Than) User Participation in Design of Learning Materials

The way we involved the practitioners in the design process was inspired by the tradition of participation as it has developed within Scandinavian systems designs. This inspiration was fairly straightforward to adopt when the learning material to be developed was regarded as a computer system of which a series of prototypes could be moulded and presented for discussion and trial with the users. The development process in both projects consisted of three main phases. In the first the basic concept for the material was developed through design and evaluation of 2–3 simple prototypes encompassing exemplary "fragments" hinting at both contents, structure and navigation in the final material. In the next phase, the full contents of the material was developed and the concept was modified in close cooperation with selected practitioners and monitored by a larger group through presentation and discussion at workshop sessions. In the last phase the learning material was tried out and evaluated in use for a longer period by the same group who had participated in the design. The involvement alternated between informal discussions on the shop floor, recording sessions, workshops and joint preparatory work outside the work area. The workshop session had a particular prominent role as they functioned as scheduled and formalised events where comments, criticism and objections to the progress of work could be voiced and formally noted. In both projects the cooperation between practitioners and designers was clearly separated from formal project management.

In the debate about participatory design different understandings of the role and nature of participation for the overall design process has been suggested. Referring mainly to the Scandinavian discussion one can say that the early contributions from the late 1970s mainly focused on the conflictual interests of different groups toward new technology, and in this light, advocated participation as a process in which the different interests could be articulated (see, e.g., Ehn, 1988). In more recent literature Ehn's notion of design as the meeting of different language games has gained considerable interest as this notion both underscores the basic differences and equality of contributions from the different participants (signalled by the label "language games" not incompatible with the idea of communities of practice discussed earlier) and puts emphasis on the particularity of the design process (signalled by the idea of a "meeting" in which mutual understanding and learning must take place).

The problem in using Ehn's conceptualisation is that it does not say very much about the roles of designers and users respectively. Why is the designer at all necessary, and who should take responsibility of organising the specific design game. It could be said that Ehn actually keeps these questions open by abstaining from any clearcut definitions of the professionalism of designers. In a recent paper he even reports how the appropriation of information technology can be successfully handed over to the users with only marginal organisational support (Ehn, 1994).

Others have taken a clearer stance in defining the roles of designers and users. For example, Kensing and Bodker (1994) see it as part of the job of the designers to analyse and expose actual work practices thereby bringing in the dialogue with the users an explicitation of often informal work practices not usually highlighted in work place discussions. With this stance they obviously fill a need for workable approaches called for by practical system designers. The problem is that it also involves the risk of pushing the users out in the periphery of the design process. There is no doubt that reading work practices from the oral descriptions of the practitioners is a highly problematic endeavour. But even though much can be said about work when applying delicate ethnomethodological tools and techniques, the involvement of designers in such an analysis will very easily result in a framing of the work practice derived from the designers' presumptions of the system to be designed rather than vice versa.

Corbett, Rauner and Rasmussen (1990) move Ehn's line of thought in a different direction. In a discussion of human-centredness in computer integrated manufacturing, they see dialogue and mutual learning between various groups of practitioners to be the core issue in conceptualising new technology. In conventional design they see this conceptualisation as monopolised by certain groups, and they suggest the use of workshop sessions bringing together and combining in different ways the insights and interests of the various groups of practitioners. In this way they follow Ehn in placing the meeting of competencies as the central arena for design, but they single out and elaborate the role of mediators or "game organisers" as important catalysts necessary to overcome limitations of common sense beliefs and orientations. Where Ehn sees the construction and reflection of the artefacts as the central theme for the dialogue between designers and practitioners, Corbett et al. talk about the construction of concepts and scenarios from which practical design can later be derived. This difference is interesting in my view because it signals a possible shift of emphasis from design as construction of physical things to design as a linguistic construct. In combination with the singling out of the role of the mediator this does also indicate a possible weakness in their understanding of design as a basically deductive process of deriving solutions from concepts (Banke and Binder, 1994).

When returning to participation in design of learning materials some of the questions raised in this discussion of participatory design has to be posed differently. First of all, what has to be designed are not tools or systems for practitioners to perform their tasks. Learning materials are basically text that can be read and reflected upon. There are no mechanistic ties between learning material and actual action, and the possibility even exists that the practitioners might simply abstain from using it. Secondly the focus on learning means that the practitioners by definition have a much more essential role to play than the designers. The design work can still be regarded as a meeting point between the communities of practitioners and designers, but the rootedness of learning and competence has as a consequence that the outcome must almost be embedded in the communities of practitioners. The designers still have a job to do by supplying skills on media and to some extent pedagogics but this contribution will clearly be subordinate to contributions from the designers. Lastly, learning makes reflection and discourse indispensable in the design work. Whereas design of tools or systems might leave the door open for various participants to pragmatically evaluate suggestions and artefacts from individual or group perspectives, the construction of text has to involve interpretation and appropriation in the domain of language, if it shall produce any kind of meaning for the participants.

These differences to the mainstream of design work within the tradition of participatory design do not in any way make design of learning materials a marginal case within this tradition. In my view it is rather so that this type of design work to an almost extreme extent, illustrates the necessity of authenticity in the process of participation. Ehn's focus on language games does in this context, gain even more relevance as not only to the media but also to the outcome of the design process which can be seen as contextualised language. Kensing and Bodker's emphasis on actual work practices is surely important but in the context of design for learning, it must be associated with the utmost concern for how insights gained with the ethnomethodological approach can gain legitimacy within the community of practice. And finally, Corbett et al.'s focus on temporary meetings between different and complementary communities should be followed up by discussions on how these meetings can result in more than temporary insights.

Creating Discourse, but What About Factory Regimes?

What has been said so far? I have tried to argue that learning means participating in communicative action. The technician, the postal worker or the machine setter all engage in action in a framework of communities that prescribe and acknowledge codes of competence without which no individual would be able to act with confidence. The ties between individual and community are the complex web of social interactions which, with an expression from Habermas is encompassed by the life world of the community. Learning is here rather as part of everyday interaction than a singular social process. As Schön says, no learning can take place without acting, and as Lave and Wenger say, no learning occurs before a learner gets legitimate access to the community. But I could add that this is just as much the case for working in general and even though this might seem to destroy the whole point, it actually opens up for a more dynamic understanding of competencies and communities as social entities that, in principle, undergo never ending transformations with or without newcomers. As to the problem of entry for newcomers, I have argued that learning depends on the richness of the community language in which the newcomer can ground and mirror his actions, and on the access to arenas in time and space where actions can reflected upon and discourses can be developed.

When turning to the question of how learning can be stimulated by the introduction of such learning materials as the computer programmes described earlier, I have argued that artefacts for learning offer both a symbolic manifestation of learning opportunities and concrete resources for reflection. Behind this argument there exists a tension between the proposed rootedness of learning and competencies and the idea that learning can be facilitated by the introduction of external learning aids. This tension gets particularly problematic when competence and community of practice are regarded as static phenomena reproducing themselves in the newcomers. I have sought to soften the tension by giving examples of how practitioners are appropriating learning materials by interpreting and reinterpreting them as artefacts as well as text, and including or excluding them from ongoing discourses in the community on roles and tasks. I maintain that this appropriation is an open-ended process which just like the appropriation of new tools or systems will leave the community at least a little different from what it was before. This means that the introduction of learning material like the POSTI system will induce changes also in the work of the competent practitioner, but it also certainly means a change which can take many directions and of which we can only say very little.

I have attempted to show how the design of learning materials involving practitioners constitutes a fruitful learning process in which the practitioners can break new ground for communicative action. I have suggested that this process should be seen as prototypical learning where the discourse evolves beyond what is already there in the community. I have also exemplified how this discourse may not be kept open when the learning materials are brought back to the workplace. This surely weakens my argument for a genuine transcendence in the dialogue among practitioners, but I think that rather than questioning the authenticity of technical discourse emerging among the machine setters, because it seemed to be cut later, we shall accustom ourselves to the volatile nature of any life world discourse.

When getting the professional task of preparing better learning aids for a particular community I believe that most of us at least for some time, will find that the accomplishment of just our task must be crucial to the future wellbeing of newcomers. Getting more distanced in time this expectation gets moderated if not by anything else than by the usually moderate results. Fischer has very nicely illustrated how a group of machinists who had been given over the task to plan their work on a team basis, actually reproduced the individualistic planning practice to which they had been accustomed for many years of a Taylorist factory regime (Fischer, 1995). I have given examples that indicate that the evolvement of new discourses that opened for new roles and competencies, although rooted in the shopfloor were rolled back by a Taylorist organisation of work. What can be concluded then: Change is not possible? Or that change of regimes takes time?

In Danish we have two sayings which can conclude my own viewpoint. The misanthropic saying is that "one bird makes no summer" which is certainly true, but for relief we also have another more optimistic saying, that "one bird in the hand is better than ten on the roof".

References

Binder, Thomas and P. Banke, Mediating between Users and Designers – User Involvement in Design of a Flexible Sewing Machine, in Kidd and Karwowski (eds.) Advances in Agile Manufacturing, IOS Press, 1994

Binder, Thomas, Designing for Workplace Learning, Copenhagen, 1994 (forthcoming)

Binder, Thomas, Mod nye læreprocesser i Industrielt Udviklingsarbejde, Institute of Social Sciences, Technical University of Denmark, 1993 (in Danish)

Böhle, Fritz, Relevance of Experience-based Work in Modern Process, paper presented at the European Conference on the Role of Research for the Social Shaping of Technology, Ravello, 13-15 October, 1993

Corbett, Martin, L. Rasmussen and F. Rauner, Crossing the border, Springer Verlag, 1990

Dreyfus, H.L. and Dreyfus E., Mind over Machine, Oxford, 1986

Ehn, Pelle and Forss Peter, Designing IT locally, Lund, 1994 (forthcoming)

Ehn, Pelle, Work oriented design of computer artifacts, Arbetslivscentrum, 1988

Fischer, Martin, Work Process Knowledge in Skilled Production and Maintenance Work, paper presented at workshop on Work Process Knowledge at Manchester University, 15-17 December, 1994

Fischer, Martin, Renate Jungeblut and Eberhart Rommermann, Jede Maschine hat ihre eigenen Marotten, ITB, Bremen, 1993 (in German)

Habermas, Jurgen, Theorie des kommunikativen Handelns, Suhrkamp Verlag, 1981 (in German)

Kensing, Finn and Bødker, Keld, Design in an organizational context: An experiment, Scandinavian Journal of Information Systems, Vol. 6, no. 1, April, 1994

Kern, Horst and Michael Schumann, Das Ende das Arbeitsteilung, Verlag Beck, 1985

Lave, Jeane and Etienne Wenger, Situated Learning, Cambridge University Press, 1991

Markert, Werner, Zur Reformulierung des Verhältnisses von Arbeit und Subjekt im Kontext einer Kritischen Bildungstheorie, in Peters (eds.), Lernen im Arbeitsprozess durch neue Qualifizierungs- und Betiligungsstrategien, Westdeutscher Verlag 1994 (in German)

Office of Technology Assesment, Worker training: Competing in the New International Economy, OTA, Washington, 1990

Orr, Julian, Sharing Knowledge, Celebarating Identity: Community Memory in a Service Culture in Middleton and Edwards (eds.) Collective Remembering, Sage, 1990

Schön, Donald, Educating the Reflextive Practitioner, Josey-Bass Publ., San Francisco, 1987

Suchman, Lucy, Plans and Situated Action, Cambridge University Press, 1990

Zuboff, Shoshona, Technologies that informate: Implications for Human Resource Management in the Computerised Industrial work place, in Walton et. al. (eds.), Human Resource Management Trends and Challenges, Harvard Business School Press, 1985

Correspondence and offprint requests to: Thomas Binder, Institute of Technology and Social Sciences, Technical University of Denmark, Building 305, DK-2800 Lyngby, Denmark. Fax: 45 45 252093.

AI & Soc (2005) 19: 229–249
DOI 10.1007/s00146-005-0337-2

ORIGINAL ARTICLE

Lauge Baungaard Rasmussen

The narrative aspect of scenario building - How story telling may give people a memory of the future

Received: 27 January 2005 / Accepted: 27 March 2005 / Published online: 12 August 2005
© Springer-Verlag London Limited 2005

Abstract Scenarios are flexible means to integrate disparate ideas, thoughts and feelings into holistic images, providing the context and meaning of possible futures. The application of narrative scenarios in engineering, development of socio-technical systems or communities provides an important link between general ideas and specification of technical system requirements. They focus on how people use systems through context-related storytelling rather than abstract descriptions of requirements. The quality of scenarios depends on relevant assumptions and authentic scenario stories. In this article, we will explore how the narrative approach may enrich the scenario 'skeleton' with 'flesh and blood', that is, living, detailed and consistent storytelling. In addition, criteria are suggested for evaluation of the quality of scenario storytelling.

Keywords Scenario stories · Narrative approach · Story-telling techniques · Socio-technical systems · Community strategy formation

1 Introduction

Well-told stories remain with us through time. They help us to make sense of what has been, what is and what might be. Stories have been used, of course, for thousands of years. However, as a deliberate tool for strategy formation and development of socio-technical systems, storytelling is quite recent, but growing very rapidly. Today it is a favoured method among an increasing number of action researchers, management consultants, planners, designers and system developers. Narrative scenario building is used for instance in planning of railway systems, air traffic control, telecommunication, the Olympic games, military planning, business systems and film-making. They may concern development of hardware, software, organisations and/or networks in different settings. Scenarios are ideal for involving people in exploring socio-technical system possibilities in complex environments. Storytelling is an excellent method weaving together the relatively certain aspects of the future

L. B. Rasmussen
Department of Manufacturing Engineering and Management,
Technical University of Demark, Lyngby, Demark
E-mail: lbr@ipl.dtu.dk

with imagination about the uncertain. Scenario building through stories can be an effective way to integrate imaginations as a systematic part of strategy formation and planning, viewing short-term preoccupations from the perspective of long-term objectives. Early signals of the coming future can more easily be picked up. " *..Scenarios give people a 'memory' of the future*" (Allan et al. 2002:186). The narrative approach allows the scenario designer to provide *holistic* views of the future. By using concrete stories to supplement abstract descriptions, it is possible to be user driven rather than discipline driven. Scenarios are for people with legitimate interests in the development of a socio-technical system. They are means to imagine what the stakeholders want as well as how systems may be developed to fulfil these needs. Even the simplest but well-told story contain the power to create in our minds an image of a possible future—so it is almost like we are there (Alexander 2004; Carroll 1995). Scenario stories are not supposed to replace analytical thinking. Instead, they may be seen as a 'bridge' between the analytically oriented planning and the creatively oriented vision making activities due to their ability to transmit both rational and creative layers of thoughts and beliefs (Moore 2000). Viewed through the lens of a well-developed story, further creative development, dissemination and transformation of the ideas behind the story may be easier and more inspiring to do. Thus, the 'softer' practice of storytelling should be applied alongside with rather than instead of analytical methods (Lindgren and Bandhold 2003).

However, it is not a question only, *how* the scenario stories are told, but also to whom they are relevant. Thus, applying storytelling as a moment of scenario building is not a question of the elegancy of the telling techniques only, but also how the ideas behind the stories reflect the needs and visions of the stakeholders. Even the most excellently developed story would not succeed to convince them, when the idea behind it is unclear or without real relationship to their basic interests or needs.

The objectives of scenario stories may vary and depend on the problem setting and the stakeholders' interests. The following examples illustrate the span of variety:

- Imagination of the specific qualities, which should be maintained or enhanced in the future, for instance in a human–computer interface design or a customer-centred contextual design. The scenario stories may focus on what people do and how they use systems in their work with concrete rather than abstract descriptions. Thus, they may counteract engineers' occupational hazard of diving into sophisticated technical details while ignoring the needs and desires of the potential users (Alexander 2004; Corbett et al. 1991)
- Specification and simulation of prospective aspects of a community as a mean to do strategy formation and planning. Instead of focussing on the economic dimension in regional development only, the narrative scenario approach can provide much more holistic descriptions of how cultural, social, environmental and economic relationships are vital for sustainable development. By introducing concrete stories, in which people act, feel and think, the strategy formation becomes more closely related to the mind sets of the regional stakeholders than relatively abstract trend analyses of the same issue. The scenario stories may contribute to activate the local people in the discussion of

visions, identity, strategies, action plans and implementation including goals, milestones, actors, oppositions and so on (Rasmussen 2004b)

- Increased employee responsibility by their active involvement in vision making and storytelling of possible futures. Organisational change may turn out to be much more successful, when top managers invite middle managers and other employees to participate in scenario workshops. Through such a collective process, storytelling may provide strong visions, reflecting its values of all aspects of its brand, recruiting practices, goals and corporate identity (Athey 2001; Rasmussen 2002).

The narrative approach may help software/ hardware designers, planners, managers, vendors, employees and citizen groups to: "... *shape strategy and help in getting others on board as they consensually validate each other's apprehension of ongoing experience*" (Boje 2002: 119).

However, in order to be able to fulfil some or all of the above-mentioned objectives, the scenario stories must be original, memorable, provocative and compelling (van der Heijden 1996/ 2004).Until now, these quality aspects of the scenario stories have not been reflected very much. Therefore, in this article it is discussed how the quality of scenario stories could be evaluated? The structure of the following sections is as follows:

Firstly, some general functions of scenario stories will be defined.

Secondly, we will go deeper into the specific steps of building enriched scenarios by using story-telling techniques.

Thirdly, we will discuss possible criteria and procedures to evaluate the quality of scenario stories.

Finally, indications will be given of how the techniques and narrative approaches of scenario building can be further improved.

2 Concepts and Functions of Stories

What is a story? According to Gabriel (2001) not all narratives can be dignified with the name 'story'. He distinguishes between short narratives and proper stories. The former are short characteristics of a person or a situation which are useful to make sense of the scenario. He calls them 'opinions' or 'proto-stories'. Purely factual narratives might better be called 'reports' or 'accounts', even though they would often be called stories in everyday speech. The difference between giving an example and telling a story is that the latter add sensuous features, feelings and thoughts, weaving the different pieces together into a wholeness, which appears to transcend the sum of the single pieces. As Ricoeur notes: "...*A story describes a sequence of actions and experiences done by a certain number of people.... These people are presented either in situations that change or as reacting to such change. In turn, these changes reveal hidden aspects of the situation and the people involved, and engender a new predicament which calls for thought, action or both*" (Ricoeur 1984:150)

The *classical elements* of stories are:

1. *The message(s):* what are supposed to be told?
2. *The tension(s):* what are the driving forces of the story?

3. *The role distribution:* who are the actors and what roles are they supposed to play?
4. *The sequence of activities:* the relationships between the events setting the story.

White (2000) and Nielsen (2004) distinguish between five different types of stories. *The great story of the community* is typically a story, which mirrors the essential values of the community often presented as an archaic fairytale. *Storytelling as a tool for leadership* typically focuses on activities which are supposed to be highly valued by the top-management. *Stories created through dialogue* may be elaborated as products of common workshops including different levels of management and/or representatives from all the levels of the company. They are used for strategy formation and planning of organisational change and/or long-term development objectives. *The personal story* may be a story of how the pioneer(s) invented and developed the community. Or it may be storytelling about how individual members of the community have contributed to its development. It may be used for branding or motivation of members of the community to follow the 'excellent' example. All five story types may be included in scenario building (Fig. 1).

Scenario stories must balance between two powers of influence: *identification* and *fascination*. The *former* means that stakeholders must be able to identify themselves with some of the actors and/or activities appearing in the scenario stories. If they do not feel or see any kind of identity, it may turn out to be impossible to motivate or involve them. On the other hand, the story must also fascinate them by being somewhat strange and unusual in order to stimulate their curiosity and perhaps their motivation to participate in the community development process. Something should be different from the present or from their conventional expectations of the future development. Fascination without some kind of identification may create curiosity but not necessarily participation, because the stakeholders may recognise it to be too far away from their

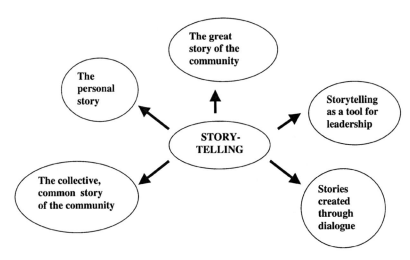

Fig. 1 Main types of stories (Nielsen 2004: 20)

mind sets. On the other side, if everything becomes known to the stakeholders, they may easily identify themselves with it. But it will most likely not stimulate or activate changes of consciousness or behaviour, because the curiosity may not be awakened.

When applied properly, storytelling offers several benefits compared to more abstract communication of values, visions and objectives related to the future development possibilities. Several writers have discussed the narrative approach as vital for creating consensus about highly valued behaviour or modes of thinking, talking or working. (Brown et al. 2004; Denning 2001; Shaw et al. 1998; Schwartz 1992).

Others have seen stories as a mean to enhance system development and strategy formation (Alexander and Meiden 2004; Lindgren and Bandhold 2003; van der Heijden et al. 2002; Schaw et al. 1998; Schwartz 1992). However, in most of this literature, the scenario stories are very seldom developed very much but mostly designed to illustrate a specific point. Still others have focussed on how stories can mediate different interests in the community (van der Heijden 2004/ 1996; Brown et al. 2004; Nielsen 2004). The successively told and retold story may enhance the process of a 'we' feeling (Waller 2003). In contrast to information about abstract rules or strategies, stories provide the core message as well as the context in which this message is supposed to be implemented. Context means having a unique and shaped frame of understanding, which makes sense to the audience. As developed by Weick (Weick 1995, 2001), sense-making is an evolutionary mode of organising. It consists of a continually social interaction, that constructs both the organisation and its environment. Both are viewed as parts of an ever-changing system. As a sense-maker, the manager focuses on certain aspects of his environment to pay attention to, while ignoring others. The sense-making is always ongoing and retrospective according to Weick. Something happens, and then we need to make sense of it. However at this point we do not agree with Weick. In our opinion, sense-making viewed in relationship to scenario building contains prospective as well as retrospective activities. This disagreement can be related to differences regarding paradigmatic views too. We prefer the 'processual' paradigm (van der Heijden 1996/ 2004) instead of Weick's evolutionary paradigm. Starting with a retrospective view of past activities and experiences, the scenario designer turn scenario building into the prospective approach of building scenarios. From there he takes again a retrospective view back to the present, also named the back-casting process. Finally, he again takes a prospective view by developing a strategy and action plan how it is possible to move from the present situation towards the future situation described in the scenario. 'Processualists' agree with the evolutionists, that most organisational situations are too complex to analyse in its entirety (van der Heijden 1996/2004), but they disagree that sense-making is retrospectively only. Instead sense-making is regarded as a continually iterative process between retrospective and prospective activities. We are going to discuss this aspect more in detail later on.

Weick uses a metaphor to describe the character of the sense-making activity, namely cartography: "... *There is some terrain that the mapmakers want to represent, and they use various modes of projection to make this representation. What they map, however, depends on where they look, how they look, what they want to represent, and their tools for representation*" (Weick 2001: 9). In a similar way, scenario builders are mapping a 'terrain' of the future from certain perspectives and by means of specifically developed tools and methods. Like in cartography, there is no 'One Best Story' of the future. For any future 'terrain' there will be an indefinite number of useful stories as well as an indefinite number of modes of representation (Weick, 2001). The task of the scenario builder as sense-maker is not to look for one true picture of the future, but to create several pictures. In doing this he uses past and present contexts, which are supposed to be of relevance for the projection of the scenario. However, it is often possible to make a choice between different possible contexts. For instance, when a leader wants to change the patterns of cooperation between the members of his/her staff, one context could be how each member of the staff contributes to the teamwork, and how it could be enhanced? Another way of defining the context may be to scrutinise, how the division of jobs has been changed through time? A third context may take the point of departure in the relationships of communication and power relationships between the leader and the staff, reconsidering the possibilities to make them more relevant in accordance with the needs of the enterprise without changing the formal division of labour. Depending on the choice of context, the suggested 'solutions' how to improve the knowledge sharing in the organisation tend to vary to a considerable extent. Similarly, the scenario building may differ due to the choice of different assumptions and scenario dimensions. Before a team is able to build consistent scenarios, the members of that team need to establish a shared context of assumptions about the environment, in which the scenarios are going to take place. Shared context means a shared understanding of external and internal worlds and how these worlds are related to each other (Holst 2004). In the absence of a shared context, the members of the scenario building team may collide in their work of creating scenario dimensions and stories.

In sum, stories can be used for many different purposes in system development:

– *Communication* of values, visions, strategies and rules related to development of socio-technical systems or communities. A story can communicate a relatively complex idea by involving the recipients in the idea more concretely and thus gradually create an 'ownership' to that idea. In addition, storytelling may enhance the participants' capabilities to express and share experiences that have been tacit until then.
– *Creative development* of new technologies, products and/or changes of communities. The application of storytelling can stimulate stakeholders to adopt multi-dimensional perspectives in socio-technical systems or strategy formation in communities and see new possible connections as well as reflecting on the implications of change in a positive way rather than just resist possible changes. Scenario stories can contribute to understand possible technological impacts in communities or societies.
– *Change or stabilisation of power relations*. Does storytelling challenge or support those in power? In some instances, stories may be created to disrupt a coalition or unsettle specific individuals or minorities. Official stories of the founders of the community starting the business in a small garage may contribute to stabilise the authority and admiration of his leadership (Allan et al. 2002). Therefore, storytelling can also be used as a mean to achieve or

maintain power, and even to manipulate with the sense-making of the stakeholders, for instance, regarding the positive or negative impacts of using a specific technology in production or as a means to facilitate social or economic services in a community. On the other hand, they may also be created as a means to diminish the image of a powerful person, for instance, stories told as jokes about the manager among members in an organisation. Or they may be applied as concrete images of alternative technology trajectories to the mainstream anticipations of technological trends. In order to try to avoid nonethical applications of stories, it is necessary to reflect and follow some ethical principles. We will come back to this aspect later on. First, we will focus on the particular techniques to enrich scenarios as part of strategy-making and planning the possible futures of the community.

3 Techniques and steps of scenario story building

Scenario stories are different from biographic stories of the past or the present. As an imagined future, the scenario story is pure fiction. On the other hand, scenario building contrasts forecasting too, because it does not pretend to predict the future, but to create several possible stories of it. Such kind of scenario stories may take the point of departure in deconstruction activity of the present and past experiences. According to Derrida (1978) the project of deconstruction is to reveal the ambivalence of a text, which can only be understood in relation to other texts. No text, including stories relying on the present or past experiences, is ideologically neutral. Instead, they are intruded by political, economic and social values. Every time a story is told in a changed context, the meaning of it may be changed too. Thus deconstruction is both a phenomenon and analysis, as pointed out by Boje: "...*It is phenomenon because 'story deconstruction' is all the constructing and deconstructing processes happening all around us. It is analysis...at two levels: the level of action and the analytical level*" (Boje 2002:18). One way to practise deconstruction is to search for voices not being expressed in the story. Another is to trace what is not told about the context or the back stage (Boje 2002). Such an analytical story deconstruction approach may result in one or several alternative 'centres' or platforms relevant for the scenario-building activity. All Western thought, according to Derrida, is based on the idea of a centre: "...*an Origin, a Truth, and Ideal Form, a fixed Point, an Immovable Mover, an Essence, a God, a Presence, which is usually capitalized and guarantees all meaning*" (Powell 1997:21). Deconstruction is not only about unmasking stories that posit an authoritarian centre, but to show several centres are in a constant state of change. These centres may be useful platforms, which expose disintegrating and reintegrating aspects and let the less visible factors come into view (Boje 2002). Such an intention is also in focus in the work of Foucault, for instance, in his detailed stories of the history of prisons (Foucault 1977/79). The development of socio-technical systems or communities may also posit a centre of powerful stakeholders with specific interests in influencing the decision making among politicians, planners or business management. Deconstruction of such a constellation may create useful platforms for other socio-technical trajectories as well.

Allan et al. (2002) suggest a matrix of four different ways of creating stories (see Fig. 2)

The *emergent* story (Wenger 1998) is the tale generated individually or collectively in a specific situation. It is not planned or anticipated, but 'grew out' of certain events or interactions in the situation. Such stories just happen and cannot be created by the mean of explicit techniques. However, a culture can be created, which stimulates members to create emergent stories.

The *designed* story (Allan et al. 2002; Wenger 1998) is planned and carefully elaborated following certain criteria and steps. For instance, scenarios are examples of designed stories. Both emergent and designed stories can be created by an individual or by a collective resulting in the matrix as illustrated in Fig. 2.

Following the deconstruction principle of focussing on the ambivalences, the first step is to open up for different kinds of interpretations of the past or present situation. When the context is a scenario workshop, the facilitator may start to listen to how the spotted ambivalences of the present are interpreted by the participants themselves. However, often it is not sufficient just to listen, because each of the participants may be unable to transcend their conventional viewpoint. In such a situation, the facilitator may initiate a creative process of letting the participants retell examples of ambivalences from different perspectives (role exchange). Or the facilitator may invite a person to tell a story related to the context of the participants but containing nonconventional viewpoints. During such a storytelling, the facilitator must practise the so-called 'double listening'. For example, Denning has pointed out that as a storyteller, he tries to generate not one but two stories in the listener:

"... One is the explicit story that the listener hears coming from the lips of the storyteller .... The other—and by far the most important—is a story that the listeners themselves will invent: a new story ... that responds to the specific features of their specific contexts, their problems, their hopes and their aspirations, in term that the listeners feel comfortable with. This second story is a creation of the

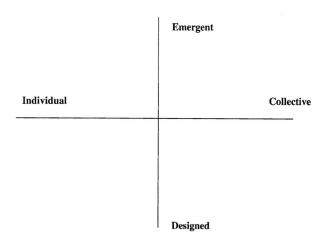

Fig. 2 Four ways of creating stories (Allan et al. 2002:14)

listeners and cannot be accurately imagined by the storyteller" (Denning 2001:129).

Here the task of facilitators is to externalise anticipations that have been 'hidden' so far. Using storytelling in this way is not only an appealing way to communicate visions or values from the storyteller to the audience. It is also a device to activate the creative imagination of the audience itself, for instance how appropriate technology may look like from their perspective, or how a sustainable life cycle may be implemented in communities. Based on this approach it may be possible to develop and select the specific frame of context of the proposed scenarios.

Before the story is ready to be told or written, several things must be clarified. *Firstly*, what are the *needs*, which the stories are supposed to fulfil in the scenarios? For instance, when the scenario describes life in a community in the period 2025–2030, in which energy is in shortage, one story may focus on the motivation of the citizens, for instance to buy software systems to optimise the use of energy for heath and electricity. Another story in the same scenario may address the needs of the local government to form an energy strategy for the community, including the development of computer-based systems, which can simulate optimal relationships between relevant input and output variables to support, for instance, the investment in public or private transport systems. A third story may take the specific needs of energy into consideration viewed from the enterprise perspective, for instance how human-centred software systems may support the employees to minimise or reduce the use of energy in production of material goods or services. Each of the suggested stories focuses on different needs, but they build on a common premise, namely the shortage of energy and an inherent conflict between interest groups how the relatively limited amount of energy should be distributed? The identified needs should be stated as concrete as possible. For instance, it is not sufficient to claim that each citizen needs a certain amount of energy. It should also be explained for which purposes they need that energy as well as possible technologies to fulfil these purposes. As van der Heijden notes: *"...The biggest mistake that scenario planners can make is to fail to take enough account of the needs of their clients. The number one rule of scenario planning is 'know your client'"* (van der Heijden 2004: 146)

The process of clarifying those needs may be a *participatory* one by the means of interviews, participatory workshops or other methods. Of course, an expert in energy consumption may be able to imagine some prospective needs of consumers and develop appropriate technology and resources to satisfy these needs. However, the collective, participatory approach has many advantages, for instance the creative imaginations of the participants, the motivation of the participants to discuss and possibly absorb aspects of the proposed scenarios as part of their own mind set. Finally, the participatory approach may enhance the general knowledge and consciousness about the issue of interest.

The scenario generation is supposed to describe several ways to fulfil the identified needs. The scenario narrative sets out a promise by offering enrichment of issues, life-like characters, events and circumstances, which move the audience towards an experience of clarification (Johnson 2000). It is a powerful means of integrating seemingly unrelated ideas and events into coherent and compelling versions of desirable futures. For instance, when a story created around the issue of energy production, distribution and consumption fulfils its promise, the audience should be able to recognize that a better state of energy transformation has been achieved compared to the present situation, for instance by implementing human centred energy saving technological systems in households, enterprises and/or public institutions. A scenario story's promise is not just fulfilled by assembling details that are as realistic as possible. It is achieved by generating details that have a purpose in resonance with the needs of its audience. For instance, the author has conducted several participatory scenario workshops, in which the participants are asked to define their needs and develop scenarios, strategies and action plans to fulfil these needs. Though the majority of the participants had never tried such an approach before, they demonstrated surprising abilities to create and combine characters and events into stories of possible futures. For instance, one of the groups started to identify the needs of unskilled women in Indian villages. Then they built scenario stories how a female teacher formed a network and established a local dairy conducted by a group of women in the village supported by ICT-mediated knowledge and distant learning. Their approach was developed from a human-centred technology paradigm focussing on socio-technical systems with a focus on the re-skilling possibilities of the dairy system. Their scenario was not constructed as a static picture, but included possible 'blocks' in form of opposing groups of vendors and traditional-minded men in the village, who opposed that women should be involved in such an entrepreneurial activity. Thus, the scenario story included a drama or a plot-line. During the three-day workshop, this group of university people and farmers was able to develop a scenario of a sustainable, female entrepreneurship in a typical North Indian village, including the impacts of using ICT to create and mediate new knowledge of practical relevance for the prospective entrepreneurs within the farming and dairy sectors in the village (Rasmussen 2003). A story designer should create characters and events, which give life to those particular ideas behind the story. Through their activities, thoughts and feelings, such characters should enrich the ideas by letting them 'breathing of life'. They should enable the audience to focus on the fulfilment of user needs supplemented by appropriate, technical novelties (Houdek and Zink 2004).

A *simple* scenario story might operate with one or a few ideas. For instance, it may describe how some citizens in the community in the period 2025–2030 minimize their use of energy in typical everyday situations for instance by implementing energy-saving technological systems, while other citizens do not (yet) fulfil the promise. Such a story consists typically of 'enlightened' in contrast to 'less enlightened' characters.

A *more reflective* scenario story might have characters, events, actions and reflections that represent different *layers of ideas*. Such stories help explore the hitherto 'hidden' side effects or easily forgotten possibilities that need to be discussed and incorporated into the strategy formation (Houdek and Zink 2004). For example, in addition to the minimizing of energy consumption, other ideas may be the use of sustainable energy sources only, the decentralisation of energy distribution, reusing systems of energy, conflict-mediating regulatory systems due to shortage of energy supply, innovation of new production and distribution technologies, in which the energy is used and controlled in more efficient ways. For instance, once the author conducted a scenario workshop in

Malaysia, one of the groups created a concrete and very detailed scenario for a specific region near Kuala Lumpur. The scenario described how the transport system in this area could be transformed to a 100% public transport system in year 2020. Both the political, economic, social and technological aspects of such a radical transformation were described as well as an action plan including actors and activities needed during a 15-year period from 2005 to 2020. Thus, the scenario story included several layers of ideas integrated into a holistic picture of the transport system in that Malaysian area.

Such a scenario story may focus on the possible conflicts between the different layers of ideas. For instance, the idea of the decentralization of the energy distribution systems may support isolationist ideas and thereby prevent a development towards more equal energy supply between different regions in the World. On the other hand, it may also create more sustainable communities less vulnerable to the intrusive effects of globalisation. The reflective and more complex scenario story may initiate more discussion about strategies and action plans than the simple scenario story. Which type of story should be chosen? It depends on the purpose. A simple scenario story may be sufficient—and perhaps even function better than a more complex story when the purpose is motivating local people to be actively involved in sustainable energy development approaches. A more complex and thoughtful story may be advisable, when the purpose is strategy formation for enterprises or communities. A rule of the thumb is that the choice depends on the issue and the audience. The story should not be designed more complex than necessary to fulfil its objectives (Rasmussen 2003). A common *mistake* is to confuse symbolic representation of ideas with the effect of a story. The scenario designer may assemble characters, which represent certain ideas and act symbolically in order to illustrate those ideas as clearly as possible. For instance, one role model may be a software engineer, who develops new energy-saving control systems. Other role models may focus on managers or employees, who are more or less convinced of the whole energy-saving approach. However, the supposed effect of the story on its audience may not be created, when the characters' actions are not arranged to create movements towards illumination of a changed situation, but merely to 'mirror' the central aspects of the ideas in a rather static and 'paradise-like' fashion. A *dramatic* way to create the desirable effect of a scenario story is to design 'blocks' and 'plots' that must be overcome to fulfil its promise. For example, in the energy scenario in the period 2025–2030, the inherent conflict is supposed to be the experienced shortage of energy in relation to the different interest groups' needs of consumption. A simple way to describe that conflict may be to write a story of conflict mediation between two or more interest groups with competing energy production and control systems. The conflict in a story is created, when the story teller creates movement towards resolution and then blocks that movement by introducing characters or events, which counteract or prohibit the main characters to act in accordance with the main promise of the scenario. For instance, fossil energy interest groups may inhibit the development of more sustainable energy systems, including the design of computer and network technologies to support those systems. Or a movement towards further sustainable development may be blocked by events like economic crisis, nature disasters or wars. Such extraneous blocks may support the creation of a dramatic effect of the story as well as helping to test the robustness .

of its movements against such kind of blocks. However, design of conflicts or blocks without relation to the fulfilment of the story's promise should be avoided, because such random, purposeless conflicts disturb the audience's focus on the main idea of the scenario story: *"..Conflict only ring 'true', when it serves a dramatic purpose. Otherwise, it is a flame that doesn't burn, an explosion with no force, heated dialogue spoken with no volume"* (Johnson 2000:56).

The blocks of a story's movement are not necessarily of physical nature. They may be about ideas or feelings in conflict or they can evolve around a struggle for understanding, or around a set of values being explored or tested. They can also be generated by focussing on what inhibit a character in the story from gaining the insights that enables him/her to overcome the obstacles, for instance ideologies, mind sets or manipulation with information, that block the movement towards fulfilment of the story's promise. The art of scenario storytelling may also concern the creation of drama that involve the audience to try to understand and perhaps overcome the blocks of affective and/or cognitive conflicts (Rasmussen 2002). Thus, scenarios of desirable futures do not necessarily need to be designed as 'peaceful paradises', which may be too boring for the audience and fail to set up those states of intense thoughts and involvement, and thereby denying the audience a prime motivation for entering the world of the story. A purposeful conflict may take the audience on a 'journey' of intense mental fights and dialogues, both of which may enhance the motivation to be engaged in the main ideas behind the stories or to oppose these ideas (Allan 2002).

How should *characters* of a scenario story be designed? To stimulate the audience's fascination of the scenario, it is vital to create characters, who are equipped with their own needs, desires and thoughts. They should not automatically respond to events the way the scenario designer would do. If all the characters in a scenario story are projections of the scenario designer's opinion, they may *"...come across as soulless, lifeless automations in the service of their creators"* (Johnson 2000:44). Such characters have nothing to resolve. They are in risk of being reactive and passive instead of shaping the moment of the story. They should have their own lives and be authentic in accordance with the story's promise and drama. They should be designed in such a manner that they are able to develop their own sense-making of the events and the environment, which they are going to enact during the movement of the story. The audience is more likely to project onto single individuals, who behave as real human beings rather than 'mannequins' (Brown et al. 2004). For instance, in the energy scenario taking place in the period 2025–2030, the main characters of the consumer scenario should not just act and reflect like the scenario designer would like to do, but be given their own enriched profile including their particular sense-making process on how to overcome blocks against the story's movement towards a more sustainable energy production, distribution and consumption.

To achieve this, the design of storylines becomes essential. A *storyline* consists of at least three events in a causal relationship. For instance, in the energy scenario, one possible storyline may be sketched as follows:

– A threatening increase of shortage of energy has inspired researchers to innovate new methods and techniques to produce and control sustainable energy. One group of engineers invents a radically new method of transforming sun energy to electricity. Another group of software developers invents a human-centred, energy-saving system allowing the consumers to adapt and control their energy consumption much more precisely than before.

- A new increase of energy consumption evolves due to this revolutionary technology
- However, this increased use of energy has a negative effect on the environment, because the use of non-sustainable products is increased too. In addition, the human-centred energy control system becomes monopolised by a multinational group of capitals resulting in steeply growing prices on this kind of technology.
- As a reaction to this development, the government decides to increase the taxes of all kind of energy consumption and to strengthen the law against monopolies.

Thus, the storyline describes events occurring within the frame of the scenario, in this case between 2025 and 2030. It is not a storyline about how to reach from the present to the scenario. But a similar narrative approach can be applied for that purpose too. While the storylines are causal relationships between events that set out a movement towards fulfilment of the story's promise, a story's *plot line* is: "*... the events that make the story advance along its storyline dramatic and compelling...As the story's events move the story along it's storyline, the events on the plot line operate to dramatically heighten that advance*" (Johnson, 2000 : 75/ 78). For instance, in the story-line sketched above, a parallel plot-line may introduce a block connected to the second bullet suggesting that the radical innovation of the new sun-transforming technology is counteracted by economic interest groups, which fight against more use of sun energy due to their own interest in wind energy or fossil-based energy production. Another plot may be introduced in connection to the fourth bullet, suggesting that the increased energy tax becomes so unpopular that an opposing political party takes over the government and decides to cut off the energy tax again, resulting in a new consumer 'bubble' of energy consumption and environmental damages. Such plots or blocks should not be introduced to entertain the audience, but to illustrate possible weaknesses or strengths of the constructed scenarios. For instance, introducing the counteracting economic interest group as initiators of a blocking event may give the scenario designer an opportunity to describe how the interest groups reflect or express their feelings and thoughts and what drives them. It may enrich the description of the characters' feelings, thoughts and actions and perhaps provoke them to react with new feelings and thoughts and come to a new understanding, all of which may help the audience to track the story's movement along its storyline (Johnson 2000).

What happens when a scenario designer is unable to make a clear distinction between storyline and plotline? The result may be a strong plotline but a weak storyline. For instance, in the energy scenario, it is possible to create a lot of plots, which are not rooted in the deeper story issues (as for example the plot about the opposing political party perhaps may seem to be). A story without a clearly elaborated storyline may be like a row of mannequins awkwardly moved around the story's stage by its author (Brown et al. 2004). Internal consistency implies that each storyline and plot-line are based on an underlying structural framework consisting of common assumptions and chosen parameters for scenario variation (see Fig. 3)

Scenarios can be constructed without a plot line—most scenarios seem to be. However, why not learn from the film makers (the place of issue for the origin of the scenario concept) and let the plot line bring more 'flesh and blood' into the story design in the scenarios?

How is it possible to *start* the story-building process? The *first* step is to *name the needs*, which are supposed to be fulfilled in the scenario. It might be about issues like human-centred interaction design, air traffic control, quality requirements of telecommunication, social welfare, education, the possible uses of new system technologies, cultural coherence, regional or local sustainability including overcoming energy shortages by innovating new kinds of sustainable energy sources. When the ideas or layers of ideas are becoming as clearly stated as possible, the *second* step consists of formulating the *premise* of the scenario story. The description of the premise should include the following *aspects* of the scenario story:

– What is the *issue* of the story?
– How is that issue *moved towards fulfilment or resolution?*
– How are the *needs fulfilled* by that movement?
– How is the premise of the story met *in accordance with the assumptions* of the scenario?

In the *third* step, the focus is on the design of the *characters* in accordance with the story's premise. To create a dramatic tension in the story's movement, one may start to create a 'white/black' constellation of '*protagonists*' and '*antagonists*' of the story's promise. The former might think and act to fulfil the story's promise, while the latter may try to block the fulfilment. Or they may provoke the protagonists to give the issue a second thought and perhaps take initiatives of revised or new actions. Other characters may serve a variety of purposes, helping either the one or the other part of the main characters to carry out their intentions. When the core features of the characters are developed, the characters should be given their 'own life', meaning that they should not just act

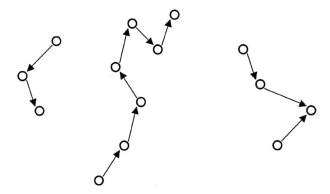

Fig. 3 Relationships between assumptions, scenario dimensions story-lines and plot-lines

as the story designers' 'soulless, lifeless automations', but be created with own needs, desires and thoughts. For instance, the protagonists in the energy scenario may also do mistakes, be in doubt or possess ambivalent feelings and thoughts. The antagonists, on the other side, may have their own interests to defend, arguments and reasons to act as they do.

When the features of the characters have been outlined, the *fourth* step is to create *storylines* and *plotlines*. At first, they may appear as disconnected fragments (see Fig. 4). Later, they may be integrated into a '*skeleton*' in which causal relationships are made clear between different events of the story (see Fig. 5):

The *fifth* step is to give the skeleton 'flesh and blood', that is, to tell the story with as many 'living' and 'breathing' details as necessary to engage the audience

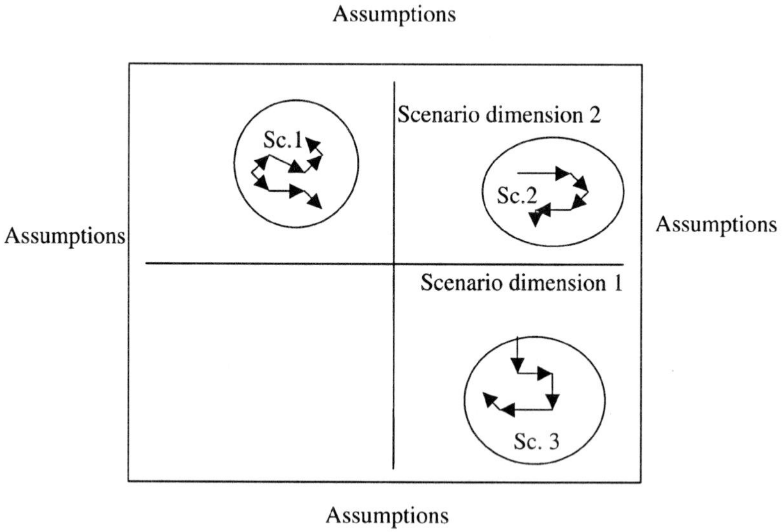

Assumptions

```
                    Assumptions
┌──────────────────────┬──────────────────────┐
│         Sc.1         │  Scenario dimension 2│
│                      │         Sc.2         │
Assumptions            │          Scenario dimension 1   Assumptions
│                      │                      │
│                      │         Sc. 3        │
└──────────────────────┴──────────────────────┘
                    Assumptions
```

Fig. 4 Configurations of storylines

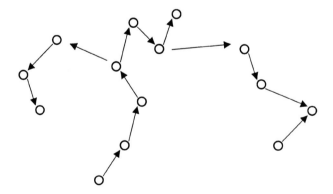

Fig. 5 Scenario skeleton

in the movement of the story through its different stages towards its fulfilment of its promise.

In order to engage the audience from the very beginning, the promise of the story should be named in the very first 'opening scenes' (Johnson 2000). For instance, in the energy scenario one character may start to illustrate a number of dramatic events in their everyday life to get sufficient amount of energy, thus *naming* that the promise of the scenario is about how to overcome shortages of energy (Fig. 6).

By naming the promise in a dramatic way, the audience may become curious how the scenario story will turn out. When the promise is clearly named and then blocked from fulfilment by a certain number of plots, the tension and the engagement can be transferred from the characters to its audience (Boje 2002; Johnson 2000). But it is important to remember, that the plots should not serve the entertainment of the audience only. They must also be directly related to the promise of the story. (Rasmussen 2003)

4 What make strong and weak scenario stories?

Scenarios are not panaceas. They do not always work. They are only as good as the *underlying idea* being conveyed. When the idea is too loose or too restricted, the scenario story may well reveal its inadequacy. Even the must elegant story from a technical viewpoint will not endure in such a case, though for a short time it may fascinate people. Thus, the first condition of making a compelling scenario is that the underlying idea makes sense to the people, who are supposed to discuss or implement it. To them the idea must be attractive or compelling. However, even when the underlying idea is recognised as being relevant, the scenario story may be inappropriate or ineffective. One reason could be that the

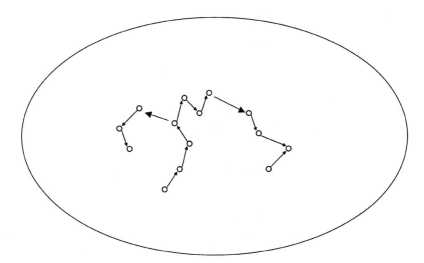

Fig. 6 Scenario enrichment

connection to the underlying idea is too weak. For instance, it may be difficult for the audience to see what the underlying idea is? After having read the scenario story, they may still ask: 'what is the point'? Sometimes a scenario story is filled with so many details that it is difficult for the audience to see the idea behind it. In such a case, it may be advisable to reduce the number of details and focus on those elements of the story, which are in clear accordance with the underlying idea (Rasmussen 2003)

Another trap is to make the scenario story too 'dry', that is, without any sensuous or emotional descriptions, for instance, in order to focus on the purely logical or rational relationships between the events and make the points as analytically clear as possible. One of the strengths of enriched scenario stories is that they may appeal to the human being as a whole creature: senses, emotions, thoughts, behaviours and so on. The scenarios should provide 'living' and 'breathing' and yet somehow strange images of the possible futures. Scenario narratives that elicit a rich imagery of thoughts, feelings, sensuous experiences and concrete activities help to engage the stakeholders in the visionary and strategic conversation regarding possible prospects of the community. The same scenario presented in tabular form may not come across of such a process so easily.

The stories should be remarkable to its audience in order to grab their attention and curiosity. Some aspects should be radically different from present and yet desirable to create fascination. They should contain novelty and surprise in directions where the ideas and visions need to be stretched. Other aspects may be similar to present and thus creating a certain amount of identification and thus making the scenario stories plausible to a 'critical mass' (van der Heijden 1996/2004). Still other aspects may be changed a little from the present, but sufficient to awake curiosity. Where do scenario designers find the creative imagination and novel insight? By reading documents (local newspapers, minutes of meetings, network documents, etc.) conducting interviews and/or participatory scenario workshops with users of the product or members of the community, it is possible to initiate a creative process. However, in most cases the scenario building may be enriched by bringing external viewpoints into the process too. Therefore, the scenario designers may want to go further than just tapping internal resources and also incorporate a wide range of outside sources in the scenario building (van der Heijden 1996/ 2004).

Traditional stories have a beginning, a middle and an end. Scenario stories do not have an end. They are placed in a certain time and space, but good scenarios are *open-ended*, inviting the audience to continue the story. 'Open-ended' does not mean that anything goes. When the scenario is told properly in accordance with an underlying idea, it should be clear when one is telling 'side-stories' or stories that are in contradiction to the underlying idea. It should not focus exclusively on the positive aspects of the idea. Ambivalences and plots may be fruitful. They may invite the audience to reflect and perhaps achieve a deeper understanding of the underlying idea and its possible implications. Therefore, the scenario story should not be told only from the perspective of a single protagonist or a 'hero' everybody can understand or emphasise with. Such a one-dimensional scenario story format may appear to seem not convincing for the more reflective part of the audience. If so, they may be tempted to create their own 'anti-story' to keep a mental distance to the protagonist version. That may of course be a creative happening, but perhaps also a counter-acting process, because it may cut the connection to the underlying idea.

The scenario story cannot be true in the sense that it is something that will happen in the future. However, it should appear *authentic* that is making sense to the audience. But how to design an authentic story that is a pure fiction? One important aspect of authenticity is the *language* used in the story. It should be as similar as possible to the spoken or written language of the relevant stakeholders. Another aspect of authenticity is the *content* of the scenario. It should be original, memorable, provocative and compelling. *Originality* means something new, different from what the stakeholders have heard before or already know about. The original aspects may focus on new ways of organising the community, new production technology, new policies, new methods of discussing or decision making, new ways of designing products or production or new planning and strategy-making methodologies. *Memorabilia* is not only a question of language, but also dependent on surprising or impressive events described in the scenario. Stakeholders tend to be impressed by stories, which combine the well known with the surprising in such a manner that a new and better possibility becomes evident. *Provocation* appeals to reflection and perhaps opposition or protests. The learning effect of a provocative scenario story may be better than a very 'nicely packed' story as long as the story does not create a fundamental antagonism, To be *compelling* is a matter of relevance in a surprising manner. For instance, the scenario stories should fascinate the audience in a way that engage them to act in accordance with the long-term objectives or the underlying idea of the scenarios. Having these characteristics, the scenario stories sometimes contain the power to break old stereotypes (van der Heijden et al. 2002; Rasmussen 2003; Rasmussen 2004b).

A number of *technical mistakes* may diminish the quality of the scenario story. *One* mistake is to design the scenario stories as 'peaceful paradises' in which the characters are moved around as complete ideal types of the designer's own idiosyncrasy. For instance, for some years ago, it was very popular to develop scenarios with all kind of futuristic technology systems in private house holds such as robots, automatic food service and so on. However, most often they were presented as ideal, static 'everyday-paradises' where the people have been released from all the boring household activities. Such kinds of 'paradises' may become engaging for a very naïve audience only, who may wish to dream rather than to act.

Another mistake may be that even when antagonistic characters are included in the story, they may be described so stereotyped that they lose their authenticity.

A *third* mistake is to design very dramatic stories in which the plot lines are strong, but the story lines are weak. Such a story may have difficulties to fulfil its promise and transfer its core ideas to its audience. Though multiple dramatic and sensory activities may be presented, they may not 'ring true', because the characters do not embody the core ambivalences of the story's premise. The dramatic actions may be perceived as pure entertainment and lack a clear connection to the scenario's assumptions and/or central ideas.

A *fourth* mistake is not to suggest the story's promise in its opening scenes. Instead of giving the audience a clear indication of the promise, a dialogue or description may be used for instance to make statements about the context of the story or its characters. Therefore, the audience may not be compelled to be engaged in the story.

A *fifth* mistake is the design of scenario stories, which pretend to be occurring in a desirable future, but really do not transcend the present state. Why should one design a scenario, when it consists of thoughts, feelings and actions, which the audiences already know about?

However, a *sixth* mistake is to do exactly the opposite: to create a scenario in which everything is far beyond the scope of imagination of its audience. That is, some aspects of the scenario must be recognizable to the audience in order to create a sense of identification, while other aspects should be new and compelling to create fascination. The balance between identity and fascination must be present through all the stages of the story.

5 Conclusions and perspectives

Storytelling is a powerful technique to provoke, engage and compel stakeholders to initiate changes of the present. Stories are products created not only by individuals, but also collectively by groups of individuals in communities. To participate in a community requires a general knowledge of these accumulated narratives. The narrative meaning of scenarios is created by the recognition that something is a part of a whole and depends on other events taking place in that whole.

"... *Because scenarios are usually developed in sets of two, three or four, in which each scenario represents an equally plausible alternative future, the scenario stories have the power to break old stereotypes. This forces the decision makers to question their broadest assumptions about the ways the world works.*" (van der Heijden et al. 2002:171).

Scenarios are applied in a wide range of socio-technical systems and software engineering. They are useful devices throughout the life cycles of system development, including local community approaches, business projects, telecommunications, transportation and human–computer interaction. However no specific discipline should have a patent or monopoly to write scenarios. The most enriched and qualified scenarios are created by multi-disciplinary groups according to the author's experiences consisting of members from a wide range of knowledge areas of relevance for the chosen issue (Rasmussen 2003). For instance, consultants or researchers are not the only groups who may write scenarios. A scenario building group may also include stakeholders like operators, system maintainers, purchasers, trainers, test engineers and so on. Likewise, in a community approach, dealing with prospective energy transformation, relevant members of a scenario-building group may be producers of different kinds of energy systems, consumers, specialists within certain kinds of energy distribution, politicians, planners and so on. The environmental, social, cultural and economic impacts on society can be described in an increasing rich and innovative way to a wide range of people not only as an easy way to communicate an idea or vision, but also as a creative tool to activate the specific knowledge and experiences from the stakeholders themselves. But of course, scenarios are not usable for every purpose. They do not replace systematic analyses.

However, the narrative techniques of shaping scenarios are far from explored or developed to the full extent. The *perspectives* of improving the narrative techniques of scenario stories are promising as well as threatening. They are promising, because the creative power, which may be released by a purposeful, narrative approach, can contribute to stimulate new modes of organisation or new technological systems more appropriate to the future needs of people. Even people, who believe themselves to be unable to tell new stories, may be astonished when they experience their creative storytelling capabilities by participating in scenario building. Scenario stories may also be used as a means to achieve or maintain power or even to manipulate with the stakeholders' sense making. Therefore, *ethical* issues should be kept in mind when using storytelling in scenario building. The objectives of the scenario stories should be transparent to everybody—both participants and non-participants. The scenario designers should openly inform the audience about the interests and objectives which are the driving forces of the scenario generation. Furthermore, they must be culturally sensitive. To be a facilitator under such circumstances demands a special sensitivity to different cultural values, customs, and taboos. It is not only one of the conditions for a successful process, it is a 'must' (Rasmussen 2003).

However, one thing is to state some general, ethical rules. Another, and much more difficult task, is to implement them in the concrete process of scenario building. Of course, ethical rules cannot prevent abuses of the narrative powers of political, economic or pathological reasons. But they may increase the awareness of the possibilities of abuses, and by doing so diminish the possible negative effects.

Well-compounded scenario stories remain with us through time. They help us to make sense of what might be. They are effective tools to integrate the imaginations of the uncertain aspects of the future with the pre-determined trends. As such, they are becoming a more and more vital part of the development of human-centred systems as part of sustainable strategies for companies or local communities. However, scenario designers still have much to learn how to create original, memorable, provocative and compelling scenario stories. In addition, the narrative aspects of facilitating scenario workshops together with co-inquirers of relevant stakeholders should be strengthened too (Rasmussen 2004a). To some extent, the interaction with professional storytellers (for instance authors, film makers, and dramaturges) may be very fruitful for scenario designers. However, at the end the latter must develop their own styles and techniques in accordance with the specific context they are supposed to deal with and be a part of. Today, we are just at the very initial steps of this learning process.

References

Alexander IF (2004) Introduction: scenarios in system development. In: Alexander IF, Maiden N (eds) Scenarios, stories, use cases–through the system development life-style. Wiley, UK

Alexander IF, Maiden N (eds) (2004) Scenarios, stories, use cases–through the system development life-style. Wiley, UK

Allan J, Fairtlough G, Heinesen B (2002) The power of the tale–using narratives for organisational success. Wiley, UK

Boje DM (2002) Narrative methods for organizational and communication research. Sage Publications, UK

Brown JS, Denning S, Groh K, Prusak L (2004) Storytelling in organizations—Why Storytelling is transforming 21st century organizations and management. Elsevier Butterworth-Heinemann, US

Carroll J (1995) Scenario-based design, envisioning, work and technology in system development. Wiley, UK

Corbett JM, Rasmussen LB, Rauner F (1991) Crossing the border–the social and engineering design of computer integrated manufacturing systems. Springer Verlag, London

Denning S (2001) The springboard: how storytelling ignites action in knowledge-era organizations. Butterworth Heineman, Boston

Derrida J (1978) Writing and difference. University of Chicago press, US

Foucault M (1977/79) Discipline and punish. Translated from the 1977 French by Allan Sheridan. Vintage Books, New York

Gabriel Y (2001) Storytelling in organizations–facts, fictions and fantasies. Oxford University press, UK

van der Heiden K, Bradfield R, Burt G, Cains G, Wright G (2002) The sixth sense. Accelerating organizational learning with scenarios. Wiley, Chichester

van der Heijden K (2004/1996) Scenarios: the art and practice of the learning organisation. Wiley, Chichester

Houdek F, Zink T (2004) Story use and reuse in automotive systems engineering. In: Alexander IF, Maiden N (eds) Scenarios, stories, use cases–through the system development life-style. Wiley, UK

Johnson B (2000) A story is a promise. Blue haven publishing, Oregon

Lindgren M, Bandhold H (2003) Scenario planning the link between future and strategy. Palgrave Macmillan, UK

Moore S (2000) Analyzing strategic activity through narrative analysis. In: Flood PC, Dromgoole T, Carroll SJ, Germen L (eds) Managing strategy implementation. Blackwell Publishers, Oxford

Nielsen KS (2004) Stories in organisations–narrative practice (In Danish). Gyldendal, DK

Rasmussen LB (2002) Identity building in organisations: proactive capability development. AI Soc 16:377–394

Rasmussen LB (2003) Action research toolkit II: the scenario workshop. In: Brandt D (ed) Navigating innovations—Indo-European cross-cultural experiences. India Research Press, New Delhi, India, pp 241–258

Rasmussen LB (2004a) Action research—Scandinavian experiences. AI Soc 18:21–43

Rasmussen LB (2004b) Sustainable entrepreneurship and quality of work. In: Garibaldo F, Telljohann V (eds) Globalisation, company strategies and quality of working life in Europe. Peter Lang, Europäische Verlag der Wissenschaften, Germany, pp 251–278

Ricoeur P (1984) Time and narrative, vol I. University of Chicago press, US

Schwartz P (1992) Composing a plot for your scenario. Plan Rev 20(3):4–9

Shaw G, Brown R, Bromiley P (1998) Strategic stories: how 3M is rewriting business planning. Har Bus Rev 76(3):3–8

Waller SE (2003) Story-telling and community visioning- tools for sustainability background paper for the state sustainability strategy, sustainability policy unit, Department for the Premier and Casinet, Australia

Weick KE (1995) Sensemaking in organizations. Sage Publications Thousand Oaks, US

Weick KE (2001) Making sense of the organization. Blackwell Publishing, US

Wenger E (1998) Communities of practice—learning, meaning and identity. Cambridge University press, UK

White M (2000) Reflections on narrative practice—essays & interviews. Dulwich Centre Publications, South Australia

AI & Soc (2003) 17: 207–224
DOI 10.1007/s00146-003-0279-5

Parthasarathi Banerjee

Narration, discourse and dialogue: issues in the management of inter-cultural innovation

Received: 29 August 2002 / Accepted: 18 September 2002 /
Published online: 23 September 2003
© Springer-Verlag London Limited 2003

Abstract Knowledge issues in the management of innovations are addressed properly when the importance of language and in particular of utterances are recognised. This is a new paradigm of management, named here as management by utterance. Unspoken knowledge is not communicated and unspeakable tacit knowledge cannot be of much use in such innovations. Knowledge can be utilised in innovations when its generation and sharing are accomplished through linguistic acts such as a narration or a drama. Discourse necessarily takes a back seat. Utterances and other linguistic forms such as narration or drama bring forth the inter-cultural issues which a manager must resolve in order that a globally diversified research, production and consumption culture remains dynamic and innovative. These inter-cultural aspects have been detailed in this paper by a description of how European and Indian cultural stereotypes understand and appreciate the same narration or utterance. It appears that cultures differ widely in their appreciations of the same management language. Moreover, such variations belittle the discourse-based styles and emphasise the foundational aspects of global communication.

Keywords Culture · Innovation · Management · Tacit knowledge · Utterance

1 Introduction

Many sciences and disciplines are interested in the voice.... There is ideology in the voice, as well as fashion, which often affects supposedly natural objects. Each year, a particular body becomes fashionable, while others go out of style. But what interests me the most in the voice, to begin with, is that this very cultural object is, in a certain way, an absent object (much more absent than the body, which is represented in a thousand ways by mass culture): we rarely listen to a

P. Banerjee
Technology & Development Studies,
National Institute of Science,
Dr. K.S. Krishnan Road, Pusa, 110012 New Delhi, India
E-mail: psb_nist@yahoo.com · Tel.: +91-11-5765380 · Fax: +91-11-5754640

voice *en soi*, in itself, we listen to what it says. The voice has the very status of language, an object thought to be graspable only through what it transmits; however, just as we are now learning, thanks to the notion of "text", to read the linguistic material itself, we must in the same way learn to listen to the voice's text, its meaning, everything in the voice which overflows meaning. The *grain* of the voice is not indescribable...but I don't think that it can be defined scientifically....one can therefore describe the grain of a voice, but only through metaphors. (Barthes 1991)

Few innovations appear these days which are based on descriptions of science alone. Innovations take up imagination and flights of fancies; they penetrate and describe anew forms of common life and, while doing so, these innovations cut across spheres of life in disjointed corners of globe made possible by the teaming up of designers and creative engineers, scientists from multiple cultures. Gone are those happy days when an in-house R and D unit could draft a master plan and could "direct" its staff towards what specific inputs they were expected to provide. Such a master plan or the matrix could describe all or almost all expected inputs beforehand because it was ordinarily based upon an extrapolation of the prior state of describable scientific and technological knowledge. An inference from the existing state of knowledge was all that would be required. With a settled meaning of scientific descriptions, with a robust R and D organisation and with a fordistic supplier's ideology on forcing a new product or a process onto a credulous consumer, a firm had but little difficulty with using a "written" communication text while managing the goal-directed innovation.

Such a written communication text was used to wield power both by the virtue of fixing up a discourse on innovation goals and by an ideology of complete scientific description: (Craig 1990; Kress 1991) "ideology....considered as a conjunct of strategies of discursive reasoning and functions of achieving power and dominance" (Shi-xu 1994). A discourse on innovation goals could set up "a grammar of motives" (Burke 1969) and consequently a teleology of ought's, that each staff of the firm in particular of the R and D unit of the firm was to share. This gives a firm its power towards making innovation strategies. A shared grammar of motives sets up a drama with a finality. Most strategy theories of firms and theories on innovation strategy implicitly or explicitly assumed a priority of shared motives, ought's and the finality of a dramatic innovational goal. Writing texts of such firm-internal goals and the ought's also turned out to be an easy task since an "algorithmic discourse" "put the literary text into logical equations" and "offers itself immediately and completely as without signified" (Barthes 1991).

This happy situation was challenged soon, however, by a state of affairs which can be adumbrated as: (a) a failure of a fordistic pushing of products mass-produced and designed beforehand with the idea that a particular utility would be served and desires fulfilled (Boyer 1997); (b) national and local cultural divergences appeared in defining both fashion, senses of utility or, in short, the emergent demand, and also in defining repertoire of scientific images, patterns and modes of creative thoughts; and (c) a new chapter on industrial organisation ensued with firms accepting globally dispersed sources and agencies of innovation, globally distributed culturally sensitive R and D and local culture-sensitised products and services. The importance of intangible assets grew in significance (Buigues, Jacquemin and Marchipont 2000) because firms now had to adopt innovations originating from several cultural sources. Qualitative and suggestive aspects of knowledge and of modes as well as approaches to innovation now appeared crucial (Banerjee and Richter 2001).

In the wake of this development, R and D as well as the technology-sourcing of large firms became globalised (Cantwell 1999; Dalton and Serapio 1995); co-produced or joint networks and networks of globalised logistics (Nohria and Eccles 1992; Duysters and Hagedoorn 2000) demanded from the incumbents the localisation of product ideas and of product marketing, which in turn compelled not only transfers of knowledge across cultural and national frontiers limited by constraints on information channels (Abo 2001) but also demanded a diversification of agencies of innovation (Mavin and Girling 2000). This was a challenge to developing a global leadership (Ajarimah 2001; Wilpert 1999) and to developing entrepreneurship within cultural milieus (Balakrishnan, Gopakumar and Kanungo 1999). Culture and values at the workplace (Sinha 2000; Chao 1990; Chakraborty 1991; Dasgupta 1997) therefore reappeared as an important parameter to reckon with and also substituted an implicit agenda of the universalisation of the management of innovation. Organisation of firms now recognised more the implicit social values which influence the creative, the innovative and the exchange behaviours of firm personnel (Sinha and Sinha 1994; Yang 1994; Kidd and Edwards 2001). In fact, quite a few innovations came up from the social networks and from the users (Uchiyama 1999) who until only recently were considered by the fordistic paradigm as a recipient of ideas on utility. All this challenged a paradigm of industrial innovation by throwing the paradigm onto a vortex of novelties.

2 The real challenge

There was however, another even more powerful challenge. Organisations hitherto had depended more on texts of written communication and on pre-designed and selected channels of information flows (O'Connor 1995; Park 2001). However, the present situation demanded face-to-face communications (Nohria and Eccles 1992) which would throw open discourses controlled by written texts and semiological information to an emotionally pervasive argument charged with rhetoric (Watson 1995; Gurevitch 2001). Diversification strategies demanded that a strategy defined and bounded by discourse be given up and be replaced with participative and forthcoming initiatives from the end-users as well as from the globally dispersed members of the organisation. Imagination rather than inferences of scientific knowledge would offer novelties, and organisational members from units in varied cultural milieus could throw up images of a future utility when they were given the freedom to talk and imagine what formal scientific knowledges they possessed. A division of knowledge between the tacit and the the codified (Nonaka, Toyama and Nagata 2000; Nonaka and Takeuchi 1995) appears to lose its significance in consequence. A codified knowledge is a written text or a text that could have been written (which includes all information passing through specified channels) while a tacit knowledge is defined as that which is not communicable—thus the knowledge system was defined in terms of what Sperber and Wilson (1986) called the "code model", such as was offered by Shannon or by Saussure and the latter semiologists. Such a knowledge avoided "speaking" and "utterance"; it avoided dialogue, narrations, humour and bliss or the pleasure of communicative engagements. Speaking is less an act driven by prior thinking than an act which accomplishes thought through acts of speaking. Thus, thinking and imagining required space for "speaking", which in turn asks for space for one's own culture and for narrations. What this speaking can achieve in narrating upon the "road to Xanadu" and in achieving dramatic significations upon the formal scientific knowledge, was beyond the scope of the "code models" of knowledge partitioned into the two halves of tacit and codified.

The age of knowledge implied much more. A transition from physical control to the control through codes or written messages saw a parallel shift of economic enterprises from the mechanical-energy driven small setups to an electromechanical setup owned by a corporation. The early years of information technology could not challenge much the corporation run by the writ of code, although slowly, and very effectively, information commenced its journey towards a non-coded semantics first, and then, what we see in the contemporary phase, a spoken language extremely rich in semantics and in suggestive powers. This is undoubtedly progress. Economic sense making and the management of such economic affairs now could hold multiple layers of meaning, inferences possibilities and suggestions. As a natural corollary to a dependence on acts of speaking and listening, issues of cultural differences surfaced. A physical control had the least meaning and a code wished to adhere to a strict meaning (or else, a rule allowing generation of reports of meaning) while a spoken language offers an infinite potential of meaning. Each cultural background offered the niceties of nuances, which were subtle yet immensely powerful. A management by speech is thus simultaneously an intercultural management. Inter-cultural issues were never before so important as it has become now. Moreover, the knowledge age demanded easy transfers of generated knowledge—an aspect best accomplished through acts of speech and of dramaturgy. The knowledge age also demanded that there remained a state of affairs which produced knowledge and innovation. In response, management by speech recognised that nothing was more ephemeral and transitory than a spoken word and yet nothing was more poignant and powerful than the word uttered. Sadly, however, this management by speech recognised that its concepts were new and novel to existing practices.

This paper is about this new paradigm-shift of innovation management. We talk about a management by speech and our context is inter-cultural space. Our background is an emergent knowledge society with its moorings sadly latched onto an earlier schema of knowledge, namely tacit-codified division. And our goal is to journey through inter-cultural spaces of knowledge-based innovations. This, we argue, is possible alone through a management by speech. In our deliberations on such a management of inter-cultural innovation, we argue how a discourse-based management gets substituted by states of affairs punctuated by utterances and narrations, novelistics and drama. We also recognise how different cultures situate themselves differently while listening to a narration or watching a performance of drama. Organisational life as we perceive it to be in the contemporary world, remains innovative through such performances alone—and these are speech performances or dramatic performances. To render our argument simpler the following discussion is limited to a comparison between two schematised representations of cultures—namely that of Europe and of India.

3 The problem and the argument

3.1 The end of a tacit-codified schema of a knowledge division

In what ways, however, do an act of speaking differ from other acts of knowing such as "learning by doing"? If cultures of the world have different answers to this question, then the schema of tacit-codified division of knowledge is seriously challenged. A learning by doing schema implicitly assumes that an apprentice employs the hand and the mind to the job while not even contemplating or communicating knowledge acquired from another person. However, anthropological evidences suggest (Geertz 1973) such a job gets undertaken in several ways in different cultures, and more often than not doing involves communicating (a "habitus" of Bourdieu 1990, also involves utterance). In other words, an act of doing things involves language for both meaning-fulfilment and for utterance. However, a tacit knowledge is by definition dumb and the codified component also belongs to the domain of signs, bereft of connotations of semantics and utterance. It appears then languaging and in particular utterance cannot belong to the domain defined by tacit, which moreover cannot also explain the multiple cultural-modes of acting on the same job.

3.2 An utterance as a possibility or as a mode of practical life

While variations in rituals or in the modes of undertaking a job can be approached from an anthropologist's perspective, utterances and dialogues cannot, however, be approached in the same manner. Cultures explain communications very differently indeed. Restricting ourselves to a comparison between the dominant and paradigmatic interpretations of an European cultural interpretation and an Indian interpretation which has very little paradigmatic force, we may observe a few landmarks. In the former culture, an utterance or an act of communication is towards a possibility. A possibility driven by fear of death (Kirkegaard 1967), by an amazement and awe at the futures of the world and which attempts to embrace truth, rationality—a sort of "universal pragmatics" (Habermas 1984, 1985; Giddens 1985; McCarthy 1985) or an "universal pragmatics" (Apel 1980). Such utterances are then acts on possibilities bound by the norms of universal or transcendental pragmatics. Speaking normatively, it is argued, defines rationality. The speech-act theories and related pragmatics also, while harping less on possibility, concern themselves with considerations of rationality (Grice 1989; Searle 1995; Burkhardt 1990). These latter pragmatics theories emphasise intentionality, and the phenomenology of awe and of possibility are replaced by intentional stances or by the reading of intentions. In short, utterance is understood, in these two strands of European thinking, as achieving possibility and/or intentionality.

In contrast, the Indian approach to utterance offers a sharply different picture. The pragmatics of speaking or communicating are maintained by the conducting of life in this practical world. It does not offer possibilities as such but it allows further acts—the latter reflecting upon several co-existent practical worlds of life. Moreover, a speech can be intentional though a hearer fails in tracing the intentionality of the speaker. The intentionality of the speaker takes a back seat in the communication and the conducting of practical life takes over defining the meaning of a speech. However, Indian theories go beyond this meaning beyond the conventions of practical life. An utterance excels when it also suggests. A suggestion is beyond what inference can bring out. An act of speech refers to denotational, indicational and suggestive meanings. Suggestion brings about blissful or enjoyable mental states in the hearer. An utterance thus appears aesthetic, and these aesthetics, it may be recalled, are not defined either by possibilities or by intentionality (Gnoli 1968; Pandey 1950; Jha 1967; Banerjee and Bhardwaj 2001). This has important bearing on narrations and the rhetoric of speaking.

3.3 Innovation as an imagination of possibilities or a suggestion on generalised meaning

Getting back to possibilities and intentionality in European thinking, we understand that a Lacanian "emergence in reality of an enormous meaning that has the appearance of being nothing at all—in so far as it cannot be tied to anything, since it has never entered into the system of symbolisation—but under certain conditions it can threaten the entire edifice" (Lacan 1993); the "imaginaire scientifique" —a scientific image-repertoire ("a language or set of languages functioning as a misunderstanding of the subject by itself", Barthes 1991) or else fantasies a la Bachelard (Bachelard 1971) offer possibilities and at the same time are challenged by intentions (Heidegger 1977; Rosenbroch 1992). Human actors, who intend or else wish possibilities about the exact knowledge of science which the actor acquired earlier, therefore in this cultural mode, read intentions or possibilities in what they are told, narrated or what they have seen. The exact knowledge of the actor is limited by such a language which yields to inferences and hence advances in knowledge appear through reasoning. However, since much of the reasoning is always immersed in the dialogues or in heard narrations, an actor conjectures on possibilities. A conjecture, as both sides of the pragmatics theorists (for example Habermas or Searle) would have us believe, must then continue to test its possibilities against the truth conditions or against the rationality considerations. In other words, these possibilities must adhere to a limiting teleology. And here dramatic elements come in (Burke 1969).

The other culture in India, however, explains the matter differently. It does not talk of a "misunderstanding" of a knowledge by itself, when the imaginative employment of knowledge acquired earlier takes place. This mode avoids a teleological account as well. As a result, a discourse structured by teleological necessity fails to carry meaning in an Indian organisation. Utterances heard or delivered carry suggestions. Such suggestions bring about changes in the mental states of the listener, who now understands some meaning other than above what can be inferred from the narration or the utterance. This "other meaning", Indian theories explain, is no longer limited by the original context of the practical world; instead, suggestions transgress the immediacy of the practical world one is living in. Thus, suggestion enables a generalised meaning or a broader meaning, which at the same time is enjoyable or pleasurable. Dialogues or utterances, not being probed for an intention or for imagined possibilities, make room to an Indian listener for suggestions or scopes. An Indian mind looks at the scientific scopes or at the suggestible utility—such a utility as would be much pleasurable.

3.4 Innovation as a goal-directed drama or as an unfolding narrative without a goal

This leads us to the third and final part of our argument. An Indian mind listens to an utterance's denoted and indicated meaning and the suggestions. The listener enjoys a state of mind endowed with generalised meaning, which in turn unfolds into another state of meaning, which again unfolds into a third, etc. In short, a narration evolves into several states, which together do not lead to a culmination. A narration unfolds and so does an innovative organisation to the Indian mind. In contrast, the European understanding as it appears, takes a dramatic structure with a culmination or a goal. Possibilities are challenged by a teleology (Burke 1969), and even if a discourse was originally absent from the scene of the talks, it appears soon and structures the utterances in the form of a drama with a culmination. Utterances in an organisation, now having left the stage where reading of organisational scientific texts (a reading of a factual fiction, see Scholes and Kellogg 1966; Macherey 1978; Davis 1996) had to confront a "deception" (Macherey 1978), leading entry either into a "novelistic" discourse ("a mode of discourse unstructured by a story; a mode of notation" Barthes 1991, also 1981) or else into a drama with a teleology. An Indian narration does not offer a singular story line. It offers several anecdotes, hyperlinked. A listener, for example, a member of an organisation, receives a generalised meaning with suggestions from one story line only to be then lead onto another narrative with a still higher generalisation rich with other suggestions. Such narratives continue, as they continue in the Arabian Nights. The organisation member accepts the story lines as the way of organisational life. The Indian theory of drama (Gupta 1954) is without a finality of events; it offers a series of hyperlinked suggestions.

3.5 Our argument in adumbration

What can these explanations about differing cultural modes (Breckenridge and Veer, 1993) of appreciating utterances in general, offer to the understanding of managing inter-cultural innovations? We argue that several dimensions of the problem are opened up. Adumbrating gains in our understanding of managing inter-cultural innovations results in: (a) organisational life, in all its aspects and particularly in its innovations, is immersed in communications of utterances, which can take up several forms from discourse to utterances including drama and narration. This life, in the context of a globally diversified organisation, cannot be guided so much by written texts and codes (of information) any longer; (b) consequently, division schema of knowledge is grouped into codified and tacit components, and management strategies grappling with this division fail expectations. Knowledge passes through verbal utterances, appreciated more as narratives and as enactments of drama; (c) engagements with utterances (and its variations such as a drama) opens up knowledge acquired beforehand to culturally given modes—as a result, even such utterances as "innovation" suggests variable meanings and varieties of future courses of actions to members who are from differing cultures; (d) since issues of management of innovations have to explore futures, such cultural mutants offer different avenues—while one culture conjures up a new utility or a new knowledge as a possibility and also as part of an intended act, another culture conceives innovation not as possibilities but as another way of conducting practical life, equally permissible and hence not challenging. The latter offers an understanding of innovation or of a new technique as offering another generalised meaning with novel suggestions; (e) images of innovations that therefore occupy the mind of both the speaker and the listener, creates through a continuous series of exchanges of communications a space of drama or of a narration. However, an organisational drama (or a narrative) assumes different structures according to cultural variations, resulting in several types of innovational structures in a global organisation.

3.6 Limits to universal claim, and an expanse of diversity

We are confronted with a problem then. Do these different dramatic structures or narratives or novelistics sum up? Would a management require a summing up of diversified structures of innovations in order to achieve a "singular goal"? But then, whose goal is it anyway? Or, would not an attempt at summing up set up again a new discourse? Otherwise, cultural pluralities could terminate the possibility of inter-cultural projects of innovations. In this paper we do not offer a specific solution to this managerial dilemma. However, recognising that a "communicative universal" (Mihayara 1995) is a cultural-specific term, we may then reject the universal solution which wishes to propose a norm of truth and possibility for all. Instead, we close our argument with the observation that the practical world of conducting life is a market-place where all cultures and all the projects of innovation meet on a common ground. This ground of practical life makes possible universal communication and management of inter-cultural innovations projects is authenticated against this proving ground alone. Such an approach allows all the cultural participants to innovations, to their free modes of utterances and their free modes of scientific imagination.

The plan of the paper is as follows: each of the above three arguments are elaborated briefly, in the following sections. A conclusion sums up the argument.

4 An end of the tacit-codified schema of the knowledge-division

Undoubtedly, language infuses through everything that is human. Any self-reflective activity takes place through the language. However, does that signify that communication too is equally pervasive? In particular, how important is communication for a project of knowledge? A pure phenomenologic sense perception can be felt and a languaging is not necessary for that feeling. It can be argued, however, that such a feeling, which is knowledge, cannot be described in terms of "tacit" knowledge (Banerjee 1997). Moreover, a self-reflection on that felt knowledge would ask for the support of language. Even more important is the fact that the person having such a felt knowledge would seek the services of not language alone but also of an utterance, in order to execute most of the practical affairs of life. Communication, therefore, would be required surely for all interpersonal acts and also for most individual acts. Utterance itself is an act, and thus a knowledge acquired through "doing" (say by hand) gets transformed in the course of the utterance proper, or else in the course of listening proper. That is in as much as "doing" is a knowledge-generating act, utterance or listening too is equally an act in knowledge-generation.

The abiding characteristic of a tacit knowledge is that it is unspeakable, or this knowledge does not do languaging. A pure unreflexive phenomenologic sense remains unspeakable till such time as the felt sense remains alone. A moment later, through reflexivity, language copulates with the sense and transforms the sense-knowledge (Russell 1993). Thus a tacit knowledge becomes a chimera or else momentary. However, languaging with oneself to render plastic imageries of the sense knowledge, is challenged further when communication is undertaken. Any communication serves a purpose in the practical world of life. Hence, spoken or heard communication transforms further this originally tacit knowledge. An organisational life rests on the dual of utterance-listening or else on viewing (such as a drama). Tacit knowledge, if any, has thus the least relevance to the organisational life.

Moreover, there are cultural variations too in apprehending knowledge. It is quite likely that the linguistic turn of twentieth century philosophy (Ayer 1984; Dummett 1996) saw its reaction in the emergence of unspeakable tacit knowledge. It came in handy for the fordistic organisation, which wished to retain and hold the worker to a specific work site (the asset-specificity of Williamson 1993). Issues of knowledge-society, worker mobility and worker turnover, and life-long learning challenged this paradigm. It is an appropriate time, therefore, to reconsider the worth of tacit knowledge.

Getting back to cultural variations on the theme of knowledge, we would benefit by informing ourselves in brief about an Indian approach to this issue. This offers a genealogy of knowledge, where acts such as "doing" or "uttering" generate a primary knowledge (that is, even a primary knowledge is suffused through language) to be captured through the sense-organs such as listening or observing, of which latter generates the next knowledge. This latter, however, gets verified or validated against the practical physical world. Next, only such a validated piece of knowledge can take flights of imagination or can appreciate suggestions, since now the mind provides the space for flights of fancy. From such a schema, "doing" and "uttering" are equivalent and are also both necessary for senses to assimilate the primary knowledge. A "listening" or a "viewing", the basic bedrock of inter-personal organisational life, can be appreciated only if such a primary knowledge is available. Finally, until such a knowledge gets validated through applications in the practical physical world, the mind does not provide the scope or space for the knowledge. Arguably, innovations in a knowledge society demand imagining or suggestiveness, which the mind alone can allow. The plasticity of knowledge and combinations of pieces of knowledge, valued much since that alone is the engine of innovation, is then made possible.

The "tacit" has its obverse in the Augustinian "code". In order that a code can be decoded, a person must have a transformer which surely the uncodable and unspeakable tacit cannot provide. That is, this schema is incomplete in itself. It is ordinarily assumed, however, in the management literature (Nonaka and Takeuchi, 1995) that social structuring of a workplace can manage the maximum transformation of the tacit into the the codifiable domain. An experience "frame" (Goffman 1974) with its proper signs is supposed to alleviate the problem of the gap mentioned above. Nonetheless, even a "frame" would require articulation and communication. Surely the dimension of utterance is missing from this perspective. No wonder all the cultures most value speaking and listening in any conceivable act (Hasan 2001). As argued above, a fordistic organisation had the wherewithal of written texts, codes—in short, instructional messages to manage not only its shop management but also its R and D. With the growing recognition that pre-conceived projects of innovations often lead to failures, companies are being challenged now to reorganise and restructure their operations towards a concurrency and flexibility (Bartlett and Ghoshal 1997), which we argue is achievable only through opening the doors to dialogues.

6 An utterance as a possibility or as a mode of practical life

This demand upon a contemporary organisation to remain innovative all the time implies that the organisation lays itself open to suggestions and possibilities. A manager is thus confronted with the quest for the best instrument that helps make an organisation always transitional. In a steady state organisation information paths are fixed and the information contents that can be accessed by a member is also fixed. A code-dependent information exchange is thus suitable for such an organisation. If now the paths are to have free passages and connectivities, and the contents are to have over and above a context-dependency a potential value beyond what the simple information-content can provide for, it is obvious that nothing other than a speech-situation can attain all this qualities. That is, utterances when allowed and when recognised as legitimate modes of communication, alone appear to be this much sought-after instrument of a manager enabling her to ride over the roller coaster of innovations.

With this recognition of utterances as the most effective instrument, a manager faces a new dilemma. The import and significance of an utterance is highly culture specific. Therefore, no sooner does the manager allow speaking out and listening to, than cultural spaces put up enclaves of niceties. Niceties, if not understood properly and not given due respect (Held 1995) create barriers to communication and hence to innovation. Otherwise, given recognition, niceties open up innovations, but on an inter-cultural level. Thus, a management employing utterances necessarily become inter-cultural. Issues of innovation are now transformed into inter-cultural issues of innovation.

Cultural relativism recognises varieties of cultures, such as sub-national or ethnic cultures, continental culture, regional or local culture, including even the culture of an individual. For the purpose of clarity and brevity, we will compare only European and Indian cultures both captured in a brief but "thick description" (Geertz 1973). With this imposed limit we observe that these two cultures explain communication differently. In the European culture a communication would be modelled after a norm of rationality or the norm of a transcendental pragmatics. An utterance in this view offers several possibilities thrown open by the speaker. In order that an effective communication takes place the listener must approach the norm. Intentions of the speaker take a back seat in this description. However, in another dominant mode of European description, intentions of the speaker and also the hearer take the centre stage. An effective communication takes place when intentions can be recognised. In contrast, an Indian description of a communication situation asserts that looking for intentions would lead to an infinite regress. A speaker's intention cannot with certainty be known. Moreover the Indian view also asserts that a dialogue does not open up possibilities which can be subjected to norms of rationality, for example, but it opens up modes of life in several practical situations of the world.

An European manager looks for dialogues amenable to norms, and since the manager recognises her norms as value-loaded (Hofstede 1980), she attempts to get over the crisis through psychological detours (as has been the wont of most management research in inter-cultural issues; see Negandhi 1975). However, a speech-dependent communication is least psychological and the norms of communication described above are cognitive and non-psychological. The manager thus needs to look for cognitive possibilities which would open up a series of potential innovations and which would sustain a condition of trust, truth and rationality (Habermas 1984). The Eastern mind looked at the same communication rather differently. An utterance conveys another practical world in existence and not in possibility. Equally, the communication situation was not searched for intentions. Instead, a hearer looks for suggestions behind the indicated meaning of an utterance. A suggestion, the Indian mind knows, is much more pleasurable.

Interestingly, a suggestion offers something which a "frame" or the context cannot indicate. A communication then offers firstly a denoted meaning, secondly an indicated meaning which is conditioned by the contextual reference or by the reference of experience, and thirdly a suggestion which is beyond both denotation and contextual indication. Communication to an Indian mind then, refers to the following three aspects together: (1) the science or a knowledge that can be inferred, hence this knowledge is of general applicability; (2) a contextual meaning which indicates specific nuances of the generalisable science or the knowledge with respect to shared organisational or cultural experience—such indications cannot be inferred since an inference will have to depend upon an identifiable intention in order to infer this indicated meaning out of several possible meanings; and (3) a suggestion, which is neither inferred nor indicated, and hence it is not a produced cognition—it is a mental state offering a generalised feeling; therefore, it is beyond context and yet it is not an inference.

In the European reckoning, too, inference serves the same function. The indicated meaning of the Indian mind, however, assumes the shape of contextual experiential or an intentional meaning. In order that this latter meaning leads the situation of communication beyond the immediacy of context or of experience or else of the intentions, the ideals of rationality or of transcendental pragmatics are invoked by the European manager. These ideals need not be resident in the utterances proper, that is, the speaker or the listener need not be intending to act rationally; although, in order that the situation of communication can take into consideration the future and the possibility of a rationality or of a science, the ideality has to be invoked by the participants in the communication. Thus, a norm is invoked in order that there remains a future of science and of a rational culture. An industrial culture (Ruth 1997) is an ideality in this sense. Such a culture proposes a norm on the possibilities of imagination. Imagination for creativity is supposed to be the foundation of an innovative organisation.

6 Innovation as imaginations about possibilities or suggestions on generalised meanings

Tacit knowledge appears to be blind to imagining. An act of imagination would require languaging with the known images, and images can be reflectively drawn from memory as well as conjured in severalties only if there are names to the images. We described above how an image may remain as a pure sense alone till such time as the senses are not named and reflected upon. A tacit knowledge, in so far as it is a pure sense without a name or without a sentence describing the state of affairs, cannot be recalled in introspection. Thus, the blind tacit knowledge cannot lead the creative insights into innovations. A gestalt is deeper than this tacit knowledge since the gestalt uses private images, much like using a private language.

A codified knowledge, as a counterpoint to the tacit, is limited by its sign-dependence (semioticity). The denotative features of such a language binds it to a mere packet of information. One cannot play with a packet of information in order to create new images—semiotics limit the coded knowledge into square boxes of a puzzle. However, denotational features of a name or of a whole uttered sentence keep free the imaginative potentiality of known knowledge. Furthermore, when spoken, such a language refers to an ambiguous set of indicative features of meaning. These are referred to the context, etc. Finally, in the Indian approach an utterance also refers to suggestions. Overall, an utterance opens up the vista of imagining on knowledge to both the speaker and the hearer. This has been possible because an act of speaking has been employed. We recognise therefore two levels: a private language and a communicative language. The former is necessary even in order that one can reflect upon and conjure fascinations on denotations; while the latter is required for communicative purposes. This later has the additional features of indicative meanings and suggested meanings (in the Indian approach) or else possibilities (in the European approach).

Undoubtedly, innovations are based upon imagining. A simple act of inference would not beget in most occasions an innovation—reason being an inference as a logical conclusion is potentially known to all. Moreover, an inference too is limited (Stich 1990) also by cultural nuances (Hutchins 1980). Innovation needs to offer a novelty in contrast. Such a novelty is then accessible only to creative imagination which in turn can happen when languages along with the associated mental states are played with—a new space is created (Bachelard 1994) now in the organisation. Dialogues, narrations and drama are thus the essentials for such a setup. Moreover, as argued above, no sooner are communicative languages recognised as the basic criterion to the management of innovation, the issues of inter-cultural aspects begin dominating the undertaking. A communication attempts to look over the private language, and therefore any utterance must wrestle with crossing over cultural defences.

Two cultures that we have referred to in this paper, however, describe imagination differently. The European culture, or, as it has been called, the "modernity", raised a purified objectivity of science at the cost of raising a large zone of fuzzy "hybrids" (Latour 1993)—an intermixture of culture and science. These hybrids constructed through a socialised discourse the edifice of scientific novelties. Hybrids encouraged imagination, however, as possibility alone, and the birth of a possibility creates a sense of "awe" (Held 1995) which gets visited by utterances of exclamations and descriptions of the social or organisational partners. These descriptions impose a discourse and eventually a norm. A possibility on imagination is thus guided by the discourse-dynamics of the hybrids. Evidently such a discourse is very culture specific. What another culture would have called an imagination, might not generate the "awe" and might not get legitimised by the current discourse-dynamics of the organisation immersed deeply in the European culture. The European manager is limited by the culture of her discourse in not recognising potential suggestions on innovations from other cultures.

Utterances do not create possibilities to an Indian hearer; instead, the mind of the latter is opened up to several distinct states of affairs. This hearer associates a particular mental state and not an "awe", with each suggestion of the utterance. A narration or a dialogue in an Indian context creates several such mental states, each of which fiddles with language-images. Imagination carries thus an alternative meaning which does not demand the imposition of discourse norm. Specifically, it does not demand an 'objective' picture of the suggested innovation, and neither does it look for the normative conditions. Perhaps the most important feature of this culture is that any narration including a drama is never conclusive or teleological. This implies that tales of innovation become a part of the organisational life.

7 Innovation as a goal-directed drama or as an unfolding narrative without a goal

An Arabian Nights story, typical to an Indian narration, simply unfolds. Each episode is punctuated by its local break, which is not a culmination, and the total narration does not offer the singular image of a cathartic build-up. Narrations are renewed and becomes a part of the life. Each event brings forth several states of mind. This sense of narration, set up through dialogues, is carried over into organisational premises. A question may naturally be asked as to how such narrations are related more to contexts of innovations than to the ordinary routine affairs of an organisation. To my understanding of the Indian psyche, any states of affairs is understood as subliminally dynamic; no states of affairs in an organisation could thus be accepted as pertaining to a routine. However, if any particular narrative event leads to a state having a large potential of economic returns, we may describe that as innovative, or to be more specific, critically innovative. Other states would also be dynamic, though holding no immediate prospect of large economic gains. Such latter states could be called uncritically innovative. Therefore any dialogue and narration, essential for letting free the imagination of organisational members, would be associated with conditions of changes—some out of which could lead to great gains in returns or in strategy.

This attitude towards changes in an organisation never, then, seek a finale. There are several dramas happening in the organisation, none of which perhaps is cathartic. Typically an Indian drama describes an attitude or a mental state – events are mellifluous and are harmonic. Both the actors and the viewers enjoy that state of mind, and it is this state which we have described as imaginative and poignant. It should be remembered that discourses fail in this culture and there are no normative binds on the course that dialogues, narrations or a drama might take. Members of the organisation become creative in a convivial spirit. The alleged failure of scientific objectivity or of rationality, that so cripples the thought of an European manager when faced with the prospect of unbound utterances and performances, does not happen to the Indian cognition which takes it with ease and pleasure. Innovation to this culture is thus intrinsically inter-cultural and part of the common (organisational) life. Each culture and each state of mind or of an organisation has thus a legitimacy. Change is typical. The jargon "change management" loses its significance.

The "uncertain dynamics of an unfolding narrative" (Czarniawska-Joerges and Jacobsson 1995) in contrast, appear as a threat to the European mind, to be counterpoised with a stabilising dimension of "role" (Goffman 1981). Much of change management literature from European culture thus refers to role management (Bartlett and Ghoshal 1997). Otherwise these uncertain narratives have been described as belonging to the "unmanaged organisation"—a "kind of organisational dreamworld in which desires, anxieties and emotions find expressions in highly irrational constructions" (Gabriel 1995). This alleged "irrationality" is understood to be subversively life-giving, pleasurable and creative sometimes. There is a sense of deception and failure of managerial authority. A manager wishes to guide the narratives through a discourse of norm-abidance because she feels threatened and is "awed" at the possibility.

Possibility is multi-faceted and multi-dimensional. To bring coherence and a unique orientation a dramatic structure in true Greek style is then assumed by the European cultural practice. This implies that a discourse fails in the event of non-compliance with the rationality-norm or the non-abidance of transcendental pragmatics. But discourse can be saved if only an organisational performance follows the structure of a drama. This is a drama with a teleology—an end or a finale. Often, a change management or an innovation is treated as a project of such a magnitude and importance as swallows up the entire organisational resource. In other words, the organisation becomes a project, and with achieving its goals naturally and logically, the organisation collapses. Moreover, partners from other cultures who do not understand such a dramatic structure also cannot share the anxieties and drives of the European manager towards innovation.

8 Conclusions: limits to universal claims, an expanse of diversity

A transition to a knowledge society demands that contemporary management switches its techniques from a dependence on codified information and its abidance to an utterance-driven management. A management based on the identification of the determinants of knowledge and on an exchange of knowledge through utterances assures a ride on the roller coaster of innovation. However, an utterance-driven generation and an exchange of knowledge immediately faces inter-cultural issues. A dialogue or a narration is evidently situated in a cultural context. Contemporary industry is both globalised and knowledge-intensive. As a result, industry today needs to recognise the paradigm shift—a shift towards the management of utterance-driven innovations. Such a management works with words, images, meanings and communication. Each culture has its own idiosyncrasies and the communicated meanings and the imaginative flights of innovative members of the organisation from across various cultures vary widely, challenging the Anglo-American pre-eminence in acts of interpretation.

These challenges are several. In this paper we used two cultural stereotypes, namely European and Indian. Use of such stereotypes certainly limits applications of our argument to a general case of multiple cultures, though we believe that certain general points too have been made. Of special importance is our argument regarding the irrelevance of a tacit-codified schema of the division of knowledge. This is a general conclusion. From this irrelevance one recognises the emerging importance of management of utterance-driven innovations. Specifically, an act of speech or of listening to or even watching the performance of a dramatic act involves cognition. An organisation in the knowledge age busies itself with cognitions alone and, thus, remains there for such an organisation but has little room for psychological values or for blind and dumb tacit sense-perceptions. Now, an organisation must manage knowledge and change through managing speech situations.

A speech situation brings about the relativism of cultural spaces inside the organisation. A single space with a discourse as its truss, fails then in eliciting the creative participation of its culturally relativised partners. What language could then be spoken and which speech situations should then be allowed by a manager of knowledge-based innovations? Could the manager substitute the discourse with rational pragmatics, and should not this be construed as culturally offensive as well as retrogressive? A communicative universal is a cultural-specific term and we may reject the universal solution which wishes to propose a norm of truth and possibility for all. Instead, we close our argument with the observation that the practical world of conducting life and business is a marketplace where all cultures and all the projects of innovation meet the ground. This ground of life and business makes possible universal communication and the management of inter-cultural innovations projects is authenticated against this proving ground alone. Such an approach allows all the cultural participants to innovations, their free modes of utterances and their free modes of imaginations about knowledge.

References

Abo T (2001) Competition and cooperation between the Japanese and British management models in the UK: international transfer problems of intangible management systems. In: Banerjee P, Richter FJ (eds) Intangibles in competition and cooperation: Euro-Asian perspectives, Palgrave, London

Ajarimah AA (2001) Major challenges of global leadership in the twenty-first century. Hum Res Dev Intl 4(1):9–19

Apel KO (1980) Towards a transformation of philosophy. Routledge & Kegan Paul, London

Ayer AJ (1984) Philosophy in the twentieth century. Unwin Paperbacks, London

Bachelard G (1971) On poetic imagination and reverie. Spring, Dallas, TX

Bachelard G (1994) The poetics of space. Beacon Press, Boston, MA

Balakrishnan S, Gopakumar K and Kanungo RN (1999) Entrepreneurship development: concept and context. In: Kao HSR, Sinha D and Wilpert B (eds) Management and cultural values: the indigenisation of organisations in Asia, Sage, New Delhi

Banerjee P (1997) Excess and necessary: redefining skill and the network. In: Banerjee P, Sato Y (eds) Skill and technological change, Har-Anand, New Delhi

Banerjee P, Bhardwaj KK (2001) Constructivist management of knowledge, communication and enterprise innovation: lessons from Indian experience. AI Soc 16(1):49–72

Banerjee P, Richter FJ (2001) Social management: situating imagination, concept, cooperation and intangible assets in the knowledge business. In: Banerjee P, Richter FJ (eds) Intangibles in competition and cooperation: Euro-Asian Perspectives, Palgrave, London

Barthes R. (1981) Critical essays. Northwestern University Press, Evanston, IL

Barthes R (1991) The grain of the voice: interviews 1962–1980. University of California Press, Berkeley, CA

Bartlett CA, Ghoshal S (1997) The myth of the generic manager: new personal competencies for new management roles. Calif Manage Rev 40(1):92–116

Bourdieu P (1990) In other words: essays towards a reflexive sociology. Stanford University Press, Stanford, CA

Boyer R, Durand JP (1997) After fordism. Macmillan Business, London

Breckenridge CA, van der Veer P (eds) (1993) Orientalism and the postcolonial predicament, University of Pennsylvania Press, Philadelphia, PA

Buigues P, Jacquemin A and Marchipont JF (eds) (2000) Competitiveness and the value of intangible assets, Edward Elgar, Cheltenham, UK

Burke K (1969) A grammar of motives. University of California Press, Berkeley, CA

Burkhardt A (ed) (1990) Speech acts, meaning and intentions. de Gruyter, Berlin

Cantwell JA, Janne O (1999) Technological globalisation and innovative centers: the role of corporate technological leadership and location hierarchy. Res Pol 28:119–44

Chakraborty SK (1991) Management by values: towards cultural congruence. Oxford University Press, New Delhi

Chao YT (1990) Culture and work organisation: the Chinese case. Int J Psychol 25(4): 583–92

Craig RT (1990) Multiple goals in discourse: an epilogue. J Lang Soc Psychol 9:163–70

Czarniawska-Joerges B, Jacobsson B (1995) Political organisations and Commedia Dell'Arte. Org Stud 16(3):375–94

Dalton DH, Serapio MG Jr (1995) Globalizing industrial research and development. US Department of Commerce, Office of Technology Policy, Asia-Pacific Technology Program, Washington, DC

Dasgupta RK (1997) Human values in management. J Hum Val 3(2):145–60

Davis LJ (1996) Factual fictions: the origins of the English novel. University of Pennsylvania Press, Philadelphia, PA

Dummett M (1996) Origins of analytical philosophy. Harvard University Press, Cambridge, MA

Duysters G, Hagedoorn J (2000) Organisational modes of strategic technology partnering. J Scien Industr Res 59(8,9):640–49

Gabriel Y (1995) The unmanaged organisation: stories, fantasies and subjectivity. Org Stud 16(3):477–501

Geertz C (1973) The interpretation of cultures: selected essays. Basic Books, New York

Giddens A (1985) Reason without revolution? Habermas's theorie des kommunikativen handelns. In: Bernstein RJ (ed) Habermas and modernity, Polity Press, Cambridge, UK

Gnoli R (1968) The aesthetic experience according to Abhinavagupta. Varanasi: The Chowkhamba Sanskrit Series Office

Goffman E (1974) Frame analysis: an essay on the organisation of experience. Harper and Row, NY

Goffman E (1981) Forms of talk. Basil Blackwell, Oxford, UK

Grice P (1989) Studies in the way of words. Harvard University Press, Cambridge, MA

Gupta CB (1954) The Indian theatre. Motilal Banarasidass, Banaras, India

Gurevitch Z (2001) Dialectical dialogue: the struggle for speech, repressive silence, and the shift to multiplicity. Brit J Sociol 52(1):87–104

Habermas J (1984) The theory of communicative action I: reason and the rationalisation of society. Heinemann, London

Habermas J (1985) Neoconservative culture criticism in the United States and West Germany: an intellectual movement in two political cultures. In: Bernstein RJ (ed) Habermas and modernity, Polity, Cambridge, UK

Hasan R (2001) Understanding talk: directions from Bernstein's sociology. Int J Soc Res Methodol 4(1):5–9

Heidegger M (1977) The question concerning technology and other essays. Harper Torch, New York

Held K (1995) Intercultural understanding and the role of Europe. Monist 78(1):5–17

Hofstede G (1980) Culture's consequences: international differences in work-related values. Sage, London

Hutchins E (1980) Culture and inference: a trobriand case study. Harvard University Press, Cambridge, MA

Jha G (1967) Kavyaprakasha of Mammata (with English translation). Bharatiya Vidya Prakashan, Varanasi, India

Kidd JL, Edwards JS (2001) Making the intangible tangible. In: Banerjee P, Richter FJ (eds) Intangibles in competition and cooperation: Euro-Asian perspectives, Palgrave, London

Kirkegaard S (1967) Kirkegaard's the concept of dread. Princeton University Press, Princeton, NJ

Kress G (1991) Critical discourse analysis. Ann Rev Appl Linguist 11:84–99

Lacan J (1993) The psychoses: the seminar of Jacques Lacan. Routledge, London

Latour B (1993) We have never been modern. Harvester Wheatsheaf, New York

Macherey P (1978) A theory of literary production. Routledge and Kegan Paul, London

Mavin S, Girling G (2000) What is managing diversity and why does it matter? Hum Res Devel Intl 3(4):419–33

McCarthy T (1985) Reflections on rationalisation in the theory of communicative action. In: Bernstein RJ (ed) Habermas and modernity, Polity, Cambridge, UK

Mihayara I (1995) Communicative universals. Monist 78(1):30–40

Negandhi RN (1975) Comparative management and organisation theory: a marriage needed. Acad Manage J 8(2):3334–44

Nohria N, Eccles RG (1992) Face-to-face: making network organisations work. In: Nohria N, Eccles RG (eds) Networks and organisations: structure, form and action, Harvard Business School Press, Boston, MA

Nonaka I, Takeuchi H (1995) The knowledge-creating company. Oxford University Press, Oxford, UK

Nonaka I, Toyama R and Nagata A (2000) A firm as aknowledge-creating entity: a new perspective on the theory of the firm. Industr Corp Change 9(1):1–20

O'Connor ES (1995) Paradoxes of participation: textual analysis and organisational change. Org Stud 16(5):769–803

Pandey KC (1950) Indian aesthetics. Chowkhamba, Banaras, India

Park YT (2001) A framework for designing technological knowledge management systems: a sector-specific approach. In: Banerjee P, Richter FJ (eds) Intangibles in competition and cooperation: Euro-Asian perspectives, Palgrave, London

Rosenbroch H (1992) Science, technology and purpose. AI Soc 6(1):3–17

Russell B (1993) Our knowledge of the external world. Routledge, London

Ruth K (1997) Learning curves in technology design. In: Banerjee P, Sato Y (eds) Skill and technological change, Har-Anand, New Delhi

Scholes R, Kellogg R (1966) The nature of narrative. Oxford University Press, New York

Searle J (1995) The construction of social reality. Free Press, New York

Shi-xu (1994) Ideology: strategies of reason and functions of control in accounts of the non-Western other. J Prag 21:645–69

Sinha JBP (2000) Patterns of work culture: cases and strategies for culture building. Sage, New Delhi

Sinha JBP, Sinha D (1994) Role of social values in Indian organisations. In: Kao HSR, Sinha D and Sek-Hong N (eds) Effective organisations and social values, Sage, New Delhi

Sperber D, Wilson D (1986) Relevance: communication and cognition. Harvard University Press, Cambridge, MA

Stich S (1990) The fragmentation of reason: preface to a pragmatic theory of cognitive evaluation. MIT Press, Cambridge, MA

Uchiyama K (1999) Reconciling the "global" and "local" by using soft systems methodology: a case of building trust relationships in South Africa. J Scient Industr Res 58(3,4):302–20

Watson TJ (1995) Rhetoric, discourse and argument in organisational sense making: a reflexive tale. Org Stud 16(5):805–21

Williamson O (1993) Calculativeness, trust, and economic organisation. J Law Econ 36:453–86

Wilpert B (1999) Leadership styles and management: universally convergent or culture-bound? In Kao HSR, Sinha D and Wilpert B (eds) Management and cultural values: the indigenisation of organisations in Asia, Sage, New Delhi

Yang M (1994) Gifts, favors and banquets: the art of social relations in China. Cornell University Press, Ithaca, NY

Rethinking the Interaction Architecture

Karamjit S. Gill[1]

[1] Emeritus Prof., Brighton University. Visiting Prof. University of Wales, Newport School of Art, Media and Design, Newport, P.O. Box. 179, Newport, kgillbton@yahoo.co.uk

Abstract. The chapter explores the design of the user interface within and across the user interaction spaces. It deals with a key issue of knowing the user from the known and unknown interaction contexts. In other words, how do we discern the reality from the actuality of user interaction? In comprehending the place and role of the user in various social, functional, and cultural contexts, we face the issue of understanding the dynamics of interactions in these sometimes overlapping and intersecting contexts. It argues that the notion of valorisation can be used to extend the concept of 'interface' from the realm of the 'separation' between the reality and the actuality, to the symbiotic realm of the actuality and reality. This symbiotic realm enables users from different realities to collaborate by pooling their knowledge and experiences, while sharing their cultural differences. In doing so, users enter into a symbiotic interaction space which facilitates the enhancing of both their common capacities (objective knowledge) and personal capabilities (tacit experiences). This perspective of seeking symbiosis between the user reality and actuality is termed here as 'valorised reality'. This concept of valorisation provides a methodological tool for bridging the gaps between "actuality" and "reality" mediated by the symbiotic interface. The concept of the cultural holon is introduced to represent the network architecture of user interactions in a local-global context. In this perspective, the symbiosis represents the possibilities, choices and alternative paths available for user interaction in overlapping and inter-linked interaction spaces.

1 Introduction

The problem and the challenge explored in the health care domain below raises issues as to how the user would interact with the diversity of professionals, carers and community organisations, and how the ICT based interface would fill the functional, social, cultural and even cross-cultural interaction gaps between user and providers of health care. All these questions are intrinsically linked with challenges of interfacing arising from the gaps (conceptual, modelling, design and application) described in the proceeding sections. As users we play different roles as individuals, members of a group, community, and society, and our interactions take place at the intersections and boundaries of the functional, social and cultural domains of our interactions. In this scenario, we encounter not just the complexity of cross-functional and cross-social interaction but also of cross-cultural communication. It is worth noting that just as the observations of one reality may vary depending upon the observer and observer context, so the observed reality and actuality of one culture may vary from those of the other culture, and same may be true of reality and actuality of the social domain, and may even be true of the functional domain. So the issue here is how to find coherence between different realities and actualities while recognising actuality-reality gaps, and in the same vein, how to find a commonality of cultural experiences while recognising cultural differences. That is to say how do we pool our shared cultural experiences (share our pooled experiences) while recognising our cultural differences and sustaining our cultural identities.

Here we introduce the concept of the 'culture of the artificial, (Negrotti 1999). This concept enables individuals (or groups) from two different cultural spaces to create a third artificial cultural space (culture of the artificial) in which to meet and share and pool their common cultural experiences for a common purpose, while recognising and accepting their cultural differences as a further resource for cross-cultural learning. We call this process, 'valorising' of cultures, which says that we make best use of our common cultural experiences while recognising our different cultural identities. While the concept of symbiosis enables the interaction in the gaps between actuality and reality, the concept of valorisation enables us to find a coherence (commonality) between cross-cultural interactions. It is worth noting that these concepts also enable learning from actuality-reality gaps and from the cultural differences. In this sense diversity becomes a tool for cross-cultural understanding and learning. The implications of this articulation of learning is that any interfacing design process dealing with actuality gaps and cross-cultural spaces should by definition be a learning process, involving both the users and designers in the process of design (Gill 2002, 2006).

When we interact with others within our own cultural space, our interactions are bounded by the social and cultural architectures, in which we live and act. However when we interact with others from different cultures, our interactions are not just bounded by architectures of both cultures but also by the intersection of these cultural architectures (e.g. Irish and Japanese cultures). But where these cultural architectures are seen to overlap (e.g. British and Irish cultures), our interactions may also overlap, sharing many common experiences and learning from differences. If we extend this cross-cultural interaction to more than two cultures, we begin to visualise interactions taking place at various levels of a web of cultural architectures, at times overlapping and intersecting. We call this overlapping and intersecting architecture a cross-cultural network architecture (Fig.1). In this architecture, each node represents a culture (or a cultural architecture) and each link represents the interaction relationship between the two cultural nodes. Depending upon the complexity of a culture, a cultural node may itself be represented as a cultural network architecture. Thus the complexity of cross-cultural interactions within cross-cultural settings depends upon the levels of hierarchy in the cross-cultural architecture, and the complexity of interactions within a culture depends upon the levels of hierarchy of the cultural architecture. Borrowing from the notion of a 'holon', we introduce here the concept of 'cultural holon' as representing a culture in the cross-cultural architecture.

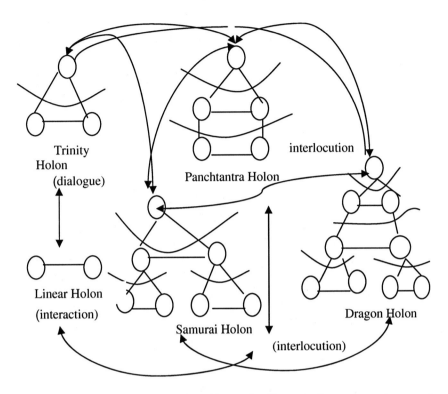

Fig 1. Holonic Architecture of cross-cultural interaction illustrating interaction and communication modes between cultural holons, each cultural holon as a simplified representation of the observed reality of interaction within a cultural structure of communication

The idea of the cultural holon is that just as the model of observation is used to represent the reality as it is observed and experienced, so a cultural holon can be used as a model to represent the architecture of a culture as it is observed in interaction. In our case we can say that the cross-cultural network architecture is a holonic cross-cultural architecture in which interaction takes place between cultural holons.

For example in this holonic architecture, cross-cultural interactions may take place at various levels of interaction, 'linear' (e.g. techno-cratic) holonic architecture dealing with interaction between two cultural interaction spaces, 'trinity' (e.g. European) holonic architecture dealing with interactions between three different cultural interaction spaces, the 'panchtantra' (e.g. Indian) holonic architecture dealing with five different cultural interaction spaces, 'samurai' (e.g. Japanese) holonic architecture dealing with seven different cultural interaction spaces, and 'dragon' (e.g. Chinese) holonic architecture dealing with nine different cultural interaction spaces (Gill, ibid).

2 User Interfacing- The Problem and the Challenge

Recently there has been increasing importance placed on strategic exploitation of new information technologies in the public administration of health (The e-Health 2003 programme of the EU). This EU programme focuses on the development of an infrastructure which will provide user-friendly, validated and interoperable systems for medical care, disease prevention, and health education through national and regional networks which connect citizens, practitioners and authorities online. It raises a question about how beneficial these IT based services would be to the citizen as the user of both health care services and health information.

In the UK, for example, the recent £6 billion NHS national programme for IT to create electronic patient records, e-booking and e-prescribing, focuses on the integration of its use by clinical and administrative personnel. This programme falls into the category of major UK public IT initiatives and projects such as the e-government, which are based on the assumption that IT systems are 'a good thing'. The complexity of the design of the proposed IT system and ambitious nature of the integrative use of this Health IT programme raises the interface problem and challenge to tackle the multi-level complexity interface between and among various levels of health care services, health care provision and health care use.

3 Interfacing Tools – A Challenge

The purpose of the interface is to bridge the gap between the medical model of health and the social model of health. The challenge is to develop multi-modal interfacing tools to support health care systems. The purpose of the interfacing tools is to facilitate interaction of users of health care professionals and carers, and participation of users of health care services and local communities in shaping health care systems. The research challenge is to transcend the techno-centric notion of 'IT as the one best solution' and develop symbiotic interfacing from the human-centred perspective. This perspective involves:

* To develop human centred models of health care, building on the interdependence and overlapping of the objective and practice based knowledge of the health care profession, and the social and personal knowledge of carers and the community

* To build a knowledge base of practice based and evidence based models of health care

* To create an interdisciplinary action research programme in collaboration with the research community and practitioners local community

* To contribute to the development of IT/multimedia supported interface tools and systems for collaboration between the health care professions and the community

4 Techno-Centric Focus of e-Health

The focus of e-Health 2003, remains essentially on the "implementation of the information technology infrastructure in health care provision". We can see a clear emphasis on technological infrastructure by the statement, "The Health Online action recognises that the first action towards exploitation of the power of information technologies in the health sector is the implementation of an infrastructure which will provide user-friendly, validated and interoperable systems for medical care, disease prevention, and health education through national and regional networks which connect citizens, practitioners and authorities online." (eEurope 2005 Action Plan for Health). The NHS national programme for IT is also rooted in the belief in the information management focus of the e-Health. Multiple links and the need for clinical and administrative personnel to use it also make it one of the most ambitious. It is worth noting that the very system, which proposes to provide an integrated health care system, has kept the input of 'doctors' and 'nurses' to the minimum (Simon Caulkin, Sunday Observer, 2 May 2004).

From this we can infer that the design of the IT systems is based on the techno-centric notion that models of technical solutions to complex industrial production and commercial information systems can also be applied to complex socio-economic problems of society such as health care. This leads to seeing the IT systems design in terms of the systems analysis methodology, which in turn shifts the focus of design of IT systems from being tools for participation, collaboration, sharing and exchange of knowledge and experiences in the health care sector, to the management of data and information on health. This focus then leads to excluding knowledge of health care, which is not amenable to explicit representation, such as the knowledge of practice and knowledge of health care use, from the design process. In other words the impoverishment of IT systems lies in their limit to deal with the complexity and richness of the practical knowledge of health care professionals and personal knowledge of users of health care systems. The implication is that the very design of IT systems exclude human interpretation and mediation of information and knowledge in varying and overlapping social and cultural contexts, the very essence of health care provision and use.

The Observer article notes that "Just 16 per cent of British (public IT) projects are fully successful, while others put the success rate even lower. This contrasts poorly with the US - where the success rate has doubled to 34 per cent over the last decade - and with the rest of Europe. The UK seems uniquely uncommitted to finding ways of improving". This lament shows the impoverishment of the techno-centric focus of complex public IT systems even on technical grounds of their design, let alone in their use in complex professional and social environments. The article further notes that large public IT projects such as the e-government project are based on " ..the self evident assumption that it (the IT system) is 'a good thing', with little evidence of benefit or payback. On a smaller scale, central specification of everything from call centres to document processing technology similarly assumes that IT is the answer - often before the real question has been identified".

5 The Problem with the Technical Solution

The faith in the 'IT as the answer' lies, in essence, in the faith in the techno-centric view of the world, in the sense that all systems can be seen as 'cause and effect' systems. In this view the technological systems should exhibit three scientific characteristics - they should be quantifiable, consistent and offer 'one best solution'. The argument then is that since health care IT systems need to be judged by this scientific criteria, their design and implementation should obey these criteria. Moreover being a national IT health system also requires consistency, transparency and universality of its use irrespective of the use context. This world view of technological systems leads to:

* Reducing the conception of health care systems to fit the technological conception of these systems

* Reducing health care knowledge to explicit, objectified and rule based knowledge to fit the criteria of consistency and certainty of the technical system

* Excluding the tacit dimension of knowledge (experiential and personal) which cannot be reduced to explicit form

* Excluding those aspects of personal knowledge and experiences (of the professionals, carers and users), as well as social and cultural contexts of health care provision and use which cannot be reduced to its mechanistic and explicit form

The consequence of this reduction is that health care knowledge is seen in terms of reducing it to data and information, in a computable form which is consistent and measurable. Thus IT based health systems are seen as another form of information systems, thereby seeing health care provision as provision of information and data to fit any use context. The implication is that the health system is then perceived as another information management system, focusing on the management of information rather than its use in varying and often uncertain and conflicting use contexts and user environments.

This technical prescription of health systems means that knowledge of health care practice and use remains either excluded from the design and evaluation of systems or at best reduced to data and information in a form that is factual, explicit, consistent, quantifiable, and amenable to computation. In other words, however complex IT systems may be from the technical perspective, they cannot deal with the complexity and richness of the social, cultural, economic contexts of health care provision, without human interfaces and human involvement, both in the design and use loops of the system.

The research challenge is to fill the gap between the technical vision of the health system and the social vision of health care systems.

5.1 Conceptual Gap

This gap essentially resides in our conceptualising of the health care knowledge system. The diagram (Fig.2) illustrates that health care knowledge varies from the tacit dimension of personal knowledge and experiential knowledge (practice based) to the objectified dimension (factual and rule based medical knowledge). In addition to this, the tacit dimension also includes the contextual (personal, social and cultural) knowledge which can only be subsidiarily known in the sense that we are aware of this knowledge only when we know the people who either have personal experience of the situation under consideration or they know other people who have similar personal experiences. In other words this knowledge is outside our own personal and experiential knowledge but we become aware of it when we get involved in the personal and community networks and meet people who have similar personal experiences.

For simplicity in the diagram (Fig.2), the knowledge of the medical model of health is seen to be rooted in the cognitive dimension and is thus represented by the factual knowledge (explicit knowing); the social model of health is seen to be rooted in the practice based dimension, and is thus represented by the experiential and personal knowledge (tacit knowing). Outside these three overlapping interacting knowledge domains (explicit, experiential, personal), we may also become aware of personal or experiential knowledge of others from our informal contacts and networking with them. In this perspective, the conceptual gaps between the medical model of health, practice based model of health, and community model of health, are mirrored by the knowledge gaps between the explicit knowing, practice based knowing, personal and subsidiary knowing. It is the awareness and understanding of these conceptual gaps that helps us to seek collaboration and interfacing between these models of health care. While evidence based practice is showing the way forward to bridge the gaps between the medical and social models of health care, there is still very little interfacing between these models and personal knowledge of users and still very little interfacing with the subsidiary knowing of health care experiences.The research challenge here is to develop a conceptual framework of health care, which finds a symbiotic relationship between the medical, practice based, personal and subsidiarily conceptions of health care provision.

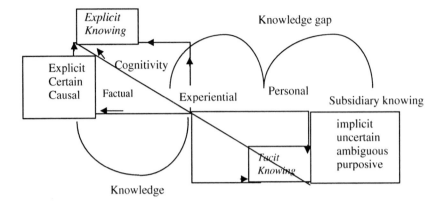

Fig 2 Shows conceptual gaps between the explicit knowing (cognitive model), experiential knowing (practice based model), personal knowing (personal experiences) and subsidiarily knowing (knowing by association with outside social/personal/cultural contexts)

5.2 Design Gap

The conception of IT health systems as information management systems leads to design, which separates the tacit from the objective, the social from the practical, and the practical from the cognitive conceptions knowledge. This conceptual formulation further leads to the separation between the systems design and system use, thereby excluding the practitioner and the user from the design process. The design of a complex health care system is thus reduced to the design of a technical system for information management. The consequence is that the design process itself excludes those practical and experiential components of health care systems, which are core elements for any purposeful and effective interfacing between the medical profession, health care professionals, carers and users of health services. The diagram (Fig.3) provides a symbiotic model of systems design, cultivating commonality of purpose and action through collaboration between the objective (factual, explicit and quantifiable) and the tacit (personal, experiential). It is the symbiotic space which provides a model for human-machine interface design for complex human and technological systems. It is worth noting that even this symbiotic interface is not sufficient to facilitate interaction and communication of the 'objective' and the 'tacit' with the subsidiary domain. One of the ways to achieve this interaction is through networking of the subsidiary domain to the other two knowledge domains. Thus a human centred design approach should incorporate human networking (for example outreach, mediation, user facilitation) in the design process.

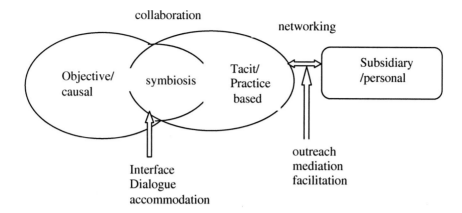

Fig 3 illustrates the evolving symbiotic space between the tacit /practice based knowl-edge(social model) and objective/causal knowledge (medical model), through collaboration. It also illustrates the possible communication of the subsidiary knowledge (outreach community) with the social model though networking and mediation.

The research challenge here is to cultivate a design culture which seeks to design machines with purpose, facilitating collaboration between the human and techno-logical systems, rather than designing 'causal' machines which seek to eliminate human involvement from the design process.

5.3 Methodological Gap

Both the conception and design focus of the health system as a causal machine for information management, fit neatly into the systems analysis methodology of sys-tems development. This linear methodology reduces the holistic health care system into measurable and quantifiable components arranged in a hierarchical order, seek-ing the 'one best solution'. The consequence is that the 'one best solution' excludes many of other equally feasible alternatives, which may provide the most purposeful and appropriate solutions. Moreover this 'best solution' may not be appropriate to many user contexts. The argument in favour of the 'one best solution' and in many cases 'the best practice' approach from the public policy perspective is that they pro-vide a consistency of data and information transactions, and thereby measurable performance for public accountability. However, it should be recognised that this view can only be valid in so far as the management of data and information is con-cerned; it leaves a gap between the use of service and management of information. Since this gap is situated in the professional practice of health care provision, as well as in the personal and social use of the health service, this gap is not amenable to technical consistency and quantitative measurement, and can only be bridged by the human interface.

The research challenge is develop a holistic (systemic) and participatory approach to the development of IT health systems, which involve the human loop at all levels of the system development.

5.4 Application Gap

While the conceptual gap can be regarded as a first order gap between the techno-centric system and the human-centred systems, the design and the methodological gaps can be considered as the second and third order gaps. These gaps are further widened when IT health systems are used in practice at various levels and layers of its application. For example there already exists a chain of knowledge and interaction gaps between the patient and the health care chain represented by the general practitioner; primary and public health carers, voluntary sector and community groups on the one hand, and the medical sector on the other hand. In addition to these gaps there also exist gaps between this health care chain and the vast majority of patient users of the NHS who do not belong to any of the special interest groups involved in the health care system. If the IT system is superimposed on this health chain, the interaction remains at the technical (data and information transaction) levels, thereby excluding interaction at the personal and experiential levels, and consequently widening these gaps much further in the health care chain. This widening of gaps leads to further increasing the break downs in health care services, which in turn are likely to lead to exclusion of many more users who are not within or associated with the formal health care chain (such as people living with mental, psychological, poverty, homeless and social problems as well as their carers), especially as these are the very excluded people most in need of these services. The breakdown and exclusion of health care provision essentially lies in our conception of the medical model of health (e.g. rule bound, explicit and consistent) and the social model of health (e.g. rule following, experiential, distributive). This conception marginalises even those primary and public health care sectors, voluntary and community networks who are concerned with the welfare of users of health, let alone the users and their home carers.

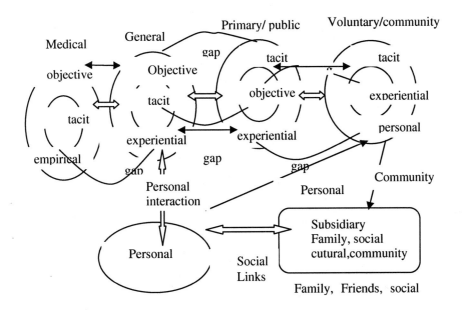

Fig.4 shows communication and knowledge gaps between various levels of health care system; illustrating knowledge gaps arising from the gaps between the objective, empirical, experiential, personal and subsidiary knowledge as well as arising from the gaps in interaction and personal and social links. For example the knowledge gap between the Medical and General practice; between the General practice and Primary/public health; between the public health/ voluntary/community groups involved in health care; links between the user of health and General practice; user and voluntary/community groups, and between (mediation/transfer) and breakdown of communication between the objective/cognitive dominated knowledge base (medical model) and the tacit (experiential/personal) dominated knowledge base of social model of health care

The diagram (Fig.4) illustrates the knowledge and interaction gaps between the medical model of health and the chain of the social model of health. Here we see that the practice of the medical model (medical/general practice) is rooted in the objectivity of knowledge, complemented by empirical and experiential knowledge. However, in this practice, objective knowledge forms the main gateway for outside interaction, while the tacit knowledge residing in the person of the medical practitioner is not amenable to outside interaction and even if it becomes available then it can be interacted by only going though the formal gateway of the objective. In other words this interaction should be seen as objective and scientific. On the other hand the social model is located in practice and therefore in the tacit dimension, complemented by the objective knowledge arising from the practice as well as interaction with the medical model. The interaction of the social model with the outside world takes place through the tacit dimension (experiential and personal knowledge). We see in this representation that interaction between the objective-objective and between the tacit-tacit in these models can take place through direct communication or through mediation. However communication between the tacit-objective domains gives rise to gaps and consequently to breakdowns as the gaps between the objective and the tacit becomes unbridgeable. In this perspective, the objective knowledge of the medical practice may not be accessible to the personal experience of the users and carers of health including the primary/public health and voluntary/community groups. In these cases the knowledge mismatch (due to knowledge gaps) leads to breakdown in communication.

The research challenge is to develop interfaces which bridge the gap between the objective (scientific) knowledge of the medical practice and the tacit (experiential and personal) knowledge of the health carers in the health care and welfare chain.

6 Conceptualising the User Interface

What are the limits of observation for the conception of the user interface? By focusing on observed reality, we limit our interaction to only one part of our observation context, thereby excluding the other part, which lies in the actuality space, the living space of our interaction. Moreover the observation may be further limited by our own limits as observers. This implies that our conceptualisation of the interaction space and therefore the conception of interface is bounded by the objectified reality. In other words the conception of the user interface accepts the separation between reality and actuality of our interaction spaces.

Here we see this separation between reality and actuality as being synonymous with the separation between the objective and the tacit domains of cultural interaction. This leads to conceptualising of interaction tools and interfaces which can only deal with first order interactions (based on observed data) and are too limited to deal with the second order interactions arising from the impact of the first order interactions, and third order interactions arising from the cumulative impact of first and second order interactions. Consider an example of the national health care system in the UK, where a patient interacts with the consultant, with the family doctor, with the community health carers, and with family and friends in different roles and in different contexts. In its simplest form of interaction, the consultant may see the patient with the objective eye (e.g. objective observations, experimental data); the family doctor with both the objective eye (e.g. patient records) and from a personal perspective (e.g. personal observations); the community health carers from functional (e.g. personal observations) and social (social contacts) perspectives; and family and friends from the personal, social, cultural perspectives. Considering culture in its broader scope (e.g. organisational culture), we can term this interaction space as a form of 'cultural holon'. We see that even in this simple interaction space, interaction takes place at different levels in diverse contexts. If the interface between the patient and others in this space is perceived only in terms of the objective reality (e.g. patient records), then we exclude the personal, social, cultural knowledge and experiences of the interaction space. This conception of the interface gives rise to a first order gap of rationality (conceptual gap) between what is termed 'actuality' (the experiencing that draws on past, present, and expectations of future) and 'reality' (the observed present). The second order gap of rationality arises from the design competency - gap between the conception and the model. The third order gap of rationality of design is technical competency, the application gap. The cumulative affect of these gaps is that it can lead to the severe breakdown and disruptions of interaction.

The tragedy of this breakdown is that the designers of the interface may not even be aware of the existence of such interfacing gaps, and they may come to blame the frailty of the human rather than recognize the limitations of the observed reality. The consequence of this conceptualisation is that it leads to designing systems and tools in the 'one best way' method rooted in the scientific rationality of 'cause and effect'. We can say this one best way conception can neither see nor hear the user of health care services (e.g. the patient and those interacting with the patient) within the holistic interaction space of reality-actuality. In other words we cannot know the user from the use context. To overcome the limitations of this one best way model of the interface, we propose a human-centred vision of the interface which is cultivated in the notion of the interdependence between the reality and the actuality. This vision forms the core of the notion of the 'symbiosis'. The symbiosis here seeks an interdependent relationship between the personal, social and cultural roles (tacit dimension) and the functional (objective) roles of the user. The notion of the symbiotic interface is thereby perceived as the "between-ness" interaction between the reality (objective world) and the actuality (tacit, practice).

7 Rethinking the Interaction Architecture

Consider a complex societal system such as UK National Health as a cross-cultural system (recognising culture in its broader socio-economic and institutional cultural sense). To illustrate the nature and complexity of the cross-cultural interaction in such a complex system, we consider exemplar models of cultural holons (Fig.1), ranging from the one-one interaction in a Linear Holon; dialogical interaction in the 'Trinity' Holon, and to interlocution in the 'Dragon' Holon. The idea of the cultural holon is that just as the model of reality is used to represent the environment as it is observed and experienced, so a cultural holon can be used as a model to represent the architecture of a culture as it is observed in interaction. Here cultural holon is seen as one of the many possible ways of modelling and representing cultural architectures. The holon here represents the interconnectedness of relationships between and among the units and whole of the interaction architecture - a model of the interaction uni-verse (Koestler 1989). For example, the 'linear' holon represents the linear architecture, which can be said to exist in highly, individualised cultural architectures (e.g. techno-centric), but of course linear architectures can be found to exist or created in almost all cultures. The 'trinity' holon representing interaction between three nodes allows for mediation by the third node in case of disagreement or conflict between any two nodes within cultural holon. It can be regarded as the minimal interaction model of a democratic dialogue. For example, to reach a democratic agreement or consensus within the Trinity Holon as a whole, an agreement or a consensus must be reached. We see that as the complexity of cultural architecture increases, we need to build more and more complex interaction architectures in order to deal with the diversity of interaction.

To illustrate the complexity and problematics of interaction between the holonic architectures (Mathews 1995), let us consider the interaction between the Linear Holon and the Trinity Holon. One possible way is to deconstruct the Trinity Holon in three linear holons, thus creating three levels of interaction between the Linear Holon and three linear components of the Trinity Holon. This is possible only if we regard each of the three linear components of the Trinity Holon as independent linear holons. This implies that interaction between the nodes of each linear component is independent of the structural links and contextual relationships with other nodes and other components of the Trinity Holon. This is to say that the only way to construct interaction between the Linear Holon and the Trinity Holon (and for that matter any other more complex holon) is to reduce the complex structure of the Trinity Holon to the level of the Linear Holon. If we follow this reductionist logic to its own logical conclusion, then what we are implying is that interaction between different cultures can take place only if we either reduce the more complex cultural architectures to map onto the technological architectures of interaction, or we reduce both the cultural architectures to a common denominator, amenable to technological architecture. This reductionist logic so inherent in the techno-centric paradigm reduces culture to a technical artefact, thereby reducing cross-cultural interaction to a technical interface. It is therefore hardly surprising that the dominant presence of the techno-centric model of interaction rooted in the rationality of the 'one best way', propagates the technological convergence paradigm, and thereby leads to a belief in technological solutions of complex societal problems. If we continue to pursue this techno-centric path, the whole socio-economic and cultural developments may not be an exception to this technological logic.

Consider the implication of reducing complex interaction architectures (e.g. panchtantra, samurai and dragon) to a linear holonic architecture. If this model of interaction, promoting direct interaction at the individual levels (e.g. internet, virtual reality), becomes a dominant interface, then the issue is how sustainable this interaction architecture is? We note that the interaction in the linear holon can only be sustained if both the nodes are always actively engaged in interaction and there is no breakdown in communication between the nodes. Although the linear architecture may be regarded as the most cost effective architecture at a direct interactional level and most explicit form of individual interaction, it remains in danger of instability and breakdown without being continuously serviced at all costs. Since this architecture has no structural mechanism for third party mediation or intervention in case of uncertainty or conflict, it therefore lacks any room for coherence necessary for even functional interaction, let alone complex forms of social, cultural or cross-cultural interactions. We are already beginning to witness the social and cultural vulnerability inherent in the linear interactive network communication structures (e.g. internet) promoting direct communication between individuals without social filtering or cultural mediating structures. For example in the UK the mantra of electronic democracy is propagating the individual interaction with various facets of governance, under the guise of equal opportunity and individual responsibility. This linear model of governance is already beginning to impoverish and ultimately dismantle the very traditional social (e.g. family, voluntary and community groups) filters, which in the past facilitated social cohesion in the form of social mediation, pastoral care, social mentoring. The consequence is that already disadvantaged groups in society are being directed to interact with governance structures using internet, excluding and alienating further those who are already being excluded from the mainstream society without the support of social filtering. There thus lies an ethical dilemma of 'governance' of using technological architectures as they impact societies and cultures.

If we regard these holons as representative models of diverse cultural architectures, then the challenge is:

a) How to design interaction architectures (e.g. cognitive, social, cultural) that facilitate collaboration within and between cultural holons related to the above challenge of developing cross-cultural models of collaboration and knowledge architectures for human development.

b) How to design communication systems that facilitate interaction and collaboration within each cultural holon; between cultural holons, recognising that interaction within and between more complex cultural holons takes place at multiple levels of hierarchy, both horizontal and vertical.

8 Towards the Symbiotic Interface

The argument on actuality draws upon Uchiyama's recent work on "The Theory and Practice of Actuality" (Uchiyama 2003) and the notion of symbiosis draws on the human-centred traditions (Cooley 1991; Gill 1996; Rosenbrock 1990). In understanding the concept of actuality, Uchiyama notes that when we play and hear music being played, we not only hear what is being played but also use our past experiences of music and sounds as well as sounds we expect to create in future to hear the music as a 'whole'. In other words we hear music as a whole, in a sort of 'time, in which the 'past' and the future are always present (and absent) in the very "now" of notes which are being played. It is this notion of the music as 'whole', which according to Uchiyama, resides 'between' real notes and us, in actuality. In clarifying the distinction between reality and actuality, Uchiyama draws upon the work of the eminent Japanese psychiatrist, Bin Kimura. Uchiyama notes that Kimura claimed that self exists in a duality of the real self and of the actual self. The 'real self' is a neomatic or 'experienced self' and the 'actual self' is neotic 'experiencing self'. In a healthy person, the real and the actual self progress in an interdependent way, drawing upon each other. However, in a schizophrenic, the actual self often becomes engulfed by the real self, leading to excessive self-reflection and disorder. It is this notion of the interdependence between the reality and the actuality, which is at the heart of the notion of the 'symbiosis' in this chapter. The notion of the symbiotic interface is also perceived as the "in-between" interaction, between the reality (objective world) and the actuality (tacit, practice).

Uchiyama draws a distinction between the way Western and Japanese participants comprehend situations. While the Western participant 'sees' the situation and relates to it as an objective observer, the Japanese participant "hears" the situation, and relates to it by feeling to be "in the situation". In the first case, the interaction between the observer and the situation is through information, and in the second case the interaction is through language. In the human-centred tradition, we call the 'information'-oriented perspective of comprehension as the 'techno-centred' paradigm of technology design and the 'language'-oriented perspective as the 'human-centred' paradigm of technology design. In the techno-centric paradigm, the situation is modelled as an explicit representation of the observed reality, and this model of simulated reality is used to design interfacing technologies. Since the model in this case is the same as the reality in the factual (data) sense, there is no gap between the two realities, and hence there is not much scope of learning, either of learning by cognition or learning by doing. In the human-centred paradigm, the situation is modelled as a symbiosis between the reality (objective) and the actuality (tacit). It is this symbiosis, which provides the "between-ness" framework for designing interfacing architectures. Drawing upon work on dialogical modelling and the definition of knowledge in terms of the objective, personal and experiential (Gill, SP, 1995), the 'tacit' is seen here as the inter-relationship between the 'personal' (feeling/experiencing) and 'experiential' (collective experience/practice).

The tacit provides a conceptual handle to articulate interdependent (symbiotic) relationships between the 'personal', the 'experiential' and the objective. It can be argued that part of the 'personal' knowledge can become part of the 'experiential' dimension over time during the process of participation in a group, and that part of the 'experiential' knowledge can become absorbed into the 'objective' dimension over time through the process of collaboration. Following the similar argument, it is proposed that part of the 'objective' knowledge can also be transferred to the 'experiential' domain, and part of the 'experiential' knowledge to the 'personal' domain. It is further proposed that this symbiotic idea of transference between 'personal' 'experiential' and the 'objective' provides an insightful framework for designing interfacing architectures for 'in-between' interactions. It is this symbiotic notion of transference and 'between-ness', which provides an interdependent relationship between cognition and action, and thus the core concept of interfacing and collaboration. In summary, the essence of the argument here is that the notion of symbiosis provides a conceptual basis to design interfacing architectures for the 'in-between' interactions. Thus in seeking interdependence between the reality and actuality, between the objective and the tacit, the 'symbiosis' provides a conceptual tool to find coherence between diversities, ambiguities and uncertainties of the human situations.

9 The User and User Interface

From the discussion above, it can be argued that the model of reality (observed/explicated) can only be weakly applied to the interaction and interfacing domains in the world of the actuality (practice). This argument is based on the proposition that in comprehending reality, we first construct a model, which represents facts as we observe them, and then use this model to design technology. However, in comprehending actuality, we experience actuality as it is practiced and experienced from within. The model of actuality thus represents the practice (tacit dimension). In other words the conceptual gap (between-ness) between reality (experienced) and actuality (experiencing), is further widened by models of their representations. We therefore need to cultivate a design culture, which overcomes the conceptual limit (due to "between-ness) and cultural errors (due to the focus on the "one best way") of the techno-centric model. This requires rethinking of the interfacing architecture for user interaction. Basically the interface architecture can be defined in the following terms (Gill 2002, 2006):

  a) Interface between the machine (reality) and the machine (reality);
  b) Interface between the human (actuality) and the machine (reality);
  c) Interface between the human and the human

where reality is defined as an objectified/explicit representation of the situation and the 'actuality' as the experience in and of the situation. The interface then is "in-between" interaction between situations.

The predominant view of interfacing tools tends to perceive the designer as the modeller of reality, and the user in terms of the user model (representation of reality). In this sense, both the designer and the user are seen as the constituents of the same reality. The argument is that since reality can be objectified and represented as a technical model, so the designer and user can also be seen as integral components of the same technical model. It is this convergence of the designer and the user in the technical realm which fails to recognise the 'between-ness" of reality and actuality, of the object and practice, and of the objective and the tacit. In this scenario we find that the interfacing (collaborating) technology design remains essentially concerned with the interface between the machine and the machine in the sense of objectified reality like (collapses into a above). It is this exclusion of the human situation (actuality) from technology design which leads to a growing concern about the place and role of the user and user communities in the debates on collaborating technologies or more properly on technologies for collaboration. For example, the information technologist may perceive the user in terms of research into human-computer interaction, the focus of the cognitive technologist may be on the cognitive models of mind, and AI scientist may regard the user in terms of knowledge mining. In a similar fashion, the philosopher may focus on the ethical dimension of the user, the sociologist on the societal dimension, the anthropologist on the cultural dimension, the engineer on the human-computer collaboration, the management scientist on knowledge management. At the same time an inter-disciplinary researcher and cross-disciplinary practitioner involved in the study of the impact of the convergence of digital technologies may see the user in terms of many social, cultural, functional and abstract roles depending upon the contexts of both the user and user interaction.

10 The User and the Actuality - Reality Gap

We can deduce from the above argument that while technical systems can be designed for interaction within the domain of actuality, we need to design human-centred systems (symbiosis between humans and technology) for interaction within the domain of actuality. In other words our faith in the technical solutions for designing user interfaces is misplaced, and we need to focus on the design of interfaces, which seek symbiotic relationship between user spaces. We therefore need to cultivate a culture of design, which overcomes the conceptual limit of reality and seeks a continuum of interaction within, between and across user spaces of interaction.

The important issue here is to recognise that conceptualising societal interaction within a particular practice (actuality) can become limited by the techno-centric model of reality. While the actuality is rooted in the past experiences and is shaped by the present reality and future possibilities, the reality is defined by the observable facts and data as of "now", the present. In an attempt to model the user interface, the designer is limited to objectifying the situation as 'observed', thereby excluding many of the possibilities of the situation as 'being observed'. We thus see a further widening of the 'actuality gap' arising from the gaps between the actuality and reality of the both the user and the designer. For example in addition to the actuality gap, our interaction experiences within our social space, especially the tacit dimension, are 'transparent' to us most of the time, while they may remain hidden to users from other contexts, thereby limiting the inclusive conception of the user interaction from a cross-user perspective. Because of the actuality-reality gap, the rich interaction experiences resulting from social and cultural contexts of users, remain excluded form design of the techno-centric systems and technologies. It is this exclusion of the 'tacit' dimension of the actuality, which limits the design of creative and imaginative applications of experiential knowledge as a learning process, and thereby impoverishes the ability of a society to shaping a holistic agenda for the knowledge society. The challenge therefore is to rethink about the appropriateness of the 'reality-centric' agenda as the dominant driving force of human development, and develop strategies and processes to mitigate its impact through societal concepts associated with actuality such as diversity, human purpose, participation, equality, social responsibility, ethics, and creativity. One way to move forward is to conceptualise knowledge in its many multifaceted roles, while recognising it is the interdependence between reality and actuality which facilitates the production, use, reproduction and creation of knowledge.

11 Valorisation of interaction spaces

In the overlapping and interlinking networked world, there is a need to create a dynamics of local-global interaction spaces in which (Gill 2002, 2006):

a) The user (self) interacts with the other user (other), and in the process they create a shared interaction space (symbiotic space), while remaining located in their own local spaces (Fig.5). It is assumed that both the local spaces belong to the same cultural space

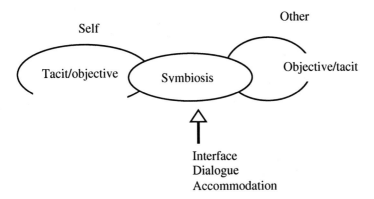

Fig 5. The evolving symbiotic space through the symbiosis between the local (tacit) and global (objective), seeking a common space of interaction within a context.

b) The user (self) belonging to interaction space A (Reality A) and the 'other' belonging to the 'other' interaction space (Reality B), create a new third interaction space (Reality C), 'space of the artificial' in order to valorise their differences and reach a common understanding. In this scenario, the common space of the artificial (Fig. 6) is evolved for seeking a common purpose, while retaining own cultural identifies rooted in local interaction spaces. This model of the space of the artificial could be adopted to create future common interaction spaces (culture of the artificial space) for interaction and collaboration of cultural holons.

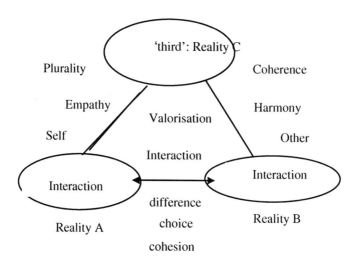

Fig 6. The creation of the space of the artificial, the third reality (common ground), for cross-cultural understanding and common purpose, created by valorization of two different realities.

In the symbiotic space (Fig.5), the objective knowledge of both the local spaces can be harmonised to form part of the common interaction space. As a result of the ongoing interaction, parts of the tacit knowledge of both the users become part of the shared knowledge, thereby becoming part of the evolving symbiotic space. At the same time part of the tacit knowledge of the users becomes part of the shared experience and ultimately part of the objectified knowledge over time, thereby expanding the objective knowledge space. Similarly the process of sharing of knowledge experiences leads to gaining new experiences in both the interaction spaces, thereby expanding the experiential (tacit) knowledge of each of the user spaces. In this scenario of a dynamic symbiotic space, both the experiential knowledge and the objective knowledge spaces expand and thereby enrich interaction.

In the space of the artificial (Fig.6), we envision a scenario in which users from two different interaction (cultural) spaces (Reality A and Reality B) come together, creating a new 'third' reality C, the space of the artificial, or culture of the artificial' (Negrotti (1999). This can be seen as finding a symbiosis of two realities (cultures) that provides a common interaction space for common purpose and mutual understanding. This 'third' culture, an artificially created cultural space, that is initially created for bringing two cultures together in a harmonious relationship, slowly takes the shape of a new 'third' cultural space. Here conflicts can be shared and resolved while respecting the diverse identities and divergences of two cultures. This 'third' cultural space enriches both the artificial (which may also be called 'virtual') cultural space and the cultural spaces (realities) of the users. In this scenario, cultural realities can be seen to be valorised through shared interaction. This 'third' reality (space of the artificial) may also be called the 'valorised reality'. The notion of valorisation emphasises making 'the best' of the differences during the process of reaching an agreement, a common purpose, or finding a common ground. Valorisation thus enables the processes of seeking cohesion of diversities (e.g. social, economic, cultural) while recognising and respecting differences. For example, in collaborating situations, participants from diverse cultures may create a new different cultural space (culture of the artificial space) in which they engage in dialogue and interlocution in finding a common ground of their differences, while at the same retaining their unresolved difference (identities) to themselves (i.e. located in the own cultural spaces). This process of 'valorisation allows for continuous enhancing of cross-cultural collaborating (or engagement) spaces while at the same enriching the own cultural horizons of participants.

This valorised cultural horizon enables us to extend the concept of 'interface' from the realm of the 'separation' between the reality and the actuality, to the symbiotic realm in which diverse cultural realities collaborate, by pooling together their praxes, experiences, knowledges and cultural resources, thereby enhancing both their objective capacities and tacit capabilities. In this perspective, the symbiosis represents the possibilities, choices and alternative paths available to human societies. This perspective of 'valorised reality' respects plurality of cultures, and seeks coherence through empathy and harmony. 'Culture of the artificial' in the sense of the transfiguration of reality (Negrotti 1999) provides a methodological handle for shaping and building of artificial landscapes by bridging the gaps between "actuality" and "reality", mediated by the human-machine symbiotic interface. The interface is viewed here as the medium for supporting communication and dialogue between and within overlapping human and virtual networks.

12 Summary

Seeing the user as an individual and a member of the group, community and society throws up a question how to conceptualise the user and the users activity contexts when designing user interfaces. If the user and the user context are perceived in terms of objectified reality, then the question is how to deal with actuality of the user and the observed (reality) use contexts which are not amenable to observed (objectified) reality. We thus encounter a problem of the gaps arising from the separation of the observed reality from the experienced actuality of user interactions.

This conception of the user within the realm of observed reality, leads to designing user interaction systems and interfacing tools, which can deal only with the first order interactions. This excludes the second order interaction (gaps between actuality and reality of the user) and third order user interactions (the actuality-reality gaps between the users from different cultural contexts). It is proposed that the way forward to deal with the actuality-reality gaps is to conceptualise the user within a symbiotic interaction space in which user interactions cover the continuum of the user interaction space defined by the multiplicity of the social, functional and cultural roles of the user.

The notion of symbiosis enables interaction in the in-between (actuality-reality gap) space. The notion of the user as a cultural holon, provides a way to perceive the user interaction in both the reality and actuality. The coupling of these notions thus provides a conceptual framework for designing symbiotic interfaces for users within the same interaction space, between different interaction spaces, and in-between interaction spaces.

The notion of the 'culture of the artificial' provides a conceptual basis to create a virtual interaction space (we term it the third cultural interaction space). This virtual space provides for evolving a shared interaction space for users belonging to two separate cultural interaction spaces, while allowing the users to interact in their own cultural specific spaces. We term this conceptualisation as the 'valorisation' of cultural interactions.

In this chapter we propose a network architecture of user interactions at various levels of interaction, 'linear' holonic structure dealing with interaction between two users, 'trinity' holon dealing with interactions between three different user interaction spaces, the 'panchtantra' holon dealing with five different spaces, 'samurai' holon dealing with seven different spaces, and 'dragon' holon dealing with nine different interaction spaces.

The proposed network structure allows for pooling of the concepts of symbiosis, holon, and the culture of the artificial, provides a cultural interaction architecture for designing user interfaces.

References

AI & Society; Journal of human-centred systems and machine intelligence, Springer-Verlag.

Caulkin, S (2005), "Why IT just doesn't compute", Business Section, Sunday Observer, 2 May 2004

eEurope 2005 Action Plan for Health, http://europa.eu.int/information_society/eeurope/ehealth/index_en.htm

Castells, M (1996), The rise of the networked society, Blackwells Publishers Ltd. Oxford

Cooley, M.J. (1987), Architect or Bee? Hogarth Press, London

Gill, K. S. (ed. 1996), Human machine symbiosis, Springer, London, 1996

Gill, K S (2002), the user in the emerging space of the digital provide, Proceedings of the Conference on" The User's Models in the Advanced Society", Venice University IUAV (Venice University Institute of Architecture) 18 -19 November 2002

Gill, K S (2006), The dance of the user in the artificial cultural space, in Negrotti M & Sato-fuka F (eds.), Yearbook of the artificial, Peter Lang, Bern

Gill, S P (1995), Dialogue and tacit knowledge for knowledge transfer, PhD Dissertation, University of Cambridge

Koestler, A, (1989), The ghost in the machine, Arkana, 1989

Mathews, J, (1995), Holonic organisational architectures, in Human Systems Management Vol.15

Negrotti, M (1999), The Theory of the artificial, Intellect Books, 1999

Rosenbrock, H. H. (1990), Machines with a Purpose, OUP

Uchiyama, K (2003), The theory and practice of actuality, Institute of Business research, Daito Bunka University, 1-91- Takashimadaira Itabashi Tokyo Japan 175-8571

AI & Soc (2000) 14:268–299
© 2000 Springer-Verlag London Limited

Towards a General Theory of the Artificial

Massimo Negrotti
IMES, University of Urbino, Urbino, Italy

1. The Icarus Syndrome

When Icarus, according to classical mythology, fell near Samo due to the melting of the wax which fixed his wings, he probably repented bitterly for not having followed the suggestion of his father, Daedalus, who put him on his guard against approaching the sun too closely. While a bird, in a similar circumstance, perhaps would have got nothing but some burn and would soon have gone down to more reasonable height, the artificial wings of Icarus did not stand the test and he suddenly died.

On the other hand, we know that Omerus, in the *Iliad*, tells us of the god Efesto, who created the first woman, Pandora, from clay; that Plato speaks us of the self-moving statue built by Daedalus himself; that the Argonauts, the famous hunters of the Golden Fleece, had at their disposal an artificial watchdog.

Furthermore, automata – reproductions of human beings very different from each other in their stuff – abounded throughout the history of human imagination, starting with the Bible up to Faust and to the RUR (*Rezon's Universal Robot*) of Capek.

It would surely be very easy to discover, case by case, the weak points of each "machine" quoted above, but what is interesting, first of all, is another question: what kind of relationship exists between these attempts to imitate nature and the technology of whatever time? In other words, is technology intrinsically intended to reproduce something existing in nature or is it developed for other targets too? After all, it is the same as we would ask ourselves: did man create technology only for reproducing nature?

A simple glance at the history of technology is enough to understand that man, designing and building objects, processes or machines, is often motivated by imitation ambitions, but, in many other cases, he aims at controlling and at dominating natural events, by means of more or less refined expedients, rather than at reproducing them. As was maintained by the mathematician Henry de Monantheuil in the sixteenth century, "... man, being God's image, was invited to imitate him as a mechanician and to produce objects which could cope with those made by nature".

In order to control natural events one needs to know them and, according to the accuracy of knowledge, we shall have technologies more or less effective, but not necessarily oriented to imitate the phenomena in question. Rather, such kinds of technologies will be able to adapt themselves to nature and to exploit its features to achieve some useful target.

Thus, the knowledge of some physical laws allows us to build machines which, like electrical or internal combustion engines, amplify our capacity for physical movement; the advent of writing induced the invention of a lot of writing tools which, today, are highly advanced thanks to computer technology; the knowledge and exploitation of other natural laws made possible the ideation, and then the construction, of systems which, like the cathode ray tube, allow the display of graphs, images, etc.

In all these examples, and in the many more which one could add, no imitation aim exists, but, rather, they exhibit an invention aim intended to make possible behaviours, effects and events which, on the basis of our pure and simple natural condition, would not be attemptable.

To sum up, close to Icarus – and to all his descendants who, up to now, constitute the world of the *artificialists* – stands out the figure of Prometheus, who, giving fire to man, rouses his invention strength, that is to say the ability to establish construction targets of objects or processes, as it were, additional and therefore heterogeneous as compared to those existing in nature.

As we know, even in doing so, unfortunately man generated dangers and disasters: Prometheus himself was the first to pay, with a tremendous torture for having taken possession of fire, which was a prerogative of the gods. Nevertheless, to imitate and to invent are two circumstances and actions different from each other, and they require analyses which are likewise different.

In the following pages, we shall aim at investigating and outlining some fundamental aspects of the first of the above technologies, namely the *technology of the artificial*. It will be conceptually separated from the second one, which we shall define as *conventional technology*, because of the fact that, unlike the latter, the former, implicitly or explicitly, assumes as its own objective: the reproduction of something existing in nature.

It is a matter of this distinction that, though it is a fact, has never been clearly defined, but it is also a matter of a separation which is very useful for trying to understand rationally a wide series of phenomena which are not just technological.

We may consider, in fact, that to imitate and to invent – that is to say, the basic human dispositions which generate respectively the technology of the artificial and conventional technology – are human turns which, on a social and cultural level, give rise to very different classes of behaviours and of activities. Imitation, for instance, exhibits a range of expressions which range from the socialisations of children to fashion phenomena, up to the spreading of cultural models (scientific, technological, ethical, religious, juridical, etc.).

Invention, in turn, reveals itself in innovative social behaviours – which, when they succeed, will be imitated, as the French sociologist Gabriel Tarde explained a century ago – and also in various typologies of economic enterprises, in exploration activities and in the generation of new ideas.

Approaching the artificial we shall concentrate on that particular field of activities which, as we said, puts at its centre, on the basis of a more general imitation "instinct", the reproduction of something existing in nature, and whose reproduction – through alternate construction strategies as compared to the natural ones – man considers to be useful, appealing or anyway interesting.

2. The Concept of Artificial: Fiction and Reality

From a linguistic point of view, the term artificial (*artificiale* in Italian, *kunstlich* in German, *artificiel* in French) covers a definitely ambiguous area which should be clarified before we proceed. In all languages, this concept seems to indicate all which, generically, is "man-made" and, simultaneously, though more rarely, something which tries to imitate things existing in nature.

As will become clear, we prefer the latter version which, however, is not of general acceptance. Nevertheless, it is a fact that, while nobody would speak of an "artificial telephone", everybody understands quite well the meaning of the expression "artificial flower". Interpreting this situation appears to us a very easy affair: though it has been never rationally defined, the concept of artificial refers properly to an object, process or machine which aims at reproducing some natural object or process. Since in nature flowers but no telephones exist , the adjective "artificial" has no meaning if we attribute it to any object invented and built by man – that is to say, an "artefact" – while it assumes full meaning when it is finalised to reproduce a natural object.

The Italian linguists Devoto and Oli have correctly defined the artificial as an object obtained by means of technical expedients or procedures which *imitate* or replace the appearance, product or natural phenomenon. In parallel, the imitation component is defined by the same authors as the capacity to get or to pursue, according to some criterion, a more or less high appearance of likelihood. The ambiguous nature of the question emerges, however, from the definition of the adjective "feigned" which, according to Devoto and Oli, defines a product obtained *artificially*, as *imitation*.

Undoubtedly people, but also many animals, are familiar with the art of imitation and of fiction (but, by the way, who would have accepted, for instance, the expression "feigned intelligence" rather than "artificial intelligence"?). Anyway, the semantic weight of this feature on the concept of artificial seems to be definitely too high.

The *perspectiva artificialis* of Leon Battista Alberti and Piero della Francesca – but also the landscape paintings of the so-called Quadraturism born in the sixteenth century and which achieved success also in subsequent periods, for instance, with Andrea Pozzo and his vault in Saint Ignazio in Rome – may be defined as "feigned", but only if one is to understand by this expression something modelled or moulded by man, as implied by the original Latin verb *fingere*.

To sum up – as we shall see more analytically later – though in every artificial object the "cheating" or "illusory" component is present for definition, it does not exhaust its constitution.

Thus, as described by Pliny the Elder, in the competition between Zeus and Parrasio the former revealed himself so skilful in drawing bunches of grapes that the birds themselves were attracted by them; Parrasio, in turn, drew a sheet which seemed to cover a painting in such a realistic way that Zeus himself was cheated from it.

In the same way, as referred to by Nicholas Negroponte, adding realism to an artificial system may sometimes have very strong effects on man too. When in the 1970s one of the first teleconferencing systems was designed in order to make the emergency procedures of the American government more efficient, a device was added to it by means of which a moving plastic head indicated the person who was speaking at each moment, for instance the President. The result was that

... video recordings generated this way gave such a realistic reproduction of reality that an admiral told
me that those speaking heads caused him nightmares. (Negroponte, 1995: 123)

In the anecdote just quoted, and also in the former ones and, overall, in the great
intellectual work done in painting during the Renaissance, it is very clear that the
"cheating" and "illusory" component of the artificial, that is to say its "fiction", is
generated at levels different from each other and with seemingly diversified meanings.
In fact, while in the case of painting the fiction is openly intrinsic to the object, in
the case of the reproduction of the President's head referred by Negroponte it is a
secondary feature of the reproduction of his presence in acoustic terms.

The famous and despairing prayer of that great sculptor who asked of his work
"Why you don't speak?" reinforces this point and the definition itself of artificial
we are supporting here. Actually, the artificial, being an attempt to reproduce nature
"through different ways", is looking for likelihood, and, if it succeeds in that, cheats
just because it is a matter of likelihood and not of identity. Nevertheless, what is
important is not the cheat in itself but, indeed, the accuracy of reproduction in the
eyes of whoever has to use or adopt it.

In this sense, as was said to us by Prof. Willelm Kolff – one of the most important
artificialists of this century, who designed the first artificial kidney during the Second
World War and who works in the field of the artificial heart – an artificial heart
tends to "cheat nature" because the blood it pumps arrives at the organs concerned
"as if" it had arrived from the natural heart. Nobody, anyway, would reduce such a
device to a "feigned" heart.

The fact is that the fiction to which common language refers is usually associated
with the artificial, thanks to some of its external or "aesthetic" appearance, like the
aspect we can perceive of theatrical scenery, the crying of a traditional doll, the
appearance of an architectural remaking by de Andrade or – but with greater prudence
because it is a matter of great art – the artificial perspective of a painting by Piero
della Francesca.

In conclusion, the term artificial implies always the work of man, his "art" in the
widest meaning, and the result cannot therefore be but to show traces of this origin:
not nature but technology, even here, in the widest sense of the word.

But this is only the *necessary* condition for speaking of something artificial. Any
artificial object, process or machine is such, in other words, because it is "man-
made", but not all that is man-made may properly be defined as artificial. In order to
be properly artificial, an object has to satisfy a second condition, namely a *sufficient*
one: that of being finalised to reproduce an object or a process existing in nature.
Even the definition of artificial as something which sets *against* the natural is upset
by the discussion we are carrying on. How would it be possible for the blood pumped
by an artificial heart to be used effectively by a natural organism if it were to come
from an object set against nature?

Rather, the opposite of the *natural* is the *conventional* artefact, that is to say the
product of conventional technology which, both in terms of material stuff and, above
all, of functions it has to accomplish, leaves nature out. Actually, a conventional
technology object only exploits some laws of nature, is subjected to natural constraints
and adds itself to natural classes of objects or anyway intervenes in the natural
world, intentionally trying to change it, sometimes giving rise to advantages and
sometimes problems of various kind but not similar to those generated by nature.

The artificial, on the contrary, cannot exist without something natural to which it refers or tries to reproduce. The artificial, in other words, has a sort of umbilical cord which links it to nature and, therefore, cannot leave it out or aim at changing it, at least in conceptual terms and of definitions, which is what we are discussing here.

3. "Copies" of Reality

Anyone having some familiarity with an electronic copier knows perfectly what we mean by the term "copy": the reproduction of a document or image from a page to another sheet of paper. The copy may be in black and white or in colour but, either way, it is nothing but a photograph, at a certain degree of resolution, of the original document.

On the contrary, if one doesn't have at his disposal such a machine nor has a camera but only a sheet of paper and a pencil, then one could "copy" the original text, make a summary of it or imitate the image, drawing a sketch of it just to give an idea of it, as we may say. If, we should have neither paper nor pencil, we could only try to memorise the relevant points of the text in question or the main traits of the image.

In all three cases, the original, after our work, remains what it was before. The only new reality will be that of the copy, of our sketch or of our memory. Furthermore, in all cases the new reality resulting from our action will reflect the materials and procedures we have adopted. The resolution of the copier, and its ink, will modify in some measure, particularly if it is a coloured ink, the aspect of the original document or image and, furthermore, in the case of an abstract of a text, our style and our choices in summarising the text or in sketching the image could even distort them.

In the third case, the "materials and procedures" we adopted will be coherent with our imitation dispositions, our memorisation abilities and related biases or habits we acquired in our experience. Nevertheless, if the original text were a mathematical or chemical formula or an analytical report on an event – that is to say, it was pure *information* – the likelihood of the copy, in terms of colours or drawing style, would be of little importance. As in the case of a train timetable, which could be written in very large characters on a wall or in very small ones in a brochure, also in the above cases the important thing is that, in the end, the original information is completely and accurately available. On the contrary, if our interest were just for the original as such, for instance for its papery, graphical or aesthetic style, then its information content would be less important. We could be tormented by the obsession, as it might be for collectors, to possess the original for its unrepeatable value, and no copy would give us sufficient satisfaction.

In other words, man can obtain copies of reality – that is to say, something identical to the original, and whose synonyms are duplication or replication – only if he has to deal with informational realities, like computer programs, but not concrete – apart from the case, which, however, concerns technological and not natural objects, of mass production where the prototype is reproduced by means of the same materials and procedures.

In the area of natural concrete objects – constituted by matter organised in whatever way – replication is possible only through natural methods and, of course, only where this is featured by nature itself, as in the case of biological cloning controlled by the DNA.

In every other area, man can only orient himself to the artificial. The artificial is not, therefore, a replication of reality, but a *reproduction*, that is to say a production oriented by a natural *exemplar*, by means of materials and procedures different from those nature uses. It has to be noted that the constraint of the materials and of procedures is not a simple foolish ambition, but an unavoidable condition. In fact, the reproduction of a natural object – let us think of a flower – through the same materials and procedures would mean falling into the class of replication, which, as we have seen, is impossible. Frankenstein, therefore, belongs to the realm of fantasy and not to that of bioengineering.

This doesn't mean, however, that man is not able to modify nature acting on its own elements. As in the case of genetic manipulation, for example – but even in the more traditional procedures of cross-breeding between animal or vegetable species – the recombination of fundamental structures of life is now within our capacity.

Nevertheless, all this has nothing to do with the artificial just because, in these activities, man places himself in nature and remains there distributing, rather like playing cards in ways not occurring in natural evolution.

In this sense, the understanding of the term artificial we are introducing here has to be separated from that – very diffused since Lucretius – according to which all is "artifice", because nature itself is able to achieve its own modifications, including those carried on by man. On the other hand, more recently the chemist Roald Hoffmann listed very effective reasons for persuading us that even the so-called natural cotton does not differ so much from other cloth generated by means of technology.

A typical field of Egyptian cotton receives several treatments with insecticides, herbicides, and chemical fertilizers. The fiber is separated from the seed (ginned), carded, spun into a yarn. For modern shirting, cotton is also treated in a variety of chemical baths, bleached, dyed. It may be "mercerized", strengthened by treatment with lye (sodium hydroxide). Optical brighteners or flame retardants might be added. Eventually the cotton is woven into cloth, cut, and sewn into a garment. It may be blended with another fiber for strength, comfort, or some other desirable property. That's an awful lot of manipulation by human beings and their tools, and to sharpen the point, manipulation by *chemicals*, synthetic and natural, going into your *natural* cotton shirt! (Hoffmann, 1997: 19–20)

These intellectual positions are quite acceptable, but, eventually, they are also largely reversible since one could maintain that, in the same way, all is natural because all is made from atoms and molecules. Such premises are of no help if one aims at understanding the possibilities, the limits and the consequences of human attempts to reproduce what he observes in the natural world; that is to say, the results of variously complex combinations of atoms and molecules already generated, in certain ways and not in others, by nature over millions of years.

The artificial, in our understanding, which is consistent with part of the historical use of this term, consists of the result of human intentional effort to pursue the same results of nature through strategies different from those nature follows, and, therefore, *lato sensu* technological. All this has nothing to do with, nor contradicts, the thesis which maintains, *at a higher level of analysis*, that all that happens in the universe is, by definition, internal to it and, therefore, natural (artificial included). Rather, even from this discussion it is possible to deduce that the artificial, if on the one hand it is debtor to nature since, without referring to it, it would have no sense, on the other is intrinsically intended to set up a new reality, a third reality made of technology inspired by nature.

In conclusion, it is reasonable to maintain that the artificial is always such as related to something which it is not and from which it draws its *raison d'être*. While nature is what it is, as it were, in absolute terms and conventional technology creates artefacts or processes more or less compatible with nature but, anyway, not present in it, the technology of the artificial generates objects, processes or machines surely technological, but "suggested" by nature. Therefore, at least ideally, the artificial should exhibit features which are not only compatible with nature but overlapping it in the most transparent way.

Conversely, as we may easily understand, a true technology of the artificial, as an autonomous body of knowledge, techniques and materials, does not exist nor is it plausible to think it could exist. Actually, intrinsically artificial materials or techniques do not exist: rather, there are and there will be natural materials recombined by man through techniques derived from conventional technology and, so to say, forced to reproduce some natural object or process. The artificialist cannot, in other terms, but exploit materials and procedures placed at his disposal by conventional technology. This is true for Icarus and the wax glue he adopted for connecting the wings to his body and for the alimentary canal of the famous duck by Jacques Vaucanson who, in the eighteenth century, became enthusiastic on hearing of the gum originating from the Indies since it appeared to him an ideal material for reproducing the internal tissues of his artificial animals.

The same is valid for current bioengineers who pay great attention to the findings coming from materials technology and from every other conventional technology, in order to find more and more suitable components for their projects of artificialisation of organic structures or processes.

The effort of the artificialist is and always will be, therefore, that of adopting materials and techniques developed by conventional technology, even asking directly some specific requests of technologists, for reproduction details of natural objects or processes.

In some measure, we are facing then a sort of paradox. Actually, on the one hand the artificial is something that, deliberately, is a function of nature which it aims at reproducing, but, on the other, it unavoidably depends on conventional technology, that is to say on a technology that, as we saw, does not set itself any reproduction target but, rather, builds objects, processes and machines which are heterogeneous as compared to nature. As a consequence, the artificial swings between nature and conventional technology without the possibility of completely overlapping either the former or the latter. In the former case, it would reduce itself to natural replication and, in the latter, it would go inexorably far from nature.

The destiny of the artificial, in whatever field it appears, cannot but bear marks of this paradoxical ambiguity which, as we shall see, is the primary logical cause of its vocation to establish itself as a *sui generis* reality.

4. The First Step Toward the Artificial: The Observation

The artificialist, that is to say the person who – engineer, artist or whatever else he could be – is attracted by the idea of reproducing something natural, is strongly characterised by a special way of living in the world.

First of all, he cannot but possess a developed disposition to observe nature, since it is just from it that he draws his working hints. Whosoever dedicates himself to the design of something artificial should be able to grasp those aspects of reality which are more likely to be reproduced, like a scientist who is sensitive to the curious or as yet unexplained aspects of what he observes or the artist who, in turn, concentrates on others who allow him to interpret them meaningfully.

Also the conventional technologist is closely related to nature and, therefore, to its observation, but his main aim is that of designing objects, processes or machines which are able to control or to modify natural events and not to reproduce them. Not uncommonly, the conventional technologist sees nature as an adversary, while the artificialist looks at nature as a project to achieve.

The four figures we have outlined below resort to four types or "styles" of observation which are present, in various measure, in every human being, but are extremely relevant, above all, in the cited professions. They are often interwoven—the figure of Leonardo is one of the best examples – but they possess their own qualities and features. For example, the evolution of the microscope was dependent, for its major improvement, on a casual observation made in the seventeenth century, when, in order to enhance its magnifying power it was assumed as exemplar of the spherical-convex shape of a drop of water. This fact was anticipated, without any subsequent development, in ancient times when it seems that spherical bottles full of water were used as magnifying tools.

The observation of the physicist or of the chemist would be concentrated, of course, on the way a drop of water forms, stabilises morphologically, or on its internal and external dynamics, while to he who was interested in improving the microscope it was relevant in terms of something natural to be reproduced. Thus, he was like a true artificialist, in the same way that Watson-Watt, the inventor of radar, drew inspiration, as is sometimes told, from the way bats detect obstacles during flight.

These two examples allow us, by the way, to underline an open truth: as technologists of the artificial always resort to conventional technology in order to realise their projects, likewise conventional technologists resort to the artificial in order to develop or to improve objects, processes or machines that, as such, do not have reproduction aims.

Anyway, it is clear that, to reproduce something, first of all one has to observe that thing and, as a consequence, observation is the first, unavoidable step every artificialist has to take.

But what does it mean to observe? As far as the observation process is concerned, its unavoidably "relative" status is a delicate point: for instance, everybody can observe the moon, but nobody can observe it in its entirety. A more relevant fact, but in another understanding of the term "relative", is that everybody can observe a landscape, but a geologist will observe it according to modalities different from those of an agronomist, a botanist or a painter.

The problem then becomes: what we observe is the reality or a part of it, an aspect, a profile which depends on the position we occupy in space or on our privileged dimension – perhaps as professionals.

In this work, we shall define an *observation level* as just the profile we observe the reality from. It is clear that the above-cited problem is of particular weight not only for philosophers but also for scientists and, in a very peculiar measure, for artificialists. When, for example, we design a human skeleton as an aid for teaching anatomy, which observation level do we assume? Usually, a plastic skeleton will not reach a molecular level or an atomic one but will place itself at the typical level of macroscopic anatomy. If we were to dissect the bones, in other words, we would not be able to observe the biological structures that constitute it in nature. On the other hand, even if an anatomy institute were to be very exigent and require that even the above biological structures were reproduced, though by means of materials different from the exemplar, soon a threshold would be reached beyond which one could not proceed, because of both our lack of knowledge and of the difficulties in rebuilding realistically the connections between the various levels.

In a different area, that of artificial intelligence, nobody could expect from a computer program able to reproduce the logical intelligence of a human being (e.g., the ability to perform correct deductions) that it would suddenly exhibit the capacity to compose poetry. Even intelligence, to sum up, can be observed and therefore described or modelled at different levels and it is intrinsically very difficult to take into account, simultaneously, more than one level.

For now, rather, we shall limit ourselves to maintaining that human beings are forced, by their own nature, to take into consideration only an observation level of a unit of time. We can move, even very quickly, from one level to another, but each time we shall modify rather radically the content of our observations, of our descriptions and of the judgments we make on what we observe. As we all know, a warm day can give happiness or, on the contrary, generate troubles according to the activity we may have planned for that day (a tour in the mountains or some chore), though it is, in itself, the same climatic circumstance.

5. Eyes and Mind: The Representations

The restriction of our observation capacities to one level only for a unit of time allows us to understand that the artificial which, at the end of the design and building process, will be achieved will in no way be the reproduction of the exemplar in its wholeness. This would be true, however, even if, deviating from the necessity to use materials and procedures different from those used by nature, we could adopt exactly the same. Though this case esulates from the field of the artificial properly said, even in the above circumstance we would be forced to use only those natural materials we would have observed and not, of course, those remaining hidden and detectable only at other levels. It is a matter, actually, of a truth very well known to all who try to reproduce some kind of fruit, flower or even their elementary derivative, by adopting the same seeds and the same procedures nature exhibits, but neglecting, or ignoring altogether, other components – like the composition of the air or the climatic dynamics – which make possible the development or production of the exemplars.

As we have already considered, the need, for definition, to use materials and procedures different from those characterising the natural exemplars introduces a decisive constraint which prevents the artificial from approaching the exemplars beyond certain thresholds.

Nevertheless, we have to clarify again some other points concerning the observation process. Very often, we argue that, in the end, we see what we "want to see", rather than the reality in its objective status. This is an issue that is well known to scientists of modern times, though in naive terms but relevant to the history of science, in their anxious, and often frustrating, search for instruments and procedures for surveying the reality "as it is". It should be enough to think of the following quotation of the founder of histology, the French scientist François Bichat, who, concerning the observation made possible by the microscope, said:

… it seems to me that this instrument is not of a great aid for us, because when men look in the dark, everybody sees it his own way. (Quoted in Galloni, 1993: 23)

Today, many philosophical doctrines deal with the process of observation in science, bringing to the extreme limit some positions that have regularly appeared in the history of thought for two thousand years, and maintain that reality doesn't exist at all, or, rather, its existence has no relevance to the moment we observe it. What is important, according to these doctrines, is our action of "constructing" the world, that is to say the disposition, of which we are slaves and masters at the same time, to give meaning to the world according to subjective premises or determined by the social culture we live in.

If we would accept completely such a position then we should deny any objective validity not only to our daily observation but also to those operated by scientists: all would be uncertain, subjective and incomprehensible. On the contrary, it is clear that, at least in the field of natural phenomena, at least those that can be precisely evaluated by means of instruments, nature has its own objective capacity to act on man, beginning with its actions on our senses – think of an earthquake. At this point, it isn't important that man himself constructs more or less founded interpretations of the event of which he was onlooker or protagonist.

If we refer to the constructivistic doctrines, it is only because they, at least, remind us of the fact that nature and its events, as we have already underlined, are not at our disposal in an "immediate" way. Our knowledge of the world is "mediated" by our mind, which enables us to form *representations* of reality. A representation is the mental reproduction of what we observe through our senses or we generate autonomously, for instance the image of a face or of a lake, but also our subjective description of the atom or of a continent, and even our "vision" of the universe or of God. For this reason, a representation is something "meta-artificial", something which preludes, as it were, the artificial: it is, in fact, a non-material construct which reproduces the world we observe and is definitely useful for surviving in it.

Without representations we would not be able to evaluate situations, to associate memories and observations: we could only rely, each time, on immediate reactions to reality like surely many animals do. Fire would burn us every time, because, within our mind, we would have no recorded notion of its features or of its effects. In practice, when we met fire we would not recognise it, and, in the same way, its symbol drawn on a wall – as a result of a collective representation – would have no meaning for us. Forming representations is a fact close to our perception and our observation and, at each level, corresponds to different classes of representation.

In forming representations the role of mind is not a passive one because, just like the choice of an observation level, the whole system of our experiences and our preferences, interests and fears acts on it. Culture itself is a powerful source of "directions" we should follow, or refuse, in observing reality and, therefore, in forming representations. For instance, the sociological or the psychological dimensions of man are today widely accepted as a reality, but it is a matter of a relatively recent fact.

Man always had, of course, what we today call a sociological or a psychological life, but the lack of representations, and then of models and theories which would appear only in the nineteenth century, specifically dedicated to these phenomena, prevented setting those dimensions as observation levels alternate to the daily, political or spiritual ones.

In the same way, as should be clear, it happened and happens permanently for many other observation levels: the subatomic or the ecological, the economical or the magnetic, the microbiological or the chemical, etc. Each of these levels is, simultaneously, cause and effect of representations which, almost referring to the same natural object or process, privilege only one profile, only one way to be or to present itself to the observer.

These considerations are true, more than ever, for all the arts. Perhaps for this reason Oscar Wilde maintained that art is nothing but a form of emphasis, of exaggeration of the reality we perceive. Though, since Aristotle, art has been assigned the role of imitating nature, *de facto* no artist can nor desire to generate copies of what he observes, but, rather, an interpretation of it according to his own poetics, that is to say to own representational modalities, or those of the school he belongs to.

The history of painting, for instance, exhibits a very wide landscape of pictorial observation levels which express very different representations: from the spirituality of the Middle Ages to the physicality of the Renaissance; from the vagueness of Impressionism to the complexity, often solipsistic, of the avant-garde.

It is through art that we can understand, by the way, to what extent mind and culture may sometimes be active protagonists in forming or in confirming many orders of representation. It should be enough to think, in the paintings of the Middle Ages, of the pictorial reproductions of God or of the devil – for instance, the chilling reproduction of the devil by Coppo di Marcovaldo in the Florence Baptistry. They demonstrate that, at the extreme limit, man is able to generate artificial objects starting from exemplars quite non-existent in nature, but, notwithstanding this, accurately represented in the cultural tradition. On the other hand, no different is how the current representation of the atom has become a true graphic symbol widely shared by scientists and lay people, with its analogy to the solar system; it is very far from being verified in its structure, in its dimensions and in its dynamics, though it is extremely useful and necessary in allowing research in the field of physics.

6. The Exemplar: Background and Foreground

As already stated, the exemplar is the object or the process which is assumed as the target of reproduction. More correctly, we should say that the artificial will consist of the reproduction of the representation. Models, even purely mental ones – in technological design as well as in artistic work – are examples of representations which function as pilot images, maps or schemes of the natural object or process which we wish to reproduce.

The choice of exemplar, however, does not constitute a simple task, devoid of ambiguities, as might appear at first sight. We all know that, speaking of an artificial heart, we refer to a well-known and recognisable exemplar, well distinguishable from all that is not a heart. Obviously, to an engineer the question is much more complex: which organic parts, vessels, muscles, subsystems, define the heart? In other words, what are the "boundaries" of a heart?

Beside the realisation of heart valves, today there are devices which act as exemplars of the left ventricle (so-called *left ventricular assist systems*) and collaborate with the natural heart of the patient. The total artificial heart, able to replace completely the natural heart, is now considered an achievable target, but many problems remain. Often they are related to the subsystem – which, therefore, has to be considered as a part of the exemplar – dedicated to generating electrical power to control the electronic circuits.

More clearly, if we would like to reproduce a given pond, how should we establish its boundaries? At a topological level, should we include in the pond even the geological structure of its bottom and of its sides or not? As far as the flora and fauna of the natural pond are concerned, what degree of likelihood should we reach, for instance, along the range that includes on the one extreme ducks and fishes and, on the other, microbiological creatures? It is quite clear that different answers to such questions will give rise to different models and concrete achievements of the pond, and these differences could reveal themselves as critical if related to our aims.

In the field of artificial intelligence this is a well-known problem and very often discussed: how should we define human intelligence as compared to other functions of mind like memory or intuition, fantasy or curiosity?

As an extreme case, we could consider that of exemplars drawn from the animal field, like a holothuria (it is also called the sea cucumber), which lives symbiotically with the small fish *Fierasfer acus*: how could we separate, first of all in representational terms and then in terms of design and of reproduction, these two entities?

It seems to us clear enough that the task of outlining an exemplar consists of an operation to be understood as always arbitrary to some extent: a true isolation of an object or of a process from a wider context which includes it or from an environment which hosts it.

Western civilisation, because of its philosophical and scientific tradition, demonstrated its ability to undertake "analyses" of the natural world, drawing great advantages from this operation. But the term analysis – which, significantly, derives from the ancient Greek "to break down" – is surely much more useful for scientific than for artificialistic aims. In fact, while the knowledge we may gain through analysis is always to be considered as valid, at least in descriptive terms and, sometimes, even in predictive ones, the reproduction of an exemplar which, in nature, behaves in a given way could require the cooperation of many parts of it. This would require, in turn, more than one observation level, and the analysis, with its usual isolation strategies, would not be able to make observable all the required levels.

In other words, the choice of an exemplar is a sort of literal "eradication" of some region of nature. All this happens as a function of the selections imposed by observation levels. A consequence of such a situation is that the behaviour of an artificial device can exhibit a good affinity to the exemplar only to the extent that the observer, or the user, will evaluate it placing themselves at a level which is the nearest possible to that assumed by the designer.

Of course, if the observer and the user had to deal with an artificial device conceived and built starting from a never-experienced observation level or extremely subjective level, then they would have to face many additional problems in order to evaluate the goodness of the reproduction.

This is true not only in the case of artistic reproduction – which is innovative by definition – but also in the scientific innovation process. Actually, the reproduction of the solar system according to a Copernican representation, by means of a mechanical device, would have not been easily understood and appreciated at the time when the Aristotelian representation of the universe was the commonly shared model.

On the contrary, under the influence of the mechanistic culture of the sixteenth and seventeenth centuries, Kepler was able to develop a three-dimensional reproduction of the universe, the famous *Machina mundi artificialis*, which was then given to the prince Friederich Von Wuerttemberg.

Thus, the definition of the exemplar is a task which, though it appears to be quite obvious in daily life when we indicate the objects or the events that surround us – or happen within us – exhibits its own complexity as soon as we try to start a work intended to reproduce it.

One of the lessons of the study of the artificial is that of bringing into the light our limits of knowing nature, which is a phase that preludes – or should prelude – the phase of reproduction.

Analysis often enables to control reality, as when, for instance, we succeed in describing with some accuracy the anatomy, physiology, ethology and perhaps psychology of a given animal, e.g. a pigeon. Thus, we can explain many of its behaviours, pathologies or abilities. This knowledge, however, is not sufficient to design an artificial pigeon, not only because it is only a small part of what we should know about a pigeon, but also because it has been achieved, unavoidably, through analytical strategies. These strategies break down reality into often very heterogeneous sectors, in accordance with the heterogeneity of the observation levels they come from, and their synthesis would require knowledge not available but through strategies up to now unknown at all.

7. What is, Essentially, a Rose?

The choice of an observation level and that of an exemplar are the first two steps in the process leading to the design of the artificial.

As soon as the problem of the delimitation of the exemplar is solved, there arises a new and decisive step. We may define this moment as the choice, or the attribution to the exemplar, of an *essential performance*.

By this expression we mean the quality, the function, the behaviour or even the aspect of the exemplar which the artificialist thinks peculiar, typical and that cannot be omitted.

In the case of the heart, cited above, there is wide agreement on what is "essential" in its behaviour, that is to say the pumping of blood. This performance of the natural heart is then essential: a project for an artificial heart cannot neglect such a feature. Actually, an artificial heart that, at the observation level we assumed, namely the physiological one, would not be able to perform the pumping of blood would be quite unrecognisable as a heart.

As far as the exemplars in bioengineering are concerned, there is rather wide agreement on what has to be considered as essential: this can be observed in the case of the heart, kidney, lung, pancreas, liver, skin and some tissue. But such an agreement is not valid in all areas of the artificial.

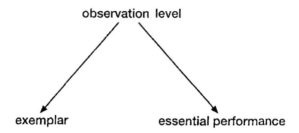

Fig. 1. The multiple selection model involved in the design of an artificial object.

In the field of artificial intelligence, for instance in the case of a rather unknown exemplar – the human mind – there are a number of options concerning its essential performance, often incompatible with each other. Intelligence itself, which at first sight might seem the essential performance of our mind, is far from being accepted by all researchers as the main mental quality, at least if by intelligence we mean the ability to solve problems. Besides other types of non-formal intelligence – like concrete or motor intelligence – we should take into account creativity, the ability to recognise objects or situations, memory, attention and many other functions.

Thus, we may state that in the field of artificial intelligence it is possible to distinguish as many schools of research or design as are the possible options concerning the essential performance of the mind, though they all have to deal, in the end, with the same exemplar.

The main schools which have difficulties in finding an overlapping point are those of the so-called symbolic artificial intelligence and those of neural networks. The former focus on the design of computer programs which try to reproduce intelligent behaviour on the basis of algorithms that simulate mental representations and knowledge through quality and numerical symbols as well as through their logical evaluation (deduction, comparison, association, calculus, etc.). The latter, on the contrary, draw hints from cybernetic works of the 1950s, and aim at designing devices whose intelligence consists of automatic recognition – neither logical nor symbolic – on the basis of suitable "training phases" of the net, of series of data very different from each other: meteorological situations, geometrical shapes, several kinds of object to be detected in ambiguous and unordered contexts.

It is important to emphasise that the choice of an essential performance is always an arbitrary action, strongly influenced by the observation level.

Even the already quoted Vaucanson was aware of this when, speaking of the digestion of his artificial duck, he defined in the following way the essential performance:

I don't pretend that this should be a perfect digestion, able to generate bloody and nutritional particles in order to allow the survival of the animal. I only pretend to imitate the mechanics of this action in three points: in the swallowing of the wheat; in soaking, cooking or dissolving it; in allowing its going out forcing it to visibly change its stuff. (Vaucanson, 1738; quoted in Losano, 1990: 91)

In the same way, two American researchers, M.A. Mahowald and C. Mead, among many who are engaged in the design of an artificial retina of the human eye, express themselves in the following way:

In building a silicon retina, our purpose was not to reproduce the human retina to the last detail, but to get a simplified version of it which contains the minimum necessary structure required to accomplish the biological function. (Mahowald and Mead, 1991)

Nevertheless,

The real vision ... will probably require that artificial retinas contain 100 times the number of pixels and auxiliary circuits, to imitate the functions of perception of the movement, and to intensify the contours performed by the amacrine cells and by the ganglion cells. Finally, these systems will also include additional electronic circuits for recognizing configurations generated by the retina. (Mahowald and Mead, 1991)

Another typical case, which is analogous to the previous one, is the attempt to reproduce the propulsion of fish by means of a robotic model:

It is almost impossible to reproduce the performances of fish simply by imitating their form and function, because a vehicle able to set up uniform and continuous flexes, having a body similar to that of a fish, is quite beyond the state of art of robotics. (Triantafyllou and Triantafyllou, 1995: 321)

Nevertheless, it is possible to imagine that

In the future, such creations which are inspired by nature, will perhaps improve their biological models for some specific task, like, for instance, the exploration of the sea-bottom. (Triantafyllou and Triantafyllou, 1995: 321)

In general terms, the question posed by the selection of an essential performance can be outlined in the following way, which will draw inspiration from the possible project for an artificial rose. In this flower, as for every other biological system – and neglecting the problems of its delimitation in space and in its structure (which we shall consider as solved) what is essential?

It is quite clear that the answer will strongly depend on the observation level we assume. The observation level at which we shall put ourselves in order to indicate the flower as an exemplar (e.g. micro, macro or some intermediate position) will induce us to attribute to it some essential performance (e.g. the shape, the colour, the perfume, some kind of behaviour, etc.) and to neglect other possibilities (e.g. the consistency of the tissues, the cell architecture, the vessel system, etc.).

A manufacturer of plastic flowers for trade is likely to select an essential performance in terms of the pure exterior aspect, while a manufacturer of educational tools will concentrate on the composition, usually only macroscopic, of the main anatomical parts of the rose. A publisher, in turn, for illustrative aims, will ask an expert in the field of graphics to outline the same parts of the rose on printed paper, while, at the opposite extreme, a painter will decide according to a much freer interpretation and range of possibilities.

It is interesting to consider that in the case of children's drawings the essential performances are never as simple and preponderant, though one often needs explanatory remarks by the child in order to understand the graphical language and the theme of the reproduction. The fact is that the ability to simplify reality begins during the age of socialisation. Thus the socialisation gives rise to the selective attitude which we develop in order to operate in the world of science, of technology and, in the end, to survive in the daily reality itself.

8. Reality Does not Make a Discount

In one of the rare works dedicated to the artificial, the biologist Martino Rizzotti, in 1984, acutely considers that:

... whatever intervention [action, technological construction, etc., NdR] involves, for its own nature, an amount of mass and energy which concerns not only the resulting object but also the environment. ... If we displace some stones we displace always some amount of mould, we crush some insect, and we lower the soil ... Even if these effects are microscopic and secondary, they appear always along with our action (Rizzotti, 1984: 34)

After having become familiar with the three main concepts of the theory of the artificial – the observation level, the exemplar and the essential performance – we introduce a principle which is decisively central to our discussion: the *principle of inheritance*.

This expression is very simple in itself but is often neglected in theory and practice. Whatever action we perform, building an artificial object or process, it doesn't limit itself to generating the effects which are predicted or planned by the project but it enables us to ascertain many others of quality and quantity which are not predictable *a priori*.

For instance, if somebody buys a car for the first time, the car will imply a series of new events which will go beyond the planned aims of the purchase. As we know, the use of a car changes our habits, induces sensations never before experienced, can affect our physical figure, implies a revision of our budget, absorbs time for its maintenance or repair, contributes to pollution, etc.

Simply, it is not possible to buy a car without its concomitant side effects: those which are known beforehand and those which will arise unexpectedly cannot be eliminated.

We could say that reality, as it were, doesn't make a discount and that a large part of the consequences of our actions are always impossible to predict. These consequences will involve several observation levels which largely are not considered when we establish our action plan.

In the case of the artificial, the inheritance principle is enabled by the subsequent selections which the artificialist should inexorably perform (selecting an observation level, isolating an exemplar, privileging some essential performance) and also, perhaps above all, by the materials and procedures he decides to adopt.

The role of multiple selections is well illustrated by the following anecdote, referred to by the psychologist of the art, Rudolf Arnheim:

The smoke detector in the new library where Mary works revealed itself so sensitive in the beginning, that for two times, when some employee lit a cigarette in the office, firemen was mobilized. Some sensitive devices artificially created by men respond to a danger sign with a reliability greater than one of the senses we are born with. (Arnheim, 1971: 53)

It is clear that no human would have acted in such an exaggerated way, but an artificial device, lacking any discriminatory capacity and privileging only the essential performance for which it was designed, is unavoidably disposed to such sudden events. The same occurs for the improperly called "errors" which often characterise computers, antitheft systems and many other control devices.

Nevertheless, the artificial exhibits its greatest exposition to the inheritance principle when it is concerned with selection of materials. This issue may be summed up in very simple terms. On the one hand, we have no *a priori* possibility to realise how many observation levels constitute natural reality or which, anyway, we could adopt in observing it. Thus, when we use some stone in a given technological project (in the field of the artificial or in a conventional technology field) we do so because some of its properties appear suitable for some aspect of the project itself. The property which would have attracted the attention of the technologist will be perceivable at some observation level, but, if we were to shift to another level, then we could discover dozens of different properties of the same stone. Some of these hidden properties could, *a posteriori*, make it easier to achieve the planned aim of the project; others, on the contrary, could reveal themselves as obstacles and others again as neutral.

The fact is that the adoption of the chosen material of that stone will *inherit* all its properties and not only the ones which attracted the attention of the designer. The inherited properties, for their part, could remain silent for an unpredictable amount of time, revealing their presence and, so to say, their "rights", in special circumstances which are in turn unpredictable. The impossibility of their *a priori* description depends, as it is easy to argue, on the number of possible interactions which the various levels of the stone could maintain with the levels of the real environment.

The number of possible interactions is, in the end, incomputable because, if we assume that whatever natural object is characterised by infinite observation levels, then its encounter with whatever real object – which is in turn characterised by infinite potential levels – will produce a quantity of possible interactions which is equal to the product by two infinite, which is an indeterminate number.

Remaining in the field of construction materials, it is well known that some marbles are more sensitive to rain and to its chemical components than others, which are more sensitive to other natural phenomena, organic or inorganic. The result is that, in all cases, after a lapse of time, the aspect and sometimes the structure itself of buildings are strongly modified by these undesired reactions. Mechanical or chemical procedures adopted for cleaning such buildings, on the other hand, raise new problems in turn. Thus, as it has been observed in some research carried out by the Masonry Conservation Research Group of the Scottish Robert Gordon University that in some circumstances buildings have been corrupted to such an extent that the stones were brought to a rapid state of decay. Actually, according to the researchers, cleaning interventions were made while ignoring the effects and the consequences of this work.

We consider here another example. A contemporary surgical room, unlike those of past centuries, is a very controlled environment. Today we know that whatever object or surgical instrument will be adopted by the surgeon, it possesses not only the desired properties (for instance, mechanical) but it brings with it other features, among them rather dangerous ones: microbiological entities, dust, metallic residuals, etc. On the other hand, and despite all precautions, no surgical room in the world may be said to be completely controlled, since, by definition, we can control only the phenomena we know of and, sometimes, not even them in total measure.

The most evident phenomenon in a medical or biological field, then, is the wide class of so-called "rejection", the immune reactions. They are true rebellions of the organism not against the essential performance that, for instance, a layer of artificial skin can exhibit towards a wound, but against some component of it which is perceived as extraneous or directly dangerous.

Dr T. Keaveny, from Berkeley, describing the problems that bioengineers face in their attempts to build and to place into the human organism artificial bones, says meaningfully:

... [the fact that] joints are trouble-free for 15 years [may be evaluated as] a remarkable record considering the harsh biomechanical and biochemical environments of the body. (Keaveny, 1996)

Because of the potential immune reactions, other researchers of the Rice Institute remember that until recently

... most research in the field [of cell transplantation, n.d.r] has focused on minimizing biological fluid and tissue interactions with biomaterials in an effort to prevent fibrous encapsulation from foreign-body reaction or clotting in blood that has contact with artificial devices. In short, most biomaterials research has focused on making the material *invisible* to the body. (Mikos et al., 1996, italics added)

A biomaterial has been defined by the American National Institutes of Health, in 1982, as

... any substance (other than a drug) or combination of substances, synthetic or natural in origin, which can be used for any period of time, as a whole or as a part of a system which treats, augments, or replaces any tissue, organ, or function of the body. (National Institutes of Health, 1982: 1–19)

The same Institute underlines that

Materials science was defined as the science which relates structure to function of materials. ... The field of biomaterials is first and foremost a materials science. (National Institutes of Health, 1982: 1–19)

and that

In evaluating safety and effectiveness of biomaterials, the material cannot be divorced from the device. ... Each biomaterial considered for potential clinical application has unique chemical, physical, and mechanical properties. In addition, the surface and bulk properties may differ, yielding variations in host response and material response. (National Institutes of Health, 1982: 1–19)

It is important to note that, though the statements by both Keaveny and Mikos were made in the second half of the 1990s, currently bioengineers are experimenting with new strategies for setting up biomaterials which may be called "hybrid". This means that the new materials aim at harmonising the artificial organ and the host environment.

By means of suitable biomaterials, they try to assign, for instance to an artificial cell, sufficient compatibility with the host organism at the surface, while maintaining the needed artificiality in its internal structure. It is a further example of an attempt to "cheat" nature, since the organism will be induced to accept the performance generated by the artificial cell without attacking it, because its interactions with the cell will be mediated by a compatible surface.

The possible extension of such a hybrid strategy to other areas of the artificial allows predictions of great interest, though not completely new, if one thinks, among the many cases we could cite, of the attempts to make a robot or the programs of artificial intelligence, something anthropomorphic (that is to say, externally similar to human beings). In all the cases in which designers resort to such interfacing strategies – between the artificial device and the natural world – their meaning should in fact be found in the effort to make compatible, at a macroscopic perception observation level, two realities heterogeneous to each other and whose interactions are controllable only within a very narrow range.

Though the issue is somewhat extraneous to our discussion, it should be very interesting, by the way, to ask ourselves what relation, perhaps very deep, would exist between the artificial and the very ancient disposition of man to build camouflage devices for altering his own identity, aspect or presence, up to the most ancient historical invention of masks in funerary Egyptian art or in Greek theatre.

What remains clear is that every attempt to reproduce a natural exemplar, and its essential performance, implies the construction of realities which are much richer than one could desire.

9. The Difficult Synthesis of the Observation Levels

The situations in which scientists and technologists act, above all technologists of the artificial, are surely made complicated by our incapacity to place ourselves simultaneously at more than one observation level.

Though scientific methodology has developed several techniques for allowing the control of more than one variable, *de facto* our theories and models are unavoidably polarised on some aspect or profile that, every time, is considered as central.

The attitude to assign to the events we observe – at a given level – some privileged and exhausting meaning is a reductive process which prevents us looking at them from other levels and at different moments.

The history of the damage or, at least, of the waste in terms of research projects, caused by these reductions or polarisations, is yet to be written, but, in the end, the human attitude producing them – that of privileging an observation level for a unit of time – seems to be definitely without alternatives. If we consider the world of the artificial, the above attitude goes along with another unavoidable constraint: that which forces the artificialist to use different materials and procedures as compared to the natural exemplar and, therefore, to introduce into the object or in the process side effects and sudden events whose frequency, intensity and quality are not predictable.

In the best cases, it is only possible to limit these effects by means of "encapsulation", that is to say isolation of the artificial from the external world, for instance the host organism. In such a way, the only interaction which can be activated between the artificial and the external world is the one we defined as essential performance, the only umbilical cord overlapping, to some extent, the artificial and the natural.

We could now ask, under what conditions and with what results, in general terms, could one design the reproduction of the same exemplar and of its essential performance at more than one observation level, or, in another version, more exemplars and more essential performances which cooperate at the same observation level?

Let us look at the case of a flower we want to reproduce at more than one observation level by means of materials and procedures different from the natural ones – for whatever aim: scientific, educational, commercial, etc. – then we would face a fundamental difficulty. We need to decide, for instance, what kind of relationship among its parts (stamens and carpels, style, ovary, stigma) we should reproduce. In other words, at what observation level (cellular, molecular, etc.) should we reproduce the relationships which characterise the flower in its whole, in order to reproduce accurately not only its structure but also its functions?

Openly, presented in this way, the problem is theoretically and practically unresolvable, since, if an artificial flower has to be a reliable reproduction of the anatomy and the physiology of the exemplar, then, if we were to succeed, we could state that we have replicated it, that is to say re-created it artificially. The analytical rebuilding, piece by piece, of a living system – but also of whatever other natural reality is complex enough – starting from its basic chemical elements, is a task which is definitely beyond our capacity and, perhaps, it is intrinsically impossible.

But the artificialists do not claim to operate in such a direction. What they pursue is, in principle, the replacement of natural materials with others which approximate them at a given observation level. Our current knowledge of organic and inorganic materials and our ability to manipulate their features – enhanced a great deal, by the way, by space technology – allows us to generate substances, physical or chemical structures, in many fields, very similar to natural ones. But this similarity is almost always recognisable at the selected observation level.

Actually, to continue our case of the flower, we are able to generate a wide range of artificial perfumes and, among these, we could select the one which is the essential performance of our exemplar. But, if our aim was that of rebuilding even only the structural and physiological subsystem which, in the flower, produces that perfume, then it would become an entirely different problem. In fact we should decide which relationship we should establish between the artificial perfume and the artificial structures we would have set up, in order to allow those structures to generate our artificial perfume.

It is important to consider that the observation levels at which the two partial artificial objects will be reproduced will be "absorbed" by a third level: that at which the relationship between perfume and anatomic–physiological structures of the flower become possible. It is just to this relationship that the two original exemplars and related observation levels will be, as it were, sacrificed. They will be remodelled in order to serve the new essential performance, which would be constituted exactly by the relationship between the two exemplars.

However, the cooperation between two artificial objects or processes poses serious methodological problems. Man, almost invariably, tries to solve them by resorting to some decision which would establish some definite point to reach.

This strategy, on the one hand, coincides with a *de facto* renunciation of the reproduction of the exemplar in its wholeness and, therefore, with its replacement with a simplified model which privileges only one observation level. On the other hand, such a strategy will imply the tacit admission that, if one desires to integrate even only two observation levels, one has to proceed, when it makes sense, to establish a third level, without the pretence that it incorporates reliably the previous two. Rebuilding an exemplar through a bottom-up strategy is, to sum up, a pure utopia.

Let us consider the design of the reproduction of the subsystem which, in the human body, supervises and coordinates vision and touch, provided we know it in a sufficient measure. Obviously all this will require setting up a model in which the relationship in question is central, assuming that the artificial devices for vision and touch are sufficiently reliable. Such kinds of model are quite plausible and actual, thanks to availability of electronic and computer technologies for implementing many types of algorithms, very flexible and even very complex.

But the critical point is dealing with the necessary adjustments we should introduce in the artificial vision and the artificial touch devices in order to coordinate these and make them compatible with the third artificial device: that which assumes as exemplar some region of our brain.

The true exemplar of such a project, in sum, would be just this region of the brain and surely not the pure "putting together" of the two partial artificial objects already available.

It is worth noting the closed analogy between the constraints regarding the combination among observation levels in the field of the artificial and the cooperation among different scientific disciplines. In fact, what we call "interdisciplinarity", when it succeeds, consists of the setting up of a new observation level rather than of a "sum" or a generic "synthesis" of two or more levels.

Biophysics and biochemistry are good examples of this kind. Both of these combine knowledge, lexicons and techniques of their disciplines, giving rise to largely autonomous new sciences, no longer easily comparable with knowledge, lexicons and techniques of the scientific fields they come from.

A final remark concerns the possibility of cooperation from two or more artificial objects or processes in the same natural organism, for instance the human body. In principle, it would seem that one should face no difficulty in putting to work together two artificial objects, say A1 and A2, which had been demonstrated to be effective as stand-alone devices. In fact, the "implantation" (to be distinguished from "transplantation", which means to place in a body a natural organ) of an artificial bone or of an artificial heart in the same organism should not give rise to any problem. But the case of the implantation of an artificial duodenum and of an artificial liver – though they are not yet available other than as experimental devices – would be a very different matter, full of snares and degeneration possibilities due to the strong functional relationship between these two organs. Even more complex, intuitively, would be the cooperation between the artificial liver, duodenum and pancreas.

The general problem is the variety of the observation levels involved and the arbitrariness which will govern the choice of the essential performance. The resulting artificial device – a true artificial subsystem – could work fine only if the assumed exemplar and its related essential performance were determinant for the functional balance of the organism.

10. Emergency and Transfiguration: i.e. "Something Occurs Always"

A famous Latin sentence says that *senatores boni viri, senatus mala bestia* (senators are good men, but the Senate is a bad beast). In general terms this sentence means that the coexistence of single entities of a given kind may give rise to a whole of a different kind, not reducible nor explainable through the "qualities" of the components considered in their individuality.

Usually this phenomenon is defined by means of the term *emergence*, coined by G.H. Lewes in 1875. Often it is a matter of a pure change of observation levels. For instance, a collection of black and white microscopic granules will appear as such under the microscope but, to the naked eye, the whole will appear grey. Notwithstanding this, in other cases, it cannot be denied that, though one remains at the same observation level, the "sum" or the "synthesis" of many objects or processes give rise to something which goes beyond of their singular features. Chemical reactions clearly exemplify this order of circumstances.

Now, the principle of emergence constitutes a foundation on which many hopes of artificialists are based in several fields. In 1987 Craig Reynolds, for instance, demonstrated that the coordinated flight of a flock of birds can be simulated without introducing into the model any central coordinator. Each simulated bird (or "boid", as Reynolds called them) follows simple rules: avoid collision with friends (*collision avoidance*), stay in step with friends (*velocity matching*) and try to stay as close as possible to friends (*flock centring*). Each bird, finally, could see only its closest friend. The simulation – which was later adopted successfully in movies – demonstrated that a flock organised in this way was able to "fly" on the monitor of the computer as a compact whole, avoiding obstacles to rejoin the flock just after them, exactly in the way it occurs in observable reality.

Other models – always formal, i.e. simulated on the computer – in the research area which is defined *artificial life* or, in short, ALife, are able to reproduce typical phenomena of living processes (self-reproduction, evolution, struggle for survival, etc.) as "emergent", not so rarely, from the coexistence of many single "agents" (cells or "cellular automata") and, therefore, from the relationships which arise among them.

Chris Langton defined ALife as

... the field of research dedicated to the understanding of life through the attempt of abstracting the basic dynamic principles which stay at the basis of the biological phenomena, in order to recreate these dynamics in different supports – like computers – making them accessible to new manipulations and experimental tests. (Langton, 1989: 32)

The spontaneous emergence, as a self-organisation phenomenon, of intelligent behaviour on the one hand or typical of life on the other, depends sometimes on reaching a sort of "critical mass", as happens in crowd phenomena or in a nuclear chain reaction, or of a threshold of suitable complexity, as occurs in the evolutive differentiation of living systems or in the emergence of intelligence in the human or animal brain.

Beyond the hope that it generates in the artificial intelligence or ALife researchers – concerning the possibility that intelligence or life could suddenly and spontaneously emerge from their models – the principle of emergence may be useful for emphasising a very simple truth. We refer to the fact that, in the field of concrete phenomena, but, in some ways – as we saw with the ALife – whatever system we build it ends invariably by giving rise to something which goes beyond the objectives of our project.

In this sense, emergence may be understood as an extension, or a particular case, of the principle of inheritance. In other words, the features, at a given observation level, of a system constituted by a certain number of components, may appear as new compared to the features of the components as such.

This happens thanks to the fact that the relationships among the components may exhibit their own qualities, that is to say just as relationships, independently of the characters of the components in question.

Experience, even everyday experience, shows us continuously how much this is true. It should be enough to think of the circumstances in which, whether or not on the basis of chemical or physical knowledge, we have to deal with reactions which produce, in a kitchen, like in a laboratory, new realities as compared to the "ingredients" we use. In the same way, in the sociological field we know well how certain collective phenomena – panic, aggression, fanaticism, etc. – are due to psychosocial relationships which often have no correspondence in individual motivations or attitudes.

Of course this fact is even more true in the technological area: the black-out which paralysed New York in the 1960s, as well as the many sudden degenerations which strike machines or systems of several kinds, belong in general to the same typology, that is to say to a class of events which emerge from a complexity that ends by following its own logic, unpredictable and therefore uncontrolled.

The artificial does not constitute anything but a particular case of this typology, of course. The point is, rather, that the quality of what may "emerge" from an artificial device – i.e., the additional performances it may exhibit as compared to the essential performances included in the project – has no reason to just consist, like a miracle, of something similar to what the exemplar exhibits in nature.

As we remarked in the previous section, the accurate reproduction, at a certain observation level, of natural organs which in the human organism collaborate to regulate some process, offers no guarantee that from their coexistence the regulation process or performance will emerge automatically. This will occur if, and only if, a precise condition is satisfied: we should know that the expected performance is a simple function (or consequence) of the essential performances reproduced by the two artificial organs.

To give a rather general example, if we reproduce accurately some performance of sunlight (say, rays belonging to a well-defined region of the spectrum which stretches from the ultraviolet to the infrared) and, simultaneously, a given quantity and quality of heat (dry, moist, airy, etc.), it is possible to get an "artificial environment" suitable for the growth of a certain tree.

In fact, we could state that such an environment will emerge from the combination of the two artificial processes in question, but it will be an emergence, as it were, guided by a project founded on sufficient knowledge to generate that phenomenon. To sum up, all science consists of a description of phenomena of this kind, though very often we are unable to give an analytical explanation.

This is what happens in the case of many drugs, several therapies and many physical products or processes we are able to reproduce by suitably combining objects or events without knowing their genesis, beyond the observation level at which we place ourselves in order to get them. Among the more spectacular cases, it would be enough to cite aspirin, for which we discover more and more effects, among the most recent being a reduction of the probability of heart attacks in diabetic patients.

The most interesting aspect of all this is, in our opinion, the fact that we only know about the successes of research and we don't consider the failures – in the sense that they haven't led to any interesting or useful phenomena. This question is very important if we keep in mind how often it happens that experimental projects intended for certain objectives lead to "emerging" phenomena of a different kind and are considered to be so interesting as to divert the research itself to these phenomena, as in the casual discovery of the semiconductivity of doped silicon. In these cases, research fails with respect to its original purpose, but it gives way to discoveries that lead to research regarding other purposes and produce very significant knowledge.

However, even in all the other cases of failure – those in which the failure is not accompanied by unexpected discoveries – *something certainly happened*. This same fact applies to the designing of artificial devices: the failure of a project in this field doesn't mean that "nothing happened", but that the performance which emerged had nothing to do with, or only to a weak and partial extent, the performance considered to be essential in the natural reference exemplar. The principle of inheritance, on the other hand, draws our attention to the case where, even if we are able to satisfactorily reproduce the selected essential performance, an unpredictable series of other performances may also be produced. This in turn means that the interactions between artificial and the natural world, including therefore interactions with human beings, will always depend on a much wider spectrum of performances than expected in the project.

Naturally, this circumstance does not imply in any way that, among the performances which emerge from an artificial object, some may necessarily be hidden which, even though they haven't been designed intentionally, may be acknowledged however as typical of the model. This possibility is obviously completely imponderable and unpredictable. It is very rare that a certain performance is the simple function of another two performances. It is more frequent that the performance in question, instead, is located at a different observation level compared to those adopted to design the two artificial objects and their relative essential performances. The essential performances of the two artificial objects and processes, in other words, can sometimes be adopted as necessary conditions but not sufficient for the emergence of a third natural performance.

Rather, what is certain is that, both in the case of the principle of inheritance as such and that of the principle of emergence any artificial object or process can only be intrinsically intended to generate a *transfiguration* of the model and its performances. Moreover, a transfiguration is even more amplified by the inevitable use of conventional technologies, which tend to control and modify the natural objects rather than imitate or reproduce them.

It is worth noting that this transfiguration is not, in itself, a negative fact. Very often artificial technology produces objects, processes or machines which exceed the performances of natural models. This is true of computers as machines which reproduce essential performances such as logical or mathematical calculations, whose speed and precision in machines are incomparably superior to man's.

However, the transfiguration could only be avoided if, in selecting an observation level, we could actually isolate our model and its essential performance from all other observation levels which distinguish natural reality. But this is obviously impossible in the real world, while it apparently becomes easy when we simulate something on a computer in a purely informational way or when, in scientific theories, we resort to abstractions by which we substitute the world with a simplified modelling of it. These are extremely useful undertakings and procedures. However, these procedures should not be confused *ipso facto* with discoveries of nature, even though at times they allow us to control it in well-defined circumstances.

11. Classification of the Artificial

On the basis of our reasoning, we can now propose a classification of the artificial objects and processes which explain the main features.

First of all, we have seen how the artificial has always led to two opposite kinds of activity depending on the *concrete* or *abstract* nature which is assumed by the "substance" by means of which the final product is designed and realised. Since man has always possessed and shown a distinct tendency to reproduce whatever surrounds him – and also whatever has a primary origin in himself, such as feelings, self-portrayals, etc. – it is not surprising that the entire history of man is intensely characterised by the invention and development of the most diverse kinds of technologies aimed precisely at the material expression, communication or reproduction of models of every kind.

Rock carvings and oral communication, the evolution of symbols and painting, the birth of music and poetry writing, up to the invention of printing and then radio and television, and the advent of informatic and telematic machines, are a few of the cornerstones which have marked man's effort to "make common" individual and collective representations, and subjective and objective models and essential performances.

In spite of their incorporation in material objects and processes – rock or paper, sound, voice or colours, electromagnetic waves or electrical signals – all forms of communication or simulation of reality can be considered as abstract artificial objects and processes for the mere reason that their purpose is not to reproduce the model concretely and materially, but to reproduce our representation of it *as such*.

For example, when we decide to communicate the images and sensations we felt while admiring a certain flower, we obviously don't have any intention or ambition to reproduce that model materially. In this case, each one of us – but also the poet or the painter, the writer or the computer simulation expert – only tries to share his own portrayal of the world, either by objective pretences ("now I will tell you how matters stand") or by openly subjective intentions ("now I will tell you how I see the world"). Whereas the scientific models and the most varied "theories" belong to the first category, the artist's "poetics" and our personal expressive styles belong to the second.

An obviously different situation arises when someone attempts a concrete reproduction of a natural exemplar. In this case we inevitably use representations (in the form of models) and therefore we introduce a subjective and arbitrary dimension. Nevertheless, our ambition is to build something concrete and realise an object or a process which we recognise, and which provides us with a common experience: a flower or a heart, skin or rain, but also, with a little more difficulty in getting general agreement, intelligence or reasoning.

Finally, we must keep in mind that even among artificial objects, processes or machines which are concrete and analytical, very often the analysis of the exemplar's structure doesn't lead to the decision to reproduce it as such – either because of its complexity, or because of its intrinsic non-reproducibility under the guidance of existing conventional technologies – whereas it is considered possible to proceed with the direct reproduction of the essential performance. In these circumstances we can say that researchers and designers provide an applicative example of the principle of *functional equivalence*. This principle comes from biology but has also has applications in human sciences. It is not rare, in nature or in social phenomena, to observe how a certain function can be carried out by a different structure from the one originally intended for such a task, for example when a social institution looks after the socialisation of orphan children by substituting the family.

In the field of the artificial we can assert that a certain high degree of functional equivalence is always present, and for this reason it is not useful to distinguish between particular classes of artificial objects. By definition, the artificial requires the use of different materials from those chosen by nature. Although the model which guides the artificialist is often homologous to a certain observation level, it is always demonstrable that it will be different on all other levels, with consequences that can be perceived in various aspects or qualities of the same essential performance.

In conclusion, the cross between the two dimensions that we have singled out – *abstract–concrete* and *analytical–aesthetic* – allows for a classification which substantially covers all the possible cases of artificial. For example, the functionality which is necessary for an artificial organ will suggest its placement in the category of concrete–analytical artificial objects or processes, whereas a doll or a puppet will have to be placed instead in the category of concrete–aesthetic artificial objects or processes.

In reality, the main benefit of such systematics – as in every other case of scientific taxonomy – will be to allow for the deduction of the general characteristics which an artificial object will have according to its placement in one category or another. Therefore we are dealing with a methodological instrument of remarkable potential importance, provided that obviously the individual categories are carefully recognised. In particular, it is plausible to maintain that the constraints imposed by the selection of the observation level, of the exemplar and of the essential performance, the problems which concern the reproduction of several performances, the principle of inheritance and the transfiguration processes, as characteristics of any artificial object or process, assume, however, different and specific features in the four categories that we have identified – a reality which the theory of the artificial has only begun to investigate.

12. A Note about Automatisms

There is a region of the "artificial kingdom" which is placed at the boundary between conventional technology and artificial technology, and it is the region of automatisms. In this vast area of designing – we can find examples going back to ancient times, for example in the Egyptian technology of the pyramids – what dominates is what we might define as the *principle of substitution*, by means of a technological device, of actions carried out by man first.

A very clear illustrative case is the invention of the throttle valve for steam intake and exhaust in machines by Thomas Newcomen in 1812. The opening and closing of the valve had to be done by an assigned person, who had to pull the cord and release it at the right moment. According to various accounts, the assigned person, probably in order to avoid a monotonous job, had the bright idea of tying the cord to the piston, so that the latter could pull the cord and release it.

As we know, the self-regulation which we are talking about was later improved by James Watt using much more complex and efficient devices. However, the main problem which concerns us regards the actual artificial nature of these kinds of inventions. The problem concerns the conceptual difference between the reproduction of something and its substitution with something else. Automatisms almost always substitute human actions by means of a technological device which allows the same results (or better results). As such, they don't intend in any way to reproduce either the exemplar (man or one of his subsystems) or the *general* natural performance which makes that action possible.

In short we could say that the people who design automatisms, even though they normally concentrate their efforts on man's essential performance, are interested in its faithful reproduction only to the extent to which such fidelity can generate a good reproduction of the actions which that essential performance allows. For example, the device which automatically opens a store door when clients enter and exit could be defined as an "artificial porter" only by strictly isolating the effect of the essential performance (opening and closing the door) but certainly not by the designer's effort to reproduce the human vision or human ability to move objects.

Likewise, *brain wheels* (gears moved by *cams*) which, beginning from the last century, have allowed the mechanical programming of machine tools, without any reproductive aim of the human mental performances. The same can be said about a thermostat which activates or shuts down a radiator or refrigerator, the automatic gear which changes velocity ratios in a car, the stabilisation circuits which operate a television set and, generally, all self-regulation devices based on *feedback*.

The computer, programmed for the administration of a firm's accounts, can be included in this category since the modalities by which it performs calculations has nothing to do with those adopted by man, just as the structure on which it is based has nothing in common with the human brain. On the other hand, in the field of artificial intelligence, programming a computer so that it produces stories or translates from one language to another means starting from an example of a human model and taking into close consideration the essential performances which are involved from time to time, while trying to reproduce their dynamics.

The most important characteristic that distinguishes artificial from automatism is its necessary contact and very close relationship with nature. Artificial, in the strict sense, confirms its close dependence on nature – though it ends with transfiguring it – whereas automatisms possess a much more marked technological–conventional inclination right from the beginning.

Although we are dealing with a distinction which can turn out to be very delicate – since any artificial object or process, as we have emphasised many times, needs conventional technology – it allows us once again to recognise the two basic aspects of this technology, from a motivational and intentional profile. The pragmatic aim of technology, which consists of its dominion over nature, is in fact pursued both by means of pure inventions and by inventions which try to produce the same effects or actions of nature without worrying about the similarity of the structures or the processes at stake. The reproductive aim of the artificial technology, on the other hand, can only be pursued by strategies which give prime importance to the exemplar and its performances. In the real artificial, in short, there is always a high degree of homology (similar structures) or analogy (similar functions or relationships) with the model and its performance, whereas automatism doesn't take these into consideration. For example, the compatibility between the materials and mechanisms of an artificial limb and the rest of the organism – thus its homology or at least its analogy with the natural exemplar and its essential performance – becomes an integral part of such a project. On the other hand, if the pragmatic aim is only to allow the patient to move a bit, any other more or less sophisticated external mechanical device will suffice, almost completely neglecting the anatomy and physiology of the limb in question.

In this sense, artificial technology can be considered an activity very much related to scientific research, in order to acquire knowledge and models on the exemplars and their performances, as well as contributing, at least hypothetically, to the advancement of this knowledge. Conversely, the technology of automatisms, although it has a common ambition with artificial technology, of not being reproductive, can, however, be defined as a substitute for nature or, more often, human actions, but cannot contribute in any way to the scientific knowledge of the exemplars or their performances, precisely because it doesn't consider their intrinsic composition.

Finally, whereas artificial technology in the strict sense of the word reveals the human ambition to re-create nature – an undertaking which obviously includes the pretence of having an excellent knowledge of it – conventional technology and automation technology are evidence of man's desire and capacity to control things and events in the natural world, by getting or without getting ideas from their way of being.

To put it into a formula, every technological device which can actually be defined as artificial acts as a substitute for something natural, whereas it is not true that every device which replaces something natural is, of itself, the result of its reproduction and therefore cannot be correctly considered an artificial object.

We must keep in mind, in fact, that many products of artificial technology have nothing in common with the world of automatisms, although they allow substitution of a natural object or process with something technological. For example, the domes in contemporary Japanese architecture (huge constructions that reproduce, among other things, alpine or tropical landscapes in which people can go on virtual vacations) are certainly artificial products and, as such, substitute their own natural models. For this reason, they do not constitute the automation of anything. The same can be said regarding various artificial organs which, being placed in the human organism, substitute one of its performances, and also many drugs which are often actually established as replications of natural substances.

13. Conclusion

The concept of the artificial and the technology which refers to it have always been a central part of human activity. It has its own characteristics which are clearly

Table 1. Classification of the artificial

	Concrete–artificial (material devices or processes)	Abstract–artificial (informational devices or processes)
Analytical–artificial (reproduction of structures)	A • organs, • cells and tissues, • robots, • virtual reality interfaced with the real world, • miscellaneous (e.g., diamonds, grass, horizon)	B • AI (artificial intelligence), • ANN (artificial neural networks), • ALife (artificial life), • GA (genetic algorithms), • …
Aesthetic–artificial (reproduction of appearance)	C • sculpture, • architecture, • imitation gadgets, • reconstructions, • …	D • drawing, • maps, • figurative arts, • simulated graphs, • descriptive virtual reality or virtual environment

distinguishable from those that describe other activities.

Despite the generic use which we commonly make of this term, almost as if it were interchangeable with the adjective "technological" or with the mere expression "man-made", the theory of the artificial shows how designing in order to produce *ex novo* and designing in order to reproduce something that exists are two definitely different processes; they demand different abilities and show strengths, difficulties and limits which in the same way are not assimilable with each other. These two activities, which we have respectively called conventional technology and technology of the artificial, end up in generating objects, processes or machines as non-natural realities.

A world made up exclusively of conventional technology objects and machines would be a world in which two realities – the natural one and the technological one – would be very distinguishable from each other, as a city is from the surrounding countryside or, better yet, a car "cemetery" compared to the landscape in which it is situated, or a watch or bracelet on a human being's wrist or a ballpoint pen held in the fingers.

The artificial creates, not always only ideally, realities which, at least at a certain observation level, should not be distinguishable from the natural context, whether it be the territory, the human body or any other natural environment. The artificial, in fact, corresponds to an ancient desire not for mere control of nature but for reproduction of nature by different strategies from its own. All this is true in motivational terms, though in teleological terms even the artificial is a matter of a form of control, but of a higher and more ambitious kind – the capability to re-create nature.

Nevertheless, as we have said, in the end both technologies create manufactures, recombinations of natural elements which, in the artificial case, have many difficulties in reaching its aims of reproducing the natural exemplars and, however, generate at the same time effects of another nature compared to the desired targets.

Perhaps it is a revenge of natural reality, but the fact is that conventional technology, with its materials and techniques, poses serious limitations to technology of the artificial. In fact, on one hand it allows, at a certain observation level, "deception" of an organism, a spectator, an environment, a living species or other structures or natural events. On the other hand, it reproposes, at different levels and often also at that assumed by the designer, its own heterogeneity with regard to the exemplar and its performances. For this reason, in spite of the artificialists' ambitions, the artificial tends to create realities which deviate more and more from nature, just as conventional technology does right from the beginning and in a deliberate way.

In short, we have noted a series of processes which decree right from the first steps not so much the failure of artificialism, as its particular physiognomy and its intrinsically autonomous development compared to the natural world which it assumes as its aim. Therefore, the culture of the artificial is a matter of a new cultural area which should be carefully known in itself and, then, integrated with the general culture we live in.

In particular, we may establish the following points.

- The artificial always derives from a process of multiple choices which, as such, prevents it from pursuing the overall analytical reproduction of the natural object

263

or process which it intends to reproduce. These choices include an observation level, an exemplar and an essential performance.

- The selection of an observation level, which also includes the possibility of its deliberate construction without direct references to the world which is perceived with the senses, leads to the formation of individual or collective representations – of the natural object or process observed – which don't necessarily respect "reality as it is". Representations may depend on a whole series of cultural premises, principles, preferences, beliefs or prohibitions which history is full of.

- The selection of the exemplar, in turn, inevitably assumes the form of an isolation, and at times a real eradication of the object or process from the natural context which hosts it. In some cases, this act doesn't have serious consequences on the reproducibility of the exemplar at the observation level one assumed. In many other cases, however, its isolation cuts off, so to speak, relationships at various observation levels with the rest of the context which it belongs to, which could be and often are vitally important in determining the characteristics of the natural object or process and, therefore, of the resulting artificial object or process.

- The selection of the essential performance is already, on one hand, bound by the selection of the observation level and the exemplar and, on the other hand, almost always makes up a kind of "bet" on the quality, function or behaviour which is considered "fundamental" in the exemplar. The principle of "functional equivalence" – between the exemplar and its theoretical model or its concrete reproduction – only guarantees that, in a few circumstances, the essential performance is sufficiently autonomous and therefore transferable.

- The emergence of properties, qualities and performances which are not explicitly planned in the design is a rule for the artificial. Anyway, this doesn't necessarily mean that whatever emerges from an artificial object or process will precisely consist of what we would expect to appear from the natural exemplar. The whole of the relationships among all the observation levels present in the exemplar have a very low probability of being exactly overlapping, because what is expected and implicit in the model which guides the reproduction is always a reality directed towards only one level, that is, on only one profile among infinite possibilities.

- The compatibility with the host context, environment and organism is usually the most crucial moment for the artificial, since it is precisely at that stage that the heterogeneity of its structure or its performances will clearly emerge. Deceit, simulation and illusion can certainly be pursued by means of various strategies, but the limits in which they are possible, inevitably rigid, strictly depend on the essential performance's autonomy with regard to the "support" which generates it in nature. At times this autonomy can be relatively high – even if indefinite – as it is when we have to deal with exemplars or, even more, merely informational performances, but it is usually very low in all the other cases of a concrete stuff.

- The synthesis or coordination of more than one exemplar or essential performance creates further problems. In fact, the "sum" of two artificial objects or processes only increases the distance of the presumably resulting object or process compared to the system made up of the two exemplars in nature. This is mainly due to the relationships, within the exemplar, among structures and processes at observation levels which are unavoidably neglected in the model which guides the reproduction. This could be called the "unavoidable price of analysis".

- Although the synthesis of two or more artificial subsystems of a natural system has been up to now almost impossible if one expects from that synthesis the same performances we get from the natural exemplar, we should not neglect the fact that, from such kinds of attempts, *always something real happens*.

- The transfiguration of the exemplar and its performances, and often of the essential performance as well, constitutes an inexorable tendency of artificial objects and processes. It is due to the combined action of the selective and heterogeneity factors mentioned above. Since nature, including human nature, is a whole which is intrinsically integrated – by physical, chemical, biological, psychological and sociological laws – even the optimal reproduction of one performance of an exemplar already represents, in itself, an anomaly because it doesn't have, and cannot easily have, natural relationships with the host context at all the levels involved when we consider it and its performances in nature. To make a final reference, artificial intelligence, distilled and "purified" by the human body, is not the prelude to the mind's reconstruction, or at least not the human mind.

From whatever perspective it is examined, the artificial is therefore a separate reality, which includes innovative effects which should be studied in depth. In fact, the density of artificial objects, processes and machines is increasing considerably, thanks to more refined technologies which allow the renewal of man's ancient ambition and utopia, and because many aspects of our existence have always been ready and available to obtain practical and imaginative, scientific or artistic benefit from those technologies.

It is likely that the dream of realising a cyborg (cybernetic organism – that is, a natural man who is improved and amplified in his performances by artificial devices connected directly to his body) will remain unrealisable for a long time, if as examples we think of the extreme characters of science fiction films. Nevertheless, already today millions of people live, work, communicate or move thanks to extensions, prostheses or implants of artificial objects of various kinds. The prospect of a more marked physical integration with the artificial is therefore not unrealistic. Rather, serious sociological, psychological and even ethical problems are already appearing on the scene. We don't know exactly what this will entail. However, to quote a very profound remark by Willelm Kolff, it is possible that in one of the next Olympic games the marathon will be won by a man equipped with an artificial heart, which is stronger and more insensitive to fatigue than the natural heart. The crucial point is this: will he be disqualified?

References

Arnheim, R., (1971). Entropy And Art: An Essay on Disorder and Order. University of California.
Galloni, M. (1993). Microscopi e microscopie, dalle origini al XIX secolo. In *Quaderni di storia della tecnologia*, Vol. 3. Levrotto & Bella.
Hoffmann, R. and Leibowitz Schmidt, S. (1997). Old Wine New Flasks. Freeman, New York.
Keaveny, T., (1996). Presentation page for the Berkeley Orthopaedic Biomechanics Research (http://biomech2.me.berkeley.edu/prosthesis.html).
Langton, C.G. (1989). Artificial Life. In Langton, C.G. (ed.) Artificial Life. Santa Fe Institute Studies in the Science of Complexity. Addison-Wesley, Redwood City, CA.

Losano, M. (1990). Storie di automi. Einaudi, Turin.

Mahowald, M.A. and Mead, C. (1991). The silicon retina, *Le Scienze/Scientific American*. 275 (retranslated from Italian edition).

Mikos, A.G., Bizios, R., Wu, K.K. and Yaszemski, M.J. (1996). Cell Transplantation. Rice Institute of Biosciences and Bioengineering (http://www.bioc.rice.edu/Institute/area6.html).

National Institutes of Health (1982). Clinical Applications of Biomaterials, Vol. 4(5). NIH Consensus Statement, 1–3 November.

Rizzotti, M. (1984). Il concetto di artificiale, Memorie dell'Istituto Veneto di Scienze, Lettere ed Arti, Venice.

Triantafyllou, M.S. and Triantafyllou, G.S. (1995). Un robot che simula il nuoto dei pesci. *Le Scienze/ Scientific American*. 3.

Young, J.Z. (1964). A Model of the Brain. Oxford University Press, Oxford.

Correspondence and offprint requests to: Massimo Negrotti, IMES, University of Urbino, Via Saffi 15, 61029 Urbino (PS), Italy. Tel./Fax: 0039 0722 2408; Email: maxnegro@synet.it

PART II

KNOWLEDGE AND COGNITION

AI & SOCIETY, VOL. 2, 99-112 (1988)

The Socratic and Platonic Basis of Cognitivism

Hubert L. Dreyfus
University of California, Berkeley, USA

ABSTRACT

Artificial Intelligence, and the cognitivist view of mind on which it is based, represent the last stage of the rationalist tradition in philosophy. This tradition begins when Socrates assumes that intelligence is based on principles and when Plato adds the requirement that these principles must be strict rules, not based on taken-for-granted background understanding. This philosophical position, refined by Hobbes, Descartes and Leibniz, is finally converted into a research program by Herbert Simon and Allen Newell. That research program is now in trouble, so we must return to its source and question Socrates' assumption that intelligence consists in solving problems by following rules, and that one acquires the necessary rules by abstracting them from specific cases. A phenomenological description of skill acquisition suggests that the acquisition of expertise moves in just the opposite direction: from abstract rules to particular cases. This description of expertise accounts for the difficulties that have confronted AI for the last decade.

KEYWORDS

Artificial Intelligence, checker program, chess, cognitivism, connectionism, expertise, expert systems, heuristic knowledge, phenomenology, Physical Symbol System, Plato, skill acquisition, Socrates

Introduction

Before we can decide whether Socrates is to blame for cognitivism we must understand what cognitivism is and what is supposed to be wrong with it. This paper has three parts: a brief account of cognitivism, supporting the claim that cognitivism treats all mental activity on the model of thinking through a problem; a phenomenology of skill acquisition, drawn from my book with my brother, *Mind Over Machine*, which seeks to show that expertise does not normally involve thinking at all; and a tentative foray into the history of philosophy which suggests that the source of the distorted view of expertise characteristic of cognitivism can be found in Plato's account of Socrates, although its implications emerge fully only in Plato's philosophy.

1 WHAT IS COGNITIVISM?

Cognitivism is not simply a theory of cognition but, as the name, cognitiv*ism*, suggests, it is the strong view that *all* mental activity is cognitive — that perception, understanding, learning and action are all to be understood on the model of fact gathering, hypothesis information, inference making and problem solving. Such a view is taken for granted by current cognitive psychologists, especially those seeking to program computers to behave intelligently. They think of themselves as pioneers of a new discipline, cognitive science, the true science of the mind, which has done for the mind what Copernicus did for the universe and Darwin did for biology.

The cognitivist assumption is so self-evident to cognitive scientists that they seldom bother to state it explicitly, let alone argue for it. For example, Jerry Fodor says in passing, as if it were obvious, that mental life is essentially thought and thought involves inference. 'Conan Doyle was a far deeper psychologist — far closer to what is essential about mental life — than, say, James Joyce (or William James, for that matter).'[1]

Lest my interpretation of this off-hand remark seems forced, we can see that Fodor's account of perception, which is least like thought, turns it, too, into detective work: 'Perception typically involves hypothesis formation and confirmation' (Fodor, 1975).[2] In general all cognitivist theories make two essential claims:

1) Our ability to deal with things intelligently is due to our capacity to think about them reasonably (including subconscious thinking).

2) Our capacity to think about things reasonably amounts to a faculty for internal 'automatic' symbol manipulation.[3]

This view is the culmination of the rationalist philosophical tradition. Descartes already assumed that all understanding consists in forming and manipulating appropriate representations, that these representations can be analyzed into primitive elements, and that all phenomena can be understood as complex combinations of these simple elements. At the same time, Hobbes implicitly assumed that the elements are formal elements related by purely syntactic operations, so that reasoning can be reduced to calculation. 'When a man *reasons*, he does nothing else but conceive a sum total from addition of parcels', Hobbes wrote, 'for REASON . . . is nothing but reckoning . . . '.[4] Finally Leibniz, working out the classical idea of *mathesis* — the formalization of everything — sought grant money to develop a universal symbol system, so that 'we can assign to every object its determined characteristic number' (Leibniz, Selections, 1951).[5] According to Leibniz, in understanding we analyze concepts into more simple elements. In order to avoid a regress of simpler and simpler elements, there must be ultimate simples in terms of which all complex concepts can be understood. Moreover, if concepts are to apply to the world, there must be logical simples in the world which the simple symbols represent. Leibniz envisaged 'a kind of alphabet of human thoughts'[6] whose 'characters must show, when they are used in demonstrations, some kind of connection, grouping and order which are also found in objects'.[7]

Cognitivism is rationalism plus the computer as a model of how this rationalist account of mind actually works. In a seminal statement of this view Allen Newell and Herbert Simon claim that the human brain and the digital computer, while totally different in structure and mechanism, have, at the appropriate level of abstraction, a common functional description. At this level, both the human brain and the appropriately programmed digital computer can be seen as two different instantiations of a single species of device — one which generates intelligent behavior by manipulating symbols by means of formal rules. Newell and Simon state their view as an hypothesis: '*The Physical Symbol System Hypothesis*. A physical symbol system has the necessary and sufficient means for general intelligent action. By "necessary" we mean that any system that exhibits general intelligence will prove upon analysis to be a physical symbol system. By "sufficient" we mean that any physical symbol system of sufficient size can be organized further to exhibit general intelligence' (Newell and Simon, 1976).[8]

If one were looking for an easy way to challenge this hypothesis one might question its most vulnerable claim: that *perception* is thought. But for the sake of this discussion I prefer to raise the stakes and take on cognitivism on the territory where it seems most plausible: its claim that *intelligent behavior* results from conscious or unconscious thinking on the model of the deliberative inference making of Sherlock Holmes. More specifically, I will focus on the case most favorable to cognitivism: the ability of experts in cognitive domains such as chess.

The issue can be focused by looking at the assumptions underlying the building of expert systems, since such systems involve a crude but consistent application of the cognitivist perspective. Building expert systems in isolable cognitive domains is the work of so-called *knowledge engineers*. What the knowledge engineers claim to have discovered is that in areas which are cut off from everyday common sense and social intercourse, all a machine needs in order to behave like an expert are some general rules and lots of very specific knowledge. This specialized knowledge is of two types: 'The first type is the *facts* of the domain — the widely shared knowledge . . . that is written in textbooks and journals of the field . . . . Equally important to the practice of the field is the second type of knowledge called *heuristic knowledge*, which is the knowledge of good practice and good judgment in a field . . . that a human expert acquires over years of work' (Feigenbaum and McCorduck, 1983).[9]

Using all three kinds of knowledge Edward Feigenbaum, the father of expert systems, developed a program called DENDRAL. It takes the data generated by a mass spectrograph and deduces from this data the molecular structure of the compound being analyzed. Another program, MYCIN, takes the results of blood tests such as the number of red cells, white cells, sugar in the blood etc. and comes up with a diagnosis of which blood disease is responsible for this condition. It even gives an estimate of the reliability of its own diagnosis. In their narrow areas, such programs give impressive performances.

And, indeed, is not the success of expert systems just what the tradition would lead one to expect? If we agree with Feigenbaum that: 'almost all the thinking that professionals do is done by reasoning . . .'[10] we can see that once computers are used for reasoning and not just computation they should be as good or better than we are at following rules for deducing conclusions from a host of facts. So we would expect that if the rules which an expert has acquired from years of experience could be extracted and programmed, the resulting program would exhibit expertise. Again Feigenbaum puts the point very clearly: '[T]he matters that set experts apart from beginners, are symbolic, [and] inferential . . . . Experts build up a repertory of working rules of thumb, or "heuristics", that, combined with book knowledge, make them expert practitioners'.[11] Since each expert already has a repertory of rules in his mind, all the expert system builder need do is get the rules out and program them into a computer.

But, plausible as it may seem, this project has not worked out as expected. Ever since the inception of Artificial Intelligence, researchers have been trying to produce artificial experts by programming the computer to follow the rules used by masters in various domains. Yet, although computers are faster and more accurate than people in applying rules, master-level performance has remained out of reach.

Arthur Samuel's work is typical. In 1947, when electronic computers were just being developed, Samuel, then at IBM, decided to write a checker playing program. He elicited heuristic rules from checker masters and programmed a computer to follow these rules. The resulting checkers program is not only the first and one of the best experts ever built, but it is also a perfect example of the way fact turns into fiction in AI. Feigenbaum, for example, reports that 'by 1961 [Samuel's program] played championship checkers, and it learned and improved with each game'.[12] In fact, according to Samuel, after 35 years of effort, 'the program is quite capable of beating any amateur player and can give better players a good contest'. It is clearly no champion. Samuel is still bringing in expert players for help but he 'fears he may be reaching the point of diminishing returns'. This does not lead him to question the view that the masters the program cannot beat are using heuristic rules; rather, Samuel thinks that the experts are poor at recollecting their compiled heuristics. 'The experts do not know enough about the mental processes involved in playing the game',[13] he says.

The same story is repeated in every area of expertise, even in areas such as medicine where expertise requires the storage of large numbers of facts, which should give an advantage to the computer. In each area where there are experts with years of experience the computer can do better than the beginner, and can even exhibit useful competence, but it cannot rival the very experts whose facts and supposed heuristics it is processing with incredible speed and unerring accuracy.

2 A PHENOMENOLOGY OF SKILLED BEHAVIOR

In the face of this impasse, in spite of the authority of the rationalist tradition and the persuasiveness of cognitivism, we must take a fresh look at what a skill is and what the expert acquires when he achieves expertise. We must be prepared to abandon the traditional view that a beginner starts with specific cases and, as he becomes more proficient, abstracts and interiorizes more and more sophisticated rules. It might turn out that skill acquisition moves in just the opposite direction: from abstract rules to particular cases. I will concentrate on chess as a cognitive skill par excellence, but will also draw on driving to show the generality of the model my brother and I propose.

Stage 1: Novice
Normally, the instruction process begins with the instructor decomposing the task environment into context-free features which the beginner can recognize without benefit of experience. The beginner is then given rules for determining actions on the basis of these features, like a computer following a program.

The student automobile driver learns to recognize such interpretation-free features as speed (indicated by his speedometer) and distance (as estimated by a previously acquired skill). Safe following distances are defined in terms of speed; conditions that allow safe entry into traffic are defined in terms of speed and distance of oncoming traffic; timing of gear shifts is specified in terms of speed, etc.

The novice chess player learns a numerical value for each type of piece regardless of its position, and the rule: 'Always exchange if the total value of pieces captured exceeds the value of the pieces lost'. He also learns that when no advantageous exchanges can be found, center control should be sought, and he is given a rule defining center squares and one for calculating extent of control.

Stage 2: Advanced beginner

As the novice gains experience actually coping with real situations, he begins to note, or an instructor points out, perspicuous examples of meaningful additional components of the situation. After seeing a sufficient number of examples, the student learns to recognize them. Instructional *maxims* now can refer to these new *situational aspects*.

I use the terms *maxims* and *aspects* here to differentiate this form of instruction from the first, where strict *rules* were given as to how to respond to context-free *features*. Since maxims are phrased in terms of aspects they already presuppose experience in the skill domain. According to Michael Polanyi, from whom I borrow the term: 'Maxims are rules, the correct application of which is part of the art which they govern. The true maxims of golfing or of poetry increase our insight into golfing or poetry and may even give valuable guidance to golfers and poets; but these maxims would instantly condemn themselves to absurdity if they tried to replace the golfer's skill or the poet's art. Maxims cannot be understood, still less applied by anyone not already possessing a good practical knowledge of the art.' (Polanyi, 1962).[14]

The advanced beginner driver uses (situational) engine sounds as well as (non-situational) speed. He learns the maxim: shift when the motor sounds like it is straining. By observing the demeanor as well as position and velocity of pedestrians or other drivers, he learns to distinguish the behavior of the distracted or drunken driver from that of the impatient or alert one. He can then apply maxims for how to proceed in various cases. No number of words can take the place of a few choice examples in learning these maxims. Engine sounds cannot be adequately captured in words, and no list of objective facts enables one to predict the behavior of a pedestrian in a crosswalk as well as can the driver who has observed many pedestrians crossing streets under a variety of conditions.

Similarly, with experience, the chess student begins to recognize such situational aspects of positions as a weakened king's side or a strong pawn structure despite the lack of precise and universally valid definitional rules. He is then given maxims to follow, such as attack a weakened king side.

Stage 3: Competence

With increasing experience, the number of features and aspects to be taken account of becomes overwhelming. To cope with this information explosion, the performer learns, or is taught, to adopt a hierarchical view of decision-making. By first choosing a plan, goal or perspective which organizes the situation and by then examining only the small set of features and aspects that he has learned are relevant given that plan, the performer can simplify and improve his performance.

A competent driver beginning a trip decides, perhaps, that he is in a hurry. He then selects a route with attention to distance and time, ignores scenic beauty, and as he drives he chooses his maneuvers with little concern for passenger comfort or for courtesy. He follows more closely than normal, enters traffic more daringly, occasionally violates a law. He feels elated when decisions work out and no police car appears, and shaken by near accidents and traffic tickets.

The class A chess player, here classed as competent, may decide after studying a position that his opponent has weakened his king's defenses so that an attack against the king is a viable goal. If the attack is chosen, features involving weaknesses in his own position created by the attack are ignored as are losses of pieces essential to the attack. Removing pieces defending the enemy king becomes salient. Successful plans induce euphoria and mistakes are felt in the pit of the stomach.

In both of these cases, we find a common pattern: detached planning, conscious assessment of elements that are salient with respect to the plan, and analytical rule-guided choice of action, followed by an emotionally involved experience of the outcome.

The experience is emotional because choosing a plan, a goal or perspective is no simple matter for the competent performer. Nobody gives him any rules for how to choose a perspective, so he has to make up various rules which he then adopts or discards in various situations depending on how they work out. This procedure is frustrating, however, since each rule works on some occasions and fails on others, and no set of objective features and aspects correlates strongly with these successes and failures. Nonetheless the choice is unavoidable. While the advanced beginner can hold off using a particular situational aspect until a sufficient number of examples makes identification reliable, to perform competently requires choosing an organizing goal or perspective. Furthermore, the choice of perspective crucially affects behavior in a way that one particular aspect rarely does.

This combination of necessity and uncertainty introduces an important new type of relationship between the performer and his environment. The novice and the advanced beginner, applying rules and maxims, feel little or no responsibility for the outcome of their acts. If they have made no mistakes, an unfortunate outcome is viewed as the result of inadequately specified elements or principles. The competent performer, on the other hand, after wrestling with the question of a choice of perspective or goal, feels responsible for, and thus emotionally involved in, the result of his choice. An outcome that is clearly successful is deeply satisfying and leaves a vivid memory of the situation encountered as seen from the goal or perspective finally chosen. Disasters, likewise, are not easily forgotten.

Remembered whole situations, therefore, differ in one important respect from remembered aspects. The mental image of an aspect is flat; no parts stand out as salient. A whole situation, on the other hand, since it is the result of a chosen plan or perspective, has a 'three-dimensional' quality. Certain elements stand out as more or less important with respect to the plan, while other irrelevant elements are forgotten. Moreover, the competent performer, gripped by the situation that his decision has produced, experiences the situation not only in terms of foreground and background elements but also in terms of opportunity, risk, expectation, threat etc. As we shall see, if he stops reflecting on problematic situations as a detached observer, and stops thinking about himself as a computer following better and better rules, these gripping, holistic experiences become the basis of the competent performer's next advance in skill.

Stage 4: Proficiency
Considerable experience at the level of competency sets the stage for yet further skill enhancement. Having experienced many situations, chosen plans in each, and having obtained vivid, involved demonstrations of the adequacy or inadequacy of the plan, the performer involved in the world of the skill 'notices', or is 'struck by', a certain plan, goal

or perspective. No longer is the spell of involvement broken by detached conscious planning.

Since there are generally far fewer 'ways of seeing' than 'ways of acting', after understanding without conscious effort what is going on, the proficient performer will still have to think about what to do. During this thinking, elements that present themselves as salient are assessed and combined by rule and maxim to produce decisions about how best to manipulate the environment.

On the basis of prior experience, a proficient driver approaching a curve on a rainy day may sense that he is travelling too fast. Then, on the basis of such salient elements as visibility, angle of road bank, criticalness of time etc., he decides whether to take his foot off the gas or to step on the brake. (These factors would be used by the *competent* driver to *decide that* he is speeding.)

The proficient chess player, who is classed a master, can recognize a large repertoire of types of positions. Recognizing almost immediately and without conscious effort the sense of a position, he sets about calculating the move that best achieves his goal. He may, for example, know that he should attack, but he must deliberate about how best to do so.

Stage 5: Expertise

The proficient performer, immersed in the world of his skilful activity, *sees* what needs to be done, but *decides* how to do it. With enough experience with a variety of situations, all seen from the same perspective but requiring different tactical decisions, the proficient performer seems gradually to decompose this class of situations into subclasses, each of which shares the same decision, single action or tactic. This allows the immediate intuitive response to each situation which is characteristic of expertise.

The expert chess player, classed as an international master or grandmaster, in most situations experiences a compelling sense of the issue and the best move. Excellent chess players can play at the rate of 5-10 seconds a move and even faster without any serious degradation in performance. At this speed they must depend almost entirely on intuition and hardly at all on analysis and comparison of alternatives. My brother, Stuart, recently performed an experiment in which an international master, Julio Kaplan, was required rapidly to add numbers presented to him audibly at the rate of about one number per second, while at the same time playing five-second-a-move chess against a slightly weaker, but master level, player. Even with his analytical mind completely occupied by adding numbers, Kaplan more than held his own against the master in a series of games. Deprived of the time necessary to see problems or construct plans, Kaplan still produced fluid and coordinated play.

Kaplan's performance seems somewhat less amazing when one realizes that a chess position is as meaningful, interesting and important to a professional chess player as a face in a receiving line is to a professional politician. Almost anyone can add numbers and simultaneously recognize and respond to faces, even though each face will never exactly match the same face seen previously, and politicians can recognize thousands of faces, just as Julio Kaplan can recognize thousands of chess positions similar to ones previously encountered. The number of classes of discriminable situations, built up on the basis of experience, must be immense. It has been estimated that a master chess player can distinguish roughly 50,000 types of positions.

Automobile driving probably involves the ability to discriminate a similar number of typical situations. The expert driver, generally without any awareness, not only knows by feel and familiarity when an action such as slowing down is required; he knows how to perform the action without calculating and comparing alternatives. He shifts gears when appropriate with no awareness of his acts. What must be done, simply is done.

It seems that a beginner makes inferences using strict rules and features just like a heuristically programmed computer, but that with talent and a great deal of involved experience the beginner develops into an expert who sees intuitively what to do without applying rules and making inferences at all. Cognitivism has given an accurate description of the beginner and of the expert facing an unfamiliar situation, but normally an expert does not *solve problems*. He does not *reason*. He does what in his experience has normally worked and, naturally, it normally works.

3 THE SOURCES OF COGNITIVISM

We have seen that it is easy to trace cognitivism back to seventeenth century rationalism. But the roots of the cognitivist account of intelligence reach much further back into our tradition. As far as I can tell, this intellectualist account grows out of two observations made by Socrates. Both were good phenomenology but, like a good philosopher, he over-generalized them. He saw that experts can often explain why they do what they do, and that these explanations reveal principles from which the behavior in question can be seen to follow rationally. Generalizing these observations, Socrates claims in the *Gorgias* that an art must have 'principles of action and reason'[15] and, in the *Laches*, that 'that which we know we must surely be able to tell'.[16] Let us look carefully at each of these claims.

The claim that a craft or *techné* must be based on principles which can be articulated by the practitioners leads Socrates to rule out of account all forms of intuitive expertise which do not seem to be based on any principles at all. Cooking, for example, is 'unable to render any account of the nature of the methods it applies'.[17] It 'goes straight to its end, nor even considers or calculates anything'.[18] Socrates holds that such intuitive abilities are not skills at all but mere knacks based on trial and error. This would rule out such experts as chicken sexors who, without being able to articulate any reasons and without, as far as anyone has been able to tell, using any features (cues) or rules, are able to sort male and female one day-old chicks at a rate of 1000 an hour with 99.5 per cent accuracy (Lunn, 1948).[19] But, since I am trying to take on cognitivism where it is most plausible, and in my story of skill acquisition I have not rested my argument on skills like chicken sexing and X-ray reading which are learned purely by apprenticeship, I will take my stand on Socrates' own ground and limit my discussion to crafts — articulable skills learned by instruction, whose practitioners do 'know many things'.[20]

Socrates shares with modern knowledge engineers the assumption that experts in a craft know principles of action and reason and that what they know they must be able to tell. In its weak form, as just stated, the claim has a basis in the experience of experts. If our account of skill acquisition is correct, some experts can at least tell the maxims of their craft. Polanyi has stressed that much can be said but that what can be said will never be the whole story: 'Analysis may bring subsidiary knowledge into focus and formulate it as a maxim . . . but such specification is in general not exhaustive. Although the expert diagnostician, taxonomist and cotton-classer can indicate their clues and formulate their maxims, they know many more things that they can tell . . .[21] According to Polanyi and our skill model, most experts can remember and state maxims or rules of thumb which help explain how they achieve their goals, but these only make sense to those already familiar with the relevant skill domain.

So far, so good. But Socrates seems to want much more. He seems to want to elicit rules or principles from experts in each craft domain that would enable *anyone* to acquire expertise in that domain. If we assume for the sake of this discussion, as Socrates assumes ironically in his dialogue, that *Euthyphro*, a religious prophet, is an expert at recognizing piety and Socrates is not, it looks like Socrates is asking for more than Euthyphro's piety recognizing maxim when he says: 'I·want to know what is characteristic of piety . . . to use as a standard whereby to judge your actions and those of other men'.[22] He seems to want a strict rule which can be used even by non-experts.

Euthyphro's first response to this demand is like that of any expert. He gives Socrates examples from his field of expertise, in this case mythical situations in the past in which men and gods have done things which everyone considers pious. Socrates then makes his usual demand that Euthyphro tell him his rule for recognizing these cases as examples of piety. And Euthyphro, like any expert examined by Socrates, produces various maxims which, if taken as definitions or strict rules, do not hold up under cross-examination. The problem seems to be that maxims have *ceteris paribus* conditions which do not detract from their usefulness to other experts but make them useless to the non-expert who wants a consistent, context-free rule, which so exhaustively captures the expertise in question as to make it accessible to any intelligent person. That Socrates demands such a rule is clear in the *Laches* where he asks Laches, presumably an expert on courage, 'What is that common quality, which is the same in all cases, and which is called courage?'[23] But no expert can formulate such definitional rules. This leads Socrates to the famous conclusion that since no craftsman, statesman or other expert can state the consistent, context-free principles which provide the rationale for his actions, no one knows anything at all.

This is where Plato came to the aid of Socrates. Perhaps experts were operating on principles they could not easily articulate, Plato suggested. Experts, at least in areas involving non-empirical knowledge such as morality and mathematics, had, in another life, Plato claimed, learned the principles involved, but they had forgotten them. The role of the philosopher was to help such moral and mathematical experts recall the principles on which they were acting. These principles would ground the knowledge of the skill. Such knowledge must be 'fastened by the reasoning of cause and effect' and 'this is done by "recollection"'.[24]

Knowledge engineers, generalizing the doctrine of recollection, now say that the rules experts — even experts in empirical domains — use, have been put in a part of their mental computers where they work automatically. Thus, Feigenbaum tells us: 'When we learned how to tie our shoes, we had to think very hard about the steps involved . . . . Now that we've tied many shoes over our lifetime, that knowledge is 'compiled', to use the computing term for it; it no longer needs our conscious attention'.[25] On this modern version of Platonic recollection, the rules are there functioning in the expert's mind whether he is conscious of them or not. After all, how else could one account for the fact that the expert can perform the task? Even Polanyi, who as far as I know was the first to see the importance of the difference between strict rules and maxims, falls for the cognitivist temptation. He tells us that: 'By watching the master . . . the apprentice unconsciously picks up the rules of the art, including those which are not explicitly known to the master himself'.[26] This is no lapse but an essential part of Polanyi's crypto-cognitivist view of the relation of maxims and strict rules: 'In performing a skill we are therefore acting on certain premisses of which we are focally ignorant, but which we know subsidiarily as part of our mastery of that skill, and which we may get to know focally by analysing the way we achieve success . . . in the skill in question. The rules of success which we thus derive can help us to improve our skill and to teach it to others — but only if these principles are first re-integrated into the art of which they are the maxims. For though no art can be exercised according to its explicit rules, such rules can be of great assistance to an art if observed subsidiarily within the context of its skilfull performance' (Polanyi, 1962).[27]

This gives the knowledge engineer a venerable task. As Feigenbaum explains: '[A]n expert's knowledge is often ill-specified or incomplete because the expert himself doesn't always know exactly what it is he knows about his domain' (Feigenbaum and McCorduck, 1983),[28] So the knowledge engineer has to help him recollect what he once knew. '[An expert's] knowledge is currently acquired in a very painstaking way; individual computer scientists work with individual experts to explicate the expert's heuristics — to mine those jewels of knowledge out of their heads one by one . . . . [T]he problem of knowledge acquisition is the critical bottleneck in artificial intelligence.'[29] Now, thanks to Feigenbaum and his colleagues, we have a new name for what Socrates and Plato were doing: *knowledge acquisition research.*[30]

But nothing has changed. When Feigenbaum suggests to an expert the rules the expert seems to be using, he gets a Euthyphro-like response. 'That's true, but if you see enough patients/rocks/chip designs/instruments readings, you see that it isn't true after all'[31] and Feigenbaum comments with Socratic annoyance: 'At this point, knowledge threatens to become ten thousand special cases'.[32] Still the generalized doctrine of recollection assures the knowledge engineer that the principles must be there in the expert's mind, the expert is simply poor at remembering them.

One important question remains: For Plato, are the unconscious principles, maxims or rules? We have seen that Socrates seems to think that experts should be able to articulate strict rules that would enable *anyone* to share their expertise. That would make Socrates an extreme cognitivist, about skills at least. But the question of Socrates's intellectualism is subject to debate. Terrence Irwin, indeed, claims that Socrates is a pure intellectualist who holds that the rules experts use must fully capture their expertise (Irwin, 1977).[33] 'A Socratic definition says what a thing is, and states an account which justified our beliefs about it', he tells us. For example, 'Socrates demands an explicit understanding of the principles guiding (not necessarily explicitly) our applications of "just" or "pious", so that we can see whether they are consistent and justifiable, and can appeal to them to project our judgements to new cases'.[34] 'The expert in a particular craft offers authoritative guidance, supported by a rational account.'[35] Alexander Nehamas, however, has argued that Socrates, the son of a stone-mason, would surely know that the rules a craftsman can articulate are not sufficiently explicit and complete to convey the craft to an outsider. 'Socrates, himself a statuary and a statuary's son (D.L. V.I.18), knew perfectly well that in ancient Athens the crafts were most often transmitted along with their "secrets within the family from generation to generation"' (Nehamas, 1986).[36]

Who is right, Irwin or Nehamas? As we have seen, Socrates does seem to hold in the *Euthyphro* that if he had Euthyphro's rules he too would be an expert on piety. Still, since we only have an example from the domain of morality where Socrates is surely to some extent already an initiate, this would be consistent with Nehamas's view that Socrates held that 'only one virtuous person can recognize another'.[37]

The same holds for the definition of courage. There is no evidence I know of that Socrates thought that a craftsman must, in principle, be able to articulate rules that would enable an outsider following these rules to become an expert at his craft.

Plato never explicitly holds this view either, but it seems to me that the doctrine of recollection as Plato uses it, i.e. not only as an account of why moral and mathematical experts cannot easily articulate their rules, but also as an account of how they learned these rules in the first place, commits him to pure cognitivism. That is, it commits him to the view that the principles underlying such expertise must be strict rules, not merely maxims. If this is, indeed, the case, Socrates and Plato would turn out to share the blame for cognitivism.

The argument is simple. If someone's knowledge in a specific domain — in Plato's example in the *Meno*, mathematics — is supposed to have acquired his expertise from scratch by seeing in another world the principles underlying the skill domain, then the principles he saw could not have been the maxims given the advanced beginner, since, as I am using the terms, maxims already require familiarity with the skill domain. Therefore, the principles the soul acquires in the other world must be the sort of strict rules defined over features which are comprehensible to a rank beginner. But then this comes to the claim that strict rules are sufficient to generate expertise, and this is precisely the pure cognitivist claim.

To sum up: What experts actually say suggests that they can at best formulate maxims which they presumably remember from when they were advanced beginners, and which can be of use to others with some skill in the relevant domain. Socrates does not seem to have contradicted this observation, but he makes two moves towards cognitivism:

1) He rules out as trial and error skills such as cooking which are learned solely by apprenticeship and which therefore do not seem to be based on principles;

2) He assumes that all true skills are based on principles which must be expressable by those who have the skill.

Plato, however, went further and provided an account of why certain types of experts were in fact so poor at articulating the principles underlying their performance, and in so doing developed the theory of recollection which committed him to the view that there were strict rules underlying certain types of expertise. Such expertise, according to Plato, was not based merely on maxim following.

Plato's account did not apply to everyday skills. It took another thousand years before Leibniz boldly generalized the Platonic account to all forms of intelligent activity: '[T]he most important observations and turns of skill in all sorts of trades and professions are as yet unwritten. This fact is proved by experience when, passing from theory to practice, we desire to accomplish something. *Of course, we can also write up this practice, since it is at bottom just another theory more complex and particular . . . .(page 8)*[40]

This sets things up for the last move which makes the rules and the elements to which they apply explicitly syntactic. Thus for modern cognitive scientists all mental activity is based upon fully rational calculations of the sort which can be implemented in a computer program.

4 CONCLUSION

A phenomenology of skill acquisition enables us to understand why the knowledge engineers from Socrates and Plato to Samuel and Feigenbaum have had such trouble getting the expert to articulate the rules he is using, and why the rules that are dredged up, when programmed, never produce expertise. The expert is simply not following any rules! He is doing just what Socrates and Feigenbaum saw and yet denied he was doing — discriminating thousands of special cases. The Socratic slogan: "If you understand it, you can explain it', should be reversed: Anyone who thinks he can fully explain his skill, does not have expert understanding.

This explains why expert systems are never as good as experts. If one asks an expert for strict rules one will, in effect, force the expert to regress to the level of a beginner and state the rules he still remembers but no longer uses. If one programs these rules into a computer, one can use the speed and accuracy of the computer and its ability to store and access millions of facts to outdo a human beginner using the same rules. But no amount of rules and facts can capture the knowledge an expert has when he has stored his experience of the actual outcomes of tens of thousands of situations.

The knowledge engineer might still say that in spite of appearances the mind and brain *must* be reasoning — making millions of rapid and accurate inferences like a computer. After all, the brain is not 'wonder tissue' and how else could it work? But there *are* other models for what might be going on in the hardware. Researchers who call themselves new connectionists are building devices that operate somewhat like neural networks. In a connectionist machine, the states of the machine often cannot be interpreted as symbols representing invariant features of the skill domain, and what are stored are not representations at all but connection strengths between neurons. Such parallel distributed processing systems can recognize patterns and detect similarity and regularity without using rules and features at all (Rumelhart and McClelland, 1986).[38]

Once one gives up the cognitivist assumption that experts must be making inferences, and admits the role of involvement and intuition in the acquisition and exercise of skills, one will have no reason to cling to the cognitivist program as a model of human intellectual operations. Those, like Feigenbaum, who boast that expert systems will soon have 'access to machine intelligence — faster, deeper, better than human intelligence', (Feigenbaum and McCorduck, 1983),[39] can be seen as false prophets blinded by Socratic and Platonic assumptions — while Euthyphro, the alleged expert on piety, who kept giving Socrates examples instead of rules, may turn out to have been a true prophet after all.

NOTES

1 Fodor, J.A. (1975). Fodor's Guide to Mental Representation: The Intelligent Auntie's Vade-Mecum, *Mind* 94, p91.
2 Fodor, J.A. (1975). *The Language of Thought*. Thomas Y. Crowell Company. 44.
3 Haugeland, John (1985). *Artificial Intelligence, The Very Idea*; Bradford/MIT Press, p113
4 Hobbes,- (1958). *Leviathan*. Library of Liberal Arts. 45.
5 Leibniz,- (1951). *Selections* edited by Philip Wiener. Scribner. 18.
6 Ibid. 20.
7 Ibid. 10.
8 Newell, Allen and Herbert Simon (1976). Computer Science as Empirical Inquiry: Symbols and Search, in John Haugeland (ed.) (1981) *Mind Design*. Bradford/MIT Press, Cambridge, Mass. 41.
9 Feigenbaum, Edward and Pamela McCorduck (1983). *The Fifth Generation*. Addison-Wesley Pub. Co. 76-77.
10 Ibid. 18.
11 Ibid. 64.
12 Ibid. 179.
13 Interview with Arthur Samuel released by the Stanford University News Office, April 28, 1983.
14 Polanyi, Michael (1962). *Personal Knowledge*. Routledge & Kegan Paul. 2nd ed. 31.
15 *Gorgias*. 501a.
16 *Laches*. 190.
17 *Gorgias*. 465a.
18 Ibid. 501a. Aristotle, on the contrary, who, as usual, stays close to the normal everyday phenomenon, sees the immediate, intuitive response, precisely as characteristic of an expert craftsman. 'Art (*techné*) does not deliberate' he says in *Physics8, Bk.II, Ch.8*.
19 *Lunn, John H. (1948). Chick Sexing, American Scientist*. 36.
20 *Apology*. 22d.
21 Polanyi, Michael. op. cit. 88.
22 *Euthyphro*. 6e3-6.
23 *Laches*. 191e.
24 *Meno*. 98a.
25 Feigenbaum, Edward. op. cit. 55.
26 Polanyi, Michael. op. cit. 53.
27 Ibid. op. cit. 162.
28 Feigenbaum, Edward. op. cit. 85.
29 Ibid. 79-80.
30 Ibid. 79.
31 Ibid. 82
32 Ibid. 82.
33 Irwin, Terrence, (1977). *Plato's Moral Theory*. Oxford University Press.
34 Ibid. 65.
35 Ibid. 71.
36 Nehamas, Alexander. Socratic Intellectualism in *Proceedings of the Boston Area Colloquium in Ancient Philosophy*. 2. 22.
37 Ibid. 30-31.
38 Leibniz,-. op. cit. 48. My italics.
39 See Rumelhart, David and James McClelland (1986). *Parallel Distributed Processing*. Bradford/MIT Press.

REFERENCES

Aristotle. *Physics*.
Dreyfus, Hubert and Stuart Dreyfus (1986). *Mind Over Machine*. Free Press.
Feigenbaum, Edward and Pamela McCorduck (1983). *The Fifth Generation*. Addison Wesley Publishing Co.
Fodor, Jerry A. (1975). *The Language of Thought*. Thomas Y. Crowell Company.
Fodor, Jerry A. (1985). Fodor's Guide to Mental Representation: The Intelligent Auntie's Vade-Mecum, *Mind 94*. 76-100.
Haugeland, John (1985). *Artificial Intelligence, The Very Idea*. Bradford/MIT Press.
Hobbes, Thomas. *Leviathan*.
Irwin, Terence (1977). *Plato's Moral Theory*. Oxford University Press.
von Leibniz Gottfried, W.F. (1677). Towards a Universal Characteristic.
Lunn, John H. (1984). Chick Sexing, *American Scientist*. 36.
Nehamas, Alexander (1986). Socratic Intellectualism, *Proceeding of the Boston Area Colloquium in Ancient Philosophy*. Vol II.
Newell, Alan and Herbert Simon (1981). Computer Science as Empirical Enquiry: Symbols and Search, in Haugeland (ed.) *Mind Design*. Bradford/MIT Press.
Plato. *Apology*.
Plato. *Euthyphro*.
Plato. *Gorgias*.
Plato. *Laches*.
Plato. *Meno*.
Polanyi, Michael (1982). *Personal Knowledge*. Routledge and Kegan Paul. 2nd ed.
Rumelhart, David and James McClelland (1986). *Parallel Distributed Processing*. Bradford/MIT Press.

AI & Soc (1989) 3: 271–296
© 1989 Springer-Verlag London Limited

Cockpit Cognition: Education, the Military and Cognitive Engineering*

Douglas D. Noble

76 Westland Avenue, New York 14618, USA

"Our final hope is to develop the brain as a natural resource . . . Human intelligence will be the weapon of the future."

Luis Alberto Machado[1]

Abstract. The goals of public education, as well as conceptions of human intelligence and learning, are undergoing a transformation through the application of military-sponsored information technologies and information processing models of human thought. Recent emphases in education on thinking skills, learning strategies, and computer-based technologies are the latest episodes in the postwar military agenda to engineer intelligent components, human and artificial, for the optimal performance of complex technological systems. Public education serves increasingly as a "human factors" laboratory and production site for this military enterprise, whose high performance technologies and command and control paradigms have also played central roles in the emergence of the information economy.

Keywords: Cognitive engineering; Education; Educational technology; Cognitive science; Information society; Military technology; Military research and development; Learning research; Problem solving; Thinking skills

Introduction

Public Education's New Mandate: How to Think, How to Learn

Problem-solving. Critical thinking. Reasoning. Learning skills. Such "higher-order" mental capacities have recently surfaced as new goals for US education.

Overnight, curriculum planners throughout the country, at all levels of

---

* This paper will also appear, under the title "Mental Materiel" in *Cyborg Worlds: The Military Information Society*, eds. Les Levidow and Kevin Robins, London: Free Association Press, (in press).

education, are designing courses in critical thinking and problem-solving. "Teaching for thinking", we are told (Costa, 1984, p. 62) "is . . . the great educational discovery of the 80s". Teachers of every subject routinely talk about "learning strategies" as their instructional focus. Articles and books promote the "new three R's: Reading, 'Riting and Reasoning", while standardized tests are revised to reflect increased intellectual expectations. Everywhere, instruction is being recodified in terms of "comprehension strategies" and 'cognitive objectives" and "metacognitive skills".

There are several reasons given by educators for this sudden new emphasis on higher-order abilities in public education. Of course, a small cadre of progressive teachers have been promoting critical thinking, logic instruction, and independent learning for years. Many others have suddenly become alarmed by the deficiencies of their students, who do not know how to learn, do not know how to think, do not know how to question what they read, do not know how to solve problems in mathematics and science. Still others have been motivated by the presence of computers, with their alleged potential to foster just such higher-level intellectual activity. Many are encouraged by a recent flurry of new research on learning and intelligence that, they are told, promises techniques to train complex cognitive functioning. Meanwhile, education leaders are heeding the call of businessmen who urge that international competition, rapid technological change, and the complexities of the information age all demand a workforce of "problem-solvers": people who can interpret information, who can learn new tasks, who can "think for a living" (Carnegie Forum, 1986).

From all accounts, a growing number of educators sincerely believe that the time is ripe for such higher intellectual expectations within public education, signaling a vigorous transition from an ineffective, deadening traditional pedagogy to an era of universal intellectual empowerment and educational excellence.

The Need for a Deeper Analysis

But things are not as they seem. In fact, this sanguine new celebration of cerebration, of intellect and learning, is for the most part a confused blend of scientific hyperbole, wishful thinking, and irrepressible ideology.

For one thing, 40% of urban high school students drop out before graduation while 25% of adults nationwide cannot read. Such statistics belie any simplistic faith that a new intellectual focus on thinking and learning skills, coupled with new technologies, will turn the nation's students, however ill-prepared, however impoverished, however disaffected, into motivated learners, let alone intelligent, reflective thinkers. Second, the sudden new appreciation of intellectual competence on the job and in school is baffling, juxtaposed beside the general derogation of intellectual competence in our society, reflected in the increase of mind-numbing service sector jobs and in the vacuous content of typical television fare.

Third, the belief in the possibility of an intellectual reformulation of education is based largely on recent cognitive research on learning and intelligence; yet there is little evidence that this research has anything to offer the classroom at this time.[2] Last, but not least, the new research on learning and intelligence underlying educators' elevated expectations has been sponsored not by the Department of Education, as one might expect, but rather, curiously enough, by the Department of Defense, which leads one to wonder what is really going on.

Clearly, the sudden celebration of intellect and learning within an educational and intellectual wasteland, a celebration largely underwritten by the military, requires a deeper explanation. Could it be that educators have unwittingly adopted the framework of a larger military/scientific enterprise that only appears to be an agenda for public education because the language – intelligence, learning, thinking, and problem-solving – is the same?

The Military Demand for Intelligent Technologies

This paper provides just such an alternative analysis of the sudden interest in the cultivation of human intellect within education. Its thesis is that this new educational impulse is in fact a derivative venture. It is both a "spin-off" of and a corollary to a much deeper and more pervasive enterprise, fueled by military research and mirrored in corporate practice. This is the enterprise to harness intelligence, both human and machine, for use within complex military and corporate technological systems. Here the promise of "expert systems" and "artificial intelligence" (AI) captures the collective imagination of generals and chief executives, for whom the interest in "understanding [and improving] how people reason . . . [is] clearly motivated by the pressing needs to make effective use of technology" (Sheil, 1982, p. 104). The new goal for education unwittingly reflects the need to fulfill this technological promise, rather than reflecting any new-found appreciation for the developed potential of enlightened, empowered human beings.

In fact, the new appreciation of intellect represents the desiccation of human intellectual potential at the very moment it appears to be celebrating it. This is because people's cognitive processes of learning and thinking, *but not people themselves*, are needed as components in the complex information systems of the military and industry. And it is because the new "higher-order" education consists in the training of cognitive procedures derived not from a deep appreciation of human ingenuity but instead from computer models of machine learning and artificial intelligence. In the "age of the smart machine", according to Shoshana Zuboff (1988, p. 309), "successful utilization of intelligent systems requires maximizing the cognitive capacity and learning ability of the work force". This in turn requires the schools to serve as both laboratory and production site, bending human minds into technologies themselves – imbued, no less than machines, with a reliable, controllable, flexible "artificial" intelligence. Human beings, already reduced to the status of "human resources", or "personnel", defined in terms of their function within institutional systems, are thus further reduced to hardly animate, mental "materiel" – cognitive processing units within the interstices of large technological systems.

The Organization of this Paper

This paper is in three parts, as follows:

Part One will consist of a brief outline of the two historical paths leading to the current scenario. First, in order to show that US education has been following military prerogatives for decades, I shall sketch the importance of military research and development in the emergence of technologies, systems and methods used in public education since the 1950s. Next, I shall trace the development, also since the mid-1950s, of a militarized science of mind, based on human cognition viewed as an information processing system. I shall show how an interest in cognitive "human factors" arose within the military context of engineering complex weapon systems, giving rise to the fields of artificial intelligence and cognitive science, as well as to a preoccupation with human problem solving.

Part Two will discuss the latest phase of military funding in cognitive science and educational technology, begun in the mid-1970s, which involves the wedding of these two military ventures. The motives of researchers and their military sponsors in this new unified enterprise are described.

Part Three will describe the new field of "cognitive engineering", born of the unification of cognitive science and educational technology. Two examples of cognitive engineering will be discussed: the amplification of intelligence through man–computer interaction, and the direct training of cognitive processes, including thinking skills and learning strategies. The question "Who is ultimately in control of these skills and strategies?" will complete the analysis.

The Conclusion will return to the role of public education in this scenario. In it, I shall suggest that public education, in its heightened emphasis on applications of new research in thinking and learning, serves unwittingly as an instrument of educational engineering. It is at once a locus of legitimation, a laboratory for developing and testing cognitive theories, and, ultimately, a site for the production of "mental materiel" for technological systems.

Part One: The background

Militarized Pedagogy: Military Origins of Educational Innovation

Although it might appear strange to suggest that impulses within public education are part of military agendas, the fact is that the US military since at least World War I has had a substantial impact on school practice. Because of its enormous budget, protected in the interest of national security, the military serves as a vanguard innovator in technological research and development. By seeding new research and by shielding the products of this research from market and democratic forces (Smith, 1985), the military permits many esoteric technological enterprises to mature. Some of these – the transistor, the chip – manage to survive later commercialization and legislative politics, while others – teaching machines, nuclear power – collapse from their own insufficiencies when they emerge from the protected military umbrella. The military nurturance and protection of educational innovations, and, as the next section will show, of artificial intelligence and cognitive psychology as well, has followed just this pattern.

In education, it is widely acknowledged that standardized testing is a legacy of Army Alpha and Beta tests originally used for selection and classification purposes in World War I; less well known are the wartime training origins of the influential "educational engineering" movement in the 1920s, which resurfaced as "educational technology" after World War II (Neumann, 1979). Since World War II, in fact, military research and development has served as the dominant incubator of educational technology, and it is the source of most of the technologies, instructional systems and learning models that have entered the schools in the last three decades.

During World War II, educators and experimental psychologists mounted a massive effort in training research and development, characterized by intensified use of behavioral objectives and task analysis, and by the use of audiovisual technologies, including instructional films, training devices, and simulations. After the war this research effort, rather than being disbanded, was intensified within a panoply of new military laboratories. These included the Air Force Personnel and Training Research Center (AFPTRC), the Air Force's RAND Corporation and System Development Corporation (SDC), the Army's Human Resources Research Office (HumRRo), and the Navy Personnel Research and Development Center (NPDRC). In addition, an "enormous body of psychological literature on learning and training was generated" (Neumann, 1979, p. 86) under contract with such military funding agencies as the Office of Naval Research (ONR), the Air Force Office of Scientific Research (AFOSR), the Army Research Institute (ARI), and the Defense Advanced Research Projects Agency (DARPA, formerly ARPA).

Educational technologies that have emerged from this military research effort include overhead projectors, language laboratories, instructional films, instructional television, teaching machines, computer-assisted and computer-managed instruction, and videodisk applications. Educational models and methods derived from this research include programmed instruction, instructional design, criterion-referenced testing, individualized instructional packages, the "systems" approach to educational administration, simulation software, skill taxonomies, behavioral objectives, the mastery learning model, and intelligent tutoring systems.[3] Anyone familiar with US education will recognize in this list a rather exhaustive compendium of educational innovations that have entered the schools, and that have fueled much of the direction of educational research since the 1960s.

These military-sponsored educational innovations reflect the distinctive needs of military training. These needs include: efficiency, particularly the shortest possible training time; task-specific performance, avoiding both "undertraining" and "overtraining"; the use of technologies and simulations, to supplant the use of instructors and actual weapon systems in training; and instructional system design, to ensure the compatibility of training to ongoing changes in mission and in weapons systems technology. All of these characteristics reflect the military need for complete control of the training process, which is viewed as a "personnel subsystem" ancillary to the design, development and implementation of complex weapons systems.

The considerable influence of military research on public schools is not a result of some Pentagon conspiracy. Rather, military educational innovations have been incorporated into public school practice and research through a convergence of efforts and motives. These include researchers seeking wider funding and laboratory opportunities, education leaders seeking ways to improve the schools and to modernize their profession, and commercial interests seeking to exploit new education markets. They also involve political leaders capitalizing on public outrage over educational failure, and a population encouraged to believe in the prestige of science and space-age technology, offering educational solutions to technological and economic threats to US hegemony.

In any event, educational agendas have been influenced enormously by the massive military research and development enterprise, although this influence is rarely discussed. So, too, have the recent cognitive thrust in modern psychology and the celebrated impulse to build intelligent machines.

Militarized Mind: The Military Origins of Artificial Intelligence and Cognitive Science

During World War II, psychologists and engineers, responding to the problems facing pilots and operators in increasingly complex weaponry, worked together to design weapons that better matched the capacities and limitations of men. Out of this human factors engineering, or "psychotechnology", came "a new view of man": "The human operator served as information transmitter and processing device interposed between his machine's displays and . . . controls" (Lachman *et al.*, 1979, p. 7). The result was a single operating unit, a new hybrid of man and machine, the "man/machine system". This new conception stimulated substantial research into the processes of human intellectual, perceptual and motor functioning: "[W]e have the human operator surrounded on both sides by very precisely known mechanisms and the question comes up, 'What kind of machine have we placed in the middle'?" (Edwards, 1985, p. 42). After the war, psychologists, biologists, and engineers began a concerted effort to provide answers to this question by applying models and metaphors from wartime developments in computers and cybernetic theory to human functioning.

The result, according to Paul Edwards (1985, pp. 1, 13), was the "militarization" of the mind and the body: "Wartime cybernetic psychology militarized the mind in theorizing . . . the antiaircraft gunner, the communications man, the airplane and submarine crewman, and the naval artilleryman . . . inserted into mechanical and electromechancial systems." With such mechanistic models and metaphors in the air, and with a growing body of empirical research on human performance, it remained for another military event to provide the context for the first concrete demonstrations of the machinery of human intellectual performance.

In 1949, in response to the first Soviet atomic bomb detonation, the US military began development of the SAGE system, a massive air defense system which eventually consisted of 23 "direction centers" across North America. Among the many research facilities involved in this effort was the Systems Research Laboratory (SRL) of the RAND Corporation, later to become the System Development Corporation. The SRL was the site of a large-scale simulation of a SAGE direction center for team training research involving radar operators.[4]

According to the account by McCorduck (1979), training director Allen Newell successfully simulated aircraft radar blips for training purposes at SRL, the first use of the computer for symbol manipulation rather than number crunching. Within the simulated training environment, Newell came to view the human operators, too, as "information processing systems" (IPS) which processed symbols just as his program "processed" the symbols of simulated radar blips (p. 127).

In the early 1950s Newell began to collaborate with RAND consultant Herbert A. Simon, whose work involved analyses of administrative decision-making in industrial organizations. Simon saw the mind as a logic machine, "which took some premises and ground them up and processed them into conclusions" (p. 127). Since signal detection by radar operators was understood as a form of complex decision-making (Did I see it or not?), Simon mapped Newell's militarized language of "information processing systems" onto a theory of management decision-making. Newell had written programs that *simulated* the symbols of radar information. Since they viewed human decision-making as another form of symbol-manipulation, or "information processing", Newell and Simon began to write programs that would *simulate* human decision-making. Their personal interests led them to start by programming simulations for playing chess and for proving theorems in mathematical logic; they then moved on to arithmetic and logic puzzles (p. 132; see also Newell and Simon, 1972).

Newell and Simon's work was part of the military endeavour to understand the "human factor" within a complex man/machine weapon system. In an early report on their work (Newell et al., 1958, p. 151), they explained, "If one considers the organism to consist of effectors, receptors, and a control system for joining these, then [ours was] a theory of the control system." They asserted that if one could simulate such complex intelligent behaviour, actually reproduce it on a computer, then one could claim to *understand* the processes behind the behavior. This was the motivation behind their work, which they called "cognitive simulation", and which was later dubbed "artificial intelligence" (AI). Although others were exploring this new research terrain at the time, Newell and Simon were the first to produce concrete examples of programs simulating intelligent behavior.

These origins of AI were also the origins of "information processing" cognitive psychology. In 1960 the psychologist George Miller and two colleagues first translated the Simon and Newell IPS into "plans and the structure of behavior" in their highly influential book by that name (Miller et al., 1960). Their efforts and others' soon replaced the opacity of the "black box" of behaviorism with the transparent "processes" of what Ulric Neisser eventually labeled "cognitive psychology" (Neisser, 1967). By now IPS cognitive psychology has swallowed up so much of contemporary psychology that the terms "cognitive psychology" and "psychology" have for many become synonymous (Knapp, 1986, p. 30).

Theories in this new psychology "represent a specific layer of explanation [i.e., computer models] lying between behavior, on one side, and neurology, on the other" (Newell and Simon, 1972, p. 876). " 'Cognition' [is] thus objectified through a new standard of psychological explanation: formal modeling [via computer programs] . . . [a] newly constructed psychological object" (Edwards, 1985, p. 22). In 1980, together with artificial intelligence and neurobiology, cognitive psychology became a part of a new science of the mind based on IPS models, christened "cognitive science" (Norman, 1981).

These origins of artificial intelligence and cognitive psychology also marked the beginning of an intense preoccupation with human problem-solving that has recently captured the imagination of educators. At SRL, Simon adopted the term "problem-solving" for what he earlier had called "decision-making"; he also used the term "problem-solving" synonymously with Newell's "information processing" (McCorduck, 1979, p. 132; Newell and Simon, 1972, p. 880). The heightened emphasis within education on complex problem-solving is a direct result of this early military human factors work in man/machine systems.

According to Newell and Simon (1972, p. 870), "the basic point inhabiting our work has been that the programmed computer and the human problem-solver are both species belonging to the genus 'information processing system' ". The recent interest of educators in AI, cognitive psychology and problem-solving relies, wittingly or unwittingly, on this view of mind as computer, which in turn stems from the view of mind as a "human factor", an "arsenal" (Simon, 1980, p. 93) of cognitive components within complex weapons systems or advanced industrial systems. According to Edwards (1985, p. 12), "cybernetic psychology began as an effort to theorize humans as component parts of weapons systems and continue[s] . . . to draw crucial models and metaphors from that problematic. Cognitive science may be read both metaphorically and literally as a theory of technological worker-soldiers."

Part Two: Educational Technology Meets Cognitive Science

A New Phase of Military Funding

The development of educational technologies and cognitive science within military man/machine research is not simply a matter of historical interest; military sponsorship of these enterprises continues to the present day, and has in fact intensified in recent years. In education, much recent research in computer-based education and computer-managed instruction (CMI) has been sponsored by the services (Ellis, 1986); the military services, particularly the Army, have been very active in videodisk research for training applications (OTA, 1982, p. 251); and practically all research on "intelligent tutoring systems", or "intelligent computer-assisted instruction" (ICAI), has been a military-sponsored enterprise (Ellis, 1986). In cognitive science, almost all research on artificial intelligence has been sponsored since the 1950s by the Defence Advanced Research Projects Agency (Bellin and Chapman, 1987; Davis, 1985), and the Office of Naval Research continues to be a prime sponsor of research in cognitive psychology.[5]

By far the most important military-sponsored efforts in educational technology and cognitive science since the 1970s have involved the wedding of the two areas into a single enterprise. As we shall see, one legacy of this union is the present emphasis in education on thinking, intelligence, problem-solving and learning strategies, which relies on research supported almost entirely by military funds.[6]

The Reasons for the Wedding of Cognitive Science and Educational Technology

Researchers in educational technology and cognitive science realized by the mid-1970s that each of their fields were at a standstill. Educational technologists recognized the limitations of behaviorist principles of learning (Gropper, 1980; Resnick, 1983) that served as the theoretical basis for programmed instruction and teaching machines in the 1960s. Early researchers in computer-assisted instruction such as Patrick Suppes began to realize that advances in this educational technology required "an explicit theory of learning and instruction" (Dreyfus and Dreyfus, 1986, p. 143), which required further reliance on the unfolding revelations of cognitive psychology.

Meanwhile, cognitive psychologists and artificial intelligence researchers also realized that they had gone as far as they could in the development of intelligent machines and in the modelling of human cognition, especially because of their inadequate understanding of human intellectual functioning in real-life situations. They recognized that "the major progress in automated . . . systems will come from a better understanding and representation of the human machine" (Towne, 1987, p. 59). AI researchers attempting to simulate such real-life human cognitive activity turned their attention from expert performance to learning processes in search of a shortcut. Simon (1983, p. 36), for one, realized that "for big, knowledge-based systems, learning [is] more efficient than programming", which quickly requires an unmanageable number of instruction steps when one attempts to simulate real-life complex behavior.

A unification of cognitive science and educational research, focused on learning and intellectual development, thus came to serve as the solution to both fields' problems; according to Roy Pea (1985b, p. 179), researchers recognized that "important advances in instructional technology and in basic cognitive science will occur as an integrated activity". Future achievements in these fields would depend on a more complete understanding of the processes of learning and of intellectual development.

Explanation of Military Sponsorship

As mentioned, the military has been a prime sponsor of this unified enterprise up to the present time; however, its interest in learning and in the development of intelligence is neither scientific nor technological, but practical, dictated by its mission.[7]

Three explanations have been offered by the military for this sponsorship: (1) the development of fully automated "intelligent systems" and "autonomous weapons", (2) the acceleration of learning and instruction in training, and (3) the "amplification" of human intelligence within man/machine systems.

(1) Total automation, in training systems and in weapons systems, has been a central theme in military research and development since World War II (Bellin and Chapman, 1987; Shaker and Wise, 1988), and is the force as well behind industry's drive for the "automated factory". The failure of this endeavour to create autonomous intelligent machines has forced the military (and corporations) to retain the "man in the loop" within complex technological systems. But one underlying focus of the new research on learning and intelligence remains this endeavour to eventually codify human intellectual functioning sufficiently to produce automated machines. In this sense, the military (and corporate) preoccupation with improving human learning and intelligence is merely an interim measure.

(2) The complexity of its increasingly esoteric weapons systems has staggered military efforts to train maintenance, troubleshooting, and operations personnel. According to Evans (1986, p. 11), learning to repair the tracks on the M-1 tank is considered equivalent in difficulty to a first-year college course, AEGIS cruiser fire controlmen spend 27 months in school, and the maintenance publications for the Navy's F-14 interceptor total 300 000 pages. And these training problems are compounded by the educational deficiencies of many new recruits (p. 12). Not surprisingly, then, the military has turned to exotic new training approaches, in conjunction with its use of sophisticated instructional technologies. McCoy (1986, p. 61) of the Air Force Human Research Laboratory, for example, contends that "the unobservable mental acts required for skillful information processing constitute important elements of technical competence across many Air Force specialities". For this reason, Wittrock (1979, p. 309) explains, "the armed services are in the forefront of applications of . . . cognitive psychology to instruction." (See also Halff et al., 1986.) Their goal is to permit direct intervention, manipulation and reorganization of these "unobservable mental acts" in order to accelerate and strengthen learning capacities.

(3) The military also needs to "amplify" and "accelerate" the cognitive processes of pilots and other operators of complex high-speed weapons systems in order to bring them "up to speed" with the systems themselves. This in turn ensures the optimal utilization of these technologies. A high performance, computer-based weapon system such as the F-14 jet fighter requires a pilot capable of split-second performance in response to the continuous flow of information generated by on-board computers. To meet such high performance specification in the "human factor", in order to make the human more "machine-friendly", the military needs to 'redesign . . . the operator" (WGBH, 1988), through an understanding of human abilities and their amplification.

In other words, the military wants to "engineer" the "human factor" just as it designs and engineers the hardware and software. According to cognitive psychologist Donald Norman (1980), "any situation in which the human mind is a relevant part of the system could use a systematic engineering application of the lessons from cognitive psychology." This engineering approach involves reorganizing human functioning based on computer models, which in turn requires a fuller understanding of the principles of learning and instruction. The urgency of this engineering project was clearly recognized early on in the development of intelligent machines. In 1964 at a symposium entitled "Computer Augmentation of Human Reasoning", Ruth Davis (Davis et al., 1965, p. 171), representing the military sponsor of the symposium, warned that "it is much easier to improve computers than it is to improve people. . . . It takes twenty years to develop a person to the extent that we are now developing the computer. And we are getting out of phase very rapidly.'

Part Three: Cognitive Engineering: Redesigning Mind

"We are going to retool our industry, and . . . we must, at the same time, retool ourselves."
J. C. R. Licklider (1982, p. 282)

For all the reasons above, a new field has emerged in the last decade called "cognitive engineering",[8] an amalgam of the "knowledge engineering" of the cognitive scientists and the "educational engineering" of the educational technologists. This new field is sometimes referred to as "AI in reverse" (Pea, 1985a, p. 77) because it ultimately involves the engineering of human learning and human intellectual functioning modeled after AI procedures. AI researchers Brown, Collins and Harris (1978, p. 108) explain: "AI has developed a variety of formalisms that in turn provide a new basis for analyzing [human] cognitive processes." Thus, although AI itself depends upon an analysis of human learning and functioning to arrive at sophisticated computer models, one central purpose of AI is to turn things around and to apply these models to improve human learning and performance.

John L. Kennedy (1962, p. 18), an early systems researcher, noted years ago: "The most important point to be made is this: the design problem [in man/machine systems] is not how to design a machine – it is how to design an organism." Cognitive science researchers, adopting this view, have often remarked on the "prescriptive" nature of their work. Simon (1981, p. 23) notes that "artificial intelligence . . . addresses itself to normative goals, and ought to. It is interested, in its applied aspects, not only in understanding intelligence but in improving it . . . We need to recognize this explicitly by speaking of cognitive engineering as well as cognitive science." Posner (1973, p. 167), another cognitive scientist, asserts that "cognitive psychology must face the problem of design, discussing not only what is but also what ought to be". Still another (Reif, 1980, p. 44) asks, "Can one design or invent modes of human information processing that can specifically enhance human cognitive performance?" Answering his own question, he concludes that one goal of cognitive science is "prescriptive": "to design . . . the information processor of interest, either a computer or a human being" (p. 43).

In 1980, the birth year of cognitive science, Simon (1981) announced that cognitive science is a "science of the artificial". By this he means that the human mind is most appropriately viewed, for scientific purposes, as a contingent, artificial "system", something that is malleable and adaptable, that could be other than what it is. He argues that cognitive science should think of human functioning "as if" it were designed; in this way one can consider "redesigning" it to suit the outer environment, which, in the case of cognitive scientists, consists of huge, complex computer systems. The redesign of human functioning, therefore, takes its cues from this environment by viewing mind as an information processing system, modeled after the computer.

We turn now to two examples of this "redesign", two central thrusts in "cognitive engineering", each substantially supported by the military: (1) the indirect "augmentation" of intelligence through the "symbiotic" fusion of mind and computer, and (2) the direct training of cognitive processes involved in thinking and learning, modeled on computer procedures and strategies.

Cockpit Cognition: Augmentation of Intellect through Man/Machine Symbiosis

Early on in the development of computers, the military was concerned with the availability of "real-time" interactivity between computers and military decision-makers, whose combat decisions could not wait for results. This led to "time-sharing", which permitted this instantaneous interactivity. Time-sharing was the first instance of "man/computer symbiosis", where the human and the computer worked as a partnership. Time-sharing was also considered to be the first computer-based "augmentation of human intellect" via the computer (Fano, 1965). This meant that the computer and human working in tandem served as an amplification of human intellectual decision-making and memory. During this DARPA-funded project, a number of leaders in the new computer field began to write and to fantasize about the further possibilities of intellectual amplification through this "symbiosis".[9] For example, Harold Sackman (1967, p. 564) a participant in the SAGE project discussed earlier, predicted that "a fundamental consequence of . . . [the idealized] maximum linkage of . . . man-to-computer communication . . . is the vast potential for the . . . realization of a far more intelligent type of human being, on the average and at most levels, than we have today.'

This idea of intellectual augmentation through symbiosis remains a potent form of cognitive engineering within the military, and among cognitive scientists and educational technologists, in the 1980s. A recent NOVA television show on pilot training (WGBH, 1988) spoke of the "magic cockpit" of the near future, in which the aircraft serves as a "pilot's associate", talking to the pilot (in a female voice) about ongoing conditions and responding to the pilot's spoken orders. Air Force spokesmen talked about the near possibility of arranging for the intelligent cockpit computers to respond to the pilot's eyesight or even his/her brain waves: "controlling by thinking is no more than 30 years away". Through this symbiosis of the pilot and the aircraft, the pilot's memory and decision-making capacities are claimed to be tremendously increased.

Such military aspirations have found their way into the thinking of researchers working at the juncture of cognitive science and educational technology. Some are captivated by similar fantasies of symbiosis. John W. Loughary (1970), an early promoter of "man–machine systems in education", predicted that laser beam technology and advances in endocrinology and biochemical control of genetics would provide the capacity to make direct changes in human learning ability. More recently, a leading Soviet proponent of educational computing recommended linking the nerve cells of teachers and students with circuitry in the computer, thereby multiplying the intelligence of both learners and teachers (Zender, 1975, p. 139). He and others also speak of implanting computer chips in the brain to augment intelligence (Pea, 1985a, p. 92). Finally, robotics scientist Hans Moravec (1988) suggests the possibility of "downloading" the entire contents of persons' brains into a computer, transforming education into the merging of computer files.

But some promoters of symbiosis in education arrive at this position via an apparently more respectable pedagogical path. Roy Pea (1985a) for example, an ardent spokesman for computers in education, has fashioned theories of his mentor, cognitive psychologist and educator Jerome Bruner, and of the Russian psychologist Lev Vygotsky, into a similar man/computer symbiosis scenario. Bruner and Vygotsky argue that human intelligence evolves as a function of its surrounding culture and the tools at its disposal. Thus, written language, musical notation and mathematical symbols have all amplified human intelligence. Pea argues that the computer can do the same: amplify, restructure and reshape human intelligence.

Computers thus can be considered new "organs of intelligence", "cognitive props", or "extracortical organizers of thought", according to Pea (1985a, pp. 88–93), which provide additional "cognitive workspace" as "adjuncts to processing capacity". But more importantly, they serve as "a mirror of the learner's thought processes by providing an external representation of internal cognitive processes" (Kozma, 1987, p. 24). Some cognitive engineers (Klein, 1985) speak of "process highlighters" and "cognitive traces" provided by the computer to the user, permitting the user to externalize his or her steps in the solution to a problem, retaining the "traces" of intermediate "processes" not otherwise available. For example, if one is graphing an equation, the computer would provide graphic representations of all early attempts, so that the student can learn from his or her mistakes and corrections in the course of solving the problem. Such transparency of one's thought processes, made possible through human/ computer symbiosis, serves to augment intellectual capabilities, according to some cognitive engineers.

Perhaps the most well-known instance of this form of cognitive engineering applied to education involves the use of "microworld learning environments", derived from artificial intelligence research, to generate powerful ideas in young children. An early leader in artificial intelligence research, Seymour Papert (1980), speaks of "mindstorms" made possible in young children through their interaction with a computer microworld utilizing the LOGO programming language. LOGO is perhaps more responsible than any other single circumstance for the introduction of computers in US classrooms. Unfortunately, early predictions that children wold arrive at "powerful mathematical ideas" through its use, or even that they would learn sophisticated forms of problem-solving and planning through their interaction with the LOGO microworld, have been disappointing (Dudley-Marling and Owston, 1988; Leron, 1985). As a result, many cognitive engineers are turning to a more direct approach (Klahr and Carver, 1980); rather than wait for the symbiosis to work its magic, they have opted instead to focus on training the reorganization and ameliorization of human intellectual processes directly.

Cognitive Process Instruction: Thinking Skills, Learning Strategies, and Metacognition

1. Thinking skills

Symbiosis is indirect; cognitive engineers have therefore focussed the better part of their attention on training higher order intellectual activity directly, utilizing the view of mind as an "informative processing system". This is variously referred to as "cognitive process instruction" (Lochhead and Clement, 1979) and "training thinking skills". Robert Sternberg a leading promoter of teaching thinking skills in schools, derived a "componential" model of intelligence, under ONR and ARI contracts, that has served as a basis for identifying the "components" of thinking that can be modified and reorganized through direct intervention (Sternberg, 1977; Keating, 1984). Another military researcher, Raymond S. Nickerson (Nickerson et al., 1985), has also been a champion of the focus within public education on training thinking skills.

This approach to education "assumes that if we can specify in enough detail the tacit processes that underlie various thinking skills, then we can find methods to teach students to master those skills" (Sternberg and Detterman, 1982, p. 173). The search for general thinking and problem-solving skills has, in the last few years, run into a problem that has also plagued AI research: namely, problem-solving and thinking is domain-dependent to a degree not previously expected (Resnick, 1987). The skills used to solve a problem in algebra, for example, may have little in common with those involved in figuring out the causes of the Civil War – or even a proof in geometry. This conclusion, still very controversial, has led to an emphasis on domain-dependent "expert systems" in AI research; such systems, though starting to be commercially successful, nonetheless represent a failure in the AI project to design flexible, adaptable intelligent machines. In cognitive engineering, then, the principal focus has been on cognitive processes that are perhaps not so domain-dependent – namely, the processes of learning.

2. Learning strategies

Learning is the central preoccupation of cognitive science at this time (Langley and Simon, 1981; Simon, 1983). As mentioned earlier, the renewed interest in learning research is a product of scientific and military interests, rather than a focus initiated by educators. Researchers in AI arrived at this new emphasis on learning in their search for efficient techniques of building flexible intelligent systems (i.e., for techniques in "machine learning"), and in their scientific quest for general "first principles", or invariants, in intellectual functioning. For reasons discussed earlier as well, the military has sponsored this research since the early 1970s; in fact, "the most ambitious recent program of research on learning strategies was funded by the Defense Advanced Projects Agency" (Rigney and Munro, 1981, p. 133), which has been responsible for the publication of many of the seminal books in the field.[10]

The study of learning processes offers more promise of arriving at domain-independent "invariants" than thinking skills; that is, learning involves more general processes than thinking does. This means that training learning skills promises to be more efficient than training thinking skills. But learning is itself rather inefficient, so the goal of the cognitive engineer is not merely to train learning skills, but, more importantly, to improve on these skills.

The military and its researchers share an interest in improving the efficiency of learning, which is typically defined by them in terms of temporal efficiency. According to Langley and Simon (1981, p. 367), "learning is taking place if solution times decrease as a person solves a sequence of [similar problems]". Simon (1983), still a key player in the cognitive fields he kindled, espouses a distaste for normal human learning, shared as well by many of his colleagues and sponsors: "Human learning is horribly slow. It takes decades for human beings to learn anything" (p. 26). Thus his goal is to search for "tricks that manage to escape the tediousness of human learning" (p. 26). He is also concerned that there is no "copy process" in human "learning programs", in contrast to computer programs, which can be copied at will: "When one computer has learned it, they've all learned it – in principle . . . Only one computer would have to learn; not everyone would have to go to school" (p. 35). Simon's frustration, and his motivation, is clear: "I find it terribly frustrating trying to transfer my knowledge and skill to another human head. I'd like to open the lid and stuff the program in" (p. 27).

The closest the new research on learning has come to such aspirations has been to focus, not on learning, but rather on "learning mechanisms" within the human "information processing system" (IPS). Here learning is viewed as the "modification of any component in the IPS" (Langley and Simon, 1981, p. 368). That is, the human being, in the language of machine learning, is an "adaptive production system". "Production systems" are discrete sets of condition–action pairs of the form "If A and B, then do C" that are the heart of AI programs; "adaptive production systems" are such systems that can add, delete, or rearrange the order of these productions automatically or through instruction (Simon, 1980, p. 87). Which is to say, they can learn. Human learning, then, is taken to be identical to machine learning: "If we are really simulating people with computers then the only way to improve people is to understand the procedures that the computer goes through and attempt to teach . . . people like we . . . teach computers" (Davis et al., 1965, p. 171).

The processes directly involved in learning are thought of as "strategies" (a military term). They are "human information-processing activities that facilitate. acquisition, retention and retrieval of representational and procedural know-ledge" (Rigney and Munro, 1981, p. 128). Examples include mnemonic devices, elaboration schemes like underlining key words in a text, looking for central ideas, and linking an idea to an analogous idea. Although these sound simply like study skills, the focus of cognitive engineering is to isolate, represent externally, and then train efficiently the internal processes and subprocesses involved in these activities. This will, in theory, equip the learner with an "armory" (Simon, 1981, p. 20) of strategies applicable to a variety of domains.

Whether or not all of this reduces to study skills when one eliminates the jargon is a controversial issue. The key difference seems to be that learning strategies are grounded in a computer model of the learner. According to Pressley (1985, p. 36), "in the best of all possible worlds, learners would have a well-developed repertoire of strategies, they would . . . know when to deploy each one, and they would know how to modify the strategies . . . Learners would keep track of their cognitive activities, with such monitoring directing strategy shifts".

The learner, then, is viewed as a processing system equipped with strategies applicable to cognitive purposes such as memorizing and comprehending texts. All of these strategies are accessible to conscious control by the learner, by the instructor, or by the instructional system. Learning strategies, then, are control processes (Snow et al., 1980, p. 307). Thus, Tessmer and Jonassen (1988, p. 41) suggest that, while "low ability learners . . . may require 'embedded' learning strategies, where cues and prompts for a student to use a specific learning strategy are actually built into the instructional materials" (p. 41), for most other learners, "the appropriate learning strategies . . . [and] the proper learning interventions are not so much provided for the learner as generated by him" (p. 34).

The question of control of learning strategies has led cognitive engineers to still another level of generality in cognitive process instruction: the "meta-level" of "metacognition," to which we now turn.

3. Metacognition

Developmental psychologist John Flavell (1977) originated the discussion of "metacognitive strategies" in the mid-1970s in describing children's knowledge of what they remember. This approach to "metamemory" soon set off a frenzy of interest in metacognitive strategies of all kinds. A decade later, Flavell (1987, p. 28) asserts that no one knows "what metacognition is, how it operates, [or] how it develops", and Ann Brown (1987, p. 105), a leader in the study of metacognition, refers to the concept as "a monster of uncertain origin". This realization has not, however, stopped cognitive engineers from applying the concept liberally throughout education.

One thing is clear. Metacognitive theory presupposes that the human mind is an IPS, and that metacognition is itself the "executive routine", as in a computer program (Yussen, 1985, p. 262; Spitz, 1986, p. 209). Metacognitive strategies occur at a level "higher" than both learning strategies and thinking skills. According to Brown (1987, p. 66), they consist of "one's knowledge and control of one's own cognitive system". For this reason, it is considered to be more efficient to train metacognitive skills than to train the particular skills for which they are responsible.

4. Who's in control?

A key question arising from the cognitive engineering of thinking skills, learning strategies, and metacognition is whether the learner or the instructional system is in control. The purposes of all three cognitive engineering approaches is to intervene in the learner's cognitive processes in order to improve them – which is to say, in order to get them to function more efficiently or otherwise appropriately. A central contradiction in the work of cognitive engineers, then, is their claim that their goal is to place the learner in control of his or her own cognitive system. Some researchers speak of transforming learners into "managers of their own cognitive resources", "information managers", even "entrepreneurs" controlling their cognitive investments (Pea, 1985a, 1985b). Others, preferring the language of the technologist to that of the capitalist, speak of "giv[ing] students the power to reprogram their own biocomputers" (Dansereau, 1978, p. 3). But we must remember the military origins of the field of cognitive engineering and so we must bear in mind that "the idea of automated control of information processes . . . has shaped more than any technology the contemporary American armed forces" (Bellin and Chapman, 1987, p. 60). Control is the name of the game, and the goal of engineering, cognitive or otherwise, is to establish control. Thus, while the emphasis of these ventures in cognitive engineering is "self-programming" and "self-monitoring", the underlying theme is self-discipline as a convenient substitute for imposed discipline. Just as "autonomous weapons" in the military "internalize" their mission and their orders, relieving some of the minute-to-minute responsibilities of the chain of command, so metacognition and learning strategies involve the internalization of external control of appropriate modes of thinking and learning. Students are set free, with their self-monitoring skills, to "match their processing resources to learning task-requirements" (Rigney, 1978, p. 200). Such is the extent of their control over their own learning and thinking.

Furthermore, the higher the level of self-control, from thinking skills to learning strategies to metacognition, the more accessible as well is the learner to external control. This is because the more general the cognitive process, the more efficient the external control. More general skills are more generic skills. The learner with most control over his or her cognitive system is most easily adaptable to a wide range of jobs. In the military, "from the point of view of the higher-order planning system, individual men are considered to be rather independent components who might, at one time or another, be required to operate in *any* man-machine system" (Kennedy, 1962, p. 18, his emphasis). The metacognitive manager, in other words, constitutes an extreme form of abstract labor.

Finally, the very accessibility to one's own cognitive apparatus, defined in generic terms, leaves one that much more open to external control: "The more transparent is the [black] box, the more efficient can be the control of its processes" (Landa, 1976, p. 51). And the potential is real. In the military, of course, with its "instructional systems design", the entire training enterprise is one of control. But as military technologies and methods of cognitive engineering enter the schools, systematic control of learning and thinking activities becomes the order of the day. In the prescient words, once again, of SAGE pioneer

Harold Sackman (1967, p. 568): "As we advance toward computer-service cultures, the educational process in society is likely to take on attributes of realtime control systems."

Conclusion: The Role of Education Revisited

"The final difficulty that . . . must be faced in the attempt to integrate the science of learning and the technology of education is that of gaining access to children of school age for . . . experimental investigations."

Arthur W. Melton[11]

Cognitive engineering is, then, a cognitive technology which combines a science of mind with a technology of learning and intelligence. While cognitive engineering depends upon the study of human learning and intelligence to develop its models, it also uses these models to redesign those human capacities – "reshap-[ing] human nature", in the words of Roy Pea (1985b, p. 169), to fit the new technological landscape.

Where does public education fit into this enterprise? For their own reasons, educators have adopted the techniques of cognitive engineering, and by now, "thinking skills", "learning strategies", and "metacognition" are all accepted entries in the educational lexicon, serving as objectives of new instructional practices. So, too, are computer microworlds and intelligent tutoring systems, designed to improve problem-solving and thinking skills through "symbiosis", steadily becoming fixtures within the public education arena.

In order to improve instruction and in order to legitimate their profession through the incorporation of new technologies and the latest applications of "scientific" research, the schools have unwittingly welcomed the Trojan horse of military prerogatives within their gates. These prerogatives include a view of human minds – of students and teachers alike – as information processing systems, layered with the procedures, strategies and heuristics of an "artificial" intelligence. They also include the idea of persons reduced to their generic cognitive components, disembodied, decontextualized and depersonalized, infi-nitely adaptable to any and all technological man/machine systems. They include as well the reduction of education to task-specific training, with its emphasis on performance outcomes and "time-on-task" efficiency. And they include, finally, a desiccated redefinition of key educational concepts – intelligence, learning, thinking – into mindless, though thoroughly self-regulated, procedures of information processing.

Of course, such models and their related methods and technologies take on new shapes once they enter the public education arena, and more often than not they are diluted as they are fitted to the bureaucratic and pedagogical preroga-tives of the schools. Metacognitive strategies, as mentioned earlier, are taught as "study skills", for example. Complaints about such dilution by researchers in programmed instruction, computer-based problem-solving, individualized learn-ing programs, and other educational innovations are legion (Popkewitz, 1982). But claims that such innovations work as planned even in the military contexts within which and for which they were originally designed are highly questionable, as Anderson (1986), Binkin (1986), Hoos (1972), Ellis (1986) and others have noted.

Whether such models and practices are inappropriate to begin with, or else lose their potency only once they enter the schools, in either case they ultimately contribute little or nothing to education or to educational change. They serve instead as massive "scientific" distractions, redirecting attention and funding away from genuine avenues of reform, approaches that might take into account the larger social, political, economic and cultural considerations that are at the real root of school problems.

To the extent, on the other hand, that such models and innovations take hold within the schools, retaining their original character and intent, they represent a militarized debasement of education. This is because, ultimately, the design and production of human components appropriate for optimal performance of technological systems – rather than the fulfilment of human potential for its own sake – is the criterion of success of such "education". In fact, as mentioned earlier, the underlying goal of military attempts to understand human capacities is the eventual replacement of human beings, by autonomous weapons and automated battlefields. This is because human limitations in cognitive processing are viewed within military technological development as the source of bottle-necks – "human errors" – in weapon systems. Thus, if education is a celebration of the potential of human beings, military cognitive research and development constitutes, at bottom, a celebration of their dispensability.

The prerogatives not only of the military but also of cognitive researchers themselves, invades the school alongside the introduction of cognitive models, methods, and technologies. According to Reif (1980, p. 45), education ought to be considered a component of cognitive engineering, with schools serving as laboratories for empirical research by cognitive engineers. The best way to understand human learning and cognition is to observe it in action – to do detailed "microanalyses" of instruction and learning processes. And the schools serve this agenda as the perfect laboratories in which to test hypotheses and to formulate new theories about learning, instruction, and intelligent technologies. "Instruction on how or what to think", say Belmont and Butterfield (1977, p. 439), "can be a potent and subtle *tool* for cognitive research". No wonder, then, cognitive engineer Reif (1980, p. 49) announces that "the time is ripe for . . . achiev[ing] a symbiotic interaction of cognitive scientists and persons interested in practical education".

In addition to their role as laboratories, schools also serve as a locus of legitimation for cognitive engineers, who are caught between several fields, with little to show as yet for their years of research. In the words of researcher David Klahr (1976, p. 331), "neither instructors nor learners could benefit from the thinking about the design of learning models. The payoff, at present, appears to be for the people who fall into the intersection of the categories of instructional designer and cognitive psychologist: 'learning engineers'."

But not only have educators acquiesced in the prerogatives of military research and of military researchers. They have also, more and more, aligned their goals with the goals of a "high technology" corporate economy that is itself, as it always has been, the inheritor of military technological imperatives. From the very beginning of industrialization, military enterprise "owing to its enduring character, its scale, and its demand for materiel of the highest quality, . . . has exerted a powerful influence in determining the institutional and technical dimensions of the modern industrial era" (Smith, 1985, p. 1). Consequences of this early influence included scientific management, mechanized production, standardization, and hierarchical organizational structures.

Since World War II, this influence has escalated manyfold, so that Daniel Bell (1967, p. 166), first ideologue of post-industrialism, recognized early on that "military technology [will be] the major determinant of social structure". The entire economic landscape of "post-industrial society", later dubbed by Bell (1981) the "information society", has been shaped by military technological enterprise, from information theory, systems analysis, nuclear energy and transistors to automation, robotization, bioengineering, and semiconductors (Hounshell, 1984; Tirman, 1984; Smith, 1985; Piller and Yamamoto, 1988). This is part of the reason why a number of noted scholars refer to the postwar US economy as a "permanent war economy" (Mills, 1959; Mumford, 1963; Melman, 1985; Lens, 1987). The "militarization of high technology" (Tirman, 1984) represents the latest phase in a century-long history of "pervasiveness of military enterprise in the American [corporate] economy" (Smith, p. 5). Because it is at the cutting edge of information technologies, and is in fact used as the protected technological R&D arm of corporate capital, military enterprise is the advance guard of the information society.

To the extent, then, that public education aligns itself with the supposed new "intellectual" requirements of the information economy, it is to that extent further saturating itself with the militarized redefinition of mind, intellect, thinking and learning that has been the subject of this chapter. Public education thus becomes not only laboratory and locus of legitimation; it also becomes the site for the actual production of "mental materiel" – for the design and manufacture of "intellectual capital" (Greeno, 1985, p. 21) needed by corporate enterprise. The production of cognitive components for complex weapon systems – mind as materiel – is also the production of cognitive components for the global systems of information technology that are transforming the character of corporate capital. Only the battlegrounds are different.

Twenty-five years ago, Herbert Simon (1964, p. 82), management theorist turned cognitive pioneer, noted that "the bulk of the productive wealth consists of programs . . . stored in human minds", and that "the principal under-utilized resources [are] . . . learning programs of the employed population". Around the same time, Jerome Bruner, cognitive pioneer turned educator, became instrumental in Federal education reform, as Headstart initiator, leader of the new social science curriculum movement, and theorist of learning and instruction. Looking back on those early years, Bruner (1983, pp. 62, 63) recently remarked, "It seems plain to me now that the 'cognitive revolution' . . . was a response to the technological demands of the 'post-industrial revolution'. You cannot properly conceive of managing a complex world of information without a workable concept of mind." He recognized that if you "develop a sufficiently complex technology, . . . [then] there is no alternative but to create cognitive principles in order to understand how people can manage it".

Elsewhere, Bruner (1985, p. 599) recently added that "it is almost the essence of the post-industrial revolution to place a high premium on the skills of the generalist, the troubleshooter, the problem-solver . . . Once 'mindful performance' becomes a practical necessity for the conduct of technology, the issue of mind and its status ceases to be governed by philosophical . . . debates." Thus, Bruner (1983, p. 274) insists, "the cognitive revolution . . . lies at the center of the post-industrial society . . . The new capital is know-how, forecast, intelligence [and] the result has been not simply a renewal of interest in how the 'mind' works, but rather a new search for . . . how mindfulness is cultivated."

This cultivation of cognitive resources for advanced technological systems is the new cognitivist agenda for the schools, and it lies at the heart of new corporate demands for employees who can "think" and "problem-solve", "reason" and "learn". In her recent book, *In the Age of the Smart Machine*, Harvard Business School professor Shoshana Zuboff (1988) calls the skills involved in this new "mind work" of corporate employees – office workers, managers, professionals and factory workers alike – "intellective skills", "abstract" skills that involve strategic planning, procedural reasoning, data processing, troubleshooting, and technical problem-solving. Zuboff's book has been highly acclaimed as the clearest expression of how new corporate information technologies, rather than deskilling or displacing masses of workers, can instead create entirely new opportunities, available to more workers than ever before, for intellectual participation in the workplace.

Motivated by such new corporate opportunities and needs for their wares, public education leaders are tripping over themselves to transform the schools, unwittingly, into a staging ground for the playing out of militarized scenarios – scenarios shaped by the requirements of advanced military weapon systems, by cognitive researchers' need for laboratories and legitimation, and by new "intellective" requirements of corporate capital in a militarized information economy.

Just as educators are being told that their longstanding desire to teach students how to think now happily coincides with the new personnel needs of multinational corporations, the ongoing, militarized degradation of education and human intelligence that lies at the lifeless heart of this happy coincidence must be kept carefully and clearly in mind . . . while we still have one.

Conclusions

The means and ends of education are being reshaped within a massive military/industrial research and development enterprise, ongoing since World War II, to engineer appropriate human factors for high performance technological systems. Most research on learning, problem-solving, and computer-based education has been sponsored directly by the military or else has been influenced by longstanding military research in the fields of human factors psychology, artificial intelligence or cognitive science. Educational practice is being increasingly viewed as "cognitive engineering," the incremental shaping of patterns of thinking and learning, themselves often modeled after their counterparts in machine learning and machine intelligence. The objective of the enterprise is the production of high performance cognitive skills adaptable to high performance information technologies. These technologies, borne of military research, are now definitive of the new production processes of the information society.

Notes

1. Machado (1981), former Minister of the Development of Intelligence in Venezuela, sponsored Project Intelligence, which, from 1979 to 1984, was conducted by the Massachusetts consulting firm Bolt, Beranek and Newman. Among the participants were Allan Collins, Jack Lochhead, Raymond Nickerson, and other individuals who play a significant role in this country in thinking skills research funded by the military. For further information on Project Intelligence, see Walsh (1981) and Nickerson (1986).
2. Critical reviews of the state of the art include Resnick (1988/1989, p. 12); Rosenberg (1987); Dudley-Marling and Owston (1988); and Resnick (1987, p. 47).
3. For evidence of the seminal military contribution to the research and development of these educational technologies, see Ellis (1986); Olsen and Bass (1982); Hitchens (1971); Lumsdaine and Glaser (1960); Saettler (1968); Blaschke (1967); and Office of Technology Assessment (1982).
4. For more information on the SAGE system and the Systems Research Laboratory, which later became System Development Corporation, see Rowell and Streich (1964); Sackman (1967); Baum (1981); and Chapman and Kennedy (1956).
5. Cognitive psychologists and scientists whose work has been sponsored recently by ONR, NPRDC, DARPA, AFHRL or ARI include: Richard C. Anderson, D. F. Dansereau, Allan Collins, John Seely Brown, Raymond Nickerson, David Rumelhart, Donald A. Norman, Roger Schank, John R. Anderson, James Greeno, Richard Snow, Robert Glaser, M. C. Wittrock, David Klahr and Robert Sternberg.
6. It must be made clear that military sponsorship of research in the 1980s is far more mission-oriented than such sponsorship in the 1950s. Military funding of "basic research" is a thing of the past; now all military funding, even for what it may call "basic research," is focussed on specific military applications (Dickson, 1984, pp. 140; Piller and Yamamoto, 1988, p. 211).

   For example, the mission of AI research by DARPA has for the first time been identified explicitly as the development of pilot associates, "intelligent surface vehicles", and battle management systems for the Air Force, Army and Navy, respectively (*Datamation*, 1984; Davis, 1985).

   The point here is this: If research in educational technology and cognitive science is substantially funded by the military, and subsequently adopted by the schools, the military purpose, or mission, of this sponsorship must be examined, and the compatibility of this mission with educational goals must be addressed. Claims that military support is unrelated to the goals of this "educational" research are no longer valid, since such research has "strong practical military implications" (Snow et al., 1980, xiii).
7. I am speaking as though the military were a monolith, with a singular motive and mission. It is not. There are many conflicting views on these projects within the military, in particular those of the opposing technocratic and "military reform" contingents. However, there is no question that the dominant dynamic in the military is the one represented here.
8. According to Donald Norman (1987), he coined the term "cognitive engineering". Others who have used this term include Robert Glaser, Herbert A. Simon, Frederick Reif, Roy D. Pea, Harold F. O'Neil, Jr, and DiVesta and Rieber (1987).
9. The term "symbiosis", applied to man/machine interaction, was first used by J. C. R. Licklider (1960), former director of DARPA's Information Processing Techniques Office, key leader in time-sharing technology, and later a prime supporter of "computer literacy" instruction (1982). John Kemeny (1972), inventor of the BASIC programming language, was another early user of the term. It is now in widespread usage, by Pea (1985) and others.
10. Among the books published by the DARPA program are: Sticht, *Literacy Training*; Dansereau, *The Development of a Systematic Training Program for Enhancing Learning Strategies and Skills*; Singer and Gerson, *Learning Strategies for Motor Skills*; Logan, *An ISD Approach for Learning Strategies*; Brown, Collins and Harris, *Artificial Intelligence and Learning Strategies*; Rigney, *Learning Strategies: A Theoretical Perspective*; O'Neil, *Learning Strategies*; and O'Neil and

Spielberger, *Cognitive and Affective Learning Strategies*.See Rigney and Munro (1981), pp. 133–134.
11. Psychologist Arthur W. Melton (1959, p. 103) was director of the Air Force Personnel and Training Research Center in the 1950s and has been instrumental in applying military training concepts to civilian education. Recently he has been the editor of the Experimental Psychology Series for Erlbaum publishers, a series which includes the first work by Robert Sternberg on his componential theory of intelligence (1977).

References

Anderson, C. L. (1986). Where did we go wrong? An analysis of the way ISD was mustered out of the Army, paper presented at AERA annual convention, San Francisco. ED 270 632.
Baum, C. (1982). *The System Builders: The Story of SDC*. System Development Corp., Santa Monica, California.
Bell, D. (1967). The post-industrial society; A speculative view. In E. Hutchings, *Scientific Progress and Human Values*. American Elsevier, New York, p. 154–170.
Bell, D. (1981). The social framework of the information society. In T. Forester (ed.) *The Microelectronics Revolution*. The MIT Press, Cambridge, Mass.
Bellin, D. and Chapman, G. (eds.) (1987). *Computers in Battle: Will They Work?* Harcourt Brace Jovanovich, New York.
Belmont, J. M. and Butterfield, E. C. (1977). 'The instructional approach to developmental cognitive research'. In R. V. Kail and J. W. Hagen, *Perspectives on the Development of Memory and Cognition*. Erlbaum, New York, pp. 430–450.
Binkin, M. (1986). *Military Technology and Defense Manpower*. The Brookings Institution, Washington, D. C.
Blaschke, C. L. (1967). The DOD: catalyst in educational technology. *Phi Delta Kappan*, 48 (5), 204–214.
Brown, A. (1987). Metacognition, executive control, self-regulation, and other more mysterious mechanisms. In F. E. Weinert and R. H. Kluwe (eds.) *Metacognition, Motivation, and Understanding*. Erlbaum, Hillsdale, N. J., pp. 65–140.
Brown, J. S., Collins, A., and Harris, G. (1978). Artificial intelligence and learning strategies. In H. F. O'Neil, Jr (ed.), *Learning Strategies*. Academic Press, New York, pp. 107–139.
Bruner, J. S. (1983). *In Search of Mind*. Harper and Row, New York.
Bruner, J. S. (1985). On teaching thinking. In S. F. Chipman *et al.* (eds.) *Thinking and Learning Skills*, vol. 2. University of Pittsburgh Press, Pittsburgh, pp. 590–599.
Carnegie Forum on Education and the Economy (1986). *A Nation Prepared: Teachers for the 21st Century*. Carnegie Forum, Washington, D.C.
Chapman, R. L. and Kennedy, J. L. (1956). The background and implications of the systems research laboratory studies. In G. Finch and F. Cameron (eds.) *Air Force Human Engineering, Personnel and Training Research*. National Academy of Sciences/National Research Council, pp. 65–73.
Costa, A. L. (1984). 'Mediating the metacognitive. *Educational Leadership*, 42 (3), 56–61.
Dansereau, D. (1978). The development of a learning strategies curriculum. In H. F. O'Neil, Jr, *Learning Strategies*. Academic Press, New York, pp. 1–29.
Datamation (1984). DARPA's big push in AI. *Datamation*, 30 (2), 50.
Davis, D. B. (1985). Assessing the strategic computing initiative. *High Technology*, 5 (4), 41–49.
Davis, R. *et al.* (1965). Potential implementation. In M. A. Sass and W. D. Wilkinson (eds.) *Computer Augmentation of Human Reasoning*. Spartan Books, Washington, D.C., pp. 151–187.
Dickson, D. (1984). *The New Politics of Science*. Pantheon, New York.
DiVesta, F. J. and Rieber, L. P. (1987). Characteristics of cognitive engineering: the next generation of instructional systems. *ECTJ*, 35 (4), 213–230.
Dreyfus, H. L. and Dreyfus, S. E. (1986). *Mind Over Machine*. The Free Press, New York.
Dudley-Marling, C. and Owston, R. D. (1988). Using microcomputers to teach problem solving: a critical review. *Educational Technology*, 28 (7), 27–33.
Edwards, P. N. (1985). *Technologies of the Mind*: Silicon Valley Research Group Working Paper 2. Santa Cruz: University of California, Santa Cruz.
Ellis, J. A. (ed.) (1986). *Military Contributions to Instructional Technology*. Praeger, New York.
Evans, D. (1986). Losing battle: the army and the underclass. *The New Republic*, 194 (26), 10–13.
Fano, R. M. (1965). The MAC system: a progress report. In M. A. Sass and W. D. Wilkinson (eds.) *Computer Augmentation of Human Reasoning*. Spartan Books, Washington, D.C., pp. 131–149.
Flavell, J. H. (1977) *Cognitive Development*. Prentice Hall, Englewood Cliffs, N.J.

Flavell, J. H. (1987). Speculation about the nature and development of metacognition. In F. E. Weinert and R. H. Kluwe (eds)., *Metacognition, Motivation, and Understanding*. Erlbaum, Hillsdale, N. J., pp. 21–29.

Greeno, J. (1985). Looking across the river: views from the two banks of research and development in problem solving. In S. F. Chipman, J. W. Segal, and R. Glaser (eds.) *Thinking and Learning Skills*, vol. 2, pp. 209–214.

Gropper, G. L. (1980). Is instructional technology dead? *Educational Technology*, 20 (1), 39.

Halff, H. M., Hollan, J. D., and Hutchins, E. L., (1986). Cognitive science and military training. *American Psychologist*, 41 (10), 1131–1138.

Hitchens, H. B. (1971). Instructional technology in the armed forces. In S. G. Tickton (ed.) *To Improve Learning: An Evaluation of Instructional Technology*, vol. II. R. R. Bowker, New York, pp. 701–721.

Hoos, I. R. (1972). *Systems Analysis in Public Policy: A Critique*. Berkeley: University of California Press.

Hounshell, D. A. (1984). *From the American System to Mass Production, 1800–1932*. Baltimore: Johns Hopkins University Press.

Keating, D. P. (1984). The emperor's new clothes: the 'new look' in intelligence research. In R. J. Sternberg, *Advances in the Psychology of Human Intelligence*, vol. 2. Erlbaum, Hillsdale, N.J., pp. 1–45.

Kemeny, J. G. (1972). *Man and the Computer*. Charles Scribner's Sons, New York.

Kennedy, J. L. (1962). Psychology and systems development, in R. M. Gagne, (ed.) *Psychological Principles in System Development*. Holt, Rinehart and Winston, New York, pp. 13–22.

Klahr, D. (1976) Designing a learner: some questions. In D. Klahr (ed.) *Cognition and Instruction: Tenth Annual Carnegie Symposium on Cognition*. Office of Naval Research, Arlington, Via, pp. 325–332.

Klahr, D. and Carver, S. M. (1980). Cognitive objectives in a LOGO debugging curriculum: instruction, learning, and transfer. *Cognitive Psychology*, 20, 362–404.

Klein, E. I. (ed.) (1985) *Children and Computers*. Jossey-Bass, San Francisco.

Knapp, T. J. (1986). The emergence of cognitive psychology in the latter half of the twentieth century. In T. J. Knapp and L. C. Robertson (eds.) *Approaches to Cognition: Contrasts and Controversies*. Erlbaum, Hillsdale, N.J., pp. 13–35.

Kozma, R. B. (1987). The implications of cognitive psychology for computer-based learning tools. *Educational Technology*, 27 (11), 20–25.

Lachman, R. *et al.* (1979). *Cognitive Psychology and Information Processing: An Introduction*. Erlbaum, Hillsdale, N.J.

Landa, L. N. (1976). *Instructional Regulation and Control* (F. Kopstein, ed.). Educational Technology Publications, Englewood Cliffs, N.J.

Langley, P. and Simon, H. A. (1981). The central role of learning in cognition. In J. R. Anderson (ed.) *Cognitive Skills and Their Acquisition*. Erlbaum, Hillsdale, N.J., pp. 361–380.

Lens, S. (1987). *Permanent War: The Militarization of America*. Schocken Books, New York.

Leron, U. (1985). Logo today: vision and reality. *The Computing Teacher*, February, 26–32.

Licklider, J. C. R. (1960). Man-computer symbiosis. *IRE Transactions on Human Factors in Electronics*, HFE-1 (March), 4–11.

Licklider, J. C. R. (1982). National goals for computer literacy. In R. J. Seidel *et al.* (eds.) *Computer Literacy: Issues and Directions for 1985*. Academic Press, New York.

Lochhead, J. and Clement, J. (1979). *Cognitive Process Instruction*. Franklin Institute Press, Philadelphia.

Loughary, J. W. (1970). Teaching technology. In A. C. Eurich, (ed.) *High School 1980*. Pitman Publishers, New York, pp. 240–251.

Lumsdaine, A. A. and Glaser, R. (1960) *Teaching Machines and Programmed Learning*, vol. I. NEA, Washington, D. C.

Machado, L. A. (1981) 'Elite babies: the weapon of the future, *The Times* (London), 30 August, no page. Cited in J. Crouse and D. Trusheim (1988) *The Case Against the SAT*. University of Chicago Press, Chicago, p. 1.

McCorduck, P. (1979) *Machines Who Think*. W. H. Freeman, San Francisco.

McCoy, T. W. (1986) New ways to train. *Air Force Magazine*, 69 (12), 55–61.

Melman, S. (1985). *The Permanent War Economy*. Simon and Schuster, New York.

Melton, A. W. (1959). The science of learning and the technology of educational methods. *Harvard Education Review*, 29 (2), 97–105.

Miller, G. A., Galanter, E., and Pribram, K. H. (1960). *Plans and the Structure of Behavior*. Holt, Rinehart, and Winston, New York.

Mills, C. W. (1959). *The Power Elite*. Oxford University Press, New York.

Moravec, H. (1988). *Mind Children*. Harvard University Press, Cambridge.

Mumford, L. (1963). *Technics and Civilization*. Harbinger Books, New York.

Neisser, U. (1967). *Cognitive Psychology*. Appleton-Century-Crofts, New York.

Neumann, W. (1979). Educational responses to the concern for proficiency. In G. Grant (ed.) *On Competence: a Critical Analysis of Competency-Based Reforms in Higher Education*. Jossey-Bass, San Francisco, pp. 67–95.

Newell, A. and Simon, H. A. (1972). *Human Problem Solving*. Prentice-Hall, Englewood Cliffs, N.J.

Newell, A., Shaw, J. C. and Simon, H. A. (1958). Elements of a theory of human problem solving. *Psychological Review*, 65 (3), 151–166.

Nickerson, R. S. (1986). Project Intelligence: an account and some reflections. *Special Services in the Schools*, 3 (1/2), 83–102.

Nickerson, R., Perkins, D. N. and Smith, E. (1985). *The Teaching of Thinking*. Erlbaum, Hillsdale, N.J.

Norman, D. A. (1980). Cognitive engineering and education. In D. T. Tuma and F. Reif (eds.) *Problem Solving and Education*. Erlbaum, Hillsdale, N.J., pp. 81–95.

Norman, D. A. (ed.) (1981). *Perspectives and Cognitive Science*. Ablex/Erlbaum, Hillsdale, N.J.

Norman, D. A. (1987). Cognitive science – cognitive engineering'. In J. M. Carroll (ed.) *Interfacing Thought*. MIT Press, Cambridge, pp. 325–336.

Office of Technology Assessment (OTA) (1982). *Informational Technology and Its Impact on American Education*. US Government Printing Office. Washington, D.C.

Olsen, J. R. and Bass, V. B. (1982). The application of performance technology in the military: 1960–1980. *NSPI Journal*, 21 (6), 32–36.

Papert, S. (1980). *Mindstorms: Children, Computers, and Powerful Ideas*. Basic Books, New York.

Pea, R. D. (1985a) Integrating human and computer intelligence. In E. I. Klein (ed.) *Children and Computers*. New Directions for Child Development, no. 28. Jossey-Bass, San Francisco, pp. 75–96.

Pea, R. D. (1985b). Beyond amplification: using the computer to reorganize mental functioning. *Educational Psychologist*, 20 (4), 167–182.

Piller, C. and Yamamoto, K. R. (1988). *Gene Wars: Military Control Over the New Genetic Technologies*. William Morrow, New York.

Popkewitz, T. S. et al.. (1982). *The Myth of Education Reform*. University of Wisconsin Press, Madison, Wisconsin.

Posner, M. I. (1973). Cognition: natural and artificial. In R. L. Solso (ed.) *The Loyola Symposium: Contemporary Issues in Cognitive Psychology*. V. H. Winston and Sons, Washington, D. C., pp. 167–175.

Pressley, M. et al. (1985). Children's use of cognitive strategies. In M. Pressley and C. J. Brainerd (eds.) *Cognitive Learning and Memory in Children*. Springer-Verlag, New York, pp. 1–48.

Reif, F. (1980). Theoretical and educational concerns with problem solving: bridging the gaps with human cognitive engineering. In D. T. Tuma and F. Reif (eds) *Problem Solving and Education*. Erlbaum, Hillsdale, N.J. pp. 39–50.

Resnick, L. (1987). *Education and Learning to Think*. Washington, D.C.: National Academy Press.

Resnick, L. (1988/1989). On learning research, *Educational Leadership*, 46 (4), 12–16.

Resnick, L. (1983). Toward a cognitive theory of instruction, in S. G. Paris (ed.) *Learning and Motivation in the Classroom*. Erlbaum, Hillsdale, N.J.

Rigney, J. W. (1978). Learning Strategies: A Theoretical Perspective. In H. F. O'Neil, Jr (ed.) *Learning Strategies*. Academic Press, New York, pp. 165–205.

Rigney, J. W. and Munro, A. (1981). Learning strategies. In H. F. O'Neil, Jr (ed.) *Computer-Based Instruction: A State-of-the-Art Assessment*. Academic Press, New York, pp. 127–159.

Rosenberg, R. (1987) A critical analysis of research on intelligent tutoring systems. *Educational Technology*, November, 7–13.

Rowell, J. T. and Streich, E. R. (1964). The Sage system training program for the Air Defense Command. *Human Factors*, October, 537–548.

Sackman, H. (1967). *Computers, System Science, and Evolving Society: The Challenge of Man-Machine Digital Systems*. John Wiley, New York.

Saettler, P. (1968). *A History of Instructional Technology*. NEA, Washington, D.C.

Shaker, S. M. and Wise, A. R. (1988). *War Without Men: Robots on the Future Battlefield*. Pergamon-Brassey's, Washington, D.C.

Sheil, B. A. (1982). Coping with complexity. In R. A. Kasschau, R. Lachman and K. R. Laughery (eds.) *Information Technology and Psychology*. Praeger, pp. 77–105.

Simon, H. A. (1964). Decision-making as an economic resource. In Seltzer, L. H. (ed.) *New Horizons of Economic Progress*. Wayne State University Press, Detroit, pp. 81–83.

Simon, H. A. (1981). 'Cognitive science: the newest science of the artificial'. In Norman, D. A. (ed.) *Perspectives on Cognitive Science*. Ablex/Erlbaum, Hillsdale, N.J., pp. 13–25.

Simon, H. A. (1980). Problem solving and education. In Tuma, D. T. and Reif, F. (eds.) *Problem Solving and Education*. Erlbaum, Hillsdale, N.J., pp. 81–96.

Simon, H. A. (1983). Why should machines learn? In Michalski, R. S. *et al*. (eds.) *Machine Learning: An Artificial Intelligence Approach*. Tioga, Palo Alto, California, pp. 25–37.

Smith, M. R. (ed.) (1985). *Military Enterprise and Technological Change*. MIT Press, Cambridge, Mass.

Snow, R. E. *et al*. (eds.) (1980). *Aptitude, Learning and Instruction*, vol. 2. Erlbaum, Hillsdale, N.J.

Spitz, H. H. (1986). *The Raising of Intelligence*. Erlbaum, Hillsdale, N.J.

Sternberg, R. J. (1977). *Intelligence, Information Processing and Analogical Reasoning: The Componential Analysis of Human Abilities*. Erlbaum, Hillsdale, N.J.

Sternberg, R. J. and Detterman, D. K. (1982). *How and How Much Can Intelligence Be Increased?* Ablex, Norwood, N.J.

Tessmer, M. and Jonassen, D. (1988). Learning strategies: a new instructional technology. In Harris, D. (ed) *Education For the New Technologies: World Yearbook of Education*. Kogan Page, London, pp. 20–45.

Tirman, J. (1984). *The Militarization of High Technology*. Ballinger, Cambridge, Mass.

Towne, D. M. (1987). The generalized maintenance trainer. In Rouse, W. B. (ed.) *Advances in Man–Machine Systems Research*, vol. 3. JAI Press, Greenwich, Conn.

Walsh, J. (1981). A plenipotentiary for human intelligence. *Science*, 214 (6), 640–641.

WGBH (1980). Top gun and beyond. NOVA Television Program (Jan. 20).

Wittrock, M. C. (1979). Applications of cognitive psychology to education and training. In O'Neil, H. F. Jr and Spielberger, C. D. (eds.) *Cognitive and Affective Learning Strategies*. Academic Press, New York, pp. 309–317

Yussen, S. R. (1985). The role of metacognition in contemporary theories of cognitive development. In Forrest-Pressley, D. L., MacKinnon, G. E. and Waller, T. G. (eds.) *Metacognition, Cognition, and Human Performance*. Academic Press, New York, pp. 252–283.

Zender, B. (1975). *Computers and Education in the Soviet Union*. Educational Technology Publications, Englewood Cliffs, N.J.

Zuboff, S. (1988). *In the Age of the Smart Machine*. Basic Books, New York.

Correspondence and offprint requests to: Douglas D. Noble, 76 Westland Ave, NY 14618, USA

AI & Soc (1998) 12:185–213
© 1998 Springer-Verlag London Limited

AI & SOCIETY

Two Legs, Thing Using and Talking: The Origins of the Creative Engineering Mind

Professor F.T. Evans

School of Engineering, Sheffield Hallam University, Sheffield, UK

Abstract: Instead of seeing technology as outside ourselves, it is argued that it is an innate human function and the main driving force in human evolution. Opportunistic 'thing using', long before stone tools appeared, was the likeliest cause of bipedalism. It also forced brain development and the emergence of creativity. The neural basis for this creative technical activity later provided the brain functions on which language could develop. This simple unifying hypothesis has interesting implications for the way that we see technology in history, and for determinist theories of the future. It also bears on the way engineers are trained, and more important, the human faculties which need to be fostered in children.

Keywords: Bipedalism; Creativity; Language origins; Palaeontology; Technology; Tool using;

1. Introduction

'The important thing is not what you know, but what you know about what you know.'[1]

This paper explores our ideas about the nature of technology. It is a word with broad uses and we usually understand it from the context where it was used – there is no single precise definition. It sometimes means the advanced products of industrial society – Space Shuttles, computers, great bridges and so on. Often there is a hint of some overall process or force shaping human life. Formerly there were resounding phrases about the great forces of nature being used for the benefit of mankind – now critical voices are pointing out dangers to the environment.[2] However, all these uses of the word treat technology as if it were a 'thing', out there, not a part of us. By contrast, it will be approached here as an inherent part of human behaviour. Kayaks

309

and flint axes have been just as much a form of technology as Space Shuttles and computers are today, or clipper ships and stage coaches were a century ago. What happened in evolution to give us the sort of mind that designs these things?

These questions will be approached under three sections. First, there will be a short consideration of how we interpret events in technology. Some historians see it as a process determined by social and economic need. Others stress the inventive role of scientists and engineers. These technical issues which interest academic historians are important because they influence our view of the world. Two points are particularly important to the issues explored in this paper. Are we justified in thinking that mankind invented technology? What part does creativity play in all this?

In the second section of the paper, the question of creativity leads into a consideration of ideas about human origins. Is there any connection between creativity and technology on the one hand, and on the other hand, key characteristics of humanity – bipedalism, tool-using and language? Finally, the third section – what significance do these ideas have for our thinking on technology or its place in human life?

2. History, Creativity – and Did We Invent Technology?

As an academic subject, the history of technology has been a slow developer. The political, economic and social branches of history have been studied for many decades and more recently the history of science has became a full discipline. Technology, on the other hand, usually gets treated as an element of other areas, as part of economic history where it touches industry or transport, or as part of military history when the development of weapons like tanks is concerned. At all events, it has been a subordinate theme – a background to events. In a lot of cases this is perfectly valid. If one is investigating the origins of the medieval English Parliament or the religious disputes of the sixteenth century, then technology played a negligible role. It seems to me, however, that in other areas of history technology itself was a decisive factor.

Take the familiar example of the fight between David and Goliath. The defeat of the heavily armed giant by a young shepherd boy is usually interpreted theologically as intervention by the deity on David's behalf. It can be seen a different way. Goliath wore bronze armour and carried a shield and spear – the weapons of a professional warrior. David, on the other hand, merely had a sling – which presumably he practised with while tending the sheep. It is not commonly realised nowadays that such a sling, which whirls the stone in a wide circle before releasing it, had an effective range of 200 yards.[3] We could therefore suggest that David had the superior, long range weapon – Goliath's spear could not kill at 200 yards – and therefore that the best explanation of his victory is the technological one.

Questions of perspective and interpretation are not just academic. They affect our whole way of seeing and doing things. We have to remember that we never perceive the world directly. We only know our sense perceptions and ideas about it. My dog, for instance, has a very different map of the world from mine, based on his superior sense of smell. He is aware of things which I cannot perceive, and this leads him to behave differently. Our behaviour is not governed by our direct perceptions, but by

Fig. 1. 'Rabbits'.

the meaning we attribute to them. Professor R L Gregory puts it that our brain **constructs** the world by the way it processes our perceptions. As an example look at Fig. 1 a rough sketch of two rabbits.

Now look at it again, expecting to see two pelicans waiting for a fish. This ambiguous drawing is well known, but it illustrated the point very well, that our expectations and ideas shape the world that we see.[4] At a more complex level, this is also true of the way in which we approach technology. It has such a profound influence on human activity that we must understand its function in our lives as well as we can. In this paper, we will be raiding a number of different academic territories – psychology, anthropology and archaeology, as well as parts of engineering and history – to synthesise a broader way of seeing technology.

Putting things simply, historians usually approach science and technology in one or other of two ways. The first way, the 'internalist', focuses on the content of technology and science. In this approach, the historian concentrates on the way that some piece of engineering or scientific work has been done. It may be the building of a famous bridge, or the development of a series of ships or steam engines. The approach may consider scientific theories, and investigate the way that physicists and engineers arrived at the ideas of thermodynamics or the behaviour of beams. In general, this internalist approach concentrates on describing the technical process itself.

The other approach takes things from a human science standpoint, and tries to explain events as a social phenomenon. Probably the best known work in this genre is T. S. Kuhn's Structure of Scientific Revolutions. This is a general description of what happens in a process of radical scientific change, when scientists exchange one mental model or 'paradigm' for another. Kuhn's interest is not in the truth or falsehood of either paradigm, but in the social interactions which accompany the shift – the period of doubt and crisis, the formation of hostile schools of thought taking radical, conservative and intermediate stances. Incidentally, the differences between the schools of internalist and externalist historians of science have led to bitter disputes – which themselves clearly illustrate the Kuhn hypothesis!

In general, then, the history of technology has been approached through its context or its content, but I would now like to suggest a third approach and look for the origins of engineering as a function of the human mind.

It seems to me that there are three levels at which technology can be approached in history. At the first level, i.e. context, it does not matter how something works. We do not need a detailed understanding of printing or steam locomotives to recognise the enormous effect that the press had on the diffusion of knowledge during the Renaissance, or railways' transformation of economic activity in the 19th century. At this level, the externalist one, we can see technology in its historical context and examine, for instance, the forces which tried to resist or to encourage change. A typical question of this kind might be about whether canal owners or landed gentry tried to hinder the building of a new piece of railway to protect their own interests.

At the second level, however, the technology itself has to be understood in order to understand events. In the 1830's the railways were challenging the canals' dominance in transport, but themselves were challenged in turn by steam carriages running on the ordinary roads. It is easy to understand how desirable such road carriages appeared, for they could use the roads just as cars and lorries do today. If we ask ourselves why railways were successful, yet steam carriages were not, we have to look at the technology. We need some idea of the engineering difficulties which steam road carriages faced.

In 1830 it was much easier to put steam onto rails than on roads. An iron railway has a hard smooth surface capable of carrying almost any weight, and a steam locomotive could haul fifty or more waggons. The railway locomotive did not need steering gear or a differential to help it round corners, and the rails were strong enough to carry a heavy high-pressure boiler. By contrast, the road steamers were hard to steer, carried only light loads, had intractable transmission problems, and their boilers blew up regularly because they had to be so lightly constructed.[5] The engineer of 1830 was simply not able to build a truly satisfactory steam carriage. The point of this example is that we need to look at the state of the technology to understand why things turned out as they did. It is an argument for studying the content or internal side of things.

The third level of understanding the history of technology concerns the creative moment when something new is coming into being. It is hard to pin down this fleeting instant between non-existence and the existence of an idea. Our brains cannot un-think a successful solution, or imagine how messy and uncertain the problem looked before the Eureka event. Inventions are like the pictures used to explain Gestalt theory. It is very hard to see them; but once seen, they are hard to forget. It takes a little time to see the cow in this picture (see Fig. 2), but once we have seen it, it leaps into view every time we look. Unless we can *unthink* our knowledge of an invention, we cannot grasp the doubts and difficulties which beset the mind of the inventor – or understand the creative moment.

Fig. 2. Dallenbach Cow.

Failing to understand the creative moment of key inventions also makes it harder to see how they change the future course of history. The 'externalist' approach to history tends to minimise the role of inventors, by suggesting that new technologies come into existence through the workings of broad social forces. This may be true of some invention; there will always be a market for a better can-opener or more efficient light bulb. Yet I find it hard to imagine a broad social force inventing anything of a more original nature. What specifically was the social pressure for the zip-fastener or 'cats eye' road-markings before their invention took place? When one examines cases like the Newcomen steam engine, Stephenson's Rocket or the Wright Brothers' Flyer, one finds that these individual inventors were years ahead of their competitors, and that things might have taken a different path without them.[6]

It is well to remember that even where there is a need, it does not make an invention predictable or inevitable. By 1700, Britain was struggling with the problem that as coal mines were dug deeper, it became harder to pump out the water flooding them. This situation did not make Thomas Newcomen's invention of the atmospheric steam engine inescapable or its success inevitable. One cannot say much with certainty about things that did not happen, but I know of no other inventor or machine at the time who had any prospect of succeeding if Newcomen had failed. As for changing the future, Newcomen was the most influential inventor in history. James Watt is more famous, but he started off with a Newcomen engine to repair, and decided to improve on it; Richard Trevithick, the pioneer of steam railways and high-pressure portable engines, started off initially trying to get round Watt's patents. The first internal combustion engines used the basic layout of steam engines. Even today, a motor car engine has the same organs as the Newcomen engine – piston and cylinder, inlet valves and timing, a means of transmitting the power to do work.[7]

Newcomen's engine was an outstanding example of an invention which was both creative and therefore unpredictable; and it changed the future so much that it has become hard to 'unthink'.

For a contemporary example, we could take the microprocessor. Who, in the early 1950's, imagined such a minute but powerful device? Nobody foresaw its industrial and administrative impact, or the way that it would put computing power into the ordinary home. Science fiction stories of the 50's would describe the captain of a space ship about to make the jump to light speed – and taking out his slide rule to make the calculations. The microprocessor was unexpected and it profoundly changed the future.

This is not an argument for believing in technological determinism. On the contrary, I think that the unpredictability of new technology gives a powerful reason for thinking that the future is undetermined. It only seems determined to the kind of mind which does not appreciate the originality and unknowable consequences of new ideas.

It is hard to ask the right questions when we think we already know the answers to the wrong ones. Externalists and internalists both assume that technology came into being by an act of human will. They assume that technology was established to meet basic human needs such as food, warmth, shelter, defence, or transport.

But perhaps we are begging a big question here. Was there ever such an intentional establishment of technology? The argument resembles the 17th century idea that the origins of government could be explained by assuming that men in the primitive natural state made some kind of Social Contract and decided to establish the state.[8] Of course this 'Original Contract' of the old political theorists was nonsense. Perhaps its is equally unreasonable to assume that in some way, at some time, technology was deliberately invented. Let us seek a different approach to our engineering origins, and look for different roots of technical inventiveness. Of course, we cannot ignore the social context or the engineering content of what mankind has built, but we must now try to get at the human behaviour and motivation which underlie them.

3. Innate Technology – An Alternative Hypothesis

What if technology is not learned, but innate – a primary activity in the most fundamental sense? I began to reach this conclusion after many years of looking at history from the wrong end.[9] For a long time, I taught my students about Henry Maudslay (1771–1831) and his wonderful screw cutting lathe.[10] I used to explain how the precision of his machines led the way towards interchangeable parts, mass production, and to building skill into the machine instead of the worker. In other words, Maudslay created some of the key elements of modern industrial production. Then it at last struck me that Maudslay made his lathe, with its accurate lead screw, by hand; and I began to see him as what he was, one of the great eighteenth century craftsman. The remarkable thing about Maudslay could not be the future – he never saw it – but how he made himself the watershed between the hand-craftsmanship of the past and the machines which began to replace it. Then I began to wonder about his clever hands and the brain that controlled them – what made human beings capable of such craftsmanship? And thence I wandered into palaeontology, human origins and the psychology of perception. What had happened in our evolution to make us inventors and craftsmen?

The quest to understand human origins has always been lively, especially now with new insights from genetics and fresh fossil evidence. Our urgent curiosity – for what question is more interesting? – leads us into speculation. The dialogue crosses many disciplines, with voices from palaeontology, microbiology, evolutionary biology, climatology and many others. Despite the efforts and some remarkable field discoveries, we have to admit that little is certain as yet.[11] We do not even know what hand-axes were used for. Davidson and Noble think that they may only be the cores left over after the desired tools had been flaked off them. Calvin thinks that they may have been a sort of thrown frisbee weapon. If there is no agreement about the commonest artefact, which had a production run of over a million years, then we are indeed groping and guessing.[12] Data exists; there is simply little agreement about what it means. The present paper uses published findings from these other disciplines to suggest a single mechanism by which key human characteristics might have emerged. The argument will focus on the cause of bipedalism and its relationship to thing using, suggesting how these may be related to creativity and the origins of language. At least the hypothesis is simple, and it seems to fit the facts.[13]

For the moment, let us consider only the minimalist viewpoint on what makes us human. True, full humanity is music and art, delight at the beauty of the world, poetry and the joy of intellectual exploration. But the simplest characteristics of humanity are that we are bipeds, tool-users, and have language. Language and tool-using set us apart from the rest of creation, and most authorities think bipedalism put us on that path. Some apes have the seeds of these talents but comparative studies only emphasise how far ahead humans have moved in tool-using and communication. Even so, it is hard to look chimpanzees in the face when we know how tantalisingly close they come to our attainments. What happened to make us human?

I think most of us have been asking the wrong questions. We are not in the situation of someone who has seen the last page of a detective story, and then knows what all the clues mean as he reads the book from the beginning. After all, the author constructed the plot and the clues with foreknowledge of what the end would be. People in history, and hominids in prehistory, did not know what the end of the story would be. Of course the past led to the present; but we shall not necessarily find the present in the past. A chicken does not look like an egg. It will be even harder to imagine the minds of long extinct creatures.

The question, 'Where did Maudslay get those hands and the brain that drove them?' can only be answered by saying that we evolved that way. My dog Paddy is very intelligent but it is unimaginable that he will ever make a lathe or build a bridge. His brain is just not organised to behave like this. From early childhood, human beings enjoy using their hands or building towers from wooden blocks. If we are to discuss how this character evolved, perhaps we should begin by imagining the time scale.

Imagine that a millimetre represents a year. Then the invention of writing is perhaps six meters away; so on this scale all true history – meaning what is written – stretches back only the length of a living room. For the first stone tools, we have to go back 2 *kilometres* to early hominids who made them. From modern man, Homo Sapiens, the ancestral line runs back, through Neanderthal and Homo Erectus, to

Homo Habilis – a tool user with a brain only a third the size of ours. He was making primitive stone chopper tools 2,000,000 years ago. That alone is enough to suggest that tool-using is not just learnt, but part of our evolutionary make up.

But we should go back further. Everybody who has tried to chip a flint nodule into a useful tool knows that it is one of the most bloodyminded and fractious materials in creation. It is impossible to believe that stone chopper tools, primitive as they seem, were the beginning. Only a creature which already knew the use of tools – whether of horn, bone or wood – would be able to make them from stone. If there is any doubt of this, let the readers try to make a cutting edge from a pebble. They will learn painfully how much is required in the way of visualisation and two-handed co-ordination! Artefacts made from biological materials like wood or bone are unlikely to survive or be recognised from such a remote past – but 'Absence of evidence is not evidence of absence'. If there were stone tools two million years ago, then we can infer that there were other tools for a long time before that. Even though no earlier non-stone artefacts have been identified, we should leave our minds open to the important possibility that things were being used and keep hoping for evidence.

Yet how far back should one go in the search for regular tool-using? Regular tool users need their hands free to use and carry things, so they have to be bipedal. 'Lucy' was a biped with an ape sized brain, 3.7 m.y.a.; so she could conceivably have used tools. Before Lucy, there is practically no hominid fossil evidence. The most remote starting point could be the separation of the hominid line from the apes. Comparative studies of DNA agree that the last common ancestor to chimp and man lived about 5 m.y.a. Chimps are able to use things that come to hand, but they are only occasional bipeds. Given our genetic closeness, splitting of the chimpanzee / hominid line presents a promising point at which to look for what makes humans more human.

4. Two Legs – Some Theories Considered

This seems to be the silly season for speculative theories about the cause of bipedalism, judging from the frequency with which they have been appearing recently. They all have to fit the scene which Yves Coppens describes so well – the drying of the Western side of the Great Rift Valley in Southern Africa: and the fact that chimpanzee remains are concentrated to the west of the Rift; and hominid remains to the east.[14] Apart from that, we have informed guess work.

An hypothesis favoured by many has been Man the Mighty Hunter – the first hominid who stayed in the plains when the forests receded, and went upright to run faster, and to see prey or dangers far off. But can we seriously believe that some newly jumped-up biped had any significant speed advantage over the predators of the savannah? Walking on two legs is mechanically difficult and requires major changes in the configuration of the bones and muscular actions used for locomotion. The vertebrae have to become load bearing. According to Lovejoy, 'Lucy' must have come at the end of a long evolution towards two leggedness.[15] It seems improbable in the first stages of the changeover that a new biped would have been faster than a quadruped.[16] Human babies strive to stand upright, but revert to crawling when they are in a hurry. Scavenging, a less flattering image of our earlier selves, is open to similar objections. Hyenas and dogs are good scavengers without abandoning four leggedness. Scavenging is at best a partial explanation.

If it was not speed, then what was the advantage of the new posture? Dean Falk seems to suggest that bipedalism was produced by the need to keep the brain cool.[17] She describes physical adaptations such as cooling holes in the cranium and more exposed pathways for blood leaving the brain, and suggests that the cooling was enhanced by going upright. Better cooling would be needed by a creature which used its brain more, especially when that brain grew larger. By the square-cube law, the surface to volume ratio becomes less favourable for cooling as the brain grows bigger. While one can see that a larger brain needed new cooling mechanisms, it is begging the question to argue that this was a cause of bipedalism. Surely the question which needs to be asked is what new activity had led to greater brain activity and the need for cooling? Other large bipeds, like ostriches and kangaroos, are certainly not noted for their brain-power – so what were the proto-hominids up to?

Another recent idea, from Nina Jablonski and George Chaplin,[18] is that Savannah dwelling apes stood upright as a display of aggression. Surely this again is a very thin cause for such a difficult bodily transformation. Chimpanzees run social lives, stylised aggression and all, without undergoing the discomforts of becoming bipedal.

The idea of bipedalism being an adaptation to the dry Savannah is challenged by a watery hypothesis – the Aquatic Ape who may have taken to the water, wading and losing his hair in the process. Elaine Morgan suggests that this could have taken place in the Rift Valley when it was an inland sea.[19] The wader's buoyancy in water would doubtless make uprightness easier. This hypothesis can also account for the high position of the breasts of the human female, and would explain a human nose which impedes the entry of water. Her argument that the detailed development of the human embryo suggests a return to the water is persuasive. Unlike any other primate, it even has a coating of wax (vernix caseosa) at birth.[20] Like other mammals which have returned to the sea, humans can control their breathing – a prerequisite of speech. The 'aquatic ape' could certainly have enjoyed a rich protein diet from shell fish and the long-chain molecules in fish oils would favour the growth of nervous tissue.

The Morgan hypothesis has the essential quality which others lack; it suggests a unique and major change of behaviour as the impulse towards bipedalism. Yet though the aquatic ape is an attractive hypothesis, it does not account for the use of tools or language. Unless the salt deposits of the Rift Valley yield up real evidence, Morgan's marine ape must remain no more than an attractive idea.

5. Two Legs – An Alternative Suggestion

These different hypotheses all depend on a two stage process to explain, first, why some apes became biped and then, second, that their hands were free for tool using to develop. But are two hypotheses necessary in the first place?

Let us consider a simpler possibility. Suppose instead that bipedalism arose because the first hominids were using their hands, which became too useful to waste on knuckle walking. Suppose that they were holding useful things. The proposition 'upright because of tools' is simpler than 'some reason for upright; and then some reason for tools.' After all, our close relatives the chimpanzees are capable of using a range of tools, like stones to crack nuts, straws to winkle out termites, and sticks to reach things. There is no fatal improbability in the idea that the first upright steps and frequent hand-use began when the new hominid line started about 5 m.y.a.

I have pointed out the difficulty of working flint, and that it seems most likely that only a creature which is already using things will have the motor skills to work stone.

Deliberately made stone tools, then, belong to a much later time. Many simpler things, however, can be used to great effect. Plain pebbles can crack nuts and seashells, or can be thrown as missiles. A dead animal offered, apart from its meat: shoulder blades to dig with; a bladder to carry water; hard, pointed horns; gut; a jawbone studded with teeth... and so on. Above all, it is necessary to imagine what power there was in a stick. It can scrape and dig, revealing new food sources like roots and bulbs; for primates have nails not claws, so they are poorly fitted for digging. The stick can extend the reach and knock down fruit and nuts. As a club it is an energy storing weapon – other animals can only store energy by charging at high speed. Furthermore, like throwing stones or using a hammer, a club requires accurate prediction of its curved path. There is no time for feed-back corrections, and Calvin considers that this required more advanced neural capacities.[21] And lastly, it might have made walking easier for a learner-biped just as it does for an ageing one.

We are not suggesting a craftsman tool-maker, an earlier claimant to be *homo faber*, but a rough opportunist; *homo bricoleur* or *thing user*.[22] He did not even need an opposable thumb. The opposable thumb is important for the precision grip in delicate operations, but the power grip is enough for grasping sticks and stones. In any case, how would an opposable thumb have come about unless it had been favoured with success? An essential feature to grasp about evolution is that a new feature does not appear before it is used. The feature only improves because it is already being used successfully. This truth is encapsulated in the saying that 'Birds do not fly because they have wings. Birds have wings because they fly.'

Primate origins left other important legacies besides the useful hand. Our brachiating branch of the primate line had acquired a particularly useful arm socket. Apes, unlike monkeys, swing beneath branches and have a much wider arm movement – handy for a prospective tool user. You can scratch behind your other ear; monkeys can't. Life in the trees also called for good binocular vision. our highly developed judgement of distance is based on a number of mental processes, not just stereoscopy; it is affected by the familiar size of things, overlapping, even colour.[23] Primates in trees needed this three dimensional mental power to recognise things every which way up. In fact, our brains are very good at rotating things mentally to compare them.[24] Even more important, the further up the primate line one looks, the more we find a tendency to learning, imitation and inventiveness.

6. The *Thing Using* Mind

Putting all these things together, we picture a creature with the potential for seeing things in three dimensions, and eventually imagining things it wanted to make. It was a creature which could adapt, not by physical evolution, but by changing its function through what it held in its hands. People turn into a different animal by picking up a hammer, a spade or a pen. In general, other animals only achieve this by physical specialisation. Aardvarks and badgers have powerful claws for digging; hoofed animals run fast and far, but they are condemned to grass eating by their single purpose feet. The first thing-user, however, has changed the rules radically, and replaced physical adaptation by changing its behaviour and adopting proto-tools. Perhaps this was the most strategically important step in the whole of evolution, at least comparable to the evolution of the eye or the backbone.

Maybe we see shadows of all this in the games that make us happy. We like swinging sticks, whether we call them golf clubs or baseball bats; we like intriguing shapes, like droodles; we like games involving positional awareness, like chess and draughts. Our *thing user* only had an ape-brain to direct its new behaviour, but the subsequent development of that brain was driven by tool using and what might be called inventive activity. If this were the case then man did not invent technology: technology invented man.

Consider what inventive behaviour needs. Some of its more obvious features are: a need for abstraction in looking at things from a new point of view; a three dimensional thought which I will call Spatial Logic; an ability to form patterns, including original and creative ones. Take these one by one.

Thing using has important psychological implications. We can suppose that *thing user* had a primate brain, well capable of three dimensional perception. But in the new behaviour things were no longer perceived in the same way as they were in a state of nature. A dog perceives a stone as a mere object. *Thing using* demands a different kind of perception. *Thing user* has to think abstractly – if it wants to crack a shell, it is the hardness and heaviness and shape of the stone that make the brain see it as a hammer. Swinging a stick involves its stiffness, hardness, length and weight; also a second order effect, that the end of the stick travels further and faster than the arm swinging it. Using things – stones, sticks, bones – implies a process of abstraction; because we are using the thing's qualities as we perceive them, and these are not the same as its original identity in nature.

The other day I was standing in a muddy ditch at Wortley Top Forge, and I wanted to clean earth off a stone; I glanced round, and found a root – straight and strong enough to scrape with. My mind had abstracted qualities – straightness and hardness – which were unrelated to root, the part of a tree that sits under the ground. This mental act took place without words – readers will know what it feels like to look round the garden shed for a piece of scrap material that will do the job.

There is also an intentionality that selects and shapes our perceptions. If I pick up a stone to use it as a hammer, it has become a hammer in my mind first. A stone becomes a hammer not only because I abstract the qualities of hardness, heaviness and shape which fits my hand, but because I want to hit something. A stick becomes different things in the mind according to desire: digger, pointer, walking aid, club – it is our perception, not the stick that changes. *Thing user* also has to make a mental pattern, akin to a gestalt perception, of what it wants to do. This is a creature which has taken a new path, replacing physical specialisation by the behavioural opportunism of an omnivore in novel conditions. This was the crucial step *thing user* took in separating from the apes. Physical evolution continued, but not towards physical specialisation for a particular niche and diet. Instead it was adapting brain and body to respond to problems by what might be called proto-technical means.

The insights of gestalt psychology and work like R.L.Gregory's on perception show how powerfully the brain processes the inputs from our eyes to give meaningful vision.[25] When one is looking for *cèpe* mushrooms in a French wood, they are difficult to see at first, but an experienced French person can recognise them in an uncanny way. Interpreters of aerial photographs develop similar skills. We are a pattern making animal. However, with invention we are not only dealing with the perception of the outside world, but a further stage, the creation of new patterns.

We not only perceive things in three dimensions; we can also imagine new things. Our brain can rotate objects mentally, literally turning things over in the mind, to see whether two things seen from different angles are identical.[26] Technical creativity requires this kind of spatial imagination, and Brooke Hindle points out that many inventors – from Brunelleschi and Leonardo da Vinci in the Italian Renaissance to Robert Fulton and Samuel Morse, in the 19th century – were also artists.[27] This is an attractive idea but it does not stand up so well in the case of England, a country short on artists but strong in engineers. Maudslay, Nasmyth, Watt, Whitworth, Clement and Parsons had splendid spatial imaginations but no artistic training. Nasmyth attached particular importance to Euclidean geometry, though admittedly artists like Brunelleschi were the first to formalise it into the rules of geometrical perspective in painting. Whether the spatial imagination is manifested in fine art, geometry or engineering, it seems likely that it owed a lot to the early hominid mind looking at a thing, and dealing with it as a spatial abstraction. Geometry, painting and invention cannot grow in minds that are not predisposed to abstract spatial thought.

Another feature associated with spatial logic is the awareness of how materials behave. Most people are not conscious of how much they know about materials. We know, without ever verbalising the thought, that we cannot push a piece of string. Your brain can instantly call up the different sensations of breaking a match-stick, and the more brittle unyielding way a stick of chalk snaps. Children can be observed learning these things about materials before they learn to talk – adults call it fiddling.[28]

Our sense of forces is also highly developed. We easily apply the right force to cracking a walnut, tightening a tiny screw, or smashing a big stone with a sledgehammer. Adolescents know how to close a door quietly, and also how to make a statement by slamming it. As Petroski says, "We are all engineers of sorts, for we have all the principles of machines and structures in our bones... We calculate the paths of our arms and our legs with the computer of our brain, and we catch basketballs and footballs with more dependability than the most advanced weapons systems intercept missiles."[29] I am not suggesting that we are born with the knowledge, but that our brains are organised to learn it very quickly. The word logic is used to imply that our wordless conceptions form a conclusion just as necessarily as the steps of Aristotelian logic do. Let the readers try a simple mental experiment, by visualising a tent pole and guy ropes. Do they see that three guy ropes will keep a tent pole upright? – you wiggle it in your head and feel that it will stand. We already have the phrase 'To see with the mind's eye.' We need another one, 'To feel with the mind's hand.'

Creativity comes when we apply our abstractions and spatial logic in a new situation. If the kitchen door keeps blowing open and a woman puts down a brick to keep it shut, then she has been creative; for bricks exist to build houses with, not shut doors. Creativity is not verbalised, not voluntary, but something which we do spontaneously. It is important to remember that all human minds are creative in this sense, and that individuals like Watt and Faraday are more gifted but not essentially different from the rest of us.

There is no explanation yet of what happens when a new idea comes. At first sight it seems paradoxical to imagine a neurological algorithm for producing new ideas. It contradicts the idea that creativity is unpredictable. Yet, logically, we have to consider that, when a creature adopts variable techniques or innovation as its adaptive strategy, presumably a genetically based capacity for creative thought must be a part of its equipment. If there were innate neural algorithms for creativity, then I suspect that they would include the capacities to abstract, see patterns, and apply metaphors from one field to another.[30]

D. A. Schon in his work on invention saw the transfer of metaphor as a principal root of invention – that we take a concept from one field and apply it in another[31]. This can happen at a very concrete level – the Inuits use a seal paw to scratch the ice near a hole, to simulate the sound of a seal and allay the fears of their prey. It is easy to think of many other examples of human beings copying or using the behaviour of an animal.

Thing using and craftsmanship are not the same thing. In much later times craftsmen come to the fore – the masons, goldsmiths or cabinet makers who set the style of a civilisation. *Thing using* is cruder and more opportunistic. We all know people who do not blush to use a sharp wood chisel as a screw-driver and I have watched with horror an antique pistol butt being used as a hammer. I meet a lot of Exploratory inventors from other countries, and I am struck by the way they will adapt things, say in a DIY shop or a workshop store, to their own purposes, well away from the original function of the thing. They bore holes in plastic plates to make wheels and use empty ball-pens to make Cartesian divers that bob up and down in a bottle of water. These are people who have never met each other before, yet their behaviour is similar. *Homo Sapiens* as craftsman comes later – we begin with homo *thing user*, and he is still around. His competitive habitat is the Egg Race.

Of course creativity is influenced by culture and circumstances or individual ability. New situations seem to trigger it – one only has to consider how the coming of railways called forth a flood of creative new bridge structures after 1830;[32] or how nearly all the modern machine tools appeared in a few decades after 1800.[33] Perhaps there are mechanisms in the brain by which new situations, new problems, new dangers switch on our creativity. But equally, culture (including education) can also inhibit creativity. Scholars are generally agreed that the mandarin system in China saw that innovation could destabilise society, so it put a stop to it. There is a story that a sheep in Wales learned that it could pass a cattle grid by lying down and rolling across. The whole flock was quickly slaughtered before this undesirable behaviour could be passed on to other sheep.

If this view of the origins of technology and creativity is correct, then we did not invent technology. Technology invented us. Its true nature is not the assembly of objects built by mankind, or the collected knowledge of all the fields of engineering. It is an element of human nature like sex and the drive to eat. Thus we see it not as something invented by society to clothe, feed and shelter us; but rather a stream that runs back to our emergence as a species. There was no sudden beginning of technology any more than there was a founding of society by some Original Compact – there, again like our chimpanzee cousins, we were a social animal and evolved ways of getting along together.

Thing user is necessarily creative. In adapting to new niches or challenges, he has replaced physical change by technical response. Dawkins says that evolution is blind;[34] we must add that technology is mind. Sometimes writers speak loosely of the evolution of technology[35] but technology is not an entity which can evolve. Artefacts do not reproduce themselves, or pass on favourable mutations. It is easy to slip into thinking like that when we look at the development of the aeroplane, from the Wright Flier to Concorde, or the line leading from ENIAC to the Personal Computer. But we are really speaking of the results of our creative thinking, for technology is exclusively a product of the brain's inventiveness. This universal human creativity is the force that takes a raw material or an existing invention, and changes or reapplies it.

7. Talking

Language is the other great defining characteristic of humanity, along with the bipedalism and tool using which I have already suggested are linked. What if language and *thing using* are linked as well? Once more, for this argument, a minimalist view of language is enough for our purposes. We must pass by the fascinating discussion about whether we can trace the existing tongues of mankind back to an original language,[36] since we are concerned with what happened before language existed. Let Chomsky's basic ideas serve for a rough working definition of language and then try to see how our 'thing user' might acquire such a thing.

1. Language is universal. Chomsky points out how easily young human children learn language. They learn not only to separate strings of phonemes into words, but they discover the rules of syntax as well. The child finds out for itself that nouns and verbs work in different ways. They quickly arrive at a competence in dealing with deep structures which are hard to express in simple rules. In Chomsky's own example, quite a young child will turn 'The man who is tall is in the room' into the question form 'Is the man who is tall in the room?' This transformation needs structural understanding, not mechanical rules, to move the second 'is' to the beginning of the sentence. 'Chomsky maintains that it is only by assuming that the child is born with a knowledge of the highly restrictive principles of universal grammar, and the predisposition to make use of them in analysing the utterances he hears about him, that we can make any sense of the process of language-learning.'[37]

2. If language is universal and the brain is not a 'general purposes' machine but specifically endowed with universal grammar, can this lead to any hypothesis about the earlier functions of this form of thought?

   Arguments for a common grammar set up neurally in the brain are often based on complex linguistic structures, like transformations and markers.[38] Perhaps we should look at simpler structures in considering language origins. One can reasonably suppose that simple statements preceded complex subordinate clauses. All human languages have verbs and nouns, and have statements with the general form **subject + verb + object**.[39] Individual languages have varying devices for expressing this. In English the word order tells us whether the man or the dog is biting or bitten; in inflected languages like Russian and Latin, the word endings tell us which is subject or object. Despite the variety, the underlying grammar is the same and – as Chomsky puts it – a Martian would think that we all speak the same language. After all, though it may seem the obvious one to us, is it the only basic structure a language might adopt? Human beings can learn other human languages and can think in them. But could there be languages we are not adapted to think in?[40]

3. Human beings use language creatively. Chomsky points out that even young children use language creatively, in the sense that they form meaningful, correct sentences which they have never heard before. Every day we make new sentences out of our grammar and vocabulary. Indeed, these can generate an infinite number of different statements.[41]

If this is a fair account of Chomsky, then language closely resembles the *'thing using'* thought discussed earlier. I suggest that the mental machinery for producing language does not originate in communication, but in the mental faculties which accompanied the evolution of the *thing using* brain. (Perhaps there was a preliminary period of gesture). Now let us compare the characteristics which Chomsky gives for language with the those needed by the *thing using* brain.

I have tried to show that the *'thing user'* has to abstract, and that the concepts in this abstract thinking can exist in non-verbal form. But words are labels we apply to concepts we have abstracted. When we grope for a word, we are seeing that the thought must exist before the word. The propensity for *'thing using'* is universal among humans. So, says Chomsky, is language. Another feature common to tool use and language is creativeness – the ability to apply the abstractions, shapes, forces and materials, in new contexts. Lastly, I suggest, the syntax of Chomsky's universal grammar is closely parallel to wordless *thing using* thought. Subject (somebody / something) + verb (action / what a tool does / operation) and perhaps object (the thing that is operated on, changed or made).

This argument is left at the simplest level, that the subject-verb-object seems like the thought of a simple *'thing user'*. R. Wallace explored a similar idea, relating areas in the brain known to support language with adjacent areas that provide our ability to map territory. He suggests that there is a link here with the brain's ability to provide markers, and to embed clauses in complex statements.[42] It seems to me that Wallace is considering linguistic forms that would appear later in language development. It is easier to believe that language was originally grafted onto simpler structures. Then, once the process started, it could spread to all the accessible functions of the brain. Such spreading of the language activity through the brain may have taken place over a long period. *Thing using*, being parallel to the simplest grammatical forms, seems a likely place to start.

There are good evolutionary precedents for this proposed transformation of organs, from one function to another. The mammals' air-breathing lung evolved from the swim bladder of fish. Fish fins have ended up as human arms and hands, and bats' wings started off the same way too.

Other clues point the same way. The neural motor areas for speech lie next to the right hand's zone, and we gesture with that hand when we talk – that is we use it for communication as well as for manipulation. Right-handed musicians can finger with their left hand, but they find it much harder to conduct with the wrong hand, suggesting that the right hand is the instrument of the individual's conceptions and intentions. [43] A possible process has been suggested by which this kind of parallel neurological equipment might evolve. J. M. Allman and J. H. Kaas have suggested that cortical areas can replicate themselves, and that the new areas can assume new functions while the original area continues to perform its initial task. [44]

Chimpanzees use simple tools, but their voice organs do not let them talk. They can however be taught to communicate by sign language, but this happens under artificial conditions, not in the wild. It therefore seems most unlikely that this brain function, supporting the unspoken language, could have evolved for communication. But it could derive from the *thing using* which they share with ourselves. If so, it supports the suggestion that the brain functions used in human language did not originate for communication, but in *thing using*.

Is *'thing using'* being forced to explain too many things here? In nature, a mono-functional behaviour often leads to multiple adaptations. Because it flies, the bird has evolved feathers, light cellular bones, as well as an aerodynamic shape and a 'retractable undercarriage'. The ocean environment led to similarly extensive changes in dolphins and whales. Limbs became fins or flippers; the skin, the shape, the breathing, the diet – all changed as they adapted from being land to sea mammals. In the case of human evolution, attention focuses more on brain function and behaviour than on physical form; but the similar principle can apply, that simple causes led to multiple complex results.

Stick using games and perception jokes like droodles have already been mentioned. More speculatively, one might consider the possibility that the origins of magic lie in the link between *thing using* and language in the brain. Magic is universal among primitive and not so primitive peoples – pronouncing the right incantations makes things happen. In many cultures, names for things and people have a far deeper significance than mere labels for communicating ideas and become taboo words. Might this be an atavistic extension of the *thing user's* thought processes into the later age of verbal consciousness? If words were descended from tools and their use, this could explain the urge to use words themselves to make things happen. Speculating further, if the likeliest early tool was the stick, then at a deep level of displacement we have the prototype magic wand.

In formal logic – from Aristotle to Descartes and Hegel – we certainly see language being used as a tool, a making of conclusions by means of words alone. If we compare them, language logic is a weaker implement than spatial logic. Aristotle's logic tells us nothing new that was not already implicit in the premises; as for Hegel's logic – his dialectic led to anything he wanted us to believe. This is not to say that Hegel had no perceptive insights; but one can jettison all the paraphernalia of thesis, antithesis, and synthesis – and the insights remain. By contrast, a good house-builder senses wordlessly where a beam is needed to strengthen an opening in a wall, or which wall bears loads. What he does is effective as well as logical – which is more than can be claimed for most verbal arguments. Fortunately for word users, arguments do not usually collapse with the same disastrous consequences as defective buildings.

8. Some Implications of the *Thing Using* Mind

Let us summarise the main features of *thing using* and Spatial Logic before looking at some implications these have for the way we think about engineering and other broader issues.

There is still not much more than 'a table top of fossils' so the hominid story between five and two million years ago remains sketchy and speculative. The *'thing using'* hypothesis is simple but it seems to fit the data we have at present from the disciplines investigating human origins.[45] It explains bipedalism more simply, by deriving it simply from to need to liberate hands for *thing using*. The new activity required the brain to work more. The substantial part of the modern human brain which is dedicated to the hands supports the suggestion that brain enlargement was substantially driven by technology.[46] Surely creativity was a necessary part of the new mental activity. Finally, *thing using* thought could have set up the neurological mechanisms in the brain upon which language might graft.[47]

Even if the early *'thing using'* hypothesis should turn out false, the following 2 million years of tool using certainly coincided with a massive growth of the brain. This fact, that the human brain has roughly tripled in size since the first known stone tools appeared, does suggest that the brain is particularly adapted to support technical activity. Tool using is as universal as language, sex and eating – and nobody would suggest that those are not genetically based.

The hypothesis also raises a question about the initial impetus towards the new activity. Evolution is good at explaining why something that already exists gets better – why flyers become better flyers, lions become better predators, and zebras get better at running away from lions. But this does not tell us what triggers off the initial direction of specialisation in the first place. What set ancestral badgers off digging and fleas biting? These are the creative moments of evolution if it is true that specialised organs follow behaviour. It is not enough to point to a new niche as the sufficient cause of new behaviour. The response to that new niche could have taken many other forms. Among wild variety of plant and animal adaptation, one sees many which are unique in the sense of being unusual, but they are not unique in the sense of being the only possible solution.

In technology, likewise, the quasi-evolutionary stages of improvement in steam engines, battleships, computers or ploughs can be followed easily. But the initial creative moment is elusive – the one we cannot 'unthink'. Obviously the new initiative solved a problem – but why that solution and not some other? Equally, in evolution, it is easier to follow the stages of new 'hardware' and we skip the question about the origin of the behaviour that led to it.

Such questions remain useful whether *thing using* appeared 2,000,000 or 5,000,000 years ago. The new perspective of seeing technology as an innate propensity changes our view of yet more questions. Cultural or economic forces remain important in studying technology, but perhaps the innatist ideas linked with *thing using* could lead to new insights. It will be a truer image if we see human technology as having a dual nature, both cultural and innate. It is partly cultural, different if the individual grows up in France, Japan or Polynesia; and partly innate, a non-verbal and creative element of being human.

Numerous other species perform quasi-technical activities, like birds and insects building nests or beavers constructing dams. Tailor birds really do sew leaves; hermit crabs really make little houses for themselves. It is not quite safe to say that, in the animal kingdom, the specific and unvarying character of such activity shows that it is instinctual rather than inventive. Termites use new materials like plastics in their nests; blue tits have learned to peck through aluminium milk bottle tops. All one can say is, yes, it is true, but human beings have made invention a habitual technique, whereas the other species do it occasionally.

Technology is not just our western technology. We must not be misled by the huge thrust which science, mathematics and social organisation have given to western invention, into thinking that this is the only viable way by which human beings adapt to their habitat. Concern for the environment is making western technology's long-term direction seem more doubtful – even worrying – and there may be something to learn from other cultures which have achieved a sustainable balance over long ages. In any case, it will always be worth remembering that inventiveness and *'thing using'* are not special to any culture but a part of human nature.

The dual nature, both innate and cultural, explains why it is found in every human culture, and is a prime means by which the group survives in its environment. Questions about the emergence of different cultures, the races, the languages and how much of this was the work of Homo Sapiens Sapiens, come later than the conjectural *'thing using'* of Lucy's ancestor. It is illuminating to go round a good museum of ethnology, in London, Paris or Cambridge, or the great Pitt Rivers in Oxford, to see the ingenuity and flavour of other cultures, and the mysterious sense of their style persisting through time.

It seems to me that we can look at things made before the great expansion of western technology, and tell where they were made, but not when. Looking at a 20th century artefact, we can say when it was made, but not where. Every part of Asia had its own fighting knives, and one immediately recognises yataghans, Cossack shashkas, Indonesian kris or Japanese swords though they might have been made at any time over the last thousand years. A four thousand year old Chinese bronze looks Chinese even today. But now, design has converged and it is not the place of origin but the date we recognise. There is no mistaking the sit of a 1950's motor car, or the look of a 60's TV or refrigerator – but they could have been made anywhere. Design – or rather technique – has largely become international. France is more retentive of its culture than most nations, but shall we ever see another 2CV? Today's little Peugeots and Renaults, even the Citroens, look like Fiestas and Metros. As manufacturing grows more competitive, with too many cars being made, it will be interesting to see where designs converge or diverge, perhaps showing parallels to evolution.

Our culture is powerful but we find things in other cultures which we could never think of ourselves. The Inuits, formerly called Eskimos, based their whole technology on materials from the seals and other creatures they hunted, for they had little stone or wood. A modern engineer marvels at their boats (bones and seal skin), or fishing tools, or powerful bows backed with sinew, or the way they make anoraks from walrus gut. This ingenuity is to be found in every culture that has not been debased.[48] In our own culture, we have lost a great deal. There are not four people left in Sheffield – that great home of cutlery – who can hand forge a blade. Populations in western countries can become de-skilled in one generation. Craftsmen and engineers used to know a hundred different timbers and where best to use them; but my modern engineering students cannot tell me which wood to use for tool handles. They do not know that ash is shock resistant, or that oak splits easily, but elm doesn't (that's why we use it for the seats of Windsor chairs – they do not split when the pegs are driven in).[49] A whole folk knowledge has been lost. Human culture is fluid and unpredictable and we should wonder what will happen to it as craftsmanship atrophies.

Supposing that all this is right – that we have evolved as tool users, with a brain adapted to learning forces and materials through our hands, and capable of three-dimensional thought. Suppose, too, that this development of the brain is linked to our creativity, and that language does not control, but merely reflects the deeper levels of thought. You have only to reflect a moment to see how far technology has diminished our skills. Artisans have become mere assemblers of factory made elements – this is true of car-makers, plumbers, electricians, and printers. This article can be set for printing from my floppy disk, and my computer replaces typesetting skills learnt formerly by long apprenticeship. In the 1960's, my first publisher, warned me that it would cost a guinea to alter a single comma in the proofs.

These are the logical consequences of those first steps. Technology or technique is liberating us from physical necessity in the same way that *thing using* freed us from physical specialisation.[50] Technology is a form of liberation. It has freed us from many kinds of drudgery, like washing dishes and cleaning dirty fire-grates. Writing freed our memories; transport has freed us from our legs. Yet it is not a simple matter. Computers free the brain from a lot of boring tasks: but virtual reality frees it from reality – which may not turn out to be so good. These are questions that we should face now. Evolution shows clearly that 'If you want to keep it, use it!' Otherwise you lose it, as with the atrophying of the ostrich's wings or the human appendix. What if technology is freeing humanity from skills and aptitudes that we should retain, that make us essentially human? One can imagine culture having a long term evolutionary effect without descending into the heresy of Lamarckism.

It is interesting to speculate for a moment about the way the culture shapes our own engineering. If there was ever a language of spatial logic, then it was Euclidean geometry. The West's continuous technological rise coincided with Geometry's rediscovery in the mini-Renaissance of the 12th century. It still astonishes many people that such an apparently abstract deductive system fits the world so well, describing levers, elliptical orbits, the six-sidedness of honeycomb alveoles, or gears. Explaining trusses in structures, one shows that triangles are rigid – can not wriggle to another shape – but that a four sided figure is not rigid. Old time engineers would often produce an answer by geometry rather than calculation, getting a square root for instance by drawing a construction based on a semicircle. This spatial way of doing mathematics suits some people better than the maths based on numbers and algebra. In my experience, students studying the aesthetics of design are often happier thinking spatially than with numerical symbols. They find Galileo's geometrical demonstrations easier to follow than the algebraic sort of explanation.

Yet are even geometry and drawing on paper a constraint on our thought? Do we limit ourselves to the design of things which we can geometrise and make on our geometrical machines? Could the engineers we train in modern methods design the

Fig. 3. Tripod.

Indian folding tripod (see Fig. 3) which is carved from one piece of wood? My own attempts to copy it showed me that the shapes are very subtle – I fabricated one from dowel and square section wood, and it just lay flat. Only then did I appreciate the sinuous curves and angles of the original. It exists, so it must be rational, yet I suspect that our methods of design cannot produce it. Perhaps our way of reasoning sets limits on our thought which we are not aware of.

This interest in the nature of three dimensional thinking led me to construct a solid version of Escher's Impossible Staircase (see Fig. 4). It was a deliberate attempt to explore the difference between thinking in two and three dimensions. I found it impossible to imagine a 3D form by distorting the flat image on the paper. I tried to imagine the paper folding over to give horizontal steps, for instance, and could not do it. With the rules of perspective we can reduce three dimensions to two. However, it does not work the other way. We cannot make a unique three dimensional form from a two dimensional image – there is an infinity of possibilities (though not all probable ones.) The problem is compounded, of course, if the two dimensional source is irrational like the Escher. When I finally persuaded my brain to work effectively, I can only describe the sensation as clicking from two dimensions to three. Perhaps we do not think enough about the difference between perceiving in three dimensions, and thinking in them; perhaps we do too much on two dimensional paper.

Designing the model gave me an interesting insight into one of the problems of teaching creativity. Creativity has many parameters. One of them is to do something new with what one has already got – a straightforward application of design skills. But a deeper creativity is to do something that one cannot do with the standard skills, to find new ways to do something. These are the things that might usually be described as impossible.

It is important to recognise that there are different forms of impossibility. One sort of *impossible* is set by the limits of nature. It really does seem impossible thermodynamically to get more energy out of a system than it contains, so engineers are very suspicious of any claims to perpetual motion. But another sort of 'impossible' depends on other constraints, the ones we impose on ourselves in a system that we

Fig 4. Impossible staircase based on the drawing by M.C. Escher. Photo: Peter Fisher.

define. We make arbitrary rules that define some things as impossible. It is impossible to built a ship that floats or a 'plane that flies using Meccano – but that is a characteristic of that construction system, not a law of nature. Creativity depends partly on recognising what is considered impossible because of the real laws of nature and what is thought impossible because of an arbitrary system or assumption. Here again, is the importance of, not just knowing, but knowing about what we know.

Much of our thinking is two dimensional, and seldom gets beyond the three dimensional level of a side, elevation and plan drawing. There are not many three dimensional mechanisms – most, like Watt's linkage, are plane solutions. The differential, like the one in the ancient Chinese South-facing Chariot, is a beautiful exception. The idea did not appear in the West until the nineteenth century. Yet it cannot be described in words. Let any reader who does not know the differential's motions ask an engineer how it works. It cannot even be sketched without imagining the paper rotating end over end.

The builders of Gothic cathedral vaults were also high order three dimensional thinkers but I do not think that they could make drawings of their vaulting. The French military engineer Vauban was another able 3D thinker. In all his works the shapes and dimensions of the bastions, tenailles, demilunes and outworks vary. Briançon, in the broken country of the French Alps, is perhaps the masterpiece – it is hard to depict even though it exists – in three dimensions. What was it like to think it out in three dimensions from a standing start? Among engines, I would nominate the little known Bishopp engine for its three dimensionality. Its inward facing truncated cones and swashing disc take some people a long time to figure out.[51]

How can this three dimensional thinking be taught, when we do so much on paper? It seems to be an intuitive rather than analytical process. Do we, perhaps, limit our thinking to what we can analyse? It is, of course, easier to teach what we can analyse.[52] Without wishing to provoke engineers, I wonder whether any of them have failed to follow up an idea because they could not see what equations to use to design it theoretically? (Newton had to invent the calculus to describe his intuition about gravity and the orbits of satellites – but plainly the intuition had come to him first.) Maybe we should see things differently and start, not from the equations, but from a mental picture.

We have to remember that whether we describe a thing in words or numbers, our description is not the same as the thing itself. Whatever my analytical or intuitive ideas are about an arch, they are not the same as that arch and miss some truth about the 'real thing'. This was brought home to me when I built a model beam out of dozens of small rectangles of plywood, held together by rubber cords running through it. It formed a beam when its ends rested on two bricks, and it bent when a weight was put on the middle. I only intended the model to show that bending, and I could have written a computer programme to show it happening on the screen. But then I put the weight nearly at the end of the beam, and instead of bending, the blocks slipped past each other. This is another kind of failure known as shear. If I had not put shear into the computer programme, it would not have shown me that effect. In other words, my conceptual model would not have been as good as the physical model.

Of course analytical methods are important and valuable. But we should remember that sometimes we assume that a thing cannot be done because we cannot calculate

Fig. 5. Wobbly Arch. The faces of the blocks are curved so the arch wobbles to a different equilibrium when the weight is added. In both cases, the thrust of the arch runs where the blocks touch.

it first. Perhaps, sometimes, we should do the thing by trial and error and then tackle the analysis. It is, after all, possible to make things before the analytical techniques for designing them exist. This picture of a 'wobbly arch' is an example (see Fig. 5).[53] The blocks forming the arch are curved, so that it rolls to different shapes as varying loads are placed upon it. A big concrete version has been built for children to walk over it – but it was designed empirically from models. So far as I know, no theoretical method exists at present for designing the shapes of the blocks.

Perhaps we could take this bow shape as a philosophical model of the problem (see Fig. 6). If we shoot an arrow with it, it becomes a beam and a stored energy problem. Use it to rotate a shaft, and it becomes a fire maker – the problem will be defined in terms of pressures and friction. Now make it a flint tipped drill and the dimensions of cutting speeds and angles take over. Add a bridge and sounding box and it becomes ancestral to the plucked and bowed musical instruments like zithers and violins. This time, you will measure the tension and length of the string and the frequency of vibration. Stand it another way, and it explains the principle of the bow-string girder. Plainly, those different ideas about the function of the bow precede any mathematical analysis.

Phenomena like these are the units or coinage of our spatial logic. They are the sort of things we shuffle in our minds when we are mulling over a design problem.[54] Equations and the optimisation of designs come later. When we invent, we think with these building blocks and they exist as concepts before we apply numbers to them.

Perhaps this is where the new Hands-on exploratories have something to offer the budding engineer. Our civilisation is becoming poorer in some respects: in tactile experience; in three dimensional perception and thought; in direct experience of shapes, materials, forces and other phenomena. What sensations does a child in a block of flats, spending its time before a television set, get to satisfy the inputs which our brain has evolved to need?

Children are escaping into the world of their computers. Instead of reacting with the physical environment, they play 'Civilisation' or the shoot-'em-up game 'Doom'. As virtual reality develops, the new artificial environment is offering false perceptions to a brain which has evolved to let us cope with reality. Our brain's accuracy of perception and understanding has been essential to our survival. It is true that simulation devices are of great value in training pilots and giving preliminary practice for all sorts of difficult tasks. But now computers can offer a harlot's reality, information without responsibility. Where is the philosophy to let us understand

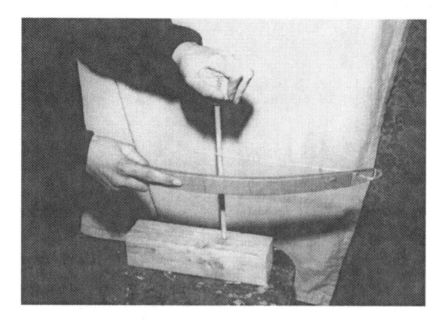

(a)

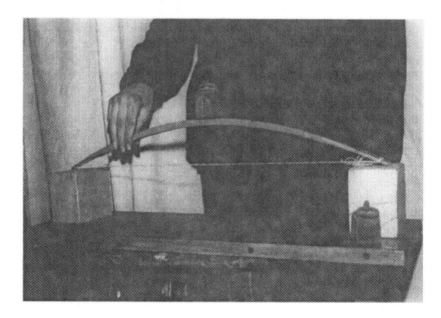

(b)

(c)

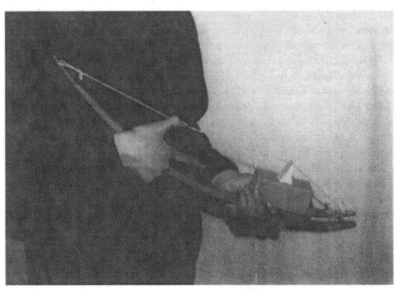

(d)

Fig. 6. The same bow: (a) Making fire (b) Bowstring girder bridge (c) Shooting arrow (d) Making music.

that gigabits alone will never make the qualitative change from information to understanding? Civilisation has always brought a contradiction between the artificial and the natural, and if the civilisation breaks down then the natural wins – it is possible to see Jean Jacques Rousseau and the *ancien régime* in France in that light.

Perhaps 'hands on' learning may help to restore a healthier sense of reality. The exploratories, by offering direct experience, real phenomena in an atmosphere of play, may turn out to be even more valuable than their founders hoped, in supplying a sense of phenomena and richness of experience, to counteract the electronic Babel.[55] We have all seen Tom and Jerry films where Tom walks over a cliff and does not start falling until he understands his predicament. Virtual reality games like Doom take us even further into an environment of false reality. Uncorrected errors augment misunderstanding, like the rumours which breed panic. Too much exposure to uncheckable electronic false reality could have analogous effects. The errors in cybernetic terms would take the form of positive feed-back.

9. Conclusion

This paper has suggested that technology has to be understood as an innate human faculty as well as the cultural phenomenon which we commonly see. Even creativity, though logically seen as unpredictable, may be an unconscious process pre-programmed into the brain and necessary to a creature which came to rely on behavioural adaptation rather than physical. This is a complex phenomenon, but a key characteristic appears to be the capacity to think in three dimensions, about materials and forces. This process is logical although it is not verbal or symbolic.

Engineering is little understood outside the members of the profession, and many English people confuse it with science. Certainly, it is not as effectively popularised as science. Perhaps the non-verbal thinking which has been described above explains why engineers are notoriously bad communicators. It is just not possible to represent the Spitfire, the Volkswagen Beetle, or the Forth rail bridge adequately in words. Yet I would maintain that these classics, and also their lesser brethren like clothes props, door bolts or sash windows, are as logical as any proposition in Aristotelian or Boolean form. One could go further, and say that some of the concepts in engineering are as beautiful and original as great poems or pictures. This is seldom recognised in Britain, and this is a sad misperception. For our culture has not made technology a part of itself.

The history of technology is more visual and tactile than most other sorts of history and you cannot do it without getting your hands dirty, getting a feel for things. Yet if the thinking of the engineer is as creative as literature or art, we should be asking ourselves why technology has not entered our general culture – why the average person knows the names of Beethoven, Van Gogh and Shakespeare, but not Newcomen, Parsons or Maudslay. Engineering could be one of the great liberal educations. For me, trained as I was in history and languages, finding out how Watt's engine worked, and how Robert Stephenson thought out the Britannia Bridge, was like coming upon the treasures of Aladdin's Cave. Engineering is too good for engineers – too few of them appreciate the richness of their subject.

If we see engineering as a natural function, not just an activity created by the needs of our own particular society, then we have an opportunity to explore its links with our biological origins and with other cultures. This point of view may also help us to build a better chain of learning for children, a gentler transition from their first toys to more mature mathematical and theoretical competence.

I have talked a great deal about evolution, but I think we must always remember that it is humanity's thought, not technology itself, which evolves. Evolution is blind: technology is mind – but my argument also implies that it may be the non-verbal subconscious mind. How can we give that non-verbal quality a fair chance in our educational system that is so dominated by written examinations? How can we give the true value to three dimensional creative thought in an educational and economic system that chiefly rewards symbol users? In biological terms it is tempting to think of the accountants and other symbol users in industry as having moved up the food chain like carnivores, leaving the engineers – creators – as herbivores to be lived off.

Here is our human mind which perceives and responds to the environment – so we have the externalists' context; and it designs things creatively – so we have the internalists' content. But most important, our heritage from the Prehistoric Engineer is creative invention which cannot be predicted, so that the future is free and undetermined. Perhaps Artificial Intelligence will one day replicate these functions, but until that possibility becomes more than philosophical speculation, it is the human mind's creativity that stands between us and extinction.

Acknowledgements

I am indebted to many colleagues and students over the years for ideas and criticism, both in Britain and France. I would particularly like to thank my wife Linda, Professor Max Hammerton of Newcastle, Professor Richard Gregory of Bristol, Dr James Stangroom (inventor), Marion Haywood, and my late uncles Douglas and Walter Jones, both inventor engineers.

Bibliography

[1]Advice to the author from the Librarian of the Seeley Historical Library, Cambridge, in 1959.
[2]Samuel C. Forman (1995), *The Existential Pleasures of Engineering*, Souvenir Press, pp. 18–19, gives some of these definitions.
[3]Manfred Korfman, (October 1973), The Sling as a Weapon, *Scientific American*, vol. 229 pages 34–42.
[4]Hanson, N. R. (1958). *Patterns of Discovery*, Cambridge University Press, 14.
[5]Evans, F.T., (January 1981): Roads, Railways and Canals: Technical Choices in 19th Century Britain. *Technology and Culture*, Vol. 22, pp. 26–34.
[6]W, Kingston, (1977), *The Creative process in Human Progress*, John Calder. Kingston offers valuable insights into the relationship between creative thinking and the process of innovation.
[7]Alan Smith, Engines Moved by Fire and Water, *Transactions of the Newcomen Society*. Vol. 66, 1994–1995, ppl-25. A useful account of the work done by others, notably Denis Papin, on early steam power.
[8]Hobbes, T. *Leviathan;* John Locke, *Treatises on Government;* J. J. Rousseau, *Social Contract.*
[9]I was guilty of whiggery as described in Professor Herbert Butterfield's book *The Whig Interpretation of History* (Cambridge University Press, 1931). The book criticises the tendency to judge past events from a later standpoint. In his words, 'What is discussed is the tendency of many historians to write on the side of Protestants and Whigs, to praise revolutions provided they have been successful, to emphasise certain principles of progress in the past and to produce a story which is the ratification if not the glorification of the present.' page v.
[10]Evans, F. T. 'The Maudslay Touch'. *Transactions of the Newcomen Society.* Vol. 66, 1994–1995, pp153–174.

[11]Roger Lewin: *Bones of Contention*. Penguin 1989

[12]Ingold, T., (1993), 'Tools, Techniques and Technology' in *Tools, Language and Cognition in Human Evolution*, ed. K. R. Gibson and T. Ingold, Cambridge. pp 337–338.

[13]For a general background to the topic of tools and language Lewin and Gibson and Ingold (vide supra) give a valuable picture. An older but impressive work is A. Leroi Gourhan *Le Geste et La Parole* (1964), translated as *Gesture and Speech*, M.I.T. Press 1993. Another seminal work is the short *Man the Toolmaker* by Kenneth Oakey, London 1972.

[14]Yves Coppens. (1994 May). East Side Story: The Origin of Humankind. *Scientific American*, vol. 270, no.5: 62–69.

[15]Lovejoy, C. Owen. (1988 Nov.) Evolution of Human Walking, *Scientific American*, vol. 259, (5).

[16]Leakey R. and Lewin R. (1992): *Origins Reconsidered*, Little, Brown and Co., ,p.90–91. offer an opposing view, that a bipedal chimp was faster.

[17]Dean Falk (1993). Sex Differences in visuospatial skills. In *Tools, Language and Cognition in Human Evolution*. ed K.R.Gibson and T Ingold. Cambridge University Press. See also the BBC Horizon programme, *Hothead*, 1994.

[18]Jablonski, N. G. and Chaplin, G. (1994 Jan.): Avant les Premiers Pas: l'origine de la bipédie, *La Recherche*, vol. 25, no. 261.

[19]Elaine Morgan. (1994). *The Descent of the Child*, Souvenir Press, London, pp156–168 offers the most recent summary of the hypothesis.

[20]ibid. 38.

[21]Calvin, W. H. (1994 Oct.). The Emergence of Intelligence, *Scientific American*, vol. 271, no 4: pp 78–83.

[22]The irregular term *thing using* has been adopted because it is more direct than 'opportunistic tool using' and perhaps it will convey more of the importance of the activity. Alternatively *homo opportunus* may be more suitable, with its connotations of 'advantageous' and serviceable'.

[23]Gregory R. L. (1976). *Eye and Brain*, 2nd ed. pp. 50–59

[24]Cooper L. A. and Shepherd R. N. (1984 Dec.). Turning Something Over in the Mind, *Scientific American*, vol. 251 no 6: 114–121.

[25]R. L. Gregory: *op. cit.*

[26]Cooper and Shepherd 1984, loc. cit.

[27]Brooke Hindle (1981) *Emulation and Invention*. New York University Press. Also see Eugene S. Ferguson: (1993) Engineering and the Mind's Eye. MIT Press. pp.41–59.

[28]K. Connolly and M. Dalgleish. 1989. The Emergence of a Tool-Using Skill in Infancy. *Developmental Psychology*, vol. 25, no. 6: 894–912.

[29]Henry Petroski (1985), *To Engineer is Human*, Macmillan, page 11.

[30]Calvin. 1994. He also makes the valuable point that trying out things mentally, comparing possible outcomes, has evolutionary value: he quotes Popper, that this permits our hypotheses to die in our stead.

[31]Schon D. A., (1967). *Invention and the Evolution of Ideas*. Tavistock Publications.

[32]Hopkins H. J., (1970): *Span of Bridges*, David and Charles.

[33]L. T. C. Rolt (1965) *Tools for the Job*. Batsford.

[34]R. Dawkins. (1988). The Blind Watchmaker, Penguin Books, London.

[35]G. Barsalla, G. (1988). *The Evolution of Technology*, Cambridge, uses this metaphor.

[36]Luigi Luca Cavalli-Sforza: (1991 Nov.) Genes, Peoples and Languages. *Scientific American* pp. 72–78.

[37]J. Lyons, *Chomsky*, Fotana, 3rd edition, 1991.

[38]Jackendoff, R. (1993). *Patterns in the Mind*. Harvester, pp. 66–82.

[39]The universality of this basic linguistic form is described by Steven Pinker (1994), *The language Instinct*, William Morrow, pp. 232–237.

[40]It will be interesting, if the language of dolphins and whales is cracked, to see whether they have the same basic syntactical structures as human languages; if they do, then the *thing using* hypothesis is weakened. I am indebted to my wife for this, and many other suggestions.

[41]J. Lyon, op. cit. pp. 24–25.

[42]R. Wallace (1989). Cognitive Mapping and the Origin of Language and Mind, *Current Anthropology*, Vol. 30, no. 4, 518–526. Ron Wallace offer a different scenario to explain the development of language. He suggests that the breakaway hominids found themselves in the new drier environment and that scavenging was accompanied by a return to sites where stone tools were used for butchering. Thus their spatial sense became more highly developed and this was located neurologically in the hippocampus. He goes on to suggest that there are strong analogies between the mental processes involved in this mental processing of spatial problems and the Chomskian deep-structure processes such as tracing (inserting a place-holder when a linguistic transformation is made) and embedding, where a sentence is built up from subordinate clauses.

Wallace's suggestion relates to complicated language structures like the ability to transform a sentence from active to passive. The idea of *thing using* thought and the subject-verb-object structure is analogous, but plainly relates to a more basic level of language formation. Furthermore, *thing using* refers to activities before the use of stone.

[43]Oldfield, R. C., (1969). Handedness in Musicians. *British Journal of Psychology.* **90**, 91–9. Quoted by K. A. Flowers in article 'Handedness', *Companion to the Mind,* ed. R. L. Gregory, Oxford. 1987.

[44]Allman, J. M. (1987) in article 'Evolution of Brain in Primates', *Companion to the Mind,* ed. Gregory, Oxford.

[45]This outline hypothesis does not aim to give a complete review of recent work in the field of human origins. For that, the collection of articles in *Tools Language and Cognition in Human Evolution* (see note 13), forms a good introductory sample. It contains useful accounts of many of the approaches to the dialogue on human origins, including tool-using and language in chimps and monkeys and the growth of cognition and skills in human infants. As a stimulating introduction to the state of linguistics and the idea of a wired in grammar, the reader may find Steven Pinker, *The Language Instinct,* Morrow 1994, or Ray Jackendoff, *Patterns in the Mind,* Harvester Wheatsheaf, 1993. Nowhere, however, so far as I am aware, is the idea put forward explicitly that *'thing using'*, distinguished from the much later stone-tool making, may be the primary activity leading to bipedalism, brain growth and the neural basis which would later accommodate language.

[46]The high proportion of the motor areas of the brain devoted to the hands is clearly illustrated by the well known homunculus diagram. See A. Leroi Gourhan *Le Geste et La Parole* (1964) (vol. 1 page 120), or page 82 in the English translation, *Gesture and Speech,* MIT Press 1993.

[47]Allan Walker & Pat Shipman (1996). *The Wisdom of Bones.* Weidenfeld and Nicolson. The authors argue strongly that the Nariokotome boy fossil (homo erectus) could not speak; and they point out that Cavalli Sforza's arguments suggest that even Neanderthal lacked language. If speech came about so late, the importance of tool using in mental development becomes even clearer. pp 210–223.

[48]C Daryl Forde (1934): *Habitat, Economy and Society.* Methuen.

[49]Evans, F. T. (1982), 'Wood since the Industrial Revolution: a strategic Retreat?', *History of Technology,* Vol. 7, pp. 37–55.

[50]English is imprecise in its ability to state exactly when we are talking about applied scientific knowledge (technology?), its systematic application (technique?), the experience of a craftsman (skill?). See Ingold, p. 433 'Tool-use, sociality and Intelligence', in Gibson and Ingold supra. Also see Jacques Ellul (1964), *The Technological Society* for a philosophical view of the stifling of creativity by technique.

[51]*Cyclopaedia of Useful Arts and Manufactures,* ed. C. Tomlinson. Plate 'Bishopp's Rotary Steam Engine or Disc Engine. (circa 1853.)

[52]Eugene S. Ferguson (1992): *Engineering and the Mind's Eye.* MIT Press. Ferguson argues that good engineering is a matter of intuition and non-verbal thinking.

[53]The model is based on H.C.Fleeming Jenkin's work. *Encyclopaedia Britannica, 9th edition,* 4, 1876: article 'Bridges' 308.

[54]Yao Tsu Li, D G Jansson, E G Cravalho (1981). *Technological Innovation in Education and Industry.* Van Nostrand.

[55]Evans, F. T. (1987), 'Designing and Making exhibits', in Stephen Pizzey, ed. *Interactive Science and Technology Centres,* Science Projects Publishing, pp. 182–188.

Correspondence and offprint requests to: Francis Evans, 14 Edgehill Road, Sheffield, S7 1SP, UK. Tel: 01142 585346; Fax: 01142 580265; Email: francis.evans@btinternet.com

AI & SOCIETY, VOL. 2, 287-301 (1988)

Rule Following and Tacit Knowledge

Kjell S Johannessen

Department of Philosophy, University of Bergen, Norway

ABSTRACT

This paper discusses the interrelationship between wisdom, science and craft from the perspective of the Wittgenstein concept of tacit knowledge. It challenges the notion of the 'rules-model' as put forward by Logical Positivists, and shows the limitation of this model for describing the tacit dimension of knowledge. The paper demonstrates the crucial role of practice in 'rule-following' in the real world. It is held that 'to follow a rule' is to practice a custom, a usage or an institutional practice. Hence, rules can only exist as a link in social life.

The dream of the 'precise' language can only be realised in a closed scientific world. It is inadequate for reflecting the user's relationship to language and its content and practice in varied 'use situations'. It is only through examples that we learn to deal with, describe, interpret and learn from the new situations.

The rule-based models which are used to acquire and describe human knowledge in syntactic and propositional forms are, in effect, an impoverishment of the description of reality. It is argued that expert knowledge and linguistic knowledge are linked together and emerge as two sides of the same subject as the pragmatic perspective of reality. The tacit dimension of expert knowledge is, in many cases, more significant than the linguistic knowledge, especially in the case of the vocational and aesthetic world.

The challenge to AI researchers, therefore, is to recognise that knowledge based systems which ignore the tacit dimension of expert knowledge not only distance the user from reality but also impoverish the learning process itself.

KEYWORDS

logical positivism, rule-following, tacit knowledge, expert knowledge, linguistic knowledge, scientific knowledge, practice

1 INTRODUCTION

The school of logical positivism has contributed, to a considerable extent, to impoverish our notions of what it means to have knowledge. The essence of this school's viewpoint can be summarised as follows: We can only possess knowledge if it can be formulated linguistically and in principle tested on the basis of experience or proved by formal methods. Everything else falls outside the domain of real knowledge. Both these requirements at first glance would appear completely natural and obvious from any modern scientific point of view. For what kind of knowledge can exist if it can neither be formulated linguistically nor proven on an empirical or formal basis? He would be thought a strange type of researcher who stood forth and proclaimed that he knew something important, but could not formulate his knowledge and could not support his findings with the traditionally accepted methods. According to Logical Positivism, knowledge can only be ascertained by fulfilling the following two conditions.

1 Our knowledge must be capable of formulation in some language or other

2 Our knowledge must, in a linguistically formulated version, be supported by experience or be proven by formal methods.

Linguistic articulation is, then, considered a requirement of all knowledge. If there are observations which cannot be presented adequately in linguistic form, they will not have consequences for scholarly work. This is because they can neither be checked nor related to scientific hypotheses or theories which are being tested. There is a similar understanding of the requirement of empirical support or formal weight of evidence as a necessary feature of everything which can properly be called knowledge. We cannot be said to know anything if we are not capable of supporting our knowledge on an empirical basis or proving it through formal methods. Without such an anchoring, the knowledge we claim to possess will appear to be loose talk or sheer fantasy.

For over fifty years researchers from widely different disciplines have been attracted by the simplicity and clarity of this view of knowledge. They find here a foundation for their understanding of themselves as practising researchers. What is simple and clear is often alluring. But one or two thoughtful souls feel a certain anxiety and nagging doubt. For it is not at all difficult to realise that such an understanding of the nature of knowledge implies a quite significant narrowing down of the areas in which ordinarily we talk about knowing something as an absolute matter of course. All forms of values, for instance, fall completely outside the area of legitimate knowledge based on this view of knowledge. The hallmark of values is precisely the fact that they cannot be either supported by empirical evidence or formally proven. Less comprehensive value norms can obviously be logically derived from more comprehensive value norms if we seek to present all the value norms of a certain type as an organised system. The fundamental norms of the system could not in that case be supported empirically or justified formally. And then we have got no further, because the logically valid deductions of less comprehensive value norms transfer only to the deduced statements the properties which the system's principles have. Therefore it will be true of the system as a whole that empirical support or formal proof cannot be used.

This observation, however, makes it clear that the logical-positivist view of knowledge is not an attempt to say anything about what we really mean by the term 'knowledge' in all its contexts. It is rather a matter of a well-founded suggestion as to how one should define limits, in an intellectually defensible way, for the use of this term. In other words, it is a case of a normative definition of the term 'knowledge'. We have already seen that this suggestion breaks with well-established opinions about what kind of relationship is it that makes it possible to have knowledge. Our acceptance of this will therefore be absolutely dependent on the quality of the reasoning which is given in support of the normative definition. For we give up quite a lot if we deprive ourselves of the right to talk about moral and aesthetic knowledge. The Bible regarded moral knowledge as the core of human knowledge. Insight into the relationship between good and evil is after all the result of tasting a fruit from the tree of knowledge. Likewise it is difficult to accept that someone who is a good judge of art does not perceive the artistic qualities on the basis of aesthetic considerations. It is not easy to see what else could form the basis of aesthetic judgments. At all events we cannot accept that aesthetic judgments can be boiled down to the following two elements: 1 I like (or do not like) this work of art; 2 So should you. Such an analysis depicts the aesthetic judgment as a combination of a subjective preference and a recommendation. This is nothing less than a ludicrous distortion of everything having to do with the appreciation of art. Nevertheless it was just such an analysis that the logical positivists championed in this field.

2 WISDOM, SCIENCE AND CRAFT

In the ancient philosophical tradition we do not find any objections to talking about knowledge in the most varied fields of experience. Aristotle is an example in that respect. In his analysis of the different qualities of the moral human being, the intellectual virtues play a central role. They all have a task to perform in this connection. What is most instructive, however, is his attempt to distinguish between practical wisdom (*phronesis*) and the two other main types of knowledge, the scientific (*episteme*) and the craftsmanlike (*techne*).[1] Scientific knowledge only deals with necessary conditions. Necessary conditions are eternal and unalterable. This distinguishes *episteme* from *phronesis* and *techne*, for they both deal with conditions which are changeable. *Techne*, however, is the sort of thing that can be bought and can be forgotten. This is not the case with *phronesis*. In a fundamental sense it can neither be learnt nor forgotten. To forget one's practical wisdom is to cease to exist as a human being. To have practical wisdom is thus to know what is the morally correct action in a concrete situation. Such knowledge is an end in itself, in the same way that knowledge about the eternal and unalterable is an end in itself. But this does not apply to the possession of *techne*. This has its goal outside itself. To have *techne* is to be able to make something based on an adequate understanding of the principle which is involved. Knowledge of this kind is primarily expressed in the choice of suitable materials and in their treatment. In other words, it has the character of a skill without any depreciation of its status as knowledge. One reason for this is that one can have a satisfactory knowledge of the thing which is to be made quite independently of actually making it in any concrete case. This is not so with practical wisdom, where the correct action can only be determined from an interplay between the action norm which is adequate to the situation and the special features of the particular situation. Practical wisdom is thus the ability to mediate between general moral principles and the multiplicity of possible courses of action that uniformity and consistency in the life of actions must take into account when facing any particular situation. Moral knowledge embraces, in other words, not only the norm which is right in a given situation, but also how it can best be applied in the concrete situation. And this is why Aristotle includes in his definition of knowledge a judgmental component as well as a non-eliminative reflection with respect to the particular situation's special character.

3 THE DREAM OF THE 'PRECISE LANGUAGE'

All this complexity in the concept of knowledge is missing in the logical positivists. We should, however, remember that they are by no means alone in having produced such a view about knowledge. The logical-positivist view of knowledge represents only the end point of a development which began as early as the renaissance with the new scientific age. Galileo asserted that nature's book is written in the language of mathematics. And from there it is not a long leap to the dream of the precise language where all this scientific knowledge can be formulated in an unambiguous way. The universal language of the logical positivists is our century's version of this ancient vision. And in that way language and knowledge are woven together in an indissoluble bond. The requirement that knowledge should have a linguistic articulation becomes an unconditional demand. The possibility of possessing knowledge which cannot be wholly formulated linguistically emerges against such a background as completely self-contradictory. Nevertheless it is this possibility of just such various kinds of tacit knowledge that is presently being explored in the philosophy of science. There has been recognition in various camps that propositional knowledge, i.e. the knowledge which is in full measure linguistically articulate, is in fact not the only form of knowledge which is scientifically relevant. Some have, therefore, even if somewhat reluctantly, accepted that it can be legitimate to talk about knowledge also in cases where it is not possible to give it an adequate linguistic form. In the following I will refer to this type of knowledge as tacit knowledge. Tacit knowledge is thus knowledge which for logical reasons cannot be articulated in full measure linguistically. There are in fact many kinds of knowledge which it would not be unjustified to describe as tacit knowledge, for example, knowledge which for various reasons we do not wish to articulate or which we are unable to formulate because of conceptual poverty. An example of the latter is our linguistic knowledge. We speak our mother tongue fluently without normally being able to formulate the rules which guide the formation of sentences. Here however it is in principle possible to formulate a theory which covers the whole system of rules which determine the sentence formation in a given natural language. We can do something equivalent as regards the sound of natural language. But when we come to the content of linguistic signs, we meet opposition. No satisfactory scientific or philosophical theory exists today which can explain how to analyse the content aspect of natural language. It is by no means sure that one can manage at all to carry out such an analytical task with the help of the concepts 'rule' and 'system'.

4 LANGUAGE AS SCIENCE

The logical positivists, however, saw no problems with formulating a language which could articulate in a fully valid way all the knowledge which a given scientific discipline considered as established. According to Carnap and his pupils this could very easily be done by specifying a language S.[2] Language S consists in the first place of a vocabulary which contains both logical constants and empirical variables. In the second place it consists of a very small number of formation rules or syntactic rules which unambiguously lay down the class of well-formed statements in S. In the third place it consists of a very small number of transformation rules which lay down clear rules for moving from one well-formed statement to another in language S. Fourthly, there is quite a small class of rules which connects some of the empirical variables with a fairly clearly circumscribed segment of the discernible reality. Such rules are often called correspondence rules. They represent the semantic system in Language S. A correspondence rule can be said to have the following form:

The symbol T can be justifiably employed if and only if the properties $P_1, P_2, P_3 \ldots P_n$ are present.

The correspondence rule represents in effect a linguistic articulation of the conceptual content which the language symbol T has in the language S. To be able to master the language S does not signify anything more than being able to create well-formed statments in S on a particular segment of the empirical reality as well as being able to derive one well-formed statement from another. And we are said to understand a statement in S if we know what is the case if the statement is true. We thus see that S is required to be a consistent extensional language where an individual statement's meaning can be given quite independent of any contextual usage. The correspondence rules will consequently be the only link between language and reality.

These days it is no news for us that the language S is radically incomplete if it is regarded as an analysis of the core of a natural language. But that is not the point in our context. I have sketched this logical-positivist interpretation of the nature of language as a reminder of how central a role the concept of a rule has for traditional philosophical linguistic analysis. It was in fact theories of this nature which constituted the philosophical context of Ludwig Wittgenstein's endeavours in the 1930s to find the way to a more adequate analysis of linguistic meaning. An especially important fruit of these endeavours was insight into the tacit knowledge which is necessarily tied to the use of language. Reflections on the users' relationship to the language and use situations are conspicuous by their absence in the logical-positivistic view of language. There it is only the logical form of the language system which is of central interest. This can be seen by reference to the correspondence rule sketched above. It has the form of a definition. The symbol T is the *definiendum* in the definition while the specification of the conceptual symbols represents the defining expression, which is normally called the *definiens*. The *definiens* lays down the only legitimate set of necessary and sufficient conditions for the use of the symbol T. The occasions on which the definition is used, the purposes of the scientist etc., are not to be taken into account.

5 TACIT DIMENSION OF LANGUAGE

Wittgenstein was especially occupied with the study of the relationship which is associated not only with the formation but also the application and teaching of the concept which is defined in a correspondence rule. If we now glance a little closer at what happens when one formulates an artificial language of type S, one discovers *inter alia* that to articulate a correspondence rule means to carry out an action. And carrying out such an action presupposes that one is already a competent user of a language where the necessary conceptual resources can in fact be found. To analyse a constructed language with the aim to increase understanding of natural language is the equivalent of studying the cart in the hope of learning something about the horse which pulls it. Such a method of approach, however, gives the impression of being both reliable and scientific. In addition it has a certain rationale insofar as one wishes to reconstruct the established scientific knowledge as an axiomatic ordered system of expression where the distinction between principles and deductive theorems plays a central role. But this is to limit the value of the study of constructed language as a means of understanding natural language. And when it is a case of the relationship between language and reality and the nature of the concepts and mode of operation, this approach is, according to Wittgenstein, directly erroneous. This is not, however, the place to develop his criticisms on a larger scale. I have done that elsewhere.[3] For our purposes the following summary is enough. Regarding the question as to how far it is possible to prove tacit components in our linguistic mastery, these are the significant points:

1 To formulate a correspondence rule is to carry out a definitional action which makes use of conceptual resources which have already been developed

2 If one is to hope to understand the nature of natural languages, one must study how the original conceptual resources were formed

3 This is best done by studying the situations where teaching or explanation of the concept occurs; because here are uncovered the basic clues which the competent language user employs in his own use of the concept

4 A definition or a semantic rule can be applied in different ways. A perfect definition gives no recipe as to how it should be used

5 We must of course make a sharp distinction between the definition itself or the rule understood as a logical form and the application it is possible to make of it

6 In addition, every definition is always applied in a space of assumptions which are not themselves visible in the definition. This is because the definitional action is done on the basis of a holistic understanding of language

7 The totality of these assumptions cannot itself assume the form of a definition. The vantage point for carrying out the definitional action would then be eliminated, and would in its turn make such actions impossible

8 In the final instance there cannot be rules as to how a definition should be applied. The application of a definition or a semantic rule is and must necessarily be performed without the support of any further rules

9 The application of a language rule in borderline cases and other more problematical cases will take place on the basis of developed judgment and with an effect constitutive of new meaning.

6 TO FOLLOW A RULE: THE 'CONCEPT OF PRACTICE'

This point by point summary of Wittgenstein's views gives a certain indication as to the direction his late philosophical work was taking. What is most striking is perhaps his turning away from dealing with rules and their logical form to investigating what it means to follow rules. In this way the application of the rule and the very nature of the situation of its user becomes the focus of his philosophical interest. This is often called the pragmatic turn.[4] Since one and the same rule can be followed in different ways, the correspondence rules cannot constitute the meaningful relationship which mediates between language and world. What guarantees that a rule is followed in the same way time after time cannot itself be a rule. It must depend upon our actions and behaviour. Wittgenstein keeps to this fundamental perspective by stating that to follow a rule is a practice.[5] This concept is one of the central elements of his later philosophy. We meet here most of the themes which dominated his thinking during this period. It is therefore not unreasonable to consider his later philosophy as a kind of practice philosophy. I understand this term to mean all philosophy which operates from the insight that there exists a complicated network of mutual constituting relations between concept formation, human reactions and activities, and what we call our reality. To learn to master a language is in a practical philosophical perspective not to learn how to formulate well-formed statements about different types of states of affairs in the world on the basis of syntactical rules and with the help of language symbol (T) which, via semantic rules (correspondence rules), is tied to a certain segment of reality. It is instead to learn to master an enormously large repertoire of situations where use of language is included in an exceedingly varied but, even so, non-eliminable way. In other words it is a matter of mastering human reality in all its complexity. It is a matter of learning to adopt an attitude towards it in established ways; react towards it; speak about it; reflect over it; investigate it; gain a foothold in it; and be familiar with it. This happens mainly because we are born into it, grow up in it and continually are trained in the established practices of linguistic involvement. This then is the background for maintaining that there exists an inner or internal relationship between the language's conceptual formations, forms of human activity and the reality which emerges as *our* reality by virtue of the concepts we have formed about it.

It would obviously be worth looking a little closer at the entirety of the established ways of acting and rules which Wittgenstein describes as practice. For this is where it is possible to come on the track of the tacit component in our understanding of language. In addition, in this way we can give some supplementary comments on the point by point summary of Wittgenstein's criticism of the logical positivists. But we should also be aware that the same criticism is directed towards Wittgenstein's earlier philosophical I as well. In fact on some points he shared the viewpoints of the logical positivists, especially concerning the emphasis on logical form and the fundamental role of the rule in the establishing of meaning in language. In his later philosophy he rejects both these opinions. He describes the situations and activities in which language is used instead of analysing and making visible the logical form of statements. This means, *inter alia*, that the pragmatic aspects of verbal communication are assigned a constitutive role in the formation of meaning. It also signifies that Wittgenstein begins to work with a much wider concept of language than reflections on the purely verbal speech suggest. In his later philosophy he includes in his concept of language such things as gestures, facial expressions, facial features in general, posture, the situation's atmosphere, situationally determined actions as for example smiling and nodding to an acquaintance as we are passing; turning one's back on somebody and going off without saying a word; standing on the quay and waving goodbye to friends; sitting in a restaurant and making a discreet sign that the waiter's presence is desired; attending an auction and making an offer with a little hand movement, etc. This extended concept of language has the aim of capturing all the means we make use of in day by day situations to make ourselves understood. Use of verbal speech demands a grasp of the use situation — whether we are sender or receiver. This means that we must master all that is significant but which does not have the character of verbal speech in a given language use situation, because a formulation does not say about itself that it is to be taken as, say, an assertion. It requires a given understanding of the existing situation it is responding to as an expression of an assertion. But the same formulation in other contexts can express quite a different thought content. Take for example the formulation: 'Laurence Olivier was convincing as Hamlet'. This can be used to communicate many different types of thought content. Let me just indicate three things we can do which are all comparatively easily expressed by this sentence.

1 We can give a description of his interpretation of the Hamlet role in the contextually implied production

2 We can express a certain interpretation of his performance in a naturalistic perspective

3 We can give an evaluation of both his interpretation of the role and his performance in it.

These are, logically speaking, very different types of thought content which must be handled in very different ways if challenged. But if we do not know the closer details of the current use situation, we will not be able to make up our minds about what is actually said. Therefore our language mastery must include knowledge about an enormously large repertoire of possible language use situations where the formation of meaning takes place in the most varied kind of ways. This brings us back to Wittgenstein's conception of practice — the rule-following behaviour. This conception draws attention precisely to the factors which are constitutive of meaning in language use situations. It emphasises *inter alia* that the very exercise of an activity is a constitutive element in concept formation. The content of the concept is thus regarded as a function of the established use of its expression. The exercise of a given practice is consequently to be regarded as a constitutive part of the concept's expression. The criterion that one has mastered a given concept is consequently that one is looked upon as a competent performer of the established procedure which incorporates the concept. This yields the following principle of conceptual mastery: The grasp a given concept gives us on the world is expressed adequately only by being practised. It is our application or practice which shows how we understand something. That is what Wittgenstein has in mind when in his characteristic style he maintains that 'practices give words their meaning' (*Bemerkungen uber die Farben*, paragraph 317).[6]

This point gives us an opportunity to make some fairly basic observations. The first is concerned with the problem of what guarantees that a principle, a law, a norm, a concept, in short everything which Wittgenstein calls a rule, is applied in the same way from one time to another and from one person to another. We have already seen that the rule itself cannot give such a guarantee. According to Wittgenstein it is the exercise of the established practice as such which gives this guarantee. This represents in fact the application of the rule.[7] And the requisite mastery of the correct application can only be acquired through a guided exercise of the established methods or practices which constitute the rule's adequate use.

7 TACIT KNOWLEDGE: THE LIMITS OF ITS EXPRESSION

The other observation is directly linked to the main theme of his paper — tacit knowledge's forms of expression and special characteristics. It is no longer problematic to talk about rules or concepts which can be formulated only incompletely as regards content, that is with the help of verbal language. The criterion for their adequate mastery lies primarily in their application. The knowledge which is built into that mastery can consequently be considered to have a partial and non-reducible expression in action. Therefore it is not possible to put into words this aspect of action that must underlie the mastery of a concept. Since it is always possible to guide the person who gropingly tries to acquire an acceptable mastery of the practices in which such concepts are 'inscribed', we also have at all times adequate intellectual control of the conceptual content. It is therefore neither contradictory nor conspicuously shocking to maintain that concepts, as well as other forms of rules, exist which can only be articulated incompletely in verbal language , but which nevertheless are fully usable tools both in our scientific management of reality and in ordinary communication. Concepts of this kind can be demonstrated in a number of different types of context. They will however be easiest to show in the aesthetic, moral and juridical fields of experience, because here the connection between building up experience, the examples' non-eliminative role in conceptual formation and judgment's constitutive function in the application can be more easily spotted than elsewhere.

It is not possible to formulate necessary and sufficient conditions for the use of the name of a certain artistic style, for instance, the term 'mannerism'. We can only learn to master this term in an adequate way if we obtain a broad first-hand experience of typical examples of manneristic paintings at the same time as we learn through expert guidance to recognise the visual physiognomy which characterises them. Here, then, we cannot manage without the requisite first-hand experience. Nor can we free ourselves from the prototypical examples, because it is they who give content to the concept in this context. And as regards some new and unknown painting from the period in question (Italian painting between 1520 and 1600), a judgmental component inevitably arises when one is to make one's mind up about whether it can justifiably be called manneristic or not. We find the equivalent in the area of morality and law. We cannot, for example, learn to master the distinction between, say, jealousy and righteous indignation as motives for action without obtaining first-hand experience about prototype examples under expert guidance. And each later application of the distinction will be indissolubly tied to a certain judgmental reaction to the situation in hand. A little later we shall also look closer at an example from the field of law where similar partial articulation is in force.

8 MODELLING POSITIVISM: TOWARDS A PRAGMATIC PERSPECTION OF TACIT KNOWLEDGE

The importance of examples, experience and judgment whose role can be only partially articulated is not confined to the concept just mentioned. We also find partial articulation where the logical positivists felt most at home, that is to say in the area of physics. When Thomas S. Kuhn maintains that the paradigm in the sense of a model solution to a fundamental scientific problem can guide research without the existence of formulated rules, theories or laws, it is this very aspect of concept formation that he has in mind.[8] Since Kuhn's exposition of these points is much more well-known than Wittgenstein's way of putting them, we can employ Kuhn's exposition to illustrate more closely the kernel of this basic point. A model solution to a basic scientific problem represents an application of a scientific theory or law. Independently of this application neither theories nor laws have any concrete meaning. The model problem solutions — by virtue of being examples of applications of theories and laws — lay down the cognitive content both in the theories and the laws. Both parts become understood in the light of their applications and cannot be wholly understood independently of them. In this sense the model problem solutions, as functions of examples of application, should be considered as constitutive for the understanding of scientific theories and laws in a scientific relation. They represent in summary the use situations for the universal statements of theoretical character in a given discipline. The model problem solutions are not only attractive because they are original and elegant — they also give promise that the same kind of procedure can be used to solve other pressing problems within the discipline. But there need not exist of course any identity between the original problem situation where the model solution is found and the undetermined field of possible future applications. The relation is more a matter of a kind of homogeneity which, according to Kuhn, can best be characterised as a family resemblance, a term he borrows from Wittgenstein. Consequently the applied theories and laws cannot be regarded as completely finished scientific products; they must rather be considered as kinds of schemata, which are bearers of an indeterminate number at any one time of future applications. Kuhn uses here as an example Newton's second law, 'K = ma', and shows how it is given different formulations when working with mutually different but nevertheless related problems. Articulation is thus necessarily a partial matter. Only relatively to the concrete problem-solving situation can there be a case of something which resembles a complete formulation of the conditions for the use of theories and laws. But also here, as mentioned, the established research practice comes in addition.

Kuhn's description gives us, however, the opportunity to investigate thoroughly what is implied by such competent exercise. The crux of the matter is, of course, the question of how we can put researchers in the position of recognising the homogeneity or family likeness which exists between the various problem situations. According to Kuhn the answer lies in looking closer at the role the model problem solutions play in the training of researchers. This is a strategy which is completely in keeping with Wittgenstein's advice to deal with the situations where the teaching or explaining of concepts take place, as we have mentioned in point (3) above. It is here the model problem solutions play a key role. Students acquire the relevant scientific concepts by learning to carry out experiments which are either part of or decided by the model solutions. This is how we get to know nature's behaviour in the relevant problem field. Expert knowledge and linguistic knowledge are thus by necessity linked together and emerge as two sides of the same subject in the pragmatic perspective which both Kuhn and Wittgenstein apply to the nature and mode of operation of the concepts. A gradual and simultaneous acquiring of both aspects takes place. In the course of this learning process the students build up a certain familiarity with the discipline's approaches to problems as they appear in the light of the discipline's model solutions. This familiarity is a fruit of experience. It also comprises training in a certain aptitude for seeing the similarities between different kinds of problem situations, even if on many points they are quite different. Thus likenesses of this type are said to have an analogic character. The initiating problem solution which the newcomers to the discipline are exposed to has as its goal, we may say, to build up the sort of experience and problem familiarity which later will make it possible for the ready trained researcher to function creatively on the research front. But the ability to display reactions which are adequate to the situation and having an eye for the analogous features in the new problem situations cannot be put into rules of method or in any other way established in verbal language. These elements represent a form of competence which is closely associated with acquiring the particular discipline's concepts, theories and laws. This sort of competence cannot be established independently of learning to master them. However, an invisible horizon of skill and familiarity remains when the discipline's concepts and theories are formulated. On the other hand neither can they be applied adequately without this sort of competence. It is therefore no exaggeration to assert that in the natural sciences too there are theories, concepts and methods which can be only partially articulated.

9 UNDERSTANDING REALITY

These are some of the more exciting observations we can make in a practice-philosophical perspective. But there are also others. We have already indicated that in this perspective human reactions and conduct are looked upon as the context and background for the formation of meaning in verbal language. By extending this observation several important points can be developed. We said earlier that to offer a definition is a linguistic act carried out from an understanding of language as method. In his lapidary style, Wittgenstein puts the point thus: 'To understand a sentence means to understand a language' (*Philosophische Untersuchungen*, paragraph 199). To understand a statement cannot be any isolated or chance happening. One must have a certain understanding of the language as a whole to be able to grasp the individual statement's meaning in a given situation. This means that a given practice cannot be thought of as an isolated monad, such as Apel and Habermas presuppose in their criticism of Wittgenstein. One cannot after all decide the identity of a given practice exclusively from the rules which more or less are completely 'inscribed' in it. If we come to a foreign culture and see two persons seated on each side of a quadrangular board which is divided into 64 squares and on the board there are placed pieces resembling chessmen, we cannot for this reason conclude that these people are playing chess. What they are doing could just as well be part of a religious or magic ritual. It is only when we see what happens, let us say, at the outcome of the activity that it is possible to decide whether it is a game or not. Practices having the character of games are integrated into the culture in ways quite different from religious and magical practices. By virtue of these contextual relations all practices are shown to be necessarily integrated entities. To establish the identity of an individual practice cannot thus be done solely on the basis of the semantic rules assumed to be immanent in it. Its relation to the surrounding practices have to be included in any reliable procedure for establishing the identity of practices. We thus see that the interrelated manifold of widely different practices makes up one single though variegated whole. Mastery of a particular practice can therefore be regarded as a fragmentary expression of an overarching and comprehensive understanding of the reality, which is common to the participants of the language community. And to have a common language is for Wittgenstein to share a form of life, because 'to imagine a language is to imagine a form of life' (PI, paragraph 19).

The totality of the actually occurring practices can therefore be said to express the common understanding of reality and thereby the form of life where this understanding is established and adhered to in the existing multiplicity of practices. We thus see that there exists a close connection between the concepts of practice and form of life in Wittgenstein. The individual practice is to be considered as a particular articulation of the whole form of life. And the concept of form of life is for Wittgenstein the concept of the given: 'What has to be accepted, the given, is — so one could say — *forms of life*' (PI, part II, p226, Wittgenstein's own emphasis). Beyond the totality of established practices there thus exists no meaningful relationship about which we can have an understanding, even if the form of life as a complex totality is historically situated and in continual movement in the sense that coinage of concepts unceasingly continues. But they are always the fruit of spontaneous and immediate reactions; they are not a result of conscious deliberations and argumentations. Wittgenstein emphasises this when he states in *Philosophical Investigations* that 'We talk, we utter words, and only later get a picture of their lives (PI, part II, p209). Here the spontaneous reaction has a verbal character, but Wittgenstein regards this as a direct continuation of our ability to react immediately and wordlessly to certain features in our surroundings. According to Wittgenstein, it is in fact in reactions of this kind that our vebal speech practices have their origin. This is established in a well-known observation from *Vermischte Bemerkungen* where it is stated that '(t)he origin and primitive form of the language game is a reaction; only from this can more complicated forms develop. Language — I want to say — is a refinement, "in the beginning was the deed"' (VB, 1977, p65).

In our later conceptual formations elements from these spontaneous reaction forms become utilised in all kinds of ways without this being reflected in the traditional model of how one indicates the content of a concept in definitional form. Both the language's general character and the forms of human reaction belong in consequence to the sphere of presuppositions which are not themselves visible in the mere definition. Forms of human reactions are, however, also connected to another side of the concept of practice, because they play a fundamental role in the handling of the examples which in a constitutive way form part of the spontaneous establishment of a practice. The indispensability of the examples emerges from the following observation in Wittgenstein's very last philosophical work, *On Certainty*: 'Not only rules, but also examples are needed for establishing a practice. Our rules leave loopholes open, and the practice has to speak for itself' (OC, paragraph 139).

That we must rely on the community of reactions which lie behind the development of the human language becomes clear when we realise that there is a limit to how far it is possible for us to explain a word's meaning with the help of other words. We come in fact quite quickly to the point where we are forced to explain the word's meaning through examples and training in its use. The latter is more fundamental than the first, and it is only the last level which interests Wittgenstein, because here we are forced to stick to the examples in certain ways which do not permit a full formulation in words. Examples should provide something which rules or descriptions are not able to do. 'One gives examples and intends them to be taken in a particular way . . . . (That is) he is now to *employ* those examples in a particular way' (PI, paragraph 71).

10 THE LIMITATION OF THE 'RULE'

The understanding of the examples lies in their correct use, i.e. in the proper reaction to them. This is the foundation of Wittgenstein's famous argument against the possibility of formulating rules for the application of rules. The point is simple, but basic. Since a definition or a rule cannot itself determine how it is to be applied, there is no point in giving a new rule to lay down how the first should be applied. For then the problem will just transfer itself to the new rule, because this also could be interpreted or followed in several different ways. It will continue thus *ad infinitum* if we try to escape this tangle by formulating more and more new rules to determine the use of the first rule. This is in other words a dead end. We must then realise that our application of rules cannot itself be determined through a rule. The application must by necessity be ruleless. That is what stops us from 'establishing a practice by rules alone'. The examples are indeed indispensable and they must function by virtue of themselves, for they must show what the rule cannot state — namely, how we should follow a certain rule. There is in fact nothing else one can use for help in those basic situations where one learns language — apart from the guidance which is given in connection with the examples. This is the deeper reason for regarding our adequate reactions to examples as a necessary condition for the meaning formation in verbal languages generally. But this situation has another and, for our purposes, rather interesting side. For what we know when we know how to apply a given rule can in its turn only be conveyed to others by the help of examples and hints about how they should be applied or followed. If a practice is dependent on our reacting adequately to the given examples for it to be established at all, there must be certain forms of reaction which in themselves are not of a conceptual nature, but which are included in the formation of concepts in all areas of life. This will be expressed *inter alia* in the kind of situation where we are able to perceive that the standard conditions for the use of a given concept are present without our being able completely to account for this knowledge by verbal means. Wittgenstein also points this out when he says in *On Certainty* that 'we recognise normal circumstances but cannot precisely describe them' (OC, paragraph 27).

In the latter case it is not a matter of various kinds of primitive reactions, but of a form of reaction which is a fruit of experience; this side of the case is also part of the concept of practice. The application of a rule can have a meaning creative effect and is often rooted in a developed judgment. Let me show this using an example from the field of law. The term 'gross negligence' plays, for example, an important role in the formulation of fire insurance policies. If a house owner has displayed gross negligence and fire breaks out, the fire insurance payment will be heavily reduced or withheld. But what is understood by this phrase? An insurance expert in an interview in the Norwegian daily press gave two examples of what the law courts have accepted as gross negligence: 1) burning rubbish close to the house walls; 2) leaving a pot with boiling fat when the cooking plate on the stove is on full. The insurance expert added that what is considered gross negligence will be the subject of discretionary judgment in every case. Such an observation is extremely interesting from a logico-philosophical point of view. It demonstrates namely that it is established beyond doubt that there is no point in formulating a general rule (concept) for what should be counted as gross negligence in connection with house fires. And this is of course quite correct. A law of this kind, that is to say a paragraph in the fire insurance policy terms, can only have effect under certain concrete conditions which can be considered as clear examples of gross negligence. These examples can then be said to be constitutive for interpreting the paragraph. They represent the only fixed points one has when it is to be applied. But because the law constitutes a sort of complete domain, the experience from similar cases could be considered valid when one attempts to apply the paragraph in a given case. And if the new application becomes legally binding, this has a significant effect on how the paragraph in question is understood. The new use will be incorporated in the class of meaning constitutive examples which establish its meaning.

11 THE SOCIAL CONTEXT

In the preceding I have tried in a sketchy way to uncover something of what is hidden behind the general notion of forming and applying a concept such as it appears from a practice-philosophical perspective. But the concept of practice also has another aspect which we have not yet discussed. Concept formation has by necessity a social character, according to Wittgenstein. To follow a rule is also to practise a custom, a usage or an institution (PI, paragraphs 198-9). Rules can accordingly only exist as a link in social life. We discover this if we try to imagine a person who is completely alone in establishing rule-following activities. An isolated individual will in fact not be capable of distinguishing between following a rule and believing that he follows it. The criterion for the correct way of following it will be lacking. What seems to be the right way will indeed become the correct application, but then the very notion of a rule will disintegrate, since we are only concerned with rules as far as we are able to distinguish between a correct and incorrect use of them. Consequently the practice, the established way of conduct, is the only intersubjective available criterion for the correct application of the rule or concept.

12 CONCLUSIONS

Here we can suitably conclude our sketch of the various aspects of the concept of practice. It should by now be clear that there is far more to knowing what a statement means than to know what syntactic and semantic rules are valid for the correct application of the statement. The last is clearly a rule-knowledge. The first, as we have seen by now, can be described as a sort of practice-knowledge. Rule-knowledge can be satisfactorily documented by formulating the rules in question. Practice-knowledge for logical reasons cannot be documented in this way. One can, however, do something analogous to documenting it by practising it. In other words, practice knowledge is displayed by a certain dexterity in employing the current statements and by a certain familiarity with the states of affairs to which the statements refer. Practice-knowledge can therefore justifiably be said to be a fundamental type of tacit knowledge. This is because neither the dexterity in use nor the familiarity with the phenomena can be articulated fully as propositional knowledge, even if both parts can be communicated directly via examples and general hints, as we have already shown. We have also shown that the dexterity in use and the familiarity with the phenomena undoubtedly possess the features that we normally ascribe to knowledge. For not only can we act as a matter of course from this sort of experience, but we also have intellectual control of it inasmuch as we have control over the learning situations where it is communicated. Since these two types of experience represent two clearly different sides of tacit knowledge, I have chosen to write about knowledge by dexterity and knowledge by familiarity. And because both these types of knowledge are necessarily linked to the acquisition and application of concepts, and concepts are necessary to articulate assertional knowledge, we can justifiably maintain that both types of tacit knowledge form a constitutive part in the acquisition of all the different kinds of propositional knowlege. Propositional knowledge rests, we can conclude, on a substratum of tacit knowledge — without tacit knowledge there can be no propositional knowledge.

Using this analysis as a starting-point, it is possible to track down tacit knowledge in all places where one can justifiably say that one possesses normal propositional knowledge. One will often discover that the tacit forms of knowledge are much more dominating than is the case with linguistic knowledge. This especially applies to vocational and aesthetic forms of knowledge. But there is no formula for proving tacit knowledge. Each area must be investigated individually.

NOTES

1 Aristotle discusses this threefold distinction in his best known work, *The Nichomachean Ethics*, book VI. In Tore Nordenstam's book, *From Art to Science: The Basis of the Humanities in a Historical Perspective*, chapters II and V, the scientific philosophical context for these three types of knowledge is elucidated historically.
2 See, for example, Rudolf Carnap, *Introduction to Semantics*. Cambridge, Mass. Chapters II and III. Anyone who makes the effort to read Carnap's own description of what he calls a semantic system will realise that the account being considered is extremely simplified, for instance, the description of rules of truth has been omitted. This is done for pedagogic reasons.
3 Here I will principally refer to my study, (1978) *Wittgenstein's Later Philosophy: An Interpretative Sketch*. Department of Philosophy Stencil Series No 42, University of Bergen. Concerning the consequences of Wittgenstein's pragmatic turn for the philosophy of science, I have outlined them in my book, (1985) *Traditions and Schools in Modern Philosophy of Science*. Bergen. Chapter IV.
4 It has taken a remarkably long time to recognise the full significance of Wittgenstein's pragmatic turn. In the 1950s and 1960s the slogan 'Meaning is Use' was frequently used. But there was little or no understanding of the dimensional depth in Wittgenstein's concern with the use situations for linguistic expressions. I have demonstrated this as regards philosophy of art in my study, (1980) *Art, Language and Aesthetic Practice*. Department of Philosophy Stencil Series, University of Bergen.
5 Wittgenstein, Ludwig (1953). *Philosophical Investigations*. Oxford. Paragraph 202. In the text it is abbreviated to PI, indicating paragraph number for the first part and page number for the second part.
6 It is this basic relationship in the use of concepts, theories and other abstract intellectual qualities which has been the origin of the pragmatic turn in the philosophy of science.
    I have tried to adapt this viewpoint to humanistic research in my article Philosophy of Science and Subject Conception: Rudiments of an Analysis of Gosta M. Bergman's Conception of the Science of the Theatre as an Independent Discipline, published in Tor Bastiniansen (ed.) (1983) *Philosophy of Science and Basic Problems in Theatre Science Research*. Theatre Science Studies No 1, University of Bergen.
    The article is also published in (1985) *Norwegian Journal of Philosophy*.20,4.
7 To show caution in this way is to make a concession to the traditional understanding of rules where one takes it for granted that the rule can be formulated in its entirety. Only under this assumption can one put rule and formulatable content on an equal basis. However it is an important point for Wittgenstein that we can also talk about rules and thus about rule-following conduct in cases where we can only partially articulate the rule with the help if verbal means. Consequently we must distinguish clearly between the type of tacit knowledge which in general is attached to the application of the concepts and the circumstance that some concepts are only partially articulable and thereby represent special types of tacit knowledge.
8 According to Kuhn's own words in the last sentence of chapter IV in (1962) *The Structure of Scientific Revolutions*. Chicago, 'paradigms can guide research even in the absence of rules', p42.

AI & SOCIETY, VOL. 2, 303-313 (1988)

Seeing and Seeing-AS[1]

BR Tilghman

Department of Philosophy, Kansas State University, Manhattan, Kansas, USA

ABSTRACT

This paper highlights the importance of inter-relationships between language, context, practice and interpretation. These inter-relationships should be of interest to AI researchers working in multi-disciplinary fields such as knowledge based systems, speech and vision. Attention is drawn to the importance of Part II, Section II of Wittgenstein's *Philosophical Investigations* for understanding the enormous complexity of the concept of seeing and how it is woven into an understanding of language and of human relations.

KEYWORDS

perception, seeing, seeing-as, natural reaction, interpretation

1 INTRODUCTION

It has long been a temptation for scientists and philosophers to seek an understanding of human beings in terms drawn from the latest scientific developments. In the wake of the triumph of mathematical physics in the seventeenth century and especially Newtonian mechanics it was thought plausible to describe human beings as mechanisms like complicated pieces of clockwork.[2] Since the middle of our century it has been the fashion to think of people as if they were computers or some form of processors of information. In our time, however, this tendency has taken a curious turn in that we now wonder whether it is machines that may be like people in being intelligent. The Artificial Intelligence program would then seem to be an attempt to understand a class of machines in what are essentially human terms. It proceeds, however, from serious misunderstandings of what those terms are. The home base, as it were, of the word 'intelligence' is its use in the description and assessment of a wide variety of human activities and capacities. A close examination of the concept would doubtless show that there is no essence or commonality to all these uses to be precipitated off and modeled in circuitry of whatever sophistication.

The burden of this paper is to show that at least one very important capacity, the capacity to perceive in certain ways, cannot be understood by analogy with the processing of information. I shall try to do this by pointing out that the language in which

353

we describe perception is considerably more complex than most theorists have allowed for and it is embedded in a background of human practices and social contexts that prevailing theory is unable to account for. It is largely by a series of indirections that I hope to find that direction out.

2 PROBLEMS AND PERPLEXITIES

Perception, that is, seeing, has puzzled philosophers and scientists alike for a long time. Perceptual psychologists are inclined to wonder why things look right side up when the image that is projected upon the retina is upside down. It does not seem to have occurred to them that a possible answer to that question is because most things are right side up. They are also perplexed because the various things that go on in the nerves and in the brain do not at all resemble what some would call our 'full consciousness of the world of objects' and this leads them sometimes to postulate complex psychological processes that intervene to convert the data of neurological input into 'the perception of the world as we know it'.[3]

Now this is no more and no less than the hoary representational theory of perception bolstered with the latest findings of physiology and neurology. What we actually experience, it is assumed, are not the things in the world, but states of consciousness or perhaps even brain states; at any rate, objects that are exactly analogous to the ideas in the mind of the seventeenth and eighteenth centuries. These states of consciousness are supposed to represent the world to us and the problem for psychology is to explain how the physical, physiological and neurological processes that intervene between the world and consciousness are able to bring it off.

At this point there is a strong temptation to suppose that if all relevant information about present optical stimulation was available and if all relevant information about concomitant neurological and brain processes and states was also available, it would be possible to predict precisely what visual perceptions a person is having. And, coming from the other direction, a complete description of the visual perception together with appropriate knowledge of the nervous system would permit a valid inference to a state of affairs in the world.

If this is how it is with visual perception, then a machine can perceive. We can think of a television set as a perceiving machine, but it is not at all necessary that the result be a visual image; any kind of representation will do so long as there is the requisite functional relation between that representation and the 'sensory' input. As a description of human perception, however, this account fails in its own terms.

This picture of perception as the end product of a series of causal processes commits us, we must notice, to complete skepticism with respect to what philosophers like to call the external world. If the only access we have to the world is through our states of consciousness, then there is simply no way to determine whether our consciousness corresponds in any way to the world or even whether there is a world for anything to correspond to. And this also applies to the very physiological data that generated the picture in the first place. Psychologists, however, seem oblivious to this disastrous implication of their theory of perception.

One mistake that might contribute to this unfortunate muddle is the assumption that physiology and neurology can tell us what perception is, that they can let us in on the *essence* of seeing. What these sciences can do, I believe, is to tell us what goes on in the nerves and brain when we see and identify causal factors that affect what we see. They cannot, however, tell us what we see, what the object of sight is, or that this experience is a true case of seeing while this other one is not.

I want to say that there is no essence of seeing. If we are to make anything of the question, 'What is seeing?' we will have to construe it as a question about the concept of seeing and that comes down to a matter of investigating how the word is actually used in our language and in our life. An important part of this conceptual investigation of perception will have to be into the relation between the physics and physiology of seeing on the one hand and the language of seeing on the other. As philosophers we cannot and must not challenge any of the empirical data unearthed by science. What we can do, however, is to challenge the relevance of that data for the questions that so many have found puzzling. But this latter is an aspect of the question that I am not going to talk about at this time.

My own field of aesthetics and the philosophy of art offers striking examples of the strength of the assumption that there is an essence of perception. Everyone agrees that works of art present us with expressive or physiognomic qualities: the flowers in a painting can be gay, a melody can be sad, and the like. But how can the qualities associated with human feeling be seen or heard? We can see the shapes and colors of the flowers, but surely not their gaiety; we can hear the musical tones and perhaps their relative pitch, but surely not their sadness. Such reflections have generated a host of theories postulating more than questionable mechanisms to explain how perceived shapes, colors and sounds can mingle with our feelings or how our feelings can be 'projected' into objects of perception. Although we may say that we see or hear these things, this species of philosophy corrects us and seeks to explain that what is going on is really seeing or hearing plus something else. It becomes clear that certain assumptions about what seeing really is are calling the sets for this kind of philosophy.[4]

3 SEEING, SEEING-AS AND ASPECT PERCEPTION

If we set these philosophical prejudices aside, however, and remind ourselves how we actually use the word, we understand right away that there is no essence of perception and that a great many different kinds of things can count as objects of sight. The place to begin in order to get some of this made clear is with Wittgenstein's *Philosophical Investigations*, especially section xi of Part II.[5] This section takes up only 36 pages, but it is some of the richest and most suggestive 36 pages ever written by a philosopher. It is also a curiously neglected section of the book. Its most famous — or should I say infamous? — character is that zoologically ambiguous figure, the duck-rabbit. Plenty of people have had something to say about the duck-rabbit, but unfortunately about little else in the section and have generally missed the greater part of what Wittgenstein was getting at. Cyril Barrett has remarked, and perhaps correctly, that there is now nothing left to do with the unfortunate creature but to stuff it.[6]

Wittgenstein begins section xi with a distinction between seeing a face and seeing the likeness between two faces. This allows him to distinguish between what he calls a perception and what he calls an aspect. If I report simply that I see a face, I am reporting a perception, that is, that an object of a determinate sort is seen. If I report that I see a likeness, then I am reporting an aspect. He goes on to talk about aspects of ambiguous figures such as the duck-rabbit, aspects of organization such as those which appear when one sees a figure in a puzzle picture, and aspects that require imagination such as those of the triangle that appear as this or that depending upon the setting that we imagine for it. He then introduces the notion of aspect-blindness and entertains the possibility that there are people who cannot see aspects or experience a change of aspect. This possibility suggests to him an important connection between perceiving aspects and what he calls experiencing the meaning of a word, which, in turn, permits him to bring in the very important concept of words having secondary senses. The discussion then modulates into further remarks about mental privacy and forms of life and concludes on the matter of understanding another person.

Space permits me to talk about only two or three of the topics in this section, but before going on I want to call attention to two things. Firstly, it is clear that for Wittgenstein there is an intimate connection between the philosophical investigation of seeing and the matter of understanding other people, and understanding other people is the basis of the very possibility of there being moral relations with other people. We must keep in mind that Wittgenstein's major concern throughout his life was ethical and that includes his philosophical concern. Secondly, it is striking that there has been no attempt of any kind that I am aware of to discuss this section as a whole and to work out the connections between these topics which are obviously of the greatest importance.

We can get a glimpse of the moral import of Wittgenstein's work right off when he talks of seeing the likeness between two faces.[7] What he is talking about here is seeing the resemblance between two members of the same family, say the son's likeness to the father. If I can see the face of my old friend in the younger edition, then I may be some way toward establishing an understanding and relationship with the lad that would not be possible with a complete stranger or if I knew only that it was the son.

An aspect is the sort of thing that can be missed and then can dawn on one. In this respect seeing an aspect is unlike seeing an object. We feel confident in being able to offer a physiological explanation of how it is possible to see an object. Light is reflected from the object and is focused on the retina whereupon the optic nerve is appropriately stimulated, and so on. We can specify what seem to be the necessary causal conditions for perception and if any one of them is lacking, if there is insufficient light or the optical apparatus is not in proper working order, the object will not be seen. This cannot do, however, for seeing aspects. Even if the conditions of observation and the condition of the observer are ideal, one may still fail to see the likeness on the duck or the rabbit aspect of the ambiguous figure. At this point Wittgenstein shifts his discussion away from causal conditions. The basis of the experience of seeing an aspect, of seeing one thing as another, he tells us, is the mastery of a technique.[8] The technique in question is usually the ability to use the appropriate language and/or make appropriate comparisons. In order to see the duck aspect of the trick figure you must be able to use the word 'duck' in more ordinary situations, be able to recognize the thing on the pond, to identify conventional pictures of the beasts, to be able to say at least that this picture is like that other thing, and so on. Let us imagine a stranger from a strange land where ducks and anything remotely like them are wholly unknown. We can say of this person that he sees a duck although he does not know what it is that he is seeing; he is, after all, looking at it in a good light, turning his head to follow it, and so on, but it would make no sense to say that he sees the ambiguous figure as a duck regardless of the light and anything going on in his nervous system. We are dealing here with a different although related concept of seeing and it is clear that to understand this concept we need to keep in mind a wider cultural and environmental context in which the person and his knowledge must be located.

For some philosophers a puzzling feature of aspect perception is the fact that when aspects are seen to change or to dawn on us our experience of the object changes and it can look quite different and yet the object itself has not changed. The temptation has been to suppose that what is actually experienced is not the physical stimulus object in the 'external world', but something such as a state of consciousness understood as a private object. Thus when I see the duck aspect flip flop and be replaced by the rabbit aspect I am actually seeing a private duck picture being replaced by a private rabbit picture. One result of this move is to conflate seeing an object as now this and again as that with seeing now this object and again that one. This move obviously assumes that there is an essence of seeing and that seeing is properly only one kind of experience.

I do not want to dwell on the confusion inherent in the private object picture of either mental life in general or perception in particular. Wittgenstein was at great pains to lay all that out in the first part of the *Investigations*.[9] Nevertheless, in section xi he does offer as neat a piece of advice as one would wish to point out the nonsense of the private object: 'Always get rid of the idea of the private object in this way: assume that it constantly changes, but that you do not notice the change because your memory constantly deceives you'.[10]

4 SEEING AND INTERPRETING

There is another move that is frequently made, designed to show that seeing an aspect, seeing-as, is not really a genuine case of seeing. It consists in the claim that what we call seeing an aspect is really a case of seeing plus an interpretation. To make clear the role of interpretation in all this I want to use the example of understanding the technical engineering drawings of a piece of machinery. When I first look at the drawing it may well appear quite chaotic and I can make little of it. I must try to figure it out. I begin by assuming that this line represents this surface of the machine, that this circle is the hole to be drilled here, and that this broken line must indicate a key slot on an interior surface, and so on. This figuring out amounts to forming a set of hypotheses that can then be either confirmed or disconfirmed by comparing the drawing with the machine itself or by going ahead to construct the thing and then seeing how it turns out. It is perfectly natural to call this kind of figuring out interpreting. And interpreting, as Wittgenstein points out, involves forming hypotheses.[11]

After a time, however, I may achieve a certain familiarity with the drawing and it no longer presents a chaotic tangle of lines to me. I may come to see the drawing as the machine it represents and I no longer have to figure out what this is or that line represents; I see it quite plainly and now I can use the drawing confidently in a way that I could not before. The organization of the drawing has dawned on me and now it all makes sense. From now on I do not have to interpret anything; I no longer have to figure anything out. The case I have just described contrasts with the case of the experienced engineer who saw the drawing correctly from the very beginning. The thing never appeared disorganized to him and there was never any question of its organization dawning on him. This man does not have to figure things out and never did. He does not interpret. What makes this kind of seeing possible is, of course, both a certain background knowledge of machinery and a knowledge of the conventions of engineering drawing.

These examples are intended to show that seeing and interpreting are different things and stand in contrast to one another. Seeing is not merely a limiting case of interpretation. Wittgenstein marks the difference by saying that interpreting is an activity, something we do, while seeing is a state.[12] One reason the distinction is of extraordinary importance, I believe, is because of the emphasis that has been put upon the notion of interpreting in so much recent philosophy of language. I am thinking primarily of the work of WVO Quine and others such as Donald Davidson whose spectrum of thought seems to dominate philosophy in the United States.

In a foreign land among exotic tribesmen whose language I speak not a word of I am at a loss to know what to make of their shout of 'Gavagai!'.[13] I do not know whether they are merely announcing the presence of the undifferentiated rabbit parts that just hopped by, anticipating hunting for Easter eggs, adoring the latest incarnation of the great god *Cunniculum*, or something quite other. I have no choice but to interpret their speech, if speech it is. I form hypotheses and utter 'Gavagai' in various situations in order to test my inferences about their 'dispositions to assent' to this or that proposition.[14] And in the fullness of time we are presumed to get on.

Let us turn now to a less exotic setting and imagine how it is that you or I often set about learning a foreign language. I arm myself with a grammar book and a dictionary. I begin to learn the basic grammatical structure and memorize verb conjugations and start to acquire a vocabulary. When I encounter the language spoken or written I have to remind myself of the person and tense of the verb and will likely have to look up some of the words in the dictionary. Doing this often involves forming hypotheses in answer to questions such as: Was that word used as a noun or a verb? Did this other word mean what I thought it did? My situation here is very much like my situation with respect to the engineering drawings; I must do a lot of figuring out. And all that is simply interpreting. After a while, however, things begin to go rather better and I no longer have to consult the grammar book or dictionary; I can now understand what I hear and read directly without going through any process of interpretation.

Now remind yourself of how it is with young children learning their native language. The child is not like the anthropologist set down upon the Cannibal Islands and perplexed about where to get a foothold although this is exactly the way that he is represented by St Augustine in the passage that Wittgenstein quotes at the beginning of the *Philosophical Investigations*. Nor is he like you and me struggling with our grammar books and lexicons. Very young children do not form hypotheses but, amazingly, they tumble to their own tongue in remarkably short order.

Nor in general do you or I have to go through any process of interpretation in our dealings with our friends and neighbors. We are able to understand one another without the aid of that kind of mediation. I pass my neighbour on a regular basis every morning and we exchange 'Good mornings'. There is no logical room here for figuring out what might be meant. But compare my experience of the other day. My ex-wife has not spoken to me for five years. We encounter one another from time to time and invariably she makes a point of looking in the other direction when we pass. But just the other morning when she approached she looked at me with a big smile and said in the friendliest voice imaginable, 'Good morning!' When it finally dawned on me what had happened I asked myself what in the world she meant by that! Is she finally mellowing or is it more than likely that she is up to something? It would be just like her. Here is the place where it is natural to talk of interpreting and of figuring things out.

Let me try to explain another reason why I think it is so important to make this distinction between understanding something, seeing or hearing it right off, and interpreting. Interpretation is a process we have to engage in when we do not understand something right way. It characteristically entails a certain hesitancy with respect to the material to be understood. I go shopping in the Cannibal Islands. If I ask the butcher's wife, who is helping out behind the counter, for some of her gavagai, I am not sure that I will get the dinner makings for the Hasenpfeffer that I came for or my face slapped. My lack of familiarity with the language has a great deal to do with how I approach the people of that land. And I am quite perplexed now about how to deal with my ex-wife.

Hesitancy does and must mark our conduct in foreign lands where we do not know the language and the customs or do not understand them very well. And it frequently marks our dealings with individuals whom we do not know. The kind of philosophical position that I am opposing here starts with the circumstance of someone, an adult someone who already speaks a language, set down in the middle of the Cannibal Islands where we can expect there to be serious problems of translation and interpretation. The sticking point is reached when it is assumed that what is true of us in that situation must be true of us across the board, even when we are speaking our native language with our family and our friends and neighbors. This kind of theory has the effect of presenting a picture of us as forever and everywhere strangers in a strange land. It is a picture that cuts off all possibility of understanding one another and of human relations in general.

5 THE COMPLEXITY OF PERCEPTION

Seeing is an enormously complex notion; the word has many different uses and many different things can count as objects of sight. Following Wittgenstein I have contrasted seeing with interpreting and it follows that if seeing is a complex concept, then so is interpreting; many different things can count as interpreting. Let's go back to my adventures with the engineering drawings. I am familiar with the conventions of drawing and know something of machinery, but I still cannot quite make out just what the drawings are supposed to be. Consequently, while I may have to interpret this line as representing this surface, I do not have to interpret the line as representing a surface; that much is obvious. But this is exactly what will have to be done for the complete beginner on the shop floor. We will have to explain to him that solid lines represent exterior surfaces and all the rest. He will have to figure out everything until he acquires more familiarity with the standard practices.

One possible source of philosophical confusion about the relation between seeing and interpreting is the fact that a description that results from an interpretation can be identical to a report of how something is seen. After a certain amount of struggle I figure out that this line is this surface and I describe it as such to the boys in the shop. The more experienced engineer picks up the drawing and tells them exactly the same thing only without having to figure it out. What allows us to say that he sees it right away without having to interpret it is simply the immediacy of his reaction and the confidence and familiarity he exhibits in using and explaining the drawing. And there is the additional fact that one can see according to an interpretation. When we offer the apprentice an explanation of the drawing it may all begin to make sense and to fall into place for him. He can now see what it is all about.

Now let us apply some of this to understanding language. I am visiting a foreign country whose language I do not speak. I find myself, let us say, in Sweden where everyone in academic circles speaks beautiful English, but out on the street it is a different matter. There I have to do a good bit of interpreting, which in this case amounts to frequent reference to my Swedish phrase book. But I note the things that I do not have to interpret. I do not have to interpret the sounds I hear people making as language. I hear intonations and rhythms in their speech that are not altogether alien. I see them going about their daily business, buying and selling in the shops, ordering meals in cafés, and so on. Of course, I cannot tell what the man at the next table is ordering, but there is no question that he is ordering something from the menu. At some point interpreting must come to an end in seeing and hearing, in an unmediated understanding of other people.

Where that point is that interpretation comes to an end varies with the situation. Consider T.S. Eliot's lines:

> The nightingales are singing near
> The Convent of the Sacred Heart,
> And sang within the bloody wood
> When Agamemnon cried aloud,
> And let their liquid siftings fall
> To stain the stiff dishonoured shroud.

Five thousand years from now an archeologist uncovers this fragment, but is not at all sure whether the marks he makes out are even pieces of language. He has much to figure out. Then there is the fellow who is learning English. For him there is no question that it is a language or even English, but he still must figure out the basic sentence structure and the verb conjugations. Let us not forget many of my undergraduate students who will not know some of the words and will have to figure them out (i.e. look them up), if they bother at all. They probably will not know who this Agamemnon chap is either. Then there are those who will seek an interpretation on the literary level: What does the tragedy of Agamemnon have to do with Apeneck Sweeney and how does the symbolism of the nightingale enter into it? What is the tone of these lines? Are they perhaps ironic? Each of these levels presupposes a starting point that needs no interpretation because it is plain to see for the person in question.

6 UNDERSTANDING LIONS AND UNDERSTANDING PEOPLE

In the middle of section xi Wittgenstein makes the remark that if a lion could talk we could not understand him.[15] This remark impressed me because it touched on something in my own experience. I recall strolling out on the High Veldt one morning, as was my wont, when I heard a growly voice say 'Good morning'. 'Good morning,' I replied from habit although I did not see anyone. I looked about to see where the voice came from and finally spied a tawny figure crouching in the tall grass. 'Oh, there you are,' I said, 'I didn't spot you.' 'Of course not,' was the reply, 'I'm not spotted, you know. You must be confusing me with my cousin, the leopard, the one that's always hanging about with that Ethiopian fellow.' I chose not to react to that and was content to express my amazement that not only could a lion talk, but talk in English. 'How did you manage to learn English?' I queried. 'A missionary taught me,' was the reply. 'He must have been a remarkable person to . . . ' 'Yes, he was very good,' my new acquaintance interrupted, and the great tongue rolled about its chops. I thought better of pursuing that one and changed the subject by asking what it was he had been in the process of eating a moment before. 'It's leg of zebra,' was the answer. 'It sat out in the hot sun all yesterday and is first rate.' 'Did you catch it?' I asked, to keep the conversation going. 'Of course not,' he replied in an offended tone, 'the girls do all of that.' 'Couldn't you help them out from time to time?' said I, from my contemporary and liberated perspective. 'Don't be ridiculous; I am a lion.' And he gazed haughtily in another direction.

Just then a lioness walked by not far from where we were and the lion followed her with his gaze. 'My my,' he murmured, did you see the way she swished that tail?' Now I must admit that one swish of a lioness's tail is pretty much like another to me, but I suggested that if he thought there may be some profit in the thing, he could follow along to see what she was up to rather than wasting his time talking to me. 'I can't go chasing off after just any lioness that walks by,' he explained, 'I have my pride, you know.' 'Say, that's pretty good,' I chuckled. 'What's pretty good?' was the matter of fact response. 'You made a pun. You see the word "pride" has two meanings and . . .' 'Of course it has two meanings,' said the lion. At this point I could see that we were divided by more than merely a taste for yesterday's zebra and I soon excused myself as politely as possible under the circumstances and went on my way.

As a matter of fact, we have no idea at all what it would be like for a lion to talk. For one thing, a lion's vocal apparatus just is not up to articulating the sounds of our languages. Nor are their paws up to using the sign language of the deaf as some apes can apparently bring off after a fashion. Nevertheless, some enterprising animal psychologist may eventually suggest a way of getting a lion to push outsize computer keys and in that way have a go at teaching him English or French, or whatever without having to worry about the thick accent. Would this tend to show that Wittgenstein's statement was false?

What divides us from lions is considerably more than taste in zebra. Lions, as I discovered, are painfully literal and have no ear for word play whatsoever. There are people like that and to some extent we are divided from them. Such people can be aware that a word has more than one meaning, but never seem to make the connection that allows the joke to go through. What is missing here is what Wittgenstein calls a natural reaction. They simply do not react as many of us do and there is no use explaining anything; no interpretation allows them to get the point.

Wittgenstein's comment that we could not understand a talking lion occurs among some remarks about forms of life and the idea of a form of life includes natural reactions. We have no inclination to lurk in the tall grass keeping an eye out for stragglers from a herd of zebra; none of us, I trust, tend to respond to the swish of the tail of a lioness. Little lions, in their turn, do not toddle after their parents trying to imitate their speech, they do not shed tears when they skin their knees, and they do not follow pointing gestures — at least I assume they do not; little pussy cats certainly do not. Nor does a lion's face display sorrow or joy, we cannot recognize smiles or frowns there. Perhaps the principle vehicle of leonine expression is the tail — it seems much like that with his domestic cousin at the fireside.

The zoologist who studies lions may be able to categorize the various swishings of the tail and other postures and correlate them with moods, sex drives, and so on, but this is not at all like the way we understand and react to our own kind. In the standard case I can see immediately that another person is angry, is in pain, is happy or is ashamed. This can frequently be seen in the person's facial expression, gestures, bodily posture, and heard in his tone of voice. These are not just bits and pieces of evidence that we must use in order to interpret or infer the presence of those various psychological states. What makes it possible to see other people so is the background of our shared form of life, the shared background of natural reactions and a common social life.

Nor must we overlook the importance of the context in which we encounter other people. There have been psychological studies in which subjects were shown photographs of people's faces and asked to identify the expression or state of mind evinced. The results are invariably very mixed. In the seventeenth century the French painter and theorist Charles Le Brun drew a series of faces illustrating the various emotions that painters could be called upon to represent. What is striking about them is that any number of them could be substituted for one another without loss.[16] What is missing in all this is any setting or context to make the emotion determinate. We must know who this person is, who these people are, what their relationship is, what is at stake in the scene, and the like. In real life as well as in painting we do not come across just faces; we encounter people in particular situations and our understanding of people cannot somehow be precipitated off and held isolated from the social and human circumstances in which they, and we, live and breathe and have our being. The idea that we can build up theoretically an account of the human being in terms of the behaviorist's 'colorless bodily movements' may be out of date now, but the related notion that we can come to understand a people's language in terms of 'dispositions to assent' to certain sentences is still very much with us. Both conceptions are equally poverty stricken.

7 CONCLUSION

We have come quite a distance from seeing the aspects of trick figures like the duck-rabbit to seeing the character of a human being. The duck-rabbit is a most congenial beast for helping us to realize that seeing and perception are far more complicated notions than either philosophy or science has been inclined to recognize. Once it has helped us to understand that complexity and to realize that there is no essence of seeing, and that psychology and neurophysiology have no special claim to the territory, we can then put it back in the hutch — or is it the bath tub? — and get on to philosophically more pressing issues, issues about ourselves.

At this point it may be useful to connect some of what I have been saying about seeing with the distinction between propositional and tacit knowledge. It is plausible, and may even be true, to suggest that we can give a 'propositional' account of what it is to see an object. With sufficient information we may be able to say that if the eye receives these light waves and if the optic nerve and brain centres are in this condition, then the person will see this object. (Note that we do not have to say that the 'perception' of the object is itself another object.) One can often explain how he was able to see an object under apparently adverse circumstances: I stood on tiptoes; I shielded my eyes against the glare, etc. Knowledge of these conditions, however, cannot allow us to determine that an aspect is being seen nor can a person explain how it is that he was able to see some aspect. For one thing, the intelligibility of aspect descriptions demands a context of previously acquired experiences which in turn implies a wider social and cultural setting. For another the fact that a person sees an aspect often has consequences for his behavior that reach through that cultural setting. The connection of aspect perception with our understanding of words and of people places it squarely in the tacit dimension. If aspect perception is to be modeled into the circuitry of a machine, then we are going to have to be prepared to describe the *life* of the machine and such things as its aesthetic judgments and its moral relations (with whom? other machines?). That, of course, is unintelligible.

Someone or other said that philosophy begins in wonder and more and more do I come to wonder how deeply concepts of seeing are woven into the fabric of our language and of our lives.

NOTES

1 This is a slightly modified version of a paper that was originally presented to the conference on *Culture, Language and Artificial Intelligence*, Stockholm, May 30-June 3 1988.
2 See, for example, Thomas Hobbes (1651). *Leviathan*, La Mettrie (1748). *L'homme machine*, and Holbach (1770). *Système de la nature.*
3 The quoted passages are taken from M.D. Vernon (1962). *The Psychology of Perception.* Penguin Books. Chapter 1. Essentially the same picture of perception can be found in any psychological work on the subject.
4 For a critical examination of this kind of theory and the assumptions behind it, see my (1970) *The Expression of Emotion in the Visual Arts.* M. Nijhoff.
5 Wittgenstein, Ludwig , translated by M. Anscombe (1967). *Philosophical Investigations.* The Macmillan Co., New York.
6 In what to the best of my knowledge is an unpublished paper.
7 Ibid. p193.
8 Ibid. p208.
9 The reader is referred to John Cook (1965). Wittgenstein on Privacy, *The Philosophical Review*, and Stewart Candlish (1980). The Real Private Language Argument, *Philosophy*, for detailed expositions of Wittgenstein's attack on the view that sensations are private objects and the language in which we describe them is a private language.
10 *Philosophical Investigations*, p207.
11 bid. p212.
12 loc. cit.
13 'Gavagai' is of Quine's coinage in his explanation of what he takes to be the problem of radical translation in (1970) *Word and Object.* MIT Press, Cambridge, Mass.
14 The expression is Quine's in *Word and Object.*
15 Ibid. p223.
16 These drawings are reproduced in Elizabeth Gilmore Holt (1958). *A Documentary History of Art.* Doubleday Anchor Books, New York. vol 2, Figure 7.

REFERENCES

Baker, G.P. and P.M.S. Hacker (1984). *Language, Sense and Nonsense.* Basil Blackwell, Oxford.
Diamond, Cora (1966-67). Secondary Sense, *Proceedings of the Aristotelian Society.* 67.
Malcolm, Norman (1986). *Nothing is Hidden.* Basil Blackwell, Oxford.
Tilghman, B.R. (1984). *But is it Art?.* Basil Blackwell, Oxford.
Wittgenstein, Ludwig (1958). *The Blue and Brown Books.* Basil Blackwell, Oxford.
Wittgenstein, Ludwig (1980). *Remarks on Philosophical Psychology.* Basil Blackwell, Oxford. 2 v.
Wittgenstein, Ludwig (1982). *Last Writings.* Basil Blackwell, Oxford. vol 1.
Wittgenstein, Ludwig (1967). *Zettel.* Basil Blackwell, Oxford.

AI & SOCIETY, VOL. 1, 25-35 (1987)

THE PRACTICE OF THE USE OF COMPUTERS
A paradoxical encounter between different traditions of knowledge

Bo Göranzon

ABSTRACT

A quotation from Shakespeare's play King Lear, 'I will teach you differences', encapsulates the spirit of this paper. The distinction is introduced between three different categories of knowledge: i) propositional knowledge, ii) skill or practical knowledge and iii) knowledge of familiarity. In the present debate on 'Information Society', there is a clear tendency to overemphasise the theoretical knowledge at the expense of practical knowledge thereby completely ignoring the knowledge of familiarity. It is argued that different forms of theoretical knowledge are required for the design of current computer technology and the study of the practice of computer usage. The concept of dialogue and the concept of 'To Follow a Rule' are therefore fundamental to the understanding of the practice of computer usage.

KEYWORDS

dialogue, French Age of Enlightenment, to follow a rule, essentially contested concepts, propositional knowledge, practical knowledge, knowledge of familiarity, epistemological error

1 PARADOXICAL VIEWS OF KNOWLEDGE IN THE AGE OF ENLIGHTENMENT

In the modern sense, applied mathematics was the creation of René Descartes. In 1637, Descartes presented a study in which he showed how, by applying abstract algebraic concepts, it is possible to formulate geometry's concrete points, lines, surfaces and volumes. He demonstrated a link between our three-dimensional world and a mathematical-logical way of thinking.

In his work 'Discourse on Methods, Optics, Geometry and Meteorology', in which Descartes presented his revolutionary mathematical theory, the word 'machine' is applied to the human body for the first time in history: 'And this will not seem strange to those, who knowing how many different automata or moving machines can be made by the industry of man without employing in so doing more than a very few parts in comparison with the great multitude of bones, muscles, nerves, arteries, veins, or other parts that are found in the body of each animal. From this aspect the body is regarded as a machine which, having been made by the hands of God, is incomparably better arranged, and possesses in itself movements which are much more admirable, than any of those which can be invented by man.'

Descartes continues with an important argument: 'Here I specially stopped to show that if there had been such machines, possessing the organs and outward form of a monkey or some other animal without reason, we should not have had any means of ascertaining that they were not of the same nature as those animals. On the other hand, if there were machines which bore a resemblance to our body and imitated our actions as far as it was morally possible to do so, we should always have two very certain tests by which to recognise that, for all that, they were not real men. The first is, that they could never use speech or other signs as we do when placing our thoughts on record for the benefit of others. For we can easily understand a machine's being constituted so that it can utter words, and even emit some responses to action on it of a corporeal kind, which brings about a change in its organs; for instance if it is touched in a particular part it may ask what we wish to say to it; if in another part it may exclaim that it is being hurt, and so on. But it never happens that it arranges its speech in various ways, in order to reply appropriately to everything that may be said in its presence, as even the lowest type of man can do. And the second difference is, that although machines can perform certain things as well as or perhaps better than any of us can do, they infallibly fall short in others, by which means we may discover that they did not act from knowledge, but only from the disposition of their organs. For while reason is the universal instrument which can serve for all contingencies, these organs have need of some special adaptation for every particular action.'

The notion that 'animals are machines' lies at the core of the Cartesian view. Descartes coined a phrase to express this opinion: Bete machine. There is a reference to this phrase in one of the earliest documents produced in the French Age of Enlightenment: *Man a Machine*, published in 1748 by Dr La Mettrie. To La Mettrie, learning to understand a language - i.e. learning to use symbols - is to become a human being. Culture is what separates man from the animals. La Mettrie means that thinking should turn from general abstractions to consider the concrete, the details. It is the models to be found in the concrete examples we meet that nurtures us in a culture. According to La Mettrie, a mind that has received poor guidance is as an actor who has been spoiled by provincial theatres, and goes on to say that the separate states of the soul are in constant interaction with the body. La Mettrie struck a chord that was to characterise the contradictory views of knowledge during the French Age of Enlightenment.

Denis Diderot, leader of the French Encyclopedia project in the Age of Enlightenment, attempted to track down the paradox inherent in the perception of the way knowledge and competence are developed and maintained. On the one hand there is the belief that everything can be systematised and formalised in a symbolic logical notation. On the other hand there is Minerva's owl which, although it first appears on the periphery of the project, when seen as a link with the current debate on technical change becomes vitally important to further development.

Denis Diderot says this: 'If I knew how to speak as I think! But as it is now, I have ideas in my head but I cannot find words for them.'

To be at once within and standing apart from oneself. To observe and be the person who is observed. But thought is like the eye: it cannot see itself. How do we shape the rhythmic gestures of our thoughts? Here we can establish a link with Ludwig Wittgenstein's philosophy of language, which is currently becoming more prominent in an international debate on technical advance.

2 ON FOLLOWING RULES

Ludwig Wittgensteins's philosphy focuses attention on the particular concrete case or example. He wishes to remind us of the complex and many-faceted logic of the example: 'It is not only a question of the errors in thinking we make when we focus only on the universal. It is also a question of the values that are lost through this intellectual attitude' says Kjell S. Johannesen.

The multiplicity of disparate activities or *practices* - following a rule in one's activities is what Wittgenstein refers to as a practice - is the focal point of his interest.

Wittgenstein perceives a concept as a *set of activities that follow a rule*, in contrast to regarding the concept as a rule, a view that characterises the earlier scientific traditions to which we have referred. In this way, the concept becomes related to its usage. The use of the concept determines its content. It is our usage or *practice* that shows the way in which we understand something.

The rule is built into the action. The concept of practice brings out this fundamental relationship. To master and coordinate actions implies an ability to be part of a practice: '. . . but if a person has not yet got the concepts, I should teach him to use the words by means of examples and by practice . . . .' *Philosophical Investigations*, §201.

'If language is to be a means of communication there must be agreement not only in definitions but also (queer as this may sound) in judgements.' *Philosophical Investigations*, §242.

We are taught a practice through examples, through models. The ability to formulate examples is vitally important. There are good examples which lead our thoughts in the 'right' direction and which refresh our minds, and there are examples which make it impossible to understand the sense of a practice. This cannot be made explicit by means of a formal description. It requires the ability to put forward the essence of a practice through examples which are followed up by teaching, by practice. We acquire a deeper understanding of the concept 'tool' by using tools in different activities. Taking part in different practices, for example when using computers, can give different opinions about the way computer usage affects the activity, while people sharing in a common practice may have varying opinions about the use of computers in this practice.

3 WHAT IS A COMPUTER?

At an international conference at Sigtuna, Sweden in June 1979 on the theme 'Is the computer a tool?', Alan Janik, the philosopher, discussed *essentially contested concepts* and the part played by these concepts in our attempts to describe reality: 'Basically, the most vexed issues which humans face involve conflicts about how we are to describe the situation we confront . . . Our evidence may be the wrong sort of evidence and our tradition may lead us to ask the wrong questions. We must be at one and the same time guided by what we take to be the substance of the issues at hand and also prepared to reconsider precisely what the substance of the issue actually is. It is always necessary to bear in mind that the most serious issues we confront concern *essentially contested concepts*, i.e disagreement over just what the substantive isues are. To prevail in the conflict is to be prepared to follow the discussion, even when it leads us into unfamiliar terrain.'

The content of the concept 'tool' is not self-evident in the same way as understanding what a computer is. There is a profusion of metaphors and parallels about computers in analogies with steam-engines, electricity, the motor-car, typewriters etc. In the same way there are numerous analogies of what a human being is in connection with the debate on technological development: man as a clockwork machine, an ant, a piano etc. A usual starting-point in the debate on computers is to compare the memory capacity of the brain to that of a computer. Here, the main function is information processing. A different starting-point is the comparison between human language and the 'language of machines'. The point of this comment is to interpret Allan Janik's discussion of 'essentially contested concepts', namely that our perception of the man-machine relationship plays a decisive part in controlling our questions on the use of computers.

4 A BOAT BUILDER ON THE WEST COAST OF SWEDEN

The conference on 'Is the computer a tool?' was also attended by Thomas Tempte, a carpenter and craftsman who for his part could see no striking similarities between computers and what he in his own 'profession' was used to calling 'tools'.

Thomas Tempte described Gösta, a boat-builder on Sweden's west coast: 'Gösta is a product of the old master-journeyman-apprentice training system in which sophisticated and complex knowledge was passed on without using words. This is not because of any aversion to transferring knowledge by means of the spoken word, but because no such tradition had been developed.

'Putting a question to Gösta elicits very precise information, often after a pause for thought. His knowledge is neither unconscious nor refined, but he is not used to passing it on in words. He demonstrates by doing the job, supplementing his example with a few words of commentary. This often takes the form of a story about a craftsman who did not do the job in a certain way, which caused him to make a mistake. One gets the feeling that he has all the answers, and this allows him to disassociate himself from the ill-judged behaviour of the offending craftsman. All this is related in the form of an anecdote.'

Here, Tempte gives an unusually penetrating description of his professional work. Nonetheless, it contains an unacceptable assumption on the nature of knowledge and how it is transferred. Tempte expresses himself from within a tradition which more or less tacitly presupposes that it is possible to express everything in words. At the same time, he describes the master craftsman as 'demonstrating, with a few words of commentary'. This is as far as one can go - providing examples and stimulating practice.

One consequence of the essential operation of following a rule is that special emphasis is placed on practice - learning. Previous experience and problem-solving - so-called sediment - is turned into a process of following rules that form the basis of the practice that we are being taught: 'Is it that rule and empirical proposition merge into one another?' Wittgenstein asks, *On Certainty*, §309, and goes on to say: 'If experience is the ground of our certainty, then naturally it is past experience and it isn't for example just my experience but other people's, that I get knowledge from.', *On Certainty*, §275.

There are many ways of following a rule. In Wittgenstein's view, guessing is of central importance to a rule system and to all forms of learning. Applying a rule is a matter of knowing what to do at the next stage. Guessing is done on the basis of examples we have been presented with and continues until we have the talent to do it correctly.

As we grow more sure - i.e. have met a large number of examples through our experience - our competence increases, and we master a practice.

5 JUDGING LIGHT IN PHOTOGRAPHY

Peter Gullers, a photographer, has reflected upon his professional work and made a penetrating description of the essential aspects of judging light in photography.

'The text of a recent advertisement for cameras said: 'Instructions for taking good pictures - just press the button'. Thanks to new technology we no longer need to know a lot about the technique of photography before we can take good pictures. The manufacturer had built a program into the camera, a program which made all the important decisions and all the assessments needed to produce a satisfactory result.

'New technology had made it easier to take photographs and photography had become very reliable and accurate in most normal conditions. When there is not enough light, the exposure is blocked or a built-in flash is activated to ensure satisfactory results.

'The program cannot be modified and no opinion can be passed on the results until later. The underlying principles are invisible - the process is soundless. Neither does the manufacturer describe how the program makes these assessments. In retrospect, when the picture has been developed, even the uninitiated judge can say that the picture is too dark, too light or blurred. On the other hand the cause of the fault is difficult to establish without a thorough knowledge of technology, or of the conditions under which the photograph was taken.

'There are numerous problem areas and the causes of these problems tend to merge with each other.

'Physiologists claim that the eye is a poor light meter because the pupil automatically adapts to changes in the intensity of light. This may be so. When faced with a concrete situation that I have to assess, I observe a number of different factors that affect the quality of the light and thus the results of my photography. Is it summer or winter, is it morning or evening? Is the sun breaking through a screen of cloud or am I in semi-shadow under a leafy tree? Are parts of the subject in deep shadow and the rest in strong sunlight? Then I have to strike a balance between light and darkness. If I am in a smithy or in a rolling-mill shop, I note how the light coming through the sloping skylights contrasts with the sooty heat of the air in the brick building. The vibrations from hammers and mills make the floor and the camera tremble, which makes photography more difficult and affects the light-metering. The daylight is enhanced by the red glow of the steel billets.

'In the same way I gather impressions from other situations and environments. In a new situation, I recall similar situations and environments that I have encountered earlier. They act as comparisons and as association material and my previous perceptions, mistakes and experiences provide the basis for my judgement.

'It is not only the memories of the actual process of photography that play a part. The hours spent in the darkroom developing the film, my curiosity about the results, the arduous work of recreating reality and the graphic world of the picture are also among my memories. A faulty assessment of the strength of the light and the contrast of the subject, the vibrations and tremors become important experiences to be called upon next time I face a similar situation. All of these earlier memories and experiences that are stored away over the years only partly penetrate my consciousness when I make a judgement on the light conditions. The thumb and index finger of my right hand turn the camera's exposure knob to a setting that 'feels right', while my left hand adjusts the filter ring. This process is almost automatic.

'The problem with automatic computer-aided light metering is that after a long period of use one tends to lose one's ability to judge light conditions. Few people can manage without mechanical or electronic light meters today.

'But it is not simply the ability to judge the light value that is disappearing. Unless one regularly makes a manual judgement of light, one's sensitivity to shades of light tends to become blunted. Our pictorial memories of past experiences are not activated in the same way unless they have been connected with similar assessments. Unless one regularly performs the actual work of producing pictures, the ability to make the best use of composition and light-modifying techniques when printing will wither too.

'The problem with the automatic meter is not only that its program does not consider whether it is day or night, or the nature of the subject, or the inexperience of the user. The most important point is that it denies me access to my memories and blunts my perceptions and my ability to discern shades of light. This intimate knowledge is not linked to what I do when I photograph, i.e. the operations I perform, but to actual memories and experiences when I take photographs and when I develop and print pictures.'

6 TECHNOLOGY AND CULTURE

Guller's example contains a cultural-critical perspective. The type of change in professional competence that Gullers points to, 'the sensitivity to shades of light tending to become blunted' is a phenomenon that takes a long time to occur. It is one of the reasons for calling attention to links with the past. Without a link with the past through epistemology and the history of ideas, a debate on the future of technological development will lack any contact with reality. It will be devoid of content and full of clichés and vague rhetoric such as 'placing the human being in the centre'.

The cultural-critical element is constantly present in Wittgenstein's thinking.

Describing a practice involves adopting a standpoint on the description of a culture. 'A whole culture belongs to a language-game.' A practice is thus at one and the same time both fundamental and relative to the culture and epoch.

In a study carried out by the ILO in Geneva comparing thirteen industrial countries and their experiences of technical change in the 1970s, a common factor emerged, namely the attention given to changes in professional qualifications. When discussing solutions to the problem of changing professional qualifications, it becomes evident that individual cultural and national characteristics become involved. The problem is a common one, but *culture and tradition* become decisive factors in the way different solutions are debated. There are culture-specific characteristics that must be observed when making international comparative studies. Why, for example, are 'isolation' and 'lack of identity' emphasised in West German studies of the use of computers? Has the computer any decisive significance in terms of the occurrence of these phenomena or are they culture-specific and can be discussed separately from the issue of computers?

7 ROUTINE PRACTICE AND DEVELOPMENT PRACTICE

We call an activity that can be described exhaustively in stated rules a *routine practice*. Here the rules are closed; they can be described in a set of essential and sufficient conditions. There is an obvious relationship to a set of rules adapted for computer technology.

An activity that is characterised by *open rules*, meaning that their expression admits of a variety of meanings, we shall call a *development practice*. It is this kind of practice that we are primarily interested in. The rules that form a development practice cannot be entirely expressed in words. As we pointed out earlier, it is essential to have good examples and to learn a practice by training. It is the following of the rules themselves that is the prism in this perspective.

At the same time, it is important to emphasise the intersubjective aspects of following rules in a practice. It is logically impossible to be the only person following a rule. A single practice can therefore not be seen as a logical place for dialogue and shared action.

8 ERROR LOCATION IN A COMPUTER PROGRAM

Per Svensson, who is responsible for developing a computer system for forest valuation, makes the following remarks on error location in a computer program: 'In the routines at the Agricultural Administration for valuing forests using EDP, error location and the correction of input data is one of the most important jobs. Programs have been written that search through input data and report any errors, controlled by given rules that are part of the program. It is impossible to make programs to locate and make a perfectly clear report on every kind of error. The input data varies far too much for this to be a practical possibility. Instead, the users must learn this work through experience. After having worked with this application for a long time, the speed with which most experienced users now locate these errors is incomprehensible to new employees. When asked 'How do you locate this error?', they answer 'I see that it is an error'. One explanation of why experienced users recognise errors when inexperienced users do not discover them is that their experience contains memories from earlier, similar cases, even if one cannot with certainty report when they occurred. This is a form of knowledge that is extremely difficult to document, but which nonetheless exists and works in a practice.

'Attempts have been made to document this particular work operation. The experience gained from these attempts is daunting. The result of the documentation was a very comprehensive catalogue of every imaginable error, how they were reported by the program and what action should be taken on them. For new users, this catalogue was both frightening and of little use, while experienced users worked quicker and more surely if they trusted their own experience and did not use the error location catalogue. Experience cannot always be documented in a usable way.'

This knowledge cannot be taught directly to others, but can be transferred to some people by using analogies and concrete examples. At the same time the individual must strive to win a deeper insight into a practice and become proficient in its use. There are different practices for error location, for example the skills mastered by flight mechanics, and in the medical care sector in professional groups such as physicians and nurses in order to make diagnoses. To be skilled in one of these practices does not mean that one can transfer this ability to another practice. Error location on aeroplanes and error location in a computer program for forest valuation are not interchangeable skills. At this level analogies and examples are not transferrable between different practices. Today, because these different activities use computer technology, there is growing interest in the possibility of moving from one activity to another if one has mastered the technology. It is this perspective that, for example, André Gorz expresses when he claims that less emphasis need be placed upon professional skills and that computer technology skills must be given pride of place. It is important to emphasise the activity-specific aspect of mastering a practice and that analogies and examples must be taken from within a practice. Of course, there may be striking examples that can be used to illustrate a number of different activities. A special talent is needed to formulate and present these good examples. There is a continuity in the mastery of error location in an activity that is accentuated in the conversion from old to new technology.

9 THREE CATEGORIES OF KNOWLEDGE

The exercise of error location involves the application of what we may call *practical knowledge*, knowledge which contains experiences obtained from having been active in a practice. At the same time there is a great deal of knowledge within this practice that we learn by examining the examples we are given by others who have been working within the practice. It is from this aggregate experience that we also build up our competence and learn from first-hand experience. The interaction between people in the same professional group is of decisive importance here. This latter kind of knowledge, knowledge that we acquire from learning a practice by examining the examples of tradition, we can call the *knowledge of familiarity*.

That part of a professional tradition that has been expressed in general traditions, theories, methods and regulations and that we can assimilate from a theoretical study of an activity, we can call *propositional knowledge*. There is a close relationship between propositional knowledge, practical knowledge and the knowledge of familiarity. We interpret theories, methods and regulations through the familiarity and skills we have gained by taking part in a practice. Allan Janik's attention to the inconsistencies in the content of these concepts is of central importance here. The dialogue between the members of a group involved in a practice contains an aspect of friction between different perceptions based on their different experiences - examples in familiarity and practical skills. Being a member of a practice and at the same time acquiring greater competence involves participation in an ongoing dialogue. Being professional implies extending one's perspective towards a broader overview of one's own skills. Being aware of anomalies - failures - is of particular importance in terms of accepting professional responsibility. The historical perspective is a central factor in the knowledge of familiarity. The paradox in this argument is that if we remove all practical knowledge and knowledge of familiarity from activity we will also empty it of propositional knowledge. These are interpretive actions that are crucial to a pragmatic perspective. What can be stored in a computer, processed in algorithms, propositional logic etc., and reported as a result in the form of a printout is raw material that has to be interpreted by the actions of a person qualified in a practice. If attention is focused on the raw material and the action of interpretation disappears, an activity will move towards chaos -

disorder - death, according to the second main law of thermodynamics.

We get a division of the different kinds of knowledge into three categories:

1 Propositional or theoretical knowledge
2 Skills or practical knowledge
3 Knowledge of familiarity

There is a clear tendency to overemphasise theoretical knowledge at the expense of practical knowledge and we tend to completely forget the knowledge of familiarity when discussing the nature of knowledge in a philosophical context. One effect of tending to ignore skills and familiarity when discussing knowledge is that one tends to assume that people who lack theoretical knowledge in given areas also lack any knowledge whatsoever of that area.

10 AN EPISTEMOLOGICAL ERROR

In a postscript to his book, *The Structure of Scientific Revolutions*, which is focused on his rejection of explicit rules and his referral to tacit knowledge for the comprehension of scientific practices, Kuhn says that when he talks about intuitions he is not discussing individual intuitions. Instead, intuitions are the tested and shared possessions of the members of a successful group and the novice acquires them through training as part of his preparation for group membership.

'When I speak of the knowledge embedded in shared exemplars, I am not referring to a mode of knowledge that is less systematic or less analysable than knowledge embedded in rules, laws, or criteria of identification. Instead I have in mind a manner of knowing which is misconstrued if reconstructed in terms of rules that are first abstracted from exemplars and thereafter function in their stead.'

In the introduction to the Encyclopedia of 1751 J.R. d'Alembert wonders how many questions and problems would be avoided if one finally established a clear and exact definition of words. This conception of an exact definition that removes all ambiguity contains the hope that in the definition there would reside a power to make our knowledge clear and explicit.

This perspective on the basis of the theory of knowledge can be used in the construction of designs in computer technology. To adopt a total view to include the use of computers is an epistemological error. The development of the practice of computer usage requires an openness to the paradoxical encounter between different traditions of knowledge during earlier epochs in the history of ideas. This requires a development of interest in the concept of education. Within the framework of the theme of Education-Work-Technology, it is my judgement that this will be a significant factor in the debate on technology, science and culture during the coming ten years.

CONCLUSION

In the autumn of 1985 and the spring of 1986 the Dialogue Seminar was held in cooperation with the Royal Dramatic Theatre, the Council for the Planning and Coordination of Research and The Swedish Working Life Center. Lectures on the following themes were published in four issues of Dialogue magazine

No 1, The world of dialogue
No 2, The inner dialogue
No 3, Dialogue and enlightenment
No 4, The unfinished dialogue.

The Dialogue Seminar investigated the concept of dialogue against the background of the emerging technological culture.

A recently-published Japanese study which reports on experience of almost two decades of transition to the so-called information society, discusses 'shadows in progress'. These experiences are summarised, inter alia, under the generic term 'functional autism'. This is a phenomenon in which people who are regularly exposed to technological environments over a long period experience difficulty in confrontation with reality, particularly in social relationships. They lose their former confidence and begin to feel restricted, as prisoners of monologue, in a calamitous confusion of people and things.

This phenomenon is not a new one. The enthusiasm for technology - what may be logically calculated - was the modernistic manifesto in, among other things, the encyclopedia project in France during the Age of Enlightenment and in Vienna at the turn of the century. These periods saw a simultaneous emergence of interest in that which cannot be directly expressed, but which, by being transformed into artistic form, becomes available to reflected thought. If we are to understand our most fundamental human needs, the artistic form of expression must be taken seriously.

Man must think the thoughts of his period whether he wants to or not. There is limited scope for what is genuinely personal. That is the principal thought of Denis Diderot, the dominant figure of the encyclopedia project. Most people who think are automatons. Originality is extremely rare. Most people are, in all respects, nothing more than copies of each other. In the preface to *Miss Julie*, Strindberg develops the same kind of idea. The weak steal and repeat the words of the strong, and then gather ideas and suggestions from one another. And the word character, which is the middle class expression for automation, implies adaptation to a certain role in life; in a word, ceasing to grow. Here, there is a connection with what the Nordic social researcher Stein Bråten calls model monopoly, which he develops in his book *Dialogens Vilkor i Datasamhället*. Stein Bråten sees competition between different conceptions as a fundamental aspect of dialogue. It provides friction with a complicated reality and can open up what Bråten calls 'the creative horizon'. The shortcoming of Bråten's arguments - and what we have given considerable attention in the Dialogue seminar - is the assumption that everything is susceptible to formulation. The much praised openness is a mentality that grows in a technological culture. The slogan of sincerity is speak frankly! Everything must be arranged, everything must be spelt out, everything must be put into words, everything must be compelled to give utterance, to announce its presence, to deliver a response. Sincerity has become the predominant virtue of our time. It is the monologue - not the dialogue - that is the form of sincerity. Denis Diderot examined the conditions for developing what Stein Bråten calls 'the creative horizon'.

Diderot's *Le Neveu de Rameau* can be interpreted as an inner dialogue on the conditions for creativity. Diderot establishes a distance to the two roles of dialogue. They are The Philosopher and representative of the logical-calculable common sense and Rameau, the vulgar Bohemian at the bottom of society who has an affinity with the deeper layers of sensitivity in his personality. Diderot examines what keeps these two different characters joined. Rameau attacks the Philosopher for retreating from a complex reality into the abstract and personal isolation. The Philospher criticises Rameau for his Salieri characteristics - becoming excited over pantomime pranks, but not being able to exercise any practical skill in his obsession. The conflict is not resolved. The agreement that is reached is that there exists a discord that cannot be bridged. The mastery of *Le Neveu de Rameau* is evinced in the fact that Diderot does not take sides in the struggle between the senses and the intellect, but retains in this play the complexity and the contradiction between different layers of one's own person. It may be possible to find a creative rhythm by maintaining the balance between the controlling common sense and what is complex and contradictory. Diderot wrote *Le Neveu de Rameau* at different periods between 1761 and 1774. In the same period, Rousseau wrote *Emile* (1762) and Voltaire wrote *Candide* (1762). The penetrating impression here is the criticism of the Utopian aspect of the encyclopedia project, the merging of all forms of human knowledge in a logical calculation. Cracks begin to show in the facade of the building. Minerva's owl begins to appear. It is the same 'shadows in development' and approximately the same time perspective in the Japanese project on the so-called information society, the foundations of which are beginning to quake; an information technology programme that is patterned on models taken from all over the world, not least in Sweden. The strength in the Japanese position, as with Diderot, is that one now demonstrates this uncertainty.

AN ANNOTATED BIBLIOGRAPHY

The introductory section on the Age of Enlightenment's paradoxical view of knowledge is a summary of an article by Bo Göranzon, *Artificial Intelligence, or the Dream of the Exact Language*, published in Dialoger magazine, No. 2 1986. The main references for this article are as follows: d'Alembert, *Introduction to the Encyclopedia*; Frängsmyr, T. (1974), *Drömmen om det Exakta Språket*, Vetenskapens Träd, Stockholm; Lindborg, R. (1984), *Maskinen, Människan och doktor La Mettrie*, Doxa.
The concept of rules is a main theme in Wittgenstein's *Philosophy of Language* and*On Certainty* and a manuscript by the Norwegian philosopher Kjell S. Johannesen entitled 'Tyst Kunskap: Om regel och begrepp'. This is to be published as a research report in the spring of 1987 as part of the theme Education-Work-Technology at The Swedish Working Life Center.
   The section 'What is a computer?' summarises the American philosopher Allan Janik's contribution, 'Breaking the ground' in Sundin, Bo (ed) (1980), *Is the Computer a Tool?*, Almquist & Wiksell International. The example of the boat-builder on the west coast is published in Tempte, T. (1981), *Arbetets Ara*, The Swedish Working Life Center. The example of light metering in photography is published in Göranzon, B. (1984),*Datautvecklingens Filosofi*, Carlssons Bokforlag. A research report within the framework of the ILO project compares experience of the use of computers in thirteen industrial countries. The Swedish contribution is published in Göranzon, Bo et al (1982), *Job Design and Automation in Sweden*, The Swedish Working Life Center. The perspective in the section on Technology and Culture is from this study.
The example of error location in a computer program is published in Göranzon, Bo (1983), 'Datorn som Verktyg', Studentlitteratur.
The division of knowledge into three categories is based upon the manuscript by Kjell S. Johannesen mentioned above.
The concluding section, An Epistemological error, contains a reference to the classic study by Kuhn, Thomas (1970), *The Structure of Scientific Revolutions*, The University of Chicago Press, Chicago. The final comment on the importance of the concept of education was inspired by the following, among others: Bergendal, B. (1985), 'Bildningens Villkor', Studentlitteratur; Lindström, L. 'Bildningsbegreppets rötter: det polytekniks bildningsidealet', published in the autumn of 1986, the Education-Work-Technology project at the Swedish Working Life Center; and

Runeby, N. (1978), *Teknikerna, Vetenskapen och Kulturen*, Uppsala. Runeby's study covers the period from 1860 to 1890 and includes a documentation of the restructuring of the educational system in relation to the breakthrough of industrialism. There is a fruitful connection to the current debate on technological change and the demand on the educational system.

AI & Soc (1993) 7:208–224
© 1993 Springer-Verlag London Limited

The Contribution of Tacit Knowledge to Innovation

Jacqueline Senker

Science Policy Research Unit, University of Sussex, Brighton, UK

Abstract: Tacit knowledge is widely acknowledged to be an important component of innovation, but such recognition is rarely accompanied by more detailed explanations about the nature of tacit knowledge, why such knowledge is significant, how it becomes codified or whether there may be limits to codification. This paper attempts to fill some of the gaps, drawing on a recent study of university/industry links in three emerging technologies. It concludes that tacit knowledge, which can only be transmitted through personal interaction, will continue to play an important role in innovation. This derives from a variety of reasons, but most significant are the complexity of systems and the emergence of new technologies.

Key words: Tacit knowledge; Innovation; Automation; Biotechnology; Advanced ceramics; Parallel computing

Introduction

Studies of innovation, technology transfer and technology diffusion identity tacit knowledge as an important component of innovation (e.g. Dosi, 1988; Rosenberg, 1976, 1982). None of these discussions provide a satisfactory definition of tacit knowledge or give a detailed, systematic account of its role in technological innovation. Nor do they provide guidance on how its importance may differ according to the industrial sector or technology being studied or how firms acquire it.

This paper is an attempt to begin to fill some of these gaps. It will discuss the methods developed by firms to capture tacit knowledge of a scientific and technological nature which is generated both within the company and that arising in external sources. It will also identify the company activities where tacit knowledge makes an important contribution to innovation and consider the processes by which tacit knowledge becomes codified.

Much of the material arises from a recent study of university/industry links in three emerging technologies – biotechnology, advanced engineering ceramics and parallel processing – which investigated all the knowledge flows used by companies in the course of innovation (Senker & Faulkner, 1992). Results from this study will be presented after proposing a working definition for tacit knowledge and reviewing literature which provides a context for the findings. This leads to a discussion of the methods by which tacit knowledge becomes codified and the limits to such codification.

Tacit Knowledge

Polanyi (1966) encapsulates the essence of tacit knowledge in the phrase "We know more than we can tell" and provides further clarification in examples such as the ability to recognise faces, ride a bicycle or swim without even the slightest idea of how these things are done. This paper, however, is concerned with the conscious efforts pursued by scientists and technologists to elucidate and/or apply tacit knowledge. I stress *conscious efforts* because the aim of scientific research is to extend constantly theoretical knowledge of the natural world. Technology, too, has a conscious aim – to develop physical devices and equipment to solve specific problems. From this standpoint, Rosenberg's description of traditional technological knowledge, accumulated in crude empirical ways, with no reliance upon science provides a good working definition for tacit scientific and technological knowledge:

...the knowledge of techniques, methods and designs that work in certain ways and with certain consequences, even when one cannot explain exactly why. (Rosenberg, 1982, p. 143).

This heuristic, subjective and internalised knowledge is not easy to communicate and is learned through practical examples, experience and practice. By contrast 'articulated knowledge' is transmittable in formal, systematic language. It has many forms, but is essentially the general scientific principles and laws acknowledged by the scientific community as supplying the foundation for its further practice. These principles and laws, which are written down in great detail in manuals and textbooks and taught to students, are closely related to Kuhn's concept of scientific paradigms: the accepted examples of actual scientific practice, which include law, theory, application and instrumentation which provide models for scientific research (Kuhn, 1970, p. 10). Other articulated knowledge is available in scientific and technical journals, in the technical specifications of materials or operating manuals of commercial process plant and research equipment.

This distinction between tacit and articulated knowledge must, however, be treated with caution. Polanyi has pointed out that:

these two are not sharply divided. While tacit knowledge can be possessed by itself, explicit knowledge must rely on being tacitly understood and applied. Hence all knowledge is *either tacit or rooted in tacit knowledge*. (Polanyi, 1969, p. 144).

Moreover, Winter (1987) has pointed out that it may be possible to teach tacit knowledge which is non-articulable; but the non-articulation of articulable knowledge may be a more severe handicap for the transfer of knowledge than tacitness itself.[1]

There are some fundamental differences between skill and knowledge. Knowledge implies understanding. The acquisition of knowledge is a purely perceptual, cognitive process. Skill implies knowing how to make something happen; it involves cognition,

---

[1] An example of the non-articulation or articulable knowledge is the non-documentation of revisions to a computer programme.

but also other aspects such as manual dexterity or sensory ability. The phrase 'tacit skills' is sometimes used in the literature. This is confusing; in some instances skills may be based entirely on tacit knowledge and in others they may rely entirely on a thorough understanding of the scientific principles involved. In most instances skills draw on a combination of tacit and articulated knowledge. This differentiation between knowledge and skills marks a fundamental disagreement with Nonaka (1992), who suggests that tacit knowledge involves cognitive dimensions (schemata, paradigms, mental models, etc.), as well as a technical dimensions (concrete know-how, crafts and skills which apply to specific contexts). Skills based on appropriate combinations of tacit and formal knowledge in specific contexts might be better defined as 'expertise'.

Although much teaching of science gives the impression that it is a mass of accomplished solid facts, the facts are of many types including techniques of manual or mental manipulation. In order to be able to do scientific research "the scientist must be an accomplished craftsman; he must have undergone a lengthy apprenticeship, learning how to do things without being able to appreciate why they work" (Ravetz, 1971, pp. 14–15). The scientist acquires an enormous variety of skills and tacit knowledge during this apprenticeship including how to assess data and information and methods for manipulating and using tools (e.g. physical apparatus, statistical techniques) including the avoidance of pitfalls involved in their use. Simple precepts may form the basis for some of this learning. but imitation and experience is the only method for acquiring the skills to formulate scientific problems and develop strategies aimed at their solution. A study of the diffusion of knowledge relating to the building of the TEA laser suggests that in new fields little of the corresponding tacit knowledge is learned during scientists' apprenticeships; furthermore, the systematic transfer of the new knowledge has sometimes been impossible, because the originating scientist may have been unaware of all the relevant parameters (Collins, 1974).

With the growth of industrial R&D during the 20th century and the widespread recruitment by firms of qualified scientists and engineers, firms have been enabled to apply scientific knowledge to solve their technical problems. It is important to recognise that the benefits gained by firms from the recruitment of university trained researchers accrue both from the formal scientific knowledge *and* the tacit knowledge and skills acquired during their training.

Technology, however, develops from a variety of sources which go far beyond the application of prior scientific knowledge. Unlike science, where the culture tends to play down the role of tacit knowledge and skills, the tacit dimension of technology is widely recognised by firms. Indeed the acquisition of tacit knowledge to support innovation is a purposive activity of much industrial development, design and testing of prototypes and pilot plant.

The development of technology builds on a long tradition where crude, empirical methods have provided the basis of much technological knowledge acquisition and accumulation, and much productive activity takes place without "a deep scientific knowledge of why things perform the way they do" (Rosenberg, 1982, p. 143). Pavitt (1987) has characterised most technology as "specific, complex, often tacit and cumulative in its development". Its basis may be technological information which is common to firms operating within the same 'technological regime' (Metcalfe and Gibbons, 1989), but individual firms also develop specific knowledge and experience relating to its products and processes. In Hall and Johnson's terminology, firms acquire system-specific technology, which is related to the tasks or projects involved in manufacturing a specific item; other firms manufacturing the same item are likely to obtain the same technology (Hall and Johnson, 1987). This even applies when such knowledge is developed by largely tacit means, as demonstrated by a study of the development of flush riveting in airplanes. Each aircraft company pursued its own innovation programme, because although books and word-of-mouth could provide some of the necessary knowledge, complete mastery required hands-on experience. "All the acquired knowledge in matters of this kind is not susceptible to codification or communication." The separate programmes resulted in widespread, simultaneous innovation throughout the industry (Vincenti, 1990).

Returning to Hall and Johnson's categorisation, firm-specific knowledge differs from system specific knowledge in not being attributable to any specific item the firm produces. Firm-specific knowledge results from the firm's overall activities (Hall, and Johnson, 1970). Firms may formalise or codify some of this knowledge for in-house use, but as it is proprietary knowledge from which firms may gain a competitive advantage, its further dissemination is generally out of the question.

Scientific knowledge, though important, may play only a minor role in innovation. Kline believes that technological knowledge has made a greater contribution to success in commercial markets than scientific knowledge and argues that:

the *content* of science bears on innovation only when it comes to the interface of technological and scientific knowledge. However, this applies to content, to the knowledge in science, and not to scientific methodology. *Both scientific methodology and the scientific view of the world are absolutely essential to all workers on technical problems everywhere.* (Kline, 1990, p. 23)

Development, design and production engineering usually make the largest contribution to innovation, as does the knowledge accumulated during the production process and from customer feedback (Pavitt, 1987; von Hippel, 1988). The importance of this knowledge is recognised in the chain linked model of innovation, which incorporates information links and feedback loops between market-findings, design, production, distribution and research (Kline, 1990). In Imai's discussion of the Japanese innovation system we get further hints as to which of these links may incorporate tacit knowledge and skills. He suggests that personal interaction is a necessity for information exchange between design, test, redesign, production and distribution and that such interactions have to be quick and dense. On the one hand, such interaction copes with the unexpected situations which frequently crop up during the innovation process; on the other, it facilitates cooperative learning for designers, production managers, marketers and machine suppliers. With regard to links with production, personal information exchange is vitally important to the upstream stage of key component and device manufacturing. Interaction, however, has little utility for final component assembly, the downstream stage, which uses traditional manufacturing.

Imai makes a similar distinction between linkages with technical knowledge, which require personal interaction and those with research, which do not. These linkages may be invoked to solve problems which crop up in the course of innovation, with recourse to research only in the event that accumulated technical knowledge fails to produce a solution. Accumulated technical knowledge may be stored in the form of a patent or as documented know-how. More often, relevant information exists randomly in society as tacit knowledge and relates to the context of a specific problem. Access is mainly through social networks, or 'know-who'. In contrast, the theoretical language used by researchers and their links through the 'Invisible College'[2] does not require personal interaction, but enables rapid exchange of information through media, such as email or fax (Imai, 1991). This view is shared by Sørensen and Levold who suggest that:

while the set-up and carrying out of an experiment may be demanding in terms of locally acquired, tacit skills, the application of the results is affected by tacit skills that are common to a much larger group of scientists. (Sørensen and Levold, 1992, p. 10)

However, following Collins, it appears that skills based on tacit knowledge are likely to be held by large groups of scientists only in relation to established areas of knowledge.

This section suggests that both scientific and technological inputs to innovation embody a considerable tacit component which can only be acquired by practical experience. Indeed, tacit knowledge and skills are particularly significant to scientific methodology and the scientific view of the world, as discussed earlier. Dependence on know-how, "a kind of knowledge which cannot be wholly formalized, nor transmitted solely through written documents" (Madeuf, 1984, p. 127), explains the impossibility of codifying technological knowledge in the form of patents, blueprints or operating manuals. The importance of know-how explains why contracts for technology transfer seldom deal exclusively with patents or intellectual property rights; and why technology payments for agreements which do not involve patents outweigh payments for those involving patents (Madeuf, 1984).

Why is Tacit Knowledge Important?

How can the persistence of tacit knowledge in innovation be explained alongside the 20th century's constantly expanding stock of scientific knowledge and growth of industrial R&D? Part of the explanation lies in the fact that industrial sectors (Pavitt, 1984) and technological regimes are embedded in very different traditions of technological change:

[Technological] Regimes differ according to the proportion of knowledge which is discovered by scientific or empirical means; they differ in the division of knowledge between codifiable, publicly available, and tacit firm, specific forms; and, they differ according to their dependence on other knowledge bases that are generated outside the industry (Metcalfe and Gibbons, 1989, p. 164).

Moreover, the direction of technological change within technological regimes is largely defined by the technology already in use. When innovations have been developed successfully on the basis of tacit, firm-specific knowledge about how to make devices work, or on the observation of empirical regularities, there is no reason for companies to change their established practices. Their aim is to improve existing technology through minor improvements based on learning-by-doing and learning-

---

[2] Imai does not use the term 'Invisible College' but this is what his discussion implies.

by-using, not to understand the nature of any problems arising. Change to established practices is only likely to occur when one firm within a technological regime gains competitive advantage through the application of scientific knowledge. Firms lacking qualified scientists and engineers on their staff, however, have restricted ability to apply such knowledge (Gibbons and Johnston, 1974).

This leads to a second reason for the continuing importance of tacit knowledge and skills. Firms or sectors lacking relevant scientific knowledge perforce depend on tacit knowledge to solve any technical problems arising. Although industrial R&D has grown rapidly during the past century, there are still many traditional sectors in the UK, such as construction, where in-house R&D is at best weak, but for the most part a rarity (Gann et al. 1992). These sectors have been characterised by Pavitt as *supplier-dominated* firms and they make only a minor contribution to their product or process technology. Most innovations derive from their suppliers of equipment or materials (Pavitt, 1984).

In some other sectors, for instance food manufacture, some of the large manufacturers involved in processing food raw materials into a state for further manufacture (e.g. flour milling or sugar refining) fit into Pavitt's categorisation of *scale-intensive* firms. Innovative large-scale producers in this sector produce a high proportion of their own process technology. However, the majority of food manufacturers are involved in the manufacture of highly processed convenience foods. These firms generally conduct little in-house R&D and are similar to *supplier-dominated* firms:

the technical potential of the food processing industry has hardly yet been exploited... The food industry struggles with the fact that the raw materials which are fed into the plant in its factories are variable, ill-defined, complex, highly sensitive to temperature, pressure, shear. oxidation/reduction, pH, and to one another, in a way that is true of few, if any, other industries...

...the food industry had to rely heavily on people with craft experience. (Edelman, 1982, p. 482)

Edelman is wrong, however, to assume that other sectors do not have to face such a high degree of complexity. Indeed the application of tacit knowledge and skills to innovation, even in companies which employ large numbers of scientists and engineers, derives to a major extent from the complexity of systems, impossible to model in a laboratory. Kline has discussed the difficulty for the physical sciences and engineering of analysing systems with even a moderate degree of complexity. He suggests that many powerful tricks have been evolved for reducing complexity in order to make analyses simpler, or even possible. Consequently he believes that there are few predictive paradigms of any reliability for complete systems, though they may exist for parts of systems. He suggests that innovation can only be created through 'observing the system, creating perturbations, and then observing what happens. That is, we control and improve such systems by open-loop feedback processes using human intelligence in a learning-by-doing mode' (Kline, 1990).

Thus, continuing dependence on tacit knowledge and skills for innovation arises from adherence to previous successful practice, from the lack or scientific or technological expertise within specific firms or sectors and, possibly most commonly, from the complexity of systems. Vicenti's (1990) observation that uncertainty diminishes as a technology becomes older suggests a fourth category where tacit knowledge is of importance. That is in the emergence of new technologies.

Tacit Knowledge in Emerging Technologies

A recent study showed that tacit knowledge is integral to innovation in emerging technologies; it sought to compare industrial linkage with public sector research (PSR) in three areas of advanced technology – biotechnology (in large pharmaceutical companies), advanced engineering ceramics and parallel processing (Senker and Faulkner, 1992). During an extensive interviewing programme, industrial researchers were asked to spell out, in as much detail as possible, the specific knowledge which they routinely utilised in the course of innovation. They were prompted to supply such information in terms of the detailed categories shown in Table 1, and, for each category, asked to identify whether such knowledge was formal and codified, or tacit in nature. They were then asked to identify the source of such knowledge – did it derive from in-house activities, from other companies or from PSR? The overall results to these questions are summarised in Table 2.

There was considerable similarity between technologies in regard to knowledge of particular fields and skills, both of which are drawn on heavily during new product development. Knowledge of particular fields is largely formal and codified and acquired during education and through reading the literature. As far as companies are concerned, formal qualifications are also evidence of researchers' tacit ability to acquire and use knowledge in a meaningful way. This attitude of mind, or Kline's "scientific view of the world", is a most important contribution to new product development. All the researchers reported that while Knowledge of particular fields is necessary for innovation, it is inadequate by itself. They also rely heavily on the skills, the learning-by-doing which takes place largely 'on the job'.

Table 1. Categories of knowledge inputs to innovation

Knowledge of particular fields	Scientific theory, engineering principles, properties etc.
Technical information	Specifications and operating performance or products, components or materials
Skills	Specific skills, e.g., programming, hardware design Research or production competence
Artefacts	Process plant Research instrumentation

Table 2. Type and sources of Scientific and Technological Inputs (STI) to innovation

Type of STI	Internal			Other companies			PSR		
	BIO	CER	PP	BIO	CER	PP	BIO	CER	PP
Knowledge of particular fields							Formal	Formal	Formal
Technical product information				Formal	Formal Some tacit	Formal Some tacit	Formal		Formal and tacit
Expertise and competence	Tacit	Tacit	Tacit						Tacit
Equipment a) Production		Tacit							
b) Research	Tacit	Tacit	Tacit	Tacit	Tacit	Formal & tacit		Tacit	Tacit

The general importance of tacit knowledge to skills is emphasized by reports of many of the researchers that most of the underlying knowledge has not yet been published or documented anywhere. Many companies are concerned to 'capture' such knowledge so that competence can be passed on to other employees. Some companies have a policy for researchers to document anything new they learn; others do not believe this possible. For instance, one had encountered major problems when trying to document a quality control programme for one of its customers.

The researchers perceive that the tacit knowledge and skills which they acquire in-house supplement and build on the formal knowledge derived from their education. It is interesting to note that in addition to absorbing formal knowledge during their scientific training, these researchers had also absorbed an attitude which failed to recognise the tacit knowledge and skills acquired at the same time. Accordingly they report that they rely heavily on the formal knowledge base at the beginning of their careers, because that is all they have, but that the expertise which they develop over time through carrying out research becomes increasingly important. Indeed, sometimes researchers forget the extent to which their work relies on formal knowledge, and one of those interviewed remarked:

I didn't realise until I began tutoring for the Open University... how much of what I learned at university is still relevant as background. I tend to take it for granted while, unknowingly, using that formal knowledge all the time.

The complementarity of the two forms of knowledge was highlighted by the experiences of two of those interviewed. The first had joined an aerospace company at school-leaving age; he subsequently took a company-funded Mechanical Engineering degree, but a further ten years had elapsed before he was a fully qualified designer. The required expertise could only be acquired by 'learning-by-doing' alongside others involved in the same task. Design rules have been codified by the company in a series of volumes, but the application of the rules and the knowledge of doing the job can only be acquired by long experience. The second researcher had also joined her company straight from school and worked as a technician for three years, before taking a degree. On the one hand the expertise she had acquired as a technician gave her an enormous advantage over other students during practicals; on the other, the formal knowledge learnt during her degree work gave her much enhanced ability subsequently with relation to company research. She gained the ability to analyse the results obtained from research, and to review and understand what had been done and why.

Turning now to technical information and artefacts, there is a difference between the three technologies in the extent to which they are used in the course of innovation, though it is not clear to what extent such differences are related to any variance between scientific and engineering applications of knowledge. Technical Information is mainly derived from other companies, and makes a significant contribution to new product development in ceramics and parallel computing. Ceramics processors and users rely heavily on materials specifications, but pointed out that it is impossible for some aspects of such specifications to be documented. This difficulty is overcome by tacit knowledge transfer from their suppliers, with whom it is therefore necessary to maintain a close relationship. Firms in parallel computing also utilise a great deal of technical information during the course of innovation. Much of this information is available in manuals or the scientific literature, for instance, in relation to components obtained from suppliers, emerging standards or architecture performance of competitive products. Here, too, companies rely heavily on tacit information which they obtain through informal interaction with users, suppliers and competitors.

Researchers involved in biotechnology could think of a few instances only where technical information makes a contribution to their work. The only example given was catalogues of companies which market molecular biology materials and give guidance on the availability and suitability of, for instance, different strains of micro-organisms or vectors.

The divergence between technologies in relation to knowledge inputs was greatest in artefacts, both in relation to the type of artefacts which were important and the source of the largely tacit information which is used. Knowledge relating to process plant makes a vital knowledge input in ceramics, unlike biotechnology or parallel computing where it has no relevance. Indeed, most parallel computing companies contract out product assembly. Ceramics processors stressed the important contribution made by tacit, in-house knowledge of process plant, much of which they design and build themselves. Their main interest is directed towards improving their processes. Process plant information is also relevant to ceramics end-users, who seek knowledge about how specific processes affect ceramics characteristics. This difference between technologies in relation to process plant appears to validate Imai's suggestion that research has little utility for interaction with traditional manufacturing, where the process is in a definite and final form and unlikely to change.

Ceramics companies also utilise knowledge inputs relating to research equipment, and those with central research laboratories may have some relevant equipment and expertise in-house. In using this equipment, they rely on their tacit knowledge about the capability of specific techniques to measure the characteristics they are attempting to capture. However, few laboratories are big enough to do everything themselves, and many small companies do not have research facilities. This explains the general tendency to contract out testing to the public sector. In so doing, company researchers not only gain access to specific pieces of instrumentation, but also to the experts with the necessary tacit knowledge to understand the results. Such interpretation provides the bulk of the information they seek and as one researcher said,

The interpretation of the results is [difficult] – it is an art in its own right and if you do not understand it properly, you can miss a lot of things out.

In biotechnology, research equipment and materials are described as a necessity, but most researchers tend to have little awareness of the use they make of knowledge inputs from this source. They have extremely well equipped laboratories, however. which suggests that the knowledge inputs from this source are taken for granted. External sources make a minor contribution to knowledge in this area, with PSR being used for training researchers in new research skills and techniques; representatives of research instruments companies also provide a useful source of tacit knowledge about machines and methodologies appropriate for specific applications.

Parallel computing, unlike ceramics and biotechnology, makes no use of PSR instrumentation. This reflects the fact that the parallel computers are the main instruments used in the development of new parallel computers. Companies use their own machines for testing, modelling and simulation work necessary to the development of new products. They also use work stations and some test and measurement equipment from other suppliers.

Industrial researchers were also asked to identify the general channels used to tap the knowledge which derived from PSR. There is a divergence between the three technologies in terms of the overall relative use of publications and personal contacts. In biotechnology, the literature is more important than personal contacts; in ceramics, contacts are marginally more important than the literature; and in parallel computing, all·researchers rely far more on contacts than on publications. It may be that in biotechnology, unlike ceramics, not only is more research being carried out in PSR, but also that much of the emerging knowledge has been codified during the last decade. Industrial researchers in parallel computing found that the literature was of little practical value because it was either too abstract or tangential to their interests

Researchers also revealed that the literature and contacts provide distinctly different types of input and are frequently used in parallel with each other. For instance, the literature is scanned to identify new developments or identify researchers with specific expertise. The limitations of the codified knowledge contained in the literature means that reading is often followed by making personal contact with the author. Personal contact is used to gain supporting information of a tacit nature – further clarification about the techniques used or an interpretation of the material contained in the literature. Informed judgement may also be sought from other personal contacts who have expertise in the field and can give an informed judgement on the relevance or significance of a specific paper. Social networks or Imai's 'know-who' are also used when researchers have a problem which they or their immediate colleagues are unable to solve. Personal contacts will often point them towards relevant published literature or experts who can solve their problem. However, the results of the study show that Imai and Sørensen and Levold are wrong to assume that the theoretical language used by researchers avoids the need for personal interaction. Theoretical language is only capable of transmitting partial information, and the application of that information also requires personal interaction for the transmission of relevant tacit knowledge and skills. This may be particularly important in relation to new technologies, but some of those interviewed said that colleagues working in established technologies also had close contact with PSR. The study therefore suggests that an important factor influencing the need for interaction is the dynamism of a particular field, or the rate at which new knowledge and techniques are emerging.

In addition to the divergence between technologies in relation to knowledge inputs and channels for seeking knowledge from PSR, the study also revealed differing recruitment strategies for research staff. The companies involved in biotechnology had strategies to recruit career scientists with PhDs and post-doctoral research experience abroad. Ceramics and parallel computing companies recruit graduates and post-graduates, but their preference is for researchers with previous industrial experience.

A partial explanation for these differing recruitment strategies is suggested by the type of tacit knowledge which companies seek to exploit in each technology which, in its turn, is affected by the type of innovation process pursued. Whereas ceramics and parallel computing firms approximate to the chain-linked model of innovation, with research closely linked with and affected by feedback from design, production and customers, pharmaceutical companies are closer to the classic linear model. New product development is strongly knowledge-led, and research is comparatively remote from the user and production. It follows that much relevant tacit knowledge in ceramics and parallel computing is developed in industry, both in-house and other companies, which explains the attraction of recruits with industrial experience.

Recruitment policy for biotechnology has to be considered in the context of intensified global competition among pharmaceutical companies. The application of biotechnology is a necessity for firms which wish to stay competitive, because it provides the potential to speed up the drug discovery process (Sapienza, 1989). Substantial worldwide support for public sector research has led to a rapid expansion of scientific knowledge along a broad front but specific expertise in many areas, for instance receptorology, is scarce. The recruitment of researchers with foreign post-doctoral experience is explained by the need to gain relevant, scarce tacit knowledge, skills and techniques associated with rapid advances in underpinning knowledge. A study in the mid 1980s found that companies needed to access scarce genetic engineering skills (Faulkner, 1986). By 1990, however, these techniques were included routinely in undergraduate courses. This observation raises a question about the process by which tacit skills and knowledge become codified.

The Codification of Tacit Knowledge

Insight into the processes by which tacit knowledge becomes codified is provided by various innovation studies, which suggest there are three main routes to codification:

1. Science push – the expansion of the public knowledge base provides the theoretical underpinning for procedures which had previously relied on tacit knowledge.

2. Technology pull – the exploration by scientists of the phenomena and problems arising in industrial products and processes and/or the practical methods developed in industry to solve problems. This research can receive Government and/or industrial support and take place in industry or PSR.

3. The introduction of automation.

While recognising that patenting also embodies a considerable codification of tacit knowledge, it is excluded from this discussion because, by its very nature, such codification represents the minimum required for legal purposes; it cannot easily be reproduced by others without access to associated 'know-how'.

The following examples show that codification of knowledge does indeed increase as a technology matures, but there are also limits to the codification of tacit knowledge. Codification arising from the science push model may be the result of strategic research specifically aimed at filling identified gaps in knowledge; it can equally well arise from blue-sky research which sets out with no strategic objective save increasing understanding. It may also be the result of investigating unforeseen but interesting occurrences which crop up during the course of research.

The rise of biotechnology is a prime example of the science-push model. The elucidation of the structure of DNA in 1953 by Crick and Watson laid the groundwork for a plethora of molecular biology studies aimed at understanding the fundamental mechanisms of biological structures. Research proliferated, especially in the US, where there was massive Federal support for this work from the National Institute of Health as well as from various medical charities. By the late 1970s, 11% of all Federally funded R&D was directed toward basic biomedical research, and the number of basic researchers such as molecular biologists, immunologists and biochemists also increased rapidly (Teitelman, 1989). The results of their research, from the late 1950s onwards, defined the basic syntax of genetic grammar, the coded information which determines the beginning and end of specific gene sequences and their functions. By the mid 1970s it had also developed a range of tools to genetically engineer the materials which make up living organisms, for instance restriction enzymes which cut lengths of DNA and ligands to recombine them. The growth of small firms from the late 1970s, which were first to exploit the potential of biotechnology, and the later adoption of biotechnology by large firms was made possible by the wealth of codified knowledge which arose from over twenty years' basic research. Excitement about the potential of biotechnology has subsequently generated worldwide support for biotechnology research, with continued rapid advances in scientific knowledge and codification.

This suggests that the science-push model operates most effectively at codifying knowledge when it is supported by significant funds for research. It should be pointed out that advances in knowledge in molecular biology and genetic engineering, funded as they were by the biomedical research establishment, concentrated on increasing understanding of animal cells based on bacterial models. By comparison, plant breeding, botany and agronomy were relatively unaffected by these advances (Kenney, 1986), and in contrast to advances in the application of biotechnology to pharmaceutical research, applications in relation to plants have been relatively slow. Emphasis has been placed on applying biotechnology to vegetables, because they are the easiest crops into which to transfer DNA; but these techniques do not necessarily work with other plant species. The techniques used to transfer DNA fragments to plants can be characterised as taking a shot-gun, 'learning-by-doing' approach, rather than the precise techniques developed for engineering specific fragments of DNA into precise locations in animal cells. Furthermore, progress to date has been made in transferring simple traits carried by a single gene only.

Many other important traits... are not well understood genetically or biochemically. Manipulating these traits requires a long-term investment in fundamental plant metabolism research in order to understand the molecular basis of these traits. (US Congress, 1991, p. 111)

There is also a general lack of codified knowledge on how to grow a whole plant through tissue culture, with a particular neglect of woody plants. Many small UK companies are involved in plant tissue culture, but each works on a different 'easy-to-propagate' species where, through experience, it has developed a great deal of expertise. These small companies lack the cohesion or financial muscle to persuade the scientific community to carry out relevant work on their behalf (Senker, 1991).

However, there are many instances where Government and/or company intervention has stimulated the codification of knowledge, in the technology-pull model. This is well demonstrated by the history of semiconductor electronics. For instance, engineers investigating the cause of short circuits in electronic equipment in the late 1940s, discovered the cause to be strong but flexible filamentary growths – so-called whisker crystals. The discovery provoked an extensive research programme into these whisker crystals, and eventually provided an understanding of the fundamental science of crystal growth. This was subsequently to prove of great value to the electronics industry.

Solid-state physics was barely on the curriculum of most universities before the discovery of the transistor in 1948. Its discovery took place in Bell Laboratories, in a small research group led by William Shockley. Because it was impossible for the Bell Laboratories to recruit people with knowledge of solid state physics, Shockley was persuaded to run in-house courses for laboratory personnel; the material used in this course was published as a book, *Electrons and Holes in Semiconductor*, in 1950. Two years later he also ran an in-house course for 30 university professors, in an attempt to encourage the establishment of university courses in transistor physics (Golding, 1971). At about the same time, Bell Laboratories, partly to contain danger from an anti-monopoly lobby, "embarked on a policy of public divulgation of its transistor knowledge... By publishing, holding seminars and licensing widely" (Braun and MacDonald, 1978). Subsequent innovations and growth of the industry were stimulated by substantial government funding, particularly military funding, for development work in industry. One estimate suggests defence customers paid for nearly half of all semiconductor research and development in the US from the late 1950s to the early 1970s (Flamm, 1988).

Automation has also been a powerful force driving the codification of tacit knowledge. It has a long history including Jacquard's automatic loom which dates back to the early years of the nineteenth century, and the player-piano. A variety of motives can explain growing interest in the automation of machines tools since World War II, including the desire for raised quality, accuracy and consistency; increased machine utilisation, productivity and control over the work force; and overcoming shortages of skilled labour. The transformation of a general purpose machine-tool into a special-purpose machine through the use of variable programs involves two separate processes: developing the equipment to read instructions and control the machine; and getting the instructions recorded in the first place. Two approaches were adopted for codifying machine tool instructions. The first, 'record playback', developed by General Electric, was based on reproducing the accumulated manual skills of the experienced metalworker and involved:

...having a machinist make a part while the motions of the machine under his command were recorded on magnetic tape. After the first piece was made, identical parts could be made automatically by replaying the tape and reproducing the machine motions. (Noble, 1979, p. 22)

Numerical control (NC), the approach ultimately widely adopted, and largely developed at MIT, depended on codification – on breaking down the specifications for a part contained in an engineering blueprint into:

A mathematical representation of the part, then into a mathematical description of the desired path of the cutting tool along up to five axes, and finally into hundreds of thousands of discrete instructions, translated for economy into a numerical code which is read and translated into electrical signals for the machine controls. (Noble, 1979, p. 23)

Nevertheless, in many cases, the effective use of NC machine tools continues to require the intervention of skilled operators to make tool adjustments, correct for tool wear and rough castings, and to correct programming errors and machine malfunctions (Noble, 1979, p. 41). In short, there are limits to the codification of tacit knowledge.

Limits to codification are exposed by attempts to produce general solutions to automation as shown by the history of the development of industrial robots. The original vision for this technology was the production of a universal replacement for human labour. In the event, families of different special-purpose robots have emerged, adapted to the needs of specific users and specific applications. Moreover, the successful implementation of robots depends on "detailed and specific knowledge about the particular situation in which it is proposed to introduce a robot, and about the technology itself" (Fleck, 1983, p. 67); besides being widely distributed throughout an organisation, much of this knowledge is tacit and uncodified. Despite these difficulties, a body of knowledge in robotics is gradually being built up by the systematisation of rules of thumb and other techniques and methods discovered through experience. This same process is also eroding gradually barriers to codification, when knowledge is advanced in the course of academic research designed to discover the underlying cause of problems experienced in the industrial use of robots (Fleck, undated). Thus codification can be an iterative process, with the development of artefacts, and observation of empirical results and problems feeding back to academic research; in time, the results of research become part of the formal knowledge system, and may be incorporated in the artefacts themselves. Developments in robotics exemplify this process; while early robots were based on the 'record-playback' principle, modern robots incorporate radical developments in software and control.

Expert systems are similar to early robots in systematising the tacit, uncodifiable knowledge of experts into sets of rules. Indeed it has been argued that in relation to computer control systems,

Only a minority of computer programs rest on mathematical control theory and on firmly established physical theories. Such programs include those that control petroleum refining plants, navigate spaceships and monitor and largely control the environments in which astronauts work. (Senker, Buckingham and Townsend, 1989)

Fleck has suggested that "the artefactual crystallisation of the non-technical is easiest where contingencies of the application domain are closely controlled and stabilised, with functions tightly circumscribed. These provisos also extend to areas where purely intellectual or mental skills are concerned" (Fleck, undated). This view is very similar to that of Kline discussed above, that the complexity of systems poses limits to the codification of knowledge. However, over time, interaction between industrial and commercial attempts to develop and use expert systems and academic research into problems arising may begin to produce a formal knowledge base for this complex area.

Conclusions

This paper suggests that scientific and technological tacit knowledge differs from general tacit knowledge in terms of the conscious and purposive efforts made to develop and apply it. Moreover, both scientific and technological inputs to innovation embody a considerable tacit component which can only be acquired by practical experience. To cope with a lack of clarity in the literature, tacit knowledge is differentiated from skills, and it is suggested that the combination of tacit knowledge and skills appropriate to a specific context might be better described as expertise. Despite rapid increases in the stock of codified scientific knowledge and growth of industrial R&D, innovation continues to rely on tacit knowledge and skills. This has various causes including adherence to previous successful practice, the lack of scientific or technological expertise within specific firms or sectors and, possibly most commonly, to the complexity of systems.

Two other causes have been identified by the case studies: the first is the emergence of new technologies, although the specific contribution and source of tacit knowledge varies between technologies. However, there are also similarities, notably the importance of the skills and experience built up in-house by company scientists and engineers over time. Secondly, dynamism in the knowledge base of established technologies may demand that researchers interact with the sources of new knowledge in order to acquire any associated tacit knowledge, skills and techniques.

Tacit knowledge arises in a variety of sources – in-house, in other companies and PSR, and transmission of this knowledge between sites ideally requires personal interaction. This explains the importance of what Imai has called "overlapping" in the chain-linked model of innovation. The largely unrecognised component of tacit knowledge in scientific advance may explain a great deal of interaction between companies and PSR. Informal personal contacts with PSR not only provide companies with opportunities to learn new experimental skills or get expert interpretations of test results from advanced scientific instruments, they also keep companies abreast of new developments or ideas, and provide value judgements about their relevance or significance.

Overlapping has another very important function; it contributes to the codification of tacit knowledge. While recognising that most codification of knowledge occurs in PSR, it is significant that iterative overlapping between firms' tacit artefactual solutions to technological problems, and PSR research based on observation of the problems arising during the use of these artefacts may be a significant arena for codifying tacit knowledge.

Acknowledgements

This paper was first presented at the PICT 'Exploring Expertise' Conference at the University of Edinburgh in November 1992. The author would like to acknowledge the financial support of the ESRC both through the Designated Research Centre on Science, Technology and Energy Policy at the Science Policy Research Unit, which enabled this paper to be written; and for the project entitled 'Public-private research linkages in advanced technologies' (ESRC award number Y 306 25 3001) conducted under the Science Policy Support Group/ESRC programme *Public Science and Commercial Enterprise* from which the empirical results derive.

References

Braun, E. and MacDonald, S. (1978), *Revolution in Miniature*, Cambridge University Press, Cambridge.
Collins, H.M. (1974) "The TEA Set: Tacit Knowledge and Scientific Networks", *Science Studies*, **4**, pp. 165–86.
Dosi, G. (1988) "The nature of the innovative process". In G. Dosi, C. Freeman, R. Nelson, G. Silverberg and L. Soete (Eds) *Technical Change and Economic Theory*, Pinter Publishers, London.

Edelman, J. (1982) "Food Chemistry and Cuisine", Chemistry and Industry, 17 July, pp. 481–483.

Faulkner, W. (1986) *Linkage between Industrial and Academic Research: The Case of Biotechnological Research in the Pharmaceutical Industry*, DPhil Thesis, Brighton: Science Policy Research Unit, University of Sussex.

Flamm, K. (1988) *Creating the Computer*, The Brookings Institution, Washington.

Fleck, J. (undated) "Configurations: Crystallising Contingency", paper prepared for special issue of the *International Journal of Human Factors in Manufacturing* on Systems, Networks and Configurations: Inside the Implementation Process.

Fleck, J. (1983) "The Effective Utilisation of Robots: The Management of Expertise and Know-how", *Proc. 6th British Robot Association Annual Conference*, IFS Publications Ltd, Bedford.

Gann, D., Matthews, M., Patel, P. and Simmonds, P. (1992) *Analysis of Private and Public Sector Funding of Research and Development in the Construction Sector*, IPRA, Brighton.

Gibbons, M. and Johnston, R. (1974) "The Roles of Science in Technological Innovation" *Research Policy*, 3, pp. 220–242.

Golding, A. (1971) *The Semiconductor Industry in Britain and the United States. A Case Study in Innovation, Growth and the Diffusion of Technology*. DPhil Thesis, University of Sussex.

Hall, G.R. and Johnston, R.E. (1970) "Transfer of United States Aerospace Technology to Japan". In R. Vernon (Ed) *The Technology Factor in International Trade*. National Bureau of Economic Research, New York.

Imai, K. (1991) *Globalization and Cross-border Networks of Japanese Firms*, Paper presented to Japan in a Global Economy Conference, Stockholm School of Economics, 5–6 September.

Kenney, M. (1986) *Biotechnology: the University-Industrial Complex*. Yale University Press, New Haven and London.

Kline, S.J. (1990) *Innovation Styles in Japan and the United States: Cultural Bases; Implications for Competitiveness*, The 1989 Thurston Lecture, Report INN-3, Dept. of Mechanical Engineering, Stanford University, Stanford.

Kline, S.J. (1990) *Models of Innovation and Their Policy Consequences*. Paper presented at NISTEP International Conference on Science and Technology Policy Research – What Should be Done? What Can be Done? Tokyo.

Kuhn, T.S. (1970) *The Structure of Scientific Revolutions*, 2nd Ed. University of Chicago Press, Chicago.

Madeuf, B. (1984) "International technology transfers and international technology payments: Definitions, measurements and firms' behaviour" *Research Policy*, 13, pp. 125–140.

Metcalfe, J. and Gibbons, M. (1989) "Technology, Variety and Organisation" In R. Rosenbloom and R. Burgelman (Eds) *Research on Technological Innovation, Management and Policy*, 4, pp. 153–193.

Noble, D.F. (1979) "Social Choice in Machine Design: The Case of Automatically Controlled Machine Tools" In A. Zimbalist (Ed) *Case Studies on the Labor Process*. Monthly Review Press, New York and London.

Nonaka, I. (1992) "Managing Innovation as an Organizational Knowledge Creation Process." Paper prepared for *(Tricontinental) Handbook of Technology Management*, Institute of Business Research, Hitotsubashi University, Tokyo.

Pavitt, K. (1987) "The objectives of technology policy." *Science and Public Policy*, 14(4), pp. 182–188.

Pavitt, K. (1984) "Sectoral Patterns of Technical Change: Towards a Taxonomy and a Theory. *Research Policy*, 13, pp. 343–373.

Polyani, M. (1969) "The Logic of Tacit Inference". *Knowing and Being*, Routledge & Kegan Paul, London.

Polyani, M. (1966) *The Tacit Dimension*, Routledge & Kegan Paul, London.

Ravetz, J.R. (1971) *Scientific Knowledge and its Social Problems*, Clarendon Press, Oxford.

Rosenberg, N. (1982) "How exogenous is science?" *Inside the black box. Technology and Economics*, Cambridge University Press, Cambridge.

Rosenberg, N. (1976) *Perspectives on Technology*. Cambridge University Press, Cambridge.

Sapienza, A. (1989) "Collaboration as a Global Competitive Tactic". *R&D Management*, 19(4), pp. 285–295.

Senker, J. and Faulkner, W. (1992) "Industrial use of public sector research in advanced technologies: a comparison of biotechnology and ceramics". *R&D Management*, 22(2), pp. 157–175.

Senker, J. (1991) *The Biotechnology Directorate's Programmes for Technology Transfer in Relation to Small and Medium Sized Firms*. Science Policy Research Unit, University of Sussex, Brighton.

Senker, P., Buckingham, J. and Townsend, J. (1989) "Some Implications of Expert Systems for Work: In T. Bernold and U. Hillenkamp (Eds) *Expert Systems in Production and Services II*, Elsevier, Amsterdam, pp. 249–269.

Sørenson, K.H. and Levold, N. (1992) "Tacit Networks, Heterogenous Engineers and Embodied Technology" *Science, Technology, and Human Values*, 17(1), pp. 13–35.

Teitelman, R. (1989) *Gene Dreams*. Basic Books Inc., New York.
US Congress, Office of Technology Assessment (1991) *Biotechnology in a Global Economy*. Washington,
    DC: US Government Printing Office, p. 111.
Vicenti, W. (1990) *What Engineers Know and How They Know It, Analytical Studies from Aeronautical
    History*. The Johns Hopkins University Press Baltimore and London.
von Hippel, E. (1988) *The Sources of Innovation*. Cambridge University Press, Cambridge.
Winter, S. (1987) "Knowledge and Competence as Strategic Assets". In D. Teece (Ed) *The Competitive
    Challenge. Strategies for Industrial Innovation and Renewal*. Ballinger, Cambridge, Mass. pp 159–183.

Correspondence and offprint requests to: Jacqueline Senker, Science Policy Research Unit, University of
Sussex, Brighton, UK.

AI & SOCIETY, VOL. 1,115 -126 (1987)

THE NURSE AS AN ENGINEER
The theory of knowledge in research in the care sector

Ingela Josefson
The Swedish Working Life Centre, Stockholm, Sweden

ABSTRACT

The nature of nursing has been the subject of discussion for the last 10-15 years. One reason is that in many countries the education of nurses has moved from teaching hospitals to the academies. This move has given rise to the question of the scientific basis for nursing knowledge.

Lately, the content of nursing knowledge has become a principal focus in the work on developing expert systems for nursing. Thus theories of knowledge and the nature of new technology are of great concern to the future of the nursing profession. The basic assumptions underlying a chosen theory of knowledge will determine the development and use of advanced technology in the future.

KEYWORDS

nursing science, expert system, propositional knowledge, knowledge of familiarity

1 INTRODUCTION

This paper explores two theories of knowledge, one with its roots in cognitive science, the other with its origin in the theory of knowledge by Ludwig Wittgenstein. The discussion is set in the context of the consequences of computerisation and the future status of the nursing profession.

Nursing science is a relatively new discipline. The models developing it are mainly based on behavioural science.

How might this theoretical orientation direct nursing education and training in the computer age?

Let me start by giving the outlines of two different theories of knowledge.

2 TWO IRRECONCILABLE TRADITIONS

In 1984 Professor Herbert Simon gave a lecture at the 20th Nobel conference. In his address, 'Some Computer Models of Human Learning', he describes the current position of research into theories of learning on the basis of cognitive learning.[1]

Simon discusses what he calls the hypothesis of 'the physical symbol system'. Put simply, it deals with the ability to recognise patterns: a human face is a recognisable

393

pattern for us. A pattern consists of a collection of configurations which we can learn to discern from one another and in which we can see similarities. They may be set in relation to each other and they may be compared with each other. Simon emphasises that a system must have this symbolic capacity if it is to function intelligently. Computers have this capacity, he says: 'We can find that out by opening the box, so to speak'.

In his lecture, Simon gives an example of mankind's ability to recognise patterns; man has a limited short-term memory. If I give you a list of six words, you can keep them in your mind long enough to allow you to repeat them back to me. But as a rule, if I give you nine words, you cannot.In cognitive science today, the prevailing opinion is that the structure of short-term memory is of decisive importance in the way experts store knowledge. The ability of experts to recognise 'cues' in a familiar situation gives them access to relevant information in their long-term memory. Simon points out that an expert's long-term memory comprises some 50 000 'chunks', and gives an example from the world of chess: you set up a chessboard with the pieces at, for example, the 20th move of a well-known game. You let the subject of the test study the chessboard for between 5 and 10 seconds and then remove the pieces.

A chess master will succeed in replacing the pieces with 90% or more accuracy. If I repeat the procedure, but position the pieces at random, the master will only manage to position six of the pieces correctly. The chess master achieves a better result in the first test because of the patterns that he knows and that are stored in his long-term memory, and because of the information he recalls through association when he sees the pattern on the chessboard. According to Simon, it is this ability, this expert tuition, that 'can be given a perfectly reasonable explanation in information-processing terms, in terms of recognition processes'.

In the subsequent discussion, Simon was asked the following question from the audience: 'Dr Simon, Descartes said that science has the perspective of studying the uniquely simple problems in material nature. Repetitive processes yield nicely to science and maths. However, unique processes, heroism, love, mercy, diverge from this adaptive model, from repetitive processes. They also seem rather non-material. How do you relate these characteristics to perfection of the non-uniqueness of human beings in nature?'

Simon answered: 'Of course, I relied on the fact that this conference is dealing with cognitive science, not with human beings in general, and I tried to be very careful in introducing physical symbol systems to say that a human being is at least a physical symbol system. Now, the human brain resides in the head, and the head, of course, is connected with the body, and the connection is thought to be important — important enough for most people to be reluctant to have the two separated from each other. In order to introduce any of the concepts of human motivation and effect, we would have to have a much more elaborate and comprehensive theory than any of us are discussing or proposing at this conference. . . . One of the reasons why it is hard to talk about things like love or heroism in connection with a computer is that a computer has none of those connections with the body and that computers, or at least computers of our generation, have almost none of the experiences that human beings store away and which are relevant to those aspects of our lives.'

A reasonable interpretation of Simon's response is that he does not regard ethics, for example, as an important aspect of an expert's knowledge.

This is the appropriate stage to introduce the philosopher Ludwig Wittgenstein, whose works are characterised by precisely the ethical dimension of knowledge.

Wittgenstein's work, *Tractatus Logico-Philosophicus*, was published in England in 1922.[2] It immediately attracted a great deal of attention, with the philosopher Bertrand Russell as its main proponent. In his foreword, Wittgenstein describes what he regards as the aim of the book: 'What can be said at all can be said clearly, and what we cannot talk about we must pass over in silence'.

In the *Tractatus*, Wittgenstein develops a formalised, ideal language whose structure, he says, reflects precisely the structure of expressed thought. He sees language as an instrument for making statements on material conditions. I quote again from the foreword: 'Thus the aim of the book is to draw a limit to thought or, rather — not to thought, but to the expression of thought: for in order to be able to draw a limit to thought, we should have to find both sides of the limit thinkable (i.e. we should have to be able to think what cannot be thought).

It will therefore only be in language that the limit can be drawn, and what lies on the other side of the limit will simply be nonsense'.

At the end of the book, Wittgenstein develops the ideas to which he will subsequently devote all his attention for a period of 25 years. He says: 'We feel that even when all possible scientific questions have been answered, the problems of life remain completely untouched. Of course, there are then no questions left, and this itself is the answer'.

This is the only book that Wittgenstein published. The other works are compilations of the very large volume of his work, the best-known being *Philosophical Investigations*, published posthumously in 1953.[3]

Wittgenstein's later philosophical work is characterised by his strong emphasis on the use of language instead of thinking in terms of the meaning of words that can be described in definitions. In the first paragraph of the book he writes: 'But what is the meaning of the word "five"?' — No such thing was in question here, only how the word 'five' is used.

Thus the aspect of action in language occupies a prominent place in Wittgenstein's philosophy: 'I shall also call the whole, consisting of language and the actions into which it is woven, the "language-game".'

On the basis of this approach, examples naturally play a crucial part in Wittgenstein's theory of knowledge.

In fact, Herbert Simon also has examples in mind when he talks about 'patterns' as being essential to the development of expert knowledge. But that is the full extent of any similarity between the two. They have divergent views of the part played by the example.

When Simon expresses his conviction that the way in which experts relate to earlier encounters with patterns can be described in the form of rules, Wittgenstein attributes this to that which cannot be expressed in language itself. Knowledge is expressed in examples. While you can point to an example, knowledge does not allow itself to be formulated in general rules.

Simon and Wittgenstein represent two disparate approaches. They are to serve as the background to a discussion on the nursing profession, a discussion which is motivated not least by developments in nursing science and in computer technology.

3 SYSTEMS THEORY IN MEDICAL CARE

'We would like to place the current issue of nurses on a different, I venture to say, higher level. It is an indisputable and purely woman's issue. Au fond, it is based on one of woman's purest and deepest attributes; that of motherliness.' (Dr Professor John Berg in an address to nurses, 1926).

These are the roots of the nursing profession; the vocation and the self-sacrificing acts of love, the value of which could not be expressed in financial terms. There is a different view of the nursing profession today, in 1987, but the financial rewards are still meagre.

In Sweden and in many other countries nursing training has taken the form of a college education in recent years. One of the reasons has certainly been that an academic training would upgrade the profession.

Nursing training in Sweden used to be carried out at a number of the large hospitals. Today, trainee nurses have become nursing students and colleges have been established for the medical care sector.

Whereas nurses' training used to be largely on an apprenticeship basis, today the scientific content of the training is emphasised. The training must be based on science.

What is the content of the discipline that is known as nursing science? This has been the subject of lively debate in the last decade. However, there seems to be a consensus that the task of a nurse is 'care', and the task of the doctor is 'cure'. These tasks require different types of knowledge. For example, it is the nurse who has the most intimate contact with the patients. Nursing science is yet another science whose direction is obscure. What research there is, is modelled on research in medicine or behavioural science.

I would like to discuss some aspects of nursing research on the basis of a seminal work in nursing science; Katie Eriksson's book *'Introduction till vårdvetenskap' (An Introduction to Nursing Science)*, published in 1983.[4] Katie Eriksson is principal of the Swedish Nursing Institute in Helsinki, and in 1982 presented a doctoral dissertation on the nursing process. Her ideas have attracted a great deal of attention in the debate on research in this area.

According to Eriksson, it is of the greatest importance that a theoretical basis is developed for nurses. This will allow nurses to become professionals, which is a prerequisite for raising the status of their occupation. A scientific approach in the profession means that nurses can develop self-criticism. She sees this as indispensable in an occupation with long traditions in which training has, for long periods, been based on the apprenticeship model. With such a historical background there is considerable risk that people develop a 'fixation with habitual and hidebound behaviour', and this is often expressed in an aversion to progress. Eriksson says that a scientific attitude means that 'applying a scientific model in solving problems becomes a challenge'. Knowledge should be developed towards a high degree of organisation and general validity, and precision must be developed in forming concepts. For 'a person who is at a higher logical level is better equipped to take responsibility, structure her working method, adapt to changes in her surroundings, be creative in her work and be less dependent on external authority'.

According to Eriksson, it is primarily the role of the theoretician that is needed in nursing science, in the absence of a basic research paradigm, this being the reason why the discipline has not succeeded in acquiring much status in the scientific world. The nurse of tomorrow should, in addition to her nursing assignments, be involved in research and development work.

In order to achieve these goals, nursing science must find models for care. The care process must be formalised in order to develop such a model. This requires the concepts to be well-defined — there is a considerable confusion of concepts in the medical care sector today. This is rooted in a lack of precision when analysing these concepts. But the theoretical concepts are important; 'They have a greater power of explanation than the observable, and therefore have a wider area of use'.

Eriksson's model is taken from systems theory. The central concepts are the system, components, relations, structure, function and information. Nursing care is the system, the components are the objective, the nursing staff, patients, patient analysis, the priority areas of nursing care, the choice of nursing intervention and process factors.

When making changes in the care system, the change that one wants to bring about is 'a change between the input and output status of the components or elements'.

In contrast to this systems model, earlier models in nursing care were largely practical, concrete and detailed. The knowledge is of the 'know-how' type. Practical nursing interventions in care are not the primary aim of a systems-theoretical model.

Eriksson summarises her care plan in four points:

1 It must specify the care ideal, the objective, i.e. the integrated person affected by nursing interventions.
2 It must contain a description of the methods that will lead to this goal.
3 It must describe how different nursing contexts affect the process of medical care.
4 A care plan must explain the assessments on which nursing interventions are based.

4 EXPERT SYSTEMS

Before I discuss Katie Eriksson's model of nursing care and the view of nurses' knowledge that it expresses, I would like to give a summary of a research project whose theory is close to that of Eriksson. The research work is on the development of expert systems for nurses. The researcher is Judy Ozbolt, a professor at the Centre for Nursing Research at Ann Arbor, Michigan. In a series of essays, Ozbolt, who used to be a nurse, has developed her views on ways in which methods could be developed to reach the objective of expert systems for nurses. My summary is largely based on the essay entitled 'A proposed expert system for nursing practice. A springboard to nursing science'.[5]

Like Eriksson, Ozbolt emphasises that, until now, nurses' knowledge has been largely developed from an apprentice model. The knowledge acquired by a nurse through practical experience made her an expert. The expert passes on her knowledge to the novice. According to Ozbolt, a regrettable result of this is that knowledge 'is often idiosyncratic in conceptualization and untested in validity and reliability'. Current information systems for nurses reflect this fact, 'the largely unsystematic nature of nursing knowledge'.

If the next generation of technology is to be an improvement, it is necessary that 'nursing knowledge be codified for incorporation into the systems'. In return, this will lead to major advances for the profession. Such systems would offer a mechanism for systematically testing existing knowledge and returning new knowledge to practical nursing. Today, nursing faces the problem of the lack of a well- developed theory of knowledge, which is an obstacle to the development of data systems that can facilitate the cognitive tasks of nursing care.

Nurses' knowledge is 'personal and idiosyncratic'. It is fragmentary and lacks cohesion, and will continue to do so until nurses find principles that permit the systematic testing of their knowledge, and a way of synthesizing and codifying this knowledge.

The problem is that nurses have difficulties in describing what they know. Even if they agree that they work on the basis of a problem-solving process, it is difficult for them to 'implement' the process, in spite of the existence of information systems that support this work.

Ozbolt asks which methods nurses use to collect 'data'. She says that four main methods are used, and refers to a major inquiry on these methods. The first two methods, *tenacity* and *authority*, are of the least value. The tenacity method perpetuates old truths and traditions 'we've always done it this way', with the attendant risk that, because there is suspicion of less traditional knowledge, false knowledge will be passed on. In its turn, the authority method implies a tendency simply to accept the knowledge of recognised authorities. This may persuade the nurse to accept invalid knowledge and be ignorant of valid knowledge.

The two foremost methods are the method based on intuition on the one hand, and on scientific knowledge on the other. The nurse uses the intuitive method when she, as Ozbolt puts it, 'reviews a mass of patient data and makes an intellectual leap to diagnoses'. There is a risk that nurses, even if they are well qualified, may disagree in their assessment, and the method in itself cannot resolve such a dispute.

Nurses' use of the scientific method is finally becoming more widespread today. It is characterised by objectivity, when assertions can be subjected to empirical tests. But even this method is problematic because researchers bring different perspectives to their work. Their knowledge cannot be synthesized in 'the growing body of knowledge'. For that reason it is difficult to introduce knowledge from research into nursing practice. If the scientifc method is to work, then nurses must themselves find suitable and applicable ways of classifying their data and diagnoses.

The chief drawbacks in the information systems for nurses today are, according to Ozbolt, that they do not provide an individualised care plan. This must be done by the nurse. Individualisation is one of the greatest advantages in using expert systems. They have 'a much richer and more complex knowledge base, one that can be used by the computer for artificially intelligent reasoning, and one that will grow with experience'. Expert systems may in the future serve as a springboard for nursing science, according to Ozbolt. The expert systems that she herself works with are based on a multivariate mathematical approach to clinical decision-making. It 'permits the incorporation of information-processing strategies experts typically used while maintaining the statistic rigour of data-based systems'. Both factual knowledge and associative information are used for drawing clinical inferences. In a later essay, 'Designing information systems for nursing practice: database and knowledge base requirements of different organisational technologies'[6], Ozbolt describes a model for nurses to apply in developing their work. The model deals with what nurses do when confronted with 'stimulus'. I do not intend to discuss in detail the argument she puts forward in the article, but I would like to highlight what I perceive as the core of her view of the future knowledge of nurses. Ozbolt applies four categories in her work. The nurse can act as a *craftsman*, as a potter works with clay. She can practice her profession as an art and be very innovative. The problem is that 'the innovations are not designed to adapt care to a unique person, since in this model the stimuli are considered to be mostly alike'. The same problems are to be found in the *routine method*, because 'clients who share a common diagnosis are expected to be more alike than different'.

Individualisation is best achieved in the *engineering* model, in which each patient is seen as a unique case. The nurse collects and analyses the patient's data to arrive at a diagnosis which includes, but is not limited to, issues that concern medical diagnosis and treatment. 'The nurse sets objectives based on knowledge and experience of what is desirable and achievable and designs an individualized care plan by selecting from a known repertoire of nursing interventions those most likely to lead to achievement of the objectives. After implementing the interventions, the nurse evaluates their effectiveness by comparing the client's subsequent condition with previous diagnoses and objectives.'

In the last model, the *non-routine* model, which is a research model, the patient is still seen as unique. The problem is that the search procedures cannot be analysed because more judgement and intuition is required in making decisions.

5 THE THEORY OF KNOWLEDGE FOR PRACTITIONERS

A recurring theme in both Eriksson's and Ozbolt's work is the inability of nurses to articulate their knowledge. Ozbolt also points out that the absence of studies of the theory of knowledge are a problem for nursing practice today.

The question is: What theories of knowledge are most likely to capture the versatility of the nursing profession?

My argument is based on eight year's experience in working life research. The essence of this work has been to interpret case studies in relation to the changes in professional knowledge as a consequence of the computerisation of different workplaces. One of these studies is of computerisation in social insurance offices. Over the past three years I have concentrated on medical care, most of the interviews having been with nurses on the subject of their professional knowledge. An exhaustive discussion on what experienced nurses perceive as the core of their professional knowledge should be an obvious starting point for subsequent discussions on which applications of technology are suitable. In the field of medical care it is often emphasised that technology should contribute to the improvement of care and this view places central importance on the theory of knowledge issues.

Half of the group of about ten nurses that I meet on a regular basis have either administrative or trade union duties. These nurses feel the greatest problem in their profession is that nurses lack adequate meansto formulate and articulate the knowledge they possess. 'A language that captures the real knowledge of nurses must be developed' has been a recurrent theme in the group's discussions over the last three years. This is an understandable viewpoint. As long as nurses are unable to describe in explicit terms what they know, they will not succeed in putting forward convincing arguments for upgrading their occupation.

Several of the people in the group felt that upgrading the theoretical training may help to improve nurses' ability to express themselves. Basically Eriksson is also a proponent of this approach.

Let us consider the question: why do nurses have difficulty in formulating their knowledge?

If, unlike the physician's profession, the basis of the nursing profession is care, then a different kind of knowledge needs to be developed in the nursing profession from that in the doctor's profession. Theoretical training inculcates important medical facts — information that is essential to the nurse. But it does not entirely prepare her for dealing with unexpected events in the care of her patients. Newly-qualified nurses usually report that a large part of their time is spent remembering the rules for practical actions such as setting up a drip-feed. This gives rise to problems in situations when nurses must act quickly. These actions must be second nature to them before they can focus their attention on the patient. Work in the medical care sector is full of unexpected complications. To deal with this degree of complexity nurses must have the ability to make a reasonable interpretation of events not covered by the descriptions in the rule book. This requires multi-faceted practical experience, through which the information acquired through formal training can be developed into knowledge. That knowledge is built up from a long series of examples which give different perspectives on an illness. Different kinds of knowledge are acquired, some of which can be described explicitly in generally applicable rules. We can call this propositional knowledge, a term which reflects the nature of the knowledge. Another equally important type of knowledge is that which becomes apparent in encounters with unforeseen complications in everyday care. This *knowledge of familiarity*[7] cannot be described in a meaningful way in general rules because its core is the ability to act with good judgement in unique situations. Propositional knowledge and the knowledge of familiarity presuppose each other and affect each other; they require many-sided, practical experience in order to develop.

When considering in their interviews what they perceive as important in their professional knowledge, the nurses mainly describe examples of a well-developed knowledge of familiarity. I have chosen to illustrate this with two examples from interviews.

A nurse aged about fifty describes her work in a post-operational ward where she has had thirty years' experience. One day a patient was admitted to her ward, a middle-aged man who had just undergone surgery. After a short conversation with him the nurse quickly realised that his condition was not normal, although the man said he felt surprisingly well. She called out the physician on duty, a young doctor with little experience who, on seeing that the patient's vital signs were normal, reproached the nurse for calling him out unnecessarily. Later in the day the patient died, and the post mortem uncovered a complication that could not have been diagnosed by an examination of his vital signs. The nurse's comment was that she noticed that something was out of the ordinary but could not explain how she had arrived at this conclusion. Previous experience of course, she pointed out, was a decisive factor.

A middle-aged psychiatric nurse describes how, shortly after qualifying, she found herself working at a hospital where the view of mental illness differed from the view inculcated by her training. Her training has given her a perception of mental illness rooted in the natural sciences. When patients became violent they were given heavy doses of medicine and were physically restrained. Psychotherapeutic principles were applied at this, her first place of work, so the patients were not bound when they became aggressive. At first she was constantly afraid of what the patients might do but, having worked in fear for a while, she began to notice that an older woman, a nursing auxiliary, was better able than others to induce calm in those around her, even in the most tense and threatening situations. Our young nurse kept as close as possible to this woman, from whom she learnt how to deal with many of the situations that she had previously found terrifying. But, the nurse told us, she never discussed this with the older auxiliary, and she commented that it was remarkable that she could learn so much from someone who had so little formal education.

Both these examples provide an indication of the content of what we call the knowledge of familiarity; the multi-faceted, reflected experience that hones the ability to notice things that are out of the ordinary and to apply experience won from previous examples as a starting-point in interpreting the unique case. The ability to deal with what are often conflicting amanuenses cannot be acquired through formal book learning, but is often developed through 'tips' given by more experienced colleagues. This requires both maturity and a knowledge of mankind.

The dilemma for nurses is that they are aware that a 'good' nurse has a wealth of knowledge of familiarity. On the other hand, this knowledge is not scientific knowledge in the sense that it can be formalised in general descriptions. It can, however, be expressed in the form of descriptive examples, but this is a different type of description from that found in the domain of propositional knowledge. In my conversations with nurses, they often emphasise that they know no-one who has been better able to give expression to the knowledge that they themselves find important than Ludgwig Wittgenstein, the philosopher. The following is a much quoted passage from his *Philosophical Investigations* that has been the subject of repeated discussions: 'Is there such a thing as "expert judgement" about the genuineness of expressions of feeling? . . . Even here, there are those whose judgement is "better", and those whose judgement is "worse".

More correct prognoses will generally issue from the judgements of those with better knowledge of mankind.

Can one learn this knowledge? Yes, some can. Not, however, by taking a course in it but through 'experience'. . . . Can someone else be a man's teacher in this? Certainly. From time to time he gives him the right tip. This is what 'learning' and 'teaching' are like here. . . . What one acquires here is not a technique; one learns correct judgements. There are also rules, but they do not form a system, and only experienced people can apply them correctly. Unlike calculating-rules.

What is most difficult here is to put this indefiniteness, correctly and unfalsified, into words.' (page 227)

6 THE CONCEPT OF PRACTICE

As I have understood it, nurses' appreciation of Wittgenstein's paragraph on the knowledge of humanity has its basis in his realisation that this is a type of knowledge that is not taught from the handbook. Nurses' personal experience has brought home to them the fact that knowledge of mankind is not easily gained. Nurses who are involved in nursing training know that courses on the knowledge of human nature generate the least interest among nurses. Instead, the students would like to have more training in, for example, anatomy, a subject based on factual knowledge. Wittgenstein's reflections on teaching and learning would, if transposed to work in the care sector, focus attention on apprenticeship. The experienced give tips to the less experienced. In another part of his *Philosophical Investigations*, Wittgenstein says this: 'But if a person has not yet got the concepts, I should teach him to use the words by means of examples and by practice. . . . And when I do this I do not communicate less to him than I know myself. I do it, he does it after me; and I influence him by expressions of agreement, rejection, expectation, encouragement. I let him go his way, or hold him back and so on.' (§208)

How are these different types of knowledge to be reconciled? It is self-evident that nurses require factual knowledge. However, what must be discussed is how the information contained in their training is to become knowledge for the nurse.

There is a difference between acquiring information, that is to say facts, and having knowledge that is rooted in a many faceted practical experience. In the latter case, knowledge has been tested and validated through encounters with unique events, and one's assessment of it is based upon similarities and disparities in comparison with previous examples. One must take an active part in work in order to acquire propositional knowledge. But the rules of propositional knowledge are not enough. Wittgenstein says:[8] 'Not only rules, but also examples are needed for establishing a practice. Our rules leave loopholes open and the practice has to speak for itself'. (§139)

A practice constitutes a whole set of rules and examples, and in the practice both propositional knowledge and the knowledge of familiarity are developed.

7 WHO DRAWS THE BOUNDARY BETWEEN MAN AND MACHINE?

Let us use this basis of the theory of knowledge in reflecting upon Katie Eriksson's and Judy Ozbolt's view of knowledge. Their work aims to make nurses' knowledge more explicit than it is today. To reach this goal the nurse must be able to develop a scientific attitude to care. This is emphasised by both Eriksson and Ozbolt. The scientific model should be a lodestar in problem solving. Knowledge should be developed towards a high degree of general application and nurses must be more precise in defining concepts. They must have a higher abstraction level. The nurse as a theoretician is, according to Eriksson, what we need most today. Seen from my arguments related to Wittgenstein's philosophy of language, it would appear that Eriksson is referring to the nurse as a better collector of information. Knowledge of mankind, the precondition to developing the ability to provide nursing care, can hardly be found in Eriksson's model. Neither is it a mark of the system's theoretical approach. This is probably the price that must be paid for choosing this type of model to improve the status of the nursing occupation. The knowledge of familiarity is not developed at a high abstraction level separated from practice. But then neither is propositional knowledge. What remains is the nurse as a carrier of information.

Both Eriksson and Ozbolt attempt to renounce the apprenticeship model that has been accepted as self-evident in the care sector for so long. It is perceived as irrevocably out-of-date and is regarded as one of the reasons for nurses' knowledge being 'idiosyncratic and impossible to validate and test'. The conclusion is that new models are needed. The strongest criticism Ozbolt makes of the traditional nurse is, however, her inability to see the patient as unique. In her opinion this is something that the expert systems of the future can help to remedy. The traditional nurses tend to regard 'clients who share a common diagnosis . . . as more alike than different'. The systematic analysis of the patient's condition by an expert system provides a different basis for interpreting it in a unique way. This requires a comprehensive knowledge base.

I began this essay by setting two views of the theory of knowledge against each other. Where Herbert Simon develops a natural sciences model to describe mankind's ability to build up knowledge, Wittgenstein emphasises the context within which knowledge develops. The actions that are carried out in an organisation are permeated by the culture and the values that mould a practice. People serving as role models and examples give knowledge its deeper content, since (as Wittgenstein expresses it in a passage I have already quoted): 'Not only rules, but also examples are needed for establishing a practice. Our rules leave loopholes open and the practice has to speak for itself'.

Seen from this perspective it is apparent that Wittgenstein's theories of knowledge capture much more of the knowledge of mankind than Simon manages to do with his model. It is possible that what Wittgenstein develops is precisely what Simon is searching for in the discussion that followed his speech: 'In order to introduce any of the concepts of human motivation and effect, we would have to have a much more elaborate and comprehensive theory than any of us are discussing or proposing at this conference. . .'

The theories behind the works of Eriksson and Ozbolt are close to Simon. However, faced with the future technical advances that await in the field of medical care, I believe that it is both important and fruitful to allow different theoretical approaches to focus on the same reality. If one objective of technology is to improve the quality of care, we must first have a conception of where the boundary between man and machine lies. It is the people who have many-sided experience from practice who are in the best position to determine which theories are best able to capture the knowledge that they consider to be important in order to do good work.

8 CONCLUSION

In the predominant nursing science the scientific model for developing nursing is pleaded for. The model of apprenticeship in learning is heavily attacked.

But science is concerned with universal, general knowledge. Nurses have until today usually seen the practical knowledge directed towards the unique patient as the main point of their knowledge. 'The most important thing in caring is to see every person as unique, but it is also the most difficult thing to cope with when you are young and lack experience', said a young British nurse whom I interviewed some weeks ago.

These are two different approaches.

There is a risk when models from, for instance, natural sciences are transferred to areas which have another character. The scientification of knowledge does not improve the quality of caring if it deteriorates the conditions for developing knowledge by familiarity.

Regarding the high esteem of scientific knowledge in our culture at the expense of practical knowledge, it is hardly surprising that nursing science aims at giving 'caring' scientific status. But if unjustified models for 'caring' serve as a basis for developing advanced technology in nursing, it might have unfortunate consequences for the profession.

A thorough discussion of nursing knowledge from different theoretical points of view should precede the development of, for instance, expert systems in caring.

REFERENCES

1 Shafto, M.(ed.) (1985). *How We Know: Nobel Conference XX*. Harper & Row, San Francisco.
2 Wittgenstein, L. (1961). *Tractatus Logico-Philosophicus*. Routledge & Kegan Paul Ltd, London.
3 Wittgenstein, L. (1953). *Philosophical Investigations*. Blackwell, Oxford.
4 Eriksson, Katie (1983). *Introduktion Till Vårdvetenskap*. Almqvist & Wiksell, Stockholm.
5 *Journal of Medical Systems* (1985). Vol 9.
6 *Computer Methods and Programs in Biomedicine* (1986). Vol 22.
7 The terms 'propositional knowledge' and 'knowledge of familiarity' were coined by the Norwegian philosopher Kjell S. Johannessen. They are developed in Wittgenstein, L. (1981). *Aesthetics and Transcendental Philosophy*, ed. by K. Johannessen and T. Nordenstam. Hölder-Pichler-Tempsky, Vienna.
8 Wittgenstein, L. (1969). *On certainty*. Blackwell, Oxford.

AI & Soc (1990) 4: 137–146

AI & SOCIETY

The Role of "Craft Language" in Learning "Waza"*

Kumiko Ikuta

Sugino Women's College, 4–6–19 Kamiosaki, Shinagawa-Ku, Tokyo, 141, Japan

Abstract. The role of "craft language" in the process of teaching (learning) "Waza" (skill) will be discussed from the perspective of human intelligence.

It may be said that the ultimate goal of learning "Waza" in any Japanese traditional performance is not the perfect reproduction of the teaching (learning) process of "Waza". In fact, a special metaphorical language ("craft language") is used, which has the effect of encouraging the learner to activate his creative imagination. It is through this activity that the he learns his own "habitus" ("Kata").

It is suggested that, in considering the difference of function between natural human intelligence and artificial intelligence, attention should be paid to the imaginative activity of the learner as being an essential factor for mastering "Kata".

Keywords: Waza; Skill; Craft language; Kata; Katachi; Habitus; Human intelligence; Artificial intelligence

Introduction

The purpose of this article is to discuss the role of "craft language" often used in the process of teaching and learning a skill of Japanese traditional performance, and also to suggest some essential points of natural human intelligence, which we should not overlook when we consider the problem of artificial intelligence.

First of all, I shall define the terms, "Waza" and "craft language". By the term "Waza", I mean a skill of Japanese traditional artistic performances such as Japanese dancing, Noh play,[1] or Kabuki play.[2] ("Waza" may also refer to traditional martial arts such as Karate,[3] Judo,[4] or Kendo[5]; surely we recognize that these have a common cognitive process in the learning with artistic performance. But in this article, I will focus the discussion on the nature of artistic performance.) And, by the term "craft language", I mean a special metaphorical language which is often used in the process of teaching a skill such as Japanese traditional performance, "Waza", different from a descriptive or a scientific language.

---

* This article is a modified English version of Chapter 5 of my book *Waza kara shiru* (Learning from Skill), Tokyo University Press, 1987, pp. 93–105.

The Goal of Learning "Waza" – "Kata" and "Katachi"

The skill of Japanese traditional performance, "Waza", has generally been construed such that it can not be taught scientifically and a learner can master it only through the activity of imitating and repeating what his teacher does. We have regarded the process of learning "Waza" as so mysterious that the people outside the world of "Waza" cannot understand it, and that we can not describe it objectively as a cognitive process. We sometimes call that way of learning "stealing in secret", *nusumu* in Japanese. In this article, I will try to make clear what the learner is supposed to "steal" from his teacher and how that "stealing" can be done successfully.[6]

We may point out that one distinctive feature of learning a skill of Japanese traditional performance is that the ultimate goal any learner tries to attain is mastering "Kata", not "Katachi". "Kata" and "Katachi" sound very similar in Japanese as you can tell and they are often confused in speech. But, in fact, these concepts are completely different and without making clear the distinct meaning of each we can elucidate neither the teaching and learning process of "Waza" nor the role of craft language, which works effectively in the process of teaching and learning "Waza".

"Katachi" is an apparent physical form of action shown by the peformer of a certain "Waza", which may be decomposed into parts and described as a sequence of procedures. For example, in the case of Japanese traditional dancing, some well-known works such as "Kikuzukushi" or "Shiokumi" can be decomposed into parts of action which can be described as a sequence of procedures by scientific language.

On the contrary, "Kata", which has been regarded as the ultimate goal of the learner to attain in learning "Waza", is not a simple collection of parts of action like "Katachi", but an artistic and personal expression of "Katachi" bearing the meaning connected with a socio-historical factor of the world of a certain "Waza", which is supposed to be mastered through the activity of imitating and repeating superficial "Katachi" with great pains.

In considering the critical difference between these two terms, it might be helpful to introduce and examine the concept "habitus", which is used by a French sociologist, Marcell Mauss (1950), in his book *Sociologie et Anthropologie*. He proposes a theory of anthropology through the analysis of physical actions man shows differently depending on the difference of culture. In discussing it, he introduces the term "habitus" as a central concept in his theory. He explains it as follows:

"Je vous prie de remarquer que je dis en bon latin, compris en France, [«]habitus[»]. Le mot traduit, infiniment mieux qu' [«]habitude[»], l'[«]exis[»], l'[«]acquis[»] et la [«]faculté[»] d'Aristote (qui était un psychologue) . . . Ces [«]habitudes[»] varient non pas simplement avec les individus et leurs imitations, elles varient surtout avec les sociétés, les éducations, les convenances et les modes, les prestiges. Il faut y voir des techniques et l'ouvrage de la raison pratique collective et individuelle, là où on ne voit d'ordinaire que l'âme et ses facultés de répétition."[7]

He insists that everyday physical actions such as eating, sleeping, walking and taking a rest, which have generally been considered just biological or physiological behaviour of man, involving no intentional teaching and learning process, do have, in fact, a socio-historical background unique to a particular culture, and that the rational cognitive process (*raison practique*) can be recognized in the learning of such kinds of action. He makes a clear distinction in the concept of "habitus" from that of "habitude (habit)". He seems to interpret the concept as a "higher grade disposition",[8] to use Gilbert Ryle's phrase, which can be mastered through the activity of "training" (the rational cognitive activity), whereas "habitude (habit)" is a "single-track disposition"[9] which can be mastered through the drill. In short, "habitus" is a composition of the parts of action disconnected from the culture or situation, but it is the culture-laden form of action, in other words, culture or situation-laden "Katachi". A new member in a certain culture begins to imitate with adoration what his elders successfully show in a certain situation, and as he does so, he gets to master a certain type of acting to such an extent that he can produce it without much consciousness.

Mauss points out the necessity of considering the human physical actions from not only the physiological, but psychological or sociological point of view. That is to say, "habitus", culture or situation-laden "Katachi" should not be considered as something that can be learnt only by imitating the apparent form of action independent of the context, but as something that is mastered only through committing himself to or indwelling inside a certain culture or situation, thereby getting to grasp the situational meaning of "Katachi" with a sense of reality. I believe, this concept of "habitus" well expresses the nature of "Kata", which is the ultimate goal for the learner to achieve in learning "Waza".

The most important matter for the learner in learning "Waza", is not the perfect reproduction of "Katachi" as a physical form of action, although it is true that he has to begin his learning by imitating and repeating "Katachi", but to "habitusize" "Katachi", in other words, to automatically reproduce "Katachi" as well as grasping the meaning of it connected with a socio-historical factor of the world of a certain "Waza", by himself with a sense of reality. Concerning the mastery of Noh play, Zeami[10] says that there would come a state for the learner, who has been engaged in imitating and repeating "Katachi", such that the consciousness with which he tries to imitate "Katachi" disappears all of a sudden. He calls such a state "Ushu-fu", while the state the learner devotes himself to imitating and repeating the form of action as "Mushu-fu".[11] It is the state of "Ushu-fu" that both the teacher and the learner should make efforts to attain in the end of teaching and learning, through committing to and indwelling in the world of "Noh", for instance. In this sense, old Japanese sayings on mastering "Waza", such as "Enter into katachi first, and then get out of it" and "Get accustomed to it rather than be taught" well point out the importance of mastering "habitus" as the end of learning.

How can "Kata" be Mastered?

If the ultimate goal of learning "Waza" is mastering "Kata", "habitus", which is not a simple automatic reproduction of the form composed of parts of physical action, then, how can it be mastered? Speaking from the point of view of the teacher, how can the teacher transmit his "Kata", not "Katachi", to the learner effectively?

I mentioned before that the learner in a certain world of "Waza" can master "Kata" through the activity of imitating and repeating "Katachi", by committing himself to or indwelling inside the world in question, just as a new member of a culture gets to learn a particular form of action by living together with other elder members, thereby getting to grasp the situational meaning of "Katachi" with a sense of reality. In addition to this process of indwelling in the world of a certain "Waza" on the part of the learner, there is what can be described as an intentional act in the teaching of "Kata", which there is not in "Katachi".

Here, we have to pay attention to the special metaphorical language which is often used in the process of teaching and learning "Waza". For example, in the case of Japanese traditional dancing, there is a form where a performer holds his right hand up with a fan. To make the learner master this form, the teacher says while showing him this form, "Hold your right hand up just as if you were trying to catch snow falling down from the sky", instead of saying "Keep your right hand up exactly at an angle of 45 degrees". Or to make the learner understand the tempo of a performance, he says "Store it, store it!" (*Tamete, tamete*) rather than saying "Keep the same form for 5 and a half seconds.

Nakamura Utaemon V,[12] recalls the method of teaching he had received from Ichikawa Danjuro IX,[13] as follows:

"I remember that the characteristic of Dajuro's teaching was that he only made keypoints rather than teaching the details of 'Katachi'. Once, he said to me when I had trouble in speaking one of my lines, 'Speak not with your mouth, but with your stomach!.' When I first heard that remark I did not understand what he was saying, but I finally realised that what he meant was that I had to notice the importance of speaking the lines only to the opposite actor. My problem was that I had tried to speak the lines to the audience so loudly that all of them could hear my voice."[14]

Nakamura Kanzaburo XVII[15] also recalled the Onoe Kikugoro's VI ways of teaching:[16]

"Kikugoro was superb at teaching and I learned a lot from him. When I played the role of Rikiya in 'Chushingura',[17] he made a good suggestion about how I could perform in the scene where Rikiya was waiting for his father Yuranosuke coming from 'hanamichi'.[18] He said to me, 'Why don't you open a hole in the curtain ("agemaku") at 'hanamichi' and try to see Yuranosuke through it.' Using his suggestion, helped me to play my role successfully."[19]

One common feature of the above examples, is that the teachers intentionally used metaphorical expressions in the process of teaching even in cases where they could express what they wanted to say to their learner in a descriptive language. For instance, Danjuro could have said, "Speak the lines less loudly than before", instead of saying, "Speak not with your mouth, but with your stomach". Also, Kikugoro could have said "To play the role of being anxious about coming of his father Yuranosuke, stare at the corner of 'hanamichi' or in the direction of the curtain." What was the practical intention of their using such metaphorical expressions in teaching?

In considering the above question, it is worthwhile citing here the analysis of jargon by Vernon Howard in his book *Artistry*. He classifies jargon into three types; theoretical jargon, gratuitous jargon, and technical jargon. He says:

"theoretical jargon consists of a set of neologisms especially coined for highly specialized theoretical concepts such as 'positron', 'valence', 'positive and negative reinforcement', 'gross national product' and the like. Gratuitous jargon is the sort afflicting such fields as politics, education and popular psychology – terms such as 'developing nation', 'underachiever', 'transactional analysis'. Technical (or practical) jargon . . . consists of a mostly ad hoc selection of metaphoric usages of terms and phrases borrowed from ordinary discourse, the special meanings of which are drawn from aspects of the skilled activities in question. The singer's vocabulary of 'registers' and 'breaks,' of 'chest' and 'head' voices, 'cover', 'placement', and 'support' to mention just a few conspicuous items, is an excellent source of examples of technical jargon."[20]

According to Howard:

"the technical jargon is an action-directed language that aims to direct, discriminate, identify and classify sensations and behaviour considered in one way or other to be essential to the correct development and deployment of a skill. . . . This feature is consistent with the primary aim of such discourse, which is to induce the relevant perceptions and actions and only secondarily to describe and explain them – whereas in science the primary aim is precisely to describe and explain, not to induce in the sense 'to provoke'."[21]

Howard calls this kind of jargon, which is often used in the process of teaching of a certain skill, "craft language".

The examples of using metaphorical expression in teaching the learner an appropriate form as I cited before, might be considered those of "technical jargon" by Howard. The teacher's purpose of using craft language is not to describe or explain the form he wants to transmit to the learner, but to provoke the same sensation as he has in the body of the learner through his imagination. And it is not until the same sensation is provoked in the body of the learner that he can grasp the meaning of "Katachi", in other words, master "Kata" beyond the activity of imitation of "Katachi". This is exactly the state of being habitualized, "Ushu-fu" by Zeami. It was the very "Kata", not superficial "Katachi", that both Danjuro and Kikugoro wanted to transmit by using craft language intentionally.

The Effect of Using "Craft Language" from the Point of View of Mastering "Kata"

Why can craft language so effectively induce or provoke sensation in the learner's body? Why can a metaphorical expression work more effectively than a descriptive one when the teacher wants to transmit "Kata" to the learner? To inquire into this problem. I would like to quote the analysis of the metaphor done by Hugh Petrie.

According to Petrie, a metaphor has two aspects, that is, "comparative" and "interactive". He says:

"one and the same metaphor can be comparative and interactive, depending on the point of view taken. An educational metaphor like, 'The atom is a miniature solar system,' is probably a comparative metaphor from the point of view of the teacher. The teacher already knows both about the solar system and about atoms and is relying upon the similarity between them which already exists in our collective understanding. But from the point of view of the student just beginning atomic physics, the metaphor, assuming it is successful, will be interactive. It will (help) create the similarity for the student. . . . Thus, the fact that the metaphor can be interactive for the student is crucial. For it may provide a way of understanding how the student's modes of representation and understanding can be changed, although granting that experience is dependent of a particular mode or scheme of understanding."[22]

The effect of craft language, to provoke a certain physical sensation in the learner's body, is grounded on the interactive aspect of a metaphor. The teacher who already knows the similarity between the metaphor and the form which is supposed to be mastered by the learner, has the intention of encouraging the learner to imagine and discover the similarity between the metaphor and the form to be mastered by himself.

Now, let us go back and consider the case of Japanese dancing. For example, receiving a metaphorical suggestion like "Act as if you are catching snowflakes falling down from the sky", may confuse the learner at first, but he may begin to imagine the scene of snow falling on a cold day, and to compare the image of catching snow with his hand with the knowledge he has stored so far through committing himself to the world of Japanese traditional dancing. And in that process of comparison between the two through his imagination, he gradually discards inappropriate properties of snow such as "white", "cold", or "melting" which have nothing to do with the dancing form itself. And he would finally reach an appropriate property of snow, which is exactly similar to the form his teacher implies. He finally understands that "lightness" or "fragileness" of snow must be the one he is supposed to express in the form of holding his right hand up. To catch snowflakes with his hand, he has to hold out his hand as gently as possible, otherwise it will surely fly away from his hand. He is convinced that though he needs to hold out his hand, it is not enough that he mechanically does so. What is important is how he holds out his hand.

As soon as he can understand what the metaphorical expression practically implies, he also can get the same physical sensation as his teacher has, in his own body, and can simultaneously grasp the meaning of "Katachi" with a sense of reality, that is to say, he can master "Kata". By intermediating craft language which has the effect of encouraging the learner to activate his creative imagination, the teacher can effectively transmit "Kata" to him. In this sense, the activity of imagination on the part of the learner, which is encouraged effectively by craft language, is an indispensable factor for mastering "Kata", not "Katachi". It is this activity of imagination that a teacher's intentional use of craft language, rather than a descriptive one practically aims for. The teacher knows from his experience that for the learner to master "Kata", he has to inquire into the appropriate form and to grasp the meaning of it by himself through activating his imagination, and that a descriptive or a scientific language does not work effectively for that purpose.

However, there is one thing we have to keep in mind in considering the effect of craft language. That is, it is not always the case that any learner, whether novice or expert, who receives metaphorical suggestions can activate his imagination. To be able to do this, he has to have already stored, both implicitly and explicitly, the knowledge about not only "Katachi", but also its socio-cultural background through committing himself to or indwelling in the world of a certain "Waza" by the time he receives such a metaphorical suggestion from his teacher. Without such knowledge, he can only imagine what the metaphorical statement literally means and he will never be encouraged to activate his imaginative activity such as comparing the literal meaning with the form he is supposed to master, and he will stay in the state of "Mushu-fu" forever.

It follows that craft language works effectively only when the learner has already been engaged in the activity of imitating "Katachi", indwelling inside the world of a certain "Waza". To those who are outside the world or have not stored enough knowledge yet, craft language means nothing or is just awkward expression at best.

Conclusion

Let me sum up what I have discussed so far.

Concerning the aim of teaching and learning "Waza", the process of teaching and learning a skill of Japanese traditional performance has been considered so mysterious and closed that the people outside the world of "Waza" hardly understand what happens there. But, in fact, what both the teacher and the learner aim for at the end of the teaching and learning is the mastery of "Kata", not "Katachi". "Kata", as distinct from "Katachi", can well be explained by introducing a sociological concept "habitus" which is a cultural or situational "Katachi". It is "Kata", "habitusized katachi", that the learner should make efforts to master through the activity of imitating and repeating the form his teacher shows. That is exactly what the learner should "steal in secret (*nusumu*)" from his teacher.

Concerning the way of how to get to the stage of mastering "Waza", in addition to the factor, on the part of the learner, of imitating and repeating "Katachi" through committing himself to or indwelling in the world of a certain "Waza", we can recognize the role of a special metaporical language intermediating in the process of teaching, different from a descriptive or a scientific one, which I here called "craft language" according to Howard. The teacher often uses craft language in the process of teaching as it effectively enables the learner to master "Kata" by encouraging him to activate his creative imagination. Through the activity of imagination as is shown in the above examples of Japanese dancing and Kabuki play, he can finally experience the same physical sensation that his teacher has and wants the learner to master in his own body. That is to say, through that activity, the learner is able to grasp, with a sense of reality, the meaning of "Katachi" he is imitating.

This process of mastering "Kata" might be drawn as shown in Fig. 1.

As this figure shows, the perfect reproduction of "Katachi" (the state of "Mushu-fu") can easily be learned through following a sequence of procedures of "Katachi" shown by the teacher, but in order for the learner to get to the state of mastering of "Kata", he has to activate his creative imagination while he is following a sequence of procedures of "Katachi", and to grasp the meaning of it by himself. Craft language effectively encourages the learner to activate his imagination, thereby enabling him to grasp the meaning of "Katachi" which is the mastery of "Kata".

Finally, I would like to say something about what the above discussion suggests concerning the general problem of human intelligence. What I intended in the discussion in this article, as I mentioned in the beginning, is not only to elucidate the cognitive process of learning a skill of Japanese traditional performance,

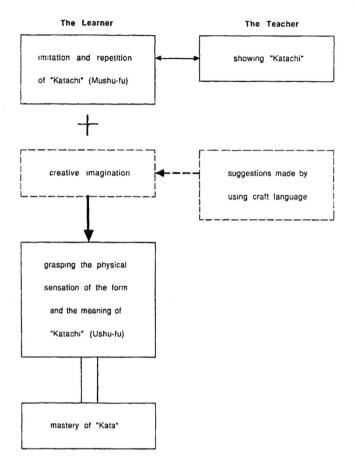

Fig. 1.

"Waza", but also to propose a new perspective, on the study of human intelligence, which has not been shed light on from the scientific point of view. Such areas as cognitive science, philosophy, psychology and AI which share the concern with human intelligence have tried to inquire into the nature of human intelligence, and in fact remarkable results have been attained especially in the area of AI today. However, although I approve of their far from small contribution to the study into intelligence, I can not hide my dissatisfaction with it from the point of view of not "artificial" but "natural" human intelligence.

As Dreyfus and Dreyfus state in *Mind over Machine*:

"Computers could then follow such rules or programs to deduce how those facts affect each other and what happens when the facts change. In this way computers came to be used to simulate logical thinking. We shall call computers used in this way 'logic machines' or 'inference engines'."[23]

"The computer, if used to simulate logical thinking, can only make inferences from lists of facts. It's as if, in order to read a newspaper, you had to spell out each word, find its meaning in the dictionary, and diagram every sentence, labelling all the parts of speech. Brains don't seem to decompose either language or images this way, but logic machines have no choice. Being unable to make inferences from images, they must decompose them into the objects they contain and into descriptions of those objects in terms of their features before drawing any conclusions".[24]

Today's computer seems to stay at the level of functioning as an analytic apparatus, that is, so to say, to stay in the stage of following "Katachi". According to the above discussion where the ultimate goal of learning "Waza" is inseparable from the matter of mastering "Kata", we cannot help concluding that human intelligence cannot satisfactorily be described as the kind that makes logical inferences by following the descriptive rules or procedures correctly, but it also involves the activity of imagination which effectively encourages our thinking. Now why should we pay attention to the aspect of human intelligence which cannot be described by descriptive rules or procedures as is shown in the above examples of learning "Waza"? If human intelligence is of the kind which can also be facilitated by such tacit factors (behind the explicit learning procedures) as commitment to the situation or creative imagination urged by craft language, we have to seriously consider the nature of such tacit factors. We should examine the meaning of human commitment to the situation or the meaning of the imaginative activity in understanding, and then consider how we can possibly apply it to the study of intelligence, whether "human" or "artificial".

The points I have proposed in this article are, in this sense, not domain-specific to the learning of Japanese traditional performance, and I am convinced that they might also be suggestive when we discuss what the nature of human intelligence really is.[25]

References

1. The oldest extant professional theatre; a form of musical dance-drama originating in the 14th century. E. O. Reishauer *et al.* (eds.) *Encyclopedia JAPAN* (1983), Kodansha International Ltd, Tokyo.
2. One of the three major classical theatres of Japan, together with the Noh and puppet theatre (*Bunraku*) (ibid.).
3. Art of self-defence that uses no weapons and relies instead on arm strides (*uchi*), thrusts (*tsuki*) and kicks (*keri*) (ibid.).
4. A form of unarmed combat that stresses agile motions, astute mental judgment, and rigorous form, rather than sheer physical strength (ibid.).
5. Japanese fencing based on the techniques of the two-handed sword of the samurai (ibid.).
6. Singleton, J. (1989). Japanese folkcraft pottery apprenticeship: cultural patterns of an educational institution. In *Anthropological Approaches to the Study of Apprenticeship*, Michael Coy (ed.), Sunny Press.
7. Mauss, M. (1950). *Sociologie et Anthropologie*, Presses Universitaires de France, pp. 368–369.
8. Ryle, G. (1949). *The Concept of Mind*, Hutchinson, p. 44.
9. Ibid., p. 44.
10. The brilliant actor, playwright, and critic who established Noh (*sarugaku*) as a classic theatrical art (1363–1443) (E. O. Reishauer *et al.* (eds) *Encyclopedia JAPAN*, Kodansha International Ltd, Tokyo, 1983).
11. Zeami, "Hanakagami", *Shinchosha*, 1976, pp. 103–104.
12. Kabuki actor (1865–1940).
13. Kabuki actor (1838–1903).
14. Nakamura, Utaemon, *Nihon no Geidan 2*, Kugei Publishing Company 1979, p. 192.
15. Kabuki actor (1911–1988).
16. Kabuki actor (1885–1949).
17. The popular 18th-century *kabuki* play. A tale of revenge based on "the forty-seven ronin incident", is a famous play shown even now in near entirety. (E. O. Reishauer, *et al.* (eds.) *Encyclopedia JAPAN*, Kodansha International Ltd, Tokyo, 1983).

18. The ramp extending into the audience toward the left side of the theatre, which serves both as a secondary stage and as the means by which the actors often make their dramatic entrances and exits (ibid.).
19. Seki, Yoko (1985). *Nakamura Kanzaburo Gakuya-banashi*, Bungeishunju Publishing Company, pp. 45–46.
20. Howard, V. (1982). *Artistry*, Hacket Publishing Company, pp. 46–47.
21. Ibid., pp. 47–48.
22. Petrie, H. (1979). "Metaphor and Learning". In *Metaphor and Thought*, Cambridge University Press, p. 443.
23. Dreyfus, H. and Dreyfus, S. *Mind over Machine* (1986), The Free Press, p. 53.
24. Ibid., p. 54.
25. For the further argument on this problem, see Kumiko Ikuta (1987), *Waza kara shiru* (Learning from Skill), Tokyo University Press.

Correspondence and offprint requests to: Kumiko Ikuta, Sugino Women's College, 4-6-19 Kamio-saki, Shinagawa-Ku, Tokyo, 141, Japan.

AI & Soc (2007) 21: 57–71
DOI 10.1007/s00146-006-0038-5

Biswatosh Saha · Shubhashis Gangopadhyay

Building a pedagogy around action and emotion: experiences of Blind Opera of Kolkata

Received: 5 May 2005 / Accepted: 24 January 2006 / Published online: 10 March 2006
© Springer-Verlag London Limited 2006

Abstract Contemporary knowledge systems have given too much importance to visual symbols, the written word for instance, as the repository of knowledge. The primacy of the written word and the representational world built around it is, however, under debate—especially from recent insights derived from cognitive science that seeks to bring back action, intent and emotion within the core of cognitive science (Freeman and Nunez in J Consciousness Stud 6(11/12), 1999). It is being argued that other sensory experiences, apart from the visual, along with desires (or intent) and emotions—like pain, pleasure, sorrow or joy—constitute equally important building blocks that shape an individual's cognition of the world around. This multi-sensory cognition colored by emotions inspire action and hence is valid knowledge. This is probably nowhere more apparent than in the world of the visually impaired. Deprived of visual sensory capability, they have to perforce depend on other senses. But the dominant discourse in wider society plays a major role in determining what they (the blind) can do. A society built around visual symbols and the written word underplays other elements of cognition and in the process undervalues them. This also gets reflected in the construction of social artifacts of various kinds, such as the educational certification system (The Braille system is an attempt to make the written world accessible to the blind through tactile signals—so that words are 'felt' and 'read.' But it is quite cumbersome. For instance, even a blind highly skilled at writing in Braille would not be able to match the writing speed of an ordinary visually endowed literate person. Effective and efficient computer-based voice–text–voice converters might solve this problem better.)-based primarily on skills over the written word. Linguistic ability becomes most valuable and at another level the written word gets salience over the spoken word. The blind hardly has a chance, therefore, except through concessions or piety. A practice built around the imagery of an empowered blind person, therefore, must depart from mainstream conceptualization—for power is derived from what one has rather than from what one lacks. It must begin by

B. Saha (✉)
XLRI Jamshedpur, C.H. Area (E), Jamshedpur, 831001, India
E-mail: biswatosh@xlri.ac.in

S. Gangopadhyay
Blind Opera, 106D Gopal Lal Thakur Road, Kolkata, 700036, India
E-mail: shubhashis_gangopadhyay@rediffmail.com

415

tapping and valorizing one's own endowments. This paper is an attempt to identify such a departure based on the experience of Blind Opera—a theatre group of the blind working in Kolkata, India. It seeks to provide an exposition in written word of an experience that can only be partially captured within the confines of a text. It is an incomplete account, therefore, and may be taken as an attempt to reach out and seek an exchange of experiences and insights.

Keywords Blind Opera · Knowledge systems · Contemporary education system · Pedagogy · Cognition · Body language · Emotional memory games · Skill formation · Action and emotion

> In a theatre auditorium in Kolkata, it is discomfortingly dark except for a beam of light in the middle of the stage. A play begins. A group of blind actors and actresses are sitting in a circle—their heads bent down touching the ground. A pensive background music fills the auditorium. Those on stage are crying—and their wail of sorrow soon overshadows the music. The audience is moved. The music changes—a slight change in rhythm changes the mood. The group on stage recovers—helped by the *common* background music that aids each of them in their *unique* journey through emotions from the depth of sorrow to joy. They hold each others hand—rhythm touches their bodies and music finds expression in their voice. They sing and dance in joy (*nache janma, nache mrityu pache pache, tata thoi thoi, tata thoi thoi... ki anondo ki anondo...*[1])—their synchronized movements choreographing into beautiful formations on stage. The audience is stunned. There is *magic* in the air. The stage is bathed in light now. For the audience that is a relief—to be in light again. But for those on stage—it hardly matters except for the warmth of the high powered spotlights that they must be feeling. The play of the blind continues...

Opening scene of Blind Opera's 'King of the Dark Chamber'

---

1 Introduction

We develop this paper on two main strands of argument building on two sets of practices of the group. Firstly, that skill formation is a multi-sensory experience and is far more effective if learning is built around action. This learning and skill formation through action is necessarily multi-sensory. We argue that this method of pedagogy (using the full sensory experience) is superior to current practices of education (especially in India now) that focuses on imparting literacy, thereby creating just an ability to dabble in some visual symbols whose connection to the actionable world often seems remote. For our purposes in this paper, it also effaces (at least to an extent) the difference between the blind and the visually endowed, if innovative techniques to tap

---

[1] A popular song composed by Rabindranath Tagore (in Bengali). Translated it would read something like—...there is dance of life and of death, one entwined with the other... dance to the beat of transcendental joy, *tata thoi thoi* (which is a simple beat or *bol* in Indian dance)

and hone non-visual cognitive capabilities of the blind are devised and perfected. This part of the paper, therefore, deals with skill formation and the pedagogy associated with it.

The second point we seek to make is that emotions constitute an important element shaping our cognition and hence learning (or education) has to take note of that. We deal in particular with a sense of stricken-ness that often characterizes socially marginalized groups. We argue that it is through a discovery of one's own emotions in memory that an emancipation is achieved—a sort of 'coming to terms.' We explore a method that partially lies beyond-linguistic reason—in music and drama and partially in a process of dialogue with the trusted. It is this emancipation that allows for a wider sense-making or a grasping of the subject's own surrounding reality. Emotions then can begin to act as springboards for action rather than as dampener of desires to act. The second strand, therefore, is not about skills but is about an attitude. The development of both of the above, i.e., skill and attitude lead to the attainment of the fruit of successful conduct of a pragmatic folk life.

The paper is organized as follows. The next section looks at practices of the group and provides a few instances of innovative techniques used to implement a 'teaching system' using multi-sensory cognition. Here we distinguish the practice of the group, rooted in traditional Indian thoughts on education, from discourses and practice of rehabilitation of the blind in Western societies. We then discuss the 'emotional memory games' and the process of dialogue involved in it, which constitute a central plank of Blind Opera's method, developing in the process a concept of trust between the teacher and student that makes such intense dialogue possible. Finally, we situate the experiment socially, speculating on supporting innovations in political economy that we think is required to sustain the initiative. We argue specifically that the experiment has to find support through local patronage mechanisms, deviating from current educational systems whose organization and administration reflects the primacy granted to the written word as a knowledge source.

2 Skill formation and the pedagogy

The dream of building up a professional theatre group of the blind is somewhat daunting, yet magical. Experience and received ideas suggest that the blind lacks an expressive body language as well as mobility. A blind person performing complex somersaults—vaulting through the air and making a perfect landing is not an image that the popular imagination about the blind can easily conjure up. Achieving complex coordinated motor movement of the body synchronized and related with the surrounding space appears difficult for the blind. Neither is blind persons too famed for expressive gesticulatory skills. Yet, theatre requires both these skills in abundance—for acting is an exercise of the mind and the body; the whole self in fact unfolds on stage. A body untrained in performing intricate movements on stage as well as forming itself into different poses and postures and a mind incapable of indulging in controlled emotions is not too effective on stage. The work of the group began,

60

therefore, as an experiment trying to explore the limits of what is possible. The group was woven around an expectation of a magic (a *chamatkar*) in the truest Indian theatrical traditions.[2]

The lack of a body language and mobility through space are important dimensions of the perceived disability of the blind as well. Lack of a body language makes communication by the blind appear stony, disinterested and mundane. It does not inspire or excite the other person engaged in a communicative dialogue, especially if it is with someone who is visually endowed, and hence the attempt at communication looses much of its import. The creative discovery of the other in a dialogue and the act of coaxing or cajoling or inducing the participant in a dialogue in a flight of fancy and such attempts involved in a communicative exercise seem difficult. The communicative difficulty arising out of a lack of body language of the blind reflects, on one hand, unfamiliarity with a widely shared repertory of signs and gestures (of the body) that the visually endowed creatively draws upon and uses while engaging in a dialogue. While the visually endowed learns such gestures through visual imitation, for the blind such a visually aided imitative learning is not possible. If alternative systems do not provide the blind access to the repertory, an adequate body language would not be developed. This lack of access to widely shared symbols, therefore, can constitute a dimension of exclusion (or lack of effective inclusion) of the blind from social communicative networks overwhelmingly dominated by the visually endowed. On the other hand, the communicative difficulty also arises from an inability of the visually endowed to appreciate signs and symbols of a non-visual nature, such as subtle differences in auditory gestures that the blind might be using in a dialogic interaction with the visually endowed. This later aspect we would further develop in course of our subsequent discussion. The point to note is that the blind whose social interaction involves, to a large extent, the visually endowed, fails to participate (as in an act) in the exercise of gestures that expresses and communicates. We argue that this external failure also probably leads to an internal cognitive failure in organizing and classifying subtle emotions and moods (and in the process further developing it), for it is through external action (in gesturing) within a social setting that an internal cognitive realization of subtlety of emotions is also

---

[2] The experiment began in 1994 within an established theatre group (Nandikar) as a project with blind boys and girls of Calcutta Blind School (a residential school partially supported by the government) financed through a Ford Foundation grant. The short project culminated in the production of a play—but Nandikar decided to discontinue the initiative thereafter. The group of blind boys and girls were, however, deeply interested in exploring the world of theatre—dabbling with stage performance had aroused that *magical* possibility amongst them. The group of theatre professionals involved with the work including the present director (the second author of the paper), also thought that the idea was promising and setup an independent outfit—the Blind Opera—in 1996 to carry on the work towards building a professional theatre troupe of the blind. While the call to explore the undiscovered world of the blind inspired, increasing discontent with developments in the world of theatre/culture that was moving away from its engagement with the life around convinced the group to seek out a departure. The work started with a group of around 30 students of Calcutta Blind School who had completed their schooling. Several of them are still with the group, while new people have also come in. The new group is more diverse with different levels of schooling (including dropouts). In general, the blind in India, after completing their schooling, enter a difficult phase because of extreme dearth of occupational openings. They are, therefore, often victims of social neglect that emanates from the closest quarters. Their lifeworld remains, as a result, stricken by horrid experiences.

achieved—for such skills[3] as gesturing are not learnt through conceptualization and a discourse but mainly through repeated action.

The other aspect that we referred to above is the difficulty in mobility that the blind experience. Difficulties regarding mobility and devising of means and methods to get over that have also been a very important concern of discourses concerning the blind in Western societies. Underlying the lack of mobility is the inability to have a visual mapping of the surrounding space and the relation of the body with other physical artifacts within the surrounding space. The mapping out of space, therefore, has to be made with non-visual cues, such as through touch or through audio cues. Exploring through these other cues, often, is a slow process and it takes time, for instance, to feel through the space around. Motion, therefore, is slow. It also induces a fear of the unknown—of new spaces or new ordering and arrangements in known space that must again be mapped, which can lead to a lack of desire to explore.

Here we make a distinction between the difficulty in navigating through new spaces or creating maps of new spaces that the blind experiences and the difficulty that the blind experiences in achieving rapid (or coordinated) movements within a known and pre-explored (through non-visual cues) space. The Western discourse around mobility and rehabilitation of the blind has concentrated thus far, primarily on the first of these two aspects through construction of several physical (external) artifacts, such as traffic signals that give out a visual and an audio signal simultaneously (or such gadgets as electronic walking sticks) that has eased the navigational problems of the blind in new spaces and have thus made social space more accessible to the blind. That, however, is not enough, particularly in cases involving problems of the later type. For instance, when Blind Opera started its work of developing stage production/enactment of theatre with the blind, one of its first innovations involved designing of such an external artifact—a thick rope that is placed at the periphery of the stage to delimit it. Before any performance begins the actors and actresses feel the space in the stage and the rope aids that process—and all through the show, the rope acts as a delimiter of all movements that are accomplished on stage—so that the inside and outside of the stage becomes clearly discernible. The innovation is remarkable for its simplicity and economy—it is hardly discernible even to the visually endowed audience. Yet this artifact does not help the movement of the blind within the bounded (and pre-explored) space—such as somersaulting during the performance. Achieving such feats, which is far more important in the context of theatre would require an adequate learning system built on non-visual cognition involving space and motion. It has to be internally driven. We would explore such a multi-sensory teaching system that can overcome the two dimensions of visual disability that we identified. While the development of these skills and its perfection is a prerequisite for theatre, a minimum development of these skills is useful (even essential) for a successful and fulfilling 'folk life' experience outside the theatrical stage. Therefore, without denying the significance of Western innovation trajectories that aim to create inclusive spaces for

---

[3] Although 'skills' generally refer to ability to dabble with the material world and achieve a desired transformation (for instance potter's skill in shaping clay to a pot), we are using skills in a wider sense while referring to gesturing as a 'skill.' A vocal musician's skill would be of a similar category, where a material object is not associated with the idea of performance of the skill.

the blind through high-tech gadgets, we argue that Blind Opera's practice is aimed at addressing facets of the problem that cannot be tackled within the Western approach. Therefore, we claim a complementarity.

2.1 Sensory skills of the blind

A group of people are sitting in a circle—some of them are blind and others visually endowed. They are all speaking at the same time—in a chaotic frenzy. The game is to decipher from the chaos the speech of the partner of each. The blind in the group succeed in their attempts—the visually endowed are most often not as lucky.

From that group, a blind girl slowly stands up—removes the anklet that makes quite a bit of noise and silently slips away. The visually endowed could see it all. Then her partner—a blind—remarks after a few minutes—"when did she leave?" Even silence could not deceive. When she left, the blind girl left a trace—the absence of a smell—that could be discerned.

The group disbands after a few more exercises. Every blind finds their partner with whom they would travel back with ease without exchanging a single word. Those who can see can seldom find their loved ones from a motley crowd just by touching them—yet the blind can discern that familiar touch of the beloved even in the complexity of a large crowd.

Even folk knowledge about the blind has long acknowledged the heightened sensory capability of 'sound–touch–smell' that the blind possess. In several mythical and poetic allusions in the Indian tradition the blind (*andha baul* or *fakir*) often led the way for they could 'sense' what the visually endowed could not 'see.' It was a celebration of the skill and capability of the blind—their heightened sense of sound–touch–smell. Just as these sensory skills of the blind are honed through repeated use in their daily living, their memory also gets sharpened through a similar mechanism. Memory serves a very important purpose for the blind even in mundane tasks as finding the way to a known place. Lacking a continuous stream of visual signals, the blind depends much more on memory of the place. While the visually endowed also recollects from memory the visual images of the place, for the blind, memory is, in a sense, used more intensely. It is therefore not too uncommon to find an average blind person to be far more capable of memorizing a long text faster and with greater retention over a longer time. Pedagogy for the blind must therefore aim to sharpen these endowments for it provides the key to their cognitive world.

2.2 Towards a multi-sensory cognition of the body and space

Developing a body language and mobility requires an exercise of the body and it starts, in a sense, from the cognition of one's own body. So knowledge of the basic anatomy and physiology of the body is essential to begin with. This knowledge is not picked up through abstract reasoning, as in memorizing or understanding a text, but it happens principally through action—an action by exercise of one's own body along with gradual familiarity with a system of naming. Therefore, it has phenomenological roots. This 'actioning' is most often imitative. Since the blind cannot imitate through visual images, alternative imitative mechanisms need to be created. Blind Opera's methods concentrate on two such modes—through sound (as in profuse verbal description of body movements) and touch (the blind imitates by touching the body movements and positions of the person whom they imitate).

This learning through imitation begins from the premise that there is motion and rhythm in everyone, driven by psycho-somatic processes—a rhythm that is primitive or pristine and natural. Yet it is through a social learning process that this inner rhythm unfolds. Blind students begin such rhythmic exercises in apparent chaos, as an untrained exercise is bound to be. Yet the work must begin from this chaotic expression rather than from an instruction of the cultivated sophisticated movements—because it is his/her own—driven by an inner cognitive state. That is why it is spontaneous and joyous. The first task, therefore, is to induce the student to participate and give expression (as in acting) to the spontaneous rhythm, however ugly it appears to an outside observer. It might be meaningless to any observer and would fail as a communicative tool but it is important to realize that it is pregnant with meaning for the actor, for it reflects the inner cognitive state. And it is full of meaning to the teacher, who has to discover the inner cognitive state of the student to engage in successful pedagogy. Teaching and learning is a process of mutual discovery by the teacher as well as the student in this method. Achieving this, that is inducing the student to engage in the spontaneous act is, however, quite difficult. It can be achieved only in an environment of trust, built up by the teacher. It cannot be induced by a fear of punishment, as in contemporary grading/marking systems in schools. Yet a disciplinary mechanism within a structure must be in place (as in the structure of games a few of which we discuss below) for pedagogy and learning to be effective. A set of injunctions from the teacher (who has power) provides the structure. It does not, however, create a fear that can throttle self-expression. The student also remains free to reveal the naiveté and ignorance and not be scoffed at or rebuked. On this chaotic expression, the teacher has to work, demonstrating, illustrating and guiding. The teacher is like the 'mirror,' whom the blind imitates by touching all over to get an image of a movement or a posture that they can then replicate. A repertory of movements and expressions slowly gets built up that the blind starts creatively drawing upon and using. We provide below, as illustration, a few of the numerous theatre games (or structured learning environments) that form the basis of this pedagogic method.

Theatre games The task of the blind in this game is to turn towards the direction of the source of a sound—it is initially told that the sound is that of gunfire. The sound can come from any direction in three-dimensional space surrounding the blind and can be located at different distances. First the game begins by slow movement of the body and then the speed picks up—the speed of turning as well as the speed of consecutive shots (or the interval between consecutive shots decreases). The body movement is achieved in several stages. It can start with a movement of the head (from above the shoulder), then it can be turning from the waist above and then turn around completely. While turning, the task of the blind is to react to the sound and its nature—to express the mood that gets created through the audio signal emanating from the gunshot. At the next stage, the blind may also react by uttering a sound, which seeks to express the own feeling. The external sound can then change in stages and at each stage the whole set of exercises are repeated. The sound can change to the growl of a dangerous animal seeking its prey, then the sound of a less dangerous animal, then an unknown person's call, a known person's call and a beloved person's call.

As the nature of the sound changes, the blind has to now react in more complex ways to that sound to express the inner emotions aroused by the external sound. The initial reactions are just bodily—though involving increasingly complex coordination of body movements. It culminates in a dialogic response, where the body language has to be only one component that must synchronize with the dialogue. As the game proceeds, the teacher observes and guides and engages in a continuous dialogue. The blind at some stage should be able to articulate (in a dialogic response to the teacher's queries) the emotions aroused within by an external sound or a dialogue. At later stages this dialogue becomes prolonged as a mutual justification is sought about the reasons for the arousal of a particular mood or emotion.

The theatre game described above illustrates several aspects of the basic pedagogic philosophy of Blind Opera. The learning system within the simulated environment of the game is multi-sensory. The basic purpose is to build up a teaching–learning method for the blind through non-visual sensory cues so that a body language gets developed. The game is structured to develop the capability to distinguish between different audio cues so that an elaborate system of classification can be developed that would enable the blind to cognize the surrounding space. A large repertory of audio signals (or sounds) in memory with the ability to draw fine distinctions between different sounds (i.e., a discerning ability) constitute a basic skill of the blind. It is this ability which aids a fuller sensory cognition of the world around—for the blind world is a world of sound, touch and smell. Similar games aim at developing and honing the sense of touch and smell so that a heightened sensory experience becomes possible. At a higher level, the game also sharpens the ability to relate between motor skills (of the body), audio skills and relating all of that to the process of recollection from the repertory in memory and the emotion aroused within. All of these coalesce at the point of action—for in action all of these skills are invoked together in the process of the act.

Secondly, in this method, learning occurs through action. The numerous theatre games that are designed regularly and played out not only makes learning interesting and fun, but it makes it more effective since the students act it out. The game creates a structured simulation of a social setting within which the action of the student (a dialogic response in the above game) occurs. This action-based learning is superior to learning systems based just on a text (or the written word), since the process of discovery of the student—in the richness of the internal cognitive world—is more effective. In action the overall cognition of a person, in its several dimensions, comes to the fore and develops along a unique path.

Finally action also effaces the difference between an external manifestation, such as a body movement denoting an expression or an emotion, and the underlying emotion. Learning through action leads to a simultaneous cultivation of the external movements—an accumulative build up of a repertory and a system of classification and differentiation of such external manifestations and a corresponding internal cultivation of underlying emotions and moods that can be finely differentiated (or classified) and hence grasped. It is through this dual movement that a cognitive grasping of the world around that leads to a fruit in the form of a successful enactment proceeds.[4] It is the explicit importance given to this internal cognitive dimension that constitutes a novelty in the practice of Blind Opera. It might be apt to recall that we argued that the Western discourse on mobility has concentrated on construction of external artifacts that aid the process of navigation of the blind. In the case of Blind Opera such an external artifact was the rope on stage that delimited—yet it was not enough to achieve movements within that bounded and known (or explored space). The differentiated movements and gestures (or body language)—such as the dance of fury, of ecstasy or the serene movement of joy or the pensive movement of sorrow—gestures that enliven a dialogue on stage (and in life as well) can be accomplished only through a system that aims at a wholesome cognitive grasping of reality.

Just as such feats are achieved through learning and doing, so can the impossible feat of a blind somersaulting—the magic of whose possibility we started the essay with—be achieved. It is a leap of faith. In one dramatic moment that is often created through a sequence, music and dialogue—pushed by a trusted teacher—a blind takes that leap. A successful accomplishment breaks a cognitive barrier—once, twice and so on till it becomes a routine—a feat in the accumulated repertory of the blind, a skill that has been learnt. When enacted on stage—it is magic for the visually endowed—for they are exposed to the product (outcome) alone. The process lies hidden in a magical mist in the mundane detail of the daily practice of the group. While these accomplishments have undoubtedly been invaluable on stage—for the purpose of theatre, it has also had a significant effect on the folk life of the students. For instance, several of the students—when they began their association with Blind Opera, would come to the place where the group worked and go back aided by an escort—normally a family member or a close friend. After around a year of involvement in Blind Opera's learning systems, they could travel alone, even in the crowded city of Kolkata—where there are hardly any special aids (as external artifacts, like signal systems) which make public space accessible to the blind.

Evolution of this pedagogy at Blind Opera based on learning through action has been influenced deeply by the long lineage of thoughts on traditional Indian systems of basic education, Rabindranath Tagore (Tagore 1961) in particular (Banerjee 1998 provides a succinct summary of the position). Briefly, basic education was sought to be built around action rather than on abstract principles or theorization (of concepts). Much of the literature emphasized skill building related to working on and transforming the material objects around (Gandhi 1962),[5] while some views within the broad tradition (especially Rabindranath among those from recent history) also emphasized skills related to performances such as music, dance and drama as a fundamental element of what basic education should seek to achieve. Clearly, the skill world was visualized as much more than a linguistic world—it was necessarily multi-sensory in

---

[4] Our argument, therefore, is in sympathy with views within cognitive science that discard a mind–body or mind–matter separation. As Clark (1997) argues, the mind is not in the brain and extends into the body and the world outside.

[5] There is a large contemporary literature on skill building of the craftsmen that share a similar concern, for instance, Gill (1996).

the first place. This basic education also needs to be distinguished from apprenticeship systems. For instance, in the practice of Blind Opera, while the basic element of say, learning of gestures, would be of benefit for everyone—an advanced learning and cultivation of the skill would be required for those who choose to specialize as performing theatre professionals. This advanced learning linked to a profession requires a working apprenticeship institution to develop. The organization has not yet been able to institutionalize such an apprentice system as would sustain continued social reproduction of theatrical skills of the blind beyond the current group of persons.

3 Drama therapy and emotional memory games

The opening scene of the play King of the Dark Chamber described at the beginning of the essay—the group of blind boys and girls making an internal emotional journey from the depths of sorrow to liberation of joy manifested externally in the wails transforming gradually to a vivid choreography of life—represented on stage an enactment of a long drawn practice of Blind Opera. It is an emotional journey that almost every student of Blind Opera has undertaken. This part of the essay explores the process that made such an experience possible in order to identify certain unique characteristics of the methods of the group. Underlying this method is the realization that emotions shape an individual's cognition and hence it plays a role in shaping the desire to act.

An individual's memory is often stricken—stricken with grief and sorrow. Emotions emanating from such grief stricken memory dampen the desire to act, to explore or to learn. It therefore, leads to seclusion or exclusion from wider social processes. This seclusion is not that of an ascetic, whose seclusion is willed, has a purpose and is a willed act. This seclusion, on the contrary is involuntary, in a sense, and leads to and arises from a sense of failure of fulfillment of desires. While such failures are ubiquitous in an individual's social existence, not being able to speak about or an inability to grasp it is what leads to a sense of stricken-ness. The grief gets overblown. The inability to engage in a dialogue leads to a failure in sense-making—so that sorrow and the emotions arising therefrom remain undiscovered. It remains clouded beyond reason, inaccessible to reason. The inability to speak out can arise for lack of a refuge of the trusted that can be acute particularly in excessively regimented systems. For the students of Blind Opera, such sense of alienation, grief and sorrow arose from the general social neglect and exclusion that they experienced—often from the nearest and dearest ones in the family and in other intimate social spaces. It may be pointed out here that it is not an external neglect alone, such as in a utilitarian view of poverty as lack of income or wealth for sustenance that causes this stricken-ness. It is the failure of sense-making of one's reality that is more important. So, symptoms of such processes can also be found in abundance in social spaces with abundant material endowment, particularly at points in history when the general sense of balance in society (and the philosophical system underlying it) is lost. This sense-making of one's reality and the failure of desires, we argue, is a social exercise and can occur only through an inter-personal process of a dialogue with the trusted. Dialogue is an action—and by acting it out an individual obtains liberation or a sense of freedom that prepares the self to again begin desiring to act. It is a cathartic act—it sort of breaks through a cognitive blind alley. This catharsis, however, is not associated with penance and is not judgmental or corrective in nature.

But, a major problem of stricken psyches is that such grief and emotions surrounding it are beyond the ambit of reason—beyond the possible ambit of a dialogue. So the first task is to break through and make such issues accessible to an inter-subjective process of dialogue and reason. This is achieved in Blind Opera's methods through simulation of events surrounding such grief in a theatrical setup (where music often plays a major role) through dialogue with the teacher (often a monologue by the teacher that guides the thought). It is a reenactment for the subject—and by this reenactment (the action) the subject obtains control over such emotions. The blind alley is torn open—action brings it out—and it becomes open to access through dialogue. The method, therefore, differs from practices of psychological counseling which can proceed only if the subject is willing to bring out such issues on the table for a dialogue of reason. In a way, it is extra-linguistic at one stage and dialogic at another.

We attempt providing below a verbal description of an emotional memory game involving one of the students of the group (incomplete though this description is by all accounts for we would in all probability fail to reproduce the emotion and the mood of the moment).

A young, talented dwarf blind girl who came to Blind Opera and got associated with one of their stage productions had a revealing experience. She was then a student at Jadavpur University (in Kolkata) and had just completed her post graduate education—all through her life she had to fight twice as hard to gain entry into educational institutions and she could prove again and again that her visual disability would not stand in the way of her education. All that fight had made her bitter, angry with the world around, particularly the world of the sighted—so easily identifiable as the 'other.' In an emotional memory game, she was talking with the teacher about all this bitterness and as she went deeper into memory and her feelings, her anger started bursting forth.

What would you choose to do if you had your way to punish this unjust world? She was asked. (Italicized part of the dialogue is by the teacher.)

I would kill... *Kill whom?* Kill all—all the sighted people, who make our life miserable.

So kill me, I am a sighted person... a representative of all the injustice meted out to you. But you are my teacher. *How does that matter—if you cannot kill me—hit me—remember it is people like me—maybe I am your teacher, yet it is sighted people like me who cause you so much pain... hit me with all your might.*

And then the teacher recounted one by one the anecdotes of pain, despair, treachery, hate—stories from her lifeworld that he had known over days of intimate interaction with the student. The group was humming a tune (generally a local folk tune that is widely shared) that captured the mood of the moment. The moment was electrifying—charged with emotions, there was music. It was a dramatic point of climax. The teacher and the student were in a trance.

And then she (the student) started beating the teacher with all the might that her little hand could muster—it was a blind fury. The humming changes. And then she broke down—in inconsolable tears. The humming changes again. She had beaten her teacher—her beloved, revered teacher. It took a month for the pain of the inflicted wound to heal.

Now that you have poured all your anger on me—has it solved your problems—what have you achieved? If now everyone else in this room decides to beat you for some wrong that you did them some day some time—how would you feel... and the dialogue continued. The girl recovered slowly. The humming of the group changes again—the group starts dancing—*tata thoi thoi..., ki anondo ki anondo, ki anondo, nache mukti nache bondho* (in Bengali; see note 1 for a translation). They hold her hand—she gets up and joins the choir. It is a catharsis—a liberating experience. None of those who watched it that day as outsiders would, probably, be able to erase it from our memory. Every student in the group, after they first experienced this kind of an emotional journey, wanted to enter the game again—to relive, reenact that experience. This experience got scripted into a play—a full stage production—where the dwarf blind girl played the lead role with élan—and it was the first time she did theatre on stage. The boundary between stage and life faded away.

Exercises in emotional memory, set within the context of simulated theatre games, have been an important aspect of the routines of Blind Opera. Several features of such games need to be remarked upon. The stricken-ness that we discussed above arises in an individual for a unique reason, a result of a unique history and a train of events—its nature, hence, differs widely. Although there might be patterns in the nature of such problems between different groups, such as between totally blind persons and partially blind persons (who still retain some very low vision), the discovery of the unique experience is very important to success of the method. Even the nature of the theatre game, i.e., what is to be played out, would depend on the teacher's understanding of the uniqueness of the student. The method, therefore, explicitly recognizes that the cognitive path to liberation is unique to an individual. As the game unfolds, there are multiple layers of movements occurring simultaneously within the subject—she is a participant in a chorus—the music that operates at the level of the subtle. At the same time she is a participant in a dialogue with the teacher—this movement is more concrete as in an unfolding of the subtle. Shared information between the teacher and the student (this information might not be accessible to others in the group and a whispering mode is often resorted to between the teacher and student) is brought to bear in this movement. And at the same time there is a cognitive movement in the subject that is unique in its detail—not fully discoverable by anybody else, even the teacher who would not know the full details of that path of journey. The method, therefore, is built around multiple layers of 'private-ness' and 'public-ness' of information. While the subtle layers bring a force to bear on the unique individual movement, it is this unique journey that is the route to liberation. While the skill of the teacher lies in operating the subtle levers, unless space is created for the unique journey through a partial discovery of certain features of that uniqueness, the method would fail. The subtle (which is the shared or general) must not dominate. The method therefore is not amenable to mass intervention systems of psychological counseling. Every participant has to be treated as unique, while maintaining a relation of tension with various layers of subtlety that are shared with groups (that differ in its extensiveness of inclusion of others), and it is in this that the success of the method lies. For the teacher, every episode is new—full of surprises in partial discovery of the unique unfolding of the subtle. Every episode, therefore, requires a creative participation of the teacher who must be motivated to take it at that rather than as a routine exercise in conduct of certain procedures from repertory.

The ignorance of the teacher about the exact cognitive path to liberation of the student poses important problems for the structure of organizing these interventions. Since there is ignorance the exact path cannot be explicated in detail—the teacher has to prod and push noting for external manifestations that would demonstrate whether the student has undertaken a sincere exploration of the depth of those thoughts. When exactly that prodding would succeed is not known a priori. Importantly, when it succeeds the full game has to be played out and nothing, such as a pre-structured time schedule must intervene. Within educational setups used to routine pedagogy in pre-structured time slots, this unique requirement to organize time poses immense problems.

We earlier argued about a two-stage process—one that is beyond-linguistic followed by a dialogic intervention. The above account mostly describes the first stage—the beyond-linguistic part that prepares the subject for a dialogic participation. Blind Opera's method differs in this respect from recent discussions and practice of pedagogy of 'marginalized' groups, such as that of the famed Brazilian educationist Paulo Freire (Freire 1972, 1995). Emancipation in Freirian method arises from a process of critical dialogue around a search for the meaning of words in the concrete context of the subject.[6] The world, including the mechanisms of oppression, unravels through this critical dialogue. However, because of its emphasis on discovery of the concrete particular context, it often looses touch with the common linking thread between the severalties of particular contexts. Blind Opera's method differs precisely here. The common link, the shared or the subtle that we identified above is a vital key to the process of emancipation. This subtle takes various forms—the humming in the episode described above or fabulous narratives of the past that are shared through a common tradition. This subtle, we also argue is what defines a society—the commonality that runs across the severalties of particularities. The emancipation is achieved by lifting the subject beyond the particularity of the context in an intense dramatic exercise—without effacing at the same the concrete particularity. The Freirian engagement with the particular therefore occurs, but without loosing sight or the possibility of emancipation offered by the subtle. The subject, therefore, becomes willing to participate in a dialogue. This willingness to engage in a dialogue is a primary indication of the subject's ability in coming to terms and countering the sense of stricken-ness and alienation. It is the first step towards acting in the pragmatic life. The dialogue with the teacher often leads to certain injunctions about the conduct of pragmatic life that has to be followed respectfully (which is possible because teacher has a power). This dialogic process, moreover, does not end during that particular interactive episode—it lingers. Blind Opera's daily practice concentrates mostly on a

---

[6] Paulo Freire developed his methods while he was engaged in adult education initiatives with several marginalized groups. His major contribution was to bring out the relation between words and the context (that gives a meaning to the word). Therefore, word or texts written by a teacher who does not share the context (and hence the meanings) of the student group often fails to evoke an interest in learning and critical thinking. Literacy becomes merely an information transfer exercise and it dehumanizes.

discovery of the cultural roots of the community through enactment of epics—so that through a series of such dramatic enactments a discovery of a common lineage occurs. Such grand narratives often become a part of the continuing dialogue—in some such narrative or epic tale a subject might find that element of emancipation. The choice of such tales by the teacher is often motivated by the need to seek such refuge in narratives—but that is never told that way. The individual has to discover the exact path to emancipation. So the dialogue is a lingering process—spaced across time, which often also escapes the confines of the present and in a flight of fancy engages with the past. As the past unfolds as a narrative, the future too unfolds as a possibility and the ground for creating an imaginative unfolding of the future seems graspable.

The second strand of our argument, therefore, has dealt with development of an attitude, rather than a skill—as we argued earlier as well. Development of the skill and attitude defines the pedagogy.

4 Conclusions: on a speculative note

The pedagogy described above is unique in several respects, as we argued above. The important aspect of that is the explicit importance given to the subject's individuality (that defines a context specificity) on the one hand along with a search and an engagement with a commonality that we argued to be the basis of the society. The target of this pedagogy, unlike most contemporary educational systems, is not to bring every participant to an average standard of performance but to seek a cognitive emancipation of each individual, although they might be placed very differently in terms of levels of consciousness and knowledge. Contemporary educational systems organized vertically under centralized administrative control are not geared to this purpose. Examination systems are, for instance, primarily oriented towards certifying certain skill levels in terms of dabbling with the written word. It would fail to evaluate multi-sensory learning systems that are oriented towards action (in this case on the theatre stage). This power of the written word, we argue as a speculative proposition, serves an important purpose of centralization and control—for it can transfer some simple information across contexts and locales much more easily. Governance then can be organized around transactions around those information. A necessary corollary of such a system is standardization and an educational system that valorizes literacy (including familiarity with written rules/laws/procedures) and hence would emphasize pedagogy around written word, which, however, seldom reaches high levels of conceptual engagement.

The written word, in a way, is inadequate in conveying richer information that needs to take recourse of multiple sensory experiences. For instance, information on pedagogic success of programs that seek to qualify students in certain standard certification tests can be developed easily and would be robust to inter-subjectivity validity tests as well—even when the people involved are located at great distances. But devising such a procedure for testing the effectiveness of Blind Opera's pedagogy would be absolutely cumbersome if it has to be administered through a bureaucratic administrative apparatus. Governance from a distance, therefore, would most likely fail. The political economy supporting such initiatives as Blind Opera probably has to be local—seeking local alliances with local patrons who can base governance on more direct experience of the work. The spread and dissemination of the practice, therefore, would require a decentralized network of several learning centers, each built on local patronage mechanisms. The network can then be linked through an apprenticeship program that would continue to generate new knowledge around the practice and transfer it at the same time to a large base of apprentices who would in turn form the nuclei of the dispersed local learning centers. However, that is a leap of faith. Over the years, the experiment of Blind Opera has been sustained by a yearly grant from government of India and small philanthropic initiatives from a local network of well-wishers. The relationship with the State bureaucratic apparatus, however, has not evolved (in fact the grant-making ministry does not even monitor the grant utilization and the work of the group). The local supporting network, in contrast, probably has to devise a shared right mechanism so as to allow the space for innovative experimenting to continue even within a dense relationship. Whether the pedagogic innovations of Blind Opera can be matched to organizational innovation required to sustain such a practice is an open question. But it is, to our mind, clear that failing the supporting organizational innovation it would probably end up with the same fate as several such initiatives, including the Santiniketan[7] experiment of Rabindranath Tagore that were made along similar lines.

Acknowledgments While the first author is a well-wisher of Blind Opera, the second author is the founder Director of the group. Authors wish to acknowledge their debts to the students of Blind Opera from whom they learnt. They also acknowledge valuable comments provided by reviewers. While only a part of it could be considered in this essay, their extensive comments would guide the authors in future work. Both authors and Blind Opera can be contacted at biswatoshsaha@rediffmail.com.

References

Banerjee P (1998) Development of skills and attitudes in basic education. Indira Gandhi National Centre for the Arts, New Delhi, available at http://www.ignca.nic.in/cd_06019.htm

Clark A (1997) Being there: putting brain, body and world together again. MIT Press, Cambridge, MA

Freeman WJ, Nunez R (eds) (1999) Restoring to cognition the primacy of action, intention and emotion. Editor's Introduction to Special Issue of J Consciousness Stud 6(11/12)

Freire P (1972) The pedagogy of the oppressed. Penguin, Harmondsworth

Freire P (1995) The pedagogy of hope: reliving pedagogy of the oppressed. Continuum, New York

Gandhi MK (1962) The problem of education. Navajivan Publishing House, Ahmedabad

Gill KS (1996) Human-machine symbiosis: the foundations of human-centred systems. Springer, Berlin Heidelberg New York

Tagore R (1961) Collected works, vols XII and XIII. Government of West Bengal, Calcutta

---

[7] Santiniketan was designed by Rabindranath Tagore as a center for higher learning, principally in fine arts and literature—and Sriniketan was built up as a twin setup to concentrate on local rural development initiatives. Both the initiatives were sought to be financed through the civil society without support from the State. After independence, though, Santiniketan was nationalized.

PART III

AESTHETICS, ETHICS, AND DESIGN

Ethics and Intellectual Structures

Howard Rosenbrock[1]

[1] Linden, Walford Road, Ross-on-Wye, Hertfordshire, UK

AI&Society (1995) 9:18-28

Abstract. In the paper, three propositions are put forward. First, that intellectual structures of wide scope commonly lead to conclusions which are ethically unacceptable; secondly that the ethically unacceptable consequences of science arise from one particular presupposition which it adopts, namely that of causality; thirdly, that causality is no essential part of science.

1 Introduction

This paper is concerned with the relation between two systems of thought, namely those of ethics and those of our science and science-based technology. These, at first sight, seem to have little contact as intellectual systems, whatever the consequences of their coexistence. Ethics is concerned with the moral principles of an individual or a group, with what is conceived to be good or bad, right or wrong, acceptable or unacceptable. It is distinct from law, which determines what is permitted or not permitted: thus, 'it is morally unacceptable for one group of people to design a technological system which condemns another group to a lifetime of trivial and dehumanised work' is an ethical statement related to technology and independent of the legality or illegality of this activity.

There is a different order of ideas and beliefs which is embedded in our technology and which arises from its basis in science. Scientific statements reject purpose, and are expressed 'objectively', that is in terms of cause and effect. They are usually taken to be true or false according to criteria based in some way upon critical observation or experiment. Truth in this sense is considered to be independent of all

Ethical considerations. 'For the scientist there is only "being", but no wishing, no valuing, no good, no evil, no goal' (Einstein, 1950, 114). Nevertheless, the pursuit of this kind of truth is wished for, and valued, and regarded as the highest good. If, therefore, we propose an ethical statement such as 'the development of the underlying science needed to make the atomic bomb is morally unacceptable' we set up a conflict.

Within the intellectual structure of science, ethical judgements of this kind have no place, while the pursuit of scientific truth must not be opposed. The nuclear physicist at Los Alamos could regard himself as a morally detached seeker after objective truth. In his search for scientific knowledge, no ethical problem could arise. Only in the use of this knowledge would ethical considerations be involved, and the responsibility for this use rested upon others, and not on himself. In some such way, we can understand the comment attributed to Enrico Fermi: 'Don't bother me with your conscientious scruples! After all, the thing's superb physics' (Jungk, 1960, 184). The discontinuity between science and ethics is usually expressed by saying that science is morally neutral: this goes beyond the rejection of ethical considerations in the pursuit of scientific knowledge by claiming that the knowledge itself is exempt from ethical judgement.

A large part of technology is concerned with detaching from the human aims which it serves, sub-problems which can be treated by the methods of science, and which can therefore inherit the scientific claim to ethical neutrality. The designers of a production system, for example, deal with problems of chemistry, or metallurgy, or mechanics, or computing and control and data transmission, or a host of other specialisations. These are all based upon science, augmented where necessary by applied research and development carried out in a scientific spirit, and they form the basis upon which the design activity is founded.

Only with great difficulty can ethical considerations be introduced into the design, and they enter as a wedge of foreign material based upon an alien system of thought, into the coherent and highly resistant body of technical knowledge. Let us propose on ethical grounds, that the production system shall respect and foster the human abilities and skills of those who work within it. The ethical requirement has no congruence with the technical knowledge of the chemist or the mechanical engineer or other technological specialist. It cannot readily be brought into a fruitful relation with this knowledge, incorporating as this does the scientific rejection of ethical criteria and a causal description of nature which excludes much of human experience. The likely outcome of this situation is easy to predict. Production systems will not be designed to cooperate with human abilities and skills in order to enhance them and make them more productive. Workers will be regarded in the spirit of Taylorism as causal devices equivalent to machines, and will be expected to perform in a machinelike way. There is ample evidence of progress in this direction, and still more evidence of the intention to progress further.

This bald outline suggests that the intellectual structure of modern science rejects any special treatment of human beings which would introduce ethical considerations, and that technology, by absorbing this outlook, becomes anti-human in its tendency.

In what follows a number of propositions will be put forward. First, that intellectual structures of wide scope commonly lead to conclusions which are ethically unacceptable: the phenomenon is not unique to science. Secondly, that the ethically unacceptable consequences of science arise from a particular presupposition which it adopts, namely that of causality. Thirdly, that causality is no essential part of science.

434

2 An Historical Parallel

For those who have lived all their lives under the influence of an unquestioned intellectual system, it is difficult to appreciate that the influence exists. What has always been familiar becomes invisible. To appreciate the influence upon us of scientific thought it may therefore be helpful to go back to an earlier period and an earlier system of thought. Jean Bodin (Hauser, 1932; Tooley, 1967; Easalea, 1980; Rose, 1980) was an elder contemporary of Shakespeare and Galileo, living in an age when the spirit of the medieval world was about to give way to a recognisably modern belief in science. Like so many in his day, he looked both forward and backward: rejecting the Copernican system; writing in favour of a limited monarchy, but basing it upon religious justification; while giving an explanation of the 16th century's inflation in a modern spirit of the quantity theory of money. He came, on more that one occasion, within reach of the Inquisition, but his published works received the Imprimatur and can be taken as representing the religious orthodoxy of his day. If one believes that the public burning to death of (mostly) women as witches, is ethically repulsive, how can one explain that a humanist and Christian such as Bodin should strongly advocate it, as he did? We can only do so by looking at the intellectual structure within which Bodin's thought was constrained. Medieval Christianity had its harsher side. The carvings over the entrance of the great cathedrals showed Christ in judgement 'so wroth that no tongue can tell' (Mirk, ca 1400), condemning the souls of transgressors for eternity to the cruel and unusual punishments described with some complacency by Dante. The soul being immortal, while the body was mortal, injury to the soul was infinitely more serious than anything inflicted upon the body; while the body was often viewed with contempt, and sometimes with hatred.

For Bodin, the world was filled with spirits, some good, some evil; they were invisible, but he could feel their touch upon his ear and hear them strike with a hammer upon a door or a stool. Witches could secure the service of evil spirits to bring down storms upon crops, and disease upon men and beasts. In so doing they inflicted bodily hardship and injury, but far worse, they could lead the souls of others to eternal torment, such as the witches themselves were doomed to suffer. With such beliefs, it is possible to understand the logic of Bodin's thought. The public spectacle of the stake and the fire would impress upon those who saw it the eternal danger to their souls and strengthen their resolution to avoid evil. While to the witch, the bodily torment was a trivial foretaste of the eternal punishment which would follow, for 'whatever punishment one orders against them by roasting and burning the witches with a slow fire, this punishment is not by a long way so great as...the eternal torments which are prepared for them, since the fire cannot last an hour, nay half an hour, before the witches are dead' (Bodin, 1580).

This conclusion seemed inescapable to Nodin. We can perhaps invent an imaginary dialogue to illustrate the grasp in which he was held by his theology:

A: M Bodin, you no doubt believe in the golden rule: 'all things whatsoever ye would that men should do to you, do ye even so to them'.

B: Most certainly: no Christian can do otherwise.

A: Then does not this rule forbid the burning of witches? For you would surely not wish that you should be condemned to burning by the witch.

B: What I advocate is just. If by God's will I were a witch, and the witch a good Christian, I should consider it just that I should be condemned to the stake.

A: But that is to suppose a different situation. The rule bids you to do to the witch what you would wish her, as she is now, to do to you, as you are now. Otherwise its force is entirely lost.

B: If the witch, as a lost soul condemned to perdition, were set over me in judgement, I should not wish to be spared, but would suffer martyrdom gladly. To accept clemency would be to cooperate with evil, and would lead to my own perdition.

A: Does it nevertheless bring the Church into disrepute when it is seen to inflict such suffering?

B: It is not the Church which does so. The Church examines a suspected witch, and if she is judged to be heretic she is handed over to the secular arm for punishment.

A: Yet the punishment will be burning?

B: Yes, and justly so.

The way in which the intellectual structure of medieval theology could lead to ethical conclusions from which we recoil will be clear. It is not religion as such that is implicated here, but rather its tendency to foster an all-embracing theology within which ethical judgments are predetermined. A similar case could be made against Marxism, which from a generous anger against the exploitation and degradation of workers in the early 19th century, led on to the penal code which filled the prisons of the Gulag Archipelago (Solzhenitsyn, 1974-78).

We should, indeed be wise to distrust all intellectual systems which claim a universal application. Distrust, however, presupposes recognition of the system to be distrusted. The account of Jean Bodin may help us to recognise the influence upon us of the intellectual structure of science.

3 The Scientific Belief System

In comparing science with medieval Christianity, or with Russian Marxism, we have to begin with a great difference. It is not, as those were, institutionalised and enforced by law. It is propagated by its own Persuasive power, like early Christianity, or like Marxism in pre-war Britain.

The persuasive power of science is felt particularly by those who have received an extensive training in its disciplines, and who form, as it were, its priesthood. A young mathematician or physicist, for example, can deduce the motion of the planets from gravitational attraction - a few pages in a modern textbook - and can compare them with Kepler's laws. The power and simplicity and generality of the methods, and their empirical correlation with careful observation, make a lasting impression. This persuasive power is one of the essential characteristics of a successful belief system. Barnes (1974) has compared scientific beliefs with the magical belief of the Azande, and points to close analogies between the ways in which the two systems are applied in practice. What he does not consider is the relative persuasive power of the two systems. We can readily conceive that a youth brought up in the Zande beliefs, might study mathematical physics and be converted to a belief in science. An attempt to convert mathematical physicists to a belief in Zande magic would seem to be a much less promising exercise. This perception cannot easily be explained away by our preconceptions - scientific beliefs have indeed propagated in a way that Zande magic has not.

One of the foundations of the scientific belief system, and indeed the weapon which it used in its contest with medieval Christianity, is the rejection of purpose and its replacement by causality. For the medieval Christian, the world was brought into being for a purpose, and was continually guided in its change with time by purposive intention - by God, by spirits, or by men and women. The scientific programme, by contrast, was to explain all natural phenomenon by a chain of causal relations. When the apple falls from a tree, it does so because it is acted upon by a gravitational force. The force causes an acceleration towards the attracting body, which is the earth. The acceleration results in an increasing velocity, and the velocity leads to a change in position. The same force of gravity acts upon the moon and causes it to accelerate towards earth. This acceleration causes the moon to deviate from its natural path, which is a straight line, and to follow a nearly circular course around the earth.

To carry out the programme of causal explanation in such terms was an immense project, unlikely ever to be completed, yet it continually gained ground from theology. Newton still believed that periodical divine intervention was needed to maintain the stability of the universe, and it was a hundred years before Laplace felt able to dispense with this hypothesis (Dijksterhuis, 1986, 491). Darwin extended causal explanation to the origin of mankind. Modem cosmology (e.g. Hawking, 1988) gives a causal description of the origin of the universe, 'after time began'. For our present discussion, the significance of this development is that in a wholly causal world, from which purpose has been banished, there can be no ethics. The working scientist, the scientist in his laboratory, so to speak, has continually stressed this. When he is explaining natural phenomena, there is 'no good, no evil', there is only the continual concatenation of cause and effect. This applies alike in the explanations of physics and chemistry and botany and zoology. Man himself, studied scientifically, is governed like a machine by causal laws: 'in science man is a machine; or if he is not he is nothing at all' (Needham, 1927, 93).

Scientists, of course, are also human beings who live in a society, and society cannot exist without ethical beliefs. The somewhat glaring contradiction is usually patched over by supposing that the scientist in his laboratory rejects all ethical considerations, but outside his laboratory he acts as a good citizen in accordance with the ethical requirements of his society. The compromise is bound to be unsatisfactory, because a very large part of the scientist's activity, the part by which he makes his major impact upon society, remains beyond any ethical control. We can invent another imaginary dialogue in a similar vein to the first.

A: You are, I believe, working as a physicist on the design of an atomic bomb.

B: My research in nuclear physics is certainly related to the bomb.

A: Is there not an ethical problem in that? I do not know what are your religious or ethical beliefs, but you probably accept the "golden rule".

B: Yes. I think it describes very well the way we should behave.

A: Yet your work, if it is successful, will result in the mutilation and death of many thousands of men and women and children.

B: My own part is a purely scientific one, in which the ethical problems do not arise. The use to which an uncontrolled nuclear chain reaction would be put is the responsibility of our political leaders.

A: The Church in earlier times disclaimed responsibility for the burning of heretics in a similar way. Surely the development of such knowledge, which is certain to be used, is itself morally objectionable.

B: I do not believe that it can ever be right to restrict the search for knowledge.

A: That is an ethically doubtful view. Would you defend the fight to acquire the knowledge which a medieval Inquisitor held, of the effective use of torture?

B: Certainly not. Knowledge of that kind could only be obtained by means that were themselves morally wrong. Science does not operate in that way.

A: But if that same knowledge of the Inquisitor could be obtained by the morally unexceptionable techniques of physiology and psychology, would the search for it be defensible?

B: Not if it arose from research directed only to that end. If it arose in an incidental way from basic research directed towards a general understanding, the case would be different.

A: So the generation of scientific knowledge is ethically defensible or indefensible according to the motives of the scientists who generate it?

B: I do not like the conclusion, but do not see how to avoid it.

A: Then accepting this conclusion, the scientist can always render his activity immune to ethical criticism by claiming that he has no thought for the possible use of any knowledge which results and is engaged only in the disinterested pursuit of truth?

B: But I insist his disinterestedness is sincere, and is not assumed for any devious purpose of that kind.

A: His sincerity, though, can be maintained only because the intellectual structure of science offers the mirage of a domain in which there is truth but 'no good, no evil'.

By retreating towards this he can disclaim responsibility for the suffering he may cause. This illustrates one part of the problem, but there is another part which is more fundamental. The assumption of causality, which science takes as basic, is itself not ethically neutral. Whatever is regarded as causally determined, as machine-like, demands no ethical considerations from us. We do not feel any moral responsibility for the way in which we behave towards a desk or a clock. We can own them absolutely, they become subject to our will, we can do with them whatever we wish, insofar as any responsibility to them is concerned. Studied scientifically, plants and animals and ecological systems are equally causal and machine-like, and only if ethical rules are imposed from outside science, by society, will they be treated in scientific research as other than machines. Men and women also are causal devices in science, and there is a continuing tension between the scientific perception of people as 'experimental material', as for example in medical research (Pappworth, 1967, xi), and the ethical requirements of society. If the consequences of the causal view were confined to the laboratory, they could be contained at the expense of some irritation among scientists over the interference by society in their pursuit of knowledge. Unfortunately the matter is less simple. Knowledge acquired by research which is governed by the causal view carries with it the consequences of this view when it is applied to the world at large. Science can acquire only that kind of knowledge which treats the world as causal, and so treats men and women (and animals and ecological systems) as machines. Laboratory experiments on genetic manipulation, for example, result in techniques which themselves imply that human beings are machines. Ethical judgements by society may reject some of these techniques, and allow others as being beneficial. But even those which are judged to be ethically acceptable carry with them the infection of the causal view. When they are applied, men and women are treated as causal devices: the caring physician, when he turns from the patient to his scientifically trained colleagues, necessarily adopts the scientific outlook, and has available to him only those techniques which incorporate this outlook. The point is clearly made by the current debate about the use of ova from aborted foetuses to treat sterility in women.

4 Technology

What precedes was intended to expose the way in which intellectual systems constrain the ethical judgement of those who accept them. It deals with extreme cases, where the issues can be stated most clearly. Those who are engaged in the development of technology cannot insulate themselves so easily as the scientist might do from the use to which the results of their work may be put, and from the ethical questions which may then arise. Nevertheless, the causal view and the accompanying rejection of ethical considerations in science, continue to exert a profound effect. The scientific denial of humanity, the treatment of human beings as machines, exerts a pervasive, subterranean influence, much as contempt for the body did in the Middle Ages. This influence can be seen in the undervaluation and rejection, in technological systems, of human ability and skill. Those parts of a production system, for example, which lie within the ambit of the hard sciences - the machines, chemical equipment, computers, etc. - are all described by their causal behaviour. It becomes difficult, in this causally-described system, to find any place for human purpose. All purpose has been translated into the causal relations which wilt fulfill it, and the machines and people alike have only to implement these causal relations (cf Nelson, 1980).

Taylorism does not have to be taught to technologists, because it arises inevitably out of the mode of thought which underlies technology. Because the human tasks in such a system are described causally, they can in principle all be performed by a machine. If some tasks are nevertheless performed by people, this is because for the present, they are cheaper than machines, and they will themselves be used as though they were machines, or components of machines to which they are subordinated. There is not seen to be, in such a system, anything which human beings can do which cannot be done as well by a machine, existing or to be invented. And machines, once invented, are perfectible in a way that people are not. The human abilities of observation, and learning, and the achievement of a purpose in the face of difficulties, are distrusted and rejected because they are not described causally, and are not congruent with the parts of the system which are described in this way.

The dogmatic implementation of such views will often lead (cf Cooley, 1987) to systems which are rigid and inflexible, and prone to failure in unusual circumstances, because the abilities of workers who could provide the needed flexibility, have been rejected. Technological development does not follow a straightforward path, and its meandefings sometimes make this criticism more obviously true. Then one sees tentative efforts, often initiated or supported by social scientists, to make better use of the human potential: the Kalmar plant, shopfloor programming of numerically-controlled machines or production islands (Brodner, 1990). Nevertheless, the steady drift of technological changes sets always in the direction of Taylorism, and the anomalous developments fall into disuse or are themselves pressed into the Tayloristic mould. It can also be objected (e.g. Friedman, 1950) that the rejection of human abilities is ethically unacceptable, because it has damaging effects upon society. To labour continually at trivialised, mechanical tasks has a dehumanising effect and damages self-respect; men and women become marginalised from society when their work is given to machines or becomes machine-like in nature.

Ethical criticisms of this kind have little effect in the research and development of new technology, which is carried on in a spirit very similar to that of the scientist: as a search for truth. Technology, like science, often claims to be value-free, and ethical considerations are projected onto 'the way it is used'. But the ways in which technology can be used are largely predetermined by what is offered for use, and the scientific ethos, acting in the way described, ensures that what is offered will embody the rejection of human purpose. Then it comes to seem that no other kind of technology is possible, and the ethical criticism of a dehumanised technology is equated to a rejection of all technology.

The examples taken here from production engineering are by way of illustration. The same points could be made in relation to a great range of activities in any industrial society, in particular, intellectual work can now be brought increasingly under the influence of Taylorism, and AI provides a rich source of further examples.

5 Equivalent Myths

The argument in Section 2, as was said before, is not directed against medieval religion as such, but against the theological structure which arose from it. In a similar way, the criticisms in Sections 3 and 4 are not directed against the body of our knowledge of nature, nor against the use of this knowledge for our own ends in technology. They are directed rather against the intellectual structure in which our sciences and technology have become embedded, with its rejection of purpose and humanity and ethics. Let us suggest that an ethically acceptable technology would not reject human purpose and abilities and skills, but would cooperate with them to make them more productive; it would not attempt to preserve old skills in a fossilised form, but would allow space and opportunity for them to develop as technology itself developed. From what kind of scientific base could we develop such a technology?

It is suggested elsewhere (Rosenbrock, 1990) that science itself would have to accommodate purpose, because a science based upon causal description can never give room for human purpose. Then the question is: can the scientific knowledge which we express in causal terms be expressed, as an equally effective alternative, in terms of purpose? We do not wish, that is, to change the content of scientific knowledge, but only the intellectual structure in which it is expressed. The answer to the question is partly clear. Classical physics can be expressed in this way by means of Hamilton's principle. So also, with some changes to the principle, can relativity, both special and general. No all-embracing generalization to cover quantum mechanics is known, but a beginning has been made (Rosenbrock, 1990, 203-219) in developing it. Supposing this development to be completed, the question would in principle be answered affirmatively, because the other sciences can (again in principle) be derived by physics. This answer 'in principle' would be sufficient for our needs, because it would allow us to see the world, not as operating mechanically by cause and effect, but alternatively, as fulfilling a purpose: not a purpose imposed from without, but one derived from experiment and observation of nature. In such a view, human purpose would not be something alien to be extruded, together with all ethical concerns which presuppose purpose, but would be something arising in ways which we do not understand, from the intimate structure of the world. Causality would be seen, not as the essential prerequisite for science, but as one alternative basis which was adopted for tactical reasons in the 17th century.

Everything that has been said before warns us that an intellectual system built upon a purposive science might carry with it the same dangers as the other systems we have mentioned. The best prophylactic is to admit that a given body of knowledge can be validly described in different intellectual structures. A causal and a purposive science, each as described above, would be equivalent for all scientific purposes. Any fact which agreed with one would agree with the other, and any fact which contradicted one would contradict the other. In such circumstances, neither the causal nor the purposive description can be regarded as a 'scientific theory' in the usual sense, because there is no scientific basis for rejecting one in favour of the other. We may call them both 'myths': not to suggest that either is untrue, for both are equally true in the normal sense of science but to emphasise the impossibility of distinguishing scientifically between them. The appropriate object to serve as a scientific theory (Rosenbrock, 1990, 49-75) is then the equivalence class to which both belong. Two distinct equivalence classes can never be equivalent, so that the ambiguity which can arise between myths is avoided.

Though they are scientifically equivalent, the causal and purposive myths give rise to quite different ethical conclusions. We could choose the purposive myth as being more ethically acceptable, while acknowledging the equal scientific validity of the causal myth. By recognising the conscious choice involved, we are protected from some of the dangers which arise when intellectual structures carry hidden ethical consequences. One stumbling block for many people in these suggestions lies in the idea of 'purpose', so it will be well in closing to say something of this. To many, purpose cannot exist without consciousness, and conscious forethought of the future. The suggestion that a physical object, say the moon, can have a purpose then seems to either be contradictory, or to savour of animism. The difficulty is partly verbal, we need not say that such objects 'have' a purpose, but only that they 'fulfil' a purpose, or more abstractly, that 'their behaviour can be deduced from a purpose'.

What is involved is only this. If we wish a train to travel over a given section of track, with its ascents and descents and its given speed restrictions, and to do so in a given time with the least consumption of fuel, we pose a mathematical problem in the calculus of variations. Given the necessary data on power of the engine, rolling resistance, wind resistance and so on, the problem can be solved. The solution then shows how the engine controls and brakes should be manipulated in order to achieve the purpose from which we started. This is a causal description, which would be implemented by an automatic controller. Mathematically, the causal description is equivalent to the purpose and can be deduced from it, and the causal relations obeyed by the train and controller are just those which will achieve the purpose. In the same way, when we say that the moon fulfils a purpose, we mean only that we can write down a prescription for its behaviour, a purpose analogous to the prescription for the train, and from it we can deduce the causal laws which will satisfy the prescription. These causal laws will be Newton's laws of motion. There is no suggestion of consciousness or forethought, though the causal and purposive descriptions differ in an essential way. The causal description shows future behaviour to be determined by the past. The purposive description shows that future behaviour satisfies a requirement in the future. The two are entirely concordant: the causal description shows how the future must depend on the past if the purpose, the future requirement, is to be satisfied. Further discussion and illustration of this point can be found elsewhere (Rosenbrock, 1992).

References

Barnes, B. (1974). Scientific Knowledge and Sociological Theory.
Routledge and Kegan Paul; see also E.E_ Evans-Pritehard (1937). Witchcraft. Oracles and-Magic Among The Azande Clarendon Press. Oxford.
Bodin, J. (1580). De La Demonomanie Des Sorciers. Jaques du-Puys. Paris.
Brrdner, B. (1990). The Shape of Future Technology. Springer-Verlag.
Cooley, M. (1987) Architect or Bee? Chatto and Windus.
Dijksterhuis, E.J. (1986). The Mechanization of the World Picture. Princeton University Press.
Easlea, B. (1980) Witch-hunting, Magic and the New Philosophy Harvester Press.
Einstein, A. (1950). Out of My Later Years. Thames and Hudson.
Friedman, G. (1950) Ou Va Le Travail Humain? Gallimard.
Hauser, H. (1932). La Response De Jean Bodin A.M. De Malestroit. Arman Colin.
Hawking, S. (1988). A Brief History of Time Bantam Press.
Jungk, R. (1960). Brighter than a Thousand Suns. Penguin Books; Jungk records, 244-255, that Fermi strongly opposed the subsequent development of the fusion bomb.
Mirk, J. (ca. 1400). Festial; quoted by C. Platt, (1981). The Parish Churches of Medieval England. 122. Seeker and Warburg.
Needham, J. (1927). Man A Machine. Kegan Paul.
Nelson, D. (1980). Frederick W. Taylor and the Rise of Scientific Management. University of Wisconsin Press.
Pappworth, M.H. (1967). Human Gunea Pigs. Routledge and Kegan Paul.
Rose, P.L. (1980). Bodin and the Great God of Nature. Droz.
Rosenbrock, H. (1990) Machines With a Purpose. Oxford University Press.
Rosenbrock, H. (1992). Science, Technology and Purpose. AI & Society 6. 3-17.
Solzhenitzin, A. (1974-78). The Gulag Archipelago. Fontana.
Tooley, M.J. (trans.) (1967). Jean Bodin. Six Books of the Commonwealth, Basil Blackwell.

AI & Soc (1995) 9:43–56
© 1995 Springer-Verlag London Limited

Organisational Spaces and Intelligent Machines: A Metaphorical Approach to Ethics

Luis Montaño Hirose

Department of Economics, Universidad Autónoma Metropolitana-Iztapalapa, Mexico

If we were only to govern our actions by the reflection of the inert world's irrevocable laws in our own consciousness, we would be completely unmoral, or to put it better, amoral; Good and Bad would lack meaning for us... A. Caso

A System is an imaginary machine... A. Smith

Abstract: This paper tackles the main changes that have taken place in the mechanical worldview of simple, self-regulating and intelligent machines, and studies their repercussions at the ethical and organisational level. These views of machines agree with the scientific, human-relations and postmodern proposals in organisation theory, in that they are in fact reflections on human nature which depend on metaphorical devices within which the machine metaphor is central.

Keywords: Organisations; Social spaces; Metaphor; Modernisation; Ethics

Introduction

The problem of ethics within organisations is an old concern. It even precedes the very formation of the discipline which studies them – Organisational Analysis. This fact is in no way surprising since every organisation which emerges into the social spectrum does so under the influence of other institutional conventions (Castoriadis, 1975), taking from these institutions a blend of values which, during a certain period of time, justify and give direction to the organisation's future conduct. In this sense, the organisation does not exist in a pure form, but in fact appears as a meeting place – and a place of confusion – where diverse social discourses coexist (Montaño Hirose, 1994). This bringing up to date of institutional spaces, similar to that which occurs in the individual subconscious over the years, is rooted in the metaphorical dimension within which individuals redefine their perception of the world, overlapping

443

it with a variety of themes. However, this metaphorical process is not confined exclusively to the sphere of institutional spaces but reaches deeper down into the great narratives which guide collective conduct.

The machine has been the central metaphor in the formal definition of organisations (Montaño Hirose, 1993). This has had a profound influence on the determination of organisational structures and processes, giving direction to important changes in the moral conception not only of organisations but also of society. Nevertheless, it is also important to show that the conception of 'the machine' in turn has undergone significant changes, in accordance with the spectacular advances achieved by science and technology, up to our current wondering about the real possibilities of constructing an intelligent machine. Two important antecedents of this project are the simple machine, present in scientific management, and the self regulating machine, central to the Human Relations School of Organisational Analysis. Without doubt, one of the fundamental aspects of the view of machines in organisations rests upon the division of labour. The latter is not, as is generally supposed, an effect of the increasing mechanisation of work, but is a result of man's conception of machines.

Thus, perhaps one of the most relevant ethical organisations, as well as the constituent elements of the metaphorical process, deeply rooted within the analytical framework of Cybernetics. These two earlier movements, Scientific Management and Human Relations – are central to understanding of so-called postmodern organisations, which incorporate the most advanced technological developments, including the possibility of the intelligent machine. This will be the subject of the fourth section. Finally, by way of conclusion, we shall outline some comments which allow Organisational Analysis to enlarge the debate. To this end we shall introduce some elements of the most significant transformations in the metaphorical process.

Division of Labour: The Forms of Solidarity

Division of labour has been widely studied. It has been treated from the beginning as a moral problem. Adam Smith, in his well known book, *An Inquiry into the Nature and Causes of the Wealth of Nations*, published in 1976, was astonished by the advances achieved by the division of labour in the already famous pin factory, and placed this in the foreground of economic analysis. Nevertheless, the author warned of the grave dangers implied in terms of the deterioration of intellectual faculties and even requested the government to intervene in the matter:

The man whose life is spent in performing a few simple operations, of which the effects too are, perhaps, always the same, has no occasion to exert his understanding, or to exercise his intervention in finding our expedients for removing difficulties which never occur. He naturally loses, therefore, the habit of such exertion, and generally becomes as stupid and ignorant as it is possible for a human creature to become. (...)His dexterity at his own particular trade seems in this manner, to be acquired at the expense of his intellectual, social and martial virtues. But in every improved and civilised society this is the state into which the labouring poor, that is, the great body of the people, must necessarily fall, unless government takes some pains to prevent it (Smith 1937: 734–735).

Nevertheless, Smith fought throughout his work for the division of labour as the source of wealth. For this author, the division precedes the development of machines, since it is the exclusive attention to a task which gives rise to the discovery of new methods of work which could be later mechanised. We can say that, from this perspective, the machine *incorporates* the functions of the human being.

From an economic point of view, it is the choice of the individual in pursuit of his own interests which causes the emergence of the division of labour. Against this view Emile Durkheim set up his proposals. For him the division of labour implies a moral basis which goes further than personal egoism, it is morality that leads to the division of labour. For Smith progress results from individual action, which can nevertheless be restrained by 'general rules' of morality, derived from the individual faculties of 'fellow feeling', reflection and imagination (Smith, 1976).

Durkheim approaches the problem of the division of labour from another ethical perspective by considering it to be one of the foundations of social order. The *Division of Social Labour*, his doctoral thesis, published in 1983, represents the first great work of this sociologist. Unlike the Scottish economist, for him the central value of the division of labour does not reside in economic achievement but in its potential as a mechanism of solidarity. This is not automatically derived from self-interest; it is the birth of a new morality, which has cooperation as its origin. The author distinguishes two types of solidarity: the mechanical, based on the similarities of individuals, and the organic, which is based on their differences. In the former, the individuals attract one another through their similarities and they find themselves linked to a common collective interest, which ensures that the individuals reproduce their fundamental similarities. On the other hand, organic solidarity, considered to be morally superior, is based on individual differentiation, and promotes more complex forms of collaboration. Cooperation, in general terms, is understood to be the distribution of roles for the carrying out of common tasks, which can be maintained by the division of simple work within which the tasks are similar, or of complex work characterised by the heterogenity of the activities to be performed. The latter implies the idea of specialisation which acquires a higher moral status; not only solidarity, but also social progress depends on it.

As for the mechanical and organic content of the forms of solidarity, the author is quite explicit. Thus, referring to the former, he says:

This word does not mean produced by mechanical and artificial means. We do not give it this name if not by analogy of the cohesion which unites within itself the elements of inert bodies, in opposition to that which constitutes the unity of living bodies. This naming has been justified by the fact that the link which thus unites the individual to society is identical to that which links the object to the person. Individual consciousness, considered in this aspect is simple dependence from the collective type (...) In those societies where this kind of solidarity is more developed, the individual does not own himself...; he is literally a thing which society makes use of (Durkheim, 1987, 141).

In its turn, organic solidarity gets its name from the analogy with superior animals in which every organ has a level of autonomy and specific functions. Durkheim establishes the superiority of the organic over the mechanical. Mechanical solidarity corresponds to primitive societies, dominated by feelings and common values. Individual rationality, incorporated into society, set itself up as the motive of progress. This improvement implied the development of a superior form of solidarity, the organic.

There are at least three criticisms to be made. Firstly, there is the concept of an evolutionism which does not take into consideration certain premodern collective forms based on the individuality of society (Starkey, 1992). Secondly, there is a clear dualism between society and individual, which has made it difficult to understand

445

the concrete forms of the social/individual, as well as groups, classes (Giddens, 1978), and organisations. Finally, the idea of a harmonious progressive social order confuses the social with the economic.

However, the economic ideal of progress based on the detailed division of labour raised its head, which left both general rules of morality and the organic nature of society out of consideration, taking up individualism – rationality and self-interested pursuits – as a source of development within society.

Scientific Management: Man-Machine or Machine-Man?

No other proposition of Organisational Analysis has met with such fierce criticism because of its mechanical nature as Taylorism (March and Simon 1958). The image of the worker reduced to a mere appendage of a machine has been a source of inspiration for the rejection of these practices. Let us remember the famous film, *Modern Times,* in which Charles Chaplin is swallowed up in the complex workings of the productive machine, not with the intention of crushing or destroying him, but of simply *incorporating* him into the machinery. This criticism is raised not only because of the economic intentions of the new practices, exploitation (Coriat, 1979), nor because of the effects of the detailed division of labour, deskilling (Braverman, 1974), nor because of the loss of meaning in the workplace, alienation (Friedman, 1963), nor because of the imposition of a new political project, discipline (Clegg, 1981), but also because of human resistance to being relegated to the inert status of a machine. In reality it is a double process of incorporation. The first consists in giving the machine a body, in copying the movements of the worker and in reproducing them, in the most efficient manner, in an inert object. In this way, every machine has an 'organic' structure, by representing an extension of the bodily functions:

The condition of possibility of using artefacts, as a last resort of machines, of mobile bodies in space, is the prior reduction of the movements of the bodily organs, mobile in space, to mechanical movements, or to movements of the human body, turn up to be artificial or contrived in terms of the way they work (Gaos, 1992, 649).

The second moment signals man's increasing dependence on machines, given the high degree of efficiency reached in terms of strength, precision, speed and capacity which machines possess in relation to some human capacities. So the relationship is inverted; the organisational capacity of the machine is such that man has to adapt himself to it, in a sense mechanise himself, generating at the same time specific forms of organisation aimed at this end. The most frequent example of this tendency can be observed nowadays in some of the most outstanding Japanese companies, where quality has ceased to represent an important problem, and where Total Quality Programmes have given way to those of Total Maintenance: i.e. total attention to the machine.

This Management, which called itself 'Scientific', was not only so because of the systematisation of tasks, as Taylor claimed, but also because deep down it shared this determined search for irreducible elements, essential material, the ultimate reality. It was also because it professed to be universal, reproducible, without any consideration for the concepts of space and time. On ethical grounds it presented a moral orientation tending to the achievement of social harmony. In the first sentence of his book

The Principles of Scientific Management, published in 1911, the author specifies the objective of management: 'To ensure maximum prosperity for the owner, together with the maximum prosperity for the owner, together with the maximum prosperity for each of the employees' (Taylor, 1972, 19). This prosperity, however, is not restricted to a mere question of salary, but is seen as an opportunity for every individual to reach his maximum efficiency in diverse spheres of life. Nevertheless, this division of labour was aimed at increasing productive efficiency to the detriment of the development of intellectual activities. A worker is not paid to think but to work – as Taylor used to say. This image of a human being reduced to the machine's condition of existence, as an object, reflects the forms taken by the organisation of production. The mechanical aspect is not exclusively due to everyday interaction with the machine but to the fact that man is the subject of a formal administration which in fact denies him the opportunities which the project of modernity had promised, i.e. access to reason.

On the other hand, we can say that to this mechanical conception of work corresponds an organic view of organisational structures. The establishment of a *Thinking Department* (Friedman, 1977), responsible for carrying out planning activities, far away from the machine room, signified another division of labour, now in terms of a wider organisational structure. The functional collaboration of both parts then came about as the primordial objective of Scientific Management, but this lacked the moral value for which Smith and Durkheim fought.

Human Relations: Towards Self-Regulation?

The School of Human Relations has generally been reduced to a code of good conduct, to a model of public relations, to the recognition of spontaneous behaviour or to the discovery of small work groups. It is true that it has also been criticised for being a poor analytical scheme (Clegg, 1990), behind which is concealed a political project capable of establishing a powerful disciplinary system, based on manipulation (Baritz, 1974; Montaño Hirose, 1985). On the other hand, it has also been integrated as a break with or as a complement to Scientific Management. In spite of it being very tempting to review all of these topics, it is necessary to limit our consideration to the Cybernetics view which underlines it (Desmarèz, 1983; Montaño Hirose, 1987), and to introduce the metaphorical mechanisms which lie at the origin of self-regulation (Montaño Hirose, 1994).

Human Relations management was built upon a systematic base very close to the Cybernetic conception of self regulation. Amidst these ideas, we must single out Joseph Lawrence Henderson. This physiologist, a professor of the Philosophy of Science at Harvard University, was as strongly influenced by the work of the French doctor, Claude Bernard as by that of the Italian writer Vilfredo Pareto, from whom he acquired the concepts of 'internal environment', and 'equilibrium'. The former is taken from Bernard and has to do with the discovery of the constancy and conservation of the composition of blood, and was evidence for an internal environment – *milieu intérieur* – which constitutes the 'condition of a free and independent life' (Henderson, 1970, 153). The latter is taken from Pareto, originally developed in a thesis on the subject of solid objects and later transferred to economics and finally to sociology.

Henderson worked out a model using these ideas, on the subject of which one of his prominent students, Norbert Wiener, commented:

There was also Professor Lawrence J Henderson, the physiologist, who combined some really brilliant ideas about the fitness of the environment with what seemed to me to be a distressing inability to place them in any philosophical structure... (Wiener, 1966, 166).

This Wienerian perspective, influenced by Henderson's developments, placed the emphasis on the concept of homeostasis, in other words on the ability of a system to resist the process of corruption and degeneration. We know that information plays a central part in the acquisition and maintenance of Cybernetic equilibrium. This is a 'negative entropy' and is a measure of the degree of system organisation (Wiener, 1969, 11). There then arises a symbiotic process: organisation as a cybernetic machine and cybernetics as an organisational conception. In this way, self regulation and organisation would appear inseparable and act as an important foundation for the Artificial Intelligence Project. The study of the organisational aspects of the machine hence became a privileged focal point in understanding the work just as it does in many of later technological developments:

Cybernetics is the first science which, after western science's advances of the seventeenth century has established its method, has brought about its operational success, and has achieved the recognition of other sciences through its treatment of a physical system, the machine, not in the operation of its constitutive elements, but in the operation of its organisational features (Nordin, 1981, 285).

Within this theoretical framework of self regulation, the concepts of internal environment and equilibrium are developed. Perhaps the most consummated proposal on the Human Relations School is that expounded by Fritz Roethlisberger and William Dickson in their well known work, *Management and the Worker*, published in 1936. For these authors, organisations consist of an alliance of dual structures – or suborganisations. 'Technical' organisation is complemented by 'human' organisation, which in turn is divided into 'individual' and 'social' organsiation. The social is then subdivided into the 'formal' and 'informal' organisations (Roethlisberger and Dickson, 1976). The first alliance accepts the distinction between material and the human fields, always emphasising their close links. The second attempts to differentiate the strictly personal from the social, finally, the third stresses the lack of connection between the planned organisation and that which in fact emerges from unexpected behaviour. So the project basically derives from an attempt to achieve an articulation between these two later organisations.

Hence an imbalance appears in this organisational duality, since the content of each of them varies in different ways and each of them requires different methods of qualitative control. So, for example, the change in the formal organisation can be very rapid and can meet few obstacles, while the informal organisation requires much longer periods of adjustment, during which time workers' resistance to change plays a dominant role. Thus Roethlisberger and Dickson implicitly raise the question of the adequacy of the forms of social organisation to meet the technological advances, in which the establishment of disciplinary mechanisms plays a fundamental role.

The relative autonomy required by the organisational system was achieved by means of the psychological process of internalisation of these external spaces. Thus, schematically speaking, we can say that informal organisation does not abstractly represent spontaneous behaviour. The authors of this movement (Roethlisberger and Dickson, 1976; Mayo, 1933, 1945; Homans, 1959) realised that cooperation, as a joint operation, was not achieved exclusively in the formal organisation but that the informal one also played a fundamental role. Informal relations represent, from our point of view, institutional spaces which the individual has internalised over the years of her/his everyday life, such as religion, school, family and army. S/he possesses a set of values, beliefs of manners of participation and of behavioural guidelines, derived from specific ethical spheres, each one controlled by diverse disciplinary mechanisms.

Thus, the individual passes daily through different social environments. When s/he enters the workplace, for example, s/he finds her/himself not exclusively in a place of work, but s/he also reproduces at the same time a set of practices from other environments. By way of example, in the company from which these studies originated, the Hawthorne works of the Western Electric Company in Chicago, employee relations policies, has been renamed *The Ten Commandments*, by the employees. However, let us not forget that the informal organisation also shelters a set of defensive practices which hinder the smooth running of the formal administration. This constant movement linking the formal and the informal organisations prevents, from our point of view, the workplace from becoming solely a productive place:

For most of the supervisors the company represents more than the 'big bosses', New York, the stockholders, or board of directors. It is more than an economic unit with merely economic functions. The company is also an entity onto which they project their greatest hopes and fears (Roethlisberger and Dickson, 1976: 368).

Organisational modernism separates the formal and the informal, not only in order to control those informal spaces which infringe the formal rules and hinder the progress of productivity, but also with the aim of taking advantage of them, rendering them the repositories of efficient disciplinary schemes. The family, the school, the prison, the church and the army are examples of social spaces with a very high disciplinary content. Through this movement we become aware of the need to anticipate open conflict through symbolic compensation (Pages *et al.*, 1979).

Thus, we find a double metaphor in this movement. Firstly, that which views the organisation as a self-regulating machine, a precursor of the intelligent machine. Secondly, a process which makes the first possible, starting with the manipulation of social environments in the organisation, whose goal is to encourage a certain type of conduct through the promotion of a set of values which would diminish the negative aspects from the outside. 'This isn't a company but a big family' is a slogan from the 1930s which exemplifies this process well. In this sense, we may say that the capacity for self-regulation was directly associated with the degree of relative autonomy reached through the 'internalisation of the external'. It was not necessary to think about adapting to the external environment since it was possible to reproduce it, in functional terms, at the heart of the company. The idea of a company as a small society is perhaps the most representative metaphoric form of this second process. It later facilitated the operation of corporate culture.

The development of the Japanese productive system of *Just in Time* was formulated in order to accommodate the needs of the market in real terms and the growing capacity of productive diversification both being results of technological innovations. It encouraged the emergence of new organisational forms which tended to overlap the formal and informal spaces of the company (Montaño Hirose, 1994). The moral values resulting from the organisational process modernisation, which originated mainly from the wider social field and were redefined in the informatal organisation, will no longer have the leading role which they once held in most industrialised countries. Nowadays, owing to the spectacular advances in technology – mainly in bid companies where the development of applied research holds a privileged position – the company has set itself up as the organisational model for all other social spaces – previously internalised. In other words it sets itself up as a promoter of wider social values. So, the school, the hospital, the state and even society itself have been the objects of profound restructurations which try to imitate the organisational forms originated in the productive model of the private sector (Ouchi, 1984).

Postmodern Organisations: An Ordered Intelligence?

Few concepts are as attractive and fashionable as that of the 'postmodern organisation'. However, this must be approached with caution so as not to fall into stereotyped ideas. The concept forms a central part of the contemporary debate about new organisational forms and their social implications (Parker 1992, 1992b; Tsoukas, 1992; Cooper and Burrel, 1988; Cooper, 1989).

The idea of social progress that strongly encouraged the division of labour, as much in its international versions (Smith, 1937) as in its social (Durkheim, 1987) and detailed versions (Taylor, 1972), now receives a new stimulus, starting from the study of industrial organisation. A new idea of organisation is proposed to substitute for the inflexibilities of the Scientific Management model. Although we could quote a whole set of characteristic elements of these new forms, we can synthesise them into one: their capacity for reprogramming, which is the basis of one of the most frequently mentioned concepts in the present process of restructuration; their flexibility.

This was the pioneering attempt carried out by Tom Burns and G M Stalker in their book *The Management of Innovation*, published in 1961. The authors suggest that the mechanical and organic managerial concepts are extreme poles of a continuum of possibilities. Both types represent rational forms of organisation. The first is characterised, amongst other things, by a specialised differentiation of functional tasks, which are constantly subject to technical improvements without any consideration of rights or obligations, and a set of technical procedures necessary to perform each task, as well as a hierarchical structure of control, authority and communication. The authors consider that this mechanical organisational form is adequate under conditions of relative stability. In contrast, the authors suggest the organic model is better when confronted with situations of change. This model is characterised, amongst other things, but the following elements: the contribution of specialised knowledge to global tasks, continual adjustment to individual tasks, a more collective responsibility and a much more open network of control, authority, and communication (Burns and Stalker, 1961; 120–121).

In this proposal, we can clearly observe the introduction of the concept of structural flexibility, preceding the discourse on post-Fordism put forward by the School of Regulation (Aglietta, 1979; Leborgne and Lipietz, 1988), and foreshadowing some of the central characteristics of the so-called 'postmodern organisation'.

Along the same lines of argument, Heydebrand sets his proposal within the context of post-industrial capitalism. This writer conceptualises the new organisational forms as the result of a transition process from an industrial capitalism to a post-industrial one. In a synthetical manner the author characterises this new form in the following way:

It would tend to be small or tend to be located in small units of larger organisations; its object is typically service or information, if not automated production; its technology is computerised; its division of labour is informal and inflexible; and its managerial structure is functionally decentralised, eclectic, and participative, overlapping many ways with nonmanagerial functions. In short, post-industrial organisations or those emerging from the transition tend to have a postbureaucratic control structure even though prebureaucratic elements such as clan like personalism, informalism and corporate culture may be used to integrate an otherwise loosely coupled, centrifugal system (Heydebrand 1989; 327).

We are currently witnessing a huge development of so-called *information technology* (Lyotard, 1989), which has substantially modified the forms taken by organisations, above all in the highly industrialised countries. On the one hand, there is the increasingly generalised use of these machines, and on the other, the high capacity they have for reducing the time of response. The introduction of industrial robots, expert systems, computer-assisted design and production, among others, have facilitated the emergence of the production system *Just in Time*. This, in turn, has required significant structural changes in the organisational field, promoting with it the materialisation of a new type of worker, called *polivalent*, who is characterised by being highly qualified in the achievement of diverse tasks and who has a high level of interaction with the machine. This polivalence is positively correlated with the development of general purpose machines, which present a higher level of productive flexiblility than their predecessors, special purpose machines. March and Simon (1958) comment that the second type gave rise to the Taylorist view of the worker as a labouring machine, whilst the first type corresponds to the modern view of the worker, i.e. computer man.

Productive flexibility, based on the high speed of response of *JIT*, facilitates the surpassing of the limitations produced by traditional systems of production, sometimes call *Just in Case*. This is based on the development of inventories as a central procedure in the combating of uncertainties, emanating from changes in demand from disarrangements in production lines caused by the difficulties of managerial coordination in the detailed division of labour.

Polivalence in no way causes harm to the division of labour in the factory. It is a question of a new modality however. This polivalence facilitates a greater rotation of posts and a continual reassignation of tasks. It provokes a greater capacity for adaptation to constant technological change, it allows the mitigation of the rigidities in order to meet production requirements. The division of labour does not reside more in the object of transformation than in organisational identification. In fact, the rotation of posts not only encourages the development of interpersonal relations which reduce the cost of interdepartmental transactions (Aoki, 1990), but it also generates knowledge of the diverse components of the organisation, achieving, not an identification with the single post or job as would be the case in the detailed division of labour, but an identification with the organisation as a whole.

Artificial Intelligence has played an exceedingly outstanding part in the aforementioned changes. As its name suggests, it is an ambitious project; undoubtedly one of the most ambitious projects that human rationality has ever been able to conceive. It is however, not a recent project since we find the first signals of it in a very distant past. One could, for example, say that the modern version of Cartesian dualism of the body and mind, is computer hardware and software (McCorduck, 1993). Nevertheless, the project is still in its first stages, and diverse contradictory positions present possible future scenarios. These vary between those which predict a realisation date of 2017 (Waltz, 1993), and those which maintain a sceptical attitude about its future (Putnam, 1993). The first group contemplates two different procedures, though not mutually exclusive: the *heuristic search*, based on the hypothesis of the *physical systems of symbols* by Newell and Simon (1972), and the theory of *neuron networks* (Waltz, 1993). In the past, the notion of Artificial Intelligence seems to have advanced more via the first procedure; perhaps its most spectacular results have been called expert systems, characterised by the handling of large volumes of information, dynamic searching processes and high processing speeds. This is far, of course, from being a true concept of AI. However, both the utilisation of these advances and the prospects of a project of such magnitude have greatly contributed to modifying not only our everyday practices but also the way in which we observe ourselves, and therefore, our own values.

In the field of Organisational Analysis we locate the proposal of March and Simon (1958) as a pioneer of a new approach. Some the Taylorist man-machine restrictions were apparently overcome by the updating of the mechanical metaphor. These authors advanced the previously mentioned concept of computer-man in order to characterise functionally the limited rational behaviour of human beings:

March and Simon do not make the mistake of claiming that the human being – the grey matter inside the skull – is built like a computer. Their basic assumption is that the human mind functions like a computing machine, just as Taylor's assumption was that the human body functions like a labouring machine.' (Kilduff 1993; 21)

Simon tried to apply the developments in this form of AI to the study of managerial decisions, basically in the field of so-called 'unprogrammed decisions'. These correspond in a big way to the decisions about which there is no archive of past experiences and in which the procedures of heuristic search acquire a significant relevance. This is made possible, as the author mentions, by the ease of imitating the logical functions of the brain which are, according to Simon, one of the most easiest to duplicate (Simon, 1977; 22).

The machine's capacity for facing new situations, the opportunity for constant reprogramming and its high speed of response have all contributed to the development of new organisational forms. Nevertheless, in spite of the fact that the metaphoric evolution of machines has known a certain continuity, it is also important to point out some basic ruptures which imply fundamental changes in social values. This, however, belongs to the concluding chapter.

Conclusions

All metaphor, as a vision of the world and startpoint of a discursive project (Foucault, 1971), establishes specific forms of behaviour. The machine has also been one of the great narratives which has left a deep imprint on the development of society and its organisations (Montaño Hirose, 1993, 1994). However, the metaphoric process has met with a whole set of accidents linked to the changes caused by the advance of technology. In this last section we will comment on three aspects which seem fundamental to this investigation.

A. Firstly, it should be pointed out that if it is indeed true that every analysed movement contains a certain mechanical view – the simple machine, the self-regulating machine and finally, the intelligent machine – each one of these assumes a certain organic form, and implies both a specific organisational form and a variation of the mechanical metaphor. The real organic metaphor in fact existed before the appearance of the mechanical option. This was one of the conditions of social existence, predominant during the Medieval era, blurred by the arrival of rationality, as Merchant reminds us:

> The image of the earth as a living organism and nurturing mother served as a cultural constraint, restricting the actions of human beings. One does not readily slay a mother, dig into her entrails for gold, or mutilate her body... As long as the earth was considered to be alive and sensitive, it could be considered a breach of human ethical behaviour to carry out destructive acts against it.' (Quoted in Capra 1982; 61)

B. On the other hand, we are currently witnessing the development of another metaphoric reversal, which, from our point of view, characterises the nature of postmodern organisation. This refers to the drastic reversal of the metaphor, which sees the company as a small society. Society no longer finds itself incorporated into the company, but the company is that which establishes itself as a social model to imitate. The advances achieved, not only in terms of productive efficiency but also in terms of speed of response and ability to adapt, have placed the company at the very heart of current social development, forcing the other social protagonists to imitate its performance. It is no longer only the school, for instance which is internalised in the informal area of the company, but it is the company which sets the behavioural guidelines of the school. The premodern duality of values par excellence, the sacred and the profane, which had a limited and partial influence over the project of organisational modernity in Human Relations, has been replaced by the duality efficiency/inefficiency (Alberoni, 1992) in the postmodern project.

C. Finally, as Baudrillard (1983) reminds us, there is an important change of those elements of the discourse that 'become more real than reality' and thus deny validating their representations, without realising the emerging absurdity of its new function. We are surely referring here to an 'hyper-real' ethical concept which could even promote irrational actions. Such are the cases, for example, of the rush of nuclear weapons production, of the *Excellence Programs*, interpreted as an endless process (Aubert and Gaulejac, 1991) and of the speed of the machine, as Goas points out:

> Such an image is that of the driver of a vehicle(...) The concept of a journey becomes an integral part of two others: that of a goal and that of a route towards it. Then the image taken to the extreme, is that of the cancellation of the route and the goal; therefore of the journey itself, it is another contradiction; it cancels itself out. (Goas 1992; 653)

Some aspects for social life, including some ethical aspects, must also be mentioned. First of all, the development of new technologies seems not to have kept its promise about the reduction of working time. High prices of new technologies and their elevated rate of obsolescence has provoked an increase of the number of hours dedicated to work – a reduction of holidays, and a growing overtime work and work done at home – because of the economic interest, by big companies, of having the greatest productivity from their investments. Spare time, which should be translated into privacy and freedom for enjoying life – music, reading, sports, family life and other activities – becomes more and more just an occasional distraction. This increasing time consecrated to work has had a very important effect not only in the living schedule but also in the manner we observe ourselves, by emphasising the workplace as the central aspect of our life, and then reinforcing the idea of the company as the model of social organisation.

Secondly, there are some ethical contradictions that derive from this metamorphical view of living organisations. We want to underline some primary aspects of self-regulating and intelligent machines. In the first case, as was already mentioned, there is a daily transit of the worker through different social spaces inside organisations. Organisation members must then reconcile different discourses which in some cases are greatly divergent, which can be emotionally destabilising. The second metaphor emphasises the speed of response to new environmental conditions through flexibility, and contracts formal and informal spaces. This trend is, however, led by the formal restrictions of production, giving rise to an ideal image of efficiency in which all organisation members are supposed to participate. This image has been quickly transferred to many other institutional spaces, for instance, the introduction of quality and excellence discourses in educational organisations.

The intelligent machine is certainly a project. We anticipate that in its future development it will face unavoidable conceptual and technical problems. It will also surely have to meet with problems of economics and implementation, which we think it will overcome because of the benefits which it promises. And not only because of those which it promises, but also because of those which it unconsciously brings about, as in the case of Biology:

The new Biology (...) borrows the fundamental concepts which have caused its theoretical advances (...) from the information sciences and artificial organisms (programmable and automated machines). (Atlan 1991; 52)

It is true that this has probably limited other projects again without realising it. The intelligent machine is probably still not a reality. However, the simple fact of announcing it modifies not only our expectations but also out ways of behaving. It deals with a project which both fascinates and terrifies us. Of all the problems in its path, there is one which worries us because it does not represent a visible obstacle. We mean ethics. Opening the doors to this discussion represents an act of 'non artificial intelligence'. Or, better still, it implies the potential to restore real meaning to the term 'artificial', not as something foreign and antagonistic to mankind, but as something produced by us for our own benefit.

References

Aglietta, Michel (1979), *Regulación y crisis del capitalismo*, Siglo XXI, Mexico,
Alberoni, Francesco (1992), *Las razones de bien y del mal*, Gedisa, Barcelona.

Aoki, Masahiko (1990), *La estructura de la economíca japonesa*, Fondo de Cultura Económica, Mexico.

Atlan, Henri (1991), *Con razón y sin ella. Intercritica de la Ciencia y del Mito*, Tusquets, Barcelona.

Aubert Nicole and Vincent de Gaulejac (1991), *Le coût de l'excellence*, Seuil, Paris.

Baritz, Loren (1974), *The Servants of Power: A History of the Use of Social Science in American Industry*, Greenwood Press, Connecticut.

Baudrillard, Jean (1983), *Les stratégies fatales*, Bernard Grasset, Paris.

Braverman, Harry (1974), *Labor and Monopoly Capital*, Monthly Review, New York.

Burns, Tom and G.M. Stalker (1961), *The Management of Innovation*, Tavistock Publications, London.

Capra, Fritjof (1982), *The Turning Point: science, society, and the rising culture*, Simon & Schuster, New York.

Caso, Antonio (1910), "La filosofía moral de don Eugenio M. de Hostos", in Conferences de Ateneo de la Juventud, Mexico. Quoted by Zea, Leopoldo (1993), *El postitivismo en México: nacimento, apogeo y decadenica*, Fondo de Cultura Económica, Mexico.

Castoriadis, Cornelius (1975), *L'institution imaginaire de la Société*, Seuil, Paris.

Clegg, Stewart R. (1981), "Organization and Control", in *Administrative Science Quarterly*, Vol. 26, No. 4, pp. 546–562.

Clegg, Stewart R. (1990), *Modern Organizations. Organizations Studies in the Postmodernist World*, Sage, London.

Cooper, Robert (1989), "Modernism, Post Modernism and Organizational Analysis 3: The Contribution of Jaque Derrida", in *Organization Studies*, 10/4, pp. 479–502.

Cooper, Robert and Gibson Burrel (1988), "Modernism, Postmodernism and Organizational Analysis: An Introduction", in *Organization Studies*, 9/1, pp. 91–112.

Coriat, Benjamin (1979), *L'atalier et le chronométre, Essai sur le taylorism, le fordisme et la production de masse*, Christian Bourjois Editeur, Paris.

Desmarzèz, Pieerre (1983) "La sociologie industrielle. Fille de la thermodynamique d'équilibre?, in *Sociologie du Travail*, No. 3, pp. 261–274.

Durkheim Emile (1987), *La división social del trabajo*, Colofón, Mexico.

Focault, michel (1971), *L'ordre du discours*, Gallimard, Paris.

Fiedman, Georges (1963), *Où ve la travail humain?*, Idées/Gallimard, Paris.

Friedman, Georges (1977), *La crisis de progresso*, Laia, Barcelona.

Gaos, José (1992), *Historia de nuestra idea del mundo*, Fondo de Cultura Económica/El Colegio de México, Mexico.

Giddens, Anthony (1978), *Durkheim*, Fontana, Glasgow.

Henderson, Lawrence J. (1970), *On the Social System*, The University of Chgicago Press, Chicago.

Heydebrand, Wolf V. (1989), "New Organizational Form", in *Work and Occupations*, Vol. 16, No. 1, pp. 13–31.

Homans, George C. (1959) *The Human Group*, Harcourt Brace, New York.

Kilduff, Martin (1993) "Deconstructing Organizations", in *Academy of Management Review*, Vol. 18, No. 1, pp. 13–31.

Legborgne, Danile and Alain Lipietz (1988), "L'après-fordisme et son espace", in *Les Temps Modernes*, No. 501, abrill, pp. 75–110.

Lyotard, Jean François (1989), *La condition postmoderne*, Editions du Minuit, Paris.

March, James G. and Herbert A. Simon (1958), *Organization*, Wiley, New York.

Mayo, Elton (1933), *The Human Problems of an Industrial Civilization*, Harvard University, Boston.

Mayo, Elton (1945), *The Social Problems of an Industrial Civilization*, Harvard University, Boston.

McCorduck, Pamela (1993), "Inteligencia artificial: an aperçu", in Graubard, Stephen R. (ed.), *El nuevo debate sobre la inteligenica articial. Sistemas simbólicos y redes neuronales*, Gedisa, Barcelona, pp. 81–101.

Montaño Hirose, Luis (1985), "Las esculas de las relaciones humanas: premisas para un debate", in Ibarra Colado, Eduardo and Luis Montaño Hirose (eds.), *Historia del pensamiento administrativo*, vol. I, Universidad Autónoma Metropolitana-Iztapalapa, Mexico, pp. 351–356.

Montaño Hirose, Luis (1985), "Las nuevas relaciones-humanas: un falso reto a la democracia", in *Ensayos críticos para el estudio de las organizaciones en México*, Universidad Autónoma Metropolitana-Iztapalapa, Mexico, pp. 63–102.

Montaño Hirose, Luis (1987), "El orden sistémico: algunos avatares del paradigma organizacional", in Ibarra Colado, Eduardo and Luis Montaño Hirose (eds.), *El orden organizacional: poder, estrategia y contradicción*, Universidad Autónoma Metropolitana-Iztapalapa, Mexico, pp. 1–58.

Montaño Hirose, Luis (1993), "De la metáfora al poder. Algunas reflexiones acera de las aproximaciones organizacionales a la educación superior", in Ibarra Colado, Eduardo (Ed.), *La universidad ante el espejo de la excelencia. Enjuegos organiacionales*, Universidad Autónoma Metropolitana-Iztapalaga, Mexico, pp. 1–17.

Montaño Hirose, Luis (1994), "At the Edge of Modernity: Boundaries Mediations and Overlappings. The Lessons of the Japanese Organization" in *Osaka City University Business Journal*, pp. 35–57.

Morin, Edgar (1981), *El Método: la naturaleza de la naturaleza*, Cátedra, Madrid.
Newel, Allan and Herbert A. Simon (1972), *Human Problems Solving*, Prentice-Hall, New Jersey.
Ouchi, William (1984), *The M-Form Society: How American Teamwork Can Recapture the Competitive Edge*, Addison Wesley Massachusetts.
Pagés, Max, Michel Bonetti, Vincent de Gaulejac and Daniel Decendre (1979), *L'emprise de L'organisation*. Presses Universitaires de France, Paris.
Parker, Martin (1992a), "Post-Modern Organizations or Post-Modern Organization Theory?" in *Organization Studies*, 13/1 pp. 1–17.
Parker, Martin (1992b), "Getting Down from the Fence: A Reply to Harimodus Tsoukas", in *Organization Studies*, 13/4, pp/ 651–653.
Putnam, Hilary (1993), "Mucho ruido por muy poco" in Graubard, Stephen R. (ed.), *El nuevo debate sobre la inteligencia artificial. Sistemas simbólicos y redes neuronales*, Gedisa, Barcelona, pp. 306–319.
Roethlisberger, Fritz and William Dickson (1976), *Management and the Worker*, Harvard University Press, Cambridge.
Simon, Herbert A. (1977), *La nueva ciencia de la decisión gerencial El Ateneo*, Buenos Aires.
Smith, Adam (1937), *An Inquiry into the Nature and Causes of the Wealth of Nations*, The Modern Library, New York.
Smith, Adam (1976), *The Theory of Moral Sentiments*, Liberty Classics, Indianapolis.
Starkey, Ken (1992), "Durkheim and Organizational Analysis", in *Organization Studies*, 13/4, p. 627–642.
Taylor, Frederick W. (1972), *Scientific Management: Shop Management. The Principles of Scientific Management*. Testimony Before the Special Committee., Greenwood Connecticut.
Tsoukas, Haridimos (1992), "Postmodernism, Reflexive Rationalism and Organizational Studies: A Reply to Martin Parker", in *Organization Studies*, 13/4, pp. 643–649.
Waltz, David L. (1993), "Perspectives de la construcción de máquinas verdaderamente inteligentes" in Graubard, Stephen R. (ed.), *El nuevo debate sobre la inteligencia artificial. Sistemas simbólicos y redes neuronales*, Gedisa, Barcelona, pp. 218–242.
Wiener, Norbert (1969), *Cybernetics. Or control and Communication in the Animal and the Machine*, Massachusetts Institute of Technology, Massachusetts.
Wiener, Norbert (1966), *Ex-prodigy. My Childhood and Youth*, Massachusetts Institute of Technology, Cambridge.

On Human-Machine Symbiosis

Mike Cooley[1]

[1] 95 Sussex Place, Slough, Berks, SL1 1NN, UK.

Abstract. Human centredness asserts firstly, that we must always put people before machines, however complex or elegant that machine might be, and, secondly, it marvels and delights at the ability and ingenuity of human beings. The Human Centred Systems movement looks sensitively at these forms of science and technology which meet our cultural, historical and societal requirements, and seeks to develop more appropriate forms of technology to meet out long-term aspirations. In the Human Centred System, there exists a symbiotic relation between the human and the machine in which the human being would handle the qualitative subjective judgements and the machine the quantitative elements. It involves a radical redesign of the interface technologies and at a philosophical level the objective is to provide tools (in the Heidegger sense) which would support human skill and ingenuity rather than machines which would objectivise that knowledge.

1 Introduction

Firstly, human centredness asserts that we must always put people before machines, however complex or elegant the machine might be. Secondly, it marvels and delights at the ability and ingenuity of human beings. It offers an insight into the way we work, and through our work the way we relate to each other and to nature. It is intended to highlight some of the problems associated with our top-heavy political structures and their total inability to respond to creative energy from below.

The central issue of our time is our overweening faith in science and in technological change. Science is shallow and arid soil in which to transplant the sensitive and precious roots of our humanity. Faith is indeed the correct work to use in this context. Science and technology are now leading edges in society – in rather the same way religion was in medieval times. Furthermore, the zealots of science and technology display much of the missionary zeal of the colonial era. Those who do not understand, or more particularly, accept the dictates of science and technology are almost viewed as lost souls who must be redeemed, are sacrificed at the stake of exclusion and unemployability. The human-centred systems movement looks sensi-

457

tively at those forms of science and technology which meet our cultural historical and societal requirements, and seeks to develop more appropriate forms of technology to meet our long-term aspirations.

2 Technology and Skill

There continues to be a widespread belief that automation, computerization and the use of robotic devices frees human beings from soul destroying routine, backbreaking tasks and leaves them free to engage in more creative work. It is further suggested that this is automatically going to lead to a shorter working-week, longer holidays and more leisure times – that it is going to result in 'an improvement in the quality of life'. It is usually added, as a sort of occupational bonus, that the masses of data we will have available to use from computers will make our decisions much more creative, scientific, and logical, and that as a result we will have a more rational form of society.

Some of the assumptions are questionable. We are already repeating in the field of intellectual work more of the mistakes already made in the field of skilled manual-work at an earlier historical stage when it was subjected to the use of high-capital equipment. The old separation between the manual and the intellectual is no longer meaningful for the study of the impact of technological change. Consequently, there is a need to look critically at technological change as a whole in order to provide a framework for questioning the way computers are used today.

In my view it would be a mistake to regard the computer as an isolated phenomenon. It is necessary to see it as a part of a technological continuum discernible over the last 400 years or so. I see it as another means of production and as such it has to be viewed in the context of the political, ideological and cultural assumptions of the society that has given rise to it. I am not at all surprised, given the questions we have asked of science and technology, the 'problems' we have used them to solve, that we now end up with the kind of systems we see all around us. I hold that we have been asking the wrong questions and therefore we have come up with the wrong answers. It is, however, extremely difficult for the public at large to intervene in this process since, instead of baffling them with Latin, the new religion confuses them with mathematics and scientific jargon. They are led to believe that there is something great and profound going on out there and it is their own fault they don't understand it. If only they had a PhD in computer science or theoretical physics they would be able to grapple with the new technological niceties. The scientific language, the symbols, the mathematics and the apparent rationality bludgeon ordinary people's common-sense. A concern that things simply are not right and could and should be otherwise is flattened into abject silence. However, those who do have the appropriate 'qualifications' are also increasingly uncertain, confused and disoriented. The discussion among physicists about the limits of their existing 'objective' techniques and the concern among computer scientists about the implications of artificial intelligence all indicate that the fortress of science and technology in its present form is beginning to show gaping cracks.

Above all this, there is a seething unhappiness among both manual and intellectua workers because the resultant systems tend to absorb the knowledge from them, deny them the right to use their skill and judgement and render them abject appendages to the machines and systems being developed. Those who are not directly involved in using the equipment are merely confused bystanders. I find a deep concern that individuals feel frustrated because their common sense and knowledge, and their practical experience, whether as a skilled worker, a designer, a mother, a father, a teacher or a nurse, are less and less relevant and are almost an impediment to 'progress'. (Cooley 1975)

3 Common Sense and Tacit Knowledge

'Common sense' in some respects is a serious misnomer. Indeed, it may be held to be particularly uncommon. What I mean is a sense of what is to be done and how it is to be done, held in common by those who will have had some form of apprenticeship and practical experience in the area.

This craftsman's common sense is a vital form of knowledge which is acquired in that complex 'learning by doing' situation which we normally think of as an apprenticeship in the case of manual workers, or perhaps practice in law or medicine.

I shall also refer frequently to tacit knowledge. This knowledge is likewise acquired through practice, or 'attending to things' (Polanyi 1962).

These considerations are of great importance when we consider which forms of computerised systems we should regard as acceptable.

It is said that we are now in, an information society. This is held to be so because we are said to have around us 'information systems'. Most of such systems I encounter could be better described as data systems. It is true that data suitably organised and acted upon may become information. Information absorbed, understood and applied to people may become knowledge. Knowledge frequently applied in a domain may become wisdom, and wisdom the basis for positive action.

All this may be conceptualised as at Figure 1 in the form of a noise-to-signal ratio. There is much noise in society, but the signal is frequently dimmed. Another way of viewing it would be the objective as compared with the subjective.

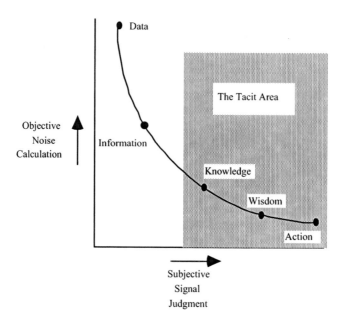

Fig. 1   The Tacit Area

Source: M. Cooley (1987), Architect or Bee?, Hogarth Press

At the data end, we may be said to have calculation; at the wisdom end, we may be said to have judgement. Throughout, I shall be questioning the desirability of basing our design philosophy on the data/information part rather than on the knowledge/wisdom part. It is at the knowledge/wisdom part of the cybernetic loop that we encounter this tacit knowledge to which I will frequently refer.

The interaction between the subjective and the objective, as indicated in Figure 2, is of particular importance when we consider the design of expert systems. In this context, I hold a skilled craftsworker to be an expert just as much as I hold a medical practitioner or a lawyer to be an expert in those areas.

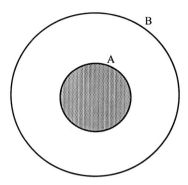

Figure 2   The limits of rule-based systems.

A   Facts of the domain
B   Expertise including tacit knowledge

Source: M. Cooley (1987), Architect or Bee?, Hogarth Press

If we regard the total area of knowledge required to be an expert as that represented by (B), we will find that within it there is a core of knowledge (A) which we may refer to as the facts of the domain, the form of detailed information to be found in a text book.

The area covered by A can readily be reduced to a rule-based system. The annulus (AB) may be said to represent heuristics, fuzzy reasoning, tacit knowledge and imagination. I hold that well-designed systems admit to the significance of that tacit knowledge and facilitate and enhance it. I reject the notion that the ultimate objective of an expert system should be so to expand (A) that it totally subsumes (B). It is precisely that interaction between the objective and the subjective that is so important, and it is the concentration upon the so-called objective at the expense of the subjective that is the basis of the concern expressed in respect of existing systems design.

4. The Acquisition of Skill

In the processes and systems that I describe in this chapter, my concern is not merely with the production, but also with the reproduction of knowledge. I frequently refer to learning by doing, for as a result of this, human beings acquire 'intuition' and 'know how' in the sense in which Dreyfus uses these. This is not in contradiction with Polanyi's (1966) concept of tacit knowledge; rather, it is a description of a dynamic situation in which, through skill acquisition, people are capable of integrating analysis and intuition. Dreyfus and Dreyfus (1986) distinguished five stages of skill acquisition:

1. Novice
2. Advanced beginner
3. Competent
4. Proficient
5. Expert

I think learning-development situations are absolutely vital, and when someone has reached the knowledge/wisdom end of the cybernetic transformation (see figure 1) and has become an 'expert' in the Dreyfus sense, they are able to recognize whole scenes without decomposing them into their narrow features. I do not counterpose tacit knowledge, intuition, or know-how against analytical thinking, but rather believe that a holistic work situation is one which provides the correct balance between analytical thinking and intuition. Broadly stated Dreyfus views skill acquisition as discussed below.

Stage 1: Novice

At this stage the relevant components for the situation are defined for the novice in such a way as to enable him or her to recognize them without reference to the overall situation in which they occur. That is, the novice is following 'context-free' rules. The novice lacks any coherent sense of the overall task and judges his or her performance mainly by how well the learned rules are followed. Following these rules, the novice's manner of problem solving is purely analytical and any understanding of the activities and the outcome in relation to the overall task is detached.

Stage 2: Advanced beginner

Through practical experience in concrete situations the individual gradually learns to recognize 'situational' elements, that is, elements which cannot be defined in terms of objectively recognizable context-free features. The advanced beginner does it by perceiving a similarity to prior examples. The growing ability to incorporate situational components distinguishes the advanced beginner from the novice.

Stage 3. Competence

Through more experience the advanced beginner may reach the competent level. To perform at the competent level requires choosing an organizational plan or perspective. The method of understanding and decision making is still analytical and detached, though in a more complex manner than that of the novice and the advanced beginner.

The competent performer chooses a plan which affects behaviour much more than the advanced beginner's recognition of particular situational elements, and is more likely to feel responsible for, and be involved in, the possible outcome. The novice and the advanced beginner may consider an unfortunate outcome to be a result of inadequately specified rules or elements, while the competent performer may see it as a result of a wrong choice of perspectives.

Stage 4. Proficiency

462

Through more experience, the competent performer may reach the stage of proficiency. At this stage the performer has acquired an intuitive ability to use patterns without decomposing them into component features. Dreyfus calls it 'holistic similarity recognition', 'intuition' or 'know-how'. He uses them synonymously and defines them as:

.....the understanding that effortlessly occurs upon seeing similarities with previous experiences.....intuition is the product of deep situational involvement and recognition of similarity.

Through intuitively organizing an understanding a task, the proficient performer is still thinking analytically about how to perform it. The difference between the competent and the proficient performer is still forced to rely on the detached and analytical way of understanding the problem.

Stage 5. Expertise

With enough experience, the proficient performer may reach the expert level. At this level, not only situations but also associated decisions are intuitively understood. Using still more intuitive skills, the expert may also cope with uncertainties and unforeseen or critical situations. Dreyfus and Dreyfus' essential point is to assert that analytical thinking and intuition are not only two mutually conflicting ways of understanding or of making judgements. Rather they are seen to be complementary factors which work together but with growing importance centred on intuition when the skilled performer becomes more experienced. Highly experienced people seem to be able to recognize whole scenarios without decomposing them into elements of separate features.

My criticism of the prevailing systems-design methodology and philosophy and my deep concerns about 'training', stem from the fact in both cases they deny us that 'deep situational involvement'. Our development tends to be constrained within the novice end of the skill-acquisition spectrum.

Later I describe those experiences, systems and machines which could reverse this approach and provide instead developmental situations to facilitate the acquisition of those attributes to be found at the expert end of the skill spectrum.

Many designers fear to discuss these concerns because they may be accused of being 'unscientific'. There is no suggestion in this line of argument that one should abandon the 'scientific method'; rather we should understand that this method is merely complementary to experience and should not override it, and that experience includes 'experience of self as a specifically and differentially existing part of the universe of reality'.

5 Human-Machine Interaction

When a human being uses a machine, the interaction is between two dialectical opposites. The human is slow, inconsistent, unreliable but highly creative, whereas the machine is fast, but totally noncreative.

Originally it was held that these opposite characteristics - the creative and the noncreative - were complementary and would provide for a perfect symbiosis between human and machine, for example, in the field of computer-aided design. However, design methodology is not such that it can be separated into two disconnected elements which can then be combined at some particular point like a chemical compound. The process by which these two dialectical opposites are united by the designer to produce a new whole is a complex area. The sequential basis on which the elements interact is of extreme importance.

The nature of that sequential interaction, and indeed the ratio of the quantitative to the qualitative, depends on the commodity under design consideration. Even where an attempt is made to define the proportion of the work that is creative and the proportion that is noncreative, what cannot readily be stated is the point at which the creative element has to be introduced when a certain stage of the noncreative work has been completed. The process by which the designer reviews the quantitative information assembled and then makes the qualitative judgement is extremely subtle and complex. Those who seek to introduce computerised equipment into this interaction attempt to suggest that the quantitative and the qualitative can be arbitrarily divided and that the computer can handle the quantitative.

Where computer-aided design systems are installed, the operators may be subjected to work which is alienating, fragmented and of an ever increasing tempo. As the human being tries to keep pace with the rate at which the computer can handle the quantitative data in order to be able to make the qualitative value judgements, the resulting stress is enormous. The crude introduction of computers into the design activity, in keeping with the Western ethic 'the faster the better', may well result in the quality of design plummeting. Clearly, human beings cannot stand this pace of interaction for long.

Taylor's philosophy (Taylor 1906) is being introduced into the field of intellectual work and in order to condition us to this subordinate role to the machine and to the control of human beings through the technology, Frederick Winslow Taylor once said, 'In my system the workman is told precisely what he is to do and how he is to do it, and any improvement he makes upon the instructions given to him is fatal to success.'

6 Why Suppress the Intellect

The more I look at human beings, the more impressed I become with the vast bands of intelligence they can use. We often say of a job: it's as easy as crossing a road, yet as a technologist I am ever impressed with people's ability to do just that. They can go to the edge of the pavement and work on the velocity of the cars coming in both directions by calling upon a massive memory bank which will establish whether it's a mini or a bus because the size is significant. They then work out the rate of change of the image and from this assess the velocity. They do this for vehicles in both directions in order to assess the closing velocity between them. At the same time they are working out the width of the road and their own acceleration and peak velocity. When they decide they can go, they will just fit in between the vehicles. The above computation is one of the simpler ones we do, but you should watch a skilled worker going through the diagnostic procedures of finding out what has gone wrong with an aircraft generator. There you see real intelligence at work. A human being using total information-processing capability can bring to bear synaptic connections of 10^{14}, but the most complicated robotic device with pattern-recognition capability has only about 10^3 intelligence units.

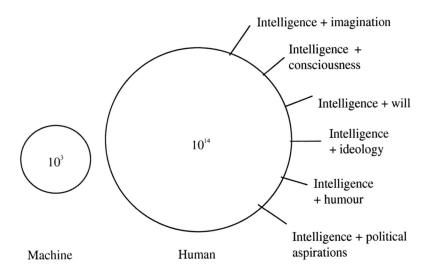

Figure 3. Comparison of units of intelligence available for toal information processing.
Source: M. Cooley (1987) Architect or Bee? Hogarth Press.

Why do we deliberately design equipment to enhance 10^3 machine intelligence and diminish the 10^4 intellect? Human intelligence brings with it culture, political consciousness, ideology and other aspirations. In our society these are regarded as subversive – a very good reason then, to try and suppress them or eliminate them altogether. This is the ideological assumption present all the time – see Figure 3 above.

As designers we don't even realize we are suppressing intellects, we are so preconditioned to doing it. That is why there is a boom in certain fields of artificial intelligence. The late Fred Margulies, former chairman of the Social Effects Committee of the International Federation of Automatic Control (IFAC), commenting on this waste of human brainpower, said:

> The waste is a twofold one, because we not only make no use of the resources available, we also let them perish and dwindle. Medicine has been aware of the phenomenon of atrophy for a long time. It denotes the shrinking of organs not in use, such as muscles in plaster. More recent research of social scientists supports the hypothesis that atrophy will also apply to mental functions and abilities. [1]

To illustrate the capabilities of human brainpower, I quote Sir William Fairbairn's definition of a millwrigtht of 1861:

> The millwright of former days was to a great extent the sole representative of mechanical art. He was the itinerant engineer and mechanic of high reputation. He could handle the axe, the hammer and the plane with the dispatch of one brought

465

up to these trades and he could set out and cut furrows of a millstone with an accuracy superior to that of the miller himself. Generally, he was a fair mathematician, knoew something of geometry, levelling and mensuration, and in some cases possessed a very competent knowledge of practical mathematics. He could calculate the velocities, strength and power of machine, could draw in plan and section, and could construct buildings, conduits or water courses in all forms and under all conditions required in his professional practice. He could build bridges, cut canals and perform a variety of tasks now done by civil engineers. (Jefferys 1945)

All the intellectual work has long since been withdrawn from the millwright's function.

7 Too Old at 24

Just as machines are becoming more and more specialized and dedicated, so is the human being, the 'appendage' to the machine. In spite of all the talk in educational circles about wider and more generalized education, the historical tendency is towards greater specialization in spite of all the talk about universal machines and distributed systems.

The people who interface with the machine are also required to be specialized. However, as indicated above, this is accompanied by a growing rate of knowledge-obsolescence. It was pointed out by Eugene Wigner, the internationally acclaimed physicist, when talking about the way our education system is going to the meet this problem of specialization, that it is taking longer and longer to train a physicist. 'It is taking so long to train him to deal with these problems that he is already too old to solve them' [2]. This is 23 or 24 years of age.

8 Lack of Foresight

One of the founders of modern cybernetics, Norbert Wiener, once cautioned:

Although machines are theoretically subject to human ciriticism, such criticism may be ineffective long after it is relevant. [3]

It is surprising that the design community, which likes to pride itself on its ability to anticipate problems and to plan ahead, shows little sign of analyzing problems of computerisation 'until long after it is relevant'. Indeed, in this respect, the design community is displaying in its own field the same lack of social awareness which it displays when implementing technology in society at large.

Undoubtedly, most of these problems arise from the economic and social assumptions that are made when equipment of this kind is introduced. Another significant problem is the assumption that so-called scientific methods will result inevitably in better design, when in fact, there are grounds for questioning whether the design process lends itself to these would-be scientific methods. (footnote)

Related to this is one of the unwritten assumptions of our scientific methodology – namely, that if you cannot quantify something you pretend it doesn't exist. The number of complex situations which lend themselves to mathematical modelling is very small indeed. We have not yet found, nor are we likely to find, a means of mathematically modeling the human mind's imagination. Perhaps one of the positive side effects of computer-aided design is that it will require us to think more fundamentally about these profound problems and to regard design as a holistic process. As Professor Lobell, the American design methodologist, has put it:

> It is true that the conscious mind cannot juggle the number of variables necessary for a complex design problem, but this does not mean that systematic methods are the only alternative. Design is a holistic process. It is the process of putting together complex variables whose connection is not apparent by any describable system of logic. It is precisely for that reason that the most powerful logic of deep structures of the mind, which operate free of the limitations of space, time and causality, have traditionally been responsible for the most creative work in all of the sciences and arts. Today it has gone out of fashion to believe that these powers are in the mind. (footnote)

9 Creative Minds

It is a fact that the highly constrained and organised intellectual environment of a computerised office is remarkably at variance with the circumstances and attributes which appear to have contributed to creativity in the arts and sciences. I have heard it said that if only Beethoven had had a computer available to him for generating musical combinations, the Ninth Symphony would have been even more beautiful. But creativity is a much more subtle process. If you look historically at creative people, they have always had an open-ended, childlike curiosity. They have been highly motivated and had a sense of excitement in the work they were doing. Above all, they have possessed the ability to bring an original approach to problems. It is our ability to use our imagination that distinguishes us from animals. As Karl Marx wrote (Das Capital):

> "A bee puts to shame many an architect in the construction of its cells. But what distinguishes the worst of architects from the best of bees is namely this: the architect will construct in his imagination that which he will ultimately erect in reality. At the end of every labour process, we get that which existed in the consciousness of the labourer at its commencement." (p.174)

If we continue to design systems in the matter described earlier, we will be reducing ourselves to beelike behaviour.

It may be regarded as romantic or succumbing to mysticism to emphasise the importance of imagination and of working in a non-linear way. It is usually accepted that this type of creative approach is required in music, literature and art. It is less well recognised that this is equally important in the field of science, even in the so-called harder sciences like mathematics and physics. Those who were creative recognised this themselves. Isaac Newton said, 'I seem to have been only like a boy playing on the sea shore and diverting myself in now and then finding a smoother pebble or a prettier shell than ordinary, while the great ocean of truth lay all undiscovered before me.' Einstein said, 'Imagination is far more important than knowledge.' He went on to say,

'The mere formulation of a problem is far more important than its solution which may be merely a matter of mathematical or experimental skills. To raise new questions, new possibilities and to regard old problems from a new angle requires creative imagination and marks real advances in science.'

On one occasion, when being pressed to say how he had arrived at the idea of relativity, he is supposed to have said,

'When I was a child of fourteen I asked myself what the world would look like if I rode on a beam of light.'

A beautiful conceptual basis for all his subsequent mathematical work. Central to the Western scientific methodology is the notion of predictability, repeatability and quantifiability. If something is unquantifiable we have to rarefy it away from reality, which leads to a dangerous level of abstraction, rather like a microscopic Heisenberg principle. Such techniques may be acceptable in narrow mathematical problems, but where much more complex considerations are involved, as in the field of design, they may give rise to questionable results.

The risk that such results may occur is inherent in the scientific method which must abstract common features away from concrete reality in order to achieve clarity and systemisation of thought. However, within the domain of science itself, no adverse results arise because the concepts, ideas and principles are all interrelated in a carefully structured matrix of mutually supporting definitions and interpretations of experimental observation. The trouble starts when the same method is applied to situations where the number and complexity of factors is so great that you cannot abstract without doing some damage, and without getting an erroneous result. More recently, these questions have given rise to a serious political debate on the question of the neutrality of science and technology and there is already a growing concern over the ideological assumptions built into our scientific methodologies.

10 Competence, Skill and 'Training'

10.1 The Origins of Design

Around the sixteenth century, there appeared in most European languages the term 'design' or its equivalent. The emergence of the word coincided with the need to describe the occupational activity of designing. That is not to suggest that designing was a new activity. Rather, it was separated out from a wider productive activity and recognised as an activity in its own right. This can be said to constitute a separation of hand and brain, of manual and intellectual work and of the conceptual part of work from the labour process. Above all, it indicated that designing was to be separated from doing. It is clearly difficult to locate a precise historical turning point at which this occurred; rather we will view it as a historical tendency.

Up to the stage in question, a great structure such as a church would be 'built' by a master builder. We may generalise and say that the conceptual part of work would be integral to that labour process. Thereafter, however, came the concept of 'designing the church' an activity undertaken by architects, and the 'building of the church', an activity undertaken by builders. In no way did this represent a sudden historical discontinuity, but it was rather the beginning of a discernible historical tendency which has still not worked its way through many of the craft skills, so that as recently as the last century, Fairbairn was able to give his comprehensive description of the skills of a millwright quoted earlier. To this day, there are many jobs in which the conceptual part of work is still integrated with the craft basis. The significant feature of the stage in question is, however, that separating manual and intellectual work provided the basis for further subdivisions in the field of intellectual work itself - or as Braverman (1974) put it, 'Mental labour is first separated from the manual labour and then itself is subdivided rigorously according to the same rules'.

Dreyfus (1986) locates the root of the problem in the Greek use of logic and geometry, and the notion that all reasoning can be reduced to some kind of calculation. He suggests that the start of artificial intelligence probably began around the year 450 BC with Socrates and his concern to establish a moral standard. He asserts that Plato generalised this demand into an epistemological demand where one might hold that all knowledge could be stated in explicit definitions which anybody could apply. If one could not state one's know-how in such explicit instructions, then that know-how was not knowledge at all but mere belief. He suggests a Platonic tradition in which, for example, cooks who proceed by taste and intuition and people who work from inspiration, like poets, have no knowledge. What they do does not involve understanding and cannot be understood. More generally, what cannot be stated explicitly in precise instructions - that is, all areas of human thought which require skill, intuition or a sense of tradition - is relegated to some kind of arbitrary fumbling.

Gradually, a view evolved which put the objective above the subjective, and the quantitative above the qualitative. That the two should and can interact was not accepted, in spite of a systematic effort and intellectual struggle to assert it. One important example of the attempt to do so was the work of Albrecht Dürer (1471 - 1528). Dürer was not only a 'Master of the Arts', but a brilliant mathematical as well, who reached the highest academic levels in Nuremberg. Dürer sought to use his abilities to develop the mathematical forms which would succeed in preserving the unity of hand and brain. Kantor (1880) points out the significance of Dürer's ability to put complex mathematical techniques to practical uses, while Olschki (1919) compares his mathematical achievements with those of the leading mathematicians in Italy and elsewhere at that time. Indeed, some ninety years after Dürer's death Kepler was still discussing his geometric construction techniques. Alfred Sohn Rethel (1978) points out, in speaking of Dürer, 'Instead of, however, using this knowledge in a scholarly form, he endeavoured to put it to the advantage of the craftsman. His work was dedicated "to the young workers and all those with no one to instruct them truthfully". What is novel in his method is that he seeks to combine the workman's practice with Euclidian Geometry'.

And further, what Dürer had in mind is plain to see. The builders, metalworkers, etc., should on the one hand be enabled to master the tasks of military and civil technology and of architecture which far exceeded their traditional training. On the other hand the required mathematics should serve them as a means, so to speak, of preserving the unity of head and hand. They should benefit from the indispensable advantages of mathematics without becoming mathematic or brainworkers themselves. They should practise socialised thinking yet remain individual producers, and so he offered them an artisan schooling in draughtsmanship permeated through and through with mathematics - not to be confused in any way with applied mathematics.

It was said that on one occasion Dürer proclaimed it would be possible to develop forms of mathematics that would be as amenable to the human spirit as human language. Thereby one could integrate into the use of the instruments of labour the conceptual parts of work, thus building on the tradition in which the profiles of complex shapes were defined and constructed with such devices as sine bars.

11 Holistic Design

Thus theory, itself a generalization of practice, could have been reintegrated with practice to extend the richness of that practice and application while retaining the integration of hand and brain.

The richness of that practical tradition may be found in the sketchbook of Villard de Honnecourt, in which he introduced himself thus:

> Villard de Honnecourt greets you and begs all who will use the deviced found in this book, to pray for his soul and remember him. For in this book will be found sound advice on the virtues of masonry and the uses of carpentry. You will also find strong help in drawing figures according to the lessons taught by the art of geometry. (Bowie 1978)

This extraordinary document by a true 13th Century cathedral builder contains subjects which might be categorized as follows:

    1. mechanics
    2. practical geometry
    3. carpentry
    4. architectural design
    5. ornamental design
    6. figure design
    7. furniture design
    8. subjects foreign to the special knowledge of architects and designers.

The astonishing breadth and holistic nature of the skills and knowledge are in the manuscripts for all to see. There are those who, while admitting to the extraordinary range of capabilities of craftspeople of this time, hold that it was a 'static' form of knowledge which tended to be handed unaltered from master to apprentice. In reality, these crafts and their transmission embodied dynamic processes for extending their base and adding new knowledge all the time. Some of the German manuscripts describe die Wanderjahre – a form of sabbatical in which craftspeople travel from city to city to acquire new knowledge. Villard de Honnecourt travelled extensively, and thanks to his sketchbook (footnote) we can trace his travels through France, Switzerland, Germany and Hungary.

He was also passionately interested in mechanical devices, and one system he designed was subsequently adapted to keep mariners' compasses horizontal and barometers vertical. He devised a variety of clock mechanisms, from which we learn 'how to make the Angel keep pointing his finger towards the sun', and he displayed extraordinary engineering skills in a range of lifting and other mechanisms to provide significant mechanical advantage. For example, he invented a screw combined with a lever with appropriate instructions – 'How to make the most powerful engine for lifting weights'.

In all this, we see brilliantly portrayed the integration of design with doing – a tradition which was still discernible when Fairbairn described his millwright.

Villard was also concerned with 'automation', but in a form which freed the human being from back-breaking physical effort but retained the skilled base of work. In woodworking, he thought of a system for replacing the strenuous sawing activity – 'How to make a saw operate itself.'

He was profoundly interested in geometry as applied to drawings: 'Here begins the method of drawing as taught by the art of geometry but to understand them one must be careful to learn the particular use of each. All these devices are extracted from geometry'. He proceeds to describe 'How to measure the height for a tower', 'How to measure the width of a water course without crossing it', 'How to make two verssels so that one holds twice as much as the other'.

Many modern researchers have testified to Villard's significant grasp of geometry. Side-by-side with this we find his practical advice to stonecutters on the building elements divisions: 'How to cut an oblique voussoir', 'How to cut the springing stone of an arch', 'How to make regular pendants'. All the latter, drawn from his own practical experience and skill, is a vivid portrayal of the integration of hand and brain.

Another 13th-Century manuscript written in the same dialect as Villard's is still preserved and can be consulted in the Bibliotheque St Genevieve in Paris. Its author likewise concerned himself with mathematical problems: 'If you want to find the area of an equilateral triangle', 'If you want to know the area of an octagon', 'if you want to find the number of houses in a circular city'.

Throughout this period, the intellectual and the manual, the theory and the practice were integral to the craft or profession. Indeed, so naturally did the two coexist that we find practical builders (architects) with university titles like Doctor Lathomorum.

The epitaph of Pierre de Montreuil, the architect who reconstructed the nave and transepts of Saint Denis, runs, 'Here lies Pierre de Montreuil, a perfect flower of good manners, in this life a Doctor of Stones.'

I have cited these sketchbooks and quoted from these manuscripts in order to demonstrate that the craft at that time embodied powerful elements of theory, scientific method and the conceptual or design base of the activity. In doing so, I am myself guilty of a serious error. I accept that a matter can only be scientific of theoretical when it is written down. I did not provide an illustration of a great church or complex struture and state that the building of such a structure must itself embody a sound theoretical basis, otherwise the structure could not have been built in the first instance.

We can also detect in the written form the basic elements of Western scientific methodology: predictability, repeatability, and mathematical quanitfiability. These, by definition, tend to preclude intuition, subjective judgement and tacit knowledge.

Furthermore we begin to regard design as something that reduces or eliminates uncertainty, and since human judgement, as distinct from calculation, is itself held to constitute an uncertainty, it follows some kind of Jesuitical logical that good design is about eliminating human judgement and intuition. Furthermore, by rendering explicit the 'secrets' of craft, we prepare the basis for a rule-based system.

12 Rules For Design

In the two successive centuries there followed systematic attempts to describe and thereby render visible the rules underlying various craft skills. This applied right across the spectrum of skills of people who were artists, architects and engineers, in the Giotto tradition, from the theory of building construction through to painting and drawing. Giotto's method was not precisely optical. The receding beams of the ceiling converge to a reasonably convincing focus, but it is only approximate and does not coincide with the horizontal line as it should, according to the rules of linear perspective. 'This method is, however, systematic and rational, factors which no doubt provided a powerful stimulus for the more fully scientific rule seekers of the subsequent centuries. Priority amongst those who preceded Leonardo in searching for precise optical laws in picture making must go to the great architect and erstwhile sculptor Filippo Brunelleschi.' (Kemp 1981, p.26)

According to Manetti, at some time before 1413 Brunelleschi constructed two drawings which showed how buildings could be represented

> 'in what painters today call perspective, for it is part of that science which in effect sets down well and with reason the diminutions and enlargements which appear to the eyes of man from things far away and close at hand'.

One of the paintings showed the octagonal baptistry (S. Giovanni) as seen from the door of the cathedral in Florence. The optical 'truth' was verified by drilling a small hole in the baptistry panel, so that the spectator could pick up the panel and press an eye to the hole on the unpainted side and, with the other hand, hold a mirror in such a way that the painted surface was visible in reflection through the hole. By these means, Brunelleschi established precisely the perpendicular axis along which his representation should be viewed.

By the use of a mirror, there was a precise matching of the visual experience and the painted representation, and this was to become Leonardo's theory of art and indeed his whole theory of knowledge (Kemp 1981). He applied the same scientific methods to his architectural and other designs. One interpretation of these events is that they represented a significant turning point in the history of design and design methodology. Thereafter, there is a growing separation of theory and practice, a growing emphasis on the written 'theoretical forms of knowledge' and in my view, a growing confusion in Western society between linguistic ability and intelligence (in which the former is taken to represent the latter). Furthermore, this is accompanied by a growing denigration of tacit knowledge in which there are 'things we know but cannot tell' (Polanyi 1962). We may cite that most illustrious embodiment of theory and practice - Leonardo da Vinci:

> 'They will say that not having learning, I will not properly speak of that which I wish to elucidate. But do they not know that my subjects are to be better illustrated from experience than by yet more words? Experience, which has been the mistress of all those who wrote well and thus, as mistress, I will cite her in all cases.' (Kemp op. cit.)

In spite of such assertions, the tendency to produce generalised, written-down, scientific or rule-based design systems continued to build on earlier work. In 1486, the German architect Mathias Roriczer published in Regensburg his deceptively named

'On the Ordination of Pinnacles'. In this, he set out the method of designing pinnacles from plan drawings, and in fact produced a generalised method of design for pinnacles and other parts of a cathedral. These tendencies had already elicited bitter resistance from the craftsmen-cum-designers whose work was thereby being deskilled.

13 The Master Masons

In 1459, master masons from cities like Strasbourg, Vienna and Salzburg met at Regensburg in order to codify their lodge statutes. Among the various decisions, they decided that nothing was to be revealed of the art of making an elevation from a plan drawing to those who were not in the guild. 'Therefore, no worker, no master, no wage earner or no journeyman will divulge to anyone who is not of our Guild and who has never worked as a mason, how to make the elevation from the plan'. Of particular note is the exclusion of those who had never [worked] as a mason. There is, as our German colleagues would put it, a Doppelnatur to this craft reaction. On the one hand, there is the negative elitist attempt to retain privileges of the profession rather as the medical profession seeks to do to this day. On the other, there is a highly positive aspect, that of attempting to retain the qualitative and the quantitative elements of the work, the subjective and the objective, the creative and the non-creative, the manual and the intellectual and the work of hand and brain, embodied in the one craft.

The pressures on the master masons were twofold. Not only was the conceptual part of the work to be taken away from them, but those workers who still embodied the intellectual and design skills were being rejected by those who sought to show that theory was above and separate from practice. The growing academic elite resented the fact that carpenters and builders were known as masters, for example, Magister Cementarius or Magister Lathomorum. The academics attempted to ensure that the Magister would be reserved for those who had completed the study of the liberal arts. Indeed as early as the 13th Century, doctors of law were moved to protest formally at these academic titles for practical people.

It would be both fascinating and illuminating to trace these tendencies through the five intervening centuries which take us up to the information society of computer-aided design and expert systems. Suffice it to say that the number of researchers drawing on historical perspectives and viewing the implications of these information-based systems, conclude that we may now be at another historical turning point where we are about to repeat, in the field of design and other forms of intellectual work, many of the mistakes made in the field of craftsmanship in the past. (Cooley 1981).

14 Separation of Theory from Practice

It is significant that J. Weizenbaum, a professor of computer science at the Massachusetts institute of Technology, uses the subtitle 'From Judgement to Calculation' in his seminal work Computer Power and Human Reason (1976) and highlights the dangers which will surround an uncritical acceptance of computerized techniques.

The spectrum of problems associated with them is already becoming manifest. They include such spectacular separation of theory and practice as to result in some of those who have been weaned on computer-aided design being unable to recognize the object they have 'designed'. Epitomising this was the designer of an aircraft igniter who calculated the dimensions on the CAD screen and then set them out with the decimal point one place to the right (which in an abstraction is very much like one place to the left). He then generated the numerical control tapes with which skilled workers on the shop floor produced an ignitor ten times larger than it should have been (Cooley 1981). Perhaps the most alarming aspect of this extraordinary state of affairs was that when confronted with the monstrosity, the designer saw nothing wrong with it.

Given the scale and nature of these problems and the exponential rate of technological change within which they are located, it behoves all of us to seek to demonstrate, as Durer did, that alternatives exist which reject neither human judgement, tacit knowledge, intuition and imagination nor the scientific or rule based method. We should rather unite them in a symbiotic totality.

15 Consumer Incompetence

Efforts to deskill the producers can only become operational if they are accompanied by the deskilling of the consumers. The deskilling of bakers, for example, can come about only if that awful cotton-wool stodge in plastic wrappers is regarded as bread by millions of consumers. Highly automated factory farming techniques are only possible if the public believes that there only two kinds of potato, 'new' and 'old', that cookers and eaters are the only forms of apples, and if it cannot distinguish the taste of free-range poultry and eggs from those produced under battery farm conditions.

The elimination of high-level skills in carpentry and cabinet-making is possible because large sections of the public do not appreciate the difference between a tacky chipboard product and one handmade with real wood and fitted joints, or between a pastic container and (say) and inlaid needlebox.

The concern for quality should not be misunderstood as an elitist tendency. Quite ordinary working-class and rural families used to pass pieces of furniture from one generation to another which, although simple, embodied fine craftsmanship and materials. A skilled joiner recently told me with great feeling how monstrous he found it that beautiful pieces of wood which could have been hand turned and carved, were being burned on a demonlition site by 'builders' who couldn't distinguish between one piece of wood and another.

Given time, more and more sections of the community will lose the capacity to appreciate craftsmanship and goods of quality. As you 'break the refractory hand of labour', you must also break the refractory will of the consumer. To do so it is of course necessary to have ranges of accomplices. These are in advertising, marketing, more generally, of the 'Waste Makers' type. The accomplices are in relation to production and consumpton and there are also partners in crime in the areas of the reproduction of knowledge. The duality of the master and apprentice, teacher and student, has now been replaced by the trainer and the trainee. In large occupational areas we no longer have education, we have 'training'.

16 Apprenticeships and Training

An apprenticeship in the classical sense was not merely a process for the acquisition of technical skills. It was far more significantly the transmission of culture, a way of understanding and respecting quality and acquiring a love of good materials. Even to this day, this cultural outlook is alive and well amongst craftspeople. Ken Hunt is a master engraver whose work is sought worldwide. He served his apprenticeship with Purdeys, the London Sporting Gunmakers, who arranged for him to work with Henry Kell, one of the specialist firms engraving the gun actions. This is how Ken Hunt described his work in 1987:

> I think engraving creates an intensely personal relationship between the work and the craftsman. It's the most lovely feeling when everything is going right: the cutting tool is working wel, the steel doesn't fight you.
>
> To me the beauty of a cut on steel with a graver is similar to the mark made by a quill pen on paper. It flows and is far removed from the straight line drawn by a ballpoint. I get so involved sometimes that I lose all track of time, and I get lost in all sorts of ideas, almost fantasies, I suppose. I find myself thinking of craftsmen centuries ago who worked metal in exactly the same way as I do now. Nothing has changed, neither the medium nor the tools.
>
> It may sound strange, but occasionally I get pieces back that I might have worked on in the sixties or even earlier, and I only have to touch them to recall exactly what I was doing and thinking when I was working on them all those years ago. Perhaps it's because each job represents and absorbs a large part of your life – maybe even your soul, who knows?
>
> Michaelangelo used to claim that all he did when confronted with a block of stone was to chip away and release the sculpture which was inside it, and I feel that too. (p.11)

Ken does not use preliminary drawings of his intended work. Nor does he have tracing on the metal which will then be simply followed by the engraving tool. 'No, I go straight in and just do it. I've got an idea in my head as how the finished work will look, but I don't believe in drawing it out carefully first.'

There is a tendency to regard such craft skills as being static and devoid of development. But the environment created by an apprenticeship encourages experimentation and innovation within a given tradition. Ken Hunt recalls that in his early days he would visit museums to admire and wonder at masterpieces from the past:

> I would stand and stare at a certain piece for ages wondering how it was done. Sometimes, I would even stay so long that the wardens would begin to eye me with suspicion! I was intrigued with everything to do with metal work, though especially gold inlaying. I eventually worked out my own way of keying gold to steel using a series of undercut crisscross lines which have a dovetail effect.

It would be unthinkable that craftspeople lie Ken Hunt would waste materials or mishandle or damage tools and equipment. All of this was integral to the totality which was embodied in a traditional apprenticeship. It was also a process by which one learned, in a very practical way the logistics of procuring such materials, treating them and forming them in a creative process which linked hand, eye, and brain in a meaningful productive process. It embodied 'design by doing' – methods of work in which the conceptual aspects of work were integrated within the overall labour process.

Apprenticeships served to develop significant skills in the field of planning and coordination, and produced quite astonishing levels of ability in the handling of materials. I marvel at St Paul's cathedral, for even given our modern means of project management and complex techniques for handling material, we may question whether anyone would be capable of constructing it today. Even if we could, what an infinitely greater task it was in the 17th century, given the limited equipment for lifting and placing the building elements into their locations.

The kind of apprenticeships those builders had, gave them a deep sense of total machines as operating systems, epitomized by the vast knowledge of the great millwrights. It is true that with the introduction of Taylorism (Taylor 1906) apprenticeships did embody the most anecdotal aspects, where considerable time was spent in making tea for others or in irrelevant activities, but that is not what we are addressing here; it is rather the great apprenticeships which produced those of the caliber described earlier.

Against this richness and competence can be counterposed 'training'. The word is very apt in the modern context. My own hierarchy of verbs in terms of competence transmission would be the following: you program a robot, you train a dog (or a soldier), but for human beings you provide educational environments. Training produces narrow, overdedicated capabilities which are generally machine, system or program-specific. With the ever-increasing rate of technological change, the knowledge required to cope with a particular machine or system may be obsolete in a couple of years' time. The trainee is then lost, and requires further 'training'. Much of what now passes for training' is nothing more than a form of social therapy. Instead of putting people on valium you put them on a training course. It is questionable whether you produce anything more than a slightly better quality dole queue. 'Training' often hides a cruel deception.

Some companies have very competent training officers who themselves have actual knowledge of the processes involved. What I am referring to here is that new brand of 'training advisers', 'training coordinators', 'training outreach workers', and 'training planners' who seem to believe that there is some separate activity called 'training' which transcends all other forms of professional knowledge. Some of the ones I have encountered seem to believe that if you've trained a Labrador to retrieve you can also train a nuclear physicist, and if you've trained somebody to make doughnuts in the catering industry, you can also train them to design a Rolls-Royce aero engine; it is, after all, just training! Because these people have no knowledge of the skills involved, they behave in a high-handed and arrogant fashion. Furthermore, because they are in a position to allocate funds, they are often able to impose their nonsense on people who could have provided a rich developmental environment. The disadvantage of using this type of 'trainer' is twofold. They don't know what they are doing and are overpaid for doing it, and, more significantly, they prevent people who do have the skills and knowledge from enjoying the experience and gaining the dignity of transmitting to a future generation.

17 A Challenge for the 21ˢᵗ Century

This extraordinary Millenium

> .....no longer will I follow you oblique like through the inspired form of the third person singular and the moods and hesitancies of the deponent but address myself to you, with the empirative of my vendettative, provocative and out direct...

James Joyce

The year 2000 marks the end of the most extraordinary millennium in human history. During it, humanity has witnessed the decline of feudalism, the growth of capitalism, and weakening of religion as the leading edge in European society. We have facilitated the emergence of Cartesian Science, the concentration of populations into modern cities and the development of 'earth-shrinking' transport systems. Above all there has been the growth of industrial society. We have allowed the great story-telling traditions to all but wither away. We have devised the means of flying, declared Jackson Pollock a great artist, bounced on the moon and killed 17 million people in just one war.

Through our science we have become the first generation of the only species to apparently have it within its power to destroy itself and life on the planet as we know it. We have become far too smart scientifically to survive much longer without wisdom.

We should reflect upon the beauty and the devastation we have wrought on our own two-edged way to the 21ˢᵗ century. The delinquent genius of our species has produced the beauty Venice and also the hideousness of Chernobyl; the playful linguistic delights of Shakespeare and the ruthlessness of the British imperialism; the musical treasures of Mozart and the stench of Bergen Belsen, the caring medical potencial of Rontgen's X-rays and the horrific devastation of Hiroshima.

The last century of the millennium has been characterized by a convulsed and exponential rate of technology change in which our speed of communication has increased to 10^7, our speed of travel by 10^3 and of data-handling by 10^6. Over the same period our depletion of energy resources has increased by 10^4 and weapon power by 10^7.

We have seen the polarization of wealth and activity. In developed countries there are computer programmes to help people diet, whilst out of the 122 million babies born in developing countries in 1982, 11 million died before their first birthday and a further 5 million died before their fifth birthday. In some countries it is more today!

At the end of the millennium we appear to stand as the masters of nature. We scrabble millions of tons of material around each year and in doing so we shift the equivalent of three times the sediment moved each year by the world's rivers. We mine and burn billions of tons of coal each years so venting the waste which includes carbon dioxide the principal contributor to the greenhouse effect.

Our agriculture, now worked on an industrial scale, causes the erosion of 25 million tons of soil each year which is 0.7% of the total arable land formed over a period of several thousand years. We put down 30kg of fertilizers per person per year to increase the crop yield, so polluting the very water we drink. In many parts of the world we have turned the soil into a craving junkie, incapable of producing without its next fix. If we continue in the present manner, we will reduce by 50% all the species of flora and fauna in less than two centuries. In fact, this is likely to be a matter decades taking into account the greenhouse effect. This will constitute a terrible reduction in bio-diversity but is also being accompanied by a reduction in diversity amongst ourselves.

Among the global issues confronting industrial society today, two are particularly pressing. They are:

1. resource depletion; and,
2. environment changes brought about by human activity.

18 Stimulus

Symbols in turn determine the kind of stories we tell and the stories we tell determine the kind of history we make remake.

Mary Robinson

The year 2000 could, and should, provide powerful stimulus to examine where, as an industrial society, we are going. To do so at the macro level, we will require the perspective of a historian, the imagination of a poet, the analytical ability of a scientist, and the wisdom of a Chief Seattle (an American Indian). We shall have to be capable of thinking holistically, working in multidisciplinary groups, coping with change and developing systems and products which are sustainable and caring of nature and humanity. Our current educational systems are fundamentally inappropriate and woefully inadequate to address this historical task.

Thus an EEC/FAST report [4] is quite unambiguous about the changes to educational activities that will be necessary. It states:

The tendency for education to concentrate on narrow specialist areas is counterproductive and must give way to holistic forms. The concern should be education rather than training. Above all, education should be the transmission of a culture which values proactive, sensitive and creative human beings.

In relation to manufacturing and industry in seems self-evident that developing the skills and competence necessary in the 21st century will require nothing short of 'cultural and industrial renaissance'.

For this to come about we will require citizens possessed not just of a knowledge but also of wisdom. It will require the courage and the dignity to ask simple questions of profound significance. Why is it that if we grow our own lettuce and repair our own car the gross national product (GNP) goes down whereas if they have a pile-up on the motorway and in the carnage scores of people are killed and piles of cars are destroyed the GNP goes up? How come we design products to fall apart after five years? What is the deranged mentality of an expert in artificial intelligence who can say:

Human beings will have to accept their true place in the evolutionary hierarchy namely animals, human beings and intelligent machines?

These are key issues as we approach the 21ˢᵗ century and our educational system should be preparing people to discuss them in an informed, creative and imaginative fashion.

19 The Industrial Future

If you look into the seed of time and say which grains will grow and which will not....

William Shakespeare

Educationalists, industrialists, trade unionists and politicians should be urged to enter into a creative dialogue with the community at large to decide what the future might be like. Such a debate would encourage human beings to perceive themselves in the dual role in society – as producers and also consumers and to recognize that they are the subjects of history rather than the objects through which it wends its painful way. The urgency of the debate is highlighted to the crisis now facing industrial societies worldwide.

There is a growing recognition that the future cannot merely be an extrapolation of the past. We cannot assume it is possible to have an ever increasing rate of production and consumption. The mass production of throw-away products based on energy, capital and chemically-intensive forms of production, whether in manufacturing or in agriculture, is no longer possible nor acceptable. The ecological damage we are doing is now making this clear to growing numbers of citizens. Furthermore, these intensive forms of production are also giving rise to political and social tensions and are contributing significantly to growing structural unemployment worldwide. In the EEC countries there are now 16.2 million people out of work and it is predicted that this will increase to some 20 million by 1996 This is inspite of the fact that there are dramatic demographic shifts taking place in Europe. In addition, 100,000 small towns and villages will cease to be economically viable.

In addition to these questions there is concern that the so-called 'lucky ones' who retain their jobs are increasingly involved in using forms of new technology which result in processes which are not only intensive and stressful for people but which frequently reduce them to mere machine appendages. The EEC report highlighted these issues and advocated Anthropocentric Systems as a more long-term sustainable alternative. The report suggests:

1　That industrial society would have to move from an economy of scale to an economy of scope and on to an economy of networking.

2　The need for a society of proactive, creative, involved citizens at all levels.

3　That society would gradually become one of 'continuous innovation', where the capacity to design and build prototypes and to have skill based, short batch manufacturing capabilities would be of growing importance.

4　That whilst during the era of Fordism a dominant mono-industrial culture based on Taylorism gave the United States important competitive advantages this would no longer be so significant and is now beginning to be counterproductive.

5   That linguistic, cultural and geographical diversity which had been perceived by some as weakness in the European situation should in future be perceived as an advantage and a source of innovation. Thechnology and educational support systems should enhance that diversity rather than diminish it.

20 A Tool Rather Than a Machine

"When the fact fails him, he questions his senses;
When the fact fails me, I approve my senses."

Robert Graves

In the Human Centred System, there exists a symbiotic relation between the human and the machine in which the human being would handle the qualitative subjective judgements and the machine the quantitative elements. It involves a radical redesign of the interface technologies and at a philosophical level the objective is to provide tools (in the Heidegger sense) which would support human skill and ingenuity rather than machines which would objectivise that knowledge.

The focus of human centredness is to design forms of technology which reverse one of the main processes of technology which is to render systems active and human beings passive. It means providing powerful analogical systems in which it is possible to programme the devices in a manner which accords with the traditional ways of working but which enhances those by providing very modern software and hardware tools. In the context of high level intellectual work (e.g. designing) it is necessary to challenge the concept of menu driven systems which frequently reduce the designer to being like a child with a LEGO set. The child can make a pleasing pattern of predetermined elements but cannot change those elements. This raises very important questions for education at every level. It further requires that the skill and competence at every level of the organisation should be changed and expanded, thereby changing the worker's perception of him or herself. For example, on the shop floor, those who functioned and thought of themselves as "machine operators" can metamorphise into 'Cell Managers'. They can take an overview of the functioning of the cell and acquire additional competencies in the field of planning, costing and systems maintenance. They can use powerful support tools such as workstations with adaptive interfaces. Such interfaces should acknowledge and celebrate traditional craft skills. It is suggested that those able to make best use of such multi media systems are those who emerge from a quasi-apprenticeship system and therefore start from a high 'competence platform'. The whole process is one in which the operator "builds on the familiar to create the new".

Part of the competence and some of the skills required to work in such environments will be the following:-

1   The ability to absorb new knowledge and transform it.
2   The ability to draw conclusions about the unknown from the known.

3   The ability to take initiatives.
4   The capacity to make decisions.
5   The ability to work as a team
6   The ability to adopt a systematic, analytical approach
7   The ability to plan independently
8   The ability to take on responsibility

Those involved in systems design will need to be competent in the design of adaptive tools which accord closely with traditions and practices of the domain area. Furthermore, they will need to be competent in the design of systems and organisations which display the following characteristics:

Coherence: The embedded meanings, if not immediately evident, at least must not be cloaked or obscure. A related concept here is 'transparence' which means rendering what is going on and what is possible as being highly visible.

Inclusiveness: The system should be inviting and tend to "invite you in" and make you feel part of a community of activities with which you are familiar and on friendly terms.

Malleability: A possibility to 'mould' the situation to suit, to pick-and-mix and sculpt the environment to suit one's own instrumental needs, aesthetic tastes and craft traditions.

Engagement: A sense that one is being invited to participate in the process and which creates a sense of empathy.

Ownership: A feeling that you have created and thereby 'own' parts of the system. A sense of belonging and even companionship as traditional craftsmen may feel with a favourite machine tool.

Responsiveness: A general sense that you can get the system to respond to your requirements and your individual needs and ways of doing things. A system which makes visible its own rules and then encourages one to learn them and to change them at will.

Purpose: Purpose is meant in the sense in which Rosenbrock (1990) describes it. The system is capable of responding to the purpose one has in mind and then encouraging one to go beyond it.

Panoramic: Most current systems tend to encourage the user to converge on narrower activities. With good embedded systems it should also provide windows or apertures through which one can take a wider or more panoramic view. This encourages the acquisition of 'boundary knowledge' and allows the user to act more effectively and competently by locating what he or she is doing in the understanding of a wider context.

Transcendence: When operating the system, the user should be encouraged, enticed and even provoked to transcend the immediate task requirements. The possibility of acquiring boundary knowledge and a macro level vision of the process as a whole should be self-evident.

Hard nosed industrialists and their compliant foot soldiers -industrial engineers- have tended to regard the type of systems described above as being at the best a diversion from "the real world of industry" or at the worst "dangerous liberal waffle". But times are changing. The crisis in many of the rigid, hierarchical large organisations is forcing a radical re-examination of much of the given wisdom. At an economic level, the multi-disciplinary report on the future of US Industry pointed out, "We have tended to treat our workforces as a cost and a liability whereas our major competitors have treated them as an asset whose skills should be ever enhanced".

Professor Hopwood (1988) has highlighted the need for accountants to re-examine their arid thinking. Thus they spend 75% of their time in dealing with direct labour costs but direct labour costs now only constitute about 10% of the total costs if one considers industry as a whole. On the other hand material, which accounts for 50% of the cost is only subject to 10% of accounting effort.

At the technical level the case is even more compelling. In machine based, hierarchical Tayloristic systems which relentlessly drive towards wall-to-wall automation, there is now a growing recognition that such systems are extremely vulnerable to disturbance. They are typically good at coping with high frequency, low impact events though bad in dealing with low frequency, high impact ones -e.g. the uncertainty of the real world. Otherwise stated, machine dependent systems are highly synchronised and co-ordinated. When one part of the system goes down, the high level synchronisation is turned into its dialectical opposite and one gets massive de-synchronisation rather in the form of catastrophe theory.

In addition to economic benefits, there may be added the long-term advantages in the form of flexibility and strategic capability for innovation. Of equal importance but less easy to quantify are social benefits such as quality of working life, dramatically improved motivation and the liberating of one of society's greatest assets, the skill, ingenuity and creativity of its people. The resultant flexibility will become paramount in coming years as there are more custom bound, short batch production runs and as an economy of networking becomes widespread. Concurrent or simultaneous engineering will further reinforce the need for systems of this kind.

21 Overstructuring

"Management is just a bad habit inherited from the army and the church".

Danny Conroy-Craftsman

A feature of modern industrial society is its over structuring. This arises within production from a mechanistic, Tayloristic view of optimum organisation. Taylor said on one occasion:-

> "In my system the workman is told precisely what he is to do and how he is to do it and any improvement he makes upon the instructions given to him is fatal to success."

The United States led in this overstructuring of industry and as a report in the late 1980s from the MIT pointed out, it is seriously debilitating because it treats human beings as liabilities rather than as assets.

Although these lessons are beginning to be understood in industry, the educational system in general and universities in particular still seem determined to pursue teaching forms which are based on factory models. When Henry Ford donated 100 million dollars to an institution which he called The School of the Future, he said (Cooley 1990)

> "I have manufactured cars long enough to the point where I have got the desire to manufacture people. The catchword of the day is standardisation".

The overstructuring reached such a level that even universities are being organised as factories within which the students are referred to as commodities, the examinations as quality control procedures, graduation as delivery and the professors as operators.

The factory model is now all pervasive. It conditions and distorts every aspect of life in the technologically advanced nations. I am not sure if it was ever true in the Shakespearian sense, that all the world's a stage. It is however certainly true that at the close of the 20th Century all the world's a factory and all of nature that surrounds us is seen as inert material for its remorseless production line.

Paradigmatic changes are already at hand and within these we will require people with the competence to cope with ill defined, loosely structured situations which cannot be defined in a unidimensional way and which embody high levels of uncertainty and unpredictability. At a design level we will have to consider a scientific methodology based on purpose and not only one based on causal explanations (Rosenbrock 1990).

22 Educate Not Train

> Any teacher who can be replaced by a computer deserves to be! David Smith

Many of the factory-like universities have ceased any pretense at education and are instead concerned with instruction. In many cases they are so highly structured that even the instruction becomes mere arid training. Training usually provides a narrow explicit machine or systems specific competence which is quicly obsolete with technological change. Education is of a much more durable quality and as one of my German colleagues put it "a state of mind". My hierarchy of verbs in these matters is that you program a robot, your train an animal but educate human beings. Education in this sense is not just that which occurs in schools or universities where so often there are those who are – as Illich point out (1971):

> Schooled to confuse teaching with learning, grade advancement with education, a diploma with competence and fluency with the ability to say something new.

Education is a subset of the cultural milieu in which it occurs. This apprenticeships in the classical sense were the transmission of a culture. They produced the giants who define our European civilisation: Leonardo da Vinci, Fillipo Brunellesci, Giotto. A great skill, as we approach the 21st century, will be to use new technologies in such a fashion as build upon the best traditions of those rich learning processes.

The human-centred community questions the given wisdom that daily advises us that we live in an informed society. We may perhaps live in a data society whereas what is required is the competence to operate at the knowledge/wisdom/action end of the cybernetic loop (Fig 1). I freely admit that it took as many years and much technocratic rambling to arrive at this rather obvious conclusion. If we had been more fully exposed to the ideas, however ill-structured, of artists or poets, this might have been more obvious. Thus in the case of Figure 1, the basic "theory" was anticipated by T.S. Elliot:

What wisdom have we lost in knowledge.

What knowledge have we lost in information.

Frequently, the big issues in society are prefigured in society by our poets and our artists and we diminish ourselves as engineers and scientists if we do not interact with them in a multi-disciplinary way. The ability to do so may be an important requirement as we approach the 21st century.

23 Imagination

It stands almost complete and finished in my mind so that I can survey it like a fine picture or a beautiful statue. Mozart.

Industrialisation has in many ways reduced and over concentrated or competences as human beings. We confer life on machines and diminish ourselves. We are gradually becoming observers of life rather than its active participants. Education in the sense in which I use it above should imbue a sense of excitement, discovery and imagination. We are far too obsessed with narrow facts, details, and exams. Exams essentially find out what people do not know rather than what they do know.

There used to be a tradition in some of the older universities if you didn't like the examination question you were set you simply ignored it and wrote your own question. Life in the widest philosophical sense should be about writing one's own questions and education should facilitate that. It should stimulate and excite our imagination and sense of discovery. The great Einstein on one occasion observed:

Imagination is far more important than knowledge

He went on to say:

The formulation of a problem is far more important than its solution which may be merely a matter of mathematical or experimental skill. To raise new questions, to look at old problems from a new angle marks the real advances in science.

This, I suggest, is the broader context in which we need to contemplate the skills and competencies for the twenty first century.

References

Braverman, H (1974) Labor and Monopoly Capital. The Degradation of Work in the 20th Century, Monthly Review Press, New York.

Bowie, T. (1959) The Sketchbook of Villard de Honnecourt. Indiana University press, 1959.

Cooley, M.J.E. (1975) The Knowledge Worker in the 1980s, Doc. EC35, Diebold Research Programme, Amsterdam.

Cooley, M.J.E. (1980) Some special implications of CAD in Mermet (ed) CAD in Medium Sized and Small Industries. Proceedings of MICAD,1980, Paris,

Cooley, M.J.E. (1981) Computerisaion – Taylor's latest disguise. In Economic and Industrial Democracy, Vol. 1. Sage: London

Cooley, M.J.E. (1987) Architect or Bee? Hogarth Press.

Dreyfus HL & Dreyfus SE (1986), Mind over Machine, Free Press, New York.

Ford, cited in Cooley, M.J.E. (1990) 'The New Shape of Industrial Culture and Technological Development'. Tokyo Keizai University.

Kemp, M. (1981) Leonardo da Vinci - The Mavellous Works of Nature and Man, J.M. Dent & Sons Ltd, London, p.26.

Hopgood in Proc. NMI Conference, London 1988.

Hunt, K. (1987) Shooting Life, Spring Issue.

Jefferys, J.B. (1945) The Story of the Engineers. Lawrence and Wishart, p.9

Kantor (1880) Vorlesunfen Uber Geschichte der Mathematik, Vol. 2, Leipzig.

Marx, K (1974) Capital, Vol.1, p.174, Lawrence & Wishart, London.

Olschki (1919) Geschichte der neusprachlichen Wissenschaftlichen Litteratur, Leipzig.

Polanyi, M. (1962) Tacit Knowing: its bearing on some problems of philosophy, Review of Modern Physics, Vol. 34, October 1962, pp.601-605.

Polanyi, M (1966) The Tacit Dimension. Doubleday.

Rose, S (1976), 'Can Science be Neutral?'. In H. Rose and S. Rose (eds), The Political Economy of Science, Macmillan, London,.

Rosenbrock, H.H. (1990) Machines with a Purpose, Oxford University Press, 1990.

Silver, RS (1975) The Misuse of Science, New Scientist, Vol.166, p.956.

Sohn Rethel, A (1978) Intellectual and manual Labour: A Critique of Epistemology, Macmillan, London.

Taylor, F.W. (1906) On the Art of Cutting Metals, 3rd edition revised. ASME.

Weizenbaum, J. (1976) Computer Power and Human Reason. W.H.Freeman&Co., San Francisco.

Endnotes

[1] F. Margulies in conversation with the author.

[2] Eugene Wigner cited in Cooley, M.J.E (1987) p.50

[3] Norbert Wiener cited in Cooley, M.J.E (1987)

[4] EEC/FAST Report, European Comptetitiveness in the 21st century: The Integration of Work, Culture and Technology.

AI & Soc (1994) 8:45–87
© 1994 Springer-Verlag London Limited

AI & SOCIETY

Open Forum

What Goes on When a Designer Thinks?

Gustaf Östberg

University of Lund, Lund, Sweden

Abstract: Design can be thought of as a model for such endeavours as are intended to result in industrially manufactured products by means of thinking and other intellectual activity. Familiarity with the thinking involved in the designing process is important, not only for those engaged in training designers, but for anyone desirous of systemizing the endeavour. One procedure for approaching an understanding of the way designers think is to describe it with the help of different metaphors. There are some metaphors for thinking about complicated and interrelated phenomena that should lend themselves to illustrating the thinking involved in design, albeit with reservations – e.g. the difficulty of allowing due consideration for what is unthinkable and indescribable in this context.

Keywords: Computerisation; Design; Metaphors; Tacit knowledge; Thinking; Unthinkables

Designing as Thinking

This paper is a contemplation of the possibilities of describing and understanding thinking and the role it plays in designer's work. The presentation proceeds from certain assumptions, namely:

- That in addition to other mental and physical activity, a certain kind of thinking is involved when designing;

- That this thinking is significant for designing and hence deserving of attention;

- That it is possible, and rewarding, to regard the thinking involved in designing as a definite and discernible phenomenon, without thereby necessarily presenting a distorted picture of design.

It is possible that these assumptions are entirely or partially incorrect, and that the solution of the problem requires other points of departure in order to do justice to the real import of design. Among other things, one should be wary of insisting on the premise that thinking can be treated in all respects as entirely self-contained and independent of other elements involved in design, especially such things as are difficult to describe as clearly and unequivocally as thinking. Nevertheless, the following exercise has seemed worthwhile, if only to determine the extent of the insight into the designer's endeavour it may provide.

The exercise involves a personally limited selection of viewpoints from the field of leaning regarding what, in more sophisticated scientific terms, is called cognition, especially the philosophical, psychological and sociological aspects of that subject. Some of what will be said here is taken from the insights that can be found even among people outside the scientific community as narrowly defined, for example creative writers, and of course from designers themselves. This personal selection is, incidentally, determined by a specific need, namely to (if possible) understand how designers and artisans treat problems dealing with materials. One particular question in this context is how designers and draftsmen use databases to obtain information about the characteristics of materials. That question cannot be satisfactorily answered without a better understanding of the thinking involved in designing and planning than we presently enjoy.

An Afterword will present some of the underlying ideas about design that have guided the reflections to which we now turn.

Not Only Thinking

It seems reasonable to assume that the ability to think is an integral part of a designer's professional competence – in addition to everything else that does not lend itself to comprehension through reason or to description in a way that corresponds to all of the implications of design. The use of *thinking* does not preclude what goes on in the unconscious and which is included, along with thinking, in what can be described as a *mental process*.

What has been referred to here as the *unconscious* for lack of a better term includes such things as feelings, imagination, intuition, visual apprehensions and other non-intellectual elements required for an activity of the kind that constitutes design as heretofore interpreted. Using an analogy from psychology, one can assert that design cannot be captured in some kind of 'behavioural thought pattern' or described as a souless 'erector set' combination of thoughts. It might in fact be permitted to go one step further and maintain that design is related to configuration, and that therefore its essence is related to, but not limited to, the concept of Gestalt encountered in psychology. (This observation is offered here without the intention of being interpreted as a profession of adherence to Gestalt psychology.)

Merely to indicate how important these elements can be to the professional competence of designers, let us briefly consider the enormous influence on our perceptions of our surroundings that we derive from impressions so fleeting that we are not even consciously aware of them. A considerable amount of our conduct

487

occurs in fact unconsciously and without planned 'thinking', in the sense usually associated with that word. It is important for an understanding of design to appreciate the relationship between 'thinking' and the unthinkable.

Hence, in turn, the importance of distinguishing between thinking activities that consist of a selection among several different impressions – whether conscious or unconscious, or 'intuitive' – on the one hand, and an endeavour that leads up to an intellectual construction composed of more or less fixed elements that are familiar, on the other. It is not the intention of the following exposition to advocate that a designer's endeavour is based on the primacy of thinking. This is not an attempt to set up a logical model or a rule book for design as merely one variety of intellectual construction.

The Difficulty of Talking About Thinking

It might conceivably be ventured that design is an existential phenomenon, and therefore cannot be treated as something that is comprehensible to reason in all its parts – which is to say, that it is nonrational. If one were, nevertheless, compelled to talk about thinking in the context of design for the purposes of understanding and education, one would have to simplify. The difficulty would then lie in not losing too much of the nonrational. Talking implies expressing oneself in metaphors. That confines one to concepts which do not always, perhaps, permit any deeper understanding. This is even more the case when one uses images. The use of both metaphors and images in the present comments is intended to add clarity, and simultaneously to trigger associations to deeper and broader notions of the implications of design.

To talk about thinking does not necessarily mean expressing any fixed and guaranteed attributes of thinking. It is more like offering descriptions of what thinking seems to be like. The existence of different descriptions is explained by the fact that the descriptions can have different aims. In scientific terms, we can briefly say that it boils down to intentionality, rather than objectivity.

Relating to the Unthinkable

It is possible to say that not everything involved in designing can be designated as thinking – and then to lay everything that is not thinking to one side. However, one cannot feel that one has treated thinking adequately unless one has taken a position on the question of the potential significance of what has been left out – the unthinkable. It is also important to try to understand how one should relate to the unthinkable in one's thinking.

The problem is mainly what cannot be verbally expressed about the thinking in design. One reason for the boundary between thinking and the unthinkable is that language has its limits. One can use language to describe what is meant by 'reality' and also, to some extent, to indicate certain connections that imply explanations. One can even express oneself about things that ought to exist in some form even though they cannot be observed.

However, it would appear to be more difficult to gain an insight into the nature and significance of the unthinkable by means of thinking as mediated via language than to understand the thinking involved in design. Of course, one can observe that something 'unthinkable' is included in design, simply because what is identified as thinking fails to satisfactorily describe or explain the course of events involved in designing, and its results. And this provides a certain grasp of the significance of the unthinkable. To reach further than that would appear to be unjustifiable. To express oneself about the nature of the unthinkable in anything like the same degree cannot be possible except with regard to specific components or in certain respects.

Simply by talking about some things as unthinkable, one has acquiesced to letting thinking and language determine one's perception of the nature of designing. Even though one may not have been beguiled into a fixed definition of the role and significance of thinking in designing, the very division into the thinkable and the unthinkable may have rendered the holistic treatment of design impossible. It can be difficult in one's thinking to relate intellectually to the unthinkable. However, this particular difficulty can be diminished by preventing one's thinking from being unduly influenced by the notion that one is dealing with discrete worlds with fixed and certain boundaries between thinking and other activities involved in design.

Computerised expert systems provide a special illustration of this problem posed by the unthinkable. We cannot entirely dismiss the possibility that such expert systems might be able to be so fashioned as to allow even the unthinkable to be a part of designing. It would seem, however, that this should not be taken for granted unless great consideration is given to the possibility that the very point of departure in linguistically mediated thinking may imply treating the unthinkable aspects of design. We cannot simply assume the likelihood of developing either a computer language or a 'natural' language that facilitates describing, or accounting for, 'reality' in such a way that the unthinkable in designing is given due recognition.

In recent years, our understanding of thinking has been enhanced by insights into the way the brain works. Among other things, it has been demonstrated that there is an interplay between what is referred to as thinking in a narrow, everyday, sense, and 'visual thinking'. The significance of other sensual inputs to thinking has also been given due recognition. There would appear to be, however, an additional step to achieving a truly informed attitude regarding the unthinkable. Among other things, we do not know very much about the extent of the conclusions we can draw with regard to design from theories and models of the way human beings perceive reality. There is a good deal of awareness of how we perceive form and colour, and of how we employ thinking and language to convey such perceptions. This is not to assume, however, that our way of producing form, i.e. design, has such great similarity with the apprehension of form that we can consequently apprehend what happens during the designing process.

Taking this background into consideration, what follows now with regard to models for thinking in the design process must be regarded as a synthesis of images of certain features of thinking. Reality does not allow the models to reflect anything but appearances.

Thinking as Navigation

A common metaphor employed when talking about thinking is 'train of thought'. This surely implies that thoughts, or mental activities, move along from one point to another. An image conveying a similar meaning, used in psychology, is that when we think, we navigate among different parts of the content of what will go into a design. But this 'navigation' occurs not only in two dimensions, as on a surface of water, but in a space made up of many dimensions.

The attempt has been made to map out how people navigate when solving a problem which involves taking various kinds of information into consideration and combining them. Several different kinds of behaviour have been identified, which can be called wandering, browsing, exploring, scanning, searching, etc. How one behaves depends on the nature of the problem and on one's own temperament.

It seems difficult to comprehend, at least in every detail, why one chooses a certain path or main direction for one's thinking in each particular case. One cannot even always anticipate where the thinking begins. As far as the selection of material is concerned, it may, for example, turn out that material selection is not the last, but rather the first, thing that happens in a particular design endeavour; perhaps one has decided to work exclusively with a particular material. It is also quite clear that in choosing a path, and in the potential of one's thinking, one is influenced by previous experiences, social circumstances and a number of similar conditions in one's life. A path that has once been tried is thus different from an unfamiliar path. Hence the way in which thinking processes a certain problem at every pause in the train of thought also depends on the external and internal conditions for the designer's thinking.

Just as sometimes happens when navigating at sea, the perception of the goal may change with time and circumstances, somewhat as in the case of Columbus. Simply reaching land may be enough.

The image of design as navigation in a multi-dimensional space can be amplified to illustrate how it may come about that the final design corresponds to a certain *style*. The course of thinking in accordance with one or another kind of behaviour depends not only on the point of departure, mobility and the obstacles that thinking encounters along the way. If one were to compare the pauses in thinking, where various problems are pondered, with the poles in a field of force, then this entire field for rational deliberation can be affected by having been exposed to influences from specific superimposed forces. This image has in mind the effects of styles, schools, paradigms, etc. Of course, thoughts always move among by and large the same problems involved in a certain design, but there may be a predilection for a certain direction.

What has been presented here through the image of navigation regarding the course of the thinking involved in design should actually be modified somewhat to accommodate more complex notions about thinking, e.g. thinking simultaneously along different trajectories. However, for the purpose of illustrating one of the more important features in the course of thinking involved in designing, this image should be sufficient.

Thinking as Vision

One of the disadvantages of the navigation metaphor is that it may convey the idea that a thought is like a particle that moves along a certain course in an array of several fixed points. One reason that this is a drawback is that thinking is not linear; it can run simultaneously along several courses, i.e. like a movement of several points at once and in different places. Another is that the thought itself need not be something as limited as a particle that finds itself in one particular place at a given moment. Furthermore, the navigation metaphor does not allow much leeway for the notion that the course of thinking can be forward and backward, or that thoughts can move on several levels.

Another metaphor may perhaps be better employed to suggest the distribution or spread of thinking over the entire area, namely vision. It is a common misapprehension, probably stemming from classical theories of perspective, that one's gaze is confined to only one fixed direction when looking at something. Actually, the gaze almost always covers a large area. That is to say that we receive impressions from more places than the one we think we are looking at. This may be similarly true of the course of thoughts, which is guided not only by forces in the immediate surroundings but by influences from afar.

Thinking as Botanising

The aspects of a designer's work that can be described – and, hopefully, also understood – with the aid of images like that just outlined are those involving the designer's overviewing and coordinating activities. On the other hand, the image does not tell us much about the thinking itself. What actually goes on in thinking when the thought, according to this image, moves about in space or a field of force with its various kinds of poles? What do 'overview' and 'coordination' imply?

There are certain philosophical concepts that would seem to be applicable for illuminating questions about the implications of thinking about dissimilar problems, for example the demands of function, economy, appearance, ergonomics, etc. By and large, we are talking about comparisons of different problems in order to ascertain what connections may exist among them in terms of what the design has in mind. Hence the task when thinking is to determine similarities and differences.

It is no doubt a common experience that the various things that have to be considered when designing – and not least the selection of material – contradict each other in many respects. Not infrequently, it appears that most of the demands are irreconcilable. Nevertheless, the result most often approximates the original goal. What has happened when considering the dissimilar demands is that, rather than setting them against one another on the level on which they are first encountered in the dimension where the thinking is going on, the thoughts move onto a higher level where there may be something in common among the demands that appeared to be contradictory at first glance.

Perhaps a different image may be useful in making it easier to understand this way of coping with the contradictions encountered in designing, namely systematic botany. Suppose you show two plants, which are related to each other but look different, to someone who is not particularly knowledgeable about botany, and ask that person to compare the plants. The first thing you will hear will involve the differences in appearance. A botanist, on the other hand, knows that behind the first appearances there may be common characteristics that make it possible to find something that relates the plants rather than separates them. Something similar may apply to thinking when confronted by apparently divergent considerations during the design endeavour.

Botanising is largely a matter of describing, hence the thinking that goes on while botanising will depend on language and its structure. One question that occurs is to what extent the systems of plants can be treated on the basis of a linguistic structure. Perhaps the answer is that the reality we visualise because it is described in language actually *has* a linguistic structure. In that case, reality can speak to us just as we can speak about it. Our speaking, or thinking, can thus be one voice in an antiphon, with all that is subsequently implied about the imprinting of our description of reality.

Thinking in Several Dimensions

When attempting to illustrate thinking in words, it is natural to employ metaphors, similes or images of human behaviour, as has been done so far. Like all attempts to put things into words, such philological resources have their limitations. When we are involved in what has been called here navigation, vision and browsing, our ideas will for example be tied to our ordinary orientation in space and time. Yet there is no prima facie evidence for assuming that thinking cannot embrace several dimensions. Thinking need not necessarily resemble something simply mechanical or electrical with only a few dimensions.

It should be possible to imagine what happens in thinking as something like the alterations in chemical systems with many variables of different kinds: temperature, pressure, concentration, etc. Of course, chemical alterations can be observed and measured in one or another variable, but we cannot produce a complete description of what happens in all respects with our ordinary dimensions. Furthermore, with regard to alterations in a chemical system, what can be best described is the immediate state of large elements in the system, whereas what characterises thinking may be what is happening on a small scale. And that may very well introduce the concept of *chaos*, which is presently being regarded in some quarters as an important contribution to how the brain processes sensory impressions.

If the notions about chaos are viable, perhaps the essential element in thinking is what happens when chaos crosses over into order. In that case, the most important aspect of design would be these transitions, while thinking, into designing in ordinary dimensions. The order implied by a certain design should then largely be determined by the paths, in several dimension, available to the organising processes in the brain.

However, a conception of order-out-of-chaos must contain something about how the ordering comes about. There are theoretical treatments of what happens during ordering which can in fact be used to illuminate practical cases, e.g. how ant-hills are constructed. Out of the chaotic pattern of the movements of ants as they build their hills in a pine forest there arises an ordered design, not only as a consequence of the surroundings and the shape of the needles. There is also an organising activity among the ants, which has been discussed within the framework of the theory of what is called self-organising systems.

The image of design thinking as a course of events involving chaos and order is rewarding to the extent that it provides an approach to the question of when *meaning emerges during the process of thinking*. At what point is it apparent that what will emerge is design and not something else? When does a pattern of thought arise that resembles design?

Association and 'Creativity'

Everyone who has followed the descriptions propounded here about thinking as a kind of movement through a system of points may understandably ask whether the issue is really that simple, and even downright ingenuous. Is it simply a matter of moving from one point to the next, or do the movements perhaps build a pattern of connections among the points, something that might be compared to associations? For many people associating is one of the crucial elements in designing, and on the basis of the images that have been used here, associations could be said to correspond to the connections indicated by the pattern of movements.

Accounts of design often include the word 'create'. If 'create' is meant making something out of nothing, it is doubtful that design has to imply creativity in that sense. To a large degree, design can be said to be a quest for a system with the aid of thinking in the way that has been described here. Associating is thus an important element, and if the associations are very extensive and complex, the result may appear to be something newly created.

Design as Speech

Some people who have studied the connection between speech and thought feel that there can be no thinking without a linguistic foundation. They base their opinion on certain similarities between thoughts and speech, but yet we know that there have always been people who were deaf, dumb and blind who could think just as well as people with unimpaired speech faculties. When it comes to thinking and design, furthermore, we must remember that design is based in no small measure on what we call 'tacit knowledge' – even in the more restricted sense which implies that knowledge cannot always be described or expressed in words.

If, consequently, there are limits on different connections between speech and thought, that fact should not exclude the possibility that language, for designers, has an important influence on thinking, in accordance with the ideas that have been presented here. The very images that have been used to describe thinking are evidence of the possibilities of language. And with regard to something like the 'paths' of thoughts – whether the ordered paths used in navigating and browsing, or the paths leading out of chaos – the concept 'path' should be eminently employable as a metaphor for language.

Using metaphors facilitates the description of both navigating and botanising; it may prove to be the case that successful thinking depends on access to metaphors. When thoughts and concepts are transformed by language into metaphors, they can be more easily passed on when navigating, botanising, visualising or ordering – whatever the image one chooses to use. And surely it is not impossible that what designing is ultimately all about is to find, or create, a form that is metaphorical.

Design as 'Metaphorising'

A lathe, for example, is for most people not merely a machine for producing objects with rotational symmetry. A lathe has a metaphorical import, and hence a lathe cannot look like something else without losing its metaphorical import. Some modern lathes have been designed as insipid boxes, and thus the important metaphorical significance is missing. In similar fashion, a certain Swedish plastic bicycle once became a commercial failure because it lacked metaphorical import, mainly, perhaps, due to its thick, ungainly spokes. Among other attributes, a bicycle should have slender spokes if it is going to suit people who regard a bicycle – through the feel in one's legs as much as through visual impression – as a mechanical extension of their bodies.

An industrial robot provides a counter example. Its design fulfils not only certain purely mechanical demands; it also expresses metaphorical significance by being an image of a human being doing mechanical work. It is no coincidence that the root of the word 'robot' has metaphorical significance.

Design and Management

As will be elaborated in the observations about industrial design in the Afterword, the designer's thinking is generally applicable to all human endeavour, and that includes other professions as well (e.g. management). What distinguishes the work of the industrial designer from that of the industrial manager is the implications of their formal positions, with different responsibilities for economy, employment, etc. But as far as thinking is concerned, their tasks are more similar than different.

Much of the content of a manager's job description could also apply to a designer. For the designer, the task is to fashion industrial products on the basis of a number of prerequisites – economy, technology, market considerations, etc. This fashioning must take into account such things as employing technology that is adopted to the consumers of the result – human beings, the marketplace, the environment, and even the production facilities. To stipulate what is essential to design, one can employ certain key words – e.g. strategy, integration, coordination, holistic approach, responsible outlook – and certain key activities – e.g. reconciling differences, enhancing communication among the firm's various departments, negotiating compromises, counterbalancing, facilitating communication, getting everyone to pull in the same direction, creating unity, merging incompatible demands, etc. Most of all this also falls within the field of responsibility of industrial management. If we want one single, comprehensive term for the activities of both designers and managers, we could say that the goal of both endeavours is 'to influence'.

One unique aspect of the designer's cooperation with industrial management, however, is that the designer's particular approach makes it possible to navigate more freely, and in other dimensions. Independent designers are also accustomed to botanising in accord with systems other than those required for industrial managers in their managing.

Cultural Imprinting

The image of the thinking designer that emerges from the more usual descriptions – those that have been offered here and those found in textbooks on design – depicts an individual human being at work. In reality, a designer is a social creature, with all that can consequently be inferred about her or his thinking. The way designers apprehend the world around them cannot help but influence the way they think, which is to say what phenomena are perceived and how that comes about.

The reference to apprehending the world in which the design endeavour transpires is meant to include, among other things, what the social anthropologists call 'cultural style'. This refers to designers' perceptions of culture as controlled, or controllable, and of themselves either as members of a team or as individuals – in varying degrees, and subject to the whims of time. Using one kind of schematisation, we can recognise different kinds of designers, for example those who regard themselves as part of a hierarchy in which their task is to function as members of a professional staff. The antithesis is a role as an individualist who is not unduly tied to precedent, but who can experiment with all feasible approaches.

There are also other kinds of sociological performance which will not be taken up here in the interests of confining the scope of this presentation. What has been said here should suffice as an indication that designers' thinking can be guided not only by the individual approach to coping with more or less logical concepts, but also by the conditions imposed by the social environs.

Education and Cultivation

Let us assume that there is an ongoing progression from 'education' to 'cultivation'. Using the images employed here, one can arrive at a simple answer to the question of the goal to which the education of professionally competent designers should lead, as regards thinking. Among other things, this training should – using the images employed here – provide the ability to navigate and to botanise. Naturally enough, and with reference to education in general, this is not to imply that learning, including the acquisition of professional competence, is concluded with the completion of formal education. One is as unprepared to set out to sea after one winter term of classroom instruction as one is to determine the species of plants only on the basis of having seen pictures of a number of flora. However, education should have provided sufficient insights to enable one to realise that the matter at hand is navigating or botanising. Lacking such insights, one can never hope to become truly cultivated.

But, with reference to what has been said about the unconscious and about culture, one must also understand how thinking is involved with, and influenced by, other than purely intellectual concerns.

One conclusion that may be drawn from what has been said about the similarities and differences between design and management is that the development of people who may ultimately find themselves in managerial positions should have included the rudiments of design, at least to the extent that they can understand the implications for the environment implied by designing. This insight has already been adopted in certain parts of the world in their attempts to revitalise industry.

In the ideal scenario, design education in general can result in the insight that most gainful employment involves a good deal of the aesthetics otherwise usually ascribed to design, more than is generally acknowledged. In that case, one should not preclude some amount of design aesthetics even in such professions as medicine or law.

An insight like this ought moreover to be useful for anyone who thinks that professional competence can be simply computerised without detriment.

Afterword (in Place of a Foreword)

Conditions for the Discourse

The question might well he raised, 'What is the point of trying to put what we call thinking in such human activities as design into words?' For a description to be clear and straight to the point requires, strictly speaking, the availability of concepts and linguistic expressions for everything one has in mind. Of course, it is possible to speak about things that can only be expressed through circumlocutions, but in that case the description will not be unambiguous and meaningful in the same strict sense of spontaneity.

Many people feel that thinking when designing involves a connection that comprises elements other than those that can be given a direct description. People customarily assume that design is largely a matter of phenomena that are intellectually almost unfathomable. In addition, thinking is presumed to interact with the other elements in such a way that something important may be lost if one describes thinking as an isolated phenomenon. It may be that what is crucial to thinking when designing never emerges at all, when everything else in the context is omitted, just because it is impossible to express everything equally directly. Furthermore, it is difficult to know how the role and significance of thinking in relation to other things can be rendered in a description in which the various aspects of design cannot be given equal evaluation.

Thus there would appear to be limits to our possibilities of producing meaningful descriptions of what goes on when a designer thinks. We must realise that this implies that every such description may suffer from mistakes and shortcomings. The scope of the significance of these imperfections depends on the purpose of the description in question. There may be a particular necessity for describing thinking that justifies an attempt. With regard to design, two conditions, or motives, have prompted the comments presented in this paper.

One is that the education of designers requires an understanding of what kind of thinking is involved. Even more importantly, such insights must be made clear to designers who may otherwise happily assume that their work deals solely with logic, calculations and dimensioning. The other motive is that when developing and implementing information for design, e.g. via computerisation, one needs to understand how information and knowledge are processed when thinking.

The difficulties of describing thinking that have here been indicated with reference to design also apply, of course, to many other phenomena in societal and individual enterprises. The fact that design has been chosen as an example for the description of thinking in similar contexts should not be interpreted as meaning that design is something unique and apart. The reason is rather that design seems to contain so much that is different from unadulterated thinking. Therefore, by attempting to describe the thinking involved in designing, one should be able to accrue much that can have more general application.

For the sake of clarity, it should be emphasised that the intention of these remarks is not to present thinking as independent of everything else, or the sole guiding principle in designing. Nor is it postulated here that sophisticated thinking enjoys precedence in all respects over everything else involved in designing.

Finally, in this general discourse on the conditions for thinking when designing, one might reasonably expect some kind of definition of what is actually meant by thinking on the whole. It would in that case be tempting to reply as Augustine did when he was asked to define 'time': "I know what time is, but if someone asks me to explain it I cannot say what it is." However, the overall context of what has been presented above should indicate what is meant by 'thinking' in this paper.

Metaphor and Rhetoric

The natural language we employ when we talk and write about design is replete with metaphors, both dead and living. The import of what we say is more than literal. We express ourselves about what goes on when a designer is at work as though it could be compared quite simply with something else we already know. Yet our choice of words reveals that we mean something more and, perhaps, something different, because words themselves are metaphors.

The metaphors of everyday language are so ingrained that we hardly notice them, and still less think about their implications other than those most obvious: the foot of the mountain, the leg of a chair, a bottleneck. Nor do we experience any difficulty whatsoever in using such common metaphors to express what we wish to say. But when we run up against phenomena with which we have not become accustomed over generations and even centuries – like design – metaphors may result in difficulties when it comes to communicating meanings and significances.

That metaphors are often used in contexts similar to design can be exemplified by the habit of referring to computers as tools, which has caused considerable difficulties for anyone seeking to understand the meaning of computerisation. In similar fashion, the concept and word 'organisation' has received different metaphorical designations according to need: machine, organism, culture, etc. All of these metaphors are more than images and models. Because they associate that which one is trying to understand with something else that is more familiar, metaphors give a meaning and a significance that extend beyond the literal.

The good thing about metaphors is that they help us enrich our conceptions with features that cannot be expressed in clear and unambiguous terms. We gain impulses and associations that allow our attention to take in more than what is most obvious.

The trouble with metaphors is that they can beguile us into focusing too much attention on phenomena that need not necessarily have any decisive significance, so that, rather than being helped, we have problems perceiving what is truly important. The way to avoid such disadvantages of metaphors is, in the first place, to be aware of this risk and, in the second place, to try to employ several different metaphors. That has been the intention in adducing a number of dissimilar metaphors in this account of the thinking involved in design.

Design and Design

As we know, design has become a rather common topic of conversation in recent years, sometimes almost to the point of satiety. It has been said that design is good for the competitiveness of industry and that, therefore, design should be encouraged. New educational programs for designers have been initiated in various places in the industrial world.

In many situations, it has become possible to talk easily about design and designers without having to offer any particular clarification of what one actually means when using these words and concepts. In certain areas, however, the meaning is sometimes stated quite firmly. In industrial contexts, which are the primary focus of this presentation, it appears that many people would like to relegate the aesthetic and artistic features to the background when describing how industrial design is unique vis-à-vis other kinds of design. The spotlight is focused instead on what is commonly agreed to be the specific goal of industrial design, namely to achieve survival and profitability through the ability to compete. Where design is concerned, this achievement is realised by giving the products a form suited to both their function and their manufacture. The form should also promote competitiveness by reflecting the identity and profile of the company and the product.

Another way to stipulate the purport of industrial design is to investigate the place assigned to it in a company's activities by looking at how it is described in the language of business economics and management. Design is customarily said to be something more than what is included in the ordinary functions in a company, such as management, administration, planning, manufacturing, distribution, marketing and sales. At the same time, it is maintained that design is closely bound up with all of these other activities.

Yet another way of characterising design is to postulate the characteristics and abilities that a designer should possess. In the industrial context, it appears to be unpalatable to mention what designers themselves stress as the crucial factor – the ability to give appearance, form or shape to something. Instead, it is said that a designer must have expertise in technology, economics and ergonomics, but that the quintessential requirement is the ability to analyse and to coordinate.

In at least one respect, however, it would seem worth the effort to force one's way beyond the worn-out locutions about the designer's role, ability and expertise. A more trenchant question one might ask is, "How can we describe what a designer *does* in his or her professional activity?" It is justifiable to pose this question when trying to understand what educational attainments should be required of a prospective designer.

It is notable that as soon as you ask a more searching question about what a certain professional activity involves, you notice how unaccustomed most people are to contemplate what working actually involves. Many people spontaneously reply with something about what a designer is, or what a designer produces, along the lines of what was said above about industrial designers. Other responses, somewhat closer to the point of the question, may deal with what we call the design process. But none or these observations about, or attitudes towards, design provide any special enlightenment for those who, with no preconceived opinions, want to acquire a better and more definite notion of what a designer should be able to do and how she or he should be able to employ their expertise. What does it mean in the actual work of design that a designer is, for example, a coordinator of other people's activities? That she or he transforms product proposals into palpable form, produces a comprehensive solution etc.?

It may be objected that the lack of understanding about what a designer actually does can indicate that the question is far too difficult to answer. The possibility thus arises that the answer will be as incomprehensible and useless as homilies about creative activity in general. What would nevertheless seem to justify a question about what a designer actually does is that an improved comprehension of the import of the designer's work can lead to better understanding in terms of education, even if the original question does not receive a response that is both crystal-clear and exhaustive.

Design as a Model for Work in General

Design is rewarding for reflections about what happens when work is being done, because design encompasses so much of everything that, to a greater or lesser degree, is involved in various occupations, especially in the business sector. Using design as a model for what goes on in work in general, one captures important features of the thinking that is involved in getting most jobs done.

One of the crucial aspects of this line of reasoning is to realise that the basis employed in our thinking is not complete or coherent, but rather a collection of sporadic impressions of reality. Design, like so many other kinds of professional activities, implies feeling our way through such fragmentary impressions in the attempt to arrive at something complete. Not everything involved in this enterprise is thinking, but thinking constitutes an important part of the effort.

Design as Life

Simply because what has been presented here about a designer's thinking is based on personal experiences within a limited area of technology should not obscure the fact that the thinking involved in design is really not a unique phenomenon that applies only to designers in their work. On the contrary, it should have become apparent by now that design is a professional activity whose composite parts can be recognised in the everyday lives of ordinary people.

Designers, in other words, are not different from other people in the sense that what they do is by definition different from what other people do. It is simply that design cultivates or emphasizes certain features in the behaviour most people reveal in their attempts to secure themselves a tolerable existence. What makes it rewarding to inspect what goes on when a designer thinks is that it yields an insight into many important features of human behaviour in general. The way human beings think is very usefully illuminated by design and by what designers do.

This is not to say that the attempt to describe, and to some degree understand, what goes on when designers think requires insights into the meaning of life. Even though design embraces more than thinking, it can be rewarding to reflect on what the thinking involved in design can help us discern about the thinking common to all humankind.

Acknowledgement

The navigation model has been developd by
Canter D., Rivers R., Storrs G., (1985) Characterizing user navigation through complex data structures. Behaviour and Information Technolgoy 4(2) pp. 93–102.
Other works dealing with parts of the subject of this paper are the following:
Cross N. (1989) Designer genes, the nature and nurture of design ability, Inaugral Lecture, The Open University.
Lawson B. (1983) How Designers Think. The Architectural Press Ltd, London.

The translation of this paper into English has been made possible by a grant from the Uddeholm Research Foundation, Sweden.

Correspondence and offprint requests to: Gustaf Östberg, University of Lund, Risk Handling, Box 118, S-22100 Lund, Sweden. Tel: +46 46 107997; Fax: +46 46 104620.

Ownership and Copyright
© Springer-Verlag London Limited
AI & Soc (2002) 16:350–365

AI & SOCIETY

Multimedia Archiving of Technological Change in a Traditional Creative Industry: A Case Study of the Dhokra Artisans of Bankura, West Bengal

David Smith[1] and Rajesh Kochhar[2]

[1]*School of Art, Media and Design, University of Wales College, Newport, UK*
[2]*NISTADS (National Institute of Science, technology and Development Studies), New Delhi, India*

Abstract: Many recent studies of technological change have focussed on the implementation of computer-based high technology systems. The research described here deals with the introduction of a new but 'low' technology into an ancient craft tradition in India. The paper describes a project to capture and archive aspects of the tacit knowledge content of the traditional cire perdue brass foundry (Dhokra) craft of Bikna village, near Bankura, West Bengal. The research involved collaboration between the Indian National Institute for Science, Technology and Development Studies (NISTADS) and School of Art, Media and Design, University of Wales, Newport, UK in the context of the EU-India Cross-Cultural Innovation Network Project. NISTADS were proposing to introduce a new fuel-efficient furnace technology in place of the traditional form used in Bikna. It was expected that the introduction of the new furnace would catalyse major changes in the entire dhokra craft at Bikna. What was not anticipated, however, was the speed and extent of this change, to the extent that the old traditional way of doing things was changed within the space of a few months. A Multimedia record of the craft and the process was developed. These technologies make it possible to develop adequate representations of skilled performance mediated by the craftsman him- or herself. Particularly valuable in this respect is the capacity of multimedia systems to use a full range of modalities of description, including video, sound, still image, conventional text and technical diagrams. This enables the presentation of very complex information in a variety of formats and contexts. The context and process of developing this knowledge archive are described.

Keywords: Cire perdue casting; India; Knowledge archiving; Tacit knowledge; Technological change; Traditional crafts

1. Introduction

This article deals with a process of technological change in the traditional *cire perdue* (dhokra) brass-making craft as it is practised by one group of families in Bikna Village, near Bankura in West Bengal, India. This change was initiated and coordinated by the Indian CSIR (Council for Scientific and Industrial Research) agency NISTADS (National Institute for Science, Technology and Development Studies). It involved replacing an ancient traditional but inefficient metal-foundry technique with another which is almost as ancient but more efficient. The impact of this apparently simple change on dhokra practice has been both profound and rapid.

Research and development carried out at UWCN (Smith and Hall, 2001) suggests that multimedia technologies make it possible to develop adequate representations of skilled performance mediated by the craftsmen themselves. Particularly valuable in this respect is the capacity of multimedia systems to use a full range of modalities of description, including video, sound, still image, conventional text and technical diagrams. This technology makes it possible to present very complex information in a variety of formats and contexts. The study is therefore part of a wider exploration of the potential capability of multimedia as a tool for ethnographic research.

The name 'Dhokra' or 'Dokra' was formerly used to indicate a group of nomadic craftsmen, scattered over Bengal, Orissa and Madhya Pradesh in India, and is now generically applied to a variety of beautifully shaped and decorated brassware products created by the *cire perdue* or 'lost wax' process. The craft of lost-wax casting is an ancient one in India, and appears to have existed in an unbroken tradition from the earliest days of settled civilisation in the subcontinent. The traditional themes of these cast metal sculptures include images of Hindu or 'tribal' gods and goddesses, bowls, figures of people or deities riding elephants, musicians, horse and rider figures, elephants, cattle, and other figures of people, animals and birds.

The first detailed study of *cire perdue* work in the Bankura District was carried out in the early 1960s by Ruth Reeves (1962). This work has been the primary source for many subsequent reports and academic theses (see, for example, Krishnan, 1976; Pal, 1978). However, there has never been a detailed audiovisual record of the craft, and this current report aims to fill this gap in the record. It documents a period during which the people of Bikna are adapting their traditional way of working to the demands and possibilities both of a new technology and a new commercial environment. It therefore provides a unique contemporary record of a historic living tradition undergoing rapid and fundamental change.

Although there is a small but increasing demand for dhokra work from urban Indian families, as well as in the tourist trade, the craft is threatened with extinction. Most of the remaining dhokra communities are extremely poor, and their economic condition has caused many families to leave the craft to find wage employment in local manufacturing centres or in metropolitan centres such as Kolkata (Calcutta). According to Sen (1994):

Perhaps the poorest craft group of West Bengal, the Dhokras are the most interesting and creative. In recent years, under the pressure of all-embracing industrialisation and changing social values, they have been forced by the loss of their natural rural market to diversify their products and are now seeking, with the help of the government and some voluntary agencies, a market among urban sophisticates, as creators of decorative ware. These efforts have met with only limited success.

Sen attributes the roots of this failure to

Greedy dealers in handicrafts [who] took advantage of the failure of the government and the voluntary organisations to provide adequate price protection for the producers.

However, as we shall show, the situation is far more complex than simply being a matter of economic exploitation.

2. The Cire Perdue Technique

The casting of finely detailed metal artefacts by means of the *cire perdue*, or lost wax, technique is almost as old as settled civilisation. The technique is simple to describe (but difficult to perfect). It involves six stages:

1. *Core-making.* A clay core is made, slightly smaller than the final intended size of the artefact. The core may be hardened by firing or sun-drying.
2. *Modelling.* A detailed wax model is built up around the core, to the thickness of metal desired in the finished object.
3. *Moulding.* The wax model is coated with a thin layer of very fine clay, which will form an impression of every detail of the model. When this layer is dry and hard, further layers of clay are added to the mould. One or more pouring channels are provided, through which molten metal can run to fill the mould.
4. *De-waxing.* The mould is pre-heated to melt the wax, and the molten wax is poured out (it may be recovered for subsequent reuse). This leaves a cavity which has the exact size, shape and surface contours of the intended artefact.
5. *Casting.* Molten metal is poured into the cavity and the mould left to cool.
6. *Finishing.* The artefact is broken out of the mould. Traces of baked clay are removed and surface blemishes and defects repaired.

There are many refinements and variations, but the above outline applies to most of the traditional styles of *cire perdue* work still extant. The sophistication of the process varies considerably, with the most advanced techniques employed in South India and Bastar in Madhya Pradesh (See Postel and Cooper, 1999: 81–97). The casting process used in Bankura appears to be the least technologically developed of all.

3. The Origins of the *Cire Perdue* Craft in India

The earliest known examples of *cire perdue* work include the famous bronze 'dancing girl' found in Mohenjo-Daro in the Indus Valley (Agrawal, 1971).

Even at such an early stage, this finely observed bronze figure already shows the highly developed creativity and mastery of the production technique typical of *cire perdue* at its finest. Lost wax casting subsequently spread, whether by communication or parallel invention, to most civilisations. The process of *cire perdue* casting has been very well documented in antiquity, and Krishnan (1976) and Pal (1978) both cite classical Sanskrit sources, such as Manasara, Silparatna and Somesvara, which give detailed descriptions (or even prescriptions), conceivably for the regulation of the craft. It was certainly pervasive throughout the Indian subcontinent, as demonstrated by an ample archaeological record, and examples exist in gold, silver, copper, bell-metal, bronze and brass.

Our specific focus here is on the production of the range of brass artefacts, commonly known as 'dhokra'. Welch (1986: 103–113) provides illustrations of examples of fine *cire perdue* dhokra work of 'tribal' origin dating back as far as the eighteenth century, from locations as disparate as West Bengal, Purulia, Maharashtra, Orissa, Bastar (Madhya Pradesh), Himachal Pradesh, Punjab and Bihar. The major contemporary centres of production are in West Bengal, Bihar, Madhya Pradesh,

Andhra Pradesh and Kerala, though the numbers of families engaged is everywhere in decline.

The craft has historically been particularly associated with the so-called 'tribal' peoples of India. Its heartland for many centuries was in the metal-rich region of Central India, covering the modern regions of Jharkhand, Orissa, Chhatsigarh and parts of Andhra Pradesh. The practice was in the hands of family groups of non-Hindu semi-nomadic artisans, called 'Dhokras'. Some of the Dhokra families appear to have migrated into the alluvial plains of Bengal, finally settling around centres such as Bankura, Burdwan, Purulia and Midnapur.

Despite its antiquity and wide geographical dispersion, it appears that the work of the dhokra makers was always marginal to the domestic economy of India, and did not achieve the importance and consequent security of, for example, the manufacture of water containers or cooking vessels. Dhokra making did not figure in Birdwood's magisterial survey of *The Industrial Arts of India* (1880), except, perhaps to be included in his rather dismissive *obiter dictum* (p. 143):

Beside the village and sumptuary arts there are the savage arts of the wild tribes ...

Sen (1994) describes the traditional dhokra craft in West Bengal and its typical products:

... they [the dhokra makers] used to move from village to village in the south-western districts, repairing old and broken utensils and selling small images of Lakshmi, her mount, the owl, Lakshmi Narayan riding on an elephant, Radha and Krishna in different attitudes, all made in a very strong and primitive folk style. These images were installed in the household shrines of newly married Hindu couples to bring prosperity and happiness. They also made and sold decorative caskets in different shapes and sizes, purchased by housewives for various purposes. They made and sold measuring bowls in different sizes. These were considered symbols of Lakshmi and were therefore highly prized by those villagers who could afford them. Ritual lamps in different designs were also popular items. Their other products included small models of animals and birds and a variety of trinkets and bells ...

4. The Dhokra Makers of Bankura, West Bengal

One of the major remaining foci for the dhokra craft is some kilometres to the north of Bankura in West Bengal. Thirty-six related families live in a close-knit clan community in Bikna village. According to Dhiren Karmakar, interviewed in September 2001, their forefathers were nomads who came from Chhota Nagpur.

The actual caste origin of the Bikna artisans is obscure. This may be due in part to a process of gradual 'hinduisation' (see, for example, Singh, 1993), though their religious practices are far from the Hindu mainstream. Worship typically involves a simple open-air 'altar', at which offerings of terracotta figures are made. The offerings depend on the seasons, and may be related to the major Hindu festivals, such as Ganesha Chatthurti.

Any attempt to clarify the relationships and history of the dhokra makers of West Bengal suffers from the incomplete and fragmentary nature of the records. No records of this artisan industry survive from pre-colonial days, and the standard documentary resources, such as Risley's monumental *Tribes and Castes of Bengal* (1891), must be seen as reflecting both the anthropological fashions of their era and, perhaps more significantly, the '*divide et impera*' priorities of colonial administration. The colonial fascination with caste and social taxonomies may stem more from a pragmatic need to create distinctions than from meaningful structures in contemporary Indian society.

There is certainly a great deal of confusion in evidence when one attempts to track the forefathers of the Bikna community through the pre-independence census data for Bengal. Mitra (1953: 2) shows that census reports reveal a tendency for caste designations to increase or decrease in number according to current thinking, leading to apparently arbitrary aggregation and subsequent disaggregation of 'caste' groups. Mitra (1953: 5) points very succinctly to the problem when he notes wryly that:

In the hands of a government which seeks to hold a country by force and guile, to rule by dividing the people, there can be few weapons as lethal as caste ...

Risley (1891, Vol. 1: 236) defines 'Dhokra' as:

A sub-caste of Kamars or blacksmiths in Western Bengal, who make brass idols.

Risley subsequently points out (Vol. 1: 388–389), regarding the sub-castes of the metal working caste of Kamars, that:

It is impossible at the present day to determine whether all of them are really derived from the Kamar caste; and it seems probable that some of them may be separate castes, which have been classed as Kamars on account of some real or supposed resemblance in their occupations.

By the middle years of the twentieth century, the Bankura dhokra makers were being described as 'Mal' or 'Malars', according to Risley (Vol. 2: 45-50):

... A Dravidian cultivating caste of Western and Central Bengal ...

which could just conceivably refer to large sections of the entire population of Bengal!

Ruth Reeves (1962) refers to the Bankura Dhokra as 'Kainkuya Mal' (which possibly derives from association with the traditional measuring vessels known in Bengali as 'kunke'). In doing so, she is following S.K. Ray's (1953) contribution to A. Mitra's ethnological analysis of the 1951 Census of India. In his treatment of *The Tribal Group of Craftsmen*, Ray asserts that:

... We can divide the Mals readily into two groups: (i) the Sanakar Mals or painters and (ii) the Kaikuya Mals or brass workers ... They have an occupational system similar to that found among the Mala of South India, namely, the Loom-Mala, the Cart-Mala, the Hammer-Mala, the Doll-Mala etc. As a matter of fact, the form of caste system that prevails among the aboriginal and backward classes of West Bengal can be called the Mala-system.

Reeves (1962: 36) also refers to the Bankura dhokra makers as 'Dheppos' described by Ray, (1953: 302) as:

... wandering artisans belonging to aboriginal stock [who] maintain a tradition of metal craft in a primitive manner ...

Ray, however, seems to imply that this latter group was not associated with the *cire perdue* tradition. In any case, earlier attempts to locate migratory dhokra makers (whatever their caste) in the region seem to have failed (see Reeves, 1962: 37), perhaps indicating that the migratory way of life had ended some time before these groups attracted the attention of the great and good. Nevertheless, the evidence of this report will show that the essential metal-founding technology used by the people of Bikna village was more appropriate to a migratory than a settled way of life, and the problem may be one of a confusion of terminology.

Mitra (1953: 1–3) helps to explain much of this confusion by detailing the changing practices in recording caste adopted by the Census of India between the 1901 Census and the first post-independence census in 1951 (when caste distinctions were legally abolished). In any case, as he points out (p. 6):

... caste has not been so immutable ... as one is too willing to imagine, but a live and pliant force, sensitive to change, as any function of society must necessarily be.

The fairly recent adoption of the 'sanskritised' caste designation 'Karmakar' by the Bankura dhokra artisans must be seen in this light, reflecting the villagers' sense of social progression and a degree of approximation to the mainstream of Hindu society in West Bengal. It may, however, be analogous to the widespread adoption of surnames by English villagers during the sixteenth and seventeenth centuries. If this is the case, 'Karmakar' might be closer in sense to the surname 'Smith' than to the location in a traditional social structure which a true caste designation might imply. However, the Dhokra Karmakars of Bikna never made eating or cooking vessels, and this would imply a historic caste limitation. Despite their apparent annexation into the Karmakar caste, the dhokra makers are still socially and economically marginalised.

5. The Dhokra-Making Tradition as Practised in Bikna Village

5.1 The Creative Process

Despite its stability over many centuries, the dhokra craft has not remained entirely static. As Sarkar (1998) points out from his analysis of the artisan Kansari (braziers) in Bengal:

... technology in Indian artisanal industry *did* change in response to market demands. If such changes appear rather timid and slow, it was because a radical transformation of the technique of production was never a pressing and unavoidable need in India.

The period of nearly four decades between the publication of Ruth Reeves' study and the initiation of this project in November 2000 witnessed a number of changes in the creative aspects of the dhokra craft as practised in Bikna. This is part of a long process of change, which Kochhar (2001) has characterised as falling into four phases:

Phase I is defined by the original Dhokra repertoire, which is simple and stark, in keeping with the makers' life style and philosophy.

Phase II came into being when the Dhokra artisans took to settled life and started making new items consistent with the demands of a food-surplus economy. Their work now included rather ornate icons of Hindu gods and goddesses. Interestingly, in their own shrines, the Dhokra artisans have retained worship of their own creations (horses, elephants etc.) in addition to Bhairon, who is a form of Shiva, and a deity consistent with non-vegetarianism.

Phase III is characterised by two major developments: patronage extended by state and socialites; and interaction with creative sculptors like Meera Mukherjee and Pradosh Das Gupta. These artists successfully imbibed in their work techniques and motifs of the Dhokra art and, once accepted as insiders, introduced the Dhokra artisans to new forms. It was during this phase that, under state patronage, the well-known Bankura Horse, a stylised, decorated horse with long upright neck and pointed ears, which hitherto had been a preserve of the Khumbkars (clay artisans), was successfully adopted for casting in metal.

Phase IV, a recent phenomenon, has been thrust upon the Dhokra artisans by the demands of the cheap souvenir market. This phase is characterised by some 'novelty' items, such as a Ganesh with an umbrella. Most of the work, however, is pure kitsch. Since the price paid to the artisans is exploitatively low, they seek to indirectly enhance their wages by compromising on the quality of the inputs as well as craftsmanship.

5.2 The Casting Technology Prior to August 2001

If the creative content of Bikna dhokra work has changed over time, their technology, on the other hand, stayed remarkably constant – at least until 2001. Beautifully adapted to the conditions of the original nomadic lifestyle, the dhokra technology did not adapt to the settled way of life.

The failure of the Bankura Dhokra Karmakars to modify their technology probably contributed to their creative and economic decline over the past 50 years.

5.2.1 Core Making

Cores were made from local clay. The fine clay-loam found around the roots of bamboo was specially favoured. The clay was dried, sieved through sacking and then mixed with uncrushed sand. This sand-rich clay was mixed with water to an appropriate consistency, and used to make suitable core figures. The cores were slowly sun-dried over 3 or 4 days.

5.2.2 Modelling

The fine detail of the object to be created is built onto the core using wax or some other suitable medium.

Ideally, wax ('*mom*') is the best modelling medium, but the Bikna Karmakars prefer to use '*dhuna*', which is based on a natural plant resin extracted from the sal tree (*Shorea robusta*) mixed with mustard oil. Dhuna becomes very plastic when warmed, but holds its shape very well, even at high ambient temperatures.

As an economy measure, many of the Karmakars had taken to using hydrocarbon pitch as an inferior substitute for mom or dhuna. This had a number of serious defects, which contributed to the decline in both creative and metallurgical quality of the final product.

5.2.3 Moulding

The completed model is covered in a layer of a very fine clay which takes an impression of all its surface details. This layer is then sun-dried.

When the first layer was dry, a second layer was built onto it. The clay used for the second mould coat was usually mixed with sand.

At this stage, one or more channels were created in the mould to allow the flow of molten brass into the space which would be left when the modelling medium had gone. Traditionally, a split bamboo rod was used to bore through the dried first layer. A large casting might need two or more channels.

The bamboo was held in place with clay, and the second coat of the mould then completed. This involved building a cup-shaped structure around the 'flow channel'. The clay of the mould was built up until the cup was held firmly in place and then the bamboo rods were removed. The cup would eventually act as a melting crucible, holding the brass for melting. At this stage, several moulds could be combined, sharing a single crucible – especially if the casting was a small one. This economised both on the labour of producing the 'crucibles', and, eventually, on fuel through minimising the number of separate items to be heated.

The final stage involved the completion of the 'crucible' part of the mould. The 'cap' of the crucible was made separately and sealed in place with clay after the crucible had been charged with brass.

The metal used was scrap brass, which had been rendered brittle by heating on the furnace and then broken up into small pieces. Recently, attempts were made to cut costs by adulterating the brass with, for example, aluminium. The result was a very inferior product and the practice only resulted in an even lower unit price for dhokra items.

A special panel was built into the crucible to provide an easily breakable 'window' to let in air so that the brass would flow into the model space.

After charging the crucible and sealing the cap, the mould was given a final coat of clay prior to firing.

5.2.4 De-waxing

The closed system moulding used by the Bikna Karmakars made it impossible to recover the wax (or dhuna), which was therefore either vaporised and burnt or else absorbed into the clay of the mould. This is vividly contrasted with the practices in Bastar and South India, where a high level of wax recovery is achieved.

The loss of the modelling medium was a serious cost inefficiency in the process.

5.2.5 Casting

A crude furnace was built in a convenient open space, using loose bricks. The fire was made using cow dung and bought charcoal. Completed moulds were laid in the fire, with the cup downwards.

When the mould was judged to be ready, it was removed from the fire using tongs or a pair of green sticks. It was inverted, so that the metal cup was at the top, allowing molten brass to run down into the mould space. The special weak 'panel' in the metal cup was broken through with a stick or other suitable implement.

The traditional furnace was inefficient in two ways. Firstly, it was wasteful on fuel. Each furnace was specially built for a single batch production. Fuel was wasted heating the furnace and the moulds to casting temperature, and there was no gain from multiple firing in the same oven, thereby conserving heat. Secondly, it was more or less impossible to control the firing temperature of the furnace. This meant that metal, particularly zinc, was lost by sublimation when the moulds were broken open. This could be seen in the colour of the fumes after opening. The loss of metal led to serious metallurgical degradation of the brass, as well as being another source of cost inefficiency. Another side effect is that many of the people of Bikna suffer from eye problems, probably due to heavy metal irritation.

Discussions with the craftsmen showed that they were aware that metal was being wasted, but felt powerless to prevent this.

5.3 Becoming an Artisan: Growing up in Bikna

Like most traditional craftspeople, the dhokra artisans of Bikna have no formal system of apprenticeship: craft training as such does not exist. The craft is, to coin a phrase, 'learned by being'. Children in Bikna grow up in an environment where the dhokra craft is everywhere around them. Every spare corner of the village is taken up by drying moulds or artefacts in various stages of preparation, and the routine of the craft is part of the daily rhythm of the village.

Small children soon learn to imitate their elders, playing with clay, making cores and eventually graduating to detailed modelling in dhuna (or pitch). The fastest learners soon become useful additions to a family team. Indeed, 13-year-old Anant, whose father is sick, supports his family by working as a wage labourer for other Karmakars.

The Karmakars agree that it is difficult to make a living at all unless the family are fully engaged in the craft, and those with small families or who have no children are at a disadvantage. This militates against extended education.

This is not to say that the Karmakars are completely uneducated. Most children manage to attend 2 or 3 years of schooling, while young women marrying into the village often have several years of elementary education. But the appeal of joining the adult world or work is very alluring and the social pressures to contribute are great.

Over the years, attempts have been made to introduce elements of formal training into the craft. The initiative in this respect has been taken by the West Bengal Crafts Commission, who have been proactive in organising creative and technical workshops for dhokra artisans.

5.4 Modelling Problems

The fact that the *cire perdue* process followed in Bikna does not permit wax recovery is a significant factor undermining the potential profitability of the craft.

The finest medium for *cire perdue* modelling is, as the name itself would suggest, beeswax (*mom*). The Bikna artisans' preferred medium is *dhuna* (a mixture of the resin of the sal tree and mustard oil). This is almost as good as wax but rather cheaper,.

Risley (1891: 48) speaks of a specific 'sub-caste' of 'Dhunakata Mal', who collected dhuna by tapping sal trees (and might therefore have supplied the resin), but both wax and dhuna are natural forest products, and would most probably have been collected by itinerant craftsmen in the course of their travels. The lack of wax recovery was therefore acceptable while the 'Kaikuya Mal' were still living as nomads.

The situation changed when the dhokra artisans settled down. Whereas artisans in other parts of India (notably in Bastar and Tamil Nadu) developed efficient means of wax recovery, the Bankura artisans did not. This added to the uncontrolled costs due to the metallurgical problems associated with the traditional furnace.

Some of the more prosperous Bikna artisans continued to use dhuna, but others tried to cut costs by replacing the dhuna with 'pitch' (coal tar). This was not a good move. Not only is 'pitch' a coarser modelling medium than either wax or dhuna, but it appears to cause 'gassing' of the molten brass in the mould, leading to pitting and erosion of the cast surface. The false economy of using pitch simply resulted in a further degradation of quality.

6. The Impact of a New Technology on the Dhokra Craft

The story of the Bikna dhokra craftspeople took a different turn, when NISTADS (National Institute of Science, Technology and Development Studies) became involved on their behalf. NISTADS funded Bengal Engineering College to design and develop a fuel-efficient permanent furnace under the management of Dr A.K. Mukopadhyay, NISTADS Resident Scientist in Bankura.

The new technology was adopted by Netai, a brazier from Petrasayer in Bankura District, West Bengal. In 1997, NISTADS helped Netai to obtain a bank loan to modernise his facilities. He was subsequently able to obtain substantial production orders for dhokra items: a fact which was well known to the Bikna artisans.

However, despite this knowledge, and despite Netai's obvious prosperity, the Bikna families made no move to adopt the new technology. It would have been all too easy to attribute this to a kind of laggard conservatism, but a field visit to Bikna and Petrasayer in November 2000 by Professor Rajesh Kochhar of NISTADS and David Smith of UWCN revealed a different, more interesting and more complex picture.

6.1 The New Furnace

Designed in collaboration between NISTADS and the Bengal Engineering College, the improved process effects substantial reduction in fuel consumption for melting brass in a low-cost furnace, of capacity 8–12 kg per batch.

The furnace lining is made with locally available burnt rice husk and clay. The rated coal/metal ratio is 1.7 in the case of single heat and 0.6 with four successive heats, as against 2.9 in the process traditionally used by the artisans.

The clay mould is also modified to facilitate open pouring from the furnace. Alternatively, the traditional clay-moulding process can be substituted by green sand moulding.

A variety of specialised tools were also introduced to facilitate effective and safe use of the furnace.

6.2 Netai Karmakar's 'Factory'

In comparison with the primitive working conditions at Bikna village, Netai's set-up was effectively a 'micro-factory'. At the time of the first field visit, the workshop was given over to batch production of brass drinking beakers, using a modern oil–sand investment moulding technique and using scrap water pots as the source of metal. A small electric grinder had been installed for finishing the products, and the business appeared to be flourishing, supporting three families in Petrasayer.

Netai still makes dhokra to order. These are mainly relatively large objects, with less fine detail than the Bikna work. Netai arranged a demonstration of dhokra casting, using an open mould rather than the traditional closed mould used in Bikna. This was an extremely interesting experience, because the clay mould was clearly too weak and 'leaked' molten brass as the metal was poured.

It seems possible that there is a real problem with the suitability of locally available clay for the construction of moulds for open casting of dhokra articles. It is worth noting that artisans in South India and Bastar reinforce their moulds with iron wire, as well as firing ('biscuiting') them before moulding (Krishnan, 1976).

6.3 Art, craft or Industry?

The reasons for the reluctance of the Bikna artisans to adopt the furnace technology with which Netai Karmakar had been so successful may be far more complex than simple conservatism or entrenched caste tradition.

First there is the issue of poverty. No detailed study has been carried out of the micro-economics of dhokra production at Bikna, but such evidence as there is points to the fact that the net money earnings of the artisans are very low indeed. They could not raise the finance to pay for a permanent furnace except by borrowing from a local moneylender at interest rates of around 2% per day.

Second is the question of the sociodynamics of the craft (See Rogers and Kincaid, 1981). Despite his evident prosperity, Netai was not regarded by the bulk of the craft community as a good role-model. His craftmanship was not admired in any case, but his location in Petrasayer, many hours' journey from Bikna, put him outside a tight-knit circle of closely related families. In fact, the Bikna people regard him not as a 'true' Karmakar like themselves, but as an inferior outsider. Netai's family certainly appear more completely 'hinduised' than the people of Bikna.

A third factor concerns the extent to which the Bikna Karmakars' sense of identity is invested in the integrity and status of their craft. Netai's success ultimately rests on the abandonment of the dhokra craft as such. Although Netai still makes dhokra items to order, the bulk of his income comes from the mass production of low-craft-content industrial items.

The identity and self-esteem of the artisans of Bikna are deeply invested in their craft. Over the years, of course, an increasing number of individuals and their families have ceased to be dhokra artisans and have moved into Bankura and other towns to work as wage labourers. Nevertheless, the core group of families at Bikna remained committed to dhokra making. Any change which effectively meant the death of the craft was almost unthinkable.

Finally, and perhaps decisively, there was an ingrained suspicion of 'initiatives'. It emerged that the Bikna artisans were owed the (for them) huge sum of 1.75 lakh rupees (1 lakh = 100,000) for goods previously supplied to official crafts emporia.

6.4 The Introduction of the New Furnace into Bikna

After the field visit in November 2000, Professor Rajesh Kochhar of NISTADS initiated a project to develop an efficient furnace for Bikna village. Dr Mukopadhyay met with Juddha and Mahdav Karmakar, two of the most senior and highly respected artisans in the village, and also arranged meetings with Netai. The object was to collaborate with the craftsmen in achieving a design which would not only be technically appropriate, but where there would be a sense of ownership.

An experimental furnace, based on Netai's, was built in Bikna during December 2000. NISTADS agreed to finance the development, but Professor Kochhar made it a condition that the furnace should be a community resource, rather than the property of a single artisan or his immediate family.

A permanent furnace needs to be protected from the weather. Fortunately, protection was available in the form of three large shelters build some years previously under a West Bengal regional development. The new furnace was built in one of these shelters.

Experience showed that the first prototype was too large and would be too expensive to operate in the long run. The design was therefore modified to create a smaller furnace. This proved to be a complete success, and over the next 3 months a further five were built, so that there were two in each of the three village shelters. All of them were used as communal resources.

It is interesting that this development has its parallels in the historic development of metal working in India. Sarkar (1997) argues that, irrespective of their origins, traditional blacksmiths were nomads, using a form of open-air furnace (*Sal*) which was very similar to the old Bikna furnace.

As these smiths settled and adopted permanent furnaces, they also developed well-built workshop structures (*Kot-Sal*). Those smiths who remained itinerant were accorded very low caste status.

6.5 How the Craft has Changed

It was expected that the introduction of a new furnace technology would catalyse major changes in the dhokra craft at Bikna. What was not anticipated, however, was the speed and extent of this change. The advantages of the new furnace were so apparent to the Bikna artisans that the old traditional way of doing things was changed within the space of a few months.

Whereas it had been anticipated that take-up of the new furnace would follow a classic technology transfer profile, the new furnace was adopted almost immediately by all of the families. Completely unexpectedly, the inefficient 'nomad' furnace was relegated to the secondary role of pre-firing charcoal for charging the new furnace, heating scrap brass (this makes it brittle and easier to break up), and, interestingly, for baking the moulds.

Other changes were significant, but relatively minor. For example, the practice of making a flow channel using a split bamboo has been replaced by the partial firing of the first mould layer, and then using a simple hand drill to bore through the clay. The 'crucible is then built up around the channel, and melted pitch or dhuna poured in to make a full connection with the inner mould.

One change in practice was particularly striking. Parts of Bikna had been wired for electricity supply at the same time as the shelters had been built. One ingenious '*bricoleur*' discovered that it was now possible to run a (rather ramshackle) lead from a mains point to drive an electric fan which could be used to speed up firing of the furnace. The effect has to be seen to be believed!

As the location of the furnace has moved from the open air to the cover of the shelters, the production process has followed suit. Most of the work is clustered around the furnaces. This allows for fuel efficiency, since as soon as the furnace is finished with one batch of moulds, it is cleared and re-charged, making use of the heat stored in the body of the furnace and reducing fuel requirements. The furnace can also be used for secondary purposes, such as baking moulds or pre-heating scrap brass.

In collaboration with Dr Mukopadhyay, the Bikna artisans have developed a range of new tools appropriate to the improved processes. However, they have not followed the example of Netai and changed over to open crucible casting. They acknowledge that this would probably be more efficient, but they feel cautious about the safety aspects of handling molten brass. Also, as Raneswan Karmakar pointed out, they are not sure whether the moulds would be suitable. Our observation in Netai's workshop suggests that this caution is probably well justified.

6.6 A New Creative Confidence

The introduction of the new furnaces has had an immediate beneficial impact on the output of the better artisans. It is now possible to maintain effective control over the casting of artefacts containing relatively large amounts of brass. New products have been created, such as the 'polybonga' (based on a popular terracotta form). This has encouraged a renewal of creative confidence, and craftsmen like Dhiren have begun to develop quite stunning works of original artistry.

Equally importantly, however, they are able to concentrate once more on the quality of their products. They see this as more important than developing new products. Dhiren Karmakar is happy making the traditional dhokra repertoire, and believes there is a market for it if high quality can be maintained. He remembers that training courses were held some years ago (by the West Bengal Crafts Commission) to help develop new products, but there was never very much demand for these. He will make them from time to time if there is an order.

6.7 New Opportunities

In parallel with the development of the new furnace technologies, NISTADS actively catalysed a range of developments intended to move the artisans' business methods in line with their new commercial opportunities. In a series of village meetings, Professor Kochhar persuaded the senior craftsmen to reactivate a defunct village Cooperative Society. This would give them access to 'soft' loans through the formal banking system, rather than high-interest 'hard' loans from local moneylenders.

In addition, a variety of commercial opportunities were opened up. NISTADS Director Professor Kochhar took advantage of the Indian CSIR (Council for Scientific and Industrial Research) Foundation Day, 26 September 2001, to raise the profile of the Bankura dhokra industry. Artisans from Bikna were invited to travel to Delhi (no minor undertaking in itself) and showcase their products.

The event was extremely successful. Substantial sales were achieved and some good orders were taken. In addition, the artisans were invited to present their wares at an event to be held at the 'Dilli Haat' craft market. It remains to be seen if this is the hoped-for breakthrough, but the omens appear to be very good.

7. The Future of the Dhokra Craft in Bikna

Despite the new sense of confidence among the older artisans, the future of dhokra making lies in the balance.

Interviewed in September 2001, Dhiren Karmakar and his relative Raneswan Karmakar were ambivalent. They felt that they themselves were better off than their fathers. The market for their products is good, and they are able to have two square meals a day, so there is no hunger any more. They do not save – they do not think in that way at all. Any money that is accumulated is spent on social events or medical treatment.

Both Dhiren and Raneswan saw a reasonably secure future for themselves in the dhokra trade. If they can get capital, they feel they can cope with changing market conditions. But they cannot accumulate capital, and rising costs cause problems, because they have to finance production by borrowing at high interest rates, which just leaves them with bare subsistence.

All the same, they feel that they are better placed than those who have left the craft to take up wage labour in cities and towns such as Bankura. Although wage labourers have more secure incomes, they do not have the prestige of the independent craft artisans, and this is important.

They also see themselves as better off than the braziers (Kansari) who traditionally made household utensils, since these articles are becoming too expensive for the market, and there is now no money at all in that trade, though previously braziers were quite prosperous.

In the end, however, they are quite clear that there is no long-term future in the dhokra trade either, and they would prefer it if the young people of the village had some other alternatives – other than becoming wage labourers.

7.1 Education and the Way Forward

Dhiren and Raneswan are agreed on the importance of education. They feel that their fathers had no power as a result of having received no education. They believe that even with just a little education, their generation is more empowered than their parents. Dhiren has four sons and a daughter. He has not been able to afford to give them a good education, and they chose to leave school and join the dhokra trade after class four.

Dhiren says that, so far, no child from the village has gone for a job (meaning high-status 'office' employment). He thinks that it will be better if future generations are able to become educated, even if that means they will leave the craft. Apart from opening up a way out of the dhokra trade, they think that educated young people would be able to keep proper accounts and be more businesslike. He sees education very much in terms of empowerment.

7.2 Anant Karmakar: The New Generation

Anant is about 13 years old. He was identified by the elder craftsmen of Bikna as the most gifted of the younger generation. His father is ill, and unable to work regularly, so Anant supports his family by working as a wage labourer for other artisans in Bikna.

Anant attended 2 years of primary school. He can read and write Bangla (Bengali), but he does not read books, and he speaks little or no Hindi. If he had a choice between working and continuing his education, he would prefer to go to school. He would like 'a job' (meaning office work) rather than continuing as a dhokra artisan.

8. Bankurahorse.com

One of the objectives of the case study described here was to develop a multimedia archive of the craft practices of the dhokra artisans. This is still in progress, but a considerable body of digital video, sound and still images has been accumulated and catalogued. It was decided that while the full multimedia package was under development, this material would be suitable for Internet access.

The domain name 'bankurahorse.com' was purchased and a web site designed by Matthew Leighfield, a Newport graduate student. The site was specifically designed to facilitate access across the low-bandwidth systems typically installed in India. This implied some reduction in functionality from what might currently be expected on the Internet, but maximised audience availability.

9. Summary and Conclusions

The ancient craft of the dhokra artisans of Bankura is in the balance. The new furnace developed under the auspices of NISTADS has eliminated a major source of inefficiency from their work, which should therefore become more profitable. In addition, a new professionalism is beginning to be apparent in the artisans' trading practices, thanks largely to the advice, support and guidance of NISTADS.

All this, coupled with the creative confidence and attention to quality documented here, means that the immediate future for the dhokra craft is reasonably assured. In the long term, however, the artisans face serious decisions about the craft. On one hand, they may choose to follow the route to industrialisation, illustrated here by the case of Netai Karmakar. On the other hand, and this is what they appear to prefer, they can develop towards a consumer market based on high-quality high aesthetic value artefacts. This could possibly be found supplying high craft content artefacts to a growing tourist and indigenous middle-class market.

The continuation and development of the dhokra industry depend on the artisans finding a stable market niche for themselves and their products. Whatever it proves to be, this market needs to be developed and supply chains established. It is easy to demonise the middle-men, but if the economic conditions of the Karmakars become less marginal and their terms of trade can be improved, then there is no reason at all why existing middle-men may not have a major role to play in this market development.

In the end, this is not simply a matter of marginal economics. The dhokra artisans of Bikna represent an ancient craft which has been in continuous production for thousands of years. The Bikna artisans are not 'primitive': they are twenty-first-century people who happen to be trapped in a cycle of poverty. Neither are they exhibits in a cultural theme park. They must be free to determine their own future. At the same time, they embody countless generations of knowledge, and this knowledge is part of the cultural heritage not only of India but of mankind. Whatever direction the craft takes in the future, it would be tragic if all this knowledge and the accumulated wisdom of millennia were to be lost.

References

Agrawal, D.P. (1971), The Copper Bronze Age of India. Mushiram Manoharlal, New Delhi.

Birdwood, G.C.M. (1880). The Industrial Arts of India. Chapman & Hall, London.

Kochhar, R. (2001). Dhokra Brass Artefacts from Bankura. Pamphlet published for CSIR Foundation Day, 2001. NISTADS, New Delhi.

Krishnan, M.V. (1976). Cire Perdue Casting in India. Kanak Publications, New Delhi.

Mitra, A. (1953). The Tribes and Castes of West Bengal. Census of India 1951: West Bengal. West Bengal Government Press, Alipore.

Pal, M.K. (1978). Crafts and Craftsmen in Traditional India. Kanak Publications, New Delhi.

Postel, M. and Cooper, Z. (1999). Bastar Folk Art: Shrines, Figurines and Memorials. Project for Indian Cultural Studies Publication VIII, Mumbai.

Ray, S.K. (1953). The Artisan Castes of West Bengal and their Crafts. In Mitra, A. (ed.) *The Tribes and Castes of West Bengal. Census of India 1951: West Bengal.* West Bengal Government Press, Alipore, 296–306.

Reeves, R. (1962). Cire Perdue Casting in India. Crafts Museum, New Delhi.

Risley, H. (1891). The Tribes and Castes of Bengal. Bengal Secretarial Press, Calcutta.

Rogers, E.M. and Kincaid, D.L. (1981). Communication Networks: Towards a New Paradigm for Research. Free Press, New York.

Sarkar, S. (1997). The Changing Face of the Craftsman: Blacksmith in Colonial Jharkand, *Calcutta Historical Journal.* **18**(2). 67–85.

Sarkar, S. (1998). Indian Craft-Technology: Static or Changing – A Case Study of the Kansari's Craft in Bengal, 16th to 18th Centuries, *Indian Journal of History of Science* **33**(2). 131–142.

Sen, P. (1994). Crafts of West Bengal. Mapin Publishing, Ahmedabad.

Singh, K.S. (1993). Hinduism and Tribal Religion: An Anthropological Perspective, *Man in India* **73**(1). 1–16.

Smith, D.J. and Hall, J. (2001). Multimedia Know-How Archiving in Aviation Industry Training. In Brandt, D. and Cerenetic, J. (eds) *Proceedings of the 7th IFAC Symposium on Automation Based on Human Skill: Joint Design of Technology and Organisation.* Elsevier, Oxford.

Welch, S.C. (1986). India, Art and Culture. Mapin Publishing, New Delhi.

Correspondence and offprint requests to: David Smith, Head of Research and Enterprise, School of Art, Media and Design, University of Wales College, Newport, PO Box 179, Newport NP18 3YG, UK. Email: david.smith@newport.ac.uk

AI & Soc (2000) 14:157–175
© 2000 Springer-Verlag London Limited

Databases are Us

Victoria Vesna

Department of Design/Media Arts, University of California, Los Angeles, USA

Abstract: In the age of information overload, the primary concern for many knowledge areas becomes the organisation and retrieval of data. Artists have a unique opportunity, at this historical juncture, to play a role in the definition and design of systems of access and retrieval, and at the very least comment on the existing practices. In this article I show how some personalities have foreshadowed and indeed influenced the current practices and huge efforts in digitising our collective knowledge. This article is an effort to broadly contextualise the current atmosphere and environment that 'information architects' are confronted with.

Keywords: Alexandria; Chronofiles; Digital libraries; Genome; Internet; Memex; World Brain; Xanadu

If we consider the invention of the printing press as the first wave of information overload, we can safely consider ourselves immersed in the second, tsunami wave. The effects of technology on human consciousness to which Marshall McLuhan pointed earlier in this century, we can easily conclude, have amplified tenfold in the face of the new technologies (1962, p.144). Crucially, we must begin to think about the relationship between consciousness and our organisation and dissemination of data. And once again we must reconsider how the organisation of data reflect our collective shifts in perception and our relation to information and knowledge. Knowledge production is undergoing radical reorganisation due to the huge amount of data being systematically digitised and made available on the Internet. This digital reorganisation means that we can anticipate the relatively fast-paced demand for creation of new systems and establishments. Artists are in a unique position to participate in this process as "Information Architects," using data as raw material.

How one moves through a physical space such as a building or a particular room is very much determined by the way an architect has conceived it. In the context of art, consider movement through the Guggenheim or the Museum of Modern Art in Bilbao – the building can be understood as a sculpture, a meta-art piece in its own right. The work presented within these spaces, in other words, cannot be viewed without a strong sense of their containers. Similarly, when navigating through various software "containers" and inputting our data, we are very much following the established parameters of information architecture. With some of the more blatant moves to create "standards" that include not only the information architecture but our online identity and the use of agents, the idea of an overarching meta-software that is planned to be commonly used by one and all is alarming. As I will show in this essay, hugely ambitious efforts are underway to digitise print-based libraries, human bodies, and finally, entire genomes.[1] How and where artists play roles in this changing terrain of digital databases cannot be considered without taking a look at these projects.

Marcel Duchamp's establishment of concept over object in art and his eventual decision to give up painting entirely in order to become a freelance librarian at the Bibliothéque Saint Geneveive in Paris not only challenged the museum system and the idea of what can be counted as art, but also drew attention to the intersections of information and aesthetics. The relationship between aesthetics and information continues to develop as the World Wide Web radically redefines libraries and museums, and many clues and opportunities await us in terms of getting familiar with the directions libraries are taking with the vast digitisation taking place. As communication media became more and more integrated into the very fabric of our societies, the creation of the artist's 'myth' and media persona is central to their output, no matter what media they may utilise. Artists continue to recognise the rich potential of information to be used as art, envisioning such things as world encyclopaedias, global libraries, and the building of personal media personas. Self documentation that ensures life of the artist's work is expanded into documentation of context and, in some cases, becomes the work itself. Buckminster Fuller's Chronofiles and Andy Warhol's Time Capsules are good examples of this practice. Visions of a World Brain of HG Wells, the Memex of Vannevar Bush, and the Xanadu of Ted Nelson are not primarily concerned with the content, but shift our attention to the way we organise and retrieve the information stored. Their work has contributed to what we know now as the World Wide Web, which acts a window to the vast collective effort of digitisation, whether organised or not. I briefly glance at efforts to revive the Library of Alexandria digitally, to make entire human bodies digitally accessible to the medical community, and to digitally map human as well as animal genomes. Finally, I glance at how artists have historically responded to archives and databases and at contemporary work, and point to issues to consider when moving towards becoming an active participant in the global in formation architecture.

---

[1] A genome is all the DNA in an organism, including its genes. Genes carry information for making all the proteins required by all organisms. These proteins determine, among other things, how the organism looks, how well its body metabolises food or fights infection, and sometimes even how it behaves.

DNA is made up of four similar chemicals (called bases and abbreviated A, T, C, and G) that are repeated millions or billions of times throughout a genome. The human genome, for example, has 3 billion pairs of bases. The particular order of As, Ts, Cs, and Gs is extremely important. The order underlies all of life's diversity, even dictating whether an organism is human or another species such as yeast, rice, or fruit fly, all of which have their own genomes and are themselves the focus of genome projects. Because all organisms are related through similarities in DNA sequences, insights gained from nonhuman genomes often lead to new knowledge about human biology.

Guinea Pig B and the Chronofile

I had the good fortune of being able to access directly the archives of Buckminster Fuller Institute, considered one of the most extensive documents of a single individual. The sheer volume of materials that he left behind is staggering, and one cannot help wondering what compels people to collect, organise and document proof of their existence and particular actions.

In 1907, Buckminster Fuller began a chronological record of his life, and in 1917, at the age of twenty two, he named it "Chronofile." Fuller conceived of the Chronofile during his participation in World War I, when he served in the Navy as a secret aide to the admiral in command of cruiser transports that carried troops across the Atlantic. After the war, he was charged with amassing the secret records of all movements of the ships and the people on them. He was impressed by the fact that the Navy kept records chronologically rather than by separate categories such as names, dates, or topics. Inspired by the Navy's cataloguing system, Fuller decided to make himself the "special case guinea pig study" in a lifelong research project of an individual born at the end of the nineteenth century, in 1895, the year "the automobiles were introduced, the wireless telegraph and automatic screw machine were invented, and X-rays discovered." (Fuller, 1981, p.128) Along with his own documentation, Fuller was keenly interested in keeping a record of all technological and scientific inventions of the time. He thought it would be interesting not to cull just attractive sides of his life, but to attempt to keep everything: "I decided to make myself a good case history of such a human being and it meant that I could not be judge of what was valid to put in or not. I must put everything in, so I started a very rigorous record." (Fuller, Dictionary. p.324, 12 July, 1962). He dubbed himself "Guinea Pig B."

In 1927, Fuller became even more ambitious. He decided to commit his entire professional output to dealing with planet Earth in its entirety, its resources and cumulative know-how, rather than harnessing his output for personal advantage; he undertook, in his own words, "to comprehensively protect, support, and advantage all humanity instead of committing my efforts to exclusive advantages of my dependants, myself, my country, my team." (Fuller, 1981, p.25)

Fuller knew few, perhaps none, would understand his professional commitment to be a practical one, but since he firmly believed that it was, he worked to leave proof behind affirming this belief, and he proceeded to do so in a scientific fashion. At the end of his life, in addition to the Chronofile, which is considered to be the heart of his archives, he left behind the Dymaxion Index, blueprints, photos, patents, manuscripts and a large amount of random elements. He saved all his correspondences, sketches, doodles made during his meetings, backs of envelopes and newspaper-edged notes–everything possible that was a record of his thought. He saved all films, videos, wire and tape recordings, posters announcing his lectures, awards, mementoes, relevant books, all he published at various stages, all indexes, drafting tools, typewriters, computers furniture, file cabinets, paintings, photos, diplomas, and cartoons. He also kept an inventory of World Resources, Human Trends and Needs, and all the World Game records. The World Game was one of the first computer game concepts whose goal was to educate global thinking. Collection of data of World Resources, Human Trends and Needs was to be used

Fig.1. Buckmister Fuller Archive, Santa Barbara, 1998

for this purpose. He assures his readers that the files includes many unflattering items such as notices from the sheriff and letters from those who considered him a crank, crook, and charlatan. (McLuhan, ed. 1967, p.75)

The output during Fuller's lifetime documented in the Chronofile is astounding: three hundred thousand geodesic domes built around the world, five million Dymaxion World maps, not to mention twenty six published books and twenty eight patents. It is important to note that he did not believe in hiring professional public relations agents or agencies, publishing bureaus, sales people, or promotional workers of any kind. Yet, towards end of his life, he did have a type of a non-profit cottage-industry operation with many working on the Chronofile. Ironically, this operation is not well documented or recorded, (see Fig.1).[2]

Collecting and archiving for Fuller did not stop with himself, but extended out to data collection of world resources as well, which became a more ambitious project with the introduction of computer technologies.

---

[2] The Buckminster Fuller Archive, located in Santa Barbara, California, consists of the following:

The Dymoxian Index, which is a detailed cross-reference and index of twenty different sections of the Fuller archives including his personal library, office inventory, and itinerary. The index was updated approximately every ten years during his lifetime and now comprises twenty volumes.

The Chronofile, which begins in 1895 and is chronologically ordered. Thirteen thousand-five hundred 5x8 cards cross-reference the Chronofile alphabetically between 1970 and 1980.

Fuller documentation on hundreds of Fuller's design artefacts, inventions, cartographic works and architectural projects including over a thousand sketches; approximately thirty five file drawers packed with published and unpublished manuscripts; transcripts from lectures and full working files of all of his major books; Fuller's photo and slide documentation on geodesic structures built around the globe by others; gifts from other artists including Isamu Noguchi, Joseph Albers, Mark Tobey, and John Cage.

Media archives are kept in a separate, environmentally controlled film vault in Hollywood. It contains approximately sixty four thousand feet of film, fifteen hundred hours of audio and three hundred hours of video.

We are going to set up a great computer program. We are going to introduce the many variables now known to be operative in the world around industrial economics. We will store all the basic data in the machine's memory bank; where and how much of each class of the physical resources; where are the people, where are the trendings and important needs of world man? (Fuller, 1965)

The Geoscope, envisioned to disseminate information about the status of the Spaceship Earth, never materialised, but the World Game, did, and it continues to be played today. Fuller is a great example of someone who progressively gets more and more ambitious to document not only himself but the world around him in the form of a database. With the advent of the computer he had plans to document all of Earth's data, and although he did not succeed during his lifetime, Fuller would be pleased to see that there is a massive collective effort to document every aspect of our lives today, from our molecular and cellular structure to all of our acquired knowledge throughout history.

Libraries/Museums, Text/Image Databasing

"The universe (which others call Library) is composed of an indefinite, perhaps infinite, number of hexagonal galleries, with enormous ventilation shafts in the middle, encircled by low railings. From any hexagon the upper and lower stories are visible, interminably. The distribution of galleries is invariable." (Borges, p.79)

Borges's Library of Babel is often summoned when describing the endlessly evolving World Wide Web and our state of information overload. The underlying history of "information overload" arrives with the introduction of the printing press and the resultant need and first efforts during the Renaissance to organise knowledge and collections. Organisation of the sudden proliferation and distribution of books into library systems happened in tandem with categorisation systems of collections being established by museums. Excellent examples in this respect are the curiosity inscriptions of Samuel Quiccheberg, considered the first museological treatise, and Guillio Camillo's Memory Theatre of the 1530s. Quiccheberg's treatise offered a plan for organising all possible natural objects and artefacts, which he accomplished by creating five classes and dividing each into ten or eleven inscriptions. This treatise allows for explorations today of the institutional origins of the museum. Camillo, on the other hand, created a theatre that could house all knowledge, meant to give the privileged who accessed this space actual power over all of creation. The structure took the form of an amphitheatre and was composed of a viewer on stage facing seven tiers of seven rows–not of seats but drawers and cabinets containing text and objects.[3]

Current cataloguing systems generally fall into two types: those treating the item as a physical object and giving it a number or code encapsulating data about its acquisition and storage, and those that communicate the intellectual content of a work and locate it within a system of such classifications. This former type of cataloguing, which begins with Diderot and D'Alembert's Encyclopédie (1751-1772), codifies and systematically delineates the relationships of all branches of knowledge.

---

[3] I learned about these historical aspects of organisation and collecting through my involvement with a research project "Microcosms, led by Bruce Robertson and Mark Meadow at University of California, Santa Barbara

The latter goes back at least as far as the Library of Alexandria (circa 100 BC), which was organised by the writer's discipline (e.g., history or philosophy) and subdivided by literary genres.

Libraries and museums have continuously intersected and impacted one another throughout their respective histories. For instance, the initial organisational system of museum collections was recorded by a librarian, Quiccheberg. Museums are essentially "object oriented" keepers of visual memory much in the way that libraries are keepers of textual memory. However, the architectures of museums determine the size and even type of collections they will accommodate, which necessarily limits their inclusiveness; rarely, for example, do museums accommodate art that involves ephemeral media. Libraries, on the other hand, accommodate the documentation of all printed matter produced by museums as well as have a close relationship to the inclusive research paradigm of academia.[4]

Digital technology is fast eroding established categories by making it possible to store all of the objects traditionally separated by media or form as bits, a continuous stream of data. As such, this technology endangers the institutions that have been established to store specific types of data and indeed the way knowledge is passed on at universities. It is becoming more and more difficult for academics to work effectively within the established departmental and specialised categories and structures of print libraries. The World Wide Web challenges the primacy of word over image by collapsing them, and further, it functions to erode the boundaries between museums and libraries, which is true of its impact on many other institutional frames as well.

Many of our current practices of cataloguing and archiving knowledge in museums and libraries are rooted in a continuous push toward specialisation and the division of the arts and humanities from the sciences. The introduction of computers, computer networks, and the consequent World Wide Web, however, has created a whole new paradigm. Organisational systems established by libraries and museums are not adequate for the vast amount of digital data in contemporary culture; consequently, new ways of thinking about information access and retrieval must be considered. Early on, Vannevar Bush pointed the way to how people may start reconsidering these activities. Once again, these ideas came directly from experiences in the military use of data.

MEMEX and the World Brain

The summation of human experience is being expanded at a prodigious rate, and the means we use for threading through the consequent maze to the momentarily important item is the same as was used in the days of square-rigged ships. (Bush. 1945)

One of the first visionaries of how computers may be used to change the way we work with information overflow in the future was Vannevar Bush, who was the

---

[4] University museums, a strange amalgam of qualities that do not approximate either the traditional library or museum, occupy a peculiarly marginalised position, and their role is yet to be defined. Outside of both the art marketplace and scholarly research and discourse, university museums are a curious entity, a floating category.

Director of the Office of Scientific Research and Development in the US and coordinator of the activities of some six thousand leading American scientists in the
application of science to warfare. His seminal "As We May Think" not only impacted
thinkers when it was published in 1945 but continues to be read today.[5] In this
essay Bush holds up an incentive for scientists to turn to the massive task of making
more accessible our bewildering store of knowledge after the fighting has ceased.
Bush makes the point that the number of publications has become so overwhelming
that it becomes difficult to keep track, remember, and recognise an important
document.

It is in "As We May Think" that Bush introduces his prophetic concept of the
Memex, or Memory Extension, an easily accessible, individually configurable
storehouse of knowledge. Bush conceives of the Memex through myriad other
technologies he describes in this essay as well: the Cyclops Camera, a photographic
device "worn on the forehead" as well as film that can be developed instantly through
dry photography, advances in microfilm, a "thinking" machine, and a Vocoder,
which he describes as "a machine that could type when talked to." He predicts that
the "Encyclopaedia Britannica could be reduced to the volume of a matchbox. A
library of a million volumes could be compressed into one end of a desk. Bush's
proposed mechanisms are based on a rational organisational system, which would
solve and control the endless flow of information.

Around the same time Bush was developing the concepts of the Memex machine,
H.G. Wells was imagining collective intelligence through his concept of a World
Brain. In a collection of scientific essays he termed "constructive sociology, the
science of social organisation" (Wells, xi, 1938) called World Brain, Wells proposes
that the massive problems threatening humanity can only be solved by well coordinated human thinking and research. In the 1995 edition of World Brain, Alan
Mayne writes a seventy page introduction on contemporary technological
developments, particularly the WWW, that parallel Wells's ideas. Without any
knowledge of computer systems, Wells proposed the World Brain as a continuously
updated and revised comprehensive encyclopaedia as a result of a systematic
collaborative effort of a world-wide group of scholars, intellectuals, and scientists.

Alongside Bush's Memex, Wells's vision was prophetic of Douglas Engelbart's
ideas of collective intelligence through the use of technology. Directly inspired by
Bush, Engelbart pursued his vision and succeeded in developing a mouse pointing
device for on-screen selection among other key innovations. Drawing on his experience
as a radar operator in World War II, Engelbart saw in his mind how computers could
visualise information through symbols on the screen: "When I saw the connection
between the cathode-ray screen, an information processor, and a medium for
representing symbols to a person, it all tumbled together in about a half an hour."
(Rheingold, 1993. p.65).

Engelbart's seminal essay "The Augmentation of Human Intellect" in turn came to
the attention of J.C.R. Licklider, who had himself been thinking about the connection
between human brains and computers. Licklider's equally visionary paper around the
same time, "Man-Computer Symbiosis," predicted a tight partnership of machines and

---

[5] Although "As We May Think" was published in 1945 (after the close of World War II), Bush had written
it much earlier, in the 1930's.

humans in which machines would do the repetitive tasks, thereby allowing humans more time to think. At the Massachusetts Institute of Technology where he was a researcher and professor as well as at Lincoln Laboratory, a top-secret DOD research facility associated with MIT, Licklider, together with his graduate student Evan Sutherland, helped usher in the field of computer graphics. Later he moved to the Advanced Research Projects Agency (ARPA) and, through his Defence Department connections, funded Engelbart's Augmentation Research Centre (ARC) at the Stanford Research Institute, which produced the first word processors, conferencing systems, hypertext systems, mouse pointing devices and mixed video and computer communications. Engelbart's ARC became the original network information centre that centralised all information gathering and record keeping about the state of the network. (Rheingold, p.72) Engelbart was particularly concerned with "asynchronous collaboration among teams distributed geographically." His work had direct influence on the research at Xerox's Palo Alto Research Center (PARC), which in turn was the inspiration for Apple Computers.

Xanadu

When I published Computer Lib in 1974, computers were big oppressive systems off in air-conditioned rooms. In the 1987 edition of Computer Lib–the Microsoft edition!–I wrote, "Now you can be oppressed in your own living room!" It has gotten far worse. (Nelson, 1974, see http:// www.sfc.keio.ac.jp/~ted/)

In 1965 Ted Nelson coined the terms 'hypertext' and 'hypermedia' in a paper to the Association of Computing Machinery (ACM) twentieth national conference, referring to non-sequential writings and branching presentations of all types. (Nelson, 1965) Five years earlier, he designed two screen windows connected by visible lines that pointed from parts of an object in one window to corresponding parts of an object in another window. He called for the transformation of computers into "literary machines," which would link together all human writing, and he saw this associational organisation of computer as a model of his own creative and distractible consciousness, which he described as a "hummingbird mind." Nelson defined hypermedia as

branching or performing presentations which respond to user actions, systems of prearranged words and pictures (for example) that may be explored freely and queried in stylised ways. They will not be 'programmed' but rather designed, written and drawn and edited by authors, artists, designers and editors.

Nelson's vision of how information may be accessed associatively using a computerised system is what completed the pieces of the puzzle that finally resulted in what we now know as the World Wide Web. This vision was Nelson's Xanadu, a next generation of HG Well's World Brain. To this day Nelson continues to work on his Xanadu project, proposing alternatives to the monolithic system being built by corporations such as Microsoft. He maintains that the Xanadu system is extremely different from that of HTML or any other popular system. The Xanadu connective structure consists of both links and transclusions, in which a link is a connection between things that are different and a transclusion is a connection between things that are the same. (Nelson, The Future of Information)

In 1998, thirty eight years after proposing the visionary hypertext system, Nelson announced the launch of a shareware software program called Zig Zag: "This is my new proposal for a complete computing world. I designed it in the 1980s, and it is beautifully implemented now. It is multidimensional; you might call it the Rubik's [cube] operating system."(Glave, 1998) Nelson also announced a public release version of Xanadu multimedia and hypertext publishing systems as well as an electronic-payment scheme called Hypercoin. In continuous development since 1960, Xanadu is based on a principle of sideways connections among documents and files. But, while Xanadu was still in development Tim Berners-Lee came up with what we know today as the World Wide Web, which completely overshadowed Xanadu.

According to Nelson, Tim Berners-Lee, designer of the original Web protocols, was unaware of Xanadu's hypertextual ideas when he started his work around 1990. On the other hand, Marc Anderseen, creator of Mosaic, the first GUI on the Web, was directly influenced by Nelson's work. With the introduction of a GUI to the vast repository of information on the Internet, the first to respond were libraries. Fuller's Geoscope, Bush's Memex, H.G. Wells's World Brain, and Nelson's Xanadu were suddenly collapsed into one huge infrastructure driven by the combined interests of corporations and academia. Because of the seemingly impossible task of organising the existing Internet into a cohesive and controllable communication network, the joint efforts of industry and academia have put plans in place for Internet 2, which, unlike the original Internet, is very much a planned enterprise.

Digital Library Projects – Ghost of Alexandria

A wonder of the ancient world, the Great Library of Alexandria was an edifice the corridors of which housed the papyrus scrolls that were the sum total of written knowledge of the ancient world. The library was constructed in the second century BC by Ptolemy I, who ruled Egypt after Alexander the Great. Unlike Alexander, whose conquests were tangible and bloody, producing the greatest empire the world had ever seen, Ptolemy's legacy was a huge archive, a place where the total wisdom of mankind could be gathered, preserved, and disseminated. The Alexandria was partially destroyed in 47 BC when fire spread from Julius Caesar's ships ablaze in the harbour and further damaged by Aurelian in 272, and then was finally demolished by Emperor Theodosius's Christians in an anti-paganism riot in 391 AD. (Twelfth-century Christians rewrote this history as an apocryphal account of the Arab General Amr destroying the library out of Koranic zeal.) Even after it was completely destroyed, the Library of Alexandria remained a legendary testimonial to the immense human drive to gather and codify knowledge (Rapaport,1996).

Ambitions to collect and archive all of human knowledge are alive and well today in the private sector as well as in universities. The private sector is focusing on laying down the foundation for the future museum and commerce systems. Universities, on the other hand, are putting their efforts towards digitising existing libraries, thereby making all of this information accessible for scholarly work. How and where these efforts will merge will be interesting to follow, particularly in light of Internet 2, which is a joint effort of industry and academia. Currently there are a significant number of networked projects digitising libraries around the world: The British Electronic Libraries programme is a three-year initiative involving some sixty projects; the G7 nations have launched similar projects; and in the US, the National Digital Library programme has been in the works since 1994. These projects promise to initiate a significant shift in the way information is stored, retrieved, and disseminated. A good example of how broad and ambitious these initiatives have become is the National Initiative for a Networked Cultural Heritage (NINCH). This organisation is comprised of sixty eight member organisations representing museums, archives, and scholarly societies, the contemporary arts, and information technology. The goal is to create an actively-maintained, international database with "deep data" on the projects developed by a geographically distributed team. Ironically, NINCH is led by Rice University in the US and King's College in the UK, which, together with the dominant language of the Internet, unfortunately reinforces the colonial legacies rather than taking this opportune time to involve marginalised nations in the process.

My personal contact with these efforts was a large-scale digital library project called Alexandria Digital Library (ADL) at UC Santa Barbara. ADL is an ambitious project connected to a larger digital library initiative. Its core is the Map and Image Laboratory of UC Santa Barbara's library, which contains one of the nation's largest map and imagery collections as well as extensive digital holdings. In addition ADL has joined forces with the University of California Division of Library Automation, the Library of Congress, the Library of the US Geological Survey, and the St. Louis Public Library, as well as university research groups including the National Centre for Geographic Information and Analysis (NCGIA), an NSF-sponsored research centre established in 1988 with sites at UCSB, SUNY Buffalo, and the University of Maine (all three sites of which are involved in the project); the UCSB Department of Computer Science; the Centre for Computational Modelling and Systems (CCMS); the UC Santa Barbara Department of Electrical and Computer Engineering; the Center for Information Processing Research (CIPR); the UC Santa Barbara Center for Remote Sensing and Environmental Optics (CRSEO), a partner in the Sequoia/ 2000 project; and the National Center for Supercomputer Applications (NCSA). There is no holding back from involving the private sector, including Digital Equipment Corporation; Environmental Systems Research Institute (ESRI) in Redlands, CA, a developer of spatial data handling software and geographic information systems; ConQuest; and the Xerox Corporation. It is awe inspiring to see how much organisation and resources, how many faculty from a variety of disciplines have a collective drive to create a system that will make data accessible and allow for some type of "control" over access and knowledge networking. If juxtaposed with a few other major efforts to "digitise all of knowledge," one begins to truly wonder what kind of role artists working with information and networks assume and indeed whether they will be able to effect coding or aesthetics in significant ways at all.

Corbis Image Library

Aspirations of a "digital Alexandria" are by no means limited to the academic world. In the private sector, the largest endeavour of this kind is pursued by the Corbis Corporation, owned by American billionaire Bill Gates. In 1995, Corbis, termed Gates's "image bank empire," announced that it had acquired The Bettman Archive, one of the world's largest image libraries, which consists of over sixteen million photographic images. Doug Rowin, CEO of Corbis, has announced that the company's objective is to "capture the entire human experience throughout history." (Hafner, 1996. p.88-90.) Microsoft is spending millions of dollars to digitise the huge resource being collected by Corbis from individuals and institutions, making it available online for a copy charge. The idea of one man, the wealthiest on earth, owning so much of the reproduction process not only makes many nervous, if not paranoid, but also contradicts the democratic potential of the medium. Charles Mauzy, director of media development for the Bill Gates-owned company, has said that the "the mandate is to build a comprehensive visual encyclopaedia, a Britannica without body text." (Rappaport, 1996)

The archive, around which all of Corbis's activities centre, consists of approximately a million digital images. It is growing at a rate of forty thousand images a month, as pictures from various realms of human endeavour–history, the arts, entertainment, nature, and science–are digitised. So far, it has largely focused on photographic acquisition, with work from such renowned professionals as Ansel Adams, Galen Rowell, Laura Dwight, Shelley Gazin, and Roger Ressmeyer. In addition, Corbis has commissioned several dozen photographers to fan out around the world to fill the Corbis catalogue–an increasingly sought-after assignment. Corbis also holds archival material from the Library of Congress, rare Civil War photos from the Medford Historical Society in Oregon, 19th- and early-20th-century photo portraiture from the Pach Brothers, as well as works from dozens of other collections. But what got the art world to finally pay attention is Corbis's amassment of rights to digital images from museums, including works from institutions such as Saint Petersburg's State Hermitage Museum, the National Gallery of London, the Royal Ontario Museum, Detroit Institute of Art, Japan's Sakamoto archive, the Philadelphia Museum of Art and the sixteen million-item Bettmann Archive, which houses one of the world's richest collections of drawings, motion pictures, and other historic materials.

In early July of 1996, Corbis, which was already online with its digital gallery, opened its archive directly to commercial customer.[6] Armed with a T1 connection and a password supplied by Corbis, these clients can access the database directly and search for images by subject, artist, date, or keyword. Once the images are presented online, they are culled; selected images can be ordered with a mouse click. Because of the shortage of bandwidth and the length of time it takes to download images averaging 35 Mbytes each, orders are sent out overnight on custom-cut CD-ROMs. All images are watermarked to ensure against further unauthorised use.[7]

This notion of delivering digital online content is one of the few constants at Corbis and has driven the company since its inception in 1989. Established as Gates's "content company," it was chartered to acquire a digitised art collection that Gates planned to display on the high-definition television screens installed at his futuristic waterfront stronghold near Seattle. But the philosophical underpinning of Corbis and its earlier incarnations–first Interactive Home Systems and then Continuum–was based on a grander notion, namely Gates's belief that just as software replaced hardware as technology's most valuable product, so too will content eventually

---

[6] Corbis online is located at http://www.corbis.com

[7] Watermarks are affixed to each online image to insure against unauthorised use; also, because the images contain a limited number of pixels, they blur when enlarged, rendering them of little use to potential image snatchers.

replace instruction sets as the basis of digital value.

In late 1994, Gates stunned the art world with an audacious 30.8 million dollar bid at a Christie's auction for one of Leonardo da Vinci's extraordinary illustrated notebooks, known as the Codex Leicester. Fears that the treasure would end up hidden away from public view were quashed when Continuum bought the rights to existing photographic images of the Codex from their joint owners, the Armand Hammer Museum of Art and Cultural Center and photographer Seth Joel. One of Corbis's first major CD-ROM productions was on da Vinci's fifteenth-century notebooks in which he visually mused about art, music, science, and engineering, sketching prototypes of the parachute, modern woodwinds, the tank, the helicopter, and much more.

Microsoft is not limited to hoarding art related images as evidenced by its TerraServer, dedicated to collecting aerial photographs and satellite images of the earth. The TerraServer boasts more data than all the HTML pages on the Internet, and if put into a paper atlas would be equal to 2000 volumes of 500 pages each. Quantities of information are becoming truly manifest and even the Internet is being catalogued and backed up for posterity.

Archiving the Internet

A fierce competitor to Corbis is Brewster Kahle, a thirty seven year old programmer and entrepreneur who has been capturing and archiving every public Web page since 1996. His ambitious archival project of digital data is to create the Internet equivalent of the Library of Congress. Kahle's non-profit Internet Archive serves as a historical record of cyberspace. His for-profit company, Alexa Internet, named after the Library of Alexandria, uses this archive as part of an innovative search tool that lets users call up "out-of-print" Web pages. Along with the actual pages, the programs retrieve and store "metadata" as well–information about each site such as how many people visited it, where on the Web they went next, and what pages are linked to it. The Web pages are stored digitally on a "jukebox" tape drive the size of two soda machines, which contains ten terabytes of data–as much information as half of the Library of Congress. And in keeping with the Library of Congress, the Internet Archive does not exclude information because it is trivial, dull, or seemingly unimportant. What separates Alexa from other search engines is that it lets users view sites that have been removed from the Web. Browser and search companies are currently busy snapping up technology that improves Web navigation. Lycos, for instance, spent 39.75 million dollars for WiseWire, which automatically organises Internet content into directories and categories. In April, 1998, Microsoft shelled out a reported 40 million dollars for Firefly, developed by Pattie Maes at MIT, which recommends content to Websurfers based on profiles they submit. (Said. 1998, p.B3.) When they encounter the message "404 Document Not Found," users can click on the Alexa toolbar to fetch the out-of-print Web page from the Internet Archive.

Kahle justifiably worries about moves for laws to be instituted that would make Internet archiving illegal. His efforts to archive the WWW implicitly addresses the fact that archiving for non-print materials is far more problematic in terms of cultural practice and focus than print materials. A good example is the documentation and preservation of television, which, in contrast to print archiving that has been a cultural priority at least since the Library of Alexandria, has relatively few archives preserved and those by relatively inaccessible places such as the Museum of Broadcasting. Although television has functioned as a premier cultural artifact of the latter half of this century, it is only now that it faces radical change that it is finally becoming clear that a lot of our heritage is in electronic form and should be well preserved as such. Even more dire perhaps is the cultural position of video art, which is fast deteriorating with no funds being allocated towards preservation and digitisation of work from the late 60's and early 70's. The work of digitisation of our collective knowledge is selective after all and seems to lean in the direction of documenting the present and not necessarily preserving the past.

Bodies as Databases – The Visible Human Project

Perhaps the most intriguing and in some ways disturbing trend of digitisation and data collection is turned on ourselves, our bodies. Dissecting and analysing bodies is ever present since the age of the Enlightenment, when the problem of imaging the invisible became critical in the fine arts and natural sciences. (Stafford, 1993)

One of the most obvious examples of this is The Visible Human Project which has its roots in a 1986 long-range planning effort of the National Library of Medicine (NLM). VHP foresaw a coming era in which NLM's bibliographic and factual database services would be complemented by libraries of digital images distributed over high-speed computer networks and by high capacity physical media. Not surprisingly, VHP saw an increasing role for electronically represented images in clinical medicine and biomedical research and encouraged the NLM to consider building and disseminating medical image libraries much the same way it acquires, indexes, and provides access to the biomedical literature. As a result of the deliberations of consultants in medical education, the long-range plan recommended that the NLM should "thoroughly and systematically investigate the technical requirements for and feasibility of instituting a biomedical images library."

Early in 1989, under the direction of the Board of Regents, an ad hoc planning panel was convened to forge an in-depth exploration of the proper role for the NLM in the rapidly changing field of electronic imaging. After much deliberation, this panel made the following recommendation: "NLM should undertake a first project building a digital image library of volumetric data representing a complete, normal adult male and female. This Visible Human Project will include digitised photographic images for cryosectioning, digital images derived from computerised tomography and digital magnetic resonance images of cadavers." [vhp.nus.sg]

The initial aim of the Visible Human Project is the acquisition of transverse CT, MRI and cryosection images of a representative male and female cadaver at an average of one millimetre intervals. The corresponding transverse sections in each of the three modalities are to be registered with one another.

The male data set consists of MRI, CT and anatomical images. Axial MRI images of the head, neck, and longitudinal sections of the rest of the body were obtained at 4 mm intervals. The MRI images are 256 pixel by 256 pixel resolution. Each pixel has 12 bits of grey tone resolution. The CT data consists of axial

CT scans of the entire body taken at 1 mm intervals at a resolution of 512 pixels by 512 pixels where each pixel is made up of 12 bits of grey tone. The axial anatomical images are 2048 pixels by 1216 pixels where each pixel is defined by 24 bits of colour, about 7.5 megabytes. The anatomical cross sections are also at 1 mm intervals and coincide with the CT axial images. There are 1871 cross sections for each mode, CT and anatomy. The complete male data set is 15 gigabytes in size.[8] The data set from the female cadaver will have the same characteristics as the male cadaver with one exception. The axial anatomical images will be obtained at 0.33 mm intervals instead of 1.0 mm intervals. This will result in over 5,000 anatomical images. The data set is expected to be about 40 gigabytes in size.

Dr. Catherine Waldby is one of the few theoreticians who have attempted to analyse the fascination with the Visible Humans online, linking it to our society of spectacle and the medical world's practice of unemotional databasing. She writes: "Medicine's use of data and data space is itself uncanny, drawing on the peculiar vivid, negentropic qualities of information to (re)animate its productions." (Waldby, C. June 2000) Making visible the invisible in ourselves, our bodies and identities, does not stop with dissecting the human flesh into millimetre pieces, digitising and posting on the net. The human genome project goes much, much further than that.

The Human Genome Project

At around the same time that the male and female bodies were being digitised and made available over the Internet, major advances were being made in the field of molecular biology, and scholars were being mobilised to map the entire human genome. The prospect of digitally mastering human genome has potential for making it possible to identify the sources of disease and in turn develop new medicines and methods of treatment. Thus, the genome project was almost immediately a focus of interest for the private sector, who saw a great possibility for profit in gene identification, which subsequently caused them to launched their own, parallel, research efforts.

Begun in 1990, the US Human Genome Project is a fifteen-year effort coordinated by the U.S. Department of Energy and the National Institutes of Health to identify all the estimated eight thousand genes in human DNA, determine the sequences of the three billion chemical bases that make up human DNA, store this information in databases, and develop tools for data analysis. To help achieve these goals, researchers also are studying the genetic makeup of several non-human organisms. These include the common human gut bacterium *Escherichia coli*, the fruit fly, and the laboratory mouse. A unique aspect of the U.S. Human Genome Project is that it is the first large scientific undertaking to address the ethical, legal, and social issues (ELSI) that may arise from the project.

One of the results of the Human Genome project is cloning DNA, cells, and animals. Human cloning was raised as a possibility when Scottish scientists at the Roslin Institute created the much-celebrated sheep "Dolly" (Nature 385, 810-13, 1997). This case aroused world-wide interest and concern because of its scientific and ethical implications. The feat, cited by *Science* magazine as the breakthrough of

---

[8] A contract for acquisition of these pixel-based data was awarded in August 1991 to the University of Colorado at Denver. Victor M. Spitzer, Ph.D. and David G. Whitlock, M.D., Ph.D. are the principal investigators.

1997, has also generated uncertainty over the meaning of "cloning," an umbrella term traditionally used by scientists to describe different processes for duplicating biological material. To Human Genome Project researchers, cloning refers to copying genes and other pieces of chromosomes to generate enough identical material for further study. Cloned collections of DNA molecules (called clone libraries) enable scientists to produce increasingly detailed descriptions of all human DNA, which is the aim of the Human Genome Project. (Human Genome News, January 1998; 9: 1-2) In January 1998, nineteen European countries signed a ban on human cloning. The United States supports areas of cloning research that could lead to significant medical benefits, and the Congress is yet to pass a bill to ban human cloning.

Much of this ambition for digitised genomes is driven by excitement for a new way of thinking and working and by a utopian vision of all information being accessible to all–the vision of a collective consciousness. But this ambition is equally fuelled by the potentially huge monetary returns it could generate. The most disturbing example is research in the field of genetics led by Carl Venter, also called the Bill Gates of genetic engineering. His claim to be able to beat the government's plan to map the entire genome by four years has even James D. Watson, the discoverer of DNA, up in arms. The rush to patent genes as they are discovered has many speculating if our bodies will truly be owned by corporate interests.

It is more than a decade since the US genetic engineering company Genentech made both medical and legal history, first with the discovery of the gene that produces insulin and then by persuading a series of US courts that it had earned the right to patent its discovery. Just as digital libraries funded by governments and developed by university consortiums have their counterparts in the corporate sector, so too in the sphere of biotechnology. The Human Genome Project is funding thousands of scientists working at universities and research labs with a generous budget of three billion dollars and climbing. But the biotech world has become a type of a battlefield, with certain private companies refusing to share the genetic codes they identified and therefore claim. The case of the *Staphylococus aurues,* a deadly bacteria that resists the strongest antibiotics, is an example of this conflict. Biotechnology and drug companies have spent huge amounts of money on decoding the genome of the *Staph*, hoping to design new drugs to combat it. But they refuse to share their discoveries or to collaborate with federal health officials, forcing them to duplicate the work at a cost of millions of dollars to taxpayers. The question is still open and mirrors the one that is always looming over the Internet: Will information be available and free in the public domain, or will it be patented and owned by the large corporate sector? (Cimons, 1999. p. A16)

Database Art Practice

Artists have long recognised the conceptual and aesthetic power of databases, and much work has resulted using archives as a deliberate base for artistic endeavours. In view of activities such as those sited above, this is rich territory for artists to work in, on many levels. Databases and archives serve as ready-made commentaries on our contemporary social and political lives. Even the places that are traditionally outlets for the work become ready-mades. The museum as an institution and the general societal attitude towards art objects can be viewed and dissected from this perspective. The gallery becomes the public face while the storerooms are its private parts, with the majority of the collection residing there. Storerooms are places where artwork resides cut off from the critical aura and in the graceless form of regimented racks. Artists have produced work that comments on these dynamics of collection and display by museums, the institutions they traditionally depend on. Let us consider some art practices in this domain before moving into how contemporary artists working with digital technologies are responding to knowledge organisation and production described above.[9]

Marcel Duchamp's Bo'tes-en-Val'se is seen as the first critique of museum practice: "[it] parodies the museum as an enclosed space for displaying art ... mocks [its] archival activity ... [and] satirically suggests that the artist is a travelling salesman whose concerns are as promotional as they are aesthetic." (McAlliter. and Weil, B, p.10). After publishing an edition of three hundred standard and twenty luxury versions of the Green Box[10], Duchamp devised a series of valises that would contain miniature versions of his artwork to be unpacked and used in museums. He commissioned printers and light manufacturers throughout Paris to make three hundred-twenty copies of miniature versions of each of his artworks and a customised briefcase to store and display them: "In the end the project was not only autobio-graphical, a life-long summation, but anticipatory as well. As an artwork designed to be unpacked, the viewing of Valises carries the same sense of expectation and event as the opening of a crate." (Schaffner, 1998, p.11).

In the 70's and 80's, artists such as Richard Artschwager, Louise Lawler, Marcel Broothers, and Martin Kippenberger have commented on museum practice using the archiving and packing practice as an anchor. Ironically, storage of fine art in many cases is more elaborate and careful in execution than the very art it is meant to protect. Perhaps anticipating the art of 'containers' of interface to data, Artschwager takes the crate and elevates it to an art form by creating a series of crates and exhibiting them in museum and gallery exhibition spaces. Similarly, Andy Warhol (an obsessive collector in his own right) curated a show at the Rhode Island School of Design that consisted entirely of a shoe collection from the costume collection, shelf and all. The show was part of a series conceived by John and Dominique de Menil, who were interested in bringing to light some of the "unsuspecting treasures mouldering in museum basements, inaccessible to the general public." (Bourdon, 1970. p.17).

Warhol's Time Capsule project, very similar to Fuller's Chronofile, consists of stored away documents of Warhol's daily life such as unopened mail and an enormous

---

[9] Curators who responded and understood artist's comments on the culture of storage, archive and preservation of art have the opportunity of participating and commenting on this practice. One of the most impressive examples of this kind of work is a recent exhibition titled *Deep Storage*, organised by Ingrid Schaffner and Mathias Winzen. This show perhaps marks the end of a certain era, of analogue archiving, and the beginning of an era of digital archiving. A few projects are included in this show which point to the next step of artwork generated by digital archiving and databasing.

[10] The green Box is actually entitled "The Bride Stripped Bare by her Bachelors, Even." The nickname is coined to distinguish the Box from Duchamp's masterpiece, a sculpture of the same title produced between 1915 and 1928, and known simply as The Large Glass.

amount of marginal notes, receipts, scraps, and other details of little or no importance. The similarity lays in the approach of not wanting to categorise the items collected or grant them any other type of specific or special significance. Warhol's obsessive collecting throughout his life time resulted in forty-two scrapbook of clippings related to his work and his public life; art supplies ad materials used by Warhol; posters publicising his exhibitions and films; an entire run of *Interview* magazine, which Warhol founded in 1969; his extensive library of books and periodicals; hundreds of decorative art objects; and many personal items such as clothing and over thirty of the silver-white wigs that became one of his defining physical features. Warhol also owned several works by Marcel Duchamp, who had a important influence on him, including two copies of the Bo'te-en-Val'ses (Smith, 1998. p.279)

Documentation of an artist's life is an investment in the future of the personae that will continue to survive in the form of information. Collecting, storing, and archiving is very much connected to time, to our anxiety over the loss of time and the speed with which time travels. We preserve the all-important self in this age of relentless movement by creating a memory bank that testifies our existence, our unique contribution, and promises to perhaps be brought back to life by someone in the future who can unpack the data and place it in a space of cultural importance. How much we leave behind, how much shelf space we occupy, is how our importance is measured. Meg Cranston makes this point in a compelling way in her piece "Who's Who by Size": Edgar Allen Poe, at six hundred-thirty three volumes, occupies sixty three and a half feet of shelf space, while Muhammad Ali, at a mere fifteen volumes, only one and a half feet. (Schaffner, 1998. p.106).

Artists working with digital media, particularly on the networks, are acutely aware of information overflow and that design of navigation through these spaces has become a demand of aesthetic practice. One of the first artists who used the World Wide Web early on with the now obsolete Mosaic browser was Antonio Muntades. Muntades's project, the File Room[11], was devoted to documenting cases of censorship that are frequently not available at all or else exist somewhere as dormant data. Similarly,Vera Frankel has created an installation that extends out onto the Web and addresses issues of collection of art, specifically of Hitler's obsession:

A particular focus of these conversations has been the Sonderauftrag (Special Assignment) Linz, Hitler's little publicised but systematic plan to acquire art work by any means, including theft or forced sale, for the proposed Furhermuseum (accent) in Linz, his boyhood town. Shipped from all over Europe to the salt mines at the nearby Alt Aussee, the burnt collection was stored in conditions of perfect archival temperature and humidity, until found by the Allies after the war: cave after cave of paintings, sculptures, prints and drawings destined for the vast museum that was never built. (Frankel, 1995)

Frankel invites other artists to contribute their own narratives, works, and bibliographies to the work, thus making the piece itself become a kind of archive whose content does not belong to one artist alone. Fear of the loss of originality and the revered artist personae is frequently connected to the endless reproductions that the digital media affords. Another source of fear for artists confronting the new technologies is the integration of individual artists into the context of other works or creation of meta-works. Of course, this is not a fear for those who have taken on a broader view of what 'originality' may mean. Ultimately, artists working with digital

---

[11] File Room is located at: http://fileroom.aaup.uic.edu/FileRoom

media necessarily work in collaborative groups and are context providers. Indeed the development of context in the age of information overload is the art of the day. This is particularly true of the current artistic practice on the net in which artists frequently coopt and summon work and data of others. One of the by products of a "global culture" is the emergence of meta-structures, which include physical architectures, software such as the browser technology that allows us to view information on the Internet via the WWW, and artworks that are meta-art pieces, including work of not only other artists but the audience itself.[12] Artists working with the net are essentially concerned with the creation of a new type of aesthetic that involves not only a visual representation, but invisible aspects of organisation, retrieval, and navigation as well. Data is the raw form that is shaped and used to build architectures of knowledge exchange and as an active commentary on the environment it depends on-the vast, intricate network with its many faces.

Fuller's Chronofile, although not without problems, is an example of a system consciously conceived without fixed categories, which poses an explicit commentary on traditional modes of categorisation through juxtaposition. Similarly, Cage, in his last exhibition piece entitled "The Museum Circle," makes a point about categorisation in cultural production and exhibition. In 1993, shortly before his death, the Museum of Contemporary Art in Los Angeles realised another version of The Museum Circle (the first being in Munich, 1991), in which more than twenty museums participated with a large number of exhibits. The Museum Circle changed its order daily according to the principle of the *I Ching*. This constant change enabled new kinds of connections to emerge and cast doubt on any "truth" the works may have revealed through their former categorisation. (Blume, 1998). And this is where I will leave off my tour of databasing our collective knowledge efforts. I believe that there is an opportunity for artists to play a vital role in the development of the evolving database culture. If we can conceptualise and design systems that in their core are about change and multiple ways of access and retrieval, we can truly anticipate a new type of aesthetic emerging.

References

Blume, E. 1998. "On the verge of Departure from Lager 1." In Deep Storage. Ed.
Borges, J. 1962. "The Library of Babel." Ficciones. Trans. Anthony Kerrigan. New York: Grove Press.
Bourdon, D. 1970. "Andy's Dish." Raid the Icebox 1 With Andy Warhol. Catalogue essay. Providence: Museum of Art, Rhode Island School of Design.
Bush, V. 1945. "As We May Think." In Electronic Culture: Technology and Visual Representation.
Cimons, M. JACOBS, Paul. 1999. "Biotech Battlefield: Profits vs. Public". Los Angeles Times. February 21.
Daniel, S. 1998. "Collaborative Systems: evolving databases and the 'conditions of possibility' – artificial life models of agency in on-line interactive art." AI & Society.
Engelbart, D. 1963. "A Conceptual Framework for the Augmentation of Man's Intellect" In Vistas in Information Handling. ed. HOWERTON, Paul. Washington D.C.: Spartan Books. London: Cleaver-Hume Press.FULLER, B.R. 1962. Synergetics Dictionary. Citing Oregon lecture #9, July 12.
Fuller, B.R. 1965. Vision '65. Keynote address. Carbondale: Southern Illinois University, October.
Fuller, B.R. 1967. "Bucky." In University of Toronto Graduate. ed. McLUHAN, M. Toronto: University of Toronto.
Fuller, R.B. 1981. Critical Path. Kiyoshi Kuromiya, Adjuvant. New York: St. Martin's Press

---

[12] Vera Frankel's Body Missing Project on the web is an extension of a video installation presented at P.S. 1 Museum, New York. www.yorku.ca/BodyMissing

Glave, J. 1998. "Hypertext Guru Has New Spins on Old Plans". Hotwired. 3.06. April 17, 1998.

Hafner, K. 1996. "Picture This." Newsweek. 24 June.

McAllister, J and WEIL, B. 1989. "The Museum Under Analysis." In The Desire of the Museum. Catalogue essay. New York: Whitney Museum of American Art.

McLuhan, M. 1962. The Guttenberg Galaxy. Toronto: University of Toronto Press.

Nelson, T. 1965. "The Hypertext". In proceedings of the World Documentation Federation.

Nelson, T. 1974. "Computer Lib/Dream Machines". Sausalito, CA: Mindful Press.

Ninch. National Initiative for a networked Cultural Heritage. www-ninch.cni.org

Rapaport, R. 1996. "In His Image." Wired, 4;11. November.

Rheingold, H. 1993. The Virtual Community: Homesteading the Electronic Frontier. New York: Addison-Wesley Publishing Company.

Rothstein, E. 1995. "How Bill Gates is Imitating Art." The New York Times. October 15. E3.

Said, C. 1998. San Francsico Chronicle. May 7.

Schaffner, I. WINZEN, M. ed. 1998. Deep Storage: Collecting, Storing, and Archiving Art. Munich: Prestel-Verlag.

Smith, J. 1998. "Andy Warhol." In Deep Storage: Collecting, Storing, and Archiving Art. Munich: Prestel-Verlag.

Stafford, B. 1991. Body Criticism: Imaging the Unseen in enlightenment Art and Medicine. Cambridge, Mass and London, UK: MIT Press.

Waldby, C. 2000. The Visible Human Project: Informatic Bodies and Posthuman Medicine, Routledge

Wells, H.G. 1938. World Brain. Freeport, New York: Books for Libraries Press.

Correspondence and Offprint requests to: Victoria Vesna Department of Design /Media Arts, University of California, Los Angeles, 1300 Dickson Art Center, Los Angeles, CA 90095, USA. Fax: 001 310 206 6676; Email: vv@ucla.edu

Recommended Reading

Sorting Things Out
Classification and its Consequences

Geoffrey C. Bowker and Susan Leigh Star 1999, MIT Press

Sorting Things Out stands at the crossroads of the sociology of knowledge and technology, history, and information science. Bowker and Leigh Star attempt to answer questions such as, What work do classifications and standards do? Who does the work? and What happens to the cases that don't fit? The authors emphasize the role of invisibility in the process by which classification orders human interaction. They examine how categories are made and kept invisible, how people change their invisibility when necessary by examining large infrastructure systems , International Classification of Diseases, the Nursing Interventions Classifications, race classification under apartheid in South Africa, and the classification of viruses and tuberculosis. The book is a result of long term, complex research that would be difficult to classify. Many notable scholars have contributed and participated in the research, it was funded by the National Science Foundation and supported by Xerox PARC. Required reading for anyone who is seriously pursuing database aesthetics and theory.

AI & Soc (2006) 20: 22–34
DOI 10.1007/s00146-005-0003-8

ORIGINAL ARTICLE

Carol Gigliotti

Leonardo's choice: the ethics of artists working with genetic technologies

Received: 10 February 2005 / Accepted: 1 June 2005 / Published online: 26 November 2005
© Springer-Verlag London Limited 2005

Abstract Working with current methodologies of art, biology, and genetic technologies, the stated aims of artists working in this area include attempts both to critique the implications and outcomes of genetic technologies and to forge a new art practice involved in creating living beings using those technologies. It is this last ambition, the development of a new art practice involved in creating living beings, that this essay will particularly take to task by questioning the ethics of that goal and the uses of biotechnology in reaching it.

Keywords Animals · Biogenetics · Ethics · Aesthetics · Ecocentricism · Anthropomorphism · Animal rights · New media

Although its source may well be apocryphal, the following quote has been attributed to Leonardo da Vinci, "I have from an early age abjured the use of meat, and the time will come when men such as I will look upon the murder of animals as they now look upon the murder of men" (Preece 2002, 93).[1] While da Vinci may not have said exactly that, his compassion for animals is well documented in his notebooks and several sources cite his vegetarianism (Clark 1977, 45). The notebooks contain numerous references to his shock and disdain for man's deliberate choice in abusing the other animals, many of whom provide him with food and labor:

> Of candles made of beeswax
> [The bees] give light to divine service—and for this they are destroyed.
> Of asses
> Here the hardest labor is repaid by hunger and thirst, pain and blows, goads and curses, and loud abuse.
> Of a fish served with its roe
> Endless generations of fish will be lost because of the death of this pregnant one.
> Of slaughtered oxen

C. Gigliotti
School of Design, Emily Carr Institute of Art and Design,
1399 Johnston Street, Vancouver, BC, Canada V6H 3R9
E-mail: gigliott@eciad.bc.ca · Tel.: + 1-604-8443800
Fax: + 1-604-8443801

[1] The quote is actually from a work of fiction written by Merijkowsky in the 1920s Romance of Leonardo da Vinci.

Behold—the lords of great estates have killed their own laborers (da Vinci, quoted in Kellen 1971, 78–79).

Vasari in describing Leonardo's exemplary character tells us how Leonardo's compassion for animals was such that he bought caged birds merely to set them free (Turner 1993, 62). Vasari, however, also has a very young Leonardo composing a painting of a monster (possibly a Medusa) modeled on dead "lizards, grasshoppers, serpents, butterflies, locusts, bats, and other strange animals of the kind" he had brought to his room. An additional story by Vasari of a much older Leonardo in Rome, describes how the artist spent his time, much to the chagrin of Pope Leo X:

> "To the back of a very odd-looking lizard that was found by the gardener of the Belvedere he attached with a mixture of quicksilver some wings, made from the scales stripped from other lizards, which quivered as it walked along. Then, after he had given it eyes, horns and a beard he tamed the creature, and keeping it in a box, he used to show it to friends and frighten the life out of them." (quoted in Turner, 62)

Much of Vasari's information about Leonardo is second hand and some of it is more than likely to have been invented (Turner, 55–68), but, together with Leonardo's notebooks, these tales of Leonardo give us some appreciation of the conflicting priorities that may have existed in Leonardo's attitudes towards animals. He was compassionate toward the plight of animals used solely for human purposes, while at times using animals himself for his own purposes. A painter, a scientist, a naturalist, a technologist, a prophet, Leonardo was both an exemplar of his time and ahead of it.

These preoccupations of Leonardo are reflective of ethical issues brought up by artists working with genetic technologies involving bacteria, plants, and animals. Many of these artists are seen or see themselves as descendents of Leonardo and his abilities to cross the disciplines of art and science. It is no accident that the leading publication of such crossover activity for the last 36 years has been the influential "Leonardo: Journal of the International Society of the Arts, Science and Technology." Held (2001) Curator of Gene(sis): Contemporary Art Explores Human Genomics, an exhibit traveling from 2002 to 2004, introduces the exhibit in this way:

> "As artists take up the tools and materials of genetic and genomic research, their experimental reflections are changing our notions of artistic practice. Many artists function as researchers, engaged in non-hypothesis-driven, open-ended investigations. Their studios are laboratories for this experience-based inquiry. In addition, artists such as Eduardo Kac, Critical Art Ensemble, Paul Vanouse, Joe Davis, Tissue Art and Culture, Jill Reynolds, Iñigo Manglano-Ovalle, and Justine Cooper, to name just a handful, regularly use biological materials in their work. In some cases, artists are creating new life forms and releasing them into the environment." (4)

Working with current methodologies of art, biology, and genetic technologies, the stated aims of artists working in this area include attempts both to critique the implications and outcomes of genetic technologies and to forge a new art practice involved in creating living beings using those technologies.

It is this last ambition, the development of a new art practice involved in creating living beings, that this essay will particularly take to task by questioning the ethics of that goal and the uses of biotechnology in reaching it. Doing so has proven to be a contentious activity, involving as it does discourse about both artistic and scientific practice, each bringing along its own linguistic and conceptual assumptions, metaphorical, and otherwise. Participants in this debate have come from what some may consider to be both "inside" and "outside" the art world: the artists themselves, curators, critics, art theorists, philosophers, cultural and political critics, theologians and scientists, and the general public.

Many of these participants, wherever their disciplinary reference-point might be, see art as one of the few environments left where uncensored thought is not only condoned, but also encouraged. As Efimova (2003), Associate Curator of the Berkeley Art Museum presentation of Gene(sis), says in her introductory essay, "...experimental art remains one of the few enclaves where imaginative, impractical, non-mundane thinking is still tolerated." (1)

---

1 Is thinking in art always radical?

The idea that art is a last bastion for radical thinking has frequently been used as a rationale for this new art practice. In an essay included in The Eighth Day: The Transgenic Work of Eduardo Kac, Machado (2003) argues this point. He contends that critiques of biotechnologies tend to take a "conservative bias" or "even dogmatic interdictions of religious order." He sees: "The more experimental and much less conformist sphere of art—with its emphasis on creation, by means of genetic engineering, of works which are simply beautiful, not utilitarian or potentially profit making..." (94) as conducive to more sophisticated discussion about genetics as well as science and technology in general. He adds, however, one of the benefits of Kac's work, The Eighth Day, is to develop science and technology "away from the unproductive dichotomy of good and bad, right or wrong, and toward a confrontation of the whole of its complexity." (95)

Two assumptions are at work in these statements by Machado and in much of the writing by both artists and critics about artists working with genetic technologies. The first assumption is that thinking in art is consistently experimental and non-conformist. While one may assume that to be true, based on some historical precedents, the assumption does not insure that all thinking emerging from art is necessarily radical. The second assumption concerns the idea that a confrontation with the complexity of a topic or issue precludes the necessity of confronting ethical choices embedded in that complexity. On the contrary, one of the main reasons for understanding complexity is the insight it may offer to ethical choice. I highlight the limits of these two assumptions because their uncritical acceptance muddies the discussion of two aspects pivotal in discourse surrounding the ethics and aesthetics of a new art practice involving living beings.

These two aesthetic aspects are most clearly delineated by art critic Bureaud (2002) in an issue of artpress that included seven essays and a "dossier" on "art bio(techno)logique." She summarizes the discourse around "biological art" as ranging from technical practices involving biological and biotechnological methods to contexts dealing with related human-centered social, political, environmental and ethical issues to human-based perspectives on immortality. Bureaud makes the point, however, that while these perspectives are essential to understanding and evaluating these works, "...analysis often fails to get as far as their artistic or aesthetic aspects." (38) While this implies that artistic or aesthetic aspects will be discussed separately from the ethical aspects of this work, Bureaud describes among the seven aesthetic aspects she has observed in this growing body of work, two characteristics or orientations, one can only see as inextricably entwined with ethical perspectives.

Fig. 1 Rabbit with skin removed
Credit: None

The first is an approach she calls the "*anti-anthropocentric art of the continuum*" including the semi-living (as in Tissue Culture and Art Projects) and transgenic organisms (as in projects by Eduardo Kac). She describes this approach as emphasizing the "permeability of the frontiers between species, the continuity that goes from the non-living to the different degrees of complexity in life forms." (38)

Catts and Zurr (2003, 2004), artists involved in Tissue Culture and Art Projects, utilize the idea of "a continuum of life" as oppositional to an anthropocentric worldview:

> "... we argue that the underlying problem concerned with the manipulation of life is rooted in the perceptions of humans as a separated and privileged life form, a perception inherited in the West from the Judo-Christian-and Classical worldviews. This anthropocentrism is distorting society's ability to cope with the expanding scientific knowledge of life. Further this cultural barrier in the continuum of life between the human and other living systems prejudices decisions about manipulations of living systems." (2)

This confusing statement can be read as both critique and support of the historic values of anthropocentrism leading to the instrumentation and destruction of living systems. Catts and Zurr, themselves, point out that much of what they are saying and doing is contradictory and this statement and much of the rest of the essay, from which it is excerpted, is evidence of this. Although they claim that their hope is to challenge "long held beliefs" about the perceived barrier between humans and other living beings, they see their involvement in actually manipulating life as "highlighting the inconsistency of the still prevalent view of the dominion of man." (3)

They acknowledge the paradoxical quality of their position:

> "...on one hand we attempt to break down specism and make humans part of a broader continuum. On the other hand, we artists-humans, are using (abusing?) our more privileged position to technically manipulate an aesthetic experiment." (17)

They insist, however, "...only when humans realize that they are a part of the continuum of life will manipulating life not be as alarming as it now seems." (17)

The absurdity of this claim is hard to miss. Humans have been manipulating animal life with impunity for thousands of years. Most do not find it alarming, but customary. If, as Zurr and Catts claim, their goal is to encourage people to understand the distortions a human centered view causes in recognizing the continuum of life, more manipulation of life forms will most certainly not contribute to that project, but only serve to reinforce it.

Kac (2000) references an anti-anthropocentric approach in his essay, "GFP Bunny:"

> "Rather than accepting the move from the complexity of life processes to genetics, transgenic art gives emphasis to the social existence of organisms, and thus highlights the evolutionary continuum of physiological and behavioral characteristics between the species." (111)

Inherent contradictions appear when reading these quotes in the context of Kac's transgenic work and his stated goals of "...a new art form based on the use of genetic engineering to transfer natural or synthetic genes to an organism, to create unique living beings." (101) Others have questioned these contradictions in essays on Kac's work. Hayles (2000) asks about Kac's Gene(sis): "Does Kac's intervention in the genetic sequences of bacteria contest the notion that humans have dominion or reinforce it? The ambiguity inheres in any artistic practice that uses the tool of the master to gain perspective on the master's house." (86)

Hayles sees the usefulness this approach might have for imagining that same drive for domination and control executed upon the future of the human. But what of the animals who currently exist under that drive? Seen through the lens of transgenic art, what future can we imagine for them?

Baker (2003), in one of the most thoughtful essays on Kac's work to date, enlists Derrida's investigations of the human responsibility to the non-human animal to help in understanding Kac's work. Derrida (2002), in "The animal that therefore I am," relates how in the last 200 years

> "...the traditional forms of treatment of the animal have been turned upside down by the joint developments of zoological, ethological, biological, and genetic forms of knowledge and the always insepa-

rable techniques of human intervention with respect to their object, the transformation of the actual object, its milieu, its world, namely the living animal." (394)

Derrida describes this as "violence that some would compare to the worst cases of genocide." While Kac judges the procedures he uses to be safe because they have been regularly employed on mice and rabbits since 1980 and 1985, respectively, Baker (2003) says, "...that is precisely the technology that has led to an increase in the numbers of animals currently subjected to laboratory experiments." (36)

And, in fact, the best estimate of current use of animals used in research in the US is 20 million, and about two million in Canada (Mukerjee 1997). According to more recent sources, however, worldwide animal use was estimated to be between 60 and 85 million animals in the early 1990s. (Rowan 1995) And though the use of animals in experimentation has decreased slightly over the last 40 years due to the diligence and commitment of a vast network of animal welfare and animals rights organizations, "...the impact of genetic engineering on animal use should be carefully monitored, given its potential to reverse the decreases in animal use seen during the 1980s and 1990s" (Salem and Rowan 2003).

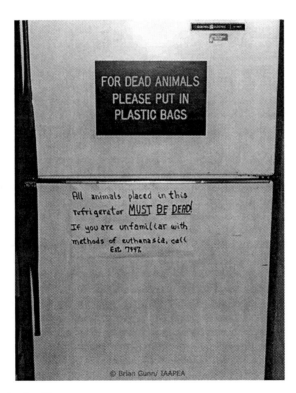

Fig. 2 Dead animal refrigerator
Credit: ©Brian Gunn/IAAPEA

How, then, do these artists see their goal of a new art practice of creating life forms as part of a world view that is anti-anthropocentric, when in fact it continues along the very traditional, conformist, and conservative paths along which are littered the bodies and lives of millions of animals?

2 Anthropocentrism, ecocentrism, and animal life

A more thorough examination of the original ideas and goals of an anti-anthropocentric worldview and associated sciences, rather than supporting the new art practice of creating life forms, allows the weakness of these artists' arguments and practice to come into view. In addition, in at least these instances, standard ideas about the dominant role played by humans are being reinforced while the truly radical notions of bio-centricism are finding support in other places.

While Kac references H.R. Mantura, and Zurr and Catts mention the work of Lynn Marguilas and James Lovelock, the wealth of material on environmental ethics from which ideas about bio-centric worldviews emerge, both in philosophy and practical ecology, have increased tremendously in the last 30 years. An important component of these truly radical worldviews exists in thinking of the *telos* of an organism, in the Aristotelian sense of the term, and can be roughly understood as the fulfilled state or end or goal of the organism. A helpful approach is to concentrate on the distinction between instrumental value, which is what we traditionally see the natural world as possessing, and intrinsic value. Taylor (1986) in his book, *Respect for Nature: A Theory of Environmental Ethics* develops a bio-centered or life centered, as opposed to anthropocentric or human-centered, environmental ethics, as well as arguing that all living organisms possess intrinsic worth. What Taylor and others like him are advocating is a "... *world order on our planet in which human civilization is brought into harmony with nature."* (308) This goal, however, is built upon cultures in which "...each carries on with its way of life *within the constraints of the human ethics of respect for persons."* (308)

Unlike some arguments based on a "deep ecology" in which a conception of individual organisms having inherent worth is not included, this understanding of environmental ethics makes integral links to necessary changes in social, political, and economic justice on a planetary scale. These changes would include the elimination of all sentient beings in any form of experimentation. As Taylor admits, these changes would require a profound moral reorientation, and the first step would be an "inner change in our moral beliefs and commitments." Respect for and consideration of the intrinsic worth of individuals of any species, far from being disconnected to these changes in our moral commitments to the human species, is fundamental to altering current compulsions for ways of life inherently devastating to much of the planet and its inhabitants. Shiva (2000) argues, "The emerging trends in global trade and technology work inherently against justice and ecological sustainability. They threaten to create a new era of bio-imperialism, built on the impoverishment of the Third World and the biosphere." (25) These trends threaten both ecological and cultural diversity. Shiva cites two root causes for the West's adherence to these obviously negative compulsions:

"The first arises from the 'empty-earth' paradigm of colonization, which assumes that ecosystems are empty if not taken over by Western industrial man or his clones. This view threatens other species and other cultures to extinction because it is blind to their existence, their rights and to the impact of the colonizing culture. The second cause is what I have described as monoculture of the mind: the idea that the world is or should be uniform and one-dimensional, that diversity is either disease or deficiency, and monocultures are necessary for the production of more food and economic benefits." (26)

For Shiva, genetic technologies are turning life, or biology, into "capitalism's lastest frontier."(28) She convincingly reasons, however:

"There is ...one problem with life from the point of view of capital. Life reproduces and multiplies freely. Living organisms self-organizes and replicate. Life's renewability is a barrier to commodification. If life has to be commodified, its renewability must be interrupted and arrested." (30)

This is being accomplished by industrial breeding, genetic engineering, and patent and intellectual property rights. Shiva, like Taylor, eloquently calls for a major shift in thought, referring to genetic engineering as based on genetic reductionism:

"A shift in the paradigm of knowledge from a reductionist to a relational approach is necessary for both biological and cultural diversity. A relational view of living systems recognizes the intrinsic worth of all species protects their ecological space and respects their self-organizational, diverse, dynamic, and evolving capacities." (129)

The fundamental goals for manipulating nature, at any level, are always grounded in human interest. Attempts by artists to make the case for biogenetic art involving living matter or beings, by and large, have come from a truly non-radical worldview, one that still posits human beings as the center and rationale of all endeavors. This should not be surprising, since this anthropocentric viewpoint matches that of both past and current genetic research upon which this art is based. Using living non-humans in experiments or for other human purposes is a generally accepted practice, one not often questioned within the discourses of science or, for that matter, within the discourses of art.[2] The worldview upon which these activities rest sees all of nature as available for human intervention.

Although the stated aims of some artists involved in these discourses are to question the anthropocentric standpoint while at the same time using the tools, methods, and assumed ideologies of biogenetics, the reality of animal use in both biotechnology in general, and in biogenetic art forms specifically, can only highlight in this work a fundamental misunderstanding of what a real commitment to anti-anthropocentric aims might mean. And it is precisely at this point where artistic practice using living beings falls short of any contribution to those aims.

---

[2]There are, of course, exceptions to this statement, including artists Sue Coe, Mark Dion, Julian Schanbel, and Britta Jaschinski, among others.

3 Theories of aesthetics and ethics and the realities of animal life

The second aesthetic aspect Bureaud mentions that is linked to ethical perspectives is "an aesthetics of attention and responsibility." Both Zurr and Catts and Eduardo Kac, insist that ethical questions are central to their aesthetic concerns. They have discussed at some length how their use of living or semi-living beings is included in that "aesthetics of care."[3] All three, however, also insist that their art practice of creating living beings offers, as Kac (2000) claims, "important alternatives to the polarizing debate" about genetic engineering, replacing dichotomy with "ambiguity and subtlety."(1) Catts and Zurr (2003, 2004) claim artists involved with this new art form are

> "...manipulating life and "inserting" life into new contexts including the art galleries. By that they are forcing the audience to engage with the living artwork and to share the consequences/responsibilities involved with the manipulation/creation of life for artistic ends." (2)

Some critics, particularly Baker in discussion about Kac's transgenic work, acknowledge the dichotomy between Kac using the techniques of animal experimentation for biotechnological investigations and his emphasis on responsibility that does not "treat an animal as an object, be it an art object or an object of any kind."[4]

Comparing Kac and Derrida, Baker (2003) says:

> "Kac, with similarly serious intentions, engages with the animal through techniques that strike many people as meddlesome, invasive and profoundly unethical." (29)

Baker believes that a more detailed reading of the connection between this engagement of Kac's, the concern of Derrida with "how to do philosophy by means of a prolonged and serious meditation on his relationship with the cat who shares his home" (32) is necessary. Baker sees the value of the comparison of the two thinkers in what it may tell us about the "relation of intentions to actions in both ethics and aesthetics." (29) I agree, but for somewhat different reasons. Both Kac and Derrida see the animal, through very thick filters, and both have disconnected their actions from their intentions. The goal for each is not an understanding of the animal for itself, but for a human-centered reason. Derrida sees the animal through the filter of "doing philosophy" and the impossibility of an excessive responsibility to the animal in the present culture, while Kac sees the animal through the filter of an acceptance of the inevitability of a biotechnological future in which his goal of the new art practice of creating living beings makes sense.

---

[3]This phrase comes from the title "The Aesthetics of Care?" a symposium presented by SymbioticA and The Institute of Advanced Studies, University of Western Australia. August 5 2002 at Perth Institute for Contemporary Arts. Catts and Zurr and their Tissue Culture and Art Project are hosted by SymbioticA—The Art and Science Collaborative Research Lab.
[4]"Interview with Eduardo Kac" Interview conducted online, with questions posted to the Genolog website, July–September 2000 http://www.ekac.org/genointer.html, pp. 3–4.

Derrida (1991), even as he attempts to outline an "excessive" responsibility that includes the non-human, builds a case for the impossibility of acting on that responsibility:

> "[A] pure openness to the [O]ther is impossible—*and certainly* in this culture. We can no more step out of carnophallogocentrism to some peaceable kingdom than we can step out of metaphysics. Put another way, a violence of a sort, "eating [O]thers," is not an option, but a general condition of life, and it would be a dangerous fanaticism (or quietism) to suppose otherwise. The issue is not *whether we eat, but how.*" (115)

Unfortunately, though Derrida's intentions are to deconstruct the general scheme of dominance in Western metaphysics and religion, he disregards something that might be helpful in being able to see animals as other than food, tools, or entertainment. He does not seem to be able to take even the fundamental step of vegetarianism. His reasons for this and arguments against those reasons are the stuff of a much longer essay, but suffice it to say, that a sense of inevitability and an inability to see or imagine outside that scheme of dominance seems to play a role in Derrida's disconnection between his intentions and actions. While his equivocation towards vegetarianism "seems to rest on the restricted, cautious assessment of its significance; one which would allow vegetarians to buy good conscience on the cheap," he misses the opportunity in a committed ethical vegetarianism, and even better veganism, for what Wood (1999) calls a "*motivated possibility of response.*" As Wood so forcefully puts it:

> "Carnophallogocentrism is not a dispensation of being toward which resistance is futile; it is a mutually reinforcing network of powers, schemata of domination, and investments that has to reproduce itself to stay in existence. Vegetarianism is not just about substituting beans for beef; it is—at least potentially—a site of proliferating resistance to that reproduction." (32)

The disconnection between actions and intentions is less overt in the case of Kac. Kac's ambivalence towards the inevitability of a biotechnological future, and in some cases his welcoming of it, clouds our reception of what his inner thoughts might be about his uses of living beings, even as he critiques the Western philosophical canon on which those uses are based. Lestral (2002) touches briefly on why this might be so in general for artists working in this vein. "We must also take into account the inglorious possibility that these artists are being manipulated—and not necessarily consciously either—by technologists and multinationals; that they are serving to legitimize practices that our cultures otherwise find it hard to accept." (45) While Lestral backs away from this conclusion, for one that he finds "more reasonable" that sees these artists as doing what artists have always done by exploring practices of their period, he questions if art can play the role of being "critical."

And while Kac's work has been effective in highlighting the complex quality of this society's involvement with biotechnology, his acceptance of a biotechnological future and his use of techniques that objectify the animal, frustrate a response that seeks to confront ethical choices embedded in that complexity and also frustrates imagining alternatives. Put another way, one cannot say they object to treating an animal as an object of any kind, and then use the very techniques of objectification to create an animal for the purpose of continuing this objectification in the form of a new art practice. What value does "confronting complexity" have if it obscures insight into a "possibility of response?"

Catt and Zurr's work suffers from the same burden, though they appropriate arguments from two of the most important animal rights philosophers, Regan (1983) and Singer (1975) to support their work with tissue cultures. Taking liberties with both philosophers' positions, they use Singer's utilitarian position that would allow experiments on animals if the experimenters also would be willing to use humans at an equal or lower level of consciousness, rather than Regan's individualist deontological position that makes a case for an end to all experimentation of non-humans. Regan argues that animals are the "subject-of-a-life" and thus have inherent value:

> "A being that is a subject-of-a-life will: have beliefs and desires; perception, memory, and a sense of the future, including their own future; an emotional life together with feelings of pleasure and pain; preference-interests and welfare-interests; the ability to initiate action in pursuit of their desires and goals; a psychological identity over time; and an individual welfare in the sense that their experiential life fares well or ill for them, logically independently of their utility for others, and logically independently of their being the object of anyone else's interests. Those who satisfy the subject-of-a-life criterion themselves have a distinctive kind of value—inherent value—and are not to be viewed or treated as mere receptacles." (243)

And in contrast to Singer's utilitarian interpretation of formal justice, and in this case Catt and Zurr's interpretation as well, Regan argues for an acceptance of the *respect principle* in relation to those who are subject-of-a-life:

> "We cannot justify harming *them* merely on the grounds that this will produce an optimal aggregate balance of intrinsic goods over intrinsic evils for all concerned. *We owe them* respectful treatment ... because justice requires it." (261)

Catts and Zurr (2003, 2004), however, seem to be filtering any understanding of their commitments and "care" for non-human beings through their fascination with the techniques of biotechnology and a confounding of what might constitute intrinsic good or evil for the animals involved in genetic technologies. Their project, "Disembodied Cuisine" investigating "the possibility of eating victimless meat by growing semi-living steaks from a biopsy taken from an animal while keeping the animal alive and healthy" (13) is an example of this. They believe:

> "That by the creation of the new class of semi-living /partial life we further shift/blur/problematise the ethical goalpost in relation to our (human) position in the continuum of life. The discussion that being generated regarding the rights of the semi-living will draw attention to the conceptual frameworks in which we humans understand and relate to the world." (17)

And to this they add: "To manipulate life is to be at home with the other that can be anything within this continuum." (17) Once again, one cannot say they do not relate to the living or semi-living as an object and then manipulate that living/semi-living being as an object. Why continue to use animals in any form as food if you wish to question the traditional view of the non-human? The continuation of such a program can only make suspect their stated goals of a "humble attempt of ethical consideration which goes beyond the 'I' the 'You' and even the 'Human' (as much as our humanness 'burden' enables us)." (18–19)

In light of the urgency of the future of the ecosystem's integrity, of which biotechnology is increasingly playing a large role, and the millions of our fellow creatures whose lives we are destroying in that process, it is important to ask, what does art contribute to that future? What responses come from those contributions? The continuation of art practices of creating life-forms through biotechnological means can only serve to implicate these practices, and artists who are involved in them, in contributing to a worldview that still values particular human needs above all else. This worldview, based as it is on the control and manipulation of nature, will continue to blind us to the more radical transformation of acknowledging that we have always been transgenic. The practices of biotechnology are misuses of that knowledge. Far more radical and creative responses to that fact may be based upon a number of increasingly influential ideas from broader areas of thought: the revolutionary idea in cognitive ethology that all living beings are equally gifted with their own worldview or a bio-centered environmental ethics that sees all living organisms possessing intrinsic worth. Appreciating and protecting the biodiversity existing already in the natural and cultural world, or what we have left of it, is part of this learning curve. Additionally, imaginative responses might be based on the enormous amount of thinking now going on in philosophy about the status of the animal. Reminiscent of Regan's Case for Animal Rights, another more recent philosophical argument along these lines, is cogently outlined by Italian philosopher, Cavalieri (2003). It is supported by much of the information and research from cognitive ethology and studies of the mind, but also rests on the major point, similar to earlier debates on the status of women and slaves, that:

> "...the shift from the condition of objects to that of subjects of legal rights does not appear as a point of arrival but rather as the initial access to the circle of possible beneficiaries of that "egalitarian plateau" from which contemporary political philosophy starts in order to determine any more specific individual right." (142)

This shift calls for a further reorganization of society, similar to ongoing shifts concerning human rights, requiring the abolition of the status of animals as property or assets and the prohibition of all practices made possible by that status. This would, of course, include the prohibition of animal experimentation of all kinds. Describing her argument as neither contingent nor eccentric but the "necessary dialectical derivation of the most universally accepted among contemporary ethical doctrines—human rights theory," Cavalieri insists the argument demands a commitment to not only avoiding participating in, but also demands, a commitment to opposing discrimination. Denying these demands would subvert "...not merely what is right, but the very idea of justice." (143)

Whether to continue to put energies toward a new art form of creating living beings or to commit to a more radical worldview that responds to the urgent cries of a disappearing natural world is the choice before the contemporary artist.

References

Baker S (2003) Philosophy in the Wild? In: Britton and Collins (eds) The Eighth Day: the transgenic art of Eduardo Kac, Institute for Study in the Arts, Tempe, Arizona

Bureaud A (2002) The ethics and aesthetics of biological art. Trans C Penwarden artpress 276:38

Catts O, Zurr I (2003, 2004) The ethical claims of bioart: killing the other or self-cannibalism. Aust NZ J Art: Art Ethics Double Issue 4(2) and 5(1):167–188. Page numbers are from http://www.tca.uwa.edu.au/publications/TheEthicalClaimsofBioart.pdf

Cavalieri P (2003) The animal question: why non-human animals deserve human rights. Oxford University Press, New York

Clark K (1977) Animals and men: their relationship as reflected in western art from prehistory to the present day. Thames & Hudson, London

Derrida J (1991) 'Eating well,' or the calculation of the subject. In: Cadava, Connor, Nancy (eds) Who comes after the subject? Routledge, New York London

Derrida J (2002) "The animal that therefore I am (more to come)," trans. David Wills, Critical Inquiry, 28(Winter)

Efimova A (2003) Introduction: Gene(sis): contemporary art explores human genomics. Berkeley Art Museum http://www.bampfa.berkeley.edu/resources/exhibit_archive/index.tml

Hayles NK (2000) Who is in control here? Meditating on Eduardo Kac's transgeneic work. In: Britton and Collins (eds) The eighth day: the transgenic art of Eduardo Kac. Institute for Study in the Arts, Tempe, Arizona

Held R (2001) Gene(sis): a contemporary art exhibition for the genomic age In: Gene(sis): Contemporary Art Explores Human Genomics http://www.gene-sis.net/new_essays.html

Kac E (2000) "GFP Bunny". In: Dobrila P, Kostic A (eds) Eduardo Kac: telepresence, biotelematics, and transgenic art. Kibla, Maribor, Slovenia

Kellen E (ed) (1971) Fantastic tales, strange animals, riddles, jests and prophecies of Leonardo da Vinci. Thomas Nelson, New York

Lestel D (2002) The artistic manipulation of the living. Trans C Penwarden artpress 276:45

Machado A (2003) Towards a transgenic art. In: Britton and Collins (eds) The Eighth Day: the transgenic art of Eduardo Kac. Institute for Study in the Arts. Tempe, Arizona

Mukerjee M (1997) Trends in animal research. Scientific American

Preece R (2002) Awe for the tiger, love for the lamb. UBC Press, Vancouver, BC

Regan T (1983) The case for animal rights. University of California Press, Berkeley

Rowan A (1995) Replacement alternatives and the concept of alternatives. In: Goldberg, van Zutphen (eds) The world congress on alternatives and animal use in the life sciences: education, research, testing. Mary Ann Liebert, New York

Salem DJ, Rowan AN (eds) (2003) The state of the animals II. Humane Society Press, Washington, DC

Shiva V (2000) Tomorrow's biodiversity. Thames and Hudson, London

Singer P (1975) Animal liberation. Avon Books, New York

Taylor PW (1986) Respect for nature: a theory of environmental ethics. Princeton University Press, Princeton, NJ

Turner AR (1993) Inventing Leonardo. Knopf, New York

Wood D (1999) Comment ne pas manger—Deconstruction and Humanism. In: Steves (ed) Animal others: on ethics, ontology and animal life. State University of New York Press, Albany

AI & Soc
DOI 10.1007/s00146-007-0097-2

ORIGINAL ARTICLE

Poetics of performative space

Sha Xin Wei

Received: 11 July 2006 / Accepted: 5 February 2007
© Springer-Verlag London Limited 2007

Abstract The TGarden is a genre of responsive environment in which actor–spectators shape dense media sensitive to their movements. These dense fields of light, sound, and material also evolve according to their own composed dynamics, so the agency is distributed throughout the multiple media. These TGardens explore open-ended questions like the following: what makes some time-based, responsive environments compelling, and others flat? How can people improvise gestures without words, that are individually or collectively meaningful? When and how is a movement intentional, or collectively intentional? This paper introduces what has been at stake behind the experimental work: subjectivation, moving from technologies of representation to technologies of performance, and the potential for ethico-aesthetic novelty.

Introduction

TGarden is a branching family of responsive playspace events and installations, with curious cousins and descendants:

X. W. Sha (✉)
Canada Research Chair, Media Arts and Sciences,
Computer Science and Fine Arts,
Concordia University, 1515 Ste-Catherine West,
Montréal, QC H3G 2W1, Canada
e-mail: xinwei@sponge.org

 Springer

{tgarden0, tgarden1, tgarden2,

{ {txoom1, txoom2,

{tgvu1, tgvu2, tgvu3, {tmtl1, ...} }

txoom3, ... },

{ trg1, trg2, ...}

}

}

What I discuss in this essay, however, are not particular playspace installations and events like tg2001, txOom or trg, that have been exhibited in North America and Europe, over the past 5 years, but some of the passionate critiques and questions motivating the TGarden, and the desired qualities of experimental experience that make some of the background and potential for such playspaces still so compelling with respect to that pre-history. Given all the heart, craft, knowledge, and energy that have been poured into making and presenting these installation-events, it is natural to ask what is at stake? Why should we, creators and participant players, care about making these playspaces? I hope this essay will encourage some of you to, as Maja Kuzmanovic put it, grow your own worlds weedily and wildly (Sha and Kuzmanovic 2002).

My interest in these responsive media spaces stems from two intertwined conversations. The first is a series of conversations about agency, language, and hybrid ontology, going back to a seminar on interaction and media (IMG) with Niklas Damiris, Helga Wild, Ben Robinson, Ann Weinstone, Alice Rayner, and other humanist scholars affiliated to Stanford University in California. For 3 years, 1995–1997, we met every week, reading gem essays smuggled out from the heart of their disciplines, recasting what insights and arguments we found into ways to articulate and maybe work with the hybrid computational/physical "interactive" media that we saw emerging around us. But we put every label and concept like "interactive" and "media," in play, and later from farther afield, "map," "system," "language," "expression," and "human" as well. I was engaged with the boundaries of language, especially with how we fleshy, mortal people could use non-linguistic writing and sketching to trace infinities like complete Riemannian manifolds, the profoundly immeasurable non-self, and the role and the power of the imaginary in our infinitely thick and dense world.

The second conversation is a specific set of challenges by two practitioners of experimental theater, Laura Farabough and Chris Salter. They came with 25 and 5 years, respectively, of experimental performance and contemporary theater, and challenged us with examples of avant-garde theatrical practice after Bertolt Brecht: guerilla theater like Farabough's Beggar's Theater and NightFire in San Francisco, Egypt, and Mexico, and the bloody and complex works of Heiner Müller, William

Forsythe, and Pina Bausch, in whose company they learned their craft. They challenged me to make palpable the ideas we were forging from what Ann Weinstone called the wild academy, to make events in which we and our participants could encounter and experiment bodily with these radicalized articulations of agency, self, desire, and action that we were so delightedly cooking up in the IMG.

This was a heady and daunting challenge, but nothing that a few tens of millions of dollars and a few dozen fearless artists and engineers could not do in 10 years. We lacked the time, the capital, and the discipline. But we did find some fearless artists. So we grew our own network of artists, from the art groups Sponge that we established in 1997 in San Francisco, and from FoAM, that Maja Kuzmanovic established with Nik Gaffney and Lina Kusaite in 2000 in Brussels.

Starting questions

Most critically, how can we make events that are as compelling for the people who encounter them as the theater by Brecht, Müller, Bausch, Sankai Juku, and Dumb Type were in their day and for their audiences? In a sense, this is a technical challenge or in other words, it is a challenge to the practice and craft of experimental performance (To what Brook (1968) called Holy Theater, as opposed to Dead Theater of typical rote and commercial performance, and different from the Rough Theater of the street and Commedia dell'Arte.) One of the questions I refined from this very broad challenge was: how can we make a responsive space and event within which initially accidental, unmarked, unrehearsed, ordinary gestures could acquire great symbolic charge? These questions were practical questions of craft, and could only be answered or explored materially, bodily, in physically built spaces and peopled events. However, the way in which we explored them was not by producing commercial shows, but by doing performance research. We made installation-events that straddled the border between closed shop studio improvisation-experiments with special audiences, and open performances with a public. As it turns out, these questions, though they were forged in a precise context of experimental performance research, resonate far outside the world of digital media art and performance. They are informed by dance, movement, textiles, fabric, musical performance, and visual art, but they also are impelled by a desire to embed such work into public space and everyday space. This is part of the ethico-aesthetic adventure of the work that appeals so much to me.

Now the same questions about the event also have a radical, micro-textural inflection. Could technologies like computational media, realtime sound and video (re-) synthesis, cheap hobbyist sensors, and the like, be added to the mise en scene of theater as Artaud (1938) dreamed to extend the theater of cruelty in a way that is relevant to us today? This theater of cruelty would create a theater that would not drop out of our consciousness as soon as we have finished consuming it but would transform those who encounter it as utterly as the plague. By cruelty, Artaud explicitly did not intend the meanness of human hurting human or animal, but the implacability and indifference of matter with respect to our human ego. Stone resists, and a tree greens, and software breaks regardless of what we say. If we desire matter to perform differently, we cannot simply legislate or script it by brandishing a pen alone, we must also manufacture a symbolic material substrate that behaves differently from ordinary matter.

Spiraling concepts

The rest of this essay will spiral up through a set of concepts: the basic kind of events that I am considering, a discussion about "representation," a question of performance, then the technologies of performance, then concepts embedded in those technologies, and finally a return of sorts to a transformed notion of event and representation (language).

Some people say that ideas are cheap, that making is hard. But we know very well that humans create and rework concepts with just as much effort and rigor and material discipline as the making of a physical installation. It is just that the young domain of media arts and sciences has not enjoyed the luxury of alloying and hammering out concepts as thoroughly as, say biotechnology or history of Renaissance Italian literature. Domains of practice that benefit from billions of dollars or centuries of investment can elaborate practices that exploit the making and composition of concepts based on antecedent literatures, intricate dependencies, and interrelationships of publication and citation, the social networks that give meaning to concepts, and procedures of evidence and argument, and generative logics indigenous to the epistemic culture.[1]

Events

The kind of events I am talking about, the kind I am interested in making are collective, co-present, embodied, and a-linguistic. These are situations to which people are invited to be physically together, face-to-face, in short, co-present. This is a basic condition of theater, too, and distinguishes theater from, for example, cinema or photography, in that the performer–actor–artist is in the same physical place as the spectator–visitor, so that the spectator can get up and physically lay a hand on the actor to interfere with the action if she or he wants to. This potential for physical contact is a condition for the collective embodied experiences needed to conduct experimental phenomenology, I believe. By design, these situations are collective, with three or more participants, three to destabilize dyadic pairing, with an eye to lowering the threshold for the improvisation of being in that space. I say embodied to mark that the fleshy bodies of the participants essentially move and act together in the co-construction of the event. The line between actor and spectator is

---

[1] I find it helpful to think in terms of inequality rather than equality or definition: concept ≠ representation ≠ abstraction ≠ concept. Also, theory ≠ philosophy ≠ model ≠ procedure (problem solving) ≠ poetry rhetoric theory. I would shy away from abstraction, model, sophist rhetoric, and art "theory's" word salad, but affirm that we need philosophy, poetry, and concepts if we want a life worth living. See Deleuze and Guattari (1994), What is Philosophy?

dissolved, so anybody may adopt the disposition of an actor as an agent of change in the event, or equally a spectator as a witness of the event.

The ambient environment will be thick with media, filled with thick sound, thick video, dense physical materials, so that people will live in a dense matter that responds and evolves in the course of their activity. All of this activity can be conducted a-linguistically, without the necessity for spoken language. On the other hand, speech is not prohibited; it is just dethroned with respect to the other modalities of co-ordination among the bodies and media in the space, again as way to estrange the speaking subject, and render more prominent the material dynamics of the lifeworld on the other side of the veil of the technologies of language.

By thickness, I refer not only to perceptual thickness—density of video and sound textures, but also to the rich magma of social, imaginative and erotic fields within which people play even in ordinary situations, situations in which we perform without first analyzing, and cutting up our experiences into analytic layers: how did I smile? How did I rest my feet on the floor? Did my voice carry or resonate well? Did I stand too close or too far from other people? Did I interrupt or listen or talk over or under other speakers? Is the light too bright? I borrow the term from Geertz's (1975) notion of a sociological/anthropological responsibility to study culture in all of its rich social patterns and dynamics without orthogonalizing it a priori into categories that we would bring to bear on that culture. So this experience should be designed in a pre-orthogonalized way by the designers, and enjoyed by the participants without requiring that they make any cognitive model of their world in order to perform in it. Why? Engineering's power derives from the portability and extensibility of standardized schemas and methods that apply globally over phenomena and life. Our engineered systems are already built on taxonomies that must be navigated by grammars and operated according to rules that discipline our thought and action—the action of power to discipline humans into docile bodies has radically evolved under the impact not only of the information technology but the epistemic matrix that encases our imaginary, for example. These taxonomies rest on fundamentalist distinctions such as signal versus noise, functional versus aesthetic, and syntactical versus non-syntactical (in relation to grammar). It is not enough to side with noise as the opposite of signal, however, or idleness (the vacation) as the opposite of wage-slavery because that still leaves in force the distinction made by the relevant schema in power.

[Representations of] lifeworld

Perhaps the principal (and only?) loci at which power grips us and with which we grip the world are the patterns and forms of the world. These regularized and normalized systematized patterns are what we call **representations**. And our most highly developed form of representation is language, which since de Saussure's (1907) semiotics has been axiomatically susceptible to regularization (and subsequent normalization) by linguistics. It is language to which most of us have been disciplined since childhood, thanks to the modern democratic impulse. That this generative power can turn to the benefit of non-elite agents is recognized as a threat by the counter-democratic forces that are dismantling the systems of public and higher education in the western nations.

It is for this reason that so much critical energy (Plato, Kant, Foucault, Deleuze, Derrida, Haraway, and so many others), has concentrated on the power of representation to constrain us to think and act in the world in certain ways but not others. I use "power" mindful of Foucault's studies of the genealogy of "madness," the "prisoner," and "sexuality" that put those categories back into play in the contingent currents of history. What is at stake is whether we can create conditions for events in which power is put in play, and its categorical fingers can be unclamped, if only provisionally from their grip upon our bodies. Power, as Foucault reminds us, is not always signed with the mark of evil (or good for that matter), it is the generative force, "the force that through the green fuse drives the flower" (to borrow from Dylan Thomas) as well as the blasting cap. To put power in play also means to unclamp the hands and collectivities that wield it against life. And if representation is the grit and grip of power, then one core way to put power into play would be to test the limits of language.

Now, mistrusting, examining, and interrogating the limits of language in fact has been one of Modernism's central concerns (Note: one modern root would be Saussure's canonical Course in General Linguistics, but of course we find antecedents in Leibniz's search for a language of mathesis universalis, and Athanasius Kircher's (1669) cabalistic formal languages.), so we are walking a path well-trodden by many, which should assure us that this concern is not peripheral or hermetic, but vital to people whenever they wonder how life is worth living.

When Wittgenstein (1922) wrote at the end of the Tractatus Logico Philosophicus, "Wovon man nicht sprechen kann, darüber muß man schweigen," (Whereof one cannot speak, thereof one must be silent), he was acknowledging the limits of what could be expressed by propositional language, of the machinery of statements with truth value that could be built with logic into the vast edifice of knowledge that could be articulated in statements like: "Creon, ruler of Thebes, forbids on pain of death anyone to bury Polyneices, who was a traitor to Thebes. Antigone has covered her brother Polyneices' corpse. Therefore Antigone's life is forfeit." or "When the appropriate conditions are satisfied, power must be exercised. Iraq has been tyrannized by a dictator. My nation is founded on principles of self-determination and autonomy. Given the pre-eminent power of my nation, it follows that, in the name of freedom, it is imperative that my nation liberate Iraq from its dictatorship."—complexes of statements that are supposed to have the same epistemic weight as: "Suppose there are only a finite number of prime integers, $p_1 < p_2 < \cdots < p_n$, where p_n is the largest prime. Then consider the integer $Z = 1 + p_1 \times p_2 \times \cdots \times p_n$, 1 added to the presumably enormous but finite product of all the prime integers. Z is not divisible by any of the primes, $p_1, \ldots, p_n$, yet Z is bigger than p_n. But it is a prime bigger than p_n, which contradicts the assumption that p_n was the largest prime integer. Therefore, there cannot be a largest prime integer, i.e., therefore, there are an infinite number of prime integers."

It would be disingenuous of me to dismiss the tremendous constructive power of propositional knowledge. Propositional knowledge is in fact part of the social/legal/economic infrastructure that makes it possible for me to walk out of this door and down the street to buy a copy of the Economist or Libération. It is part of the technoscientific apparatus that allows me to type this essay without thinking about the galaxy of electronic and logical procedures that are being performed to stabilize and transmit my words to you. My purpose is not to diminish the scope and depth of propositional knowledge, which in effect is all we can state about ourselves and our experience, but to play at the limits of propositional language, of language, of sign in general, in fact at the meeting place of sign and matter, which is the symbolic.[2] That is what led me to consider creating playspaces of responsive media saturated with symbolic potential in distributions of desiring matter. That is why I thought of the TGarden and its precursor installation-events as phenomenological experiments.

Wittgenstein, who like A. N. Whitehead cut his teeth on logic and the foundations of mathematics, so he knew profoundly what he was talking about, also wrote in the Tractatus: "*[Die] Ethik nicht aussprechen lasst. (Die Ethik und Ästhetik sind Eins.)*" Ethics cannot be expressed. (Ethics and aesthetics are one.) (1922, point 6) With this, Wittgenstein expressed several deep insights with characteristic compactness. Even given the rich and ever more complex web of knowledge that can be expressed in propositional language, such as law and morality—social norms—and computer science, matters of ethics and aesthetics cannot be expressed in propositional language because such language cannot express value. Recognizing this, Wittgenstein (1958) closed his project on the logical foundation of knowledge, and wrote the Philosophical Investigations, surgically deflating the illusions of the conventional theories of meaning one-by-one until we are left standing at the door to the only source of meaning, which is life, practice, the lifeworld. Meaning, Wittgenstein observed, cannot come from any set of rules, from correspondence to the world, or from appeal to transcendental objects. (That last observation is pretty obvious after Descartes and Kant.) Meaning comes from contingent use, meaning comes from practice in life. But the lifeworld is external to the span of what language can contain in itself.

Derrida (1976, p. 158) wrote, in Of Grammatology: "*Il n'y a pas de hors-texte*" (There is no outside-text), meaning not that the world is entirely contained inside the semiotic, but that we cannot ground language's meaning by having it represent faithfully something in a transcendental or exterior world. Context determining the meaning of a text can only be expressed in language itself, so it would be delusional to attempt to ground meaning by believing language homologously represents or faithfully points to some ultimate reality, whether that be the Bible, genes, memes, or bits.

So, after Wittgenstein and Derrida, it would be quixotic to try to simplify our lifeworld by reducing how we make meaning and symbolic charge to one thin layer of the world or another, so let us skip by the monuments of cognitivism, and move into the lifeworld, the other to language.

---

[2] I thank Patrice Maniglier for teaching me this concept of the symbol.

Reality and the imaginary

What can we do in the lifeworld, then? And what would it take to unmoor power-that-controls and put it in ethico-aesthetic play?

One of the basic distinctions we have to address here is the issue of Reality. There is much talk about reality as if it were something pure that we could contaminate, and therefore save. But even if corporate and state power require the conceit that reality is pure and must be protected by opposing it to the virtual, we do not. As Baudrillard (1994) observed in Simulation and Simulacra, it is exactly at the moment that our symbolic machines have become so powerful as to threaten to destabilize capitalistic power that power tries to distinguish reality from virtuality, and re-inscribe reality so ferociously. Why? The virtual is that which is not actual, but could be, and understood this way is identical to the potential, a mortal threat to the power that would control. In fact, reality, as Latour (1993) so thoroughly and persuasively argued in "We Have Never Been Modern", is always and everywhere radically, inextricably mixed with society and nature, word and thing, symbol and substance. In fact, it is useful to think of reality as everything that is not logically self-contradictory, like a four-sided triangle, and include the virtual as part of this reality.

So, Reality = Potential + Actual. The actual is what is in the here and now, what is the case, whether as configurations of physical matter, or as symbolic patterns like law, business, or systems of value like emotional relations, fashion, and aesthetic tastes. The potential is what is not the case, but could be, and the imaginary is the collective or individual envisioning of that which is not the case, and of transforming the potential into the actual. So, reality is always already mixed. The challenge is not to define, brand, or package mixed reality, but to mix reality, just as the deepest challenge is not to define the human, or the citizen or the psychological or cognitive subject (as AI aspires to do), but to human (adapting from Ann Weinstone[3]).

Therefore, what I will do is not just putter around synchronic representations of mixed reality which can be much more than written language, of course, including any map, diagram, schema or any sign system whatsoever, but bracket the operation of [Representation of], and move to the arena of improvising, performing, practicing in symbolic, desiring, embodying matter. What in the world could that possibly be like? How can we work not instrumentally but poetically with such material magmas and stay clear of formalizing, disembodying, and dessicating reductions to the informatic or cognitivist abstractions of the lifeworld?

Felix Guattari's decades of work with schizophrenics in his clinic La Borde, while deeply informed by the tradition of psychoanalysis of Freud and Lacan, parted from psychoanalysis in a most radical way. Guattari left behind psychoanalysis' aspiration to be scientific, to discover the truth about the subject's world, and recognized instead that all forms of expression are actually also simultaneously forms of content, that every one of us co-creates the world and co-adapts to the world. Guattari (1995) recognized that the schizophrenic is as much a co-structuring

---

[3] Anne Weinstone, essay, personal communication (Stanford 1995).

agent as the doctors and nurses who ostensibly run the clinic. One of the most illuminating examples in Chaosmosis tells about families who come as a group to sessions in which actors introduce extra characters in filmed events. The participants must revise, improvise, enact, and re-enact their relations for each other and for later viewers. There are vocal and manual gestures or movements whose meanings are not pre-defined or evident but arise organically from exfoliating in the world in a signifying process that Guattari (and Deleuze) called pathic subjectivation. The subjects later reviewed these events, and narrated to themselves what they saw themselves doing. This is radically different from the subjectification imposed according to schema by an analyst who announces to his patient: "By the power invested in me from my training as an analyzed Analyst and interpreter of the DSM-IV (2000), the standard reference of psychiatric disorders, I declare, 'You are schizophrenic.'" It is one of Guattari's clearest examples of ethico-aesthetic play in the magma of a-signifying semiologies, and of improvisation over rehearsal and experience sedimented over the lifetime and (acknowledging Lacan) beyond the lifetime of the ego. This is not theatrical role-playing, nor everyday activity observed in the wild behind a screen, nor purified laboratory interrogation. There are no blueprints or recipes for any of this kind of playful, rigorous work, and in fact it would be a terrible betrayal to make a method out of this.

Much of this articulation has come to me only after many years of working dumbly, so to speak, so I have enjoyed the pleasure of traces of recognition in these writers who wrote incandescently out of the crucible of their own experiences. Guattari and Artaud resonate well with how I have tried, in very preliminary and partial ways, working with autonomous people and the means at hand, to nurse art research in a studio-lab I established, called the Topological Media Lab (TML).[4]

Responsive media research at the Topological Media Lab

Given these concerns, as I have described them, what is interesting is not so much a matter of taxonomy, and schemas and classifications or standards and protocols, although those are necessarily part of the robust construction and operation of our playspaces, but the dynamics of processes that stir, up, shape, and unshape the material patterns that constitute the lifeworld. The early exercises, studies, and installation-events by Sponge[5] dealt with particular questions, in performance research, such as the following: How to make events that were experientially as powerful as works of avant-garde theater but without resorting to verbal/written language, erasing the distinction between actor and spectator, and relying on thick, physical/computational ambient media. TGarden:TG2001 as built by FoAM[6] and Sponge was an installation-event that marked a transition and a bifurcation from performance research into a strand of public installation-events and a strand of studio-laboratory research in the TML. I started this atelier-studio-laboratory after

---

[4] Topological Media Lab, http://topologicalmedialab.net.

[5] Sponge, http://sponge.org.

[6] FoAM, http://f0.am.

leaving Stanford for Georgia Tech in 2001 to take stock of, and strategically extend some of the technologies of performance according to a particular set of ethico-aesthetic heuristics inspired by continuity, human performance (e.g., the violin), human play (e.g., in water and sand), and non-electronic matter like clay, smoke, or rain. I wanted to make responsive media synthesis engines and gestural instruments, and choreography systems that would allow participants to experimentally co-structure, not interact (!), with co-evolving ambient life in the "real-time" of perceptually concurrent action and the specious present.[7] The media engines and instruments that we have developed fall naturally into the areas of calligraphic video, gestural sound, softwear (active materials made of fabric and other soft woven or non-woven matter), and audio-visual instruments (such as DMX-controlled theatrical instruments).

Media choreography

Media Choreography names how, in the approach taken by the TML, the creators of a playspace put all the media together using continuous dynamics and quasi-physics, rather than rules, databases, and procedural logic. This is both an aesthetic and an operational heuristic. Media choreography is a way to relate the synthesis of all the different streams of media in concert with the activities of the people in the common playspace, such that the behaviors (to use an overly anthropocentric term) of the media and the people co-structure one another, and evolve over time according to pre-arranged strategies and latent predilections, contingent activity, and memory of past activity. I appealed to continuous dynamical systems on several grounds:

1. People's experience of the world is continuous.
2. People have sedimented a huge amount of experience with the physical world, so we should leverage it by using quasi-physics models.
3. I wished to see how we could move away from the Judeo–Christian technology of ego-centrism and anthropocentrism.

A most important common feature of the media choreography of this family of playspaces, from tg2001 (TGarden) to trg, including Time's Up's A Balanced Act, is that the creators specified not a fixed, discrete set or sequence of media triggered by discrete visitor/player actions, but rather a potential range—a field—of possible responses to continuous ranges of player actions. But in this family, behavioral tempers, or to use less animistic terms, climates of response evolve over macro-scopic periods of time (minutes), according to the history of continuous player activity.

A subtle difference between an information theoretic approach to scripting the behavior of a system and the TGarden's quasi-physical approach is that the latter bets on a radically modest approach to computational media as dumb matter. By dumb I mean (1) free of language, even the formal procedural programming

---

[7] Regarding the specious present, see James' (1890, p. 573) principles of psychology; see discussion in Meyer's (2001) irresistible dictation.

languages that are operationalizations of the logic that I relinquished early in this essay; (2) free of intelligence, the cognitivist approaches of symbolic artificial intelligence; and also (3) free of representations of abstract structures like hidden Markov statistical models or 3D polyhedral geometry.

One particular research strategy I am exploring in the TML is to use continuous dynamics to sustain superposition of contingent and composed potential behavior, and expose these intertwined dynamic processes to the players not through words or discrete tokens, props, or characters, but via the richest available temporal textures of sound and visual imagery. The research heuristic is that this way we can leverage people's bodily intuition by having them play in the media, rather than look at representations of some squiggly shapes projected at some remove from their own flesh. (Representation would rear its head.) To let people play immersed in media, we could have them step into a warm pool of water laced with honey, so why use computational media? Computing the quasi-physics allows the creators to inject a physics that changes according to activity and local history, and respond in ways that resemble but are eerily unlike any ordinary matter. This is analogous to the alienation effect of theater but not at the level of whole bodies: characters, actors, spectators, plot. Instead, what continuous, dense, topological dynamical systems afford is a micro-fine alienation effect at the level of substrate media such as calligraphic video, gestural sound, and kinetic fabrics imbued with uncanny physics.

A word on method, design heuristic

Indeed it would take a lot of work to build up to macroscopic objects and actions from relatively homogeneous textures and simple dynamics. But I would say that it is not "hard" (the adjective used by Tim Boykett in Riga[8]), but strange and un-idiomatic for all of us who have been trained to the aesthetics and logic of whole bodies and macroscopic human-scale objects like words, props, characters, and conventional game action. After all, to render a character in a novel or play from the raw material of alphabetic text and grammar, takes an enormous amount of hard-earned psycho-social knowledge, literary apparatus, and wordcraft.

However, this apparent inefficiency is in fact endemic not only to "bottom-up" simulations but to all simulations and simulacra. As Maturana and Varela (1980) pointed out, to be as dense as life, a simulation of an autopoietic system can never operate any faster than that autopoietic system, and can at best run at the speed of life—so much for the cybernetic fantasy of mastering and replacing the lifeworld by a transcendental, superior simulation of life.

One significant difference between trg and the earlier TGarden, txOom, and tgvu experiments, is that in TGarden and tgvu, the metaphorical behavioral state topology is independent of media state topology, whereas in trg, what the player sees is identical to the behavioral topology. TGarden's state engine evolves through a rather sparse topological landscape with few valleys and peaks, whereas the visual

---

[8] Tim Boykett, talk, Space and Perception, International Symposium on Mixed Reality, RIXC Media Space, May 20–21, 2005, Riga, Latvia, http://rixc.lv/sp/en.html.

and sound fields are synthesized as densely and temporally finely as possible and as necessary to sustain a rich experience, with micro-dynamics of response that we do not attempt to trace using the state engine.

The reason for decoupling the dynamical metaphorical state engine from the media engines was in fact to decouple the evolution of the behavioral response "climate" from the dynamics of the visual and sonic textures, which has to be as rich and tangibly responsive to the players' actions as possible. It seems artistically and compositionally useful to keep these dynamics decoupled from one another.

My concern at least in the context of this essay is precisely with what possibilities a micro-phenomenology, free of ego and anthropocentrism and indeed of any fixed, a priori objects, can offer toward fresh and refreshing improvised play. Aesthetically, at least for TGarden, this play should take place immanently in as dense an ambient medium as that of ordinary life. So the best approach would be to start with ordinary matter and real fleshy people in common space, and judiciously augment the everyday matter with just enough computational matter to give the event a strange and marvelous cast. This approach, which I nickname "minimax" design: maximum experiential impact for minimum computational technology, resonates with the poor theater's choice of a minimalist technology of mise en scene relative to cinema, a minimalism which in fact is constitutive of its magic.[9]

As for theoretical approach, my long term interest in the TGarden and its sibling responsive playspaces extends beyond the actual events themselves to the mixing of ideas and conflicting ideological commitments from different epistemic cultures. I would not take the space here to pursue this sociologically or anthropologically, but it would be liberating to practice our arts and sciences in a more reflexive way.[10]

The week after the 'Space and Perception' conference at RIXC in Riga, I participated in a symposium focused on Deleuze, Whitehead and the Transformations of Metaphysics (Note: with Isabelle Stengers, James Williams, Mick Halewood, Steven Meyer, and about 20 other philosophers, Proceedings of the Royal Flemish Academy.) There I realized how to articulate that one could use mathematics as poetry rather than as instrument or measure, or a replacement for God, or an intellectual battering ram. (I must confess, however, to deriving some pleasure from reading Badiou's (2004) fearless and fierce polemic about mathematics = ontology.) I agree with Badiou that mathematics is substance, and not merely a description of substance. Shaping mathematics as poietic material in fact differs in kind from using mathematics to describe the universe as physicists see it. Part of trg's charm is its attempt to make palpable a concept of the world (recent quantum field theoretic cosmology) by forcibly identifying it with the perceptual field—a cosmic ambition. The artists could only begin to approximate this by restricting trg to a very compact physical duration and place in Kibla, and by making allegorical simulations in software. Allegory makes the world of difference between depiction and enaction, perception and phenomenology.

---

[9] See Grotowski's (1968) towards a poor theater.

[10] Stengers (2003a, b) has retold the stories of seven scientific disciplines in a way that presents the partial and provisional messiness of science as it is actually practiced. Telling science in this way has both cosmological and political implications, hence the title of her books: Cosmopolitiques.

As for experimental phenomenology, I am trying to discover and mix together mathematics as materials that are adequate to life. It could be sharply different sorts of poetic matter: continuous topological dynamics, geometric measure theory, or even fancier stuff like non-commutative algebra and etale cohomology. But I choose to start with the simplest symbolic substances that respect the lifeworld's continuous dynamism, change, temporality, infinite transformation, morphogenesis, superposability, continuity, density, and value, and is free of or at least agnostic with respect to measure, metric, counting, finitude, formal logic, linguistics (syntax, grammar), digitality, and computability, in short of all formal structures that would put a cage over all of the lifeworld. I call these substances *topological media*. Simplicity here is not a requirement of the theory (no Occam's razor here) but merely an acknowledgement that I do not understand enough about the lifeworld to bring out fancier stuff yet, of which there is so much more up the wizard sleeves.

The fundamental difference in this approach is to use mathematics as substance in a workmanlike way, patching here and there to see what values ensue, as a trellis for play, rather than a carapace, but always sensitive to whether the poetic material accommodates transfinite, incommensurable, immanent passion. Totalizing carapaces like Wolfram's computational equivalence principle, which at bottom is a transcendental atomic metaphysics founded on making counting sacred, would hammer us into a very sparse ontology. And to a hammer everything is a nail.

What's at stake?

I approached the branching family of playspaces represented by TGarden, txOom, tgvu, and trg as phenomenological experiments of a certain kind, as events based on gesture and movement, rather than language, for people face-to-face in a common place, playing and improvising meaningful micro-relations without language, in thick responsive media. I see these as opportunities for ethico-aesthetic play, to borrow and adapt Guattari's concept of the coming into formation of subjectivity, to engage in biopolitics, radically dispersed into tissue and molecular strata, and reaching far beyond the computational media arts, meeting with experimental impulses in dance, movement, textiles, musical performance, experimental theater, but also the most speculative initiatives in urban design, science studies, and philosophy. But the ambition here is to conduct even the most philosophical speculation by articulating matter in poetic motion, whose aesthetic meaning and symbolic power are felt as much as perceived.[11] I shift the emphasis from spaces of representation to spaces of experience, hence the TML's emphasis on technologies of performance, and on live event.

If we grant ourselves the power and opportunity to experiment with the world at all scales, in all strata, and relinquishing all schemas for an object-oriented ontology, to what extent can the blackboxed modes of work, operation, representation themselves be continuous and transformable sans metric, i.e., topological?

---

[11] See Gendlin (1997) on felt meaning.

Art all the way down?

If art puts the world in play, puts questions in motion via human and material experience, then art practice could be a mode of material and speculative philosophy. But working in a plenist, unbifurcated world (working with White-head's concept of nature recovered whole from the many dualist knives of modernism and postmodernism), I wonder to what extent we can truly suspend, float, and dissolve all distinctions that fracture our being in the world, including the distinction between art and craft. Under capitalism, modern art practice is well served by a distinction between the artist and the executant, the director and the designer, art and craft, theory and practice, and in exchange much commodity art pretends to nothing more than a clever permutation or anamorphic mirror of the actual. But art all the way down could put all relations in play, which implies that how it is produced is as important as what is produced. Therefore it must risk dissolving those distinctions of modern art. FoAM is a good example of an a-modern art organization that tries to work this way with limited access to knowledge and financial capital. However, with the rising star of engineering buoyed by a particularly crude version of pragmatism, there has been of course the counter-cultural revolution aimed to turn the tables on high art, but very often this threatens to merely flip the duality upside down, and manacle art to the categories and norms of engineering and design.[12] Given that one of engineering's norms is modularity, I ask, can we alchemically open and critically transform all these blackboxes: "interaction," "program," "information," "bit," "sensor," "cpu," "linguistics," "market," "design," "industry," "body," "ego," "citizen," "machine," and, "human."...? Art all the way down means there is no layer below which the socio-technical magma becomes mere machine and craft, the level of the technician who executes the artist's desire. But on the other hand, this means also that we do not reduce conceptual rigor and passionate dreams to a willfully dematerialized, a-historical, anti-intellectual naiveté. It means, for example, that to explore the erotics of the formation and dissolution of object from field has consequences not only at the level of co-present bodies but also at the level of programming language, drawing model, and graphics and dynamics engines.

Can the material process of making things collectively be radically non-denumerable, countless, non-computable, non-dimensional, infinite, and yet remain also immanent, embodied and continuous? Can we make playspaces that evoke not puzzle-solving behavior, but ethico-aesthetic-erotic play, and marvel, or vertigo, or elation? To respect the open, unbounded lifeworld, such a space should not be useful or therapeutic. In fact, that was Guattari's point about psychoanalysis, too. The point would not be to help the participant construct a narrative analogous to the hermeneutic objective of classical psychoanalysis—"This is what the patient's

---

[12] There is a profound difference between discrete approximations to continuous things and things that are discrete from the get go. One example is the definition of flow by mean curvature, a project that Brakke (1978) tried to carry out but could not complete due to deep technical lacunae that could not be patched until Ilmanen's (1994) work 20 years later. Elevating the discrete and the computable to universality, via for example Wolfram's principle of computational equivalence or Newell and Simon's (1976) symbol processing hypothesis excludes more life than it includes.

phobias/psychoses/dreams mean," nor to effect a cure—therapy's arrogant stance with respect to its patient: "You are sick. We will fix you." In a playspace, a participant would not read, interpret or recount a dream—a participant would *be* a dream.

Why not just enclose a volume of ordinary space and repeat some experiments like the action art of 40 years ago? With our techniques, a playspace could be charged with latent magic, a heightened potential for charging gestures with symbolic power. A playspace could become a theater for the alchemical transformation of hybrid matter, but not a space for cognitive games, inducing puzzle-solving behavior, nor a bath of raw qualia. An alchemical theater would avoid having "users" and "system" building models of each other. (In the human, such models would be cognitive models.)

Our typical model of interaction has been of humans and their proxies engaging in an action-reaction ping-pong. And interaction design, even in its most enlightened mood has been centered on the human (viz. human-centered design), as if we knew what a human was, and where a human being ends and the rest of the world begins.

Since the beginning of the Enlightenment, the automaton has fascinated those members of our species who cannot themselves bear children. One of the most celebrated such automata was the Turk, a chess playing machine unveiled by Wolfgang von Kempelen in 1770, and toured through the courts of Europe (Standage 2002). In fact, this chess playing automaton turned out to be powered by a human dwarf hidden inside the box. This piece of automata history is in fact emblematic of the genealogy of the concept of the software agent as a homunculus, from the ENIAC to the fictive Hal 9000 in "2001," to the agents of Sim City and the customer call center program that can interpret telephonic speech as well as John Searle's Chinese Box.

But this anthropocentrism is not confined to engineering, of course. Look at Viola's (2003) beautiful series of video works, The Passions. If we really take seriously the challenge to pursue art all the way down, and if we are willing to put in play, in suspension, all the putative atoms, objects, and subjects of the world, then I ask you this question: to whom do you owe allegiance: Homo Sapiens Rex, or the world?

Apart from the totalizing and dematerializing power of the Judeo–Christian God, and of informatic and logico-linguistic schemas, essentially the only ethico-aesthetic choice in the West is to start with the self, with Homo Sapiens. We witness the disastrous global ecological and economic consequences of this choice. However, given topology as a way, even a rigorous and precise way, to articulate living, non-denumerable, dense, non-dimensional, open, infinite, and continuous matter, one has the option of choosing the world instead. I use these adjectives precisely for their interwined technical and poetic values. But this is not going to be a cure-all, a recipe for success. It is an approach to design, a way to think about living in the world, how to shape experience, a disposition with respect to the world, rather than a methodology or a technology.[13]

---

[13] This will be the subject of a book on the genealogy of topological media. For a spirited and beautifully motivated introduction to the mathematical study of proto-metric substance, see Jänich's (1984) Topology.

Enactment and enchantment in living matter

Thomas (1934) wrote:

The force that through the green fuse drives the flower
Drives my green age; that blasts the roots of trees
Is my destroyer.
And I am dumb to tell the crooked rose
My youth is bent by the same wintry fever.

The force that drives the water through the rocks
Drives my red blood; that dries the mouthing streams
Turns mine to wax.
And I am dumb to mouth unto my veins
How at the mountain spring the same mouth sucks.

The hand that whirls the water in the pool
Stirs the quicksand; that ropes the blowing wind
Hauls my shroud sail.
And I am dumb to tell the hanging man
How of my clay is made the hangman's lime...

Allow me to suggest a reverse-allegory and use a piece of the world to stand in for some concepts. This is a patch of sod that I cut out of the earth under a tree outside the RIXC building. Representations, words, are like the blades of grass, individually well formed, discrete. I can pull up this piece of sod and turn it over to reveal the root structure underneath. Yes, there is a network of roots as we can plainly feel running our fingers through the dirt. However, I draw attention past the blades of grass and their contingently formed roots to the dirt and the moisture in between the roots. It is the continuous, nourishing, dark, loamy stuff in between the discrete structures that materially constitutes the Earth. This moist earth is always and everywhere in continuous transformation. Our discrete structures, our words, syntax, grammars and schemas and methodologies are the blades and at best the roots. And yes, they are our best ways to grip the earth. But though they are a common supra-individual resource, they are not transcendental. They can only take form in and draw meaning from the earth, and become earth when their life cycle is finished.

Archimedes said, "Give me a place to stand, and I shall move the World." But what if there is no place to stand inside a bubbling chaosmotic soup of infinite inflation? To what extent can we alchemically open and critically transform all of modernity's blackboxes such as market, machine, or human if we do not have a place to stand in this age of globalized empire and permanent war?[14] Is there any possibility for an immanent resistance for us not as non-docile bodies, but as

---

[14] See Hardt and Negri (2000), empire and Multitude (2004).

 Springer

resistive and desiring flesh? Yes, I believe, yes, if we take reality already as an amalgam of the potential and the actual, dematerializing, for example by becoming fictive, and rematerializing under the incessant quickening action of our imagination. This affords openings for life in the mud-filled interstices of our technology.

A most immanent mode of resistance and weedy generation in those muddy interstices of our technologies of representation is play. Play could be the make-belief, the as if, making fictive, becoming other than what is the case, the art that drives the green fuse all the way down and up again. But in recent years, play has been harried by many who would classify it, barely escaping the nets of those taxidermists who would like to stuff play into the carcass of game. What our playspaces could offer us are not allegories of other worlds, whether cosmological, or political, or religious, or psycho-fictive, but events affording playful processes that open life up to more life. Let me close by suggesting a few senses of play that may merit more careful consideration. There's the play of water lapping against the side of the boat, making the lazy slapping sound that evokes sunlight and fish in the clear water just beyond the reach of your fingers. There's the play, the empty space, between the teeth of interlocking gearwheels, without which the entire assembly of gears would lock up; the teeth guarantee discrete synchrony, but it is the gap that allows movement to be born. And yet, that gap is never a vacuum because the world's structures are always and everywhere part of the substrate magma of the world. There's play in the sense of continuous, infinite dimensional variation from any given trajectory that invites arbitrary degrees of novelty. And there's play as the infinite deferral of definition, a passionate sense-making that develops ever more virtuosity re-enchanting the world.

References

American Psychiatric Association, Task Force on DSM-IV (2000) Diagnostic and statistical manual of mental disorders: DSM-IV-TR. Washington, DC

Artaud A (1970) The theatre and its double: essays (1938). Calder & Boyars, London

Badiou A (2004) Theoretical writings. Translation by Ray Brassier, and Alberto Toscano. Continuum. London, New York

Baudrillard J (1994) Simulacra and simulation. University of Michigan Press, Ann Arbor

Brakke KA (1978) The motion of a surface by its mean curvature. Princeton University Press, Princeton, NJ

Brook P (1968) The empty space. Atheneum, New York

Deleuze G, Guattari F (1994) What is philosophy?. Columbia University Press, New York

Derrida J (1976) Of grammatology. Translation by Gayatri Chakravorty Spivak. Johns Hopkins University Press, Baltimore

Geertz C (1975) The interpretation of cultures: selected essays. Hutchinson, London

Gendlin ET (1997) Experiencing and the creation of meaning: a philosophical and psychological approach to the subjective. Northwestern University Press, Evanston, IL

Grotowski J, Barba E (2002) Towards a poor theatre (1968). Routledge, New York

Guattari F (1995) Chaosmosis: an ethico-aesthetic paradigm. Indiana University Press, Bloomington

Hardt M, Negri A (2000) Empire. Harvard University Press, Cambridge, MA

Hardt M, Negri A (2004) Multitude: war and democracy in the age of empire. Penguin Putnam, London

Ilmanen T (1994) Elliptic regularization and partial regularity for motion by mean curvature. Amer Mathematical Society, Providence

James W (1983) The principles of psychology (1890). Harvard University Press, Cambridge, MA

Jänich K (1984) Topology. Springer, Berlin

Kircher A (1669) Athanasii Kircheri...Ars Magna Sciendi, in Xii Libros Digesta, Qua Nova & Universali Methodo Per Artificiosum Combinationum Contextum De Omni Re Proposita Plurimis & Prope Infinitis Rationibus Disputari, Omniumque Summaria Quaedam Cognito Comparari Potest. Amstelodami, apud J. Janssonium áa Waesberge

Latour B (1993) We have never been modern. Harvard University Press, Cambridge, MA

Maturana HR, Varela FJ (1980) Autopoiesis and cognition: the realization of the living. D. Reidel Pub. Co., Dordrecht, Holland

Meyer S (2001) Irresistible dictation: Gertrude Stein and the correlations of writing and science. Stanford University Press, Stanford, CA

Newell A, Simon HA (1976) Computer science as empirical inquiry: symbols and search. http://doi.acm.org/10.1145/360018.360022. Commun ACM 19(3):113–126

de Saussure F (1986) Course in General Linguistics. (Cours de linguistique generale, 1907). Ed. by Charles Bally and Albert Sechehaye, Albert Riedlinger & translated by Roy Harris. Open Court, LaSalle, IL

Sha XW, Kuzmanovic M (2002) Sustainable arenas for weedy socialityldistributed wilderness. In: Proceedings of the CPSR directions and implications of advanced computing symposium in Seattle (DIAC), pp 113–119

Standage T (2002) The mechanical Turk: the true story of the chess-playing machine that fooled the world. Allen Lane, London

Stengers I (2003a) Cosmopolitiques I: La Guerre Des Sciences; L'invention De La Mécanique, Pouvoir Et Raison; Thermodynamique: La Réalite Physique En Crise (1997), vol 1. La Dcouverte/Poche, Paris

Stengers I (2003b) Cosmopolitiques II: Mécanique Quantique: La Fin Du Re'Ve; Au Nom De La Fle'Che Du Temps: Le De'fi De Prigogine; La View Et L'artifice: Visages De L'émergence; Pour En Finir Avec La Tolérance (1997), vol 2. La Dcouverte/Poche, Paris

Thomas D (1934) 18 poems. The Fortune Press, London

Viola B (2003) The passions video installations. http://www.getty.edu/art/exhibitions/viola/

Wittgenstein L (1958) Philosophical investigations, 3rd edn. MacMillan, New York

Wittgenstein L (1994) Tractatus logico-philosophicus (1922). Routledge, London

AI & Soc (1995) 9:29–42
© 1995 Springer-Verlag London Limited

AI & SOCIETY

Ethics is Fragile, Goodness is Not

Fernando Leal

University of Guadalajara, Mexico

Abstract: This paper first illustrates what kind of ethical issues arise from the new information, communication and automation technology. It then argues that we may embrace the popular idea that technology is ethically neutral or even ambivalent without having to close our eyes to those issues and in fact, that the ethical neutrality of technology makes them all the more urgent. Finally, it suggests that the widely ignored fact of normal responsible behaviour offers a new and fruitful starting point for any future thinking about such issues.

Keywords: Skills; Deskilling; Communication; Control; Privacy; Identity; Ethical neutrality; Discourse; Responsibility

> *Graham*: Harry doesn't know any better. He's never thought of anybody but himself.
> *Billie*: Who does?
> *Graham*: Oh God, Billie, millions of people do.
>
> Born Yesterday, the film

Although the prestige philosophers once enjoyed in general society is pretty worn out by now, a kind of secret hope sometimes lingers that they may still be able to offer good advice or even answer the big questions about what the good life is (Williams, 1986). This hope is bound to be disappointed for several reasons, not the least among which is that there are no ethical recipes and never have been. On the other hand, even if I would like to maintain that there is some useful work for philosophers to do in our increasingly complex societies, if only we pull ourselves together and dare see what is in front of our eyes, nonetheless I would also like to persuade my readers that they should not wait for philosophers to build an ethical theory free from any possible objection or immune to abuse. Ethical issues always arise in concrete settings and nobody is better qualified to attend to them with the required subtlety and feeling for detail than the persons directly acquainted with those settings. Remote managers and bureaucrats, let alone philosophers, are in comparison rather like the proverbial elephant in the china shop. But doesn't ethical knowledge and moral thinking require professional skills? All classical moral philosophers, most famously among them Immanuel Kant, didn't think it did.[1] And they were right. Only the insidious dualisms mushrooming in our modern industrial life could produce the absurd idea of "ethical expertise".[2]

The particular subject of this paper is the new information, communication and automation technology, or ICA technology for short; and its argument runs as follows: (1) ICA technology is related to a lot of ethical issues, some of which are wholly new and all of which are at least partly new; (2) we may embrace the popular idea that technology is ethically neutral or even ambivalent without having to close our eyes to those issues, in fact the ethically neutrality of technology makes them all the more urgent; and (3) the starting point for a new thinking about them has to be the widely ignored fact of normal responsible behaviour.

Dr Frankenstein's Ethical Legacy: Five Examples

Different writers may want to classify the ethical issues arising from ICA technology in different ways (see e.g. Ermann *et al.*, 1990). My favourite five categories are all in terms of *loss*: what we are losing are skills, communication, privacy, control and last but not least, our own sense of self (or our identity, to use the more fashionable expression in the social sciences). Although each one of these complex ethical issues can be said to be a direct consequence of (some use of) ICA technologies, it could be argued that there are also causal connections between some of them, which reinforce the original impact of technology. Figure 1 suggests some of those further connections, which I hope to explore in a future publication. For lack of space, the following shall be a very brief review of the issues when considered in isolation.

Perhaps the most widely publicised ethical issue is that associated with the concept of *deskilling*. Ever since Bravermann published his famous book there has been a great debate as to whether ICA technology has effectively destroyed the old skills of workers by first incorporating them in ever more sophisticated systems and then letting these be run or supervised by unskilled operators (Wood, 1982, 1989). But the arguments purporting to show that technological developments are unethical show a great deal of diversity. The simplest argument just says that through ICA technologies, job are lost, unemployment rises and more people become welfare dependent and their lives lose the meaning associated with working. On the other hand, it is also said that automation creates a new kind of dualism: some people get the more interesting work of, say, designing the systems, whereas other people have to perform the unskilled jobs, such as entering data routinely into computers or thoughtlessly following the instructions issued by the system at ever higher speeds (Garson, 1988). This dualism is considered to be bad in itself, because it reinforces old or fosters new divisions in society, some of which are based on differences of class, race or gender. But it also has the consequence that the particular jobs in the lower ranges are soul-destroying, inhumane, and debasing. A yet different line of argument says that the products of such new division of labour tend to be of a much poorer quality than in the good old days. This might be considered bad in itself, but it has yet another consequence which is sometimes mentioned, viz that the standards of excellence of the consumer or end user become lowered in the process. Finally, at a slightly more philosophical level it might even be argued that creating systems, such as expert systems, which incorporate the knowledge and skills of real people

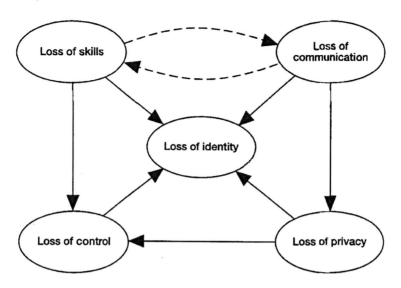

Fig. 1. Some causal connections between the five identified complex ethical issues arising from the new ICA technology. (The dotted lines are rather more tentative than the continuous ones.)

coping with real situations effectively destroys such knowledge and skills (Cooley, 1987; Dreyfus and Dreyfus, 1986). Some argue that this is bad in itself, whilst others point out the terrible consequences which might ensue if in the future there should be a shortage of energy preventing the new systems from working properly. As far as I can see, these are the arguments purporting to show the unethical consequences of deskilling. There are of course, other people who claim it is all very much exaggerated, and that automation actually eliminates only jobs which were uninteresting in the first place, and also that all deskilling is accompanied by processes of reskilling, whereby new knowledge and skills are born into the world (Wood, 1982, 1989; Hirschhorn, 1984; Ropohl, 1985). Wherever the truth may lie, moral philosophers manage to keep very quiet about these debates.[3]

New *communication* technologies have arguably a paradoxical effect in that they either change the actual process of communication or even destroy it (see Ord, in this issue). This sort of problem was probably first experienced when the very first communication technology appeared, viz, writing (Havelock, 1982). We know that writing and reading are acquired tastes and demand the development of special skills to cope with them. These skills go hand in hand with the creation of new codes, registers and jargons; written language is very different from spoken language, a fact which has a particular effect upon ordinary human communication by speech. And this effect becomes even more marked when writing is supported by printing. We all know from United Nations reports, how widely spread functional illiteracy is, even in industrial societies, and what the consequences for education, training, and cultural division and discrimination are. Now the temporal distance between the invention of writing and the invention of printing embraces more than two millennia, whereas the distance between the invention of printing and the development of new communication technologies span only about three centuries. First, we had the telegraph, the gramophone and daguerreo type, then the telephone, the radio, and moving pictures, later the television. And now we have all these as enhanced by satellite communications, plus the personal computer, the modem, the fax, the email, the video, and so on. Communication and thereby human life itself has been changing at an incredible pace. It can be argued that our very being, character and personality are changing. There is talk also of new varieties of artificial 'autism', and of the inability to cope with so much information as is being produced by the minute. There is talk of the effects of visual violence on the souls of children and young people. There is talk of visual and acoustic pollution in our towns and cities. All these and other things can be said to be very relevant to ethics, but they have been and still are by and large, ignored by our moral philosophers.

A third complex issue has to do with *privacy* – or rather the loss thereof. It has been known for many years that ICA technologies allow for a rapid transfer of information, some of which used to be the property of individual people in the old days. Thus you subscribe to a journal and in some mysterious way you start receiving all sorts of offers from all sorts of people who know who you are, where you live and what you do. This may be mildly annoying in some cases, and words like 'junk mail' have been coined to talk about them. Yet, quite a few people are worried about what might happen if some of this private information ends up in the wrong hands. There is a new mistrust growing in industrial societies about answering polls and surveys. New laws have been passed to prevent the worse, but it may not be enough. When communication technologies enter into the picture, you even see things like sexual harassment via electronic mail. Finally, at the workplace, we find quite a lot of monitoring of people's work. The new managers are capable of not only counting one's keystrokes and phonecalls, but also listening in when one is talking to clients to see whether one is really following the instructions of the newest expert system; why they can even analyse one's general patterns of performance! Up to a few years ago, this sort of monitoring affected workers only on the shopfloor or at the counter, then it reached middle management, but recently, it has begun to affect the work of the big bosses themselves. They don't like it naturally, but they were rather naive if they thought they were going to be exempt. Absolutely no job is safe from this kind of sophisticated surveillance. So the invasion of privacy is something moral philosophers should be worrying about, but they don't seem to be much interested.

The invasion of privacy is of course, only the beginning. The information gained about people, can of course, be used to manipulate and control them (Garson, 1988, Ermann *et al.*, 1990). On the other hand, people are supposed to *control* things themselves and this is becoming increasingly difficult because of the sheer complexity of some of the tasks assigned. First of all, a breakdown in power supply might disrupt the functioning of the new system and thereby cause lots of trouble, sometimes suddenly forcing operators to take desperate steps to remedy the situation for which they are scarcely prepared. When such things happen at critical moments, such as during heavy traffic in sophisticated transport systems, accidents may occur resulting in loss of lives and property (for further elaboration of this problem, see Shipley, this issue). Yet it has been powerfully argued that human beings are not 'biologically designed' to cope with these or similar situations which are becoming increasingly common in the 'nonstop society'. The new ICA technology makes it possible and even imperative at least under capitalism, for workers all over the world to labour under extremely stressful conditions and at times of the day which may run counter to their own internal clocks. This creates an unprecedented danger which the economy does not address, preferring as it does to invest in systems rather than in people (Moore-Ede, 1993). And if it escapes the economy, it is no wonder that it also escapes professional philosophy.

Finally, one of our most cherished values has to do with our *sense of self*. It can be argued that all the things listed above have an impact on our identity going well beyond the changes they effect in the ways we communicate and gather or transfer information, and even beyond the ways we work (hence the middle position of the 'loss of identity' circle in Fig. 1). Namely, it can be argued that the very fact that our computers and systems are so clever makes for comparison. On the one hand, people can get quite intimidated by ever more complicated software, faulty design of control buttons, or levers, and hard to read instruction manuals (Norman, 1989). Their self confidence falters and they may be prey to depression and stress. But there may be a more direct probably deeper and partly independent influence of ICA technologies on our sense of self. Comparison between people and systems produces, as we know, the so called computer metaphor, which is a sophisticated elaboration of the older machine metaphor. Now the machine metaphor as such was rather harmless in comparison. After all, it is difficult to feel jealous of a motorcycle or a car because they can run faster than us or of an airplane because it can fly and we can't. But when machines start to think, or at least, when we believe they do, it is far more difficult to retain our poise. We are tempted to describe ourselves in a new way. The point, is of course, that according to some authors, this redescription is all wrong and has tremendous ethical implications. It has even been argued that the unethical aspects of information, automation, and communication here briefly reviewed, are ultimately dependent on the computer metaphor; that we could never design the jobs we are designing or pry into people's lives the way we do or suffer the television programmes we suffer it we didn't think of people as machines, and particularly as computers (Rosenbrock, 1989, 1990, and this issue). If this is so, then a certain loss of identity will not only be influenced by the above mentioned four losses but will actually have an impact upon them through the peculiar kind of technology we have (Fig. 2 is a possible partial representation of this). For the purposes of this essay, it doesn't matter whether these claims are true or not.[4] The important thing is that our smartest pundits and gurus working in artificial intelligence and cognitive sciences – and of course, also their philosophical allies – do not give a damn about ethical issues. So their use of the computer metaphor can be safely described as ethically neutral. This leads us to the general question of the ethical neutrality of technology.

Is Technology Neutral?

A thesis that has been defended by politicians, business persons, scientists and engineers is that 'there is something wrong with the tools per se', or to put it in a terminology which has become familiar from an old debate in the social sciences, that technology is value-free. The social science debate actually didn't revolve around a statement but rather around the demand that social science should be value-free, a

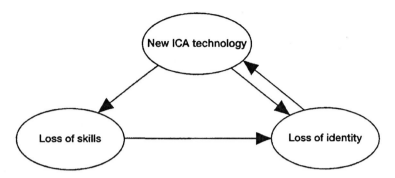

Fig. 2. Possible causal connections between loss of skills and loss of identity in relation to the new ICA technology.

demand which was designed to prevent political commitments interfering with scientific objectivity. I suppose the thesis as related to technology could be also framed as a demand that technology should be value-free, because politics would otherwise prevent it from *working*. So working in technology would be the equivalent of objectivity in science. Sham technology which doesn't do what it is supposed to do but only benefits politicians is not what we want. We want it to work, but of course, how we use it is a completely different thing: we can use atomic technology to kill people or to cure cancer. This is up to us and the politicians.

Regardless of whether it is a statement or a demand, the following discussion might become easier if we refer to the above thesis as *neutralism*. By far the most popular argument against neutralism counters that there are at least some technologies, like those specifically pertaining to nuclear weapons, which can only used wrongly. In as much as this argument depends on the further premise that nuclear weapons are inherently destructive, one could argue that it is just a particular application of the standard philosophical argument against neutralism, viz, that our technologies embody our values, whether we are aware of the fact or not. In a parallel fashion, some people might be prepared to argue that, say, expert systems will destroy existing knowledge and skills however we design them. Thus nuclear weapons and expert systems would be ethically wrong in themselves. The counter-argument would of course be that expert systems may destroy knowledge but do not have to. We can find a better use for them and design them so that human life and work is enhanced instead. If we generalise this position, we would then say that any technology can be used both *rightly* or *wrongly*. This corresponds to the most popular form of neutralism; but it seems to me to be a bit too strong. Maybe there are inherently bad technologies after all. And anyway I don't want to go into debates as to whether the atom bomb or experts systems are capable of ethically impeccable application. So I propose to settle for a weaker version, viz that any technology can be used *wrongly*. According to the standard philosophical jargon we might call this position weak *neutralism*.

Now, enemies of neutralism, as I mentioned before, want to insist that technologies have inbuilt values. Although they usually have in values they disagree with, unless they are totally opposed to any kind of technology, they necessarily imply that there might be technologies which embody the right values. An example might be a computer program built in such a way as to save effort when completing our annual income tax return. The point is that such a program may eventually be used to deskill people, to destroy valuable knowledge or even to put an innocent person in prison. It is clear that both the good and the bad guys can use practically any technology for their own purposes, which will eventually result in good and bad (or wrong) uses made of it. In fact, technology is not only independent of the high ethical standards and integrity of its designers or inventors, it is also independent of the moral qualities of its users, because, as we know, any action can have bad consequences for all or some of the people affected by that action. Indeed, given the vulgaries of human intentions and the reality of unintended and perverse effects, I suggest that we have to accept that weak neutralism is true.

However, there is a further consideration emerging from an unprejudiced acceptance of weak neutralism. Even weak neutralism presupposes that we can distinguish good and bad consequences of technology. The question is whether we can do that in a way that really satisfies everyone involved. I said before that any action can have bad consequences for all or some of the people affected by that action. But what very commonly happens is that some actions have good consequences for some people and bad consequences for others. This is a question which has to be addressed when considering the ethical issues raised by technology.

Barbara Garson's book, *The Electronic Sweatshop*, (1988) is an impressive source of examples of job design and expert systems which destroy skills and cause anxiety, stress and loss of self confidence. Some of her cases have to do with ICA technology and some do not. But even these latter, she argues, obey the same kind of logic. For Garson, a certain kind of job design is always the harbinger of technological changes: you first change the job, then you introduce the systems. Her case is powerfully argued and profusely illustrated, so that one wonders whether she can see any positive effect accruing from ICA technology. She presents findings from interviews with all sorts of people and at all levels, who either explicitly articulate their anger at the workplaces made possible by ICA technology or else unwittingly in some other way betray the horror of those new jobs. But there is a very interesting exception – her interview with former secretary Sophia Crandall in Chapter 7. The topic of this chapter is the changes in the office which started taking place in the 1980s, when the personal secretaries of managers were separated from the latter and integrated into a secretarial department of their own – a rearrangement of jobs made possible by the introduction of word processing. Managers who thus lost their 'office wife' and personalised assistance, and quite a bit of status, complained just a little bit louder than the secretaries themselves who became more strictly monitored and controlled under the new system. But then Sophia Crandall's interview makes visible a hitherto unnoticed aspect of the new arrangements in the office. She says that managers resent the fact women have their own department, usually run by one of them instead of by a male, so that bosses can no longer impose extra-official duties on secretaries or harass them any more. The secretarial department on the other hand, gives women a new sense of their own power and importance with respect to the general output of the company; at the same time, they now have more control over their own time and duties than they ever had when 'monogamically' attached to just one manager.

This relatively simple example proves that we shouldn't be too quick in judging whether a given consequence of the new ICA technology is good or bad. There may be cases in which a group of people will find that ICA technology has displaced them or made their work more difficult; whereas another group of people will instantly welcome it because it benefits them enormously. Recent ethical theories which say moral philosophy should be based on what is called 'discourse' (Habermas, 1983) are relevant here. By that we mean a kind of discussion which does not seek to control or manipulate other people but to bring genuine differences of opinion to full expression; reasoning instead of force is then used to achieve some form of reconciliation which respects as fairly as possible all interests involved in a given situation. There is of course, no unique method for reaching agreement or even compromise, say in the workplace, when the system gets very complicated (Cropanzano, 1993). And the deeper one looks, the more complicated things get. Thus, most conflicts and controversies which have a moral edge are doubtless connected with the relatively simple clash of particular personal or corporate interests, but it is becoming increasingly clear that at least some of them have to do with a deeper struggle between different or even incompatible value systems. The most obvious of these differences emerge from the multiethnic and multicultural nature of today's societies, which is caused by global communication as well as by migration; migration being in its turn not only caused by politics but also by economic factors connected with technological progress.[5] Less obvious but immensely important are the differences within what would appear to be a single culture, as was first argued by Macchiavelli in the 16th century (Berlin, 1955), then by Montesquieu and Stewart in the 18th century (Hirschman, 1977), and more recently by several authors writing from quite diverse perspectives (see, e.g. Hampshire, 1989; Klein and Eason, 1991; Jacobs, 1993).[6] Clearly, 'discourse' isn't easy and we shouldn't be naive about that or believe good will is all we need. Tolerance and good judgement are rare skills, which we will have to cultivate much farther before we can make any real progress. In this context, I think that we still have much more to learn from the kind of discourse which Socrates introduced into general philosophy. But a discussion of this topic would go far beyond the limits of this paper.[7]

But can ethical reasoning and ethical discussion deliver goods by themselves? In trying to promote them, we may easily forget the most important lesson which weak neutralism can teach us. Bad consequences of our actions and our use of tools may be just a contingency we have to learn to live with, but the same thing is true of ethics as long as we think of it as a kind of *theory*. It makes no difference whether the inventor or user of a new technology is not just an ordinary human being but actually a moral philosopher, even a professor of ethics. Even if the theory be somehow part of a master plan underlying our technology, weak neutralism warns us that such a technology, like any other one, is liable to misuse of one sort or another. Yet, technologies are not always misused. We have not yet said anything about why this should be so, although it is, in my opinion, the other half of the ethical story and by far the most vital one.

Normal Responsible Behaviour: A Neglected Quantity

Third World countries are famous for a kind of corruption which seems to be endemic to the social system. There may or may not be a significant difference in the amount of corruption actually existent in a Third World country such as Mexico, and first world country such as Britain, but bad reputation has at least one consequence which often escapes notice. I was once teaching logic to a group of high school students in Mexico, when something they said made it clear to me that they actually thought that nobody in our country abides by the law. I was amazed by the idea and spent the rest of the hour trying to prove by means of examples that such a state of affairs could simply not be true, that social life is impossible unless the majority of people's actions are in conformity to the written law and also obey all sorts of implicit norms and rules. Thus I pointed out to them that they would have been unable to come to school if it hadn't been for a bus driver who for the most part obeyed public regulations; in fact, it was necessary for most people driving that morning to do so; otherwise the traffic would have been in chaos. I also pointed out to them that even before going out to take the bus, all sorts of other people would have had to do their jobs, starting with those who collected the garbage from the streets and their own parents who woke them up and prepared breakfast for them, and ending with the farmers who produced the food their parents then prepared, the merchants and grocers who made sure that food was of good quality, transported it across the country and put it on sale in the right places, and so on. After an hour or so of describing all those things, they had to accept that, in spite of all the corruption there might otherwise be, such a statement as 'nobody abides by the law in Mexico' is simply outrageous. Most people must just be doing their duty most of the time, even in Mexico.

Simple as this statement might appear to be, no moral philosopher has given it the weight it should have. As the celebrated zoologist, J Z Young (1951), once said, it is not rationality or consciousness which make us the peculiar biological species that we are but rather that intricate network of cooperation, on a steadily increasing space-time scale, which constitutes social life. What I am calling 'cooperation' seems to have two aspects, a collective aspect and an individual one. The collective aspect is what social scientists commonly refer to as cooperation but which I would prefer to call 'coordination' (Argyle, 1991). Coordination ranges from the intricacies of face-to-face conversation to the complexities of telecommunications and from simple localised division of labour in a workshop to the international transfer of capital and human resources. It is an amazing thing to look at and trying to understand how it works can be very difficult indeed. But it does work, and it does make us human. On the other hand, there is an individual aspect of cooperation without which coordination would not be possible. I propose to call this 'normal responsible behavoiur'.[8] Of course, it could equally well be argued that normal responsible behaviour is also impossible without coordination. I am ready to concede that; but the fact is that coordination is something which at least social scientists are ready to recognise and research into, whereas normal responsible behaviour is receiving much less attention than it should. However that may be, the fact that coordination and normal responsible behaviour necessitate each other and are mutually dependent does not affect the argument.

I would like to suspect that normal responsible behaviour should be the centrepiece of ethical consideration. There was a famous writer who once said that all great literature is about a human misfortune, and that nobody writes about happiness because it is so terribly boring. A similar gestalt effect applies to normal responsible behaviour. It is always bad conduct which makes the headlines (no news is good news, as they say). The result is that we become blind to the normality of cooperative social life, viz to that which happens most of the time. We are obsessed with evil, sin and human error. This is as true of literature as it is true of moral philosophy and social science. And goodness strikes us only under the guise of heroism, even it is a tragic failure. I don't want to dismiss heroic deeds, but I think that we need heroes only insofar as the system has broken down. Thus we should be thinking more of how to design systems so as to make heroism as unnecessary as possible. But we can only do that if we pay sufficient attention to normal responsible behaviour.

To push my argument a bit further, I would like to say that normal responsible behaviour embodies *human goodness* at its best. Normal responsible behaviour is very robust and very reliable, so reliable in fact that badly designed systems are sometimes prevented from breaking down only because responsible human operators save the situation by doing the right thing at the right time.[9] But of course, normal responsible behaviour as all things human, is not infallible. It works most of the time but not always. And one of the reasons why it sometimes doesn't work is the way we design the system (Moore-Ede, 1993, and almost all contributions in this issue). To see this more clearly, I think we have to go into a bit of philosophising, for which I offer my apologies in advance.

My main thesis then is that the embodiment of human goodness in normal responsible behaviour makes it invisible to the usual ethical theorising and psychological or sociological analysis. As far as I can tell, there was only one philosopher who actually tried to make the right connection here, viz Socrates, who having been a skilled craftsman himself, pointed out again and again that human goodness was akin to a skill. This point was partially recovered by Aristotle when he distinguished the practical philosopher from the theoretical philosopher. The theoretical philosopher is a person who can think her way through mazes of argument, dissect pros and cons, and come up at the end of all this with a neat well-grounded logical solution to some philosophical question, say how movement is possible, what ultimate component of matter there are, or whether the universe has a beginning in time. The practical philosopher, by contrast, is a person who has become wise, i.e. who hasn't just thought about philosophical problems or knows the right solutions to such problems, but a person who *incarnates* philosophy in all her *dealings* with the social and political world around her; a person who enacts philosophy, who makes it work in the real world. The problem is that this insight was drowned by Aristotle's own vision of the good life as contemplative and intellectual. In fact, we scholars and scientists have inherited this prejudice, which in some way or other infects all current models underlying cognitive science and their practical applications within the new technology (Shipley and Leal, 1991; Leal and Shipley, 1992).

What I therefore would like to suggest is that we should reassess Socrates and even perhaps go beyond him in saying that goodness is not just a skill among others, but that is an integral part of all human skills, effectively embedded in any one of them. I don't think that we can extricate ordinary goodness from ordinary skills. Of course, there is slipshod craftsmanship, skills *can* occasionally be misused, and ordinary goodness as embedded in a skill is far from infallible. However, a familiar point from the psychology of skills is that skills are not supposed to hit the target all the time but only most of the time (Singleton, 1978). I want to suggest that what is true of ordinary skills is also true of human goodness. In fact, there is bound to be the case if my suggestion that they belong together is anywhere near the mark. The important thing is that such limited success is usually enough. Being able to hit the target most of the time doesn't make ordinary skills and ordinary goodness fragile, except if the system puts inordinate pressure upon them. Which leads to the importance of keeping the reality of normal responsible behaviour in mind when applying the new technologies.

One of the old philosophical dreams was the attainment of absolute certainty and absolute perfection. The whole history of philosophical thinking can be read that way (Dewey, 1929). Now the form in which such certainty and perfection was to be attained was the theoretical form. Practice and experience was just too accidental and variegated to serve the purpose of such a magnificent dream. Our own century has seen such revolutions in theory that it is nowadays as commonplace to think of theories as fallible and replaceable. But it hasn't quite taught us to think of ordinary human experience and practice, of ordinary human judgement and skill, in one word of ordinary human *goodness* as the only genuine article. I think that by doing so we might yet be able to design better systems – systems, that is, which better enable people to do what they would try to do anyway. Doctors, psychologists and ergonomists are fond of depicting themselves as in a perpetual struggle with engineers to protect human operators from unnecessary hazards (Oborne *et al.*, 1993; Moore-Ede, 1993). This is of course largely, although not completely true. On the one hand, some engineers have put up a valiant fight to advance human-centred technology (Rosenbrock, 1989, 1990; Cooley, 1987, this issue; Eason *et al.*, this issue). On the other hand, the truth is that *most* people involved in human factors, whether they are engineers or not, have the deplorable habit of describing the human operator as a worrisome 'source of error' and/or 'the weakest link' in the system; consequently they constantly strive to 'close the loop' and 'design the man out' of the system. At the same time, however, designers and consultants implicitly and even unthinkingly take for granted what I've been calling normal responsible behaviour. When all is said and done, this means that they rely on the common decency of human operators, who will indeed do their sometimes desperate best to protect the health, safety or even life of the people immediately affected by any malfunctioning of their precious systems. I wonder how many of them really obey the Golden Rule of putting themselves in other people's shoes.

Conclusion

In conclusion, if technology is ethically neutral in the sense that it is liable to misuse, then ethics under the dispensation of powerful new technologies is a very fragile thing indeed.[10] This makes ethics all the more precious – meaning by 'ethics' not only ethical theory in the abstract but also the 'moral' structures and the inbuilt 'values' of say, technology.[11] Nevertheless, I want to insist here that it is ethics and not human goodness which is fragile, as has recently been suggested (Nussbaum, 1986). Believing in the fragility of goodness comes, I think, from the strong influence that the tragic vision of humankind and human life still has upon our imaginations.[12] As against this tragic vision, I would like to insist that people – ordinary real people

– do not normally lead tragic lives and so their goodness is a firm rock upon which we can build and use ever better technologies.

Acknowledgements

Part of the above material was used in a seminar I gave on 'Language, Ethics, and the Philosophy of Work', at the Organisational Studies Area (Department of Economics) of the Metropolitan University in Mexico City in November 1993. My heartfelt thanks go to all participants and especially to the organisers, Dr Luis Montano and Eduardo Ibarra, for their helpful comments. I am also very grateful to Dr Rene Saran and Dr Patricia Shipley for reading the first draft of this paper and improving both its form and its content. The Society for the Furtherance of the Critical Philosophy (London) provided financial assistance and a congenial environment which allowed me to finish the work in leisure.

Notes

1. When someone else tried to criticize Kant by saying that his 'categorical imperative' was only a formulation of common human knowledge, he replied that he never intended it to be anything else, and that it would be ridiculous to try to pose as a moral master to humankind, as though ethics was something a philosopher could invent from scratch (Kant 1786, Preface).
2. These dualisms have been explored in recent papers by the guest-editors of this special issue (Shipley & Leal 1991, Leal & Shipley 1992; see Shipley, this issue).
3. The reader will remark that this as well as the next four paragraphs reviewing the ethical issues arising from ICA technology always finish by indicating that contemporary moral philosophy is guilty of neglect. This theme is developed further in the introduction to this special issue.
4. Thus, Kenneth Gergen has interestingly argued that we shouldn't mourn the loss of a "stable center of identity" – by losing it the world stands a fair chance to get rid of self-righteousness, bigotry and jingoism. For a popular summary of righteousness, bigotry and jingoism. For a popular summary of Gergen's ideas, see "The decline and fall of personality" in Psychology Today, vol. 25, no. 6, November–December 1992, pp. 59–63.
5. People working at what might be called the 'cultural interface' – social workers, educators, and so on – thus acquire a particular relevance in helping us to sort things out and achieve 'discourse'. Like engineers, doctors and ergonomists in system design, those persons are best qualified to think about ethical issues arising from ICA technology in their particular workplaces.
6. I suspect that the distinctions between the right and the good, or between duties and virtues, or between justice and care, are "splits of (ethical) truth", if i may be allowed to use a phrase used in classical German philosophy. This would explain the increasingly acrimonious tone of many recent debates in moral philosophy, in which people tend to conceive of each other as ethical morons. But this whole subject goes beyond the scope of this paper.
7. The contributions by Eason et al. and Ord to this issue are in the context exemplary, as observed in the introduction to this special issue.
8. This theme is explored in several chapters of Oborne et al. 1993, even if the term 'normal responsible behaviour' does not explicitly appear in any of them (see also Shipley & Leal 1991, Leal & Shipley 1992).
9. Notice that I am not asking the question why (most) people are (for the most part, most of the time) good. I don't know the answer to that question and probably on one else does. However, it is not necessary either to ask that question or to answer it in order to see that (a) as a matter of fact, people are good; (b) things in general run relatively smoothly for everyone because people are good; (c) people "save the situation" very often *because* they persist in being good despite inhuman arrangements; (d) everyone would be better served if people should be enabled to persist in being good without having to "save the situation", i.e. if inhuman arrangements would be improved. That is all we need to know.
10. A good example is genetic screening as presented by Sanmartín in this issue.

11. It should be clear by now that by 'ethics' I understand a framework or structure within which things are done. Such a framework is constituted by ideas, values, precepts, codes, and whatnot; and so is an *intellectual* structure, or rather several intellectual structures, in Rosenbrock's sense of the word (see his contribution to this volume). Calling such a structure "fragile" means first of all that it is liable to abuse at any given time. One example among many is the value shift in hospital life examined by Ord in this issue.

12. "Only in very wicked world would decency inspire awe", says quite justly Mary Mothersill (1984) when criticizing Kant's temporary lapse into estheticizing ethics. Anyone can succumb to this ever present temptation; and maybe it is a good thing, too, or even avoidable when dealing with literary works or art (such as those Nussbaum analyzes in her beautiful book); but we should resist it when discussing real-life issues.

References

Argyle, Michael (1991) *Cooperation: the basis of sociability*. London: Routledge.

Berlin, Isaiah (1955) *Against the current: essays in the history of ideas*. London: The Hogarth Press.

Cooley, Mike (1987 *Architect or bee? The human price of technology*. New edition. London: The Hogarth Press.

Cropanzano, Russell, ed. (1993) *Justice in the workplace: approaching fairness in human resource management*. Hillsdale, NJ: Lawrence Erlbaum Associates.

Dewey, John (1929) The guest for certainty: a study of the relation of knowledge and action. London: Allen & Unwin.

Dreyfus, Hubert L. & Dreyfus, Stuart E. (1986) *Mind over machine: the power of human intuition and expertise in the era of the computer*. New York: The Free Press.

Ermann, M. David, Williams, Mary B. & Gutierrez, Claudio (1990) *Computers, ethics, and society*. New York: Oxford University Press.

Garson, Barbara (1988) *The electronic sweatshop: how computers are transforming the office of the future into the factory of the past*. New York: Simon & Schuster.

Habermas, Jürgen (1983) Theorie de Kommunikativen Hadelins. Frankfurt: Suhrkamp.

Hampshire, Stuart (1989) *Innocence and experience*. Harvard University Press.

Havelock, Eric (1982) *The literate revolution in Greece and its cultural consequences*. Princeton, NJ: Princeton University Press.

Hirschhorn, Larry (1984) *Beyond mechanization: work and technology in postindustrial age*. Cambridge, MA: The MIT Press.

Hirschman, Albert O. (1977) *The Passions and the interests: political arguments for capitalism before its triumph*. Princeton, NJ: Princeton University Press.

Jacobs, Jane (1993) *Systems of survival: a dialogue on the moral foundations of commerce and politics*. London: Hodder & Stoughton.

Kant, Immanuel (1786) *Critik der practischen Vernunft*. (Critique of Practical Reason.) Hartknoch: Riga.

Klein, Lisl & Eason, Ken (1991) *Putting social science to work: the ground between theory and use explored through case studies in organizations*. Cambridge, UK: Cambridge University Press.

Leal, Fernando & Shipley, Patricia (1992) 'Deep dualism' *International Journal of Applied Philosophy*, 7, 33–44.

Moore-Ede, Martin (1993) *The 24-hour society: the risks, costs and challenges of a world that never stops*. London: Piatkus.

Mothersill, Mary (1984) *Beauty restored*. Oxford: Clarendon Press.

Norman, Donald A. (1989) *The design of everyday things*. New York: Doubleday.

Nussbaum, Martha (1986) *The fragility of goodness: luck and ethics in Greek Tragedy and philosophy*. Cambridge, UK: Cambridge University Press.

Oborne, D.J., Branton, R., Leal, F., Shipley, P. & Stewart, T., eds. (1993) *Person-centred ergonomics: a Brantonian view of human factors*. London: Taylor & Francis.

Ropohl, Günter (1985) *Die unvollkommene Technik*. Frankfurt am Main: Suuhrkamp.

Rosenbrock, Howard (1990) *Machines with a purpose*. Oxford: Oxford University Press.

Rosenbrock, Howard, ed. (1989) *Designing human-centred technology: a cross-disciplinary project in computer-aided manufacturing*. London: Springer-Verlag.

Shipley, Patricia & Leal, Fernando (1991) 'The active self: beyond dualism.' *Newsletter of the British Psychological Society, History and Philosophy Section*, 13, 4–16.

Singleton, W.T., ed. (1978) *The analysis of practical skills*. Lancaster: MTP Press.

Young, J.Z. (1951) *Doubt and certainty in science*. Oxford: Clarendon Press.

Williams, Bernard (1986) *Ethics and the limits of philosophy*. London: Fontana.

Wood, Stephen, ed. (1982) *The degredation of work?* London: Hutchinson.
Wood, Stephen, ed. (1989) *The transformation of work?* London: Routledge.

Correspondence and offprint requests to: Dr F Leal, Paseo de los Robles 4169–4, Guadalajara JAL 45110, Mexico.

Contributors

Satinder P. Gill
School of Computing, Middlesex University, Hendon, London NW4 4BT, UK.

Satinder Gill is a Senior Research Fellow with the School of Computing, Middlesex University, and is a member of the Centre for Music and Science, Faculty of Music, University of Cambridge. She has a BA (Hons) degree in Philosophy, Politics and Economics, University of Keele, UK, and received her PhD on 'Dialogue and Tacit Knowledge for Knowledge Transfer' from the University of Cambridge in 1995. Her research is on Knowledge, Communication, and Technology, focusing on the pragmatic dimension of communication, in particular gesture and speech coordination in interaction and the phenomenon of entrainment. As an interdisciplinary researcher, she is concerned with the Human-System Interface and her current work with musicians, artists, and performance arts, explores the relation between the analog and the digital. She has been a Research Scientist with NTT's communication Science Laboratories in Japan, and has held a joint position with CKIR, Finland (Centre for Knowledge and Innovation Research) and CSLI (Centre for the Study of Language and Information), Stanford University, USA. Since 2004, she has been collaborating with the Topological Media Lab (first at Georgia Tech), at Concordia University, Canada. At Middlesex University, she is the Coordinator of the EU funded Research Coordination Action: ETHICBOTS "Emerging Technoethics of Human Interaction with Communication, Bionic and Robtic Systems". Her previous research positions have included: Visiting researcher with the Swedish Centre for Working Life, Stockholm, Visiting Research Fellow with the Institute of Technology and Education, Bremen University, and Visiting Researcher with IMES, Department of Sociology, University of Urbino.

Jacob Mey
Department of Linguistics, University of Southern Denmark, DK-5230, Odense M, Denmark.

Jacob L. Mey is Professor Emeritus of Linguistics at the University of Southern Denmark. He has taught at the University of Oslo, the University of Texas at Austin, Georgetown University, City University of Hong Kong, Tsukuba University, Universidade de Brasília, and many other institutions of higher learning throughout the world. His research interests concern all areas of pragmatics, with an emphasis on the social aspects of language use, the pragmatic impact of computer technologies, and the pragmatic use of linguistic/literary devices. His publications in these areas include Whose language? A study in linguistic pragmatics (1985), Pragmatics: An Introduction (1993; second edition 2001). His most recent publication is As Vozes da Sociedade (The Voices of Society; in Portuguese; 2002). Among Jacob Mey's other main interests are the theory of literature and poetics. These interests have recently culminated in his book: When Voices Clash: A study in literary pragmatics (2000). Jacob Mey is co-founder and chief editor of the monthly Journal of Pragmatics (since 1977). He also edits the semi-annual RASK: International Journal of Languages and Linguistics and is Area Editor for Pragmatics in the second edition of the 14-vol. Encyclopedia of Language and Linguistics, to appear November 2005.

Renate Fruchter
Department of Civil and Environmental Engineering, Department of Civil and Environmental Engineering, Terman Engineering Center M4, Stanford University Stanford, California 94305-4020.

Renate Fruchter is the founding director of the Project Based Learning Laboratory (PBL Lab), lecturer in the Department of Civil and Environmental Engineering, and thrust leader of "Collaboration Technologies" at the Center for Integrated Facilities Engineering (CIFE), at Stanford. She leads a research effort to develop collaboration technologies for multidisciplinary, geographically distributed teamwork, and e-Learning. Her interests focus on R&D and larger scale deployment of collaboration technologies that include Web-based team building, synchronous and asynchronous knowledge capture, sharing and re-use, project memory, corporate memory, and mobile solutions for global teamwork and e-Learning. In addition, she has established in 1998 a strong research effort focusing on the impact of technology on learning, team interaction, and assessment. She is the leader and developer of the innovative "Computer Integrated Architecture/Engineering/Construction Global Teamwork" course launched in 1993, at Stanford, engaging universities from Europe, Asia, and USA.

Daniel Memmi
Department d'Informatique, UQAM, C.P. 8888 Succ. C.V., H3C 3P8, Montreal, QC, Canada.

Daniel Memmi received a M.A. in Linguistics from the University of Chicago, a Ph.D. in Linguistics from the University of Paris-VII, and a Ph.D. in Computer Science from the University of Paris-Sud. He was researcher in computer science with C.N.R.S. in Paris and Grenoble from 1980 to 2004. He has since been associate professor in computer science at UQAM in Montreal, Canada. During his career, he has worked mostly on natural language processing and expert systems, using both symbolic and connectionist techniques. His present interests include text analysis, collaborative information retrieval, social networks and virtual communities.

Carl Martin Allwood
Department of psychology, Lund University, Box 213, SE-221 00 Lund, Sweden.

Carl Martin Allwood is professor of psychology at the Department of psychology, Lund University, Sweden. Allwood's research investigates conditions for the development and application of human understanding in various social contexts. His studies of human-computer interaction (HCI) include analogical thinking in HCI, training on application programs, users' manuals, and how different aspects of the system development process affect the usability of the software product. Other research areas are theory of science and science studies (including the anthropology of knowledge), studies of metacognitive realism in confidence judgments of memory performance (for example in forensic contexts) and decision making in every-day life work contexts. He has published about 60 articles in international scientific journals and edited two books "Decision making: Social and creative dimensions", 2001 (with Marcus Selart), and "Creative knowledge environments", 2004 (with Sven Hemlin and Ben Martin).

Jan O Borchers
RWTH Aachen University, 52056 Aachen, Germany.

Jan Borchers is full professor of computer science and head of the Media Computing Group at RWTH Aachen University. With his research group, he explores the field of human-computer interaction, with a particular interest in HCI design patterns, new post-desktop user interfaces for smart environments, ubiquitous computing, interactive exhibits, and time-based media such as audio and video. Before joining RWTH, he worked as assistant professor at Stanford University and ETH Zurich. He received his Ph.D. in computer science from Darmstadt University of Technology in 2000, and his B.Sc. & M.Sc. (Diplom) in computer science from the University of Karlsruhe in 1995, with some time at Imperial College London. He co-organized or participated in most of the HCI Design Patterns workshops at conferences such as CHI, INTERACT and ChiliPLoP since 1999, and is the author of "A Pattern Approach to Interaction Design" (Wiley), the first book on HCI design patterns.

Casper Jensen
Copenhagen Business School, Department of Organization, Kilevej 14a
2000 Frederiksberg, Denmark.

Casper Bruun Jensen received his Ph.D. from Information and Media Studies at the University of Aarhus and is currently an assistant professor at Department of Organization and Industrial Sociology, Copenhagen Business School. He has published in Configurations, Qualitative Research, Science, Tehnology and Human Values and Social Studies of Science. A volume co-edited with Kjetil Rödje and entitled Deleuzian Intersections in Science, Technology and Anthropology is forthcoming on Berghahn Press. Casper's current research focuses on ICT in development and development and the environment.

Thomas Binder
Center for Design Research, Royal Academy of Fine Arts, School of Architecture
Philip de Langes Allé 10, DK-1435 Copenhagen K, Denmark
Thomas Binder is senior researcher at the Danish Center for Design Research. His research includes empirical studies of design discourse and situated everyday practices of designers, and experimental explorations of the relations between designed artefacts, place and space. Thomas Binder has been studio director at the Interactive Institute in Malmö, Sweden and has been part of the user-centered design group at the Danish company Danfoss. Thomas Binder has been the chairman of the Nordic Design research conference and the Participatory design conference. He holds a Ph.D in Science and Technology studies from the Technical University of Denmark.

Lauge Rasmussen
Industrial Management, Technical University of Denmark, Manufacturing Engineering & Management, Matematiktorvei, DTUI - Building 303, DK-2800 Lyngby, Copenhagen, Denmark
Lauge Baungaard Rasmussen is sociologist and Associate Professor in organisational development, strategy and planning methods at the Department of Manufacturing Engineering and Management at the Technical University of Denmark. He has participated in several international research programmes and networks, that include, ESPRIT, Comett, FAST, CAPIRN, EU-India cross-cultural innovation network, RLDWL. He teaches engineering students organisational development and concepts and methods of strategy and planning, such as scenarios, future creating workshops, SWOT, Causal mapping, Balanced scorecards, Interactive Planning. Lauge Rasmussen is Member of the Advisory Board of the journal, AI & Society.

Parthasarathi Banerjee
National Institute of Science, Technology and Design Studies (NISTADS), Pusa Gate, Dr.K.S.Krishnan Road, New Delhi – 110012, India.
Parthasarathi Banerjee is currently acting as Director of NISTADS, New Delhi and has been associated with the AI & Society since 1992. His interests range from philosophical issues of aesthetics and cognition, to history and institutions of ideas and knowledge. He professionally researches issues of business strategy, technological innovations and ethics of business and technology. Banerjee has written/edited nine books, several research reports, more than a hundred papers, and organized numerous conferences and remained associated with several international journals and fora. He has a special interest in Indian philosophy and ideas. In the areas of innovation, his recent two books are: 'Biomedical innovation in India', New Delhi, 2007 and 'Indian Software strategy', London, 2005. Dr. Banerjee has been teaching in areas of business strategy and has been with SUNY, Binghamton; Ecole Polytechnique, Paris; EHESS, Paris; University of Tokyo, Tokyo, among others.

Karamjit S. Gill
University of Wales, Newport School of Art, Media and Design, Newport, P.O. Box. 179, Newport.
Karamjit S Gill is Professor Emeritus, University of Brighton, Honorary Professor, University of Urbino (Italy), and Visiting Professor at University of Wales,

Newport and Waterford Institute of Technology, Ireland. He is the founding Editor of the international journal AI & Society, and the founding Series Editor of the Human Centred Systems Society Book Series, leading to the publication of 400 journal articles and 25 books. These two publications have played a key role in establishing the human centred system field as a mainstream area of postgraduate education and applied research. He has coordinated a number of European and international R&D networks, including research links with Japan, India, and China. His research interests include cross-cultural innovation, knowledge architectures, trans-disciplinary networking, soft technology, security and social citizenship, social mentoring, and culture, enterprise and social innovation.

Massimo Negrotti
IMES, University of Urbino, Italy.

Massimo Negrotti has been a Full Professor of Sociology of knowledge at the Universities of Parma and Genoa, and is presently Director of the IMES-LCA (Lab for the Culture of the Artificial) at the University of Urbino. His main areas of interest are cybernetics, methodology and the culture of the artificial. Since 1980 he has carried out theoretical and empirical studies on the AI researchers and pracititioners in Europe and in the USA. He has presented his findings on both of the above subjects at several conferences and lectures in Europe, USA and Japan, and has published widely in Italian and in international books and journals. He is currently working on the socio-cultural and techno-methodological premises and regularities of naturoids, conceived as a general area of research within which technology tries to reproduce natural exemplars.

Hubert Dreyfus
Department of Philosophy, 314 Moses Hall 2390, University of California, Berkeley, CA 94720-2390

Hubert Dreyfus received his PhD from Harvard University and taught philosophy for ten years at MIT before moving to Berkeley where he has been a Professor of Philosophy since 1968. He thinks of himself as an applied philosopher reflecting on the bearing of the work of existential thinkers such as Søren Kierkegaard, Martin Heidegger, and Maurice Merleau-Ponty on current cultural developments such as the attempt to create artificial intelligence, and the effect of the Internet and various technologies that facilitate disembodied action at a distance, on everyday human interactions. Dreyfus's publications include: What Computers (Still) Can't Do, Being-in-the-World: A Commentary on Division I of Heidegger's Being and Time; (with Stuart Dreyfus) Mind over Machine; The Power of Human Intuition and Expertise in the Era of the Computer; and, most recently, On the Internet.

Douglas D. Noble
76 Westland Avenue, New York 14618, USA.

F.T.Evans
FT Evans passed away in 2004.

Kjell S. Johannessen
Department of Philosophy, University of Bergen. Øvre korskirkeallmenning 10, 5017 Bergen, Norway.
Kjell S. Johannessen is Professor of Philosophy at the University of Bergen. Although he maintains a comprehensive field of philosophical engagement, his publications are for the most part within the areas of the Philosophy of Art, the Philosophy of Language and the Philosophy of Science. Johannessen is primarily known for (a) his "praxis"-interpretation of Wittgenstein's *Philosophical Investigations*, (b) shaping the theoretical foundations for what is internationally referred to as the Bergen School of Aesthetics; and (c) his contributions to the analysis of what in the Philosophy of Science is called "tacit knowledge". Johannessen has written or edited 17 books and contributed about 50 articles to international, Nordic and Norwegian journals and anthologies. A list of central publications within the aforementioned areas can be found at: [www.skapende.no]. Johannessen was previously Vice-Chancellor of the Nordic Summer University and before that leader of its program committee. He worked many years as editor of *Norsk filosofisk tidsskrift* (Norwegian Journal of Philosophy) He has also, in cooperation with professor Bo Göranzon, for many years led a doctoral course in the Philosophy of Science at Kungliga Tekniska högskolan (The Royal Institute of Technology) in Stockholm and Arbetslivcentrum (Stockholm) supporting local and international cooperation and exchange between educational institutions and business.

Ben R. Tilghman
1602 Brandon Woods Court, Lawrence, Kansas 6640, USA.
Ben Tilghman was born in St. Louis, Missouri in 1927. BA and MA from Washington University and Ph.D from the University of Washington. He taught at Reed College, Western State College of Colorado, the University of Wyoming where he became head of the newly organized philosophy department. He was head of the department at Kansas State University from 1967 to1980. He retired in 1994. His publications include The Expression of Emotion in the Visual Arts, Language and Aesthetics, But is it Art?, Wittgenstein, Ethics and Aesthetics, Introduction to the Philsophy of Religion, and Reflections on Aesthetic Judgment and Other Essays.

Bo Göranzon
Department of Skill and Technology, School of Engineering and Management, the Royal Institute of Technology, S-100 44 Stockholm.
Bo Göranzon is Professor at the Royal Institute of Technology. He is also Director of Artistic Content of the Dialogue Seminar with the Experimental Theatre Dialogues. This is a joint Royal Institute of Technology and Royal Dramatic Theatre project. He is on the Editorial Board of the Dialoger Journal and is Research Fellow of Clare Hall College, University of Cambridge, UK. His publications of sixteen books include, Göranzon, Bo and Florin, Magnus, *Dialogue and Technology: Art and Knowledge*, Springer-Verlag, 1991, and Göranzon, Bo (ed.), *Skill and Technology: Practical Philosophy*, Springer Verlag, 1996.

Jaqueline Senker
SPRU Science and Technology Policy Research, Freeman Centre, University of Sussex, Brighton BN1 9QE, UK.

Dr. Jacqueline Senker is Senior Fellow at SPRU Science and Technology Policy Research, University of Sussex. Her research has identified tacit knowledge as a crucial element that drives university-industry research links. She has published widely on this topic, as well as on changes to European public sector research and the development of biotechnology. She is co-author of Knowledge Frontiers: Public Sector Research and Industrial Innovation in Biotechnology, Engineering Ceramics and Parallel Computing, Oxford University Press, 1995 and editor of Biotechnology and Competitive Advantage, Edward Elgar, 1998.

Ingela Josefson
Södertörn University College, 141 89 Huddinge, Sweden.

Ingela Josefson is Vice-chancellor of Södertörn University College, and is Stockholm. She is also professor in work life research and adjunct professor in practical knowledge, at Bodö University College, Norway. She has a PhD in linguistics. Her field of research is on the tension between theory and practice in vocational education (or: in education).

Kumiko Ikuta
Graduate School of Education, Tohoku University, 6-3 Nishi Minemachi, Ota-ku, Tokyo, Japan, #145-0075.

Kumiko Ikuta is Professor in the Graduate School of Education, Tohoku University. Her academic field is the Philosophy of Education and Cognitive Science. She has an MA degree in Education from the Graduate School of Keio University, 1972. Her chief works include: *"Learning from Skill (Waza)"*, The University of Tokyo Press, 1987; *"What are the Implications of the Teaching and Learning Method of Traditional Japanese Artistic Performances?"*, *'Kampf oder Dialog der Kulturen ?'* *Bildung und Erziehung* PP.429-439 53.Jg.Heft4/Dezember 2000; *"Reconsidering of the Concept of Skill:Focus on the Concept of 'Waza' as an disposition([Saiko] Kyouiku niokeru "Gino"gainen:Keikousei tositeno"Waza"gainenniChumokusite)"* *'Kyoikuotou Kyoikugaku'* PP.11-32, Keio University Press 2006.

Biswatosh Saha
Indian Institute of Management Calcutta, Diamond Harbour Road, Joka, Kolkata 700104, West Bengal.

Biswatosh Saha currently teaches at Indian Institute of Management Calcutta. An enginner by graduate training, he moved into social science mainly because of an interest in social effects of technology, including problems of innovation. His current teaching and research interests include areas such as Strategy, Power - innovation. His association with the co-author has led to a very interesting exploration of Indian theatre traditions, many aspects of which are not too widely known. He can be contacted at biswatosh@iimcal.ac.in

Shubhashis Gangopadhyay
C/O: Mr N.Halder, 138K Bhattacharya Para Roa, Kolkata 700063, West Bengal, India.

Shubhashis Gangopadhyay lives and works in Kolkata, India. He is a playwright and a dramatist. He founded and directed Blind Opera, a theatre group of the blind. His numerous productions and plays, all in Bengali (the regional language of Bengal) represent his sincere and earnest interest in trying to understand his own times and his surroundings in the light of the long Indian theatre and cultural traditions that run with several departures through Bharat, Kalidasa, the Bhakti traditions (in medieval times) to Rabindranath Tagore in early 20th century. It is an attempt to understand one's own roots and search for its emancipatory potential. He can be contacted on phone at 919830273306. Emails to biswatosh@iimcal.ac.in will be immediately passed on to him.

Howard H. Rosenbrock
Linden, Walford Road, Ross-on-Wye, Hertfordshire, UK.

Howard Rosenbrock, born in Ilford, England in 1920, graduated in 1941 from University College London with a 1st class honors degree in Electrical Engineering. He served in the Royal Air Force Volunteer Reserve (Signals) in 1941-46, and from 1947-62 worked at the GEC Research Laboratories, taught high school physics, worked for the Electrical Research Association, John Brown & Co Ltd. and Constructors John Brown, latterly as Research Manager. His Ph.D. was obtained for research done in industry in that period. In 1962 he joined John Coales's Control group at Cambridge University, spent 1963-64 at MIT and in 1966 was appointed to a chair in Control Engineering at UMIST, where he set up the interdisciplinary Control Systems Centre. He received his D.Sc. for research in Control from London University in 1963.He has received a number of awards including an honorary doctorate of Salford University (1987), IEE Premium, Heaviside Premium and Control Achievement Award (all IEE), Control Systems Science and Engineering Award (IEEE), Oldenburger Medal (ASME), Moulton Medal (IChemE), Sir Harold Hartley Medal and Sir George Thompson Gold Medal (Inst. Meas. & Cont.) and the Nordic Process Control Award. He is also a Fellow of the IEE and the IChemE, Hon. Fellow of Inst. Meas & cont., Fellow of University College London, Fellow of the Royal Academy of Engineering, and Fellow of the Royal Society.

Luis Montaño Hirose
Universidad Autónoma Metropolitana-Iztapalapa, Posgrado en Estudios Organizacionales. Edificio H. Cubículo H063. Av. Rafael Atlixco N° 186 Colonia Vicentina. Código Postal 09340, México D. F. México

Luis Montaño Hirose is professor of Organization Studies at the *Universidad Autónoma Metropolitana* (UAM), México. He studied his PhD in Organization Sciences at the *Université de Paris IX-Dauphine*, France, and has been invited professor at *Osaka no Machi Daigaku* (Osaka City University), Japan, *Ecole Polytechnique*, France, and *Ecole des Hautes Etudes Commerciales*, Canada. Professor Montaño has produces several books, including the most recent *Los Estudios Organizacionales en México*. He was Director of the Organization Studies Posgraduate Programe at UAM and President of the Mexican Research Network in Organization Studies.

Mike Cooley
95 Sussex Place, Slough Berks, SL1 1NN, UK.

Mike Cooley grew up in the West of Ireland and then studied engineering in Germany and Switzerland. His PhD is in Computer Aided Design. He has held senior posts in both the aerospace industry and the public sector including Director of Technology at the Greater London Enterprise Board. He has been a visiting Professor at universities worldwide and his work is published in over 20 languages. He has broadcast on TV and radio in several countries since the 1970.s when he had become internationally known as an initiator of the Lucas Plan for Socially Useful Technology. Mike was Chief Consultant for a UN technology project and was Chairman of the EU/India Scientific Committee. He is currently Chairman of the AI & Society Advisory Board. His distinctions include the Freedom of Detroit, the Keys of Osaka and in 1981 the $ 50,000 Alternative Nobel Prize which he donated to socially useful production.

Gustaf Östberg
Professor, Emeritus of Engineering Materials, University of Lund, Box 118, Lund 22100, Sweden.

David Smith
Newport School of Art, Media and Design, University of Wales, Caerleon Campus, PO Box 101, Newport, NP18 3YG, Caerleon, Wales.
Originally educated as a marine biologist, David Smith's convoluted career track has included researching fish physiology, lecturing in Malawi, site labouring in Rescue archaeology and heading up the Centre for Evaluation of IT in Education (CITE) at the UK National Foundation for Educational Research. David has held research fellowships at Huddersfield Polytechnic and Southampton University, and has published widely in both conventional and multimedia formats. After six years in the Multimedia Industry, David joined the then Newport School of Art and Design as Course Leader, to design and set up new undergraduate and postgraduate courses in Multimedia. He is now Associate Dean of Research and Enterprise in the Newport School of Art, Media and Design, University of Wales, Newport. He is Director the School's Applied Research and Consultancy Centre, and is engaged in a range of consultancies and projects for public sector and corporate clients. He is an active researcher, developing multimedia-based ethnographic techniques to research and archive craft traditions, both in High-Tech Industry and rural India. He is or has been involved in a number of international research projects including 'ITHAC' (MEDIA Plus), the Anglo-Irish 'HUCIS', the EU-India Cross-Cultural Collaboration Programme and the Institute for People-Centred Computation (IP-CC).

Rajesh Kochhar
Institute of Pharmaceutical Education and Research, Mohali, Punjab, India.
An astrophysicist by training, Prof. Rajesh Kochhar has published across a number of disciplines: Theoretical astronomy, history and sociology of modern science and technology, civilizational history of astronomy, ancient Indian history, and globalization-era science policy. He is particularly interested in the use of science, technology and education for inclusive growth. He is a former director of India's National Institute of Science, Technology and Development Studies, New Delhi. He is a Jawaharlal Nehru fellow and a Fulbright scholar. Currently he is professor of

Pharmaceutical heritage at National Institute of Pharmaceutical Education and Research, Mohali, Punjab.

Victoria Vesna
Department of Design|Media Arts, UCLA. Broad Art Center, Rm. 2275, Box 951456, Los Angeles, CA 90095, USA.
Victoria Vesna is a media artist, professor and chair of the department of Design | Media Arts at the UCLA School of the Arts. She is also director of the recently established UCLA Art|Sci center and the UC Digital Arts Research Network. Her work can be defined as experimental creative research that resides between disciplines and technologies. She explores how communication technologies affect collective behavior and how perceptions of identity shift in relation to scientific innovation. In her most recent installations she is concerned with the environment -- "Mood Swings" deals with the environmental effects on mental health and was exhibited in University of Washington, in a festival in Berlin and Castellon, Spain. "Water Bowls" aims to raise consciousness around the issues of pollution of our global life source and was exhibited in Beijing, Los Angeles and will be exhibited in Spain and Zurich. Other notable works are Bodies INCorporated, Datamining Bodies, n0time and Cellular Trans_Actions. Victoria has exhibited her work in 18 solo exhibitions, over 70 group shows, published 20+ papers and gave a 100+ invited talks in the last decade. She is recipient of many grants, commissions and awards, including the Oscar Signorini award for best net artwork in 1998 and the Cine Golden Eagle for best scientific documentary in 1986. Vesna's work has received notice in numerous publications such as Art in America, National Geographic, the Los Angeles Times, Spiegel (Germany), The Irish Times (Ireland), Tema Celeste (Italy), and Veredas (Brazil) and appears in a number of book chapters on media arts. She is the North American editor of AI & Society and editor of Database Aesthetics to be published by Minnesota Press in July 2007.

Carol Gigliotti
Emily Carr Institute, 1399 Johnston Street, Vancouver, BC V6A 2A5, Canada.
Dr. Carol Gigliotti (http://www.carolgigliotti.net/) teaches Media as well as Environmental Ethics at Emily Carr Institute in Vancouver, BC, Canada. She has been presenting and publishing about ethics and technology for the last 15 years. Recent activities include: a presentation entitled "Wildness and Technology" at the 2007 Planetary Collegium in Montreal; speaking at 2006 Kindred Spirits Symposium at Indiana University, an essay in the June2005 issue of Parachute on "Artificial life and the lives of the non-human," guest-editing a special issue on "Genetic Technologies and Animals" for the January06 issue of the journal AI and Society. She is presently working on a book, entitled "Wildness and Technology" and is Co-Chair of the Research B Cluster at University of British Columbia's innovative Centre for Interactive Sustainable Research.

Sha Xin-Wei
Fine Arts and Computer Science, Concordia University, EV06-769, 1515 Ste-Catherine West Montreal, Quebec, H3G 2W1, Canada.
Sha Xin Wei is Canada Research Chair in media arts and sciences and Associate Professor in Fine Arts and Engineering & Computer Science at Concordia Univer-

sity, where he directs the Topological Media Lab. After obtaining his PhD from Stanford in Mathematics, Computer Science, and the History and Philosophy of Science, Sha joined the faculty of Literature, Communication and Culture in Georgia Tech. Dr. Sha has been Visiting Scholar at Stanford University, Harvard University, and MIT. His work has been recognized by the Rockefeller Foundation, LEF Foundation, Creative Work Fund, and the Fondation Langlois. Sha is an associate editor of the Experimental Practices book series (Rodopi Press), and is writing a book about poiesis in topological media.

Fernando Leal
Department of Philosophy, University of Guadalajara, Paseo de Loma Larga 5016-5, 45110 Zapopan, Jal, Mexico
Fernando Leal is Professor of Philosophy and Social Science at the University of Guadalajara (Mexico). He currently works on the interface between ethics, economics and politics, on the history, philosophy and methodology of the social and cognitive sciences, and on the application of linguistic theory to the study of neurodevelopmental disorders. He co-edited *Person-Centred Ergonomics: The Brantonian View of Human Factors* (London, Taylor & Francis, 1993). He has just finished a book-length dialogue on the nature of values (*A Dialogue on Good and Evil*, forthcoming in Spanish).

Printed in the United Kingdom
by Lightning Source UK Ltd.
131636UK00007BA/15/A